A Hi̇stο̇ *ο̇le*

A HISTORY OF
THE OSAGE PEOPLE

Louis F. Burns

THE UNIVERSITY OF ALABAMA PRESS
Tuscaloosa and London

Copyright © 2004
The University of Alabama Press
Tuscaloosa, Alabama 35487-0380
All rights reserved
Manufactured in the United States of America

Originally published by the author in 1989

Typeface: Bembo

∞

The paper on which this book is printed meets the minimum requirements of American National Standard for Information Science–Permanence of Paper for Printed Library Materials, ANSI Z39.48-1984.

Library of Congress Cataloging-in-Publication Data

Burns, Louis F.
    A history of the Osage people / Louis F. Burns.— [New ed.]
        p. cm.
Includes bibliographical references and index.
    ISBN 0-8173-1319-2 (cloth : alk. paper) — ISBN 0-8173-5018-7 (pbk. : alk. paper)
1. Osage Indians—History. I. Title.
    E99.O7.B85 2004
    978.004′9752—dc21

                                                                            2003007997

British Library Cataloguing-in-Publication Data available

To my wife, Ruth, who is
my greatest fan, my severest critic,
and *Wa ta Nontsa.*

Contents

Illustrations   ix

Preface to the New Edition   xi

Preface to the First Edition   xiii

PART ONE: THE ASCENT OF THE OSAGE PEOPLE, 1200–1803
1. Osage Origins   3

2. The Osage Empire   23

3. Osage Relationships with Euro-Americans, 1675–1803   87

PART TWO: ERODING THE OSAGE CIVILIZATION, 1803–1850
4. Coming of the Americans   139

5. Treaties and Land Cessions   147

6. The Indian State and Removal   172

7. The Effects of Removal   186

8. Osage Culture and United States' Policy   198

9. The Search for Comprehension   218

PART THREE: FACING THE FOUR HORSEMEN, 1850–1865
10. Pestilence Strikes the People   233

11. The White Man's War Visits the Osages   246

PART FOUR: THE EURO-AMERICAN AFFLICTION, 1865–1875
12. The Outcasts   271

13. Osage Land Cession of 1865   281

14. The End of Indian Treaty-Making   292

15. The Drum Creek Treaty   300

viii / Contents

16. The Osage Removal   314

17. The Final Move   335

PART FIVE: THE ROAD TO ACCOMMODATION, 1875–1906
18. Farewell to the Past   357

19. Bluestem and Cattle   368

20. Constitutional Government and Allotment   390

PART SIX: STANDING IN TWO WORLDS, 1906–1989
21. Black Gold   417

22. Indian Influences and the Modern Indian   445

23. Epilogue   486

Notes   497

Bibliography   529

Index   541

Illustrations

Fig. 1. Osage Tribal Organization   5

Fig. 2. Woodland-Osage Comparative Designs   8

Fig. 3. Two *Ho E Ka* Snares   13

Fig. 4. The Relative Location of the Osage Empire in the United States   26

Fig. 5. Osage Expansion, 1500–1800   31

Fig. 6. The Osage Domain and Routes to the Far West   36

Fig. 7. Osage Government: Gentile Government   39

Fig. 8. Osage Government: Three Groups of Bands   42

Fig. 9. Osage Villages and Camps in Missouri   46

Fig. 10. Osage Villages and Camps in Kansas   57

Fig. 11. Osage Villages and Camps in Oklahoma   65

Fig. 12. Osage Trails in Missouri   73

Fig. 13. Osage Trails in Kansas   76

Fig. 14. Osage Trails in Oklahoma   78

Fig. 15. Cultural Contrasts   88

Fig. 16. French and British-American Forts, 1730–1757   100

Fig. 17. Missouri River Trade, 1775–1776   105

Fig. 18. Assignment of Traders, 1794–1795   108

Fig. 19. Location of Indian Nations, 1803   112

Fig. 20. Population of Louisiana, 1771   120

Fig. 21. Cherokee Strip and Outlet   162

Fig. 22. Cessions of 1808   167

Fig. 23. Cession of 1818   169

Fig. 24. Cession of 1825   170

Fig. 25. Osage Age Groups in 1878   178

Fig. 26. Emigrant Indian Groups of the Northeast and Old Northwest and Their Respective Populations, 1829   184

Fig. 27. Emigrant Nations on Former Osage Domain in Missouri   187

Fig. 28. Emigrant Nations on Former Osage Domain in Kansas   188

Fig. 29. Emigrant Nations on Former Osage Domain in Oklahoma   190

Fig. 30. Osage-Cherokee Problems   192

Fig. 31. Kiowa Calendar   216

Fig. 32. Harmony School, 1824–1825   221

Fig. 33. Osage Missions   222

Fig. 34. Known Osage Epidemics   239

Fig. 35. Estimates of Osage Population   243

Fig. 36. Kansas Territory   249

Fig. 37. Kansas in 1862   252

Fig. 38. Kansas Population Growth   266

Fig. 39. Leases of 1893   375

Fig. 40. Leases of 1898   376

Fig. 41. Leases of 1900   377

Fig. 42. Leases of 1901   378

Fig. 43. Leases of 1904   380

Fig. 44. Leases of 1905   382

Preface to the New Edition

Several improvements have been made in this Osage history. Most of Part One has been almost entirely omitted in order to enable the reader to start right off with the Osages. The appendices have also been deleted. Since the botany section, added originally as a point of interest, was general and not Osage specific, it was not needed here. The biographical section has been reluctantly left out to conserve space.

A number of corrections were necessary. An incredible amount of archaeological developments have occurred in the past decade, and the same is true of Indian literature. This new information has been added.

Most of the additions are clarifications. Transmitting a thought from one person to another can be tricky. Rereading something years after it was written often allows one to see the need for clarification. A significant addition is a redesigned population (1878) graph (Fig. 25) that allows the reader to view the entire graph on one page. The use of story in lieu of myth in this account must be justified. There are, of course, distinctions among myth, legend, and folk tales. However, that myth is sometimes taken as a fable is a deep concern. Myths should always be taken as a part of sincere religious devotion.

In the haste to get the history into print, its original preface omitted an important recognition, that is, not giving acknowledgment to a dear, sweet man, Dr. Abraham P. Nasatir, who gave us a whole day of his valuable time. If the Spanish period in the Osage history has special merit, it is because of the late Dr. Nasatir. The first preface acknowledges my wife Ruth as my helper for forty-four years. Now, in 2002, I must thank her for fifty-seven years.

As a final note, I would like to stress again the lessons of the Osage experience as exposed in the history. The first lesson is that of being adaptive to change—this is the only constant. The second is to love the earth, for it is all we have.

In the Osage *Ne ke A Tun ka* (Great Words of the Ancient People), there is a thought we have paraphrased in American-style English:

To touch the earth is to touch the past, the present, and the future.

We hope this account of the Osage experience, bought at such a terrible price, will encourage each of us to keep in touch with the earth, for the earth is truly our past, present, and future.

Preface to the First Edition

When a person becomes rash enough to undertake the writing of history, it behooves him to explain his views about it. Defining history is no easy task. It may be a simple chronicle of events or it might be an intricate web of human intrigue. Whatever history might be, it cannot be the same as the actual event or experience. Obviously, to write an action or perform deeds of yore on paper is not possible. Thus, history through necessity must capture only the essences of the past, and in doing this it becomes interpretative.

All history, therefore, is interpretative. This places a terrible burden upon the writer of history. One must try to rise above backgrounds and truthfully and faithfully reflect the past of those who are no longer alive to defend themselves. This is especially difficult because it is easier to condemn than it is to praise.

If one condemns, it should be for a constructive reason. Praise is a reward for something above the ordinary, and it too should be used constructively. A writer of history must try to exercise restraint and seek moderation in the presentation. The lure of overstatement and understatement is always with us. With these thoughts in mind, I would like to express a few of my goals.

The writing of this history began long ago in the idle hours of my childhood. It started as a boyhood dream and simmered in the mind of a young man. Through maturity, it began to solidify and now in my "golden years" it has become a reality. This history was over three-hundred years in the making and a lifetime in the writing.

Along the way, decisions about interpretation and presentation were made. Very early, it was decided that the Osage viewpoint would prevail—it would hold the center of the stage. If I have erred, I have tried to err on behalf of the Osages. Some will accuse me of being biased in favor of the

Osages. My answer is, "It is time for some bias in favor of the Osages—there has been so much bias against them."

Another priority is to avoid the "Lo! The poor Indian," practice, which seeks to point to the great evils committed against Indians. If this were all it did, it would not be so repulsive, but it also points the accusing finger at all who have descended from those people who treated Indians so shabbily. It is an outright bid for sympathy and relieves one of the need to comprehend. The Osages do not need or want sympathy, but they desperately need understanding.

It would be misleading to allow the reader to think this history is the work of a single person. A glance at the bibliography will show a legion of contributors. I have carefully tried to credit these contributions in the footnotes. I cannot possibly list all those who assisted in the writing of this history, but I would like to mention a few. Maude Cheshewalla often discussed the Osage People with me. Her store of Osage life and culture was remarkable. She will be mournfully missed in the days ahead. Mr. Joe Revelette placed us heavily in debt for the collection of papers he accumulated during his terms as a council member. Chief Sylvester Tinker has over the years discussed many Osage matters and has filled in many blanks. No one can imagine how much my wife of forty-four years has helped. Specifically, the index is all Ruth's work but her help went far beyond this.

If some of the things about the organization and presentation of this history seem strange, this is not accidental. I deliberately tried to establish a different pattern for Indian histories. However, to avoid any misunderstandings, I would like to explain what I was trying to do.

The history opens with a prologue and ends with an epilogue. In every history there are lessons to be learned. The prologue is meant to alert the reader to the central theme running through the chronicle of events, that is, survival in its array of costumes. The epilogue returns to this theme in order to see how the Osages fared as a result of the Ordeal and what we as a country should learn from their experience. This is a simple fundamental question and it has a simple fundamental answer.

The drama that unfolds in Osage history is exciting. Before our eyes we see a proud but disciplined people rise to become the most potent force in mid–America. Equally vivid is the soul-rendering erosion of all they had. Their lands, their culture, their pride, their discipline, and their population were gone. Only shreds and tatters remained. Yet they did not despair. Money came in undreamed torrents, but it could not buy what was gone. Facing reality, these remnants turned to the present. Again, rising from the ashes of their past the Osages are seeking through excellence to become "the people."

A History of the Osage People

PART ONE

The Ascent of the Osage People, 1200–1803

I

Osage Origins

THE PREHISTORIC OSAGES

Introduction

While there is considerable amount of disagreement about Osage origins, it is clear the Osage people originated east of the Mississippi. According to Osage traditions, as interpreted by J. Owen Dorsey, the Osage (Dhegiha Sioux) homeland was the Chesapeake Piedmont.[1] Recent archaeological findings seem to indicate that both the Dhegiha Sioux and Chewere Sioux were the Indian-Knoll and shell mound culture of Kentucky and Tennessee. While this would not necessarily negate the Chesapeake concept, it would tend to trace their westward migration. The Indian-Knoll theory makes a definite connection with the Folsom culture.[2]

Shell Mound Culture

Sizable numbers of so-called shell mounds can be found along the Ohio River and lower reaches of the Tennessee River. We say "so-called" because shells actually make up a small percentage of the mounds. The surviving artifacts show that the phase was primarily a hunting culture that used mussels and gathering to supplement their diet.

Quapaw legends clearly link the Quapaw and other Dhegiha Sioux (Osage, Quapaw, Ponca, Omaha, and Kansas) with the Indian-Knoll. This, in turn, almost certainly indicates a descent from the Folsom and Clovis cultures because the lower levels of the mounds and the nearby rock shelters and caves are proven to be from the Folsom culture. Because the occupation seemingly was continuous from around 8000 B.C. to A.D. 1300, some justification for a claim for this descent exists.[3]

A combination of archaeology and the body of Chewere/Dhegiha stories and legends leave little doubt that both the Dhegiha and their near kinsmen the Chewere Sioux (Missouria, Otoe, Iowa, and Winnebago) remained primarily Archaic throughout most of the Woodland period. That is, while they almost certainly adopted many Adena, Hopewell, and Mississippian traits, the Archaic culture remained the base culture of both the Dhegiha and Chewere. Some Dhegiha and Chewere undoubtedly became a part of the late Mississippian Oneota people. Certainly, de Soto's expedition clearly shows that in the mid-1500s the Quapaw exhibited Mississippian Southern culture.

It seems probable that the Hopewell phase encompassed several different Indian groups instead of being composed of only one people. Doubts certainly exist when the manner of Hopewell expansion is considered. The original Hopewell people differed from the western extension or Illinois Hopewellians. The core Hopewell estate group did not expand through conquest and the forced adoption of conquered groups but instead accepted other groups who wished to join them and absorbed them into their culture without coercion. However, the Illinois Hopewellians evidently expanded through conquest and forced adoption.[4] The Osages clearly followed the practice of the Hopewell estate core group in this particular matter.

Figure 1 shows the five subdivision mergers of the Osage people, based on their stories, legends, and ceremonies. These sources show that the new groups were accepted in every case without coercion. As a matter of known practice, each new group was given the position of greatest honor, and rites of the new group were given precedence over the rites of the mother group. Sometimes a new line of worship was instituted. Each of these new amalgamations entailed a *move to new country*. This Osage expression means a change to an untried organization, which may or may not involve an actual physical move into a new land area. Another aspect of this expression involves a concept alien to the European mind. This concept involves the practice of a powerful majority submitting themselves to the unknown ways of a weaker minority so the minority will feel comfortable with the merger.[5] In *The Prince,* Niccolò Machiavelli advises his Prince to allow conquered people to live under their usual laws and habits as much as possible. The Osages went much farther than this, and changed their own laws and habits to accommodate the new people.

The Mississippian Phase

The Mississippian phase of the Late Woodland culture probably arose from remnants of the Hopewell phase. Mississippian mounds built on the flood plains along the middle Mississippi River and lower ends of the Illinois, Ohio, and Tennessee Rivers indicate these areas as places of origin for this

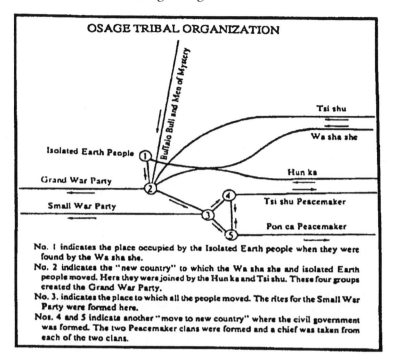

Fig. 1. Chart showing mergers and organization of Osage government. This chart was drawn by Red Bird to illustrate the story of creating the Osage tribal government (from *36th Annual Report,* BAE, Smithsonian).

culture. Artifacts from these areas suggest influences from Mexico at about A.D. 900.[6]

After A.D. 1200 the Mississippian influence spread to the lower Mississippi and the Southeast.[7] Of special interest to this history is the expansion along the Arkansas River. The mounds at Spiro, Oklahoma, lay in the historic Osage territory, including the mounds on the north side and near the mouth of the Arkansas. What is called the Long-Nosed God cult of the Southeastern Mississippian is of interest because of its Caddo connection. The Caddo also occupied the area of the Spiro Mounds in historic times, and evidence indicates that the Long-Nosed cult came to the Southeastern Mississippian through the Caddo.

Osage stories tell of the search for the Isolated Earth People. Descriptions of their village and customs fit the Caddo better than any other known culture. Yet the stories clearly say the Isolated Earth People spoke the same language. While the stories indicate no particular time span, they do maintain a sequence of events. Under this sequence, the Isolated Earth People entered the Osage Tribal Circle between the Earth and Sky people. That is, they joined the *Wa sha she* (Water People) and *Hun ka* (Earth People) before the *Tsi shu* (Sky People).[8] We have some indications that the *Wa sha she* and *Hun ka* were Ohio Hopewellian. There is also a story of a Chewere (Iowa, Missouria, Otoe) association.[9] The Osage name for the Iowa is *Pa Ho tse* or Snow Head. The story relates that the Iowa left the others (Dhegiha and Chewere) during a snow storm. Since the Chewere are known to have moved west from the Great Lakes, this would seem to indicate the *Wa sha she* and *Hun ka* also followed this route from the upper Ohio. Thus, the Isolated Earth People seem to be from the northern Caddo instead of southern Caddo, if they were not Dakota Sioux. Stray bands of Caddoean Pawnee were known to have entered North Central Illinois.

Like other Woodland cultures, the Mississippian phase was characterized by mounds. These mounds were different from the Hopewellian mounds in two respects. They were larger and they were pyramidal rather than conical. Monks Mound at Cahokia, Illinois, was started in A.D. 900 and took two-hundred-fifty years to build. Its base covers eighteen acres, and it rises one hundred feet above its base.[10] The tops of the pyramidal mounds were flat, and wooden houses for temples or housing of leaders were built on the flat area. Often, these mounds were erected on the four sides of a central square in major ceremonial centers. Ceremonial centers featured satellite villages and maintenance of eternal fires, both of which are also features found in the Mayan culture.[11] While food production was very like the Hopewell phase, the Mississippian people practiced a more intensive corn culture with improved varieties of corn.[12]

Mississippian pottery shows improved techniques over the Hopewellian pottery, and the resemblance to Mexican ceramics is more pronounced. New artistic capabilities are also evident in engravings and painting. More than anything else, the socio-religious-political system of the Mississippian shows a revolution in Hopewellian ways. This tightly organized system was structured around new religious beliefs and ceremonies[13] resembling those of the Mayan. It is possible that a Mexican group of Indians may have established a colony among the late-Hopewellians and formed the nucleus of the Mississippian phase. However, they may have come to the Mississippian peoples indirectly through the Caddo people.

The Mississippian phase reached a climax in the 1500s, after which their ceremonial centers were neglected and the population dispersed. Although religious and political institutions were altered, they became weaker in spite of these efforts. We cannot be certain what caused the fall of the culture.

However, such a sudden large population loss often suggests epidemics, possibly from diseases transmitted by Europeans.[14] Tatters of the phase remained to be recorded by de Soto and early French explorers.[15] Of special interest to Osage history is a possible invasion from the northeast. If such an invasion did occur, it would have driven many Mississippian groups into Iowa. There the fragmented groups could have amalgamated into the Oneota aspect.[16] Archaeological studies by Carl H. Chapman, Brewton Berry, and John Mack seem to place the Dhegiha in the Upper Mississippian phase. They do not separate the Big and Little Osages, but their report does reflect differences between the two Osage groups. These historians also felt the Osages could have belonged to the Oneota aspect as well as the Chewere. The pottery at the Little Osage site in the Bend of the Missouri most closely resembled the Orr focus of the Oneota aspect, but differed in some fine details.[17] This viewpoint is also reflected by other authorities.[18]

Archaeologists rely on the hard evidence of artifacts. Anthropologists, ethnologists, and sociologists add theories that are based on the knowledge of humans. While stories and legends are indeed soft evidence, they do sometimes provide a degree of guidance in the search for truth. Two factors from the stories, legends, and ceremonies of the Osage strongly suggest a connection with both the Hopewell and Mississippian phases of the Woodland culture.

The comparison of Woodland designs with Osage designs are shown in Figure 2.[19] A question arises about the circle with a black dot in the center. In the desert culture, a circle with a dark dot in the center indicates a campsite. However, this particular design was from the Woodland culture of Missouri and could have had at least two other meanings. It could mean *O ke sa* or Midheaven, where the people acquired souls; *O ke sa* was midway between the second and third Upper Worlds. *O ke sa* also symbolized the origin of all human life and the place where the soul must return when the physical body dies. A second possible meaning requires some explanation. The Osages had no design to represent the concept of the Isolated Earth, although the idea is included in their ceremonies. This concept argues that the earth is a celestial body apart from the other heavenly bodies. (This is much like the old Ptolemaic theory.) As a matter of interest, all Osages claim origins in the four upper worlds, except the Isolated Earth People who claim origins on earth. Since the Dakota Sioux also claim origins on the earth, this could indicate the Isolated Earth people were from either the Dakota or some other Siouan group whose views differed from the views of the Dhegiha.

The Four Winds or Breath of Life symbol is well known, since it is not

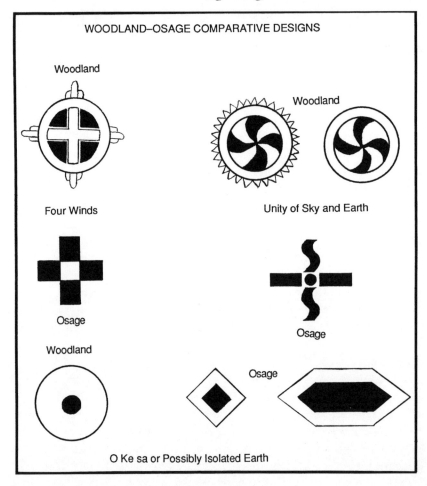

Fig. 2. The comparative designs have the same basic meanings.

exclusive to the Osage. On the other hand, the Striking the Earth symbol is distinctively Osage. It expresses the unity of sky and earth, which makes life on earth possible. The wavy lines of the Woodland design superimposed on the sun has the same meaning. In the Osage design, the sun is represented by a small round shape in the center, and the sun's path is shown as straight bars. Benefits of the sun are shown as wavy lines.[20]

A second Woodland cultural influence on the Osage is a Mayan morning prayer. The Osages were noted for their morning devotions at sunrise. To Euro-American ears, this sounded like a funeral with wailing and weeping. Yet, prayers were recited to greet the sun and its life-giving rays. It was these prayers that stirred memories of departed loved ones and evoked the wails and tears. The Osage sun prayers at dawn express much the same thoughts as the Mayan dawn prayer.[21] "Look at us, hear us! . . . Heart of heaven, Heart of Earth! Give us our descendants, our succession, as long as the sun shall move. . . . Let it dawn, let the day come! . . . May the people have peace . . . may they be happy . . . give us good life . . . grandmother of the sun, grandmother of the light, let there be dawn . . . let the light come."[22]

Certainly, the Osage obsession with a long life, both as individuals and through descendants, is well known. For example, the red cedar is symbolic of individual old age and the red oak symbolizes a long life through many descendants. *Pe se* or acorns of the red oak are likened to a profusion of descendants. White and pale blue are symbolic of the clear day which, in turn, refers to a long peaceful life. Since these concepts are associated with the *Tsi shu,* the fourth group to join the Osage, they almost certainly came from the Mississippian phase.

The Prehistoric Age

In many respects the Prehistoric Age actually reaches back to the Adena phase of the Golden Age. That is, both the Golden Age and the Prehistoric Age begin at the close of the Archaic Age. This last Paleohistoric period of the North American Indian represents a parallel line of development to the Woodland and Desert cultures. Whereas the Golden Age cultures turned more and more away from the hunt and toward agriculture, the Prehistoric Age tended to retain many ways identified with the Archaic Age. At first, the Prehistoric trend involved a few isolated bands of hunters. Possibly, their ranks were increased by descendants of Ice Age hunters who followed the game northward as the glaciers retreated. These descendants could have been invaders of the Woodland and Desert cultures. In any event, all through the Golden Age there were small independent groups who developed their own languages and were basically hunters.

Aside from these small groups—who apparently never attached themselves to the major cultures—were other groups. Any society has dissident factions who, for reasons of their own, sever their connections with the society and strike out on their own. Such rebel groups tend to increase as a culture falters and loses its vitality. Other groups may have found the free life of seminomadic hunting more attractive than sedentary village life. These factors would create many diverse groups, such as existed when Europeans first met the North American Indian.

The Osages were always drawn to the hunt by the attractions it offered. They were also cognizant of the advantages offered by the agricultural Woodland cultures. They could never abandon the free life of the hunt for the regimentation of agricultural life, yet they could accept some advantages offered by both. The Osages may have acted as suppliers of raw material to the main Woodland centers. They apparently always, right up to historic times, lived on the fringes of the Woodland cultures. Their easy adaptation and utilization of trade with Europeans suggests the possibility of trade experience.

With the exception of three of the six Little Osage bands, the Osages have traditionally sought out hill country that adjoined a major river. This runs counter to the Woodland practices, where the flood plains were the preferred terrain. Most of the people in the three Little Osage bands that differed in terrain preferences were Those Who Were Last to Come. That is, it is all but certain that they were from the Arkansas River Mississippians. Nearly all these Little Osages were also Heart Stays People.[23]

Several accounts stress a close association of the Osages with the Mississippian Illinois Indians. The earliest of these accounts was written in 1682 by Father Zenobius Membré, who was with the La Salle Expedition: "There had been several engagements with equal loss on both sides, and that, at last, of the seventeen Illinois villages, the greater part had retired beyond the river Colbert [Mississippi River] among the Ozages, 200 leagues from their country, where a part of the Iroquois had pursued them."[24]

The known Osage tendency to fight any invasion of their territory seems to have been replaced in this case by a rare amity toward the Illinois. It is the only such case recorded where the Osages sheltered a large group of distressed alien Indians. They did allow the Wichitas to hunt in their territory during the Civil War, but they did not shelter them from other Indians.

A second account was written in 1721 by Sieur Deliette, a nephew of Henri de Tonti.[25] It is well to mention that this description of a calumet included Missourias and Osages, which suggests that the Osages were Little Osages. Deliette described the singing of the calumet by the Osages in great detail. This is the only recorded account of Osages singing a calumet among any other Indian people. The rarity of Osages sheltering the Illinois and the singing of a calumet among them show a strong association between these two peoples.

A third account, written by Thomas Nuttall in 1819, also notes this strong relationship. Nuttall was correct in linking the Quapaw and the Osage together by language: "The friendship which they [Illinois] cultivated, about a century ago, with the Osages, and the Arkansas [Quapaw], who are the same people, and some incidental resemblances between them, lead us to believe them commonly related by language and descent."[26] Nuttall was also correct in noting their close relationship to each other. In addition, a close relationship existed between the Osage and the Illinois.

A discrepancy of twenty-seven years exists between Nuttall's estimate of one hundred years of amity and Membré's account in 1682. However, Osage stories and legends indicate Those Who Were Last to Come joined with the Osages sometime between 1600 and 1682. Another part of Nuttall's account indicates the Illinois were also on amicable terms with the Quapaw.

In describing de Soto's trans–Mississippi route, Houck mentions a battle between the Casquins (Kaskaskias) and the Capahas (Quapaws).[27] Apparently, this battle took place slightly north of New Madrid, Missouri. The battle was with the Cahokia and Kaskaskia bands of the Illinois that the Osages and Quapaws were on friendly terms with at a later date. Although other Illinois such as the Peoria and Weas lived near the Osages in the 1850s, no special animosities or amity appear in the records.[28] The Quapaw and Illinois evidently reconciled their differences between 1539 (de Soto's Expedition) and 1719 (if we use Nuttall's estimate; 1682, if we use Membré's account). The Membré account is more likely to be accurate since it was closer to the event in time.

One other matter touched upon by Houck is interesting. Houck places de Soto on the upper White River at a Caya (Kansas) village.[29] Identification of these Indians is credited to Schoolcraft. While we have the highest regard for both Houck and Schoolcraft, we cannot agree to this identification. Without a doubt Caya does refer to *Kon za* or Kansas, but it would seem to apply to the Osage or Quapaw *Kon za* clan instead of to the Kansas or Kaw tribe. Many Little Osages from this original *Hun ka* clan broke off from the Little Osages around A.D. 1500 and moved up the Missouri to form the Kansas tribe. This new tribe settled above the mouth of the Kansas River and obviously did not hunt or dwell on the Arkansas. Most of the remaining *Kon za* clan were with the Pomme de Terre River Big Osages, who established numerous villages between the headwaters of the Pomme Terre and White Rivers in Missouri. We find it difficult to associate the Kaw tribe with the upper White River, which was deep within Osage home territory and not adjacent to or near Kansas tribal areas. This is the only reference available that reported the Kaw being so far south.

It had to be the Big Osages or Quapaw of the *Kon za* clan—who remained with the Osages and had from the first formed around the Grand *Hun ka* Chief—that was mentioned in the de Soto account. They later supported the leadership of young Claremore II and his uncle Tracks Far Away (Big Foot) who was the Grand *Hun ka* Chief by the late–1700s. Only the Spanish records mention these Grand *Hun ka* Chiefs and the Pomme de Terre bands.[30] The Spanish records, however, omit the Black Dog Band which was one of the Pomme de Terre bands.

OSAGE STORIES AND LEGENDS RELATING TO THEIR ORIGINS

Introduction

Before the discussion of the Osage stories, some explanations are necessary. First and foremost, paraphrases and not actual interpretations will be given. Most of these stories are recorded in Osage, in literal translation, and in free translation by the Bureau of American Ethnology. Secondly, each of the twenty-four clans had different versions of these stories. Although they agree in essence, they vary in some details. Another related problem arises because some parts of these stories were the exclusive property of a particular clan. Sometimes, these special parts could not be recorded because their owners would not sell them and, thus, they have been lost. A third item is a caution. These stories and comments must not be taken as proof of anything. They are presented as possible clues in Osage prehistory.

A final observation in regard to Osage oral stories must be made: The circumstances under which these stories were related and recorded is of vital importance to their accuracy. For example, if a story was given without charge at any time, especially in the dead of winter, it should be suspected of being of questionable authenticity. Osage stories were not given free of charge by the Little Old Men, who were the true keepers of Osage stories and legends. Something had to be given in return for the story. In January and February, the Guardians of One's Word were inactive. Thus, an Osage could and often would tell some big whoppers. However, when the Guardians were active, an Osage would be as truthful as his ability, knowledge, and courtesy allowed.

The innate courtesy of the Osage sometimes created unreliable information. If a slight acquaintance seemed eager for some bit of information, an Osage would extend himself to tell the person what he wanted to hear. It was considered a duty to do this rather than to disappoint an acquaintance. Stories recorded by the Bureau of Ethnology were paid for and were related by the Little Old Men to trusted friends. Any deviations from the centuries-old wording—which sometimes happened because of memories that had faded from lack of use—were either noted and paraphrased by the Little Old Men or omitted rather than give a false story.

Genesis

According to the Panther (Puma) clan version of the Osage genesis story, the beings who became Osage originated in the fourth or lowest upper world. They had no bodies, no souls, nor communication or intellect. As they ascended through the third upper world into the second upper world, they

TWO HO E KA (SNARES)

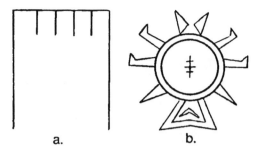

a.   b.

Fig. 3. a. The elk's forehead, which represents the horizons of the earth and the four winds. b. A stylized black widow spider whose web was also a snare for all life.

acquired souls. This point, midway in the upper worlds, is called *O ke sa* (Midway). In the second upper world, they acquired intellect, and in the first upper world they acquired communication.

Although the people now had souls, mind, and communication, they still felt incomplete because they had no bodies. Since bodies could not exist in the upper worlds, they realized they would have to descend to the earth. After asking the various manifestations of *Wah kon ta* for help, the people finally asked *Hun ka Ah hu tun* (*Hun ka,* Having Wings) to lead them below where they could have bodies. Assuming the form of eagles, the people soared downward and alit in seven trees.[31] All the earth below the branches was covered with still water. After some time, *O pon Tun ka* (Big Elk) came to their aid. Four times he threw himself upon the still waters until the soil of the earth appeared. Big Elk then called for the four winds, the breath of *Wa kon ta,* to come dry the land. He called first the wind of the rising sun. Then he called loudly over the lands of the earth for the cedar wind (north wind). He called for the wind from sundown and the warm winds of the south. Once the winds were gathered, the Elk endowed them with the breath of life and commanded them to blow over the earth.

Again, the huge elk threw himself upon the ground. He left hairs on the ground which became grasses and useful plants. Food animals would feed on the grasses, and other plants furnished the people with food wherever they wandered. Now the elk gave the people his last gift: "Take my forehead, for I have made a snare for all life; none can escape from it." This refers to the dark outline on the elk's forehead, which is shown in Figure 3(a).

The Ancient Osages considered the earth to be a snare or trap which held all physical life. Only by death, which freed the soul from the physical body and allowed it to escape, could a creature of earth escape the snare. The Milky Way was likened to the spirit path which led the way back to *O ke sa*. For three days the soul lingered here on earth, then it started the long journey back to *O ke sa* where it had come from.[32]

Wa kon ta brought the sky and earth together so that physical life such as plants and animals could exist on earth. Rains and the warm sun's rays came from the sky and the earth nourished and sheltered all the physical bodies. Therefore, all physical life was confined to the earth, for only there could it find such things in the proper combination.

We do not attach any symbolism to the four upper worlds. In the version just given, the trees stood in still waters, but in the Black Bear version they stood amidst huge boulders. This indicates a mixed woodland and grassland. The elk was not confused with the moose, who was a swamp animal. The elk has the *Ho e ka* etched in black on his forehead; the moose does not have this marking. Thus, a temporary standing of water seems probable. This was a condition common to the glacial climates. Stress placed on the size of the elk suggests a prehistoric elk. In ordinary usage the elk was called *Wa tso Ta Cee* (Yellow Animal) or *O pon* (Elk). The addition of *Tun ka* (big, huge, great) to *O pon* signifies an extraordinary elk.[33]

Forming the Confederation

Figure 1 shows the merging of five subdivisions to make up the Osage people. The *Hun ka* (Earth People) joined the *Wa sha she* (Water People) who were the original Osages. We do not have the stories associated with this event because they have been lost in time. Yet, we know from the wording of the *Wa ho pe* songs that this was true. These two people, the *Wa sha she* and *Hun ka,* formed the ancient fourteen fireplace organization. They had seven *Wa sha she* and seven *Hun ka* fireplaces. A moiety of War (*Hun ka*) and Peace (*Wa sha she*) existed. Traditionally, the *O su ka ha* (Those Who Make Clear the Way) clan of the *Wa sha she* led the people in their wanderings. It was members of this clan who first met the Isolated Earth People. One look at the new people's village discouraged the Osages from entering. Only one member of Those Who Make Clear the Way clan would enter the village. Human bones lay strewn about mingled with animal bones. Excrement and accumulated debris were scattered throughout the village. The stench was almost unbearable.[34]

A breakthrough occurred during the visit between the two headmen. First, they marveled at the fact that they spoke the same language. Then the *Wa sha she* mentioned that he was *Hun ka* (of the earth, in this sense) and the other leader covered his mouth (surprise) and said he too was *Hun ka* (of the earth). After some discussion, it was agreed that they would all make a *move to new country.* That is, they would reorganize and become one people. An actual move to a new area was part of the agreement along with the abandonment of the unsanitary practices of the Isolated Earth People. One other concession was made by the new people. Their leader had mentioned that they used the four winds to destroy all life. Since the Osages did not believe in destroying life, the Isolated Earth people also agreed to abandon this practice. The two groups then formed a union for mutual defense.

Two Houses of Mysteries were created. One, called the Little House of Mysteries, was placed in charge of the Isolated Earth People. Ironically, or maybe wisely, this was the House of Peaceful Ceremonies. For example, the Isolated Earth clan always conducted the naming ceremonies. The other house was called the Big House of Mysteries and it was placed in charge of the Black Bear or Radiant Star clan. All ceremonies of war, which included the hunt since it too involved taking life, were held in this house. Generally, throughout the ceremonial songs, the expression, "it has been said," refers to the house of peace and the expression, "it has been said in this house," refers to the house of war.

As Figure 1 shows, the *Hun ka* had joined the *Wa sha she* and then broken off again before meeting with the Isolated Earth People. As the same diagram shows, they rejoined in time for this new organization. Possibly the *Hun ka* objected to accepting the Isolated Earth People into the tribal circle. This could account for giving the house of war to the *Hun ka* instead of the Isolated Earth. In the new tribal circle, the Deer and Fish clans of the *Wa sha she* were counted as one fireplace in order to make a place for the Isolated Earth. The *Hun ka* remained as seven fireplaces on the War side of the circle. Although the *Tsi shu* are shown as joining the circle at this time, we believe they joined after the basic organization was formed but before the new liturgy evolved.

It seems probable that the *Tsi shu* refused to join the others at first because of the dominant role in the new government given to the Isolated Earth and the *Hun ka.* However, the four ceremonial pauses before the actual attack of a war party or hunting party testify to the *Tsi shu* presence in this new alliance. The War Party in Great Numbers (or Grand War Party) was a part of this new organization, and it also included the *Tsi shu.*

The legends tell of a long time of almost continuous warfare and internal strife. Confusion reached such a critical point that the *Wa sha she* led another *move to new country.* In this reorganization, the Houses of Mysteries were left in the same hands, except the Panther (puma) clan joined with its kindred Black Bear clan as vice-chairman of the house of war. Authority to initiate war movements was vested in the Black Bear, *Hun ka* clan; the *Wa sha she* division; the *Tsi shu* division; and the Isolated Earth division. It should be noted, that the *Hun ka* were represented by a single clan, but the other divisions were represented by division. This reorganization severely curtailed the powers of the Isolated Earth People. This was probably done to satisfy the *Tsi shu*. The subordination of the *Hun ka* division power to one clan could have served the same purpose. It cannot be determined with certainty that a power struggle was going on among the divisions. However, the stories seem to imply that compromises were made to ease hurt feelings.

Without a doubt, this first reorganization brought a much needed period of order and peace to the Osage. Apparently, it eased internal strife among the divisions and provided an effective military response. However, the military organization eventually became increasingly burdened with time-consuming ceremonies, which tended to hamper its quick response to hostile intrusions. By 1500, the ceremonies had become so cumbersome that a reorganization was necessary, yet a full reorganization did not occur until after 1600. About this same time, a final group merged with the Osages. These people were called the *Tsi ha she* (Those Who Were Last to Come).

The story of creating the Hawk *Wa ho pe* or Hawk Shrine throws light on the *Tsi ha she* and the second reorganization.[35] The Old Men, having determined the hawk was suitable for use in a new war ritual as an emblem of courage, began to make a Hawk Shrine. As they were working on the last shrine in the House of Mysteries, they were startled by a sudden clap of thunder. A *Sho ka* (messenger) was sent to see what had made such a great noise. He soon returned and reported Man of Mystery had made the noise.[36] All the Little Old Men agreed that Man of Mystery was a desirable person, so he was invited to join them and he was promised the finished shrine would be given to his keeping. With this invitation and promise, Man of Mystery descended and alit on the ridgepole of the House of Mysteries.

Almost immediately there was another terrifying noise outside the door. As the messenger threw aside the door flap, there stood a huge enraged buffalo bull. He pawed the earth and bellowed, "I am Buffalo Bull, lift up your heads."[37] Terrified, the Ancient Men threw the sacred emblems toward the angry bull. Seeing this, he immediately became quiet and friendly. As a result, the Men of Mystery and Buffalo Bull clans became joint keepers of the Hawk *Wa ho pe*.[38]

It seems clear that the *Tsi ha she* had brought the Small War Party and Little Shrine ideas to the Osages. Equally clear is that the original intent was to assign control of the Little Shrine to one of the more powerful subdivisions such as the *Tsi shu*. This story illustrates the argument that ensued as a result of that intent. A significant fact is that the Small War Party and Portable Shrine concepts are typically Algonquian.

Three classes of small war parties were created under this third military government. All three could be created *outside the House of Mysteries.* This meant they could be formed without the time-consuming ceremonies of the Grand War Party, which often consumed seven to fourteen days. In addition, frequent ceremonies were held while the war party traveled. The first class of Small War Parties was made up of warriors from only one of the Grand Divisions. A second type of small party consisted of warriors of at least two clans from either of the two Grand Divisions. Finally, a Small War Party could be formed by warriors from a single clan. It was under this last reorganization of the military branch of government that the Osages first met the white man. The Black Bear and Panther clans that gave the Spanish and Americans so much trouble on the Arkansas River were Small War Parties of the third class.

Along with the military reorganization, the Little Old Men, who had now become the controlling power of the Osages, also reorganized the gentile system. The *Wa sha she, Hun ka* and Isolated *Hun ka* became subdivisions of the *Hun ka* Grand Division. This division represented the lands and waters of the earth. A second Grand Division was composed of the *Tsi shu* and the *Tsi ha she* subdivisions, which represented the sky.

Government Organization

Weaknesses in the civil government did not become evident for several generations. Even when the problems were recognized, more generations elapsed before solutions were formulated and implemented. To keep the civil government separated from the military government, two new clans were created from older clans. These new clans were denoted as gentle or peacemaker clans. Each of the two Grand Divisions (moieties) had one peacemaker clan. A hereditary line of Chiefs was established for both the Sky and Earth Grand Divisions. The Osages were at least two centuries ahead of the British in one concept: Grand Division Chiefs were like the later British Prime Minister and the Cabinet members. Often the British Prime Minister is described as a *peer among equals.* That is, the two Chiefs were equal in theory, but the *Tsi shu* Grand Chief was dominant in practice. This was especially true after contact with Euro-Americans, since the Grand Sky Chief became spokesman for the Little Old Men. The Grand Earth Division Chief was with the Claremore bands and was considered to be no more than a band chief by Euro-Americans.

To forestall any seizure of total power by either or both Grand Chiefs, the Ancient Men carefully outlined the duties and powers of the Chiefs. The twelve rules for the Chiefs were well understood by the people. We will only touch on two of these, but mainly they were provisions to allow the Grand Chiefs to keep the internal peace and to save the lives of captives (internal sovereignty). In no way were the Grand Chiefs given any war powers or power to meddle in external affairs (external sovereignty). Apparently, this was modified slightly after contact with the white man. The Grand *Tsi shu* Chief was given the office of spokesman for the *Ne ke a Shin ka* (Little Ancient Men) much as the Prime Minister speaks for the British Cabinet. Evidently, none of the Euro-American peoples were aware of this until the late–1800s. By this time, the *Ne ke a* were fading away as an effective force in Osage government.

The eleventh rule for the Grand Chiefs involved the hunt, which in Osage minds was almost identical to warfare.[39] It was the obligation of the Grand Chiefs, who shared the responsibilities, to designate the route, the campsites, and departure times to and from the Grand Buffalo Hunts. While traveling, the Chiefs served on alternate days. Once they arrived on the hunting grounds a ceremonially appointed Director of the Hunt took charge. This *chief* served only for the term of the one hunt. No permanent war or hunt *chiefs* were ever permitted in Osage government; the term of office was always limited to one specific engagement.

It seems strange that no early observer associated the so-called *soldiers* to their proper place in the Osage government. The twelfth rule for Chiefs spells out the role of one class of *soldiers*. To aid the Grand Chiefs in the enforcement of their duties, each Chief was empowered to select five assistants called *Ki he ka Ah ke ta* or Chief Protectors. These *Ah ke ta* had to be selected from any of ten clans, but the Chief was not required to select his five Protectors from his own Grand Division. Chief Protectors were always from the following clans: *HUN KA* DIVISION: Black Bear *or* Panther, Little Male Deer, Elk, *Hun ka* Having Wings, and Isolated Earth; *TSI SHU* DIVISION: Men of Mystery, Buffalo Bull, Elder *Tsi shu,* Elder Sun Carriers, and Buffalo Bull Face. The five *Ah ke ta* formed a special council when a Chief died or became incompetent, and it was their duty to select a new Chief based on heredity and qualification.

In the interest of enlightenment we must mention two other types of Protectors or *soldiers*. In warfare or the hunt, the Director of the Attack is called *Wa na she* and his assistants are called *Wa na she Shin ka* or Little Soldier. The other class of Protector was especially important in relations between the Osages and Euro-Americans. This was the *Moh shon Ah ke ta* or Protector of the Land. These *soldiers* had the office of protecting the Osage domain against uninvited intruders. If an intruder harmed any animal in the Osage domain, it was the duty of the *Moh shon Ah ke ta* to kill the intruder. Failure to comprehend this Osage custom cost many Euro-American lives. To the Osages, there was a difference between being invited to hunt and trap and doing it without being invited. Other Indians knew that their heads could rest on stakes if they hunted without permission in territory claimed by the Osage. White men would have killed anyone who slaughtered their livestock and stole their grain, but they could not understand why Osages killed hunters and trappers for doing the same thing. The decapitated head placed on a stake to warn intruders away horrified Europeans, who apparently could not read plain signs. While we have made no actual count, Spanish records report a modest estimate of over a thousand white and Indian hunters and trappers that were slain as intruders in the Osage domain. In the American period almost as many immigrant Cherokees lost their lives for the same reason, and they should have known better.

We would be giving a false picture of the Osages if we did not mention the other side of the coin. If other people, Indian or white, asked for permission to hunt for food, the Osages nearly always gave their permission, and none of them was harmed or mistreated. An outstanding example of this occurred during the Civil War. A centuries old enemy, the Wichita, were starving and asked for Osage permission to hunt in Osage territory. Permission was given to these enemies because their need was great. No Wichita was harmed or insulted until the emergency was over and the Wichita had returned to their own territory. The hostilities then resumed as they had existed prior to the emergency. The Wichitas knew and respected the Osages as the Osage knew and respected the Wichita. Both were people of great honor.

Technological Developments

We have digressed somewhat from comments on the stories to show the function of the *Ah ke ta*. Several of the stories deal with technological developments, among them, the club, knife, and the bow.

Younger Brother, the messenger, went forth five times and brought back a different colored flint each time. He brought back red, blue, yellow-streaked, black, and white flint, but each kind was rejected as unsuitable. On the sixth journey, Younger Brother found the round-handled knife, which was accepted as the ceremonial knife.

Again, Younger Brother was sent forth; this time he was seeking material for a ceremonial club. He brought back the smooth bark hickory, the red oak, and the dark-wood tree (red bud), but none of these was suitable. On his fourth trip, he brought back the willow, which was accepted as the proper material for the ceremonial club.

They took the round-handled knife from its honored resting place. As they did this, they noticed the knife was awe-inspiring and mysterious. So, they decided to make Awe-Inspiring and Mysterious Knife personal names. Now they lifted the knife and cut four strips from the willow, one for each of the four winds. When they finished carving, the long club was shaped like the back of a fish.

This story gives us clues as to its location. It had to be near outcrops of limestone because of the availability of so many colors of flint.[40] The trees also give us clues. The exact location is a problem however, because both the limestone and trees mentioned cover all the regions the Osages inhabited, from Pennsylvania through the Ohio Valley and west to Kansas.

More light is thrown on the knives in another story. The Black Bear clan was custodian of the four symbolic knives. These knives were called *Moh he Se e pa blo ka* (Round Handled Knife); *Moh he Sop pe* (Black Knife); *Moh he Hun ka* (Sacred Knife); and *Moh he Shu tsy* (Red Knife). These knives were originally assigned to the first four divisions. That is, the Water People, the Earth People, the Isolated Earth People, and the *Tsi shu*. After Those Who Were Last to Come merged with the Osage, the knives were reassigned. The first two knives were reserved for the *Hun ka* subdivision. Both the *Wa sha she* subdivision and the *Tsi shu* Grand Division shared the other two knives.

When a warrior used a knife to behead an enemy, the knife he used was considered to be mystically converted to one of the four symbolic knives. Thus, the warrior could count his act as a war honor. In ceremonies, these knives are often alluded to as *Wa pa he* or Pointed Sharp Weapons.

Perhaps one of the most frustrating things about these stories is trying to fix a time and place for the event. Certainly, the arrow stories present this problem. The Black Bear clan gives us the story of a strange people and arrows. When Little Brother came to the fourth far off valley he beheld the seven bends of a great river, wrapped in a cloud of smoke from many fires. Through the smoke he saw seven villages, one for each bend of the river. He cautiously crept closer so he might observe unseen the people of the villages. After noting the tattoo marks on their foreheads and jaws and the closely cut hair of their foreheads, he then slipped away unseen by these strange people.

His manner of approach betrayed his excitement as he reached the outskirts of his village. Noting the excitement of their Younger Brother, the Elder Brothers ran to meet him. Radiant Star (Black Bear) related his news as all the *Hun ka, Tsi shu,* and *Wa sha she* gathered about him.

The *Tsi shu* were not ready for war since they did not have a good supply of weapons. The *Wa sha she* did have a good supply of weapons, especially arrows. With the consent of all, the Little Ones went to war with these strange people (they were probably the Iroquoian Cherokee) and eventually defeated them.

Another isolated fragmentary myth throws more light on this story. The

Elder *Wa sha she* clan of the *Wa sha she* subdivision, conferred upon the *Hun ka* clan of the *Hun ka* subdivision the power and authority to organize war parties. A subclan of the *Hun ka* clan found the foe, when the tribe as a whole began its warlike career. At that time, the Elder *Wa sha she* offered the *Hun ka* the use of their seven mystic arrows with which to *lay low* the foe. These mystic arrows were pointed with the antler tips of seven deer.

The two stories, one from the Black Bear and the other from the *Wa sha she,* stress two different points of view. One stresses the importance of finding the enemy and the other stresses the importance of the arrows. In the Black Bear version, we are told the *Tsi shu* received the arrows, but in the *Wa sha she* version it was the *Hun ka*. This version might have been the *Hun ka* (Black Bear) covering up the fact that they were also unprepared. Each of the twenty-four clans had their own version of the stories they shared, thus, each version presented their clan in the best possible light.

Other Stories and Legends

One must be cautious about the seven bends and seven villages in the arrow story above. In the Osage mind, seven bends of a river symbolized life. That is, each life has seven crises. Thus, the seven bends and seven villages represent that this event was the first crisis in the life of the Osage people. We can be sure it was on a notably large river, that the people wore tattoos on the forehead and jaws, and that they wore short hair at the brow. Possibly, these could have been Iroquoian Cherokee or even Caddos.

It is evident in these—and all the early stories, regardless of which clan related them—that the *Wa sha she* was the mother group. They are always the ultimate source of solutions. It is pure belief, but to us this suggests the *Wa sha she* were Adena people. In later stories the *Tsi shu* become the dominant group, and this seems to indicate they were from one of the later Woodland cultures, possibly Hopewell or Mississippian. Both the *Wa sha she* and *Tsi shu* were more inclined toward peace than the *Hun ka*. This is not to say they did not make war, but that they tended to seek peaceful solutions in preference to warfare. The *Hun ka* always chose warfare as a solution to problems. For this reason, they are thought to be either Sioux or Plano at their roots, although they could have been Iroquoian or Algonquian. Commentary has already been made earlier on the Isolated Earth and *Tsi ha she* people, and there is no need to repeat concepts of their origin again.

A great many sources have given location legends, although disagreement as to their reliability has been raised by Carl Chapman. Because of its bearing on Osage prehistory, this problem is worth investigating. There are two basic sources for the location legends. However, we have some indication that the legend about living at the forks of the Ohio was given before 1754 and, therefore, could not have originated with the French and Indian War. The earliest legend we can document comes from George Sibley, factor and Osage Agent at Fort Osage. A second comes from H. Owen Dorsey of the BAE. The body of literature concerning the original Osage homeland is based primarily on these two sources. A confirming source comes from linguistic studies (discussed later in this chapter). In essence, Chapman makes a good point in suggesting the Osages could have migrated from the southwest.[41] Any discussion of Osage origins must keep this possibility in mind.

We believe Dorsey and the Osage stories and legends are correct, but until strong proof is found, no one can be certain where the old Osage homeland was located. We can theorize that all Siouan people may have come from New Mexico and moved northeastward with the Folsom or Plano cultures. This could account for Chapman's belief that they came from the south or southwest. One fact is very clear from the historic record; the Osages had a decided preference for dissected plateau terrain on a sizable river with a vegetative cover of prairie and woodland. The Austin area of Texas is the only area southwest of the historic Osage homeland to have such terrain. To the south of the Ozark Plateau the country flattens and originally lacked prairies. The northwest also lacks such terrain.

On the other hand, the Chesapeake Piedmont–Blue Ridge area is almost identical to the Missouri Ozarks. Along the Ohio Valley one finds this same terrain. In the Austin area one notes some vegetative parallels, but the many references to the vegetation in well-authenticated stories and legends rule out this area. Pawpaws, red bud, red oak, chestnuts, and many other plants point to the Piedmont and Ohio Valley.

In addition to the historic preference and the stories, the Osage language reveals their prehistoric homeland. The language is rich in woodland, prairie, inland water, and dissected plateau words. Coastal, desert, mountain, and dry land vegetative words are either rare or absent. Inland waters are well represented, for example, *Ne*=river or water; *Tse*=lake; *Moh ne ski Ski ka*=marsh; *Ka he*=creek; and *Ne ta pa*=Pond. In use, these terms are further refined by suffixes such as *Shin ka*. For example, the Arkansas River was called *Ne Shu tsy* (Red River) and the Little Arkansas River was called *Ne Shu tsy Shin ka* (Little Red River). Plant names positively indicate the Ohio Valley, since many plants in the Osage lexicon are not native to the areas north, south, or west of Missouri. When one adds the animal names, the focus becomes even more centered on the Piedmont and Ohio Valley.

2

The Osage Empire

GEOGRAPHIC SETTING

Climates

Climate is often defined as average weather in a given region. Certain special climates are an advantage to any culture because climate affects the food supply and the energy of humans. Fortunately, the Osages were blessed with a variety of climates at the peak of their empire. We are not aware of any other North American Indians whose territory encompassed a greater variety of climates on such a large scale. This does not include the many small isolated climatic areas; this work considers only major climatic regions in our discussion. The Osage domain included three types of continental climates and one subtropical climate. These four climates were: (1) Long Summer Humid Continental; (2) Subhumid Continental; (3) Dry Continental; and (4) Humid Subtropical.[1]

Each climate produced distinctive vegetative zones and thus provided the Osages with a diversified food supply. Vegetation in the Long Summer Humid Continental climate is characterized by vast hardwood forests with a dense undergrowth. Grassy openings (prairies) are scattered throughout the region. Hardwoods such as walnut, hickory, pecan, chestnut, hazelnut, and oak were a source of nuts for the People of the Middle Waters. Berries and papaws grew in the undergrowth and at the edges of prairies. Ox bow lakes, left as remnants of old river courses, supplied lily roots and potatoes. Prairies were especially abundant in deer, elk, and sometimes buffalo. The hills, with their caves, sheltered many bears. When all the various factors involved are taken into consideration, the Humid Continental climates of the world are the most favorable climates for human activity. At the present time in man's history, peoples of these climates control the entire world.

Vegetation of the great Subhumid and Dry Continental climates are usually classified as steppes or grasslands. In the Osage domain, these vegetative areas are called the tall grass region and the short grass region. The Grand Osage Prairies and Flint Hills lie in the tall grass region of the Subhumid Continental climate. Today, these tall grass areas produce outstanding beef cattle, but in the 1700s they produced the best buffalo meat in North America. The big and little bluestem grasses of these areas feed on decomposed limestone soils, which make them exceptionally nutritious.

As the Indian frontier advanced, the great southern buffalo herds were forced westward into the Dry Continental climate or short grass region. Here, the Great Plains lie in the "rain shadow" of the lofty Front Range of the Rocky Mountains. Moisture-greedy westerly winds clutch the available moisture and create a dry condition on the Central Plains. Thus, the vast steppes of Asia are duplicated in North America. Most of the domestic grazing animals of the world originated in the Asian, African, and North American steppes. It was this short grass region that furnished the mainstay of the Osage diet until after 1880 when the last survivor of the southern buffalo herd was killed.

South China lies in a Humid Subtropical climate which supports one of the world's heaviest populations. In the Osage domain, this climate was found along the southern borders in Oklahoma and Arkansas. Such climates produce a profusion of plants useful for food and industry. Today, these climatic areas are characterized by large-scale production of specialized plants. Rice in the Orient and cotton in the American South are typical examples. The Osages made little use of this area other than as a barrier to southern invasion or as a source of plunder from raids. Exotic plants native to the Humid Subtropical climate do not appear in the Osage language. While this is a simple, verifiable observation, it is a strong indication that the Osages did not migrate from the south. This would also suggest only an indirect contact with the Mississippian culture at Spiro, Oklahoma, although the mounds there were located within the Osage domain in historic times.

Another significant observation is the fact that all the main Osage villages were located in the Humid Continental climate. From this core area, as recorded in history, they expanded south and west into other climatic regions. Even after they had added vast areas of other climates to their domain, they continued to live in the Humid Continental climate, although the Claremore bands lived on the extreme southern boundary of that climatic zone. From their bases in the Humid Continental climate, the Osages could control territory in other climatic regions.

We do not want to make any exaggerated claims about the role of climate on human activity, but we must acknowledge some effects of climate.

Anyone who has experienced the surge of vigor on a crisp fall day and the lassitude of a warm spring day is aware that weather affects our energy. The frequent shifts in weather so characteristic of the Humid Continental climate apparently stimulate the peoples of this region. Thus, they tend to be energetic and intellectually active. This, in turn, tends to drive them to excel in whatever they undertake. There is no doubt that the Osages excelled in most of their ventures. Their achievements in creating their empire testify to this fact. Certainly, their diet was varied and abundant. When all five of the elements of the physical environment are considered, the Osages still stand out as an energetic, mentally active people.

Elements of the Physical Environment

Yet, the other elements of the physical environment must also be taken into account. Aside from the number one element of climate, the other elements are: (2) Relative location on the earth; (3) Land forms; (4) Bodies of water; (5) Soils and minerals.[2] These four geographical factors, combined with a favorable climate, placed the Osages in a favorable position to achieve excellence.

Assuming outside social or technological factors do not intrude and, in effect, cancel the geographic factors, a nation may possess all these factors but one and still never rise to the status of a great power because of this missing factor. One of the most critical factors in a nation's rise is its relative location in relation to other nations, the sea, certain land forms, or a multitude of other geographic relationships. The Osage compact core area in west central Missouri was very favorably located for the time preceding 1800. After 1800, with the coming of the Euro-Americans, political, social, and technological changes radically reduced the geographic advantages which had favored the Osages before that time.

In 1907, at a meeting of the American Historical Association, Miss Ellen Churchill Semple set forth some principles of the relation of geography to history. Among other comments, she made the following statement: "The location of a country is the supreme geographical fact in its history. The dispersion of people over a wide, boundless area has a disintegrating tendency, while the opposite result follows concentration within a restricted national base. A people situated between two other peoples generally form an ethnical and cultural link between the two. . . . [Concentration] means opportunity for widening territory and the exercise of a widespread influence, but it also means danger."[3]

Centrally located as they were on the major mid–American rivers (see Fig. 4), the Osages were surrounded by a large number of different peoples.

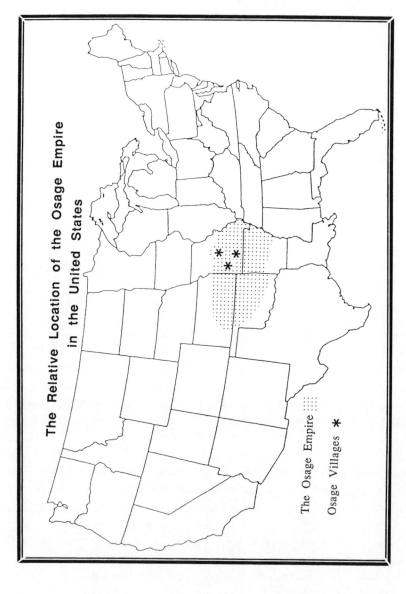

Fig. 4. Notice the central location of the Osage villages.

Thus, they had the means to acquire a wider range of ideas than would be available to a more isolated people. The general cultures of the Northeastern tribes and Southeastern tribes differed from each other. Differences between those to the north of the Osages and those to the south also existed. Indians to the west differed from those of the northeast, southeast, north and south of the Osage homeland. Because of this, the Osages were cosmopolitan in many facets of their culture. Since virtually all the North American Indian cultures were basically continental cultures, this made the midcontinent location of the Osages especially significant.

The location of the Osages at the northwestern edge of the Ozark Uplift was also a great advantage. Uplifted plateaus, such as the Ozarks, are among the most rugged land forms known to man. History records that a handful of Spartans seriously delayed a vast Persian army at the narrow pass of Thermopylæ. In the battle of Saratoga, Benedict Arnold and Daniel Morgan, with only a brigade and one rifle company, defeated General James Burgoyne's army at Freeman's farm during the American Revolution. These are only two examples of how rough terrain can enable a small force to repel a large force. An invading military force is always at a disadvantage in terrain such as the Ozarks. Utilization of the Ozark terrain gave the Osages security from an invading force large enough to inflict severe damage upon them.

On the north boundary of the Osage domain the Missouri River flowed, and, on the east, the Mississippi formed a barrier. To the land-bound Indians, these rivers were formidable barriers. Even those who used the dugout canoes were unable to cross these barriers with enough men to overcome the Osage military force. On the south, the Arkansas River formed a lesser barrier to invasion, but the Ozarks precluded an invasion from the south. Only to the west lay an open invasion route. Even here, a retreat into the Ozarks would have forestalled a fruitful invasion.

The fortress, which was their homeland, provided a secure base for Osage expansion. It is worth noting that this base also lay across three of the four routes to the American West—the two river routes of the Missouri and Arkansas Rivers and the ancient Continental Trail. For over a century and a quarter, the Osages denied the effective use of these routes to Euro-Americans. Only the western portion of the Continental Trail which lay beyond Osage territory was ever used by Euro-Americans to reach the Far West. Historians of the American Frontier rarely take notice of this well-developed, all-land route to the American West that existed centuries before Columbus discovered America.

While the west offered an invasion route, it also offered an expansion route. The northern and eastern nations could not successfully invade the Osage domain, but by the same token, the Osages could not expand into their territory. Lack of buffalo to the south caused the Osages to shun the area except to plunder the less energetic southern nations. To the immediate west, the Caddoean peoples had been firmly established for at least two hundred years. Their culture was very different from the stereotype of the Plains Indians.

On the prairies and plains that lie between the 95th and 100th meridians and between the Canadian River and the Kansas River watershed are many river valleys. In effect, these form a different geographic province from the Great Plains that surround them. It was in these valleys of the Plains that the Caddoean peoples built their stockaded grass lodge villages and tilled their crops. They were not the nomadic, tepee dwelling buffalo hunters so often pictured. They did hunt buffalo and other game, but they were predominantly sedentary farmers.

Therein lies an important distinction between the Siouan Osages and the Caddoean Pawnee, Wichita, and Tonkawa. The Osages cultivated food plants, but they were primarily hunters. Behind the Osages lay centuries of experience in warfare. Among the Caddos, warfare was a matter of "forting-up" until an attack was abandoned; they had little experience in aggressive warfare.

Combined with the Osage expansion from the east was an expansion from the west of Caddoean territory. The horse gave mountain peoples, such as the Comanche, Kiowa, Cheyenne, and Lipan Apache, the mobility they needed to move onto the Plains. Like the Osage, these people were hunters and well experienced in warfare. Therefore, they too expanded at the expense of the Caddoean people.

By 1750, the Osages had driven many of the Caddoean people south of the Red River. The mountain people had slowed Osage expansion at roughly the 100th meridian. At its legally recognized size, the Osage empire included half or more of Missouri, Arkansas, Kansas, and Oklahoma. It was bounded on the east by the Mississippi. The north boundary followed the Missouri River across Missouri and then the northern limits of the Arkansas River watershed. On the south, the Arkansas and Canadian Rivers formed the boundary. East of the 100th meridian was undisputed Osage territory. West of the 100th to the Front Range was disputed territory, as was the area south of the Arkansas and the Canadian.

Soils and minerals were both diverse and plentiful in the Osage domain. The Missouri, Neosho Grand, Verdigris, and Arkansas Valleys contain some of the richest farm soils in America. While the limestone bedrock lies too close to the surface for farming on the Flint Hills, the bluestem grasses of this region more than rival the famed Kentucky bluegrass as a grazing region. It was the presence of this grass that drew the buffalo, who grew sleek and fat on rich bluestem. These in turn, drew the Osages westward from the Ozarks.

Minerals and rocks useful to the Osages were abundant in the finest quality. Flints, cherts, crystalline quartz, jasperoid, sandstone, pipestone, and clays were easily found. Possibly the largest concentration of flint and chert in the world is found in the Ozarks and the Flint Hills. The purest, clearest natural quartz crystals ever seen by man were found in the Osage domain. Missouri grindstones are world famous, as are the novaculite sharpening stones. Black pipestone was found in Neosho County, Kansas. Firing clays of kaolin, volcanic, and other clays are plentiful in the old Osage domain, as the many ceramic industries of today testify.

The largest lead and zinc mining district in the world, as well as large coal seams, lies near the center of the old Osage empire. The productive Mid-Continent Oil Field lies under their lands. At Magnet Cove Arkansas, thirty-two different minerals, including the nation's largest barium mine are found in a fifteen square mile area. Osages had discretionary control of the Murfreesboro, Arkansas, area, where the only diamonds in North America are found.

More useful to the Osages were the many calcite and other gypsum deposits found throughout their domain; with these they could bleach deerskins. Salt was so valuable in Roman times that it was used as money to pay the legions. From this practice we get the word salary, Latin for salt. Many saline springs and the Great Salt Plains gave the Osages a surplus of salt.

Apparently, plants and animals were available to the Osages in a greater variety and profusion than to other Indian people. Roger Ward Babson, a twentieth-century economic statistician, located his *Golden Triangle* near Eureka, Kansas, which was near to the center of Osage civilization, deep within their lands. He claimed everything humans needed for survival was obtainable within this triangle.[4] No wonder they called their domain "the center of the earth." Such great gifts of *Wa kon ta Ke* (The Mysterious Being of the Universe) were not ignored by the Osages. They considered themselves to be caretakers appointed by the Mysterious Being to protect these gifts.

Because of a favorable combination of geographical factors, the Osages became the dominant force in mid–America. This and their institutions made the Osages a force that shaped the history of the American West. For over one hundred years, they blocked the westward expansion of the European powers. As late as 1800, they still had the military power to destroy all European settlements on the Middle Waters. Even after they were overwhelmed by a deluge of Euro-American intruders and migrant Indian nations from the east, they still could divert the tide of western movement to the north and south of their domain. It was no accident that in 1893 the American Frontier ended within the bounds of the old Osage empire.

OSAGE EXPANSION

Introduction

There were three Osage core groups. The northernmost group was the Little Osages who lived between Malta Bend and Glasgow in Missouri. Apparently, the mother group of the remaining Osages were those who had their permanent villages along the Osage River in Missouri. Through most of recorded history, before 1822, this group lived near the junction of the Little Osage and Osage Rivers. Between 1775 and 1796, the third group consisted of random bands of Osages who tended to live on the headwaters of the Pomme de Terre, Niangua, Sac, and White Rivers in Missouri and Arkansas. It was these random bands that formed around Town Maker (Claremore II) in the late–1700s. By 1800, they were known as the People of the Oaks or the Claremore bands. However, they were also called the Arkansas bands. Their villages were located on the lower Neosho-Grand River and the Verdigris in Oklahoma. From these villages, Osage expansion extended southward and westward. Generally, the Arkansas bands pushed southward as far as Natchitoches, Louisiana, and southwestward to Lawton, Oklahoma. The Little Osage and Osage River bands pushed as far west as the Front Range in Colorado and southwestward as far as the Texas Panhandle. This is not to say that they established firm control as far as these extreme areas, but only that their war parties probed as far as these extremes. Spanish records show the Osages sometimes raided as far southwest as Santa Fe.[5]

Osage expansion into the south and west took place between 1700 and 1800 (see Fig. 5). Accounts of Coronado's Expedition in 1541 tell us the Caddoean peoples occupied the area included in Osage expansion. While Euro-American accounts frequently refer to these Caddo as Wichita, Osage oral history accounts, with few exceptions, refer to them as Pawnee. Since the Osage names for geographic features also reflect a Pawnee presence, we will follow the Osage custom.

By 1700, the Osages had made the Kansas part of the Neosho–Grand Valley their own. At about this date, they had reduced the easternmost Pawnee stronghold and were probing the east bank of the Arkansas River near Newkirk, Oklahoma. The Pawnee stronghold at the junction of the

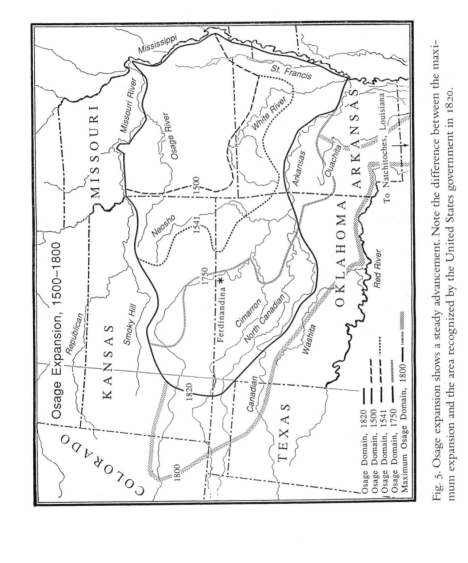

Fig. 5. Osage expansion shows a steady advancement. Note the difference between the maximum expansion and the area recognized by the United States government in 1820.

Fall and Verdigris Rivers (Neodesha, Kansas) had held the Osages back for sometime.

This fort or stronghold was at a strategic point on what was later called the First Buffalo Trail by the Osages. The section between the Vernon County, Missouri, villages and the Pawnee fort was merely a feeder trail to the main Continental Trail. From the Pawnee fort, the First Buffalo Trail followed an alternate Continental Trail to the Arkansas River, crossing near Newkirk, Oklahoma. From this crossing, the First Buffalo Trail went westward to the Salt Plains. However, the alternate Continental Trail followed the Arkansas River upstream to the Wichita villages at the mouth of the Little Arkansas River, where it rejoined the main Continental Trail.

Wars of Expansion

Bluff War

Characteristically, the Osages fought the Caddo peoples in "bluff paint." That is, the upper half of the face was black or red and the lower half yellow. Bluff war, among the Osages, consisted of baiting an enemy to fight; the most common bait was insults. Since the Caddo did not speak Osage, and because conversations were delivered at a long bowshot between the two parties, "finger talk" was used.[6] Oral Osage has no curse words or foul language. However, finger talk could be used to convey extremely vile, insulting concepts.

At first glance, bluff war may seem to be a poor strategy for territorial conquest. But no one who is aware of the Osage knowledge of human character would doubt the effectiveness of bluff war. They were well aware of the Caddo tendency to seek shelter in their palisaded villages at the first sign of an unfriendly war party. Osage boys sometimes amused themselves by pretending to be a war party, just to see the panic they created, but for a real war party, it was not an idle game. Anytime an Osage put black or red (depending on the Grand Division) paint on any part of his face an enemy could easily lose his life or face capture and being sold as a slave to the Southeastern tribes. The latter alternative was often used since the Osages did not believe in taking any form of life needlessly. Osage warriors knew the effects of repressed anger and wounded pride as the result of repeated insults. They also knew that if the pressure became too great, the Pawnee would come out to fight. Such action led to death or capture of the Pawnee. If they were killed, their heads were cut off and placed on stakes as a warning to other Pawnee to leave or die. In time, the harassed Caddo moved away to salvage the remaining shreds of their abused pride, to save their lives, or to escape slavery. Each move made the next move easier to justify.

Through the strategy of bluff war, the Osages gained a large portion of Caddo territory with very little loss of life on either side. Some idea of the Osage feeling in this matter can be gained from the name they gave to Pond Creek in present-day Osage County, Oklahoma. It was called Poor Pawnee Creek because the Osages killed a stray, half-starved Pawnee on this creek. They were so ashamed of themselves for killing the Pawnee needlessly that they always paid honor to him when they passed his grave by placing another stone on the grave. In the Osage mind, this *was* the poor Pawnee's creek.

Ferdinandina

In the area near Newkirk, Oklahoma, a cluster of Pawnee villages stood at the historic crossing (called *Ta Ka ha* [Deer Creek]) of the alternate Continental Indian Trail. The French built a stockaded trading post here in September of 1719 and named it Ferdinandina.[7] This post was a barrier to the Osage advance as long as it existed. The Osages could have destroyed the post, but diplomacy of the time dictated otherwise. Destruction of Ferdinandina would have cut off the supply of trade goods and guns entering the eastern borders of their domain. Not only was Ferdinandina a barrier to their westward expansion but it was also a breech in the Osage blockade of trade goods to the Indian nations of the Plains. So Ferdinandina had to be either eliminated or reduced to a post of no consequence.

With typical Osage "searching with the mind," they conceived a strategy to reduce Ferdinandina without rupturing relations with the French. Since an open assault on the post would disrupt trade with the French, this was to be avoided until a later time. Between the establishment of Ferdinandina in 1719 and its fall in 1757,[8] the Osages concentrated their expansion southward. They crossed the Arkansas River between Arkansas Post and Ferdinandina at many points. River traffic between these two points was severely disrupted and the Caddoean peoples were pushed to the south side of the Red River. By 1749, the Osages had virtually cleared the Caddo out of the area between the Red River and the Arkansas-Canadian Rivers in Oklahoma and western Arkansas. French traders of the Caddo followed them and founded the twin villages of San Bernardo and San Teodoro on the Red River.[9]

Ferdinandina never became a major trading post because its shipments of hides and tallow as well as trade goods were often seized by the Osages. This was an overriding factor in the decision not to reopen Ferdinandina after the Osages took the post in 1757. By this time the post was so unimportant that the French ignored the seizure. This would have been the attitude of the French even if France had not been involved in the French and Indian

War. The French could ill afford to alienate the most powerful military force in mid–America over an insignificant trading post. The Osages were well aware of this when they seized the post. Their strategy had ultimately yielded their objective.

Maximum Expansion

With the capture of Ferdinandina, the Osages again turned their expansion to the west. The Great Salt Plains were firmly in Osage hands by 1760. By 1770–1775, they had a good claim as far west as the 100th meridian and north to the Arkansas–Smoky Hill River divide. They also had dominion as far south as the Canadian River and down the Red River as far as Natchitoches. Most of the Caddoean peoples of the South-Central Plains had been compacted into the area between the Red River and the Gulf of Mexico.

As we have already mentioned, the Osages tried not to take life unnecessarily. During their expansion, many Pawnee were captured. Some of these captives were adopted and became Osage; many more were traded as slaves to the Cherokee and Muskhogean nations in the southeastern United States. The French made no effort to stop this slave trade but in the waning days of Osage expansion, the Spanish caused this trade to cease.[10] Contrary to reports that the Osages had slaves, they did not hold any slaves. Their captives were either adopted or sold and rarely killed, but they did not keep slaves.

At the southwest edge of the Osage domain were the Southern Cheyenne. In the Texas Panhandle, the Comanche barred Osage expansion. To the west were the Kiowa and Apache of the Plains (Lipan Apache). Bluff war was not very effective against any of these people. Like the Osage, they had a long tradition as hunters, and they were experienced in warfare. When the Osages went to war against these people they customarily wore black paint. Both black and red symbolized the merciless fire that consumed all in its path. If an Osage wore black or red paint over the entire head or body, it meant an all-out, no quarter war. One of the Little Osage chiefs had the valor name of Chetopa (*Tsi Tó pa* [Four Lodges]). He led a war party that killed every man, woman, and child in four lodges of Kiowa. Their heads were left in brass buckets as a warning to refrain from hunting in Osage territory or trading with people who brought trade goods south from the Platte River route.

The Kiowa and Apache gave way before this ruthless warfare. They sought shelter in the Wichita Mountains of southwestern Oklahoma. While this was Cheyenne territory, the need of the Kiowa and Apache was great and the Cheyenne needed the extra warriors to hold back the Osages. Thus, the three nations combined to stem the expansion of the Osages into the Southwest.

Although the Osages took insignificant amounts of territory from the Cheyenne or Comanche, they halted the eastward movement of these people. On November 27, 1868, the Osages brought a crushing blow to the Southern Cheyenne. Under the leadership of Tally and Hard Rope, the Osages led George A. Custer and the 7th Cavalry to the camp of Black Kettle. In an unusual act, Custer heeded the advice of his Osage scouts and struck the Cheyenne at dawn. From Custer's description of the Osage face paint we know that the Cheyenne had killed an Osage from the sky division. From movements prior to the engagement we also know they had hunted in Osage territory without permission. The destruction of the Black Kettle band was complete.[11] It was at this battle of the Washita that Custer acquired his reputation as an Indian fighter. Without the Osage scouts, Custer and the 7th Cavalry would not have been alive to fight at the Little Big Horn. There is a story among the Osages that a single Osage scout was with Custer on the Little Big Horn. The story claims that when Custer ignored their advice, the Osage and a Delaware scout pulled their blankets over their heads and slipped away before the Sioux struck.

Place in United States History

Effect on Louisiana Purchase

In a one hundred twenty-five year period, 1678–1803, the Osages performed a feat no other American Indians duplicated. They stopped the westward expansion of the Euro-American peoples and simultaneously tripled the size of their own domain. One may expect that a people of such great capability would have some significant effect on the history of the United States.

It is significant that Cape Girardeau and Ste. Genevieve, Missouri, tasted success before St. Louis. Both were located on branches of the Continental Trail while St. Louis was not. The Continental Trail was the shortest, most direct route to the far west. This trail ran from the Atlantic Seaboard through the Osage domain and on to the Rio Grande settlements and the Pacific. As late as 1825, the Santa Fe Trail skirted the northern and western fringes of the Osage nation so it could follow the Continental Trail on into Santa Fe. Zealous protection of the Osage domain had diverted the flow of trade and westward movement to the north and south of the Osage territory even before the Americans had appeared on the scene. These routes had been restricted in their use by the Osage blockade on the lower Missouri

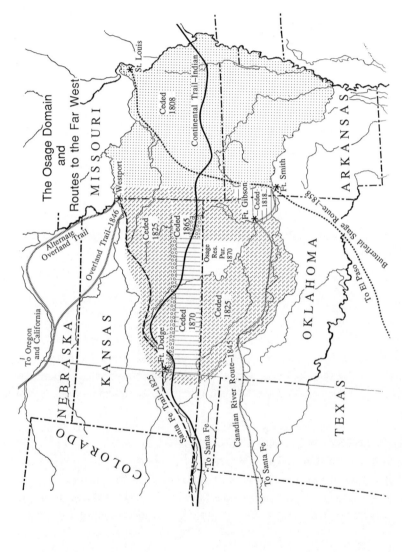

Fig. 6. Note that the trails were used only after the Osages ceded the area.

and Arkansas Rivers. Thus, neither France nor Spain had been able to open overland or river routes to the Pacific. They also did not establish a foothold in the areas west of the Osage empire or within the Osage domain. While other factors may have had some effect on this situation, the Osage effect cannot be denied (see Fig. 6).

One can only speculate on the fate of the United States if either France or Spain had been able to establish a firm control over the Osages. At the very least, the United States would have been confined to the area east of the Mississippi, for either France or Spain would have controlled the Mississippi. Quite possibly, the very existence of the United States would have been doubtful. However, because of the Osage nation, neither France nor Spain became firmly established on the Middle Waters. Hence, the vast reaches of the American West was available to the United States when she was best able to capitalize on it.

Natural Rights Philosophy

Some Americans are not aware of the origins of natural rights philosophy and the role this has had in the creation of the United States. The idea of humans living in harmony with themselves and nature stimulated the philosophers of France and England. From reports of Indian cultures, they conceived a line of thought that was different from any other line of thought in the history of Western civilization. After the passing influence of the American Indian, however, Western philosophy reverted to the traditional trend of Western thought regarding the individual's relationship to the State. Thomas Jefferson summed up the trend of natural rights thought when he wrote, "men are endowed by their creator with certain inalienable rights." Thus, American Indian governmental practices became the base for American government.

In 1725, Bourgmont took a group of Little Osages and their kindred Missourias to Paris, France. We cannot document that Charles de Montesquieu actually visited with these Indians. However, it is inconceivable that he would miss the opportunity to question them since he was in Paris at the time. In 1748 he published *The Spirit of Laws*. Coincidence or not, in this work, he describes some core principles of Osage and Missouria government.[12] Because of their significance to our subject, we include four quotes from *The Spirit of Laws* that touch upon Osage ideas.

> The law of nations is naturally founded on this principle, that different nations ought in time of peace to do one another all the good they can, and in time of war as little injury as possible, without prejudicing their real interests.

Virtue in a republic is a most simple thing: it is a love of the republic; it is a sensation, and not a consequence of acquired knowledge.

These people enjoy great liberty; for as they do not cultivate the earth, they are not fixed: they are wanderers and vagabonds; and if a chief should deprive them of their liberty, they would immediately go and seek it under another, or retire into the woods, and there live with their families. The liberty of the man is so great among these people that it necessarily draws after it that of the citizen.

The division of lands is what principally increases the civil code. Among nations where they have not made this division there are very few civil laws.

The institutions of these people may be called *manners* rather than *laws.*

Among such nations as these the old men, who remember things past, have great authority; they cannot therefore be distinguished by wealth, but by wisdom and valor.

No one has ever made a better summary of the basic Osage governmental principles than Montesquieu. In times of peace, the Osages traded with their neighbors and helped them. In times of war, they tried not to take life unnecessarily. The Osages have a love for each other. This takes the form of caring, and, as Montesquieu states, it is a matter of feeling and not of the intellect. Although it is sometimes called the tribal bond, it is more accurately called love.

Land allotment was opposed by the Osages; they were the last Indians in Oklahoma to allot their lands. Early visitors always mentioned how well-mannered the Osages were. They did not interrupt each other in speech and treated each other with courtesy. In the last paragraph of the last quote, Montesquieu seems to be describing none other than the Society of Little Old Men. Since the existence of this society was not generally known to Euro-Americans until the late–1800s, one wonders where Montesquieu got this information, if not from the Osages.

American frontier historians universally point out that the strongest support for the American Revolution came from the frontier. But how can one account for such widespread support from a generally illiterate people who had little comprehension of governmental principles and scant exposure to natural rights philosophy? The only logical answer lies in their close acquaintance with the American Indian. In fact, more than one Euro-American joined the Indians to escape the restrictive laws of Western civilization and live the freer life of the Indians.

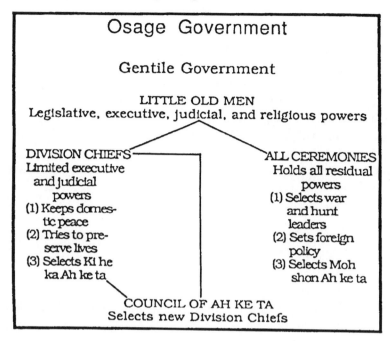

Fig. 7. This first part of Osage government shows the gentile government, which was the only government that applied to all the people.

OSAGE VILLAGES AND CAMPS

In order to fully grasp the importance of Osage villages in the lives of the people, some background about Osage tribal organization is helpful. The gentile organization, physical divisions, and overlapping bands of the Osage were among the most intricate in North America. To a great extent, this complicated organization was a result of the large number of Osage people. This group probably constituted one of the larger nations in North America to function as a single unit.

The most influential group among the Osages was the *Ne ke a Shin ka* or Society of Little Old Men (see Fig. 7). They controlled the gentile organization, the religious ceremonies, and were the living libraries of Osage history. From the position of actual power, the next in importance were the individual band chiefs, who existed outside the gentile system. When one considers prestige and respect as a measure of importance, the Gentile Division Chiefs must be considered more important than the band chiefs. Although physical divisions stood between the gentile organization and the bands, they were separate from both. The physical divisions had probably existed before the people had formed into bands.

Without any doubt, the twenty-four clans and their numerous subclans that made up the gentile system were the oldest units of tribal organization. Likewise, they were the glue that held the Osage people together as one people. It was the blood ties of mutual kinship within each clan and its subdivisions that kept the Osages a united people. The gentile rule against marriages within a clan or its subdivisions linked the twenty-four clans together through marriages. That is, one could not marry within his or her own clan or subclans, nor could one marry within his or her own subdivision without some exceptional reason. There were two Grand Divisions and five subdivisions, so it was easy to follow these rules. In many ways, the gentile organization functioned as a national or central government. Representation in the gentile council (Little Old Men) was acquired by achievement and ability, except that a member's widow took his place when he died. Such women had to be intelligent and capable because none of the Little Old Men would have married her if she had been otherwise. In effect, this council was an unicameral legislature with a considerable amount of executive and judicial powers, especially in external matters (those matters concerning relationships with other nations).

The executive branch of the gentile government was vested in two moiety or division Chiefs. While these Chiefs possessed both executive and judicial powers, they were strictly limited to internal peace-keeping functions. Each Chief selected five *Ah ke ta Ki he ka* (Chief Protectors). When it was necessary to select a new Chief because of death or incompetence, these five *Ah ke ta* formed a Council of *Ah ki tas*. As many as twenty *Moh shon Ah ke ta* or *Moh shon ka shay* (Protectors of the Land) may have existed at any given time. Chief Protectors and Protectors of the Land were the only standing military force permitted. The duty of the Protector of the land was to conserve and protect resources, especially from intruders.[13] In carrying out the function of their office, these soldiers often upset Euro-American plans.

Physical Divisions formed the next layer of organization. No real function for this layer of government has been recorded. Some intermediate role is suggested because of the alignment of the Physical Divisions. It seems that formerly this layer may have acted much as provincial governments. Sometime in the Osage past they were caught in a great sudden flood. In seeking safety, the clans were dispersed. Those who stayed on low hummocks on the flood plain and survived were called Heart Stays People. Some climbed trees to save themselves and were named Tree Sitters. A third group found salvation on the slopes of a nearby hill and were called the

Down Under People. The first two groups and about half of the third group moved away from the others and in time were called Little Bone Osages. Others found safety in a thorny, bushy side valley which caused them to be called the Thorny Bush People. The final group succeeded in climbing to the top of a forested hill. These Osages were called Upland Forest People. The Thorny Bush, Upland Forest, and many of the Down Under People were known collectively as Big Hills. These people were also sometimes called Big Bone Osages. As time passed, the bone was dropped from the Little Bone Osage and Big Bone Osage names.

Since the great flood divided the clans by spreading their members among the various Physical Divisions, a precedence was established for bands to also cross clan lines. At one time after the flood, the Little Osages and the Big Osages apparently had established governing units for each group. Certainly, the Little Osages had a head chief over all the Little Osage bands, as has been mentioned in written history. For all practical purposes, many of the twenty-four clans were represented within each of these two groups. An Osage band usually consisted of members from two or more clans. In some respects the Bear and its kindred Panther clan could be considered as a single-clan band, but in accuracy it was a two-clan band.

Bands were led by a chief who was selected by the people he led. Those who did not choose to follow this chief simply moved to a band led by a chief they wanted to follow. This voting with the feet caused some mobility among the various bands. Careful formal limitation and checks which were exercised with Division Chiefs did not apply to band chiefs. A band chief's power was limited only by the people he led. Since he led only by the consent of the governed, if he abused his power, he had no people to lead. The consent of the people he led could be withdrawn simply by their choice to follow another leader (see Fig. 8).

These band chiefs were the masters of local government. More often than not, the band chiefs were very capable and did an outstanding job of taking care of the people in their bands.[14] What characterizes the Osage government is its outstanding trait of caring for its people. This reciprocal caring between the people and their leaders ties the Osages to each other even today. Osages walking in the world today and working at a chosen profession, trade, or craft may appear to be just ordinary American citizens, but these people know in their hearts that they belong to a people who care about them; the person *is* Osage. This is not a matter of blood quantum, but it is a matter of the heart and conviction; it is the tribal bond. Osages have always throughout time had this caring bond with each other. No Osage has ever walked alone. If one grasps the complexities of the preceding explanations, the importance of communication among the Osage villages will be

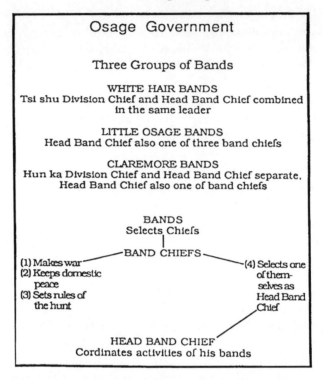

Fig. 8. Part two of Osage government shows the three groups of bands and band government. These governments applied only to the members of a particular band.

appreciated. It is the association with each other that creates the tribal bond. Osage warriors admired the wolf's ability to stay away from his home for long periods of time. This the warriors could not do. They were very attached to their homes and associates.

Types of Communities

There were four basic types of Osage communities. The villages of the Gentile Division Chiefs represent the first type. Originally the Division Chiefs lived in the same village with the *Tsi shu* (Sky) Chief on the north side and the *Hun ka* (Earth) Chief on the south side of an east-west street. Lodges of the Division Chiefs were always in the middle of the villages, and the same was true of the band chiefs. References to the House in the Middle always refer to the dwelling of a Division Chief. Apparently, at some time near 1800, the Division Chiefs started living in separate villages—the Sky Chief lived with the White Hair bands and the Earth Chief lived with the Claremore bands. However, one must be aware that

Town Maker (Claremore II) was a head band chief and was not the Earth Division Chief. Since he was from the Sky Peacemaker clan, he could not be a Grand Earth Division Chief. An Earth Division Chief, by law, had to come from the Ponca Peacemaker clan, and, conversely, a Sky Division Chief had to come from the Sky Peacemaker clan.

Band villages were a second type of community and they varied greatly in size. Both the Division Chief villages and the band villages were as permanent as the fuel, water, game, sanitation, wild food plants, and tillage area allowed. A third type of community was semipermanent because they were used only for the seasonal grand hunts. Under normal conditions, the Osages engaged in three grand hunts each year. The spring and fall grand hunts took place out on the Plains to kill buffalo.[15] In the early winter, a third grand hunt took place for bear, deer, and elk. Groups of hunters entered caves to take bears that were in early hibernation and, thus, still in prime condition. These grand hunts differed from other hunting in that they were highly organized and systematic, involving all able-bodied persons in a group. Individual hunts were not permitted during a grand hunt. That is, hunting outside the organized grand hunt was not allowed. Free or individual hunting was encouraged at other times, however.

In a semipermanent community the framework of the wickiups were left in place and reused on the next hunt. Hide covers were carried from camp to camp. The fourth and last type of community was tepee communities. The Osages rarely used tepees. In most instances, they were used only when the Osages hunted west of the 100th meridian. Here, materials to construct wickiups were hard to find and the portable tepee became a necessity. These tepee communities left little, if any, sign of their passing, except a ring of stones or sod. Locations of any of these tepee communities cannot be pinpointed since their signs did not last longer than a year.

Migration Concept

Before we can discuss the location of Osage village sites we must explain a problem these sites reveal. If we accept the idea that the Chesapeake Piedmont was the Osage homeland and that they entered Missouri from the Ohio Valley, a possible inconsistency must be resolved. According to legends, the Dhegiha and Chewere moved west together. Since the Chewere moved west between the Great Lakes and the Ohio River, this would suggest that the Osages entered Missouri from north of the Ohio Valley. Yet, both historic accounts and village sites tend to suggest a southeastern Missouri entry.

Due to the close relationship between the Dhegiha and Chewere we believe they were once a united people who started west together. A split, possibly at or near the mouth of the Wabash or Illinois River, may have sent the Chewere westward into Iowa while the Dhegiha moved southwestward down the Mississippi to the site of Kaskaskia, Illinois. Although only the Osages have the flood tradition and the other Dhegiha have none, we believe the sudden flood was on the Ohio. That the other Dhegiha groups were located above the flood plain in the Ohio or Kentucky highlands is very probable. It is unlikely that the Osages would have been caught in an ordinary flood situation. The legend states very clearly that the flood was sudden and unexpected.

Although the Ohio is notorious for flooding due to rain storms from the southwest that move upstream, it is certain that the Osages were aware of this and would have taken steps to protect themselves. Two situations in the Ohio Valley could have caught the Osages unprepared. One is the reflux of water due to an earthquake and the other is the breaking of an ice dam. No mention is made of the earth shaking in the myth so the breaking of an ice dam at the forks of the Ohio seems to be a likely cause of a sudden and unexpected flood. While the Missouri River has ice dams, they are not so severe as those on the Ohio.

We know the Little Osages and the Big Osages lived apart from each other after the flood. It is also known that the Little Osages had a closer relationship with the Missouri and Illinois than the Big Osages had with these tribes. Likewise, there was a closer relationship between the Big Osages and the Quapaw than there was between the Little Osages and Quapaw. With this background, it seems reasonable to suggest that the two Osage groups may have entered Missouri at two different points.

In view of the splintering taking place among the Dhegiha and Chewere, it is not unreasonable to suppose the Little Osages elected to live on the north side of the Ohio Valley. Nor would it be out of character for the Big Osages to move along the south side of the valley with the Quapaw. I do not suggest that the Little Osages ever severed their gentile relationships with the Big Osages. From their own legends, the Up River People (Omaha and Ponca) apparently followed about the same route as the Chewere. No obstacle seems to exist to the belief that the Little Osages and the later Kansas splinter could have followed a route slightly south of these people.

As a matter of observation, in most sudden flood situations, fewer people reach the highlands than those who do not. Yet, the historic record shows the Big Osages outnumbering the Little Osages more than two to one. On the surface, this suggests a sizable decimation of the Little Osages because the numbers should at least be equal. Almost without exception, the Osage *Kon za* clan members are Big Osages. Since there are very few Kansas clan members among the Little Osages, it seems apparent that the *Kon za* clan members and their followers splintered off from the Little Osages and reformed as the core of the Kansas nation.

Archaeological evidence reveals that the Little Osage sites on the Missouri River and in Vernon County, Missouri, show a strong relationship to the Orr focus of the Oneota aspect. Yet the Big Osage sites show very little, if any, relationship to the Oneota aspect. This appears to be a clear indication that the Little Osages had experienced a closer contact with the Oneota than had the Big Osages. Thus, there is some justification for suggesting that the Little Osages may have entered Missouri between the mouths of the Des Moines and Missouri Rivers, but the Chain of Rocks crossing near St. Louis should not be ruled out.[16]

It is doubtful that the concept of dual Osage migration routes will resolve the inconsistencies of some villages on the Missouri and others far to the south. However, maybe it will open a new line of investigation. Certainly, it leaves us free to pinpoint the known Osage village and campsites without further consideration of this inconsistency. For organizational reasons the sites will be presented by states, beginning with Missouri.

Villages and Camps in Missouri

H. R. Schoolcraft found three Osage winter hunt camps on Swan Creek in northeastern Taney County, Missouri, which he visited in the winter of 1818. Although they were vacant, he estimated that each camp could have accommodated about one hundred able-bodied males. Another Osage camp was at the junction of Swan Creek and the White River.[17] No positive identification exists of any permanent villages on or near the upper White River. Certainly, such a village site must exist, and possibly more than one. Clearly the Osages extensively used a well-established trail on the left bank of the White River. They frequently used this route to reach Arkansas Post throughout the Spanish period and slightly into the American period. As the trail neared the mouth of the White River on the Mississippi, the Osages would cross the narrow divide between the White River and the Arkansas River, which placed them at the door of Arkansas Post (see Fig. 9).

A possibility has been suggested that as trade developed between the Osages and Euro-Americans, the Osages could have moved outward from the heartland of the Missouri Ozarks.[18] This would seem to produce some sizable old villages between the heads of the Sac–Pomme de Terre–Niangua Rivers and the head of Swan Creek. In the outward movement, one or two bands should have moved lower down on the White River to be nearer to Arkansas Post. Several villages have been found on the Pomme de Terre and Niangua. Yet, every indication suggests these sites predate contact with the white man.

Fig. 9. Note the center cluster of villages with smaller clusters to the north and south.

It seems likely that the Big Osages crossed the Mississippi near Cape St. Anthony, Missouri, and followed the Continental Trail (Virginia Warrior Path) to the Pomme de Terre, Niangua, White River divide. They apparently established villages in this vicinity and northward along the Pomme de Terre, Sac, and Niangua Rivers. The Osages called the Pomme de Terre, Big Bone River, from which the name Big Osage is derived. In this way, they would have had closer contact with the Little Osages, who with the Missourias acted as a barrier between the Sac-Fox and the Big Osages. By the time of Joliet and Marquette's visit in 1673, the bulk of the Big Osages were evidently on the lower Sac, Pomme de Terre, and Niangua Rivers and along the Osage River between the Sac and Niangua Rivers.[19]

From a defensive viewpoint, this movement placed the Big Osages in a position to observe the Sac and Fox yet still have the protection of the Ozarks at their backs. However, some bands of Big Osages were still in southwest Missouri and northwest Arkansas as late as 1775. Among these were the Grosse Côte (Big Hill) and Black Dog bands, which moved to Spring River near Baxter Springs, Kansas, between 1775 and 1777.[20] The Little Osages were guardians of the "northern marches," and the Arkansas bands were the guardians of the "southern marches."

We have verbal assurances that an important Osage village was located in what is called Gladstone Cove on the Lake of the Ozarks.[21] Certainly, the projectile points and scrapers found at this site seem to be Osage. This site is about twelve miles northeast from the mouth of the Niangua River between Laurie and Gravois Mills, Missouri. The village was possibly the northeastern-most Big Osage village. For that reason and because of its location on the best Sac and Fox invasion route, this village would be vitally important to the Osages. Quite probably, the chief of this village would be a major chief.

Although no Osage village site has, to our knowledge, been reported either on or below Rocky Ridge near the mouth of the Pomme de Terre River, there had to be either a village or camp in this area. Albert Koch is credited with finding large prehistoric bones at this site in 1840.[22] A report from an Osage village near this site led him to the discovery. This would be only a few miles below the present Pomme de Terre dam.[23] While over twenty-five sites were found in a survey of the *Pomme de Terre* Valley before the dam was built, only one shows evidence of being Osage.[24] Evidently, traces of the Osage villages had either washed away or were buried in silt. The Osages called the Pomme de Terre River by two names. One was Potato River, which would be pomme de terre in French, and the other was an older name which translates to Big Bone River. It was this latter name that led Albert Koch to his discovery in 1840. It is also the source of the Big (Bone) Osage term that came from the Osage name for the river that flowed past their village.

Three Osage village sites are given by John Swanton.[25] One was near the mouth of the South Grand River.[26] In this vicinity, near Warsaw, Missouri, the South Grand and Pomme de Terre join with the Osage River. As nearly as the name given, Tanwakanwakaghe, can be deciphered, it would be, *To won Kon ka He* (Go to Meet the Victors Town). Go to Meet the Victors is a traditional woman's name, but the clan cannot be identified with any certainty.

The other two villages are at or near the junction of the Sac and Osage Rivers. They might have been the same village, but one is given as being *at* the mouth of the Sac River and the other was located *near* the mouth of the river. Intapupshe or *En Ta pu Pshe* (Teach to Grind Corn with Stone) was given as being above the mouth of the Sac River. Nikhdhitanwan or *Ne ka To (do) he To won* (Good Man Town) was apparently at the mouth of the Sac River. Good Man is a title of earned respect, so it gives no clue as to a clan name. Evidently, the other Sac River village was noted for its corn grinding facility, perhaps because of possible stone outcrops at this site.

Franquelin's map of 1684 shows an Osage village at the mouth of the

Osage River.[27] I believe this would be a Little Osage village. If our concept of dual Osage migration routes has any validity, it would be natural for the Little Osages to arrive at the mouth of the Osage River via what was later called the Sac and Fox War Trail or by following the Mississippi and Missouri to the mouth of the Osage River. The Sac–Fox War Trail ran from the mouth of the Des Moines River near Keokuk, Iowa, to the mouth of the Osage River. The terrain of this site would have better suited the Little Osages than the Big Osages.

Pressure from the Sac and Fox probably forced a move from the exposed mouth of the Osage River. Quite possibly the Sac and Fox were a motive for the Kansas splinter leaving the Osages. Apparently, a large number of Heart Stays Little Osages had established their village among the Missouria in the Bend of the Missouri River.[28] It seems likely that the Osage River Little Osages had included a sizable number of *Kon za* clan members. After the splintering of the Kansas, the remaining Heart Stays, Tree Sitters, and Down Under People of various clans would be forced to relocate because they were not large enough to stand alone against the Sac and Fox. Evidence shows the Little Osages composed of Heart Stays, Tree Sitters, and Down Under People attached themselves to the Big Osages before 1800.[29]

From the names and identifications given in the Spanish records, we know the Little Osages of Van Meter State Park were Heart Stays People, Cahokian, and Kaskaskian.[30] After they moved from Saline County, around 1777, they and about half of the Missourias (80–100) divided into three bands and lived for a time at present-day Jefferson City before they settled on the Neosho in Kansas, which was before 1785.[31] After Fort Osage was opened, one or more bands would live near the fort for a year or two at a time.

The Down Under Little Osages with the Heart Stays and Tree Sitters had also formed into three bands by 1777. These three bands came to be considered as a part of what was called the White Hair bands by 1800. Jesuits at Osage Mission distinguished between the two Little Osage groups by calling three of the bands White Hair Little Osages and the remaining three bands Little Osages.[32]

At the heart of the Osage empire were the Vernon County, Missouri, villages. Apparently, there were at least four Osage villages clustered around the junction of the Marmaton, Little Osage, and Osage Rivers.[33] One of the villages was located on the left side of the Little Osage River opposite the mouth of the Marmaton. This was the site occupied by the White Hair Little Osages, although there may have been one or two others that stood on the flood plain. The known village was a large village covering about thirty acres.

The other three known village sites seem to have been Big Osage sites. One of these was located on the right side of the Marmaton about five miles above its mouth. It was about fifteen acres in extent. Another site was the well-known Halley's Bluff site on the right side of the Osage River and about two miles below the junction of the Osage and Little Osage Rivers. By tradition, this was the village of White Hair I. Approximately three miles south of White Hair's village was another village which covered about thirty acres.[34]

A feature of these villages is that they were all above the flood plain. The same is true of the Saline County Little Osage site. While such locations are to be expected of the Big Osages and possibly the Down Under Little Osages, the Saline County Little Osage (Heart Stays) village represents a departure from custom. Possibly the need to defend against the Sac and Fox overrode the Heart Stays, Little Osage custom of building villages on the first river terrace. This may also explain why only one Little Osage village site, the Van Meter Park site, was found in the Bend of the Missouri, because traces of others were washed away from the terrace. This same situation could explain why only one Little Osage village has been found in Vernon County. There should have been three sizable Little Osage villages in the Vernon County area.

Villages in Kansas

Black Dog's Band

Osage villages were clustered along the Neosho-Grand and Verdigris in Kansas from 1785 to 1870. Another cluster was on the lower Neosho-Grand and Verdigris in the early part of this period, but since these were in Oklahoma they will be discussed later. Semipermanent camps extended as far west as Wichita, Kansas, and tepee camps as far as the Front Range in Colorado. Since the latter camps left no trace, we cannot give their locations.

As near as can be determined, the three Little Osage bands and the Big Osage Black Dog Band settled in Kansas about the same time. It is likely that the Black Dog band under the leadership of Black Dog's father located near Baxter Springs, Kansas, as early as 1775 but no later than 1795. The Black Dog Museum places the completion of the Black Dog Trail between Baxter Springs and the Salt Plains as being in 1803. Eighteen hundred would be a more accurate date. Black Dog I was between 67 and 70 years old when he died in 1848. This would place his birth between 1778 and 1781. He was sixteen years old when he became band chief, which would place the date between 1794 and 1797. Since his father moved to Baxter Springs at least two years before his death, this would place the location in Kansas at 1792 or 1795. Allowing for adjustments in the Gregorian calendar, the date could not have been later than 1794. This is not an unreasonable date since the Little Osages were on the Neosho by 1785.[35]

Black Dog's village at Baxter Springs was well located. By following Spring River to its headwaters, a link-up with both the Continental Trail and the north-south Osage Trace could be made. This trace connected the White Hair bands with the Claremore bands and continued southward to the Red River and Natchitoches. The trace later became famous as the Sedalia–Baxter Springs Cattle Trail (sometimes called the Shawnee Trail). This Osage Trace was the south half of the military road connecting Ft. Leavenworth with Ft. Gibson and Ft. Smith. The trace continuation south from Ft. Smith was part of the Butterfield stage route. All permanent Osage villages were on the Arkansas River drainage system after 1825 and remain so today.

Intruders

After 1808, an increasing number of Euro-Americans came into contact with the Osages in Missouri. The strain of trying to shun these contacts and, thus, avoid open warfare, greatly affected the Osages. The Osages considered Euro-Americans to be rude in manners and offensive in odor. In all fairness it should be said that the intruders were, in many respects, outcasts of their own culture and were not noted for cleanliness or manners. Greed for land and personal possessions was not a new experience for the Osages, but they had never seen it practiced on such a large scale before 1810. The Euro-Americans' seeming lack of respect for each other in speech and action shocked the Osage sense of order and caring for each other. American frontier settlers have been described as "keeping the Sabbath and everything else they could get their hands on." Being unfamiliar with the "claims game," the Osages, until 1865, filed no claims for the theft of such Osage property as game, furs, hides, livestock, and the plundering of their burials. Yet, innumerable exaggerated claims were filed against the Osages, and most of these unfounded claims were paid by treaty provisions. Only rigid restraint by the Little Old Men and the band chiefs prevented an all-out war against the intruders.

Under this turmoil and suppression of anger, many individuals and bands, after 1808, began a movement from Missouri. Some moved to Kansas between 1808 and 1820, but many more joined the Claremore bands in Oklahoma in this period. Very few of the White Hair bands remained in Vernon County, Missouri, after White Hair I died. Between 1820 and 1825 a massive migration from Vernon County to Neosho County, Kansas, took place. In the fall of 1822 (and before the Treaty of 1825), White Hair II led what was left of his Vernon County bands out on the Plains to hunt buffalo. They never again returned to Missouri to live but instead built new villages on the Neosho-Grand.

The abrasion of intruders upon the Osages caused them to accept a buffer zone between themselves and the intruding settlers. The Treaty of 1825 provided a strip twenty-five miles wide east/west and fifty miles long north/south between the Osage villages and the west boundary of Missouri. This strip was called the Osage Neutral Lands until it was given to the Cherokees, and then it was called the Cherokee Neutral Lands. The buffer zone experiment was possibly the first and only time the idea was tried in Euro-American and Indian relationships. It never worked because intruders settled on the Neutral Lands illegally, and the United States made no effort to enforce the treaty agreement.

White Hair III

White Hair III divided his time between those of his people in Vernon County and those on the Neosho. We have ample evidence to show that the bulk of White Hair's people had left Vernon County by 1822, although White Hair himself moved in that year. W. W. Graves quotes from the Harmony Mission Journal for September 5, 1822[36]: "The most of White Hair's people have gone on their fall hunt. It is understood that they do not intend to return to their late residence but to establish themselves sixty or seventy miles from this station." On September 26, 1822 the Union Mission Journal reported, "Mr. August P. Chouteau with a party of Indians from White Hair's village called here. A boat of his had arrived at the mouth of Grand River [Neosho-Grand] with goods to trade with the Indians. He intends to form an establishment on this river above this place and states that White Hair's people have left their town with the intention of moving to this river."[37] Then on October 17, 1822, the Union Mission Journal stated, "Last evening arrived a company of White Hair's Indians. This is the first visit from that part of the nation. It appears that they are in an unsettled state and have not selected a place for their new home."[38]

Black Dog II

Over four-hundred members of the Black Dog band were the first Big Osages to settle on the drainage of the Neosho-Grand in Kansas. In the fall of 1803, the Black Dog band joined with the Claremore bands and left Kansas.[39] However, they returned to Kansas in 1826 and stayed in Kansas until all the Osages left in 1870.

Although his second Kansas village was about five miles below the Village of the Pipe, south of Oswego, Black Dog I died while visiting at his old Big Cedar village in present-day Claremore, Oklahoma. Leadership of his band was disputed after his death. Black Dog II was slow to assert his right to the chieftainship, and the result was that his band was split into two factions. One faction followed Black Dog II, and the other followed Wolf, a Cherokee member of the band. After his father's death, Black Dog II moved his village to Pumpkin Creek on the Verdigris. Wolf led his part of the Black Dog band to live with the Cherokees. But, in order to draw Osage annuities, which the government refused to pay his band as long as they lived with the Cherokee, Wolf returned to Kansas and settled on the Verdigris.

Little Osages–Little Bear

On the Neosho-Grand, the Little Osages and the White Hair bands built villages from Owl Creek on the north to below Labette Creek on the south. The Little Osage villages at the north limits of the reservation were probably the oldest of these villages. Little Bear's Little Osages settled near the mouth of Owl Creek in Allen County, Kansas, in about 1823. Earlier the Little Osages had lived near the Burlington Crossing in Coffey County, Kansas, having settled there prior to 1785. After the Treaty of 1825, Little Bear had to move south from Owl Creek because it was in the Sac and Fox reservation.

Little Bear was head chief of the three Little Osage bands during the 1820s and until his death in 1868. The other two bands were led by Nishu-mani or *Ne shu Moie* (Traveling Rain) and Numpevale or *No pa Walla* (Thunder Fear). Little Bear was a member of the *Hun ka* (Earth) Night People clan, while Traveling Rain and Thunder Fear were from the *Tsi ha she* (Those Who Were Last to Come) Men of Mystery clan. Around 1828, Little Bear's village was located where Chanute, Kansas, now stands. At this same time, Traveling Rain and Thunder Fear had their villages about five miles downstream from Chanute near the mouth of Big Creek.[40]

As more and more intruders settled illegally in the Osage nation, Little Bear led the Little Osages to the area around Thayer, Kansas.[41] These were the last Little Osage villages in Neosho County and on the Neosho-Grand watershed. By 1865, they had relocated their villages in Wilson County, Kansas, west of Thayer. These villages were on the north fork of Chetopa Creek, which is in the Verdigris drainage system. After the Treaty of 1865 (Canville Treaty), Little Bear again moved his people, and two of the bands settled near the mouth of Chetopa Creek on the Verdigris. Chetopa, who had replaced one of the other band chiefs, settled in the north vee between the Verdigris and Chetopa Creek. The other band settled in the south vee opposite the Chetopa band. Little Bear built his last village near the old Pawnee Fort at the junction of Fall River and the Verdigris. This village was very close to present-day Neodesha in Wilson County, Kansas. These were the last homes the Little Osages had in Kansas.

For the sake of accuracy, we want to mention that, although his descendants use the Little Bear name as a surname, Little Bear is a convenience interpretation. Little Bear would be *Wa Shin ka* in Osage, but this is usually given as *Wa Sop py Shin ka* (Little Black Bear). The Jesuits rarely used the Little Bear convenience. They spelled his name in such ways as Mintson Shinka, Mitsoshinka, Miciao-shinka, and Micio-Shinca. These spellings translate as *Me tso Shin ka* or Little Grizzly Bear, which was his correct name as a member of the Night People clan.

White Hair Chiefs

A great deal of confusion exists about the White Hair line of succession. While tracing the White Hair line of *Tsi shu* chiefs is not too difficult, tracing the descent of *Hun ka* chiefs is difficult. In May of 1794, the Spanish gave White Hair I a small medal and called him a counselor.[42] Since *Gra Moie* or Arrow Going Home (Claremore I) died late in 1794 or early in 1795, he was alive when this happened. Yet the Spanish records note that White Hair I had replaced Town Maker (Claremore II) in 1796.[43] This clearly establishes Claremore I's death as sometime between May of 1794 and 1796. It is also clear that White Hair I was established as Grand *Tsi shu* Chief by 1796. Pike's date of 1800 is an estimate, while the Spanish records were on-site observations and should take precedence over Pike's date. Pike's account is the one most commonly used, however. The six-year difference in dates has led to incorrect conclusions as to why White Hair I was chosen over Claremore II, which will be dealt with later.

We also have some indication that White Hair I was the son of the Grand *Tsi shu* Chief who preceded Claremore I. This same source gives the unlikely information that White Hair I was uncle to Claremore I.[44] This relationship would have to be in European kinship terms. An Osage uncle was the mother's brother; the father's brother was called father, not uncle. If White Hair I was Claremore I's Osage uncle, he would have been from some clan other than the *Tsi shu* Peacemaker clan and could not have been a Grand *Tsi shu* Chief. Since White Hair I was clearly younger than Claremore I, plainly he was not likely to be brother to Claremore I's father. It is probable that White Hair I was uncle to Claremore II (in European terms) and brother to Claremore I. The difference between Osage kinship terms and European kinship terms could easily confuse Euro-American recorders.

Conflicting stories about the White Hair name is also evident. Francis La Flesche gives White Hair as a personal name that refers to the sacred white buffalo.[45] Another story relates that White Hair I led an Osage war party to aid the Illinois Indians in the battle against General Arthur St. Clair. This battle was fought on the Wabash River, November 4, 1791, and it was the worst defeat the Americans ever suffered at the hands of Indians. More than nine hundred Americans were killed and wounded. White Hair I, in trying to take a scalp, ended up with a "scratch" (white wigs worn by the soldiers of the time). He often wore the "scratch" and took the valor name of White Hair. We believe both stories are true because it suited White Hair's purposes to take a valor name that was also a traditional name. Incidentally, White Hair I's original, traditional name was *Gra to Moh se* (Iron Hawk).

White Hair I's oldest daughter, Pahushan, married Noel Mogray (Mongrain) who was half Osage and half French.[46] Jean Baptiste Mogray, an older son of this marriage, became a major chief in the White Hair bands. White Hair I died in 1808 and was buried near his village in Missouri. At this time, George White Hair could not have been more than four or five years old since his burial record gives his age as about forty-eight years in January of 1852. A footnote in *Tixier's Travels on the Osage Prairies* casts some light on the question of White Hair descent.[47] As the editor points out, Pike's report indicates White Hair I had a grown son in 1806. This grown son became White Hair II, but he was such a bad chief that the Council of *Ah ki ta* replaced him with White Hair III, who was George White Hair's father. Houck claims White Hair I died in 1808. Bradbury in his *Travels* states White Hair was six years old in 1811. Lastly, De Mun's Journal claims White Hair was a grown man in 1816. To add our own comment, it is difficult to reconcile Iron Hawk (White Hair IV) as cousin to George White Hair without an adult White Hair between White Hair I and George White Hair. Thus, the White Hair descent would run from White Hair I to White Hair II to White Hair III to George White Hair IV and then to Iron Hawk. As subsequent events indicate, this was the likely line of succession. It seems that it was White Hair III who led the Vernon County, Missouri, bands to the Neosho River in 1822.

George White Hair became White Hair IV in 1833 upon the death of his father White Hair III and moved his village downstream from where his father had located. This move also indicates that George's father was indeed White Hair III. It is possible that Fr. Bax erred in estimating George White Hair's death age as forty-eight years in 1852 and that Bradberry could have underestimated George White Hair's age as six in 1811. However, a two or three year difference is not a serious error in estimating age; it is near enough to be almost conclusive. It seems quite clear that George White Hair was fourth in the line. It is likely that White Hair III was also called George Whitehair.

George died without a son of his own blood although he had an adopted son who was a minor when George died. White Hair III, George, had two brothers, although neither was immediately acceptable as Chief. These brothers were *Tcio cio anca* or *Tsi shu Wa ti an ka* (Saucy *Tsi shu*) and Little White Hair.[48] Saucy *Tsi shu* was chief of Elktown (at the junction of the Elk and Verdigris Rivers) but he was passed over by the Council of *Ah ke tas,* possibly because he was allied with the Claremore bands or, as Fitzgerald states, "because he was wild and mischievous." Little White Hair was, in 1852, chief of Littletown (Oswego, Kansas; however, he was later chief of the Village of the Pipe) but since he was in poor health, he was passed over.

George White Hair's cousin, Gratamantze or *Gra to Moh se* (Iron Hawk) was selected as the fifth White Hair Chief.[49] It should be explained that "cousin," as used here, is a European term. The Osages had no cousin term; in Osage relationships, Iron Hawk was brother to George White Hair. That is, he was the son of George's father's brother. Iron Hawk died of scurvy on March 12, 1861, at the age of 48.

Little White Hair replaced Iron Hawk as Grand *Tsi shu* Chief and thus became the sixth White Hair Chief. He was also the last hereditary White Hair Chief. Upon his death on December 24, 1869, Isaac Gibson, the Osage Agent, appointed *Wa tse Ki he ka* (Star Chief) as Governor of all the Osages and, thus, brought an end to the ages-old practice of selecting Division Chiefs. Star Chief is better known by such names as Joe *Pawnee No Pa she* (Not Afraid of the Pawnee), Governor Joe, and Big Hill Joe. Star Chief was the last hereditary Grand *Hun ka* Chief.

Grand Hun ka Chiefs

As near as we can trace the descent of the Grand *Hun ka* Chiefs, it appears to be as we have outlined in the following paragraphs. Jean Lafon was mentioned in Spanish records in 1786 and again in 1794 when he was killed returning from New Orleans.[50] While his French name was sometimes translated as The Fool, we think a more accurate interpretation would be The Farther End. This in turn easily translates to *Ko she Se gra* or Tracks Far Away. The Spanish mention that Claremore I and Lafon were the two main chiefs. Since Tracks Far Away is a Ponca Peacemaker name and Claremore I was the Grand *Tsi shu* Chief, apparently Jean Lafon was the Grand *Hun ka* Chief.

Both Claremore I and Jean Lafon were opposed to the presentation of a small medal to Grande Piste (Big Track). Big Track's name was also Tracks Far Away and he was apparently son to Jean Lafon. His father would definitely be opposed to his son leading the Big Hills to the Arkansas and any medal that recognized his leadership of the splinter bands. Yet, after the death of Jean Lafon, clearly Cashesegra (the Spanish spelling) did become Grand *Hun ka* Chief and thus placed the Grand Division Chiefs in different villages, the very thing his father had tried to prevent.

It appears that Tracks Far Away II was probably followed by another of the same name who was commonly called Mad Buffalo (the Cherokee called him Skiatook). The U.S. government imprisoned him, and as a consequence another Grand *Hun ka* Chief was chosen. *Pawnee No Pa she I* (Not Afraid of the Pawnee is a valor name; his real name was Star Chief) was the fourth *Hun ka* chief, starting with Jean Lafon. On Joseph *Pawnee No Pa she*'s (Star Chief II) baptism record this was also the name given for his father, and his mother's name was given as *Waco Ki he ka* (Woman Chief).[51] We cannot determine if *Pawnee No Pa she I* was the son of Tracks Far Away II or Mad Buffalo. However, since Joe *Pawnee No Pa she* was eleven years old when he was baptized on November 1, 1848, his father would have been a very young adult when Tracks Far Away II died, so it would seem that he would be Mad Buffalo's son. It would seem Joe's father was fifth in the historic line of Grand *Hun ka* Chiefs and Joe himself would have been the sixth.

We must mention one other background. From about 1850 to 1897, a sizable band of Quapaw lived near the Osages. The bulk of these lived in a village between the mouths of Labette and Cherry Creeks. All the rest lived in Beaver's Town.[52] In the 1850s, some Quapaws lived on the Canadian River of Oklahoma. The remainder lived in the Neutral Lands or with the Osages. During the Osage allotment process in 1906, a few Quapaw were given lands in the southeast corner of the Osage reservation. Others were forced to their own reservation in Ottawa County, Oklahoma, by the United States government. This action was a prelude to forcing the Osages to allot their lands in 1897. However, Osage resistance to these efforts by the United States government delayed the allotment of their lands until 1906–1907.

White Hair Villages

Records are often confusing in their references to White Hair villages along the Neosho-Grand in Kansas (see Fig. 10). While there might have been other reasons for the confusion, two factors were reasons enough to cause a great deal of confusion. First, one must bear in mind that villages were abandoned and new ones built because of changing conditions, such as sanitation and the need for firewood. Second, there were four different White Hair Chiefs that served between 1822 and 1869. We will try to locate and date the various White Hair Villages in this time span.

White Hair II established his village on the Neosho-Grand in 1822.

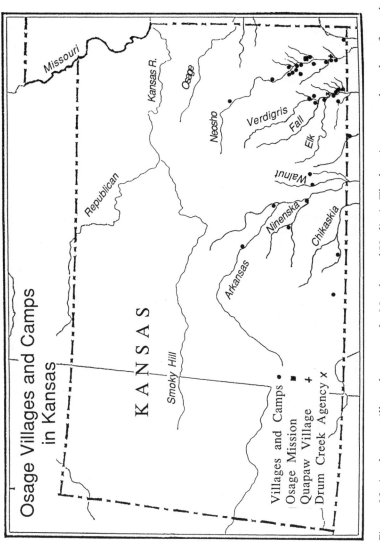

Fig. 10. Notice the two village clusters on the Neosho and Verdigris. The hunting camps show three favored hunting areas.

W. W. Graves locates this first White Hair Village as being in Section 16, Township 28, Range 19, or across the Neosho west of Shaw, Kansas. Since White Hair II died here in 1833, this was White Hair's Town from 1822 to 1833. George White Hair was third in the line. Graves positions his town in Section 2, Township 29, Range 19 or across the Neosho opposite Boudinot Mission, which was near the mouth of Four Mile Creek.[53] This would be on the right side of the Neosho on Ogeese Creek about six miles down river from the first White Hair Village. The first village site was established about 1822 and the second site existed by 1830 when Boudinot mission was built. This second site was George White Hair's Village of residence until his death; he was buried January 24, 1852, at about 48 years of age.[54] The village was inhabited until 1865, but it was White Hair's place of residence only between 1833 and 1852. Fr. Ponziglione describes George White Hair's house as a double cabin near a large saw and grist mill.[55] The Osages burned the house and mill probably because of their dislike for these symbols of Euro-American life. Fr. Ponziglione says they were burned because they did not pay their expenses. Articles 2, 4, and 10 of the Treaty of 1825 provided for the construction and operation of White Hair's cabin and mill.

This White Hair village had several names. It has been called Nion–Chou Town or Neosho Town. Another name which is sometimes used in early accounts is Manrinhabotso or *Mo he Ah Gra* (Reaches the Sky). This name refers to the wind reaching the sky and it is a traditional name of the Isolated Earth clan.[56] White Hair I's grandson, Jean Baptiste Mogray (Mongrain), was chief of this village, but because George White Hair resided there it was also known as White Hair's Town. The village was the center of the United States government's activities. In addition, it had a trading post owned by the Chouteau's Western Division of the American Fur Company.[57] Melicour Papin was the agent for his Chouteau cousins. In later years this post was moved to the Heart Stays village (Little Town), which was sometimes called Papin's Town because the trading post was relocated there.

The selection of Iron Hawk shifted the White Hair chieftainship to another village. This village was often called Little Town and it stood very near the present site of Oswego, Kansas. We identify this as Iron Hawk's town because of baptism records and a description by A. T. Andreas.[58] Confusion arises because the Jesuits used two Little Town names. However, they sometimes distinguished between the two by calling one the Little Town Below and the other Little Town. The Jesuits often called the Oswego village, Nantze Waspe or *No tse Wa spe* (literally Quiet Heart, freely translated as Heart Stays). John Mathews established a trading post near this village. Since this village was also called Papin's Town, it is possible that Mathews bought the post from the Chouteau owners. White Hair IV (Iron Hawk) was a White Hair Little Osage and became Grand *Tsi shu* Chief early in 1853. Thus, Little Town was White Hair's Village from 1853 to March 12, 1861, when Iron Hawk died.

Little White Hair became Grand *Tsi shu* Chief upon the death of Iron Hawk. His Osage name was given by Fr. Ponziglione as Owassoppe or *Wa Sop pe* (Black Bear).[59] At first glance, this may seem to be a name of the Bear or Night people clans, but in fact, it was a traditional name of the *Tsi shu* Peacemaker clan. Tixier wrote in 1839–1840 that the chief of Naniompa or *No ne O pa* (Pipe) was Old White Hair, uncle of the present chief.[60] Yet, Fitzgerald states that Little White Hair was chief of Little Town and brother to George White Hair.[61] There appear to be two conflicts in these sources, one of relationship and one of villages. "The present chief" in 1839–1840 was George White Hair and the uncle term had to be an error of misunderstood relationship. A similar mix-up existed between the two brothers, Gra Moie (Claremore I) and his only brother White Hair I. The only way "old White Hair" could have the White Hair name and be uncle to George White Hair was to be a brother of Claremore I and White Hair I. There is no record of such a brother; even if a third brother did exist, he would have been some years older than the life expectancy of an Osage male, which in 1839 was about fifty years. Claremore I and White Hair I had no known brothers, but their oldest sister married White Plume, the well-known Kansas (Kaw) Chief. Another sister married an Osage, but nothing more is known of this sister or her descendants.

While Fitzgerald is apparently correct in calling Little White Hair a brother of George White Hair, Tixier seems to be correct in placing him as chief of the Village of the Pipe. We believe Fitzgerald was referring to the Little Town Below, which was also the Village of the Pipe. It is possible that before this time (1839–1840) Little White Hair was chief of Little Town (Little Town does not refer to the size of the town but to the fact that it was a Little Osage village). Another possibility was the nearness of the Village of the Pipe to Little Town. The Village of the Pipe was only five miles downstream from Little Town; this is why the Jesuits called it the Little Town Below. The Quapaw village was across the Neosho on the left bank and the Village of the Pipe was on the right bank. Five and one-half miles downstream from the Village of the Pipe, and also on the right bank, was the village of Black Dog I. White Hair V occupied the Village of the Pipe until 1865. He then moved to the Verdigris in Montgomery County, Kansas, where he died in 1869. Thus, from 1861 to 1865 the Village of the Pipe was White Hair's Town.

The pipe material found at this village needs discussion at this point. To call the pipes made of this material a calumet pipe is an abuse of Osage custom. All Osage calumet (peace and friendship) pipes were made of catlinite, which is red. The red of the sunrise was the symbol of life. *Sop pe* or dark is often interpreted as black, but it means any dark shade or color. This black or dark pipe material is symbolic of war, death, night, and the unknown. Thus, pipes made of this dark pipestone had a different use than as a calumet, although pipes of this material may be given as a gesture of friendship to a bereaved friend.

There were many Osage villages visited by the Jesuits, as shown in the Osage Mission Records.[62] Most of these were called by the chief's name at the time of the entry into the records and any given village possibly had two or more chiefs between 1847 and 1865. Thus, it may appear that more villages existed than is justified by the actual number of Osage villages on the Neosho-Grand in Kansas. Since locating these villages accurately is virtually impossible, the locations given are only approximate and errors are very probable.

We know from the Jesuit records that Owl's Village was located on Big Creek, probably near the mouth. This village was composed of White Hair Little Osages. It seemingly went out of existence around 1850. However, Owl could have died and been replaced by *Wa she Pe she* (Bad Temper) of the Winds clan. This chief was also called Bad Bird. Owl (*Wa po ka*) was spelled Woipoka and Oipoka by the Jesuits.

Two villages were located close to the Mission (today's St. Paul, Kansas). These were Little Town Over the River which was also called Little August (Ogeese Capitaine) Village and Over the River. This town was three miles southwest of the Mission and across the Neosho (west side). The second nearby village was Briar's Town. This village was probably on Flat Rock Creek two or three miles northeast of the mission. Briar's Town had many names: Tzewha-changi, Beaver's Town, Mill's Town, Inshapiungri, Cucici-nica's band, and Wochaka Ougrin.

Claremore Villages

Black Dog I's village has already been given as being five and one-half miles downstream from the Village of the Pipe and on the same side of the Neosho. It would seem that confusion about Belle Oiseau or Pretty Bird is rivaled only by the White Hair confusion.[63] Tixier mentions this village as belonging to Belle Oiseau or Shinkawassa. Pretty Bird is *Wa shin Log ny* in the Osage language. *Wa shin* and sometimes *Wa Shin ka* mean bird; *Log ny* means good, handsome, or pretty. There is no way one can make "pretty" out of *Shin ka Was sa*. Yet, this is close enough to *Shin ka Wa sa* (Dark Eagle) so as to be a certainty. There is little doubt that Tixier, like many before and after him, confused Pretty Bird (Belle Oiseau in French) with Black Dog, whose traditional name was Dark Eagle. This name belongs to the Mottled Eagle clan. Anyone who speaks Osage could easily verify these names. Tally and Pretty Bird often represented Black Dog because they were his best friends. Tixier undoubtedly met Pretty Bird and mistook him for Black Dog. From his description it is evident that he never met the seven-foot-tall Black Dog.

Between 1865 and 1870, all the Osage villages were on the Verdigris in Kansas. The Agency was relocated near the mouth of Drum Creek about four miles downstream from Independence, Kansas. Two miles southwest of the Agency was Governor Joe's Village. About seven miles downstream, between the Verdigris and Big Hill Creek was Tally's Town (Black Dog's band). Two miles south on Claymore Creek stood Claremore's Village. Wolf's Village (also a Black Dog band) was two miles south of Claremore's Village, on Pumpkin Creek. Black Dog's Town was on the west side of Onion Creek, near its mouth, until Tally moved it to Big Hill Creek.

Claremore's Town was called Townmaker's Town, Grema's Town, and Gemond's Town. To the Osages, the town was Pasuga or *Pa shon O gre* (Those who Came to the Bend of the River), which the Jesuits spelled as Passu Ougrin. This was the name of their old village west of Claremore, Oklahoma, next to Claremore's Mound.

Tally's Town was also called Sanze Ougrin or *Son tsa O gre* (Those who Came to the Upland Forest). Most of Claremore's bands were Upland Forest Big Hills while the White Hair Big Hills were Thorny Bush People. Black Dog's Town (Tally's Town) was also called Passoni Tanwha by the Jesuits, which translates to Pasona Town (*Ho tse Tun ka* or Big Cedar). Pasona was Black Dog I's old Village at present-day Claremore, Oklahoma.

Hunting Camps in Kansas

As one would expect, there were many Osage buffalo hunting camps in Kansas. It should be kept in mind that there were more en route camps than actual hunting camps, that is, camps spaced a day's journey apart between the Vernon County, Missouri, Neosho-Grand and Verdigris villages and the hunting grounds. When traveling to and from the buffalo hunts, it was customary to erect a camp on both sides of major stream crossings. The Osages almost universally ended a day's travel on a stream and on the side that was in the direction of travel. Thus, a sudden flood in the night did not delay their next day's travel.

In identifying these buffalo hunting camps, we were forced to realize that time was an important factor. Most of the Kansas camps were being used by the Osages by 1750. The Oklahoma camps could not have been used very extensively until after 1757, which was the year Ferdinandina fell into Osage hands. Most of the Kansas camps were used heavily until 1860. The slavery controversy in Kansas interrupted their full use until 1865, but the intruder problem still hampered a complete use of the camps. Removal and the disappearance of the southern herd eventually halted Osage buffalo hunts in Kansas.

A favored buffalo hunt camping area of the Little Bear and Nopawalla bands of Little Osages was along the Little Arkansas from its mouth northward and west on the Arkansas. A major camp was near the Indian Cultural Center at Wichita, Kansas.[64] The Osages had driven the Wichitas from this area between 1720 and 1750. During the Civil War the Osages gave the Wichita permission to stay here because they had asked for permission to wait out the war here. Their need was great and they were an honorable people so the Osages gave their consent.

Two Black Dog sites were at Oxford and Bluff City, Kansas.[65] The Oxford hunting camp was below the Ninnescah mouth and the other camp was on Bluff Creek at Bluff City. After 1803, the Oxford camp was used by the Little Osages. This was a very desirable site since it was at an excellent crossing on the Arkansas. Buffalo were plentiful in the area because of lush, rich grass. In addition, they were attracted by the Salt Plains to the southwest.

George Sibley visited two Osage buffalo camps in Kansas while on a tour during August of 1811.[66] He reported a Little Osage camp below the forks of the Ninnescah in Sedgwick County, Kansas. Another camp, which was used by the Big Osages, was near Caldwell, Kansas, on Bluff Creek. This camp was probably used by White Hair's Big Osages, because Sibley places the Claremore bands in an Oklahoma camp on the same tour in which he mentions this camp being used by the Big Osages.

Several other Osage camps have been recorded. Without a doubt there were Osage hunting camps in Barber County, Kansas.[67] Another reported camp was about thirty miles west of Wichita.[68] This would place the hunting camp on Smoots Creek on the upper Ninnescah in Evan township of Kingman County, Kansas. En route camps were located on Grouse Creek about two miles north of Dexter, Kansas.[69] This seems to be true in view of the known en route camps given in the same source as being on Timber Creek in present-day Winfield, Kansas. About fifteen or sixteen miles, the distance between Dexter and Winfield, would be an easy day's travel for a Grand Hunting Party, which usually made fifteen to twenty miles a day through the Osage Prairies and up to thirty miles a day on the Plains.

Quite probably the last Osage buffalo hunting camp in Kansas was about eighteen miles southeast of Medicine Lodge, Kansas. Specifically, this was

Section 36, Township 34, Range 10, of Barber County, Kansas. On or about August 7, 1874 a band of Osages led by Big Wild Cat were camped near Cedar Springs. There were twenty-nine men, women, and children in the hunting party. A group of Indian haters from Medicine Lodge fell on this band, killing four Osages and looting the camp.[70] The Osages had reserved the right to hunt in this area in the Removal Act of 1870 and had every right under United States law to hunt in this area. The Governor of Kansas protected the murderers by mustering them into the militia and back-dating their papers. Evidently, the men had found times hard and needed an excuse to draw militia pay. It is ironic that Big Wild Cat was one of the scouts who made George A. Custer's campaign against Black Kettle a success (Battle of the Washita, 1868). It was in the Washita campaign that Custer became known as an Indian fighter.

This incident and the subsequent lack of justice was a major cause of Osage discontent. Discontent, which had almost reached the point of retaliation upon Medicine Lodge, led to placing the Osages under martial law. This is the only time they were subjected to this indignity. Ultimately, as an outgrowth of the Crime at Medicine Lodge, all Indians in Oklahoma and Indian Territories were confined to their reservations to control the growing discontent on the reservations. It was against this background that the northern Cheyenne "jumped" their Oklahoma reservation and subjected Kansas to its last Indian war in 1875. The Medicine Lodge Indian haters brought upon themselves and Kansas the "Indian Scare of 1875" by their attack on peaceable Osage hunters.

Villages in Oklahoma

On the surface, it appears there were fewer villages of the Claremore bands than there were of the White Hair bands. Nearly all the Claremore bands were Big Osages but the White Hair bands included at least four Little Osage villages. Clearly the Claremore bands had a majority of the Big Osages. The apparent difference in the number of villages is not a good measure of the number of people involved because the villages varied in population. From the debatable population figures available, it seems evident that each of the three largest Claremore villages were larger than any single White Hair village. By weighing the available information, it would be reasonable to state that the size of the Claremore bands were about equal to or slightly larger than the White Hair bands.

All the known Osage villages in Oklahoma prior to 1870 were located either on the Verdigris or the Neosho-Grand. In all but one or two exceptions, the villages were between the two rivers, although they might have been closer to one than the other. Black Dog's band was somewhat of a "wild card." That is, he joined the Claremore bands in 1803 and left them in 1826 to settle twelve or thirteen miles downstream from Oswego, Kansas. Thus, for a period of about seven years, 1826–1833, Black Dog was not attached to either the Claremore bands or the White Hair bands. Black Dog's independence indicates the probability that the Black Dog band would have formed a fourth Osage group if the Euro-Americans had not appeared on the scene. It was not that Black Dog felt a need to form an independent group, but it was a natural drift toward independent status.

Black Dog rarely caught the attention of visitors because he tried to avoid them. However, his good friends Tally and Pretty Bird frequently represented him. For this reason, Euro-Americans often mistook Tally's office to be chief counselor to Claremore. In fact, Black Dog was chief counselor to Claremore and Talley was chief counselor to Black Dog. While Black Dog II was away during the slavery controversy, Tally acted as head chief of the two Black Dog bands.[71]

The earliest known Osage village in Oklahoma was at the Three Forks (the junction of Neosho-Grand, Verdigris, and Arkansas) (see Fig. 11). This was Tracks Far Away's (misinterpreted as Big Track) village, which was between the Neosho-Grand and the Verdigris, opposite what was later Fort Gibson.[72] The misinterpretation, Big Track, is the best known and most widely used interpretation of Cashesegra. The phonics are so good, it is difficult to understand how the name could be so badly misinterpreted. Cashesegra is clearly Ka she Se gra which unmistakably translates to Tracks Far Away. Equally clear, in the name alone, is that it refers to the genesis myth of discovering the first buffalo.

This story relates that Little Brother traveled many valleys and discovered the tracks of "big foot" (an Osage name for the buffalo). He hurried back to the village to relate his news. The Elder Brothers could see from the grass stains on his legs that he had traveled far and his manner showed he had exciting news. When Little Brother told of finding these tracks far away, the people decided to adopt Tracks Far Away as a personal name in honor of the event. Thus, Tracks Far Away became a personal name of the Ponca Peacemaker clan. Possibly the Osage appellation of "Big Foot," for buffalo tracks, led to the interpretation of Big Track.

The significance of the role played by Tracks Far Away was lost because of the misinterpretation. Tracks Far Away was the Grand *Hun ka* Chief, which means that under Osage law he stood equal to Claremore I (Arrow Going Home) and his successor White Hair I (Iron Hawk). It has been claimed that Tracks Far Away usurped the authority of young Town Maker (Claremore II). This could not be true, since Tracks Far Away was the Grand *Hun ka* Chief who stood above any band chief. There were severe restric-

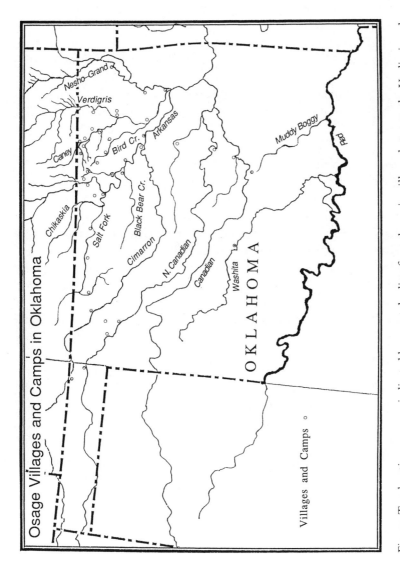

Fig. 11. Two hunting areas are indicated by camps leading from the main villages between the Verdigris and Grand Rivers.

tions on this supreme Grand *Hun ka* office, which precluded interference with a band chief. Town Maker was a band chief with only the restriction of the consent of his band on his actions. There can be no doubt that Tracks Far Away had a considerable amount of influence on Town Maker, since he was Town Maker's uncle. In Osage relationships, the only uncles were the mother's brothers; the oldest of these was *the* uncle. *The* uncle was responsible for his nephew's education and training. Therefore, Tracks Far Away did exert a considerable amount of influence over young Town Maker. Euro-American observers, however, recorded what they thought they saw and did not consider the complexities of Osage life.

The best-known Osage village in Oklahoma was Claremore's Village. This was near the Verdigris, between Claremore's Mound and the river. It was twenty-eight miles west of Union Mission and had a population of three thousand living in about three hundred lodges (at about 1820).[73] Around this main village were several smaller villages. The Osages called this village Pasona or Those Who Came to the Bend of the River. They also called their later village in Kansas by the same name. Town Maker (Claremore II) died here in 1828. Claremore III (Town Maker II) son of Claremore II moved Pasona to Kansas in about 1833.

Another well-known Osage village in Oklahoma was the Grosse Côte or Big Hill Town.[74] This village was located on the Verdigris in present-day Nowata County, Oklahoma. It was probably about eight miles east of Nowata, Oklahoma, on the right side of the Verdigris. The chief of this village in 1822 was Sing ah Moineh which seems to be *Moh en ka Shin ka* (Little Clay).[75] This name is a reference to the mythological crayfish that gave the Osages the four sacred colors of clay. The crayfish was the Little Earth Maker and the elk was the Big Earth Maker. Little Clay and Little Earth are names of the Elk and Crawfish clans.

As was explained above, Black Dog avoided greeting visitors. His village was not as well known as Claremore's Village or even the Big Hill Village. Yet, it was a sizable village and had some features that illustrate the greatness of Black Dog I. This village was at the site of the present Woodlawn Cemetery in Claremore, Oklahoma.[76] Both this village and the later two Kansas villages were all called Pasuga or Big Cedar. Black Dog had three great engineering feats among his achievements: (1) constructing the Black Dog Trail, the first improved road in Kansas and Oklahoma; (2) constructing a well-planned racecourse at Claremore; (3) constructing a concealed cave at Claremore which could hold a year's supply of food and all of the almost five hundred people in his band.

It was this cave that spared the Black Dog band from the cruel calamity that fell upon the Claremore band at Pasona. In the fall of 1817, a force composed of Cherokees, Delawares, Choctaws, Chickasaws, Koasati, Tonkawa, Comanche, and white men, which totaled nearly six hundred men—three times larger than the total of old men, sick persons, and young children in the village—struck Claremore's village. They judiciously selected a time when all the able-bodied adults were away on the Plains hunting buffalo. With only the old, ill, and very young to oppose them, it is not surprising that this "brave" force was able to slaughter or capture most of the Osages in the Claremore band in this atrocity that is often presented as the "Battle of Claremore's Mound."

Seeing the smoke and hearing the sounds of this "battle," the Black Dog people hid in the cave. When the victorious force sought to slaughter the residents of Pasuga, they found no prey. Although they looted and burned the village in their rampage, not one life was lost nor were any children taken. Black Dog's foresight had saved his people; thus, they were available to feed and aid the few survivors of Pasona. When the Osages retaliated for this assault on their helpless ones, the United States government supported the Cherokee because they viewed them as "civilized" and the Osages as wild, trouble-making buffalo Indians.

Black Dog's achievements were not limited to engineering. Among the various Osage bands, none emerged from the severe epidemics as well as Black Dog's people. He did not know what caused the people to sicken, nor did he know how to cure the stricken. However, he did know that isolation on the High Plains lessened the strength of the epidemic. At the first sign of an outbreak, Black Dog led his people out onto the Plains. Medieval Europeans could not conceive of a better way to cope with this problem, and they had a great deal more experience with it. Black Dog died while visiting his old village site at Claremore on March 24, 1848, twenty-two years after he had moved back to Kansas. He was buried in the cave he had engineered so many years before. With both Claremore and Black Dog among the Arkansas bands, these bands had two of the strongest leaders that existed among the Osages.

Aside from Black Dog's village there were also two small church-related villages. There were two branch missions called Hopefield in Oklahoma and one in Kansas. These missions did not exist in the same time span. Hopefield number one was on the west side of the Neosho-Grand about five miles upstream from Union Mission. An Osage village headed by Monepasha or *Moh ne Pa she* (Not Afraid of the Gopher) was at this site.[77] (The Osages, generally, greatly feared the pocket gopher because they believed it was capable of great harm. The root words, *Moh* and *Ne ka* or earth man, possibly have some connection with this belief. However, this appears to be a valor name instead of a traditional name.) This band was not among the original

Claremore bands. They came from the White Hair bands when Hopefield number one was founded in 1823.

A second Hopefield mission was established on the Neosho–Grand. Along with the establishment of this branch mission came a small band of full-bloods and mixed-bloods. This village was also on the west side of the river near Cabin Creek about four miles upstream from the Chouteau-Revoir (Revard) post on the Saline.[78] Apparently, these were also White Hair people and some mixed-bloods who lived with them. Given time, it is possible that these Osages would have become farmers. The three Hopefield Missions were the most successful farming missions ever established among the Osages.

Camps in Oklahoma

As in Kansas, the Osage buffalo camps in Oklahoma far exceeded the number of villages. We do not pretend that the camps described below are in any way a complete catalog of camps. However, the campsites given do allow some idea of the length and breadth of the Osage buffalo hunting range. They also indicate, to some extent, routes to these hunting grounds.

One of the southern camps was located in Pontotoc County, Oklahoma.[79] This camp was in the northeast corner of the county on the south side of the Canadian River. It was located about fifteen miles south and slightly west of Holdenville, Oklahoma. A monument at Mates Springs west of Allen, Oklahoma, on Highway 12 marks the site. This camp was used by both the Claremore bands and Black Dog in the 1830s.

Another camp was reported in 1819.[80] This was an en route camp located across the Arkansas opposite Sand Springs, which is in the Tulsa, Oklahoma, area. It is a point of interest that near this same site Fort Arbuckle was established, to cover the heavily used Osage buffalo trails that passed along the north and east side of the Arkansas in this area. From this point, it followed the Arkansas to the mouth of the Cimarron. Lt. Wilkinson, while returning from an exploration of the Osage hunting areas in Kansas in 1806, found Tracks Far Away (Big Track) in a camp between Tulsa and the mouth of the Verdigris.[81] This en route camp was on the same trail.

In August of 1811, Major Sibley made a tour of the Osage hunting grounds and visited a hunting camp of the Arkansas bands near Medford, Oklahoma, on the Salt Fork.[82] He traveled from this camp, some thirty miles west of the Salt Plains, to Salt Rock on the Cimarron in Woodward County, Oklahoma, with a party of Osage hunters. From this account, it is evident that Osage buffalo hunters often ranged great distances from their hunting camps.

Albert Pike in 1832 reported finding the Claremore bands hunting on

the Washita in what is probably Grady County, Oklahoma, which was probably as far southwest as the Osages established hunting camps.[83] There were
reportedly about thirty lodges in the camp, which would indicate a party
of more than five hundred people. This area was very close to Cheyenne
territory, if not actually in their country. However, a party of this size would
have little cause for alarm despite their nearness to the Cheyenne. It was
unlikely that the Cheyenne would attack a party this large but, certainly,
the hunters would need to be alert.

We have personal knowledge of three Black Dog en route camps. At one
site, the Joe Boulanger site, Black Dog's marks are still on a large rock. The
hearts and horse pictographs were used to denote campsites on the Black
Dog trail (second Osage buffalo trail). This site is on the Caney River,
southwest of the old Joe Boulanger home and across the river from the old
Paul Herard home.

Another Black Dog campsite is one-half mile south of Elgin, Kansas, in
Osage County, Oklahoma, on the Caney River. This is the famous *Gra to
Me Shin ka* (Little Hawk Woman) site. The ancient elm trees which once
sheltered Black Dog's people are still standing. For many years, it was a favored picnic spot. We boys often swam in the Bass Hole, which was a deep
pool below the Black Dog Crossing.

A final en route camp in this general area was located on Pond Creek in
Osage County, Oklahoma. This Pond Creek was called Poor Pawnee Creek
by the old Osages, not the Pond Creek west of Ponca City, Oklahoma. Black
Dog's camp was a half mile upstream from the Pond Creek bridge on Highway 99. This site was later, after 1870, the location of Strike Axe's Little
Osage Village. It was also the site of the ration station for his band. We have
not located the Osage villages in Oklahoma after 1870 because they came
so late in time.

TRAILS

Many trails used by the Osages were ancient before the Osages used them.
Without a doubt, Indian feet walked upon them before the time of Christ.
A few may have even been used over three thousand years ago. Of course,
the Osages opened new trails as the need arose. One feature stands out in
the network of Osage trails—there were more east-west trails in use at any
given time than there were trails that ran north and south. That is, at any
given point in time, more east-west routes were being used than north-
south routes. This pattern in the network of transportation still prevails in
the United States today. One can only conclude there was a greater east-
west movement than north and south movement.

We do not wish to over theorize, but in view of this prevailing movement of Indian peoples east and west, as their trails bear witness, there is a well-established pattern. Frontier historians stress the westward movement of the Euro-American people. Geographers note the east-west dominance in transportation, and geopoliticians note the westward orientation of the American nation. Since each offers theories for this phenomenon, there can be no harm in suggesting another. This pattern was not created on this continent by Euro-Americans. Euro-Americans merely followed the pattern already established by Indians. The American Indians had created it long before Europeans appeared in America. Such patterns across continents are created by continental cultures. Coastal cultures, such as those of Europe, are characterized by inland routes from the seas and waterways. Typically these are short routes that favor no particular direction. This is the pattern that was followed in the early settlement of the Atlantic Tidewater region.

These Osage trails show another pattern that Euro-Americans often overlook or misunderstand. In our research, we have frequently encountered statements to the effect that Osage trails followed the highlands. Facts do not support such statements, which are obviously assumptions based on Euro-American backgrounds. Euro-American trails generally followed the highlands because they used wheeled vehicles. In this way, they could avoid the torture of crossing innumerable small streams. Possibly, the defensive advantage of holding to the high ground was also a consideration. Euro-Americans reckon distances from hill to hill or ridge to ridge partly as an outgrowth of this practice.

The pattern of Osage trails shows conclusively that, generally, they follow the stream courses. Furthermore, the left side of a stream is more often followed than the right side. Osage myths support this practice of following streams by invariably giving distances as so many valleys traveled. Since Osage trails ran along north, south, east, and even west flowing streams, the left bank preference does not seem to be a physiological factor since in many cases the two sides match physically. Botanical factors must be ruled out for the same reason. Therefore, the cause for this preference must be a cultural factor.

We can find no ceremonial factor that would justify a left bank preference. However, one custom may have some bearing on the preference. In peace, the lodges were faced to the east with the peace division to the left and the war division to the right. In war, these positions were reversed. This reversal took place in both war against humans and hunting since both activities took lives. West was the direction of death; east was the direction of life. Likewise, the left was the side of life and the right the side of death. Symbolically, a war or hunting party always left the village going west, even if they were ultimately going east or some other direction. Thus, in symbolism, they were always on the left bank when they traveled to the hunt or war and still on the left bank when they returned since they were at peace and the directions were reversed back to normal or peace again. We doubt, though, that this is the reason for the left bank preference. It is more likely that the pattern was established by a much earlier people and the Osages merely followed the practice by habit.

The network of Osage trails also shows an interconnecting system of trails that tied the various villages to each other. Feeder trails also joined to the major trails and connected various points within the empire. These connecting and feeder trails enabled the Osages to keep in close touch with each other and to rapidly reach anywhere in their empire in a surprisingly short time. The Osages knew their trails very well, but any invading force would find them to be death traps.

In general, the trails were wide enough for several persons to travel side by side. However, in narrow valleys they tended to be single file paths. The Black Dog Trail was a minimum of eight horsemen side by side in width. All brush, trees, and large stones were cleared to this minimum width. Ford approaches were ramped downstream on both sides. This was indeed a well-engineered and well-constructed road. Years later, wheeled vehicles and even cars could travel over it.

These Osage trails were not always single routes. That is, any single trail often had many alternate trails. These alternate or branch trails were used for a variety of reasons such as defensive measures, floods, and the search for a particular plant food or drug en route. Wild fires and wood supply also affected the alternate routes selected. Even the seasons affected the choice of routes, for plants of different uses came at different times of the year. If scouts suspected enemy ahead, ambushes could be avoided by taking an alternate route. These branches tended to go in the same general direction as the main trail and ultimately rejoined it. The trails clung to the river courses and valley as long as the terrain and destination permitted. When a trail ascended to a highland, it descended as soon as possible into another valley. Highlands left the people exposed to the elements and the eyes of a possible enemy. In the valleys, they had the stream at their back and trees for shelter. Most Osage villages and camps were located near stream mouths or in bends of a river so they only had one side to defend, the stream forming a barrier on the other sides.

Far out on the Plains, these same practices were followed. There are streams on the Plains and most of these furnished both wood and water as well as shelter from other men and the elements. Strict rules were enforced to prevent unnecessary exposure on the great swells of the Plains. Guards were posted on high points overlooking the scene of the hunt. This was to forestall a surprise attack by an enemy and to protect the hunters. Rules of the hunt forbad any hunter to pursue a buffalo out of the sight of these guards. Any hunter who broke these rules was whipped with a whip. These whips were later used as quirts or horse whips. While the pursuit of a buffalo was permitted in a free hunt, it was not permitted in an organized hunt. Only in the absence of the women was free hunting permitted, since the men's first duty was to protect the camp. Their second duty was to "make meat." Only after these duties were met, could recreational hunting take place.

We will follow the same pattern with the Osage trails that we followed with the villages. That is, we will start with Missouri and then go to Kansas and lastly Oklahoma. Arkansas will be discussed in connection with the other states.

Osage Trails in Missouri

The so-called Virginia Warrior's Path is what we choose to call the Continental Trail. This trail started on the Atlantic Seaboard in Virginia. It followed the Potomac River to the Potomac Gap where it crossed over to the Monongahela River, which it followed to the Forks of the Ohio. Braddock followed this route only to meet defeat at the hands of the French and Indians at Duquesne (Forks of the Ohio). This trail then followed the Ohio, primarily on the Kentucky side, to the Mississippi.

Although the point of entry into Missouri is debatable, the most likely point is Cape St. Anthony or possibly Gray's Point. In any event, the trail did seek the highlands for about seventy-five miles and then followed headwater valleys across southern Missouri until it arrived between the headwaters of streams feeding the Osage and White Rivers. It then left Missouri about due west of Carthage. We will continue this trail across Kansas later. It is very probable that the Big Osages, and possibly both the Big and Little Osages, entered Missouri by this route (see Fig. 12).

A Sac and Fox War Trail, as it was called later, led from the mouth of the Des Moines River almost straight south to the mouth of the Gasconade River on the Missouri. There it joined with an Osage trail, which forked at the mouth of the Osage River. Another branch of the trail followed the Missouri to its mouth and had a branch that led to St. Louis. One of the forks at the mouth of the Osage River followed the Missouri to the Little Osage Village in the Bend of the Missouri and continued on to Kansas City (at the mouth of the Kaw/Kansas River). The other fork at the mouth of the Osage River followed that stream to the Big Osage villages on its upper reaches.

Fig. 12. Compare the length of east-west trails with the length of north-south trails.

A very unusual highland trail started at the mouth of the Niangua River and went eastward to St. Genevieve. We say it is unusual because it primarily followed the highlands. Osages customarily followed the streams, but special circumstances may have caused an overland route to be followed or the route was adopted from an earlier people. It is even possible that this route was developed by Euro-American traders. At the Meramac River, a branch of this trail went northeasterly to St. Louis. Apparently, there was a trail that skirted the west bank of the Mississippi between the mouth of the Missouri and New Madrid. This trail may have continued on southward.

Without any doubt, trails followed the Niangua, Pomme de Terre, and Sac Rivers to connect the Osage River with the Continental Trail. These trails united at the headwaters of the White River. From there a trail followed the White River to its nearest point to the Arkansas River where it crossed the divide and was at the door of Arkansas Post. The trail then continued southward to the Saline River and Red River at Natchitoches, Louisiana. We have scant indication that the Osages used this approach to Natchitoches to any extent. For the main part, they approached Natchitoches from the northwest.

Two Osage trails led southward from the Missouri River and met on the South Grand River near Clinton, Missouri. One of these starts near the mouth of the Lamine River and follows this stream to the Grand (south of the Missouri River). The other branch started at Fort Osage on the Missouri and followed the Grand southward. From the junction of these branch trails, the trail crossed to the Osage River and then to the Vernon County, Missouri, villages. This trail continued southward via the Marmaton and Spring River to a point east of Neosho, Missouri. Continuing southward into Arkansas, it followed the Illinois River south to the mouth of the Canadian River on the Arkansas River. We will come back to this trail later.

Before we leave these Missouri trails we would like to mention that on our map (Fig. 12), we took the liberty of placing the trail skirting the Missouri River on the south side instead of on the north side. This was done as a convenience to avoid crossings. As a matter of accuracy, the trail for the most part clung to the north or left bank. Sufficient data was not available to date these trails. Also, these trails are not absolutely accurate—that is, they only show approximations and should be used only with this understanding.

Osage Trails in Kansas

In Missouri the Continental Trail west of Carthage, Missouri, was left in the map on the headwaters of the Spring River as it entered Kansas. The trail crossed Cherokee County, Kansas, and entered Labette County about four miles south of Oswego, Kansas. It followed Labette and Spring Creeks northwesterly across Labette County. The trail crossed the extreme northeast corner of Montgomery County, Kansas, and entered Wilson County at the southeast corner. After passing about one-half mile north of Neodesha, it followed Fall River for a few miles then went straight west to Elk County. From here, it followed the Elk River and its North Fork across Elk County and left the county in its northwest corner. It followed the Hickory Creek branch of the Little Walnut and Four Mile Creek of the Walnut River across Butler County, Kansas.

In Sedgwick County, it passed north of Wichita to the Quivera (Wichita) villages. From this point it followed the Arkansas to Gray County, Kansas. It left the Arkansas in Gray County and caught the Cimarron near Cimarron, Kansas. From here, the Santa Fe Trail followed the Continental Trail into Santa Fe and the Rio Grande settlements of the Desert Cultures. The later California Trail, as laid out by Lieutenant Randolph B. Marcy, probably followed the Continental Trail on out to the Pacific. Coronado seems to have followed Marcy's Canadian River route into Oklahoma then turned northward into Kansas.

There were five Osage entry points into Kansas from Missouri. The first was at Kansas City (Kaw's mouth), next was the Marais des Cygnes–Osage River, third was the Little Osage River, fourth was the Marmaton River, and lastly Spring River.

The latter was the Continental Trail (fifth entry), but it had a branch at Neodesha which went southwest instead of northwest. This section was an alternate Continental Trail which led to the Pawnee villages at Ferdinandina (near Newkirk, Oklahoma). The alternate route branched at Grouse Creek in Cowley County and went to the Pawnee villages on the Walnut near Arkansas City. It then followed the Walnut River north to Timber Creek (Winfield, Kansas) where it turned west and crossed the Arkansas at the mouth of the Ninnescah. Here the two rejoined and followed an alternate trail that paralleled the Arkansas from Ferdinandina to Wichita. These sections with a part linking Osage Mission and Neodesha made up the First Buffalo Trail of the Osages. The Osages used this trail at an early date from their Vernon County, Missouri, villages and it served as a war trail as well as a buffalo trail. They followed the Marmaton to Bourbon County, Kansas, and the Neosho to the Osage Mission Area (this route was the fourth entry point) (see Fig. 13).

The third entry followed the Little Osage River into Kansas. It crossed to the Neosho and followed that river northwesterly to Council Grove in Morris County, Kansas. At the Burlington, Kansas, crossing this trail crossed the second entry trail. The second entry trail followed the Marais des Cygnes–Osage River into Kansas and crossed to the Burlington Crossing. From there it went southwesterly to Wichita.

At the Kaw's mouth (Kansas City), the trail from the Little Osage village on the Missouri followed the Kaw (Kansas) and Wakarusa Rivers southwesterly to Council Grove. Perhaps more significantly, a north-south trail ran from the Kaw's mouth (first entry) to Fort Scott and on south along the Neosho-Grand to Three Forks on the Arkansas. This later became the basis for the Military Supply Road between Fort Leavenworth and Fort Scott. Eventually, the Military Road was extended to Fort Gibson at Three Forks and Fort Smith downstream on the Arkansas.

Before we leave Kansas and go to the Osage trails in Oklahoma, we must trace the Black Dog Trail. Like the Continental Trail (fifth entry), this trail

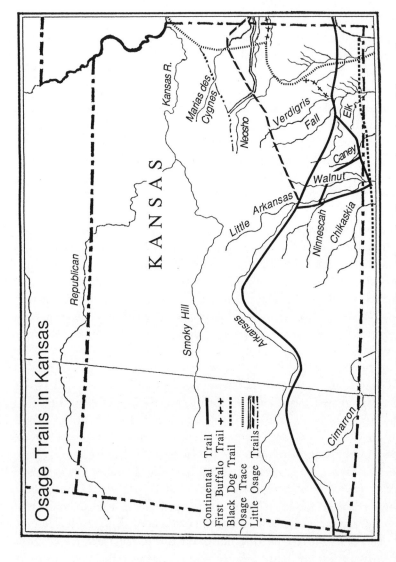

Fig. 13. Notice the branches in the Continental Trail and how the Osages used portions of these trails as hunting trails.

led from Spring River. It started east of Baxter Springs, Kansas, and roughly followed the 37th parallel (Kansas-Oklahoma state line) to the extreme southeast corner of Chautauqua County, Kansas. Here it dipped southward to the Caney River and followed it to Elgin, Kansas, where it followed Buck Creek. It continued west by following the west fork of Buck Creek and then crossed over the divide to the headwaters of Elm Creek. At the junction of Elm Creek and Salt Creek, the trail turned due west to the Arkansas River, which it crossed at Ferdinandina. Here the trail branched, with the north fork going up the Arkansas to the Ninnescah. The other fork continued west to the Salt Fork, which it followed to the Salt Plains.

An alternate route was to follow the Caney River to Ozrow Falls near Cedar Vale, Kansas, and then to follow the alternate Continental Trail either to the Ninnescah or Ferdinandina crossings of the Arkansas. To the Osages, the Black Dog Trail was also known as the Second Buffalo Trail.

Osage Trails in Oklahoma

General Trails

There were two significant north-south Osage trails in Oklahoma. One entered Oklahoma from two points of the Kansas border. The other followed the Illinois River into Oklahoma from Arkansas. By following the Neosho-Grand and Spring River into Oklahoma, the Osages could follow the Neosho-Grand to Three Forks. This trail then followed the Arkansas to Sand Springs, Oklahoma, and then turned south and a little west to the mouth of Little River on the Canadian. From here, it continued south to the headwaters of Muddy Boggy, which it followed on down to the Middle Boggy and then to the Red River, and on to Natchitoches.

The Illinois River trail followed this river to Webber Falls near the mouth of the Canadian on the Arkansas. It followed the Canadian and its southern feeder streams south to the Middle Boggy where it joined with the trail described above. By continuing down the Red River, the Osages could come upon Natchitoches from the northwest. These two trails were the basic routes followed by the later military roads as well as the Sedalia and Baxter Springs cattle trails (see Fig. 14).

We have traced the First and Second Buffalo Trails under the Osage Trails in Kansas. The Third Buffalo Trail left the Claremore Villages between the Verdigris and Neosho-Grand then followed Bird Creek northwest to the Elm and Salt Creek fork. From this point, it followed the Second Buffalo Trail to the Plains. A branch of this trail followed Salt Creek south, and then, north of Fairfax, Oklahoma, it turned west to cross the Arkansas above the mouth of Red Rock Creek. By following Red Rock Creek, the trail reached the Plains.

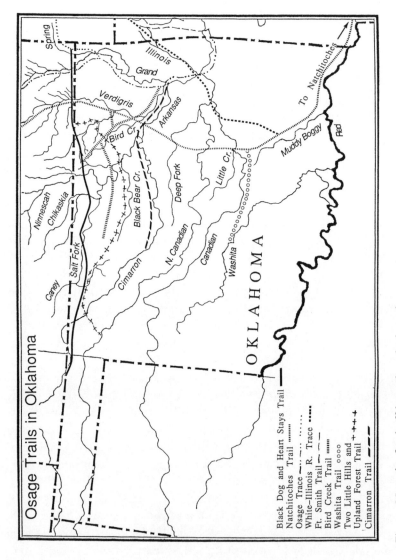

Fig. 14. Note the five buffalo trails and where they terminate.

Early American explorers were very familiar with the Fourth Buffalo Trail, since they often used portions of it. This trail ran upstream from Three Forks along the Arkansas River to the mouth of the Cimarron River. It then followed the Cimarron out to the Plains. A branch of the north-south Neosho-Grand River route turned west at the Canadian River and eventually crossed to the Washita River and thus reached the hunting grounds in Southern Oklahoma.

Francis La Flesche recorded a detailed description of three Osage hunting trails.[84] He numbers these trails 1, 2, and 3. To avoid confusion with the four Osage Buffalo Trails which are also numbered, I have named La Flesche's three trails. His first trail will be called Two Little Hills Trail, his second trail, Heart Stays Trail, and the third trail has been named The Upland Forest Trail. All these trails start in Kansas, but they are mainly in Oklahoma. This location would date the trails as being used between 1822 and 1870. The distance between camps has been included in parentheses, the first number indicating the distance between camps and the second number denoting the distance from the starting point.

Two Little Hills Trail

The Two Little Hills Trail starts at a village called *Wa ha Ka U le* (meaning undetermined), which was located near *Pa se Shin ka Lo pa* (Two Little Hills). This was probably Saucy *Tsi shu's* village at the junction of the Verdigris and Elk Rivers two and one-half miles north of Independence, Kansas.

Camp number one was called *Pa le Wa kon ta Ke Ka ha* (Medicine Man Creek) and was near Coffeyville, Kansas. A strange Indian was found dead in a cave at this place (distance 16 mi, 16 mi).

Next, was *Pe tse Moh kon Ka ha* (Fire Medicine Creek) or *Ne Pe she* (Bad Water). Smoke was seen rising from this creek in all seasons. This second camp was probably at the junction of Cheyenne Creek and the Little Caney (distance 20 mi, 36 mi).

Kon za Wa ha pe was the name of the next camp (a Kansas Indian won a footrace at this place). This was the third camp on the Two Little Hills Trail. It was probably at or near the junction of the Caney River and the Little Caney a little south of Copan, Oklahoma (distance 15 mi, 51 mi).

The fourth camp was at Bartlesville, Oklahoma, in the Johnstone Park. Its name was *U su E ha Shin ka* (Little Mouth Forest). Once there had been a large bend in the Caney here, and the river had almost bypassed the bend. Thus, the Little Mouth name and the mouth had a wooded area on it—hence, the name Little Mouth Forest (distance 12 mi, 63 mi).

Ne Log ny (Good Water) was the next camp. Nelagony Creek passes by the old depot at Nelagony, Oklahoma, which was the old campsite. Evidently, the trail had led up Sand Creek to Okesa, Oklahoma, where it cut over to Nelagony. This was the fifth camp on the Two Little Hills Trail (distance 17 mi, 80 mi).

Pawhuska, the present Osage Capital, was the sixth campsite on this trail. Its original Osage name was *Ne ah he He sko pa* (Deep Ford). For many years, Pawhuska was called Deep Ford. This campsite was near the cemetery and the ford crossed Bird Creek above Clear Creek (distance 8 mi, 88 mi).

The seventh camp was near Fairfax, Oklahoma. Its Osage name was *Ne ske le Ka ha* (Saltwater Creek) (distance 25 mi, 113 mi).

Ne Shu tsy (Red River) was the Osage name for the Arkansas River. This was the site of the eighth camp, which was on a small creek named *Mo she Scah* (I am White). This crossing was about midway between the mouth of the Salt Fork and the mouth of Red Rock Creek (distance 12 mi, 135 mi).

La Flesche and the rest of us are confused on the next two camps, numbers nine and ten. He gives no tenth camp. He gives the name *Ne Shu tsy Shin ka* (Little Red River) for the Salt Fork. This should be *Ne ske le Ne* (Saltwater River) because the Little Red River was the Osage name for the Little Arkansas River. It is possible, though, that this was also another Osage name for the Salt Fork. However, the Cimarron was also called *Ne Shu tsy;* early accounts call it the Red Fork. The trail crossed the Salt Fork at about White Eagle, Oklahoma. We will pick up La Flesche's numbering of the camps with number eleven but it was really the ninth camp.

La Flesche's eleventh camp was northwest of Ponca City, Oklahoma, on the Bois de Arc Creek. The Osage name for this camp was *Moh tse Sta Ka ha* (Bow Wood Creek). Today it carries the Osage name in French (distance 20 mi, 155 mi).

La Flesche did not give the twelfth camp, but it had to be on the Salt Fork near Pond Creek, Oklahoma. These distances from camp to camp varied with the difficulty of travel; they were in more open country now and travel was much easier (distance 35 mi, 190 mi).

The thirteenth campsite had two names, *Son tse Shin ka* (Little Upland Forest) and *Ne ne Po sta* (Shooting Springs). This campsite was on the east edge of the Salt Plains. Actually, there were two campsites that were very close together so their names were often used interchangeably. However, those who traveled on the Two Little Hills Trail customarily used the wooded area and those who moved on the Heart Stays Trail used the spring site. It must be kept in mind that while we divide these trails, campsites and other trails were often combined as alternates to the route we are tracing (distance 20 mi, 210 mi).

Ne ske le U su U gra in a literal translation means Salt Lowland Forest, but in a free translation it would mean Salt Plains. At this fourteenth camp, the Osages often gathered rock salt. It was located at the west edge of the Salt Plains near Cherokee, Oklahoma (distance 15 mi, 225 mi).

At the fifteenth camp, ten Pawnee warriors were killed in the woods. The Osages called this camp *Ho tse He Pa se* (Cedar Tree Hills), but they probably had another name that referred to the slaying of the ten Pawnee. This camp was probably on Eagle Chief Creek south of Alva, Oklahoma (distance 20 mi, 245 mi).

The sixteenth camp also had two names, *Ah le Pa se Shu tsy* (Red Hill Top) and *Mo ha Pa se Shu tsy* (Red Cliffs). This was also a camping place on the Heart Stays Trail. It was on the left bank (east side) of the Cimarron River across from the Alabaster Caverns State Park in present-day Oklahoma (distance 20 mi, 265 mi).

At the seventeenth camp, they were far out on the Plains. This camp was called *Tsi She pe a go* (Buffalo Range). Osages describe this place as a large basin with a gap like a door at the west edge. Gate, Oklahoma, is at the site of this door or gate in the basin. This camp was probably at Doby Springs between Buffalo and Gate, Oklahoma (distance 35 mi, 300 mi).

To shon He (Papaw Bark), was the eighteenth camp. The papaw was very useful to the Osages. The bark was used for thread and the fruit was used for food. It was considered to be a sacred tree. To find the papaw this far out on the Plains seems strange. However, it was very convenient having the bark available here because the Osages would cut buffalo ribs off the carcass, flatten them, and then sew them together with papaw thread. The entire blanket of ribs was then thrown over a rack for drying. This camp was very likely on Horse Creek north of Gate, Oklahoma (distance 25 mi, 325 mi).

The full meaning of the name of the nineteenth and last camp, which the Osages called, *Ne ske le Ka ske pe,* cannot be determined. From what can be determined about the name, it seems they must have found rock salt here. The camp was probably on the Cimarron near where it enters Oklahoma from Kansas north of Mocane, Oklahoma. This was the westernmost camp found in the records. However, indirect evidence indicates they hunted much farther west than this location, but these were probably tepee camps and left no trace (distance 20 mi, 345 mi).

Heart Stays Trail

The name of the village where the Heart Stays Trail started was *No tse Wa spe* (Heart Stays). This was at present-day Oswego, Kansas, on the Neosho-Grand River.

Although the first camp on this trail was omitted by La Flesche, we would place it near the west side of Chetopa, Kansas (distance 10 mi, 10 mi).

Wa se Tun Ho e was the Osage name for the Verdigris River. They obtained green paint here near Coffeyville, Kansas. This was the second camp on the Heart Stays Trail (distance 25 mi, 35 mi).

The name of the third camp was *Ka he Kon se ha* (Two Creeks Running Parallel to Each Other). Clearly, this should be between the Little and Middle Caney west of Caney, Kansas; however, the campsite was near the southeastern corner of Chautauqua County, Kansas (distance 20 mi, 45 mi).

The fourth camp was also a camp on the Black Dog Trail. We have a variety of names for this camp, *Ne ha Ka ha* (Falls Creek), *Gra to Me Shin ka U su* (Little Hawk Woman's Grove), and *Gra to Me Shin ka* (Little Hawk Woman). Falls Creek is a small intermittent stream which flows north along the west base of the north spur of Tinker Hill. It enters the Caney River just below the ford into what is called the bass hole. Little Hawk Woman's Grove is still standing on the left side of the ford; the river curls around the grove on the south and east side. The Little Hawk Woman campsite was adjacent to the grove. This is one-half mile south of Elgin, Kansas, in Osage County, Oklahoma.

The fifth camp was named *Mo shon Ah ke ta Ka ha* (Protector of the Land Creek). Today, the Osage name has been changed to Acker Creek. It was in Range 7E, Township 29N, Section 21 of Osage County, Oklahoma (distance 20 mi, 85 mi).

Two names were applied to the sixth camp, *Ne scah Lo scah* (Place Between Two Rivers), which is now called Beaver Creek, and *Tsa non sa Che ha pe* (in effect, place where a fence was built to protect against buffalo). There is a story that the buffalo stampeded through this camp at one time, so an earthen wall was built around the campsite to prevent it happening again. This camp was located in the fork of Spring Creek and Beaver Creek—Range 6E, Township 29N, Section 19, Osage County, Oklahoma (distance 10 mi, 95 mi).

La Flesche was again confused at the Arkansas River. He omitted the seventh camp entirely and placed the eighth camp far down Elm Creek near its junction with Salt Creek. This might have been an alternate camp on the Two Little Hills Trail or some other trail, but it could not have been on the Heart Stays Trail because it was too far off the course of the trail. Although La Flesche also confuses the ninth camp, we can with certainty place it at the old Pawnee Deer Creek villages on the Arkansas River at the Ferdinandina crossing. We will retain La Flesche's numbering of the camps insofar as possible (distance 20 mi, 115 mi).

Both the Two Little Hills Trail and Heart Stays Trail shared the camp on Bois de Arc Creek northwest of Ponca City, Oklahoma. This was the tenth camp on the Heart Stays Trail (distance 15 mi, 130 mi).

From La Flesche's naming of the ninth camp on the Heart Stays Trail and the eighth camp of the Two Little Hills Trail, we deduce he means the Salt Fork instead of the Little Arkansas. To further confuse the matter, when he discusses the Heart Stays Trail, he gives this as the ninth camp on the Two Little Hills Trail. To maintain his camp numbering, we will label this camp ten B on the Heart Stays Trail. This was near Pond Creek, Oklahoma, on the Salt Fork (distance 15 mi, 145 mi).

The name of another camp was *U pa le.* The meaning cannot be ascertained, but it is a personal name. The son of this man was wounded in battle, and the old man remained at this place caring for his son. A creek was named for him. This was the eleventh camp. Apparently, this was also near Pond Creek, Oklahoma, but more to the north so it must have been an alternate camp (distance 20 mi, 150 mi).

La Flesche omitted the twelfth camp altogether. Clearly he was badly confused in this general area and never had a chance to get it straightened out. He gives the thirteenth camp as the Little Upland Forest, as well as Shooting Springs. These were both camps on the Two Little Hills Trail and Heart Stays Trail. The distance traveled tells us there could not have been another (twelfth) camp in this area. This trail had now reached the east edge of the Salt Plains (distance 20 mi, 160 mi).

Moh sa He (A Thicket of Arrow Wood) was the name of the fourteenth camp. Probably, this was on the west edge of the Salt Plains on the Salt Fork (distance 15 mi, 175 mi).

An Osage man of the *Lo Ha* (Buffalo Back) clan died at the spot where the fifteenth camp was located. Although the meaning of the name has been lost, the Osages called it *Moh en ku ah ha.* Possibly, this was near Alva, Oklahoma, on the Salt Fork (distance 20 mi, 195 mi).

The sixteenth camp was again shared by the Two Little Hills and Heart Stays Trails. This was the Red Hill Top or Red Cliffs already mentioned. The sharing of campsites saved the labor of erecting wickiup framework (distance 20 mi, 215 mi).

A departure in the two trails occurs at this point. The seventeenth camp was called *Ho tse He Ka he* (Cedar Tree Creek). This camp was about midway between Alabaster Caverns State Park and Woodward, Oklahoma (distance 15 mi, 230 mi).

Ne ne Po sta (Shooting Springs) was the eighteenth and final camp on the Heart Stays Trail. There were two springs about fifteen miles apart in this area. One was clear and sweet and the other was black and bitter. The springs had a movement that caused the Osages to call them shooting springs. In all probability, this camp was in or near the Boiling Springs State Park, Oklahoma (distance 15 mi, 245 mi).

The Upland Forest Trail

Son tse U gre (The Upland Forest) was a name of Claremore III's village on the Verdigris River. It was the starting place of this last Osage trail.

La Flesche omitted the first camp but it would almost positively be near Coffeyville, Kansas (distance 10 mi, 10 mi).

It is very noticeable that The Upland Forest Trail covered more in a day's travel than the other two trails. The second camp is given as being on the Arkansas west of Hominy, Oklahoma. Even the Osages could not make such a trip from west of Coffeyville in one day. La Flesche omits the third camp and places the fourth camp south of Bartlesville. We have changed his camp numbering to conform to geography and reality. The second camp was the Little Mouth Forest at Bartlesville, Oklahoma. This was the fourth camp on the Two Little Hills Trail (distance 40 mi, 50 mi).

We have changed La Flesche's second camp to the third camp. This site was called *Pa hu Te pa* (Round Hills) and was on the Arkansas River near Blackburn, Oklahoma, and west of Hominy, Oklahoma (distance 45 mi, 95 mi).

Wa Sop pe U tsy (Where Black Bears are Plentiful) is called Black Bear Creek today. This was about eight miles northwest of Morrison, Oklahoma (distance 30 mi, 125 mi).

The fifth camp on this express trail was probably near Enid, Oklahoma. It was called *Tse le Ke he* (Big Lake) (distance 30 mi, 155 mi).

We cannot fully translate the name for the sixth camp, but *Shon tse Lu Sop pe,* the Osage name for this camp, has something to do with castrating a horse or animal. This was on the extreme headwaters of Turkey Creek northwest of Enid, Oklahoma, near Helena, Oklahoma (distance 23 mi, 178 mi).

Hu lah Ki he ka Ka ha (Eagle Chief Creek) was the seventh camp. It was on Eagle Chief Creek south of Alva, Oklahoma (distance 30 mi, 208 mi).

The final and eighth camp of The Upland Forest Trail was called *Tse He Tun ka* (Bed of Big Lake). This was near Boiling Springs State Park, Woodward, Oklahoma (distance 35 mi, 243 mi).

CONCLUSIONS

This summary of the routes followed by the Osage trails shows an extensive system over which the Osages moved in war and peace. It is not surprising that so many of these routes became major roads in later times. What is surprising about these routes is that none of them came into use as major routes as long as the Osages controlled them. This is true of the network of route density in Missouri, Kansas, and of one route in Oklahoma. Interstate

44 utilizes many Osage routes in both Oklahoma and Missouri that touch on network centers. Railroads earlier had touched the Kansas centers. However, it is significant that the network center of these trails in Osage County, Oklahoma, has no modern major routes and that no part became a major route.

Either by an accident of history or by design, all major routes of travel skirted territory held by the Osages. The routes that evolved came after the Osages no longer controlled the area. Such consistent practices almost always indicate something more than accidents of history. One may argue that the Missouri and Arkansas Rivers offered natural routes to the West. This is true enough, but it is significant that these routes were not available until the Osages were removed from the Missouri by the Treaty of 1808 and from the Arkansas-Canadian by the Treaty of 1818.

We would also like to point out that the shortest, fastest, most direct route lay through the Osage country. Even as late as the 1850s, this route was so little used by the California gold miners that it has all but escaped the attention of Frontier historians. Only a few pioneers mention using it in going to and from the gold fields. Surely, there must have been some reason for this bypass practice in United States history.

One may also wonder why the former Kansas home of the Osages north of their present purchased reservation filled so rapidly. By the same token, the lands of Indians to the east, south, and southwest also were quickly settled. By 1892, the only lands left available for homesteading lay in the Cherokee Outlet west of the Osages. This was their hunting grounds long before the Cherokee dared to cross the Mississippi. It was the last Osage hunting ground. Here the Great American Frontier ended in 1893. Only the million and one-half acre Osage reservation remained to be settled.

After 1893, some small pocket areas here and there throughout the west remained unsettled; however, these were almost universally undesirable because of aridity and other natural reasons and were also areas set aside as national reserves. The Osage reservation was desirable land. By 1900, the Euro-American culture had swirled around the Osages for two hundred and twenty-five years. While the Osages had been influenced by the majority culture, they still held it at an arm's length away. It is this hard-core of Osage culture that turned the grinding land hunger of Manifest Destiny around their domain instead of through it. First, they fought with bows and arrows, then with guns. However, they always fought with their wits. It was 1925, after two hundred and fifty years of conflict, that the Osages were finally overwhelmed. The last of the fighting Indians had finally been inundated with Euro-Americans, but they still fought for their rights in the courts and in the halls of Congress. Their vast domain had been reduced to an underground reservation of petroleum—the land was gone. In the Osage language the land is called *Moh shon* and the Earth is called *Hun ka,* which means the Sacred One. The Great Creator brought the sky and earth together to make the land, which made life on Earth possible. He did this as the last act of creation, and then he said "*O pah*" ("It is finished").

3

Osage Relationships with Euro-Americans, 1675–1803

CONTRASTS

Introduction

There is no doubt that the Osage culture differed from the culture of Western civilization. Equally evident is that these differences were a source of friction between the two cultures. The Osages could clearly see the superiority of Western trade goods to their own. However, they considered the other cultural aspects of Western civilization to be inferior to their own (see Fig. 15).

Land ownership concepts evolve from a diversity of geographic and cultural sources, but a decisive factor is the role land plays in food production. A culture that obtains its major food supply from the hunt will have a different concept of land ownership than a culture that acquires its food from agriculture. Each culture benefits from its own type of land ownership. A hunting culture benefits from communal ownership of land simply because game animals do not arrange themselves evenly over the land. Open ranges on the early cattle ranching frontier were used for the same reason, but enclosure (fencing) eventually ended open ranges. The enclosure laws of England were enacted to encourage production of wool for the growing textile industries, but these laws destroyed the common grazing areas and displaced large numbers of farmers. Many of these displaced farmers came to the American colonies hungry for lands of their own.

Like land ownership, the Osage economy differed from that of Euro-Americans. An economy based on hunting and a limited agriculture cannot support a population as large as an economy based on agriculture, trade, and manufacturing. European justification for seizing lands owned by Indians was based upon this so-called highest use argument.

Some technologies are visibly superior. Muskets and rifles clearly have

CULTURAL CONTRASTS	
OSAGE CULTURE	WESTERN CIVILIZATION
Land Title	
communal–all lands owned in common by all the people	communal–public domain or crown owned royal–owned by monarch private–owned by individuals or the church
Land Policies	
Acquired lands by merging with owners, displacement, or annihilation of owners.	Acquired lands by purchase, merger, displacement, annihilation, or subjugation of owners.
Occupied lands in villages, hunting camps and by maintaining patrols of Protectors or hunting parties.	Occupied lands by farming and in communities.
Economies	
Food supply came from hunting, gathering, and supplemental agriculture.	Food supply came from intensive agriculture and herding.
Simple manufacture including tanning and utility articles	Highly developed manufacturing of varied articles
Trade by direct barter of simple articles	Trade by medium of exchange for varied products
Religion	
Highly developed and tolerant	Highly developed but intolerant

Fig. 15. Cultural comparisons

advantages over spears and bows. The advantages of technologies such as fertilization of fields to increase production are not immediately evident. The Osages were quick to see the advantages of the visible technologies that could readily be fitted into their culture. In time, they adopted some of the less evident technologies, but only those they could use with little adjustment to their culture. Their core culture remained intact throughout the period of 1675–1803.

Western people rarely visualize Indians as having well-defined policies. The Osages had a set of policies which they followed with great consistency, such as their fixed policy of opposition to intruders. Their distinction among three types of intruders was clearly defined. A traveler or party who crossed Osage territory uninvited but who used only what was necessary in their passage was one type of intruder. Uninvited individuals or groups who plundered the resources were a second type of intruder. The third type of intruder was those people who settled on Osage lands without invitation.

Another notable Osage policy was to take no major action without first evaluating the situation. For this reason, Osages frequently remained out of sight and observed a situation before they took a major action. This policy is so deeply ingrained into the Osage character that it is often mistaken for an inherited trait. It is easy to confuse the policy with the general Indian reserve and sense of order so often noted by Euro-Americans.

If the Osages were not the most *deeply* religious Indians in North America, they were close to being the *most* religious. Until 1850, they refused under any circumstances to abandon their religion and accept the Christianity of Western civilization. As a matter of policy, they respected the rights of others to believe as they wished, and they reserved the same rights for themselves. For hours and with great respect they would listen to Euro-American ministers expound their faith, but they did not abandon their own faith.

Land Policies

A major contrast between the Osage land policies and the policies of Western nations hinged upon the concept of subject areas. Having an alien people subject to their rule, by force or otherwise, was unknown to the Osages. Their practice was to adopt alien individuals and to either merge with whole groups or to force them to move out of the desired area. Failing in these measures, the conquest was either abandoned or a total war was undertaken. But the idea of subjugation was never used.

Trade with the Euro-Americans made a new Osage land policy mandatory. Under this policy, Euro-Americans were permitted subsistence and distribution bases in Osage territory. Yet, these were carefully observed, and periodic bluff raids were used to limit their size. Trading posts were encouraged near their villages and eastern borders. Posts to the west and southwest were discouraged.

Osage land title was held by occupation, conquest, and the ability to enforce one's own claim. Euro-American trade bases were on Osage lands either by consent or invitation. Enforcement of Osage territorial claims were violent, graphic, and effective. Intruders of the second and third types were killed on or near the spot of violation. Their heads were cut off and placed on stakes. Indians usually had no difficulty in reading these graphic signs—the evidence of violation and the results were both there as plain as day. Since decapitation was an especially serious matter in most Indian religions, it was an effective deterrent among Indians. However, Euro-Americans either did not read signs very well or chose to ignore them. Thus, the effectiveness of enforcing territorial claims was weakened, and in the process Euro-Americans blamed the Osages for the consequences of their own trespassing.

The discovery of the Americas presented a dilemma for the Western colonial nations. Their desire to claim these new lands as their own conflicted with the fact that the lands were already owned and occupied by native nations. By mutual consent of the major colonial powers of Europe, the Western nations accepted their claims as valid among themselves. Although they disputed the claims made to some specific areas, the right to claim and attach American lands to their empires was never disputed. Under these arrangements, the native nations were in almost the same situation as the overseas provinces of the Roman Empire, who operated under their own laws and rule in subjection to the approval of the Roman government.[1] Thus, the Osage nation, in the European mind, was a subject nation or province of, first, France, then Spain and the United States.

As far as the Indian nations were concerned, these arrangements were mere theory until the European nations were strong enough to impose this agreement upon the Indian nations. Each of the three major colonial powers (Spain, France, and England) used their own individual means to impose their overlordship. Spain used the sword and cross very effectively in establishing themselves as the supreme ruling power in their claimed areas. France accepted alien peoples as they are and imposed their rule through trade. England used trade and massive agricultural settlement to slowly ease Indians out of their lands and onto other Indian lands. Indian resistance was crushed by forces from a firmly settled base. This latter stage was inherited by the United States. This discussion refers to the actual practices, which differed from the official policies.[2]

The extinguishment of land title—like establishment of overlordship— was a departure from official policy.[3] It seems clear that the Western powers were officially attempting to justify the seizure of Indian lands, leaving the actual seizure procedures to those present on the scene. This is strong evidence that Western civilization was evolving a new concept in government, which was later called imperialism. Eventually, two concepts that evolved from the Indian land seizure experience pushed the United States into the leadership of Western civilization. These were Manifest Destiny and Economic Imperialism. While it would be interesting to pursue the evolution of these concepts, our purpose here is to contrast the Osage and Euro-American concepts of land ownership.

Officially, all lands not physically occupied by Indians were considered to be Crown or Royal property.[4] In actual practice some form of compensation was even paid for what appeared to Euro-Americans to be *unused, va-*

cant, or *waste lands.* The truth is, however, that all Osage lands were *used;* they were seldom *vacant,* and *waste lands* produced game animals which were used for food. Osages lived on their land in villages and hunting camps. Since their lands were heavily patrolled by special Protectors of the Land and hunting parties, all Osage lands were occupied. In practice and officially, areas not physically occupied by villages were available to be purchased, or in some way compensation was to be paid.

Clearly, if this policy of extinguishing the Indian land title was implemented—and it was—it would ultimately compact Indians into an increasingly smaller area. Equally evident is the eventual destruction of all hunting cultures. Amidst the turmoil created by this policy, in 1889, the Commissioner of Indian Affairs stated this solution to the dilemma (one that was not resolved in colonial days nor later): "The Indian must conform to the white man's ways, peacefully if they will, forcibly if they must."[5] A more enlightened view, if not a solution, was expressed by Eric Thompson, "This disintegration of native culture before the advance of 'civilization' is sad, for material advances do not bring greater happiness or compensate for lost spiritual values."[6] Our purpose here is not to cry, "Lo! the poor Indian," but to show contrasts in viewpoints. If the Osage people are to continue to "stand in two worlds," they must keep one foot anchored in their past and keep the other foot planted in the majority culture. The two bases must balance or the people will totter and fall.

Economies

Compared to those of Western civilization, the Osage economy was not sophisticated, but when compared to the economies of their neighbors, it was well advanced. In 1675 to 1800, their neighbors were other Indian nations and scattered settlements of Euro-Americans. The Euro-American neighbors of this period had a very inferior economy. It is a small wonder that these fragmentary representatives of Western civilization did not impress the Osages.

Osages procured their food supply from three sources. The hunt supplied a large amount of meat and raw materials for some manufacture. It is probable that the gathering activities were next in importance to the people. From these they not only garnered a large supply of vegetable foods but also other raw materials of the economy. Agriculture was the third source of food, but it stood more as a supplementary source instead of a primary source.

Before the opening of large scale fur trading, the Osage traded some peltries and buffalo robes to their eastern neighbors. Catlinite (red pipestone) from their northern neighbors was exchanged for black pipestone. Fine pelts, abrading stones, and some finished leather clothing were traded to their southern neighbors for sea shells from the Gulf of Mexico. However, the greatest volume of trade was with their western neighbors. This was primarily a food trade of Caddo corn for Osage berries, nuts, and potatoes (these were not the so-called Irish potato but a wild legume related to the Peruvian potato).

After the fur trade with Euro-Americans opened, the Osages became trade entrepreneurs or middlemen between the Euro-Americans and the tribes to the west. The Osages quickly learned the dangers of food poisoning from foods cooked in brass or copper pots and pans. These they traded to the Caddo people and they kept the cast iron pots for themselves. Trade knives and hatchets were normally traded without grips or handles, but some handles were added by the Osages before they were traded to the Caddoeans. Bow wood of Osage Orange (Bois de Arc, Hedge, Bodark) was in great demand.

Osage Orange is probably the best bow wood in the world. It surpasses the English yew, lemon wood, hickory, and ash as bow wood. Two types of Osage bows were made and traded by the Osage. The long flat bow was often six feet or more in length and almost universally made of Osage Orange. A short "horse bow" of three to four feet in length was also made. This was usually rounded on the outside and flat on the inside with rawhide thongs wrapped side-by-side across the length. Smooth bark (pig nut) hickory was a favored wood for these bows, although some were made of Osage Orange or ash.

Aside from handles and bows the Osages were also proficient in other manufacturing. Furs in their homeland were good but not as fine as those taken farther north. The pelage (thickness and texture of the hair) of Osage furs was thinner and coarser than northern furs. To compensate for this, the Osages had developed better tanning methods. Even in their treatment of raw peltry, the Osages used better preparation. This might have had some bearing on the fact that Euro-American free trappers and brigade trappers never operated in Osage territory. Instead of free trappers, the post system prevailed on the Lower Missouri and Arkansas Rivers. Only on the Upper Missouri and in other cold climates did the free and brigade trappers obtain better prepared peltry. Yet, in candor, it must be noted that the Osages discouraged such Euro-American trapping.

In contrast to the Osage economy, Euro-American food procurement was primarily through agriculture with herding as a secondary source of food. The primary distinction here is the presence of domestic animals. Osage agriculture could not be as extensive or intensive as Euro-American agriculture because of the absence of draft animals. Likewise, herding as a source of meat could not exist, because the Osage had no domestic herd or flock animals. This was all a matter of availability and not of superiority, however.

Euro-American trade was not only more diversified than Osage trade, but it had the advantage of a medium of exchange. The evolution of this superiority to the Osage shows the advantage of a maritime culture over a continental culture. Creating a medium of exchange is a peculiar aspect of maritime cultures. Typical of continental cultures, the Osage used direct barter in trade. In direct barter a trader must find someone who not only has something the trader wants, but the owner must also be willing to trade it for what the trader has to offer. A medium of exchange such as gold and silver has a standard of acceptable value and, therefore, is widely accepted in exchange for any trade goods. Obviously, this provides a greater flexibility in trade than direct barter, since a trader simply has to find what he wants and trade a medium of exchange for it.

Mediums of exchange have been in use since the Phoenicians introduced them into the trade of Western civilization. However, their use in large scale trade and role in the rise of national states did not appear until vast amounts of gold and silver came to Western civilization through Spanish imports from the Americas. In 1492, the total gold and silver supply of Western civilization was slightly less than $200,000,000 or about two dollars per person. By 1600 there was an 855 percent increase in these metals; in 1700 a 1,984 percent increase; and in 1800 a 3,786 percent increase. Using 1934 as a comparison year, Western civilization had about $32 billion in gold and silver. This would be nearly $40 per person.[7]

The changes brought to Western civilization by the huge increase of gold and silver also affected the Osages. While a minority of Europeans enjoyed a relatively high living standard in 1500, the vast majority of Europeans had a wretched living standard. By contrast, all classes of the Osage were better fed, better clothed, and better housed than the average European in 1500. The infusion of gold and silver with a five-fold increase of available land caused a revolution in Western civilization. While this European revolution improved the condition of the average European, it had a reverse effect on the condition of the Osage.

In matters of trade and the rise of the national states, American gold and silver brought about the practice of mercantilism. Abundant land destroyed feudalism and brought about individualism. It is ironic that their beloved land held the foundation for the ultimate destruction of the Osage culture. The resources of their land fed the mercantilism of national states and the surface of their land fueled the flames of land hunger in the former European serfs.

We must review the principles of mercantilism to see how this affected the Osage people. A basic premise of mercantilism is that gold and silver are wealth. One of the secondary premises is that the wealthiest state will also become the most powerful state. The third premise is that in order to acquire gold and silver, a nation must have colonies to supply raw materials so the mother country can be self-sufficient. This meant the mother country would be able to sell more than it bought in foreign trade and thus acquire a favorable balance of trade that would be paid in gold and silver. Implementation of these premises caused this practice to be called Imperialism because it required the possession of colonies.

A discussion of the fallacies in this economic theory would lead us far from our purpose. However, it should be evident that it was the ultimate desire for gold and silver that propelled Spain, France, and England into colonialism. By the same token, it brought first the French and then the Spanish into trade relationships with the Osage. Thus, we find the French and Spanish concentrating on the two resources of the Osage that gave the highest return for the amount invested. These were products of the hunt plus lead and zinc ores. Furs, hides, and tallow were the main products of the hunt that French and Spanish traders desired. Lead and zinc mining held no interest to the Osage of this period as long as the mining did not interfere with the game animals.

The rising, growing middle class in Western civilization could now afford the furs of nobility. But, it was not the need for furs that created a fur market. Rather, the prestige of wearing furs created the fur market. Even the poor could now afford to wear buffalo hide shoes and light their cottages with tallow candles. Their old wooden sabots were discarded, along with their saucer lights. Under the demand for hunt products, the Osage began to deplete their supply of fur and game animals. Through expansion, they were able to defer the effects of the trade in hunt products until 1860, but poverty and lowered living standards with roots in the 1600s struck them in the 1800s.

In our urban-industrial culture, it is sometimes difficult to comprehend the land hunger of Euro-Americans between 1500 and 1910. One must bear in mind that in 1500 land was the basis of all wealth. With only minor exceptions, the land was owned by the nobility, either the nobility of the church or the temporal nobility. The vast majority tilled soil they did not own and were serfs or peons. Both serfdom and peonage are forms of slavery that tie a human to the land. When the land changes ownership the estate includes the serfs or peons.

Occasionally a kindly lord would give a loved serf a few acres of land, and thus a small class of yeoman farmers came into existence. It is small wonder, then, that a five-fold increase in land area whetted the land appetite of European serfs. They now had hopes that someday they would be yeomen or even lords. Land ownership meant more than land possession—it included position, political influence, and protection of laws. Once they arrived in America, no human power could deny these immigrants land ownership, and thus the largest number of middle class farmers in history was created. It is with good reason that land and property are called *real estate.*

A growing decrease of game and the "not to be denied, would-be land owners" destroyed the Osage culture. Yet, this came after the French and Spanish period, and it will be dealt with in later chapters. The contrast in the economies of the Osages and Western civilization show the potential conflict of the two. No doubt, both cultures borrowed portions of the other's culture while rejecting other selected portions.

OSAGE RELATIONSHIPS WITH FRANCE

Foreknowledge

No documentation shows any contact between the Euro-Americans and Osages before they were mentioned at Detroit in 1712. But judging by the number of grown-up mixed Osages-French during du Tisné's visit in 1719, there had been undocumented contacts in the late–1600s. It is probable that both Coronado and de Soto met separate bands of Osages in the early–1540s. The surviving descriptions of Osage legends certainly indicate they did. One of Coronado's descriptions fits the Osages better than any other Indians, and this description was given in sight of the mountains (hills with blue haze) to the east (the Osage Hills or Flint Hills?)[8] De Soto apparently met some Osages and mistook them for the Kansas. Long before Radisson mentioned them in 1659 and Marquette eleven years later, the Osage knew of the Euro-American presence. It would have been entirely in keeping with the Osage character if they had remained unseen while observing the white men.

The Osage watched new developments very carefully. It was their custom to learn as much about anything unusual as they could. Once they had a good assessment of the situation, they formulated a strategy to deal with it. They had both the horse and horse technology almost as soon as the Kiowa because they got both from the Kiowa by trade. Since they had a close alliance with the Illinoian Cahokia and Kaskaskias, it is probable that they had even traded with Euro-Americans while disguised as Illinois Indians.

By 1712, the Osages were well prepared to meet the French. It is important to note that they were not identified as Osages until they arrived at Detroit. In the best account of this battle, we are told the Ottawa and Pottowatomie met a large war party of Illinois reinforcements. The Osages were a part of this party, but this fact did not emerge until they arrived at Detroit.[9]

Like most Indian wars, this started as bluff war. A group of Maskoutin Indians were using bluff war on an Ottawa chief. In retaliation, the Ottawa and Pottowatomie struck the Maskoutin's winter camp in April of 1712. After a three-day battle in which they suffered many casualties, the Maskoutins retreated to Detroit and joined their Sac and Fox allies. At this point, the Ottawa and Pottowatomie met the party of Illinois, which included the Osage. With this additional force, the allies (the Osage friends) struck the Sac and Fox stockade at Detroit. In the sixteen-day battle, the Sac and Fox side lost about a thousand men, women, and children. This is the heaviest battle loss to an Indian group that we have found in the records.

Dubuisson, the French commander at Detroit, tried to prevent the battle. After failing to get cooperation from the Sac and Fox, he threw his support to the allies. While this turned the Sac and Fox against the French, it strengthened the French standing among the allied nations. As a note of interest, from this time the French turned to the south instead of to the west. This led them to Fort Duquesne (Pittsburgh, Pennsylvania) at the Forks of the Ohio, Vincennes at the mouth of the Wabash, Kaskaskia near the mouth of the Ohio, and Cahokia opposite the mouth of the Missouri and New Orleans, as well as posts on the Red and Arkansas Rivers.

After the battle at Detroit a young French officer, Entienne Veniard Bourgmont, deserted his command and went with the Osages to their village in the Bend of the Missouri. Apparently, he lived with a woman of the Elk clan and had several Osage children.[10] Bourgmont later married a Missouria woman. Upon his return to France, the King not only overlooked his desertion, but appointed him Commandant of the Missouri. Bourgmont was promised royal titles if he would do two things. First, he was to construct a fort on the Missouri and, second, make alliances with the western nations (Pawnee, Wichita, Kansas). Fort Orleans was built in the Bend of the Missouri, on the left bank, in the summer of 1723.[11]

During 1724, Bourgmont carried out the second part of his mission. With Osage and Missouria guides, he explored as far west as Salina and Junction City in Kansas.[12] This greatly added to the knowledge of the American West that had been accumulated by Western civilization. Upon his return to the Bend of the Missouri, Bourgmont departed for Paris, taking some Osages and Missourias with him. Their arrival in Paris, 1725, created a sensational swell of curiosity. Because of this visit and a later visit the Osages became well known in France.

Before 1725 the relationship between the Osage and the French on the Missouri was reasonably amicable. However, an incident on the Red River in 1719 was not as amicable as relationships on the Missouri. The dream of reaching the western nations, New Mexico, and maybe the Pacific led the French to a decision. They decided to send Bernard de la Harpe up the Red River guided by Caddoean scouts.

In the Kiamichi Mountain area of Southeastern Oklahoma, La Harpe found that it did not pay to bypass the Osages. The reaction of the Caddo when they met an Osage war party clearly indicated Osage control of the Red River route.[13] It is evident from the success experienced by Bourgmont and the failure of La Harpe that any move to develop a route to the west must be made with the consent of the Osages.

Although the Osage blockade was effective, there were times when they failed in their attempts to prevent passage through their territory. Certainly, Charles Claude du Tisné, in the spring of 1719, managed to proceed to the west despite Osage objections.[14] Not wishing to lose the profitable French trade, the Osage allowed du Tisné to proceed with a severely restricted amount of trade goods instead of killing him. The Mallet Brothers also slipped through the Osage barrier and reached Santa Fe in 1739.[15] Stung by these breaches of their blockade, the Osages stiffened their resistance. In the winter of 1741–1742, Fabry de la Bruyére, who was guided by the Mallets, attempted to reach Santa Fe. Low water stalled the expedition about one hundred and fifty miles upstream from the mouth of the Canadian River in Oklahoma.[16] The Osages harassed the Bruyére party, delaying them and frustrating their efforts to secure horses. Because of this harassment, Bruyére could not obtain horses, so he turned back.

To a limited extent, one can judge the effectiveness of the Osage defense of their territory by the accounts of the chroniclers. Between 1675 and 1860, these accounts, with notable exceptions, describe the Osage with bitterness and in unflattering terms. Their word, their honor, and their achievements are cast to fit into the mold of the recorder. This is clearly a case of "whose ox is being gored." From the Osage viewpoint, the French, the Spanish, the Americans, and the emigrant Indian nations were intruders upon the Osage domain. Naturally, in the defense of their lands and their rights as protectors of the land, they frustrated the intentions of those who sought to use the Osages and the Osage domain for their own benefit.

One must bear in mind that those persons writing about the Osages were mainly frustrated intruders or those who had limited association with the

Osages. They were seldom impartial observers without any vested interests. Since the Osages and those who knew them better than anyone else left few written records, the picture of the Osages hangs unbalanced. It is sad that a few modern writers parrot this bias by accusing the Osages of being liars, whiners, treacherous and bloodthirsty. When the evidence is weighed on the scales of fairness and impartiality, such accusations only serve to show the Osages outwitted, outfought, and outmaneuvered the "superior" recorders and their friends. This unwillingness to admit that "wild savages" beat them at their own game is an effort to fit the Osages into the crass mold of their own cultural bias.

Accommodation with the French

Antonine Crozat had a monopoly of all trade in French Louisiana between 1712 and 1717. Being unable to finance the development of Louisiana, Crozat turned his monopoly back to the King. In August of 1717, John Law received the monopoly of trade in Louisiana.[17] Law was at least one hundred years ahead of his time in the field of finance. He was mercantilistic in his belief that money was wealth. Yet, despite this belief, he issued paper money based on real wealth such as land and resources. His downfall came when he resorted to the dangerous practice of issuing watered stock. In effect, this devalued French currency and caused a collapse of French finance, thereby retarding the development of Louisiana.

Law's vigorous efforts to develop his Louisiana trade monopoly caused the French explorations we mentioned earlier. While the exlorations irritated the Osage, his colonizing and efforts to stop the slave trade in captured Caddos more than antagonized them. French-Americans who were on the scene realized this and continued the slave trade. The colonial settlement never flourished and a new spirit of working together developed between the Osage and the French after Law's "Mississippi Bubble" broke in 1720. Law's company was finally abolished in 1731.

While there were irritations between the two cultures, the Osage tempered their attacks slightly and the French overlooked most of the incidents. One must carefully distinguish between the official French policy and the implementation of that policy by those French who were dealing directly with the Osages. These were two entirely different matters. Officially, any Indians that did not comply with French policies were to be exterminated. French realists on the scene realized there was no feasible way the Osages could be exterminated. They also realized that moves in that direction could easily lead to their own extermination. Instead, they tried to placate the Osages and to play down the killing of an occasional *Coureurs de bois* or *Bohéme*.

The effectiveness of this realistic policy is shown by the loyalty of the Osage to the French. Not only did they intermarry with the French, but they also supported them in the Seven Years War (French and Indian War). We must explain that in the Osage culture, as in Western civilization, marriages between the cultures was not considered desirable. It was an extraordinary gesture on the part of an Osage family to give consent to an Osage-French marriage. Usually, these were third daughter (*Ah sin ka*) marriages. Yet, if the Frenchman was held in great esteem among the Osage, a marriage with the second daughter (*We ha*) or more rarely the first daughter (*Me nah*) was permitted. Children of these marriages were accepted as Osage if they lived by Osage customs and laws. If they did not do this, they were considered to be "nobodies." That is, they were beings without bodies, a nonperson. They could live with the Osage or anywhere they wished, but they were not considered to be Osage.

French and Indian War

The French and Indian War (Seven Years War) was the last of the wars in the struggle for colonial empire in North America. France, England, and Spain fought three other wars before the French and Indian War. In America, these wars were called King Williams' War, Queen Anne's War, and King George's War. Of these four intercolonial wars, the French and Indian War was the only one that started in America.

As their first line of defense, the French had built a string of forts from the Great Lakes to the Forks of the Ohio (see Fig. 16). The Osages were involved in battles at two of these forts, Niagara on the Great Lakes and Duquesne at the Forks of the Ohio. The British built a corresponding string of forts east of the Appalachian Crest. Generally, except for the Iroquois, the Indian nations—including the Osage nation—supported the French.

General Edward Braddock had been a successful general in the European wars, but he had no experience in fighting American-style wars. The fact that there was a difference in the style of warfare in Europe and that of America clearly shows an Indian influence on the Euro-American culture. European armies of the 1750s used volley fire as their basic style of firearm use. Muskets, which were the standard military firearm, had a smooth bore. Hence, the projectile tended to be erratic. By firing in a series of volleys, the effect was much like a large shotgun in that a great number of projectiles were sent toward a target at one time. Although some would miss hitting a mark, many would strike some mark. These projectiles were lead balls over one-half of an inch in diameter (.69″). If they struck any part of a human body, they did a considerable amount of damage.

Indians had little use for muskets in battle since a bowman was more

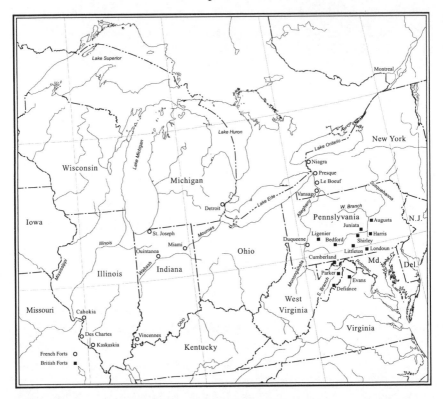

Fig. 16. Notice the concentration of forts along the Ohio headwaters.

accurate and faster than a musketman. A rifle differs from a musket in that the bore has spiral grooves running the length of the bore. This gives the projectile a spin which yields pinpoint accuracy. (Fletching on arrows perform the same function.) The rifling also lessens the need for a large projectile. For bowmen and riflemen, it is more logical to fire from cover than to fire from an exposed position. Osages and other Indians customarily used fire in motion. That is, they would fire from cover and immediately move to another covered position. Thus, the return fire would be directed at the first position. This had the added advantage of causing the enemy to overestimate the size of the force they were facing.

Braddock was no different from most military commanders of his time, including George Washington. These commanders clung to the musket and volley fire because the bow required constant practice and the rifle required more time to reload as well as a greater skill in its use. Not until the Battle of New Orleans in 1815—when 126 riflemen, fighting Indian-style, destroyed two regiments of highlanders—did the armies of Western civilization adopt the rifle as a standard military weapon. During World War II, in the rain forests of the Southwest Pacific, we were taught to use fire in motion as if it was a new concept, although it was combined with saturation fire (a type of volley fire).

Chetoka or *Tsi Tó ka* (Whetstone) related that a large war party from his Little Osage village participated in the Battle of Duquesne.[18] Apparently, they were supplied with powder and ball at Fort Des Chartres and were gone about seven months. Most of the party was from the Mottled Eagle clan.[19] One can almost see Braddock's army, in their red coats with white cross belts, forming into lines of four ranks across the glade. At the other end of the glade, the French regulars stand at the ready in their green coats. Suddenly, a sword is raised and dropped; volley after volley are exchanged. The French break ranks and take cover behind the trees. Slowly the red ranks march across the glade. Then a withering rain of aimed projectiles strike the British ranks. Again and again the ranks close and fire volleys into the wooded shadows, yet the British melt away like butter on a hot rock. The Osages, who admired bravery, took many scalps, for scalps from such men were greatly honored.

Some Osage stories relate that the Osages went on to Fort Niagara and there again fought the British. After the defeat of the British at Duquesne and Niagara, Indians from all over the old Northwest flocked to the aid of the French. No evidence exists to show that the Osage participated in the later battles. However, they had aided the French when it was desperately needed, before other nations allied with the French. Apparently, though, the Osages used the freedom from conflict with nations on their eastern borders to expand their southwestern domain and were too busy to render further aid to the French.

Transition to Spain

Under the terms of the Treaty of Paris, 1763, France ceded all of Louisiana to Spain. Spain was slow to take over the territory, so the Spanish period ran from 1765 to 1803, but actual Spanish control was not established until 1769. In the transition period, the French commander at Fort Des Chartres (mouth of the Kaskaskia River), Louis St. Ange de Bellrive, refused to turn the fort over to the Spanish. He held it for the British, who took possession of the fort in May of 1765.

The Osages were intensely loyal to the French. This was evident in an incident that occurred at Fort Des Chartres while the British were being installed there. An Osage chief was visiting St. Ange when he saw a British officer. It took St. Ange and the interpreter's best efforts to keep the Osage from tomahawking the British officer.[20] While their dislike of the British was intense, the Osages also had a great dislike for the Spanish. They had experienced direct and indirect encounters with the Spanish earlier—in the Southwest and in Texas near Natchitoches—and had already formulated a dislike for them. It is fortunate for the Spanish that most of the French remained in Louisiana. These French were the ones who traded with the Osages, although there were a small number of Spanish traders. Osage contacts with the Spanish were often over some matter involving Osage conflict with Spanish policy. Such meetings had a tendency to cause more malice toward the Spaniards.

When the British took possession east of the Mississippi many French moved west of the Great River. St. Ange moved his soldiers and many residents of the nearby village of Kaskaskia to the newly founded St. Louis. One of these soldiers was Nicholas Royer dit Sansquartier, and one of the residents of Kaskaskia was Jean Baptiste Janot/Jeanot dit La Chapelle. Both became the ancestors of many Osage mixed-bloods.[21]

The French had introduced trade goods from Western civilization into the Osage culture. They had intermarried with the Osages and thus established blood ties. As a result, a mutual trust and friendship developed between the Osages and the resident French. However, we must in candor note that the *Coureurs de bois* and *Bohémes* were not included in this relationship by either the Osages or the regular French inhabitants and traders. The Spanish never grasped this distinction in Osage-French relationships.

IN SEARCH OF ACCOMMODATION WITH SPAIN
Spanish and Osage Character
Spanish Colonizing Policies

Whereas the French official policy toward the Indian was harsh and the application enlightened, the Spanish official policy was enlightened and the application was harsh. The *Requerimiento* is a classical example of the contrast between Spanish policy and Spanish practice. This statement of conciliation and assurances was a requirement of all first contact between the Spanish and Indians. It was to be read to the Indians by the Spanish leader and witnessed by a priest. Too often it was read in whispers among the Spaniards in the darkness before a dawn attack or, as some reports say, it was read to the trees around them.[22]

Spain used three methods to "civilize" Indians. Perversion of the *Requerimiento* led to outright enslavement of the Indian or extermination, which was the first method. A second method was the *encomiendo* system. Again, the official intent was to Christianize and "civilize" the Indian. Under this system, a landowner would agree to "civilize" an Indian in return for his labor. However, it more often led to virtual enslavement or peonage. The final method was the mission system, which was well intentioned, but it too led to a form of benign peonage. This is why so many Indians oppose sainthood for Fr. Junípero Serra. The Osages were well aware of these practices and wanted no part of them.

Characterizations

Fortunately for the Spaniards, they did not make any serious effort to implement these practices with the Osages. Insofar as their character and culture permitted, they generally tried to continue the former French practices. Cervantes's *Don Quixote de la Mancha* gives us an excellent insight into Spanish character and culture. José Ortega adds to these insights in his *Meditations on Quixote*.[23] More than these great works, the letters exchanged between the Spanish Governors and Lieutenant Governors of Louisiana reveal the Spanish character. They often tilted with the Osage windmill in their reluctance to face realities. Not once in three printed and bound volumes of their letters did they mention the unusual size of the Osage. It would seem that the Spanish ego could not bear to acknowledge that the Osages were a larger people than themselves.

The Osage, like the Spanish, were a proud people. While they displayed a generous amount of egotism, this was tempered by a humility that was absent in the Spaniard. Both peoples were devoted to their religious beliefs. Osage and Spaniard alike were idealistic in their religion. Possibly the arrogance arising from the confidence in their abilities and successes generated a friction between the Osage and Spanish. It is amazing how alike many of their traits were. Yet, the Osages were realists in all cultural matters other than religion. It was the Osage humility that baffled the Spanish mind. The frequent switch from arrogance to humility was incomprehensible to the Spanish. Like most Euro-Americans, the Spanish would have difficulty in understanding why an Osage would mourn the death of an enemy he had slain. This contrast in the arrogance of taking a human life and the humility of mourning for taking the life was at the root of much of the Spanish distrust of the Osage.

Spanish Failure

Many factors worked against the Spanish in their relationships with the Osage. Possibly the essential factor was the Spanish viewpoint that the Osages were rebellious subjects. From the Osage viewpoint, they were the subjects of no one, and the Spanish intruders were tolerated only as a means to acquire trade goods. Spanish embargoes of Osage trade caused punitive Osage responses because they removed the only reason the Osage tolerated the Spanish. Trade goods destined for other tribes were looted. After one attempt by the Spanish to exterminate them, the Osages' only response was simply to steal their farm horses. As a result, the Spanish subjects in the Illinois Country nearly starved to death because they could not raise their food. Only by lifting the extermination attempt and trading for Osage food could the Spanish save their toehold in the Illinois District.

Love, fear, and consent are needed to conduct an orderly government. The most successful governments are those based on love and consent with a touch of awe growing out of respect. Frederick the Great once became incensed at the bowing and scraping of a servant. He beat the servant with his cane and angrily shouted, "Love me, don't fear me!" It seems the Spanish tried this policy with the Osages and failed. The Osages' fear of losing trade was the only means the Spanish had to bring the Osages under their rule. They never had the love and often lost the consent of the Osages. The inability of the Spanish to enforce an embargo removed any fear of the Spanish on the part of the Osages.

The Fur Trade

Factors in the Trade

Among the various factors affecting the fur trade of mid–America, the single most important factor was the Osage nation. While this has been discussed by several authorities, none has stated the role of the Osages better than Carl H. Chapman.

> The Osage Indians were the most important of the tribes living in the western part of Spanish Illinois [Upper Louisiana] during the Spanish rule. They played several roles in the unfolding of the historical scene in the central Mississippi-Missouri Valley area and the prairies to the southwest. They were suppliers of hides and furs to St. Louis and Arkansas Post; they were barriers to overland travel and trade between the Spanish territory bordering the Mississippi and Missouri rivers and that of Mexico and New Mexico; they were buffers against the English during the American Revolution. They were indomitable in their position of power.[24]

It is easy to see why the Osages presented such a problem to the Spanish fur trade. They were the largest suppliers of furs, and at the same time they were the greatest barrier to enlarging the fur trade.

The Spaniards introduced two new practices in the fur trade of the Middle Waters. First, they worked through French fur traders and second they encouraged Indians from the east side of the Mississippi to move to the

MISSOURI RIVER TRADE, 1775–1776		
Nations	Number of Traders	Trade Goods (value in pounds of furs)
Omaha	2	5,000
No. Pawnee	1	1,800
Pawnee	2	1,200
Otoes	2	4,000
Kansas	2	7,500
Missouri	2	4,000
Republican	1	3,000
Little Osages	2	7,200
Big Osages	7	15,000
TOTALS	21	48,700
TOTAL OSAGE	9	22,200

Fig. 17. Notice that almost half of the total trade was with the Osages.

Osage territory and trap furs.[25] French traders were well established in the trade before the Spanish acquired Louisiana. While some Spaniards, such as Lisa and Vasquez, entered the trade during the Spanish period, their number was quite small. A distinction among the traders must be made. Legitimate traders were respected by the Osages as long as they did not try to trade with the Indians of the west. Thus, in the absence of a Spanish embargo, fur trade was allowed to the northwest up the Missouri (see Fig. 17). Other types of traders were the *Coureurs de bois* (Runner of the Forest) and *Bohéme* (vagabond-outcast). These traders ignored the embargoes, which was agreeable with the Osages, but when they trapped furs in Osage territory or traded with the western tribes the Osages killed them. The majority of this type of trader operated along the Arkansas River.

Emigrant Indians were especially odious to the Osages, because they knowingly violated Indian custom. Not only did they deplete Osage game supplies, but they did this under the protection of the despised Spaniard. Even though the Southeastern Indians disliked the Spanish (as did all the Indian nations), they were especially adept at feeding the Anglo-American vanity. The Osages held this practice in great contempt as being unworthy of an honorable people. This was a view generally held by most peoples of the Plains who had a tradition of warfare, and it is an important distinction between the Plains and woodland peoples. We will return to this matter in a later chapter.

In Spanish Louisiana, there were three fur and hide trading centers. These were St. Louis in the Illinois district, Arkansas Post in the Arkansas district, and Natchitoches in the Red River district.[26] Officially all Osage trade was to be through St. Louis. This was a satisfactory arrangement for the Little Osage and White Hair bands, but it was not accepted by the Arkansas bands. In part, it was the search for a convenient trading outlet that unified the scattered Osage bands that dwelt on the Arkansas drainage. The desire of the Spanish at Arkansas Post for this share of the Osage trade made the various embargoes difficult to enforce. Natchitoches was a hide, tallow, horse, and cattle trading center. Red River residents raised tobacco for sale in New Orleans and, therefore, had many horses. Horses attracted the Osages like a magnet.

It is possible that the Spanish might have been able to rigidly enforce an Osage trade embargo by forcing their traders at Arkansas Post to comply. However, it is doubtful that this action could have been effective. The Osages would have supplied themselves with trade goods destined for other nations. In effect, they would have shut off all Spanish fur trade on the Missouri, Arkansas, and Red Rivers. Thus, Spain would have been harmed more than the Osages. The British were a further threat to Spanish embargoes.

The Osages disliked the Spanish, and their dislike of the British was equally as great. Yet, they would trade with the British if it became necessary because they were realists in trade. Certainly, the Ducharme incident showed British interest in the Osage trade. Jean Marie Ducharme and a party of British traders attempted to trade with the Osages during one of the many Spanish embargoes. Although the Spanish intercepted and confiscated the boatload of British trade goods, it did not entirely stop the British from trading with the Osages.[27]

No matter how one looks at the Spanish in the Mississippi Valley, one gets the impression that they were engaging in a holding action. They wanted a buffer between the British-American settlements and the Mexican provinces of Texas and New Mexico. However, it seems likely that they wanted to hold Louisiana for future development as well. The problem was how to finance the holding period. There can be little doubt that the fur trade was expected to pay the expenses for financing the administration of Louisiana. Therefore, we need to examine the value of that trade.

Some idea of the value of the fur trade in the 1775–1776 season can be gained from the assignment of traders and the amount invested in trade goods. A total of 97,000 livres was invested in the Missouri trade.[28] If we take twenty cents as the value of a livre, this would be a total of $19,480 invested in trade goods. Profits usually ranged from 100 percent to 200 percent of the amount invested in trade goods.

We will take 100 percent as our figure for estimating the value of the Missouri trade in 1775–1776. On this basis, the Missouri trade would amount to $1,948,000 and the Osage part of this trade would amount to $888,000. By applying the same basis to the 1794–1795 season, the amounts would be $3,500,000 for the total Missouri trade and $1,920,000 for the Osage trade alone.[29] Clearly, the Osage trade accounted for half or more of the Missouri trade. No figures are available for the Arkansas trade, but the Osage portion of this trade would be at least half. These figures are not impressive in terms of modern dollars. However, it would take more than twenty modern dollars to equal a dollar value in the late–1700s. The Spanish were excellent administrators and kept passport records. Every trader was required to have a passport to trade with an Indian nation. A typical passport listed, first, the name of the Lieutenant Governor issuing the passport. This was followed by the name(s) of the major leader(s) and the nation they were authorized to trade with. Then the names of the employees of the trading party were listed. Bans, such as supplying other traders and trading with other nations were specified in the passport. The passport was visa stamped or signed at Fort Missouri (see Fig. 18).[30]

The Vasquez Affair

Competition for the Osage trade was nearly as important in the Spanish fur trade as the value of the Osage trade was in preventing an effective embargo of the Osages. There were several incidents that illustrate this point, but none shows the rivalry between St. Louis and Arkansas Post better than the Vasquez Affair. St. Louis had all the Osage trade, but Arkansas Post wanted the Osage trade on the Arkansas drainage.

In a letter dated December 29, 1786, Jacobo du Breuil, Lieutenant Governor of Arkansas Post, wrote to Governor Estevan Miró about an alleged story told by Benito Vasquez.[31] We use the term *alleged* because the story may or may not have been told by Vasquez. Despite subsequent testimony to the contrary, the St. Louis trader was capable of such an act. In du Breuil's letter, he claimed that Vasquez had told the Osages that an army was coming to Arkansas Post to make war on them. Vasquez purportedly warned the Osages not to go near Arkansas Post or they would be killed. Brucaiguais or *Bro Ki he ka* (Chief of All), who was also called Caigues Tuajanga or *Ki he ka Wa ti an ka* (Saucy Chief), was from the *Tsi shu* Peace Maker clan. Chief of All had signed the Peace Agreement of 1785 but had allegedly broken it by attacking the Caddo on the Red River. Since the Spanish were demanding Chief of All as a hostage for this act and the Osages had not given him to the Spanish, obviously the alleged Vasquez story would be believed by the Osages.

Since this story came to du Breuil from Francisco Martin, who got it

ASSIGNMENT OF TRADERS, 1794–1795		
Nation	Traders	Shares
Big Osage	Coliere, Ceret, Roubidoux, Andreville, Montardy, Dubreiul, Pierre Chouteau, Papin, Chavin, Sanguinet, Clamorgan, Boleduc.	12
Little Osage	Roy, Marié, Lefleur, Pratt.	4
Kansas	Benito Vasquez, Bernard Sarpy, Durocher, Zenon Trudeau.	4
Republican	Auguste Chouteau	1
Otoes	Reilhe, Lavalé.	2
Pawnee	Yostie	1
Caddo	Leconte	1
Loups	Labadie	1
Omaha	Vincenes, St. Sire, Hubardau.	3

Fig. 18. Several Osage mixed-blood families have ancestors among these traders.

from Chief Cogisiguedes or *Ko ke Se ke ta gra* (Approaching Foot Sounds), one may suspect that the Osages could have "planted" the story. This would be a typical Osage tactic to confuse an enemy and to take the pressure off themselves. Approaching Foot Sounds had agreed to turn Chief of All over to Francisco Martin, but he had slipped away from him near Arkansas Post. A Quapaw woman told du Breuil that the Osages feared they would be seized and burned if they surrendered. This also suggests an Osage hand in the origin of the story. The Quapaw would look upon their part as a joke on the disliked Spaniard. Such "inside jokes" were dear to the Indian heart.

Francisco Cruzat, Lieutenant Governor at St. Louis, set about refuting the story when Governor Miró asked him to investigate the Vasquez Affair. In a letter dated July 29, 1787, Cruzat reported his findings to Governor Miró.[32] Cruzat points out that the testimony, under oath, of the traders who were with Vasquez, denies any knowledge of such a seditious story. He further points out that Chief of All and Approaching Foot Sounds had departed from Claremore I's village (Halley's Bluff in Vernon County, Missouri) before Vasquez had arrived there. As a further note, he adds that Martin was noted for bearing unreliable tales. Cruzat's astuteness is revealed when he attributes the origin of the story to the Osages.

Any one of the three parties involved—the St. Louis traders, du Breuil, or the Osages—could have started the story. However, we agree with Cruzat and attribute the story to Osage tactics. Regardless of who originated the story, the Vasquez Affair shows the maneuvering going on in the Spanish fur trade. This three way action, combined with the threat of British entry into the Osage trade, caused the failure of the Spanish embargoes against the Osages. As a result, the Spanish never brought the Osages under their rule.

Three of the traders who gave testimony in the Vasquez Affair left descendants among the Osages. One of these was Santiago Chovin/Chavin, who was a native of New Orleans and was forty-five years old in June of 1787. Another was Carlos Tayon who used the dit names of Michel, St. Michel, and Mikles among the Osages. He was a native of the Illinois country and in June of 1787 he was twenty-seven years old. A final attester was Josef Rivar (or Joseph Revard), who was a native of Three Rivers, Canada, and in June of 1787 was fifty-two years old. This Joseph Revard was a direct lineal ancestor of Major General C. L. Tinker on the maternal side.

The Problem People

Conflict of Objectives

Spain had a serious conflict in objectives between the Red River district of Louisiana and the Texas district of Mexico. To preserve the buffer status of Louisiana, it was necessary to promote trade. While this placed Louisiana as a buffer between the British-Americans and the Mexican districts of Texas and New Mexico, it placed firearms into the hands of the Lipan Apache and Comanche. Thus, the Texas and New Mexico districts could not bring these nations under their control.

The Osages were fighting the Comanche and Lipan Apache on their western and southwestern borders and were aware of their source of firearms. Their incessant raids on Natchitoches served two purposes: it supplied them with horses, and it hampered the trade with the Lipan Apache. While these raids harmed the development of trade in the Red River district, they tended to aid the Texas and New Mexico districts. Thus, these districts were able to put a more effective force in the field against the Comanche and Lipan Apache. This is exactly what the Osages wanted, for it placed the Comanche and Apache between two opposing forces.

Under Governor Francisco Hector Carondelet, Natchitoches suffered the loss of most of its tobacco market. This created a large number of traders who had been tobacco producers. These traders were unlicensed and scattered, so it was difficult to supervise them. While some of these former tobacco raisers traded with the Osages, the others either traded into Texas or directly with the Cheyenne, Comanche, and Lipan Apache. This aroused the Osages, and many traders were killed. The Osages could not allow this trade to undermine their own trade.

St. Louis was rapidly becoming the gateway to the West while Natchi-

toches was withering under conflicting policies and Osage attacks. The
Osages had no particular interest at stake on the northern reaches of the
Missouri. So long as they had a sufficient supply of trade goods, they allowed the Upper Missouri trade to proceed without molestation. However,
trade that involved their western and southwestern territory was certain to
attract their opposition. Pedro Vial arrived in St. Louis on October 6, 1792,
from Santa Fe, New Mexico. He confidently stated that the road to Santa
Fe was open, and it could be reached in twenty-five days.[33] Vial did not
consider the objectives of the Osages, so his road to Santa Fe did not become a reality until thirty-three years later, in 1825.

The development of a Missouri route to the Pacific was progressing very
well, and the Spanish might have been able to reach the Pacific by this route
if they had not insisted on placing embargoes on the Osages. These on again,
off again embargoes led to intermittent blockades of the Missouri River by
the Osages, which prevented any consistent, sustained efforts to reach the
Pacific via the Missouri. Jefferson was aware of these problems before he
sent Lewis and Clark on their expedition. The Lewis and Clark Expedition
was successful because it was a large brigade, the largest to ascend the Missouri up to that time. Jefferson's idea was to send a party so large that even
the Osages could not stop it. This idea did not escape the St. Louis fur traders, as the larger fur brigades after the expedition show. It is worth observing
that half of the original Lewis and Clark Expedition was sent back when
they reached the Mandan villages.

The message from the Osages to the Spanish was clearly trade with us
but do not trade with our enemies. Apparently, the Spanish either did not
interpret the message correctly or they chose to ignore it. We believe the
Spanish ascribed the Osages' acts of opposition to being willful acts of an
ignorant savage people. We doubt, however, that their response would have
been much different if they had fully realized why the Osages opposed
them. Both the Osages and the Spaniards had objectives in the West. The
Osages attained a portion of their objectives, but Spain failed in her ambitions. Spain became so embroiled in trying to subdue the Osages that she
neglected other problems and more important objectives. The Osages, Comanche, and Lipan Apache dealt Spain more problems than any other Indians the Spaniards had intercourse with in North America.

Danger of War

The Little Osages in the Bend of the Missouri had aroused Spanish anger
by killing five hunters in the spring of 1772 on the St. Francis and Arkansas
Rivers. Then to add insult to injury the Big Osages killed three hunters and
made captives of two more. From the Spanish viewpoint these acts were

a "lack of cooperation, . . . hostile attitude, overbearing procedure, and . . . failure to keep peace or submit to reason."[34] No consideration was given to the Osage viewpoint that these poachers were violating Osage territorial rights. Not only were they poaching game food, but they were, in effect, stealing trade furs and thus depriving the Osages of the trade benefits.

The Osages were an orderly people, and they did not take to violent actions without good reasons. The poaching and stealing activities far exceeded the consent of the Osages. The consent or permission given by the Osages to Euro-Americans was for the establishment of trading facilities but no more. The Euro-American view that the Osages were subject to their rule and that they had no title to unoccupied territory was never accepted by the Osages in the French or Spanish period. Yet, the Spaniards proceeded as if, in fact, they were masters of the Osages and Osage territory.

Given the cultural yardstick of Spanish standards and the conflicting standards of the Osage culture, it is easy to see why the Spaniards were so angry with the Osages. Equally clear is the reason why the Spanish never really reached an accommodation with the Osages. Lacking the financial means and military force to impose their rule upon the Osages, their only viable recourse was to accept the situation and adjust to it. The French, as realists, had adjusted to the situation. However, the idealistic Spanish were so dedicated to their concept of how things should be that they could not adjust to the situation that prevailed. In the poker game of Louisiana, Spain held one ace and six losers; she discarded her ace and held losers against the Osage nation's full house.

Between 1782 and 1791 the major thrust of Osage actions was centered on the Caddos, Kichais, Pawnee, and Arkansas Post.[35] However, this is not to say that no actions occurred elsewhere in the Osage empire. The Mississippi settlements, the Missouri area, and Natchitoches also felt the Osage presence. In March of 1785, a conference was held at New Orleans between the chiefs of the Arkansas Osages and the Caddos. "A peace was agreed upon but quickly broken by the Osages who, without provocation, attacked the Caddos and Kichais."[36]

Although this account does not tell where the fight took place, it does relate that the Caddos and Kichais were returning from a hunt. The Osages would not have attacked these people unless they had hunted in Osage territory. Thus, it was the Caddos and Kichais who broke the peace agreement. Since the Spanish did not recognize hunting territory rights, they considered the attack as an unprovoked violation of the agreement. The Caddo were well aware they had violated Indian law and the spirit of the agreement. They sought revenge on the Osages and hoped to acquire Osage hunting rights by claiming the attack had no provocation.

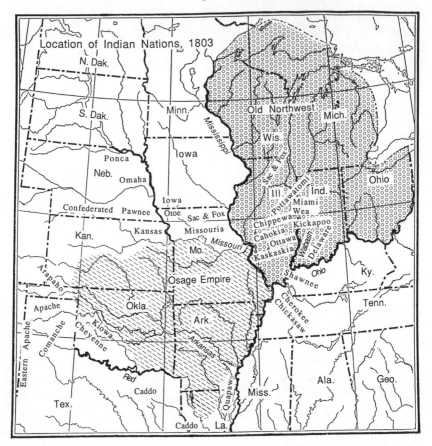

Fig. 19. Notice that the Osage Domain was only slightly smaller than the Old Northwest. Practically all the nations around the Osages warred against them to acquire Osage lands.

The Spanish, acting on misconceptions they were all too willing to accept, placed another embargo on Osage trade and encouraged Indian nations to the north, south, and east of the Osages to make war on them. Councils were held where powder and ball were distributed, but the Spanish Indian allies had a realistic view toward the Osages and only a few token raids were made by them. These raids were not large enough to use up the powder and ball (see Fig. 19).

As a result of these Spanish actions, the Osages showed their naked power. In 1789, they struck the Kichais near Natchitoches and forced them to move nearer to the Little Caddos. Earlier in 1788, they had forced the Great Caddos to seek safety among the Little Caddos. Undoubtedly, there were seizures of trade goods and illegal trading going on all through this period. The Spanish were becoming alarmed, and with more than a little justification because the Osages were without a doubt considering forcing them out. Spanish actions had weakened the restraint of the Little Old Men. It took all their waning power to restrain the band chiefs. Fortunately for the Spanish, the desire for trade goods outweighed the Osage hatred for the *E spa lo* (Spaniard).

The Spanish wanted to exterminate the Osages but the cost, which had been estimated at twenty thousand pesos without any guarantee of success, caused them to temper their desire.[37] At the close of 1791, no solution had been found for the Osage problem, and it had now become more critical than it had been in 1782 at the beginning of Governor Miró's administration. Nerves were wearing thin under the constant threat of Osage attacks. In a fit of childlike frustration a Spanish Commandant on the Arkansas wrote, "It is cruel that a nation so cowardly, of so little consequence, and an enemy of nearly all its neighbors, does us so much wrong and deprives the province of the immense resources that it might withdraw from the lands where they claim to dominate. This nation would not long exist if the Caddo, their irreconcilable enemy, and the Arkansas were aided."[38] While this statement has the usual lies about the Osages, it does reveal the Spanish blindness to reality. They were aware of Osage territorial domination but refused to admit it. Idealism again shows in the dream that the Caddo and Quapaw could overpower the Osages. Over the previous century, the Osages had so completely defeated and demoralized the Caddo that they were useless as an effective fighting force against them. The Quapaw were a kindred people to the Osages. While they and the Osages often warred against each other, neither wore black paint in these clashes. Their conflicts were more of a family spat than war. It was advantageous for the Quapaws to make the Spaniard believe they would war on the Osages. Both the Osages and Quapaw knew that Quapaw thrusts into Osage territory were moves to convince the Spaniard that they were enemies of the Osages.

From Uneasy Peace to War

The American Revolution created a threat to the Spanish in Louisiana. Due to the immediate need to deal with this threat, the Spanish put Osage matters in the back of their minds. Therefore, an uneasy peace prevailed between the Osage nation and Spain between 1775 and 1782. While this period of peace had conflicts and counter conflicts, these were not as severe as they became in the period between 1782 and 1794.

Shifting powers on the east bank of the Mississippi had no immediate effect on the Osage or the Spanish. However, as more and more American settlers moved west along the Ohio and Tennessee Rivers, their presence created a threat to both. The British were trying to trap out and trade for as many furs as possible in the northern part of the Old Northwest. This was eventually ended by the War of 1812. Yet before that time, the British exerted a growing influence in the Old Northwest (the area between the Ohio and Great Lakes, west to the Mississippi) and northern Louisiana. Without any doubt, the Osages participated to a limited extent in this growing trade.

Spanish administration in Louisiana always labored under a shortage of adequate funds and military force. The American Revolution forced the Spanish to realize how vulnerable they were without Indian allies. They, like other Euro-American powers, sought to use Indians as pawns in the struggle to keep their colonial empire. What the Spanish (and, for that matter, all the Euro-American governments) did not take into consideration was the aims and needs of the Indians. Euro-Americans always did, and still do, tend to consider all Indians to be the same, and, therefore, they established a uniform policy toward the Indian nations. This always has been and still is a mistake, because Indians differ greatly and no single uniform policy can ever solve Indian-related problems.

It was Spanish policy to use the Southeastern nations as a buffer between the Americans and the Floridas (East and West Florida) as well as the lower Mississippi. This policy suited the Osages since the Spanish discontinued the practice of encouraging the Cherokee, Choctaw, and Chickasaw to move to the west side of the Mississippi. This was to keep them available east of the Mississippi. Spanish policy demanded that the Indian nations west of the Mississippi act as a bulwark against the Americans on the east and the British on the north. However, in order for them to be an effective force they had to bring about peace among the western Indian nations. Unfortunately for the Spanish and possibly for themselves, the Osages blocked these Spanish efforts to bring about peace.

It was not the intent of Osage policy to block the Spanish peace efforts. Their policy was to protect their land, and in doing this they upset Spanish plans. Osage religion, custom, and practice all dictated that intruders who hunted in Osage territory without permission must be killed. In a long letter from du Breuil of Arkansas Post to Governor Cruzat in October of 1786, amid a long list of so-called atrocities committed by the Osages and plans to wage war against them with Osage enemies, a revealing remark is made. "They [the Osage enemies] promise good support to the Caddo immediately upon the withdrawal of the hunters of this district who are scattered on the branches of this river."[39] Since the compaction of so many nations south of the Arkansas made game scarce on that side, it is clear that the hunters were on the north side in Osage territory. Failure to recognize these acts as provocations of Osage rights doomed the Spanish peacekeeping gestures. Under the Biblical injunction, "If thine eye offends thee, pluck it out," the Spanish tried to exterminate the Osages.

Osage Response

As the Spanish drew closer to openly declaring a war of extermination against them, the Osages responded to the embargoes and the sending of other Indians to war on them. The Spanish paid dearly for fumbling the matter of Osage relationships. Throughout the Spanish period, the Osages continued to kill Spanish subjects. We place the burden of blame for these acts of the Osage at the Spaniards' doorstep because they were supposedly the more civilized and advanced of the two sides, as well as being the intruder.

Osage actions in the south and southwest were as follows: Five traders killed on the Washita River; seven Frenchmen killed near Arkansas Post; a hunter killed on the Arkansas near the mouth of the Poteau; four Frenchmen killed on the Poteau; trappers robbed above the Poteau; three Frenchmen killed and robbed near Natchitoches; and two Frenchmen killed in the Pawnee country.[40] Santiago Traver, a hunter, was killed on the Arkansas and three others robbed on the White River.[41] Baptiste Le Duc, a creole, was killed on the Arkansas.[42] This Le Duc was either a mixed-blood Osage or married to an Osage. In either case, he was considered to be a traitor by the Osages.

Actions around Natchitoches were especially alarming to the Spanish. By the spring of 1788, the Osages were attacking near the outlying cattle ranches of Natchitoches.[43] From Quachita (French spelling for the Osage *Wa she Ta* [Fat Deer]), which was a post up the Red River from Natchitoches, four more killings and beheadings were reported.[44] The Osage pressure on the Caddoean peoples became so great that the Tonkawa, Tawakoni, Kichai, and Yscanis relocated near San Antonio, Texas.[45] Bodies of two men and a woman were found within sixty leagues (180 miles) of Natchitoches, and their deaths were attributed to the Osages.[46] Letters reporting these incidents were bitter in their views of the Osages.

Osage responses were not limited to the Arkansas, Red, and Washita Rivers. The Mississippi settlements also felt the Osage presence. Ste. Genevieve was the subject of several Osage raids, but other areas were also affected. Settlers were attacked on Canteen Creek, twelve miles north of St. Louis. A man and a boy were killed on the Meremec.[47] Citizens of Ste. Genevieve complained that the Little Osages had struck their villages for seven or eight consecutive years and that they no longer had horses enough to till their fields.[48] The house of Sieur Gratiot was looted by the Big Osages only six miles from St. Louis. At this same time, the Little Osages killed and be-headed a hunter near Ste. Genevieve.[49] Manuel Perez, Lieutenant Governor at St. Louis, reported horses stolen by the Little Osages at St. Louis and Ste. Genevieve.[50]

These are only a small sample of Osage responses that have been docu-mented. Undoubtedly, only a fraction of the incidents were reported in the existing documents. We omitted most of the incidents involving Indians friendly with the Spanish. Interestingly, in the Illinois district (St. Louis to Ste. Genevieve) very few Euro-Americans were killed. In each isolated case, they were hunting and had been beheaded. This district experienced looting and horse stealing but very few killings. Evidently, it was the Osage intent to harass but not kill in this district. Since they did not trade on the Arkan-sas, that area experienced more killing of Euro-Americans.

The contrast between the Illinois district and the Arkansas-Natchitoches districts show a favorable treatment to the Illinois district. Since Osage trade goods came through the Illinois district, the Osages did not want to be too severe in their actions in this district. Thus, they employed harassing actions that inflicted economic hardships on the inhabitants and would somewhat demoralize the settlers. These were strategies the Osages had used for cen-turies and apparently they worked against the Euro-Americans as well as they did against Indians.

Arkansas and Red River districts did not share in the Osage trade mo-nopoly held by the Illinois district. Thus, the Osage restraint against killing Euro-Americans in the Illinois district did not apply to these two districts. However, in truth, there were more free or independent hunters and trappers in the Arkansas and Natchitoches districts than in the Illinois district. This fact meant that Osage hunting rights would be more frequently violated in these districts. For this reason, more Euro-Americans would pay for these violations by losing their lives.

One other factor contributed to the contrast between the treatment of the Illinois district and the other two districts. The Little Osage and Osage River Big Osages were conducting the campaign in the Illinois district. It was the Arkansas bands who conducted the campaign in the southern and southwestern districts. The Little Osages had primarily three war clans: the Mottled Eagle, Men of Mystery, and Buffalo Bull. These were secondary war clans and as such favored the harassment strategy over killing. Big Osages on the Osage River also had many people in secondary war clans. However, they also had the two Division Chiefs whose duty it was to keep the peace. In the late–1700s this condition changed with the Earth Division going to the Arkansas bands.

While the Arkansas bands had some people who were members of secondary war clans, the majority were members of the Bear and Panther clans, the two leading war clans of the Osage people. Thus, in general, killing took precedence over harassment in their campaigns. To say that the leading war clans always preferred killing or that secondary war clans always chose harassment would be misleading. We are indicating tendencies instead of absolute preferences.

It seems that these three factors—trade consideration, independent hunting and trapping, and the distribution of war clans—caused a difference in Osage actions in the three districts. A historian must seek cause and effect relationships and interpret their significance as clearly as possible. Apparently, the Osages were telling the Spanish, we approve your presence for trade purposes, but we forbid hunting and trapping by intruders in our territory. Evidently, the Spanish were telling the Osages, you are rebellious subjects and if you do not keep the peace we will exterminate you. The conflict in these messages is obvious. It was time for the Spanish to "put up or shut up."

The Osage-Spanish War

Petitions and Speeches

Most of the agitation for war against the Osages came from Arkansas Post and Natchitoches. This is understandable because they had been hardest hit by Osage actions. The St. Louis traders stood to lose a rich fur trade if Spain went to war against the Osages. Neither Arkansas Post nor Natchitoches legally shared in the Osage trade, so they had little to risk and much to gain if the war subdued the Osages. These posts wanted a share of the Osage trade, but they wanted even more to be able to trade with other Indians in peace.

A petition of hunters and inhabitants of Arkansas Post dated May 8, 1789, is an example of many pleas for an Osage war.[51] This petition was signed by twenty Euro-Americans who asked for permission and help to make war on the Osages. Obviously, the post was suffering from poverty due to Osage depredations against them. The signers were in an excellent position to know they had absolutely no chance to inflict any significant harm to the Osage. To be candid, this seems more of a ploy to secure relief from poverty than a sincere desire to go to war against the Osages, and it is the first time in Osage history we have noted this ploy being used. In the American period, the American intruders developed this device to a fine art form with more creative variations.

Realizing that embargo hurt themselves more than the Osages and only brought an increase of Osage attacks, the Spanish were constantly seeking other means to subjugate the people. On October 8, 1789, Perez wrote to Governor Miró about actions he was taking.[52] Perez was demanding that the Osages deliver to him the Indian that had killed a Euro-American. Furthermore, when they delivered the accused, the Osages were to execute the Indian in Perez's presence. We give Perez an "E" for effort, but he must have known that in 1789 no Osage would be turned over to the Spanish for execution. Positively, an Osage would not kill another Osage for the Spanish, because his own life would be forfeited upon his return home. Perez was sure the Osages would not comply with this demand, although the Quapaw had earlier met such a requirement. As an alternative, he planned to seize an Osage chief as a hostage.[53]

Perez included a copy of the letter he had sent to the Osages so the Governor could see what he had written. It is interesting that Perez opens his letter with a reference to the blue sky. Either Perez or an advisor had some knowledge of Osage customs. The clear blue of a cloudless day, in the Osage idiom, meant peace and a long life. His concluding paragraph was not mentioned in his cover letter to Governor Miró. In this paragraph, Perez threatened the Osages with an embargo, encouraged other Indians to attack them, and threatened an attack from all sides.

Osage reaction to the Perez demands was typical: they ignored them. On March 7, 1790, Perez wrote that no chiefs had made an appearance.[54] He reported that there had been a heated discussion of the matter among the Osages and then it was dropped. Perez probably suspected that the discussion was about the question of making war on the Spanish instead of about whether to meet his demands or not. He immediately points out how powerful the Osages are and the need to temporize. Also, he points to the need for tact since the available force permitted little else. The Osages were a proud people and the insult Perez had sent in his letter to them was certain to inflame their war spirit. Perez had a better comprehension of the Osage problem than most of the Spanish officials in the Mississippi Valley. However, it seems he had received some sound advice from the French traders at St. Louis. He was in the midst of some of the most astute Frenchmen in the American Fur Trade, the ones who had made St. Louis the gateway to the West. These men had created the spirit of St. Louis, and Perez was deeply influenced by this spirit.

Problems of Fighting the Osages

One of the major problems plaguing the Spanish was the problem of population. If we are to believe later records, the Osage population was between 8,000 and 10,000 people. The Osages all through the first half of the 1800s claimed their population had remained at these levels despite conflicts in the

French, Spanish, and American periods. We believe the Spanish consistently underestimated the Osage fighting force as being from 700 to 1,200 men. We would estimate that to 1850 the Osages had at least two thousand prime-age warriors and could field another 1,000 young and aged warriors, although they would be less effective than the prime-age men. Most Osage women were skilled in the use of the bow and constituted a reserve force. The remaining elderly and very young had some fighting potential, as they demonstrated against the Cherokee in the so-called Battle of Claremore's Mound. If we take the minimum figure of eight thousand people, the Osages were indeed a formidable force.

By comparison, a census of Louisiana taken in the fall of 1771 shows a total male Euro-American population of 1,507. The total population including women and slaves totaled 11,344.[55] Since male Euro-American population figures include all ages, it is doubtful if the Spanish could muster more than 800 to 1,000 effective white male fighters. They would be facing at least 1,200 to 2,000 fighters trained from childhood and seasoned in actual combat. It is doubtful if this pitifully small Euro-American force could have stood up in combat with the Osage secondary force of old warriors and young boys.

The Spanish realized they could not rely on their available Euro-American manpower. However, they hoped against their misgivings that they could entice their Indian allies to attack the Osage. This was not feasible for many reasons, not the least of them the general Indian dislike of the Spaniard. We have mentioned that the Spaniards had forced the Quapaw to give up one of their people and slay him in Spanish presence. Such acts may satisfy one's thirst for power, but it surely would not generate any great love for the Spanish in Quapaw hearts. The Caddoean peoples had been thoroughly demoralized by the Osages for over a hundred years. They held the Osages in such awe that they were useless to the Spanish in an Osage war.

The Indian nations east of the Mississippi, impacted by the advancing American frontier, thirsted for Osage lands or, more accurately, the game upon the land. However, the Spanish did not offer them land or game, only powder and ball. Even the offer of land would probably not have been enough to induce these Indians to plunge deeply into the Osage homeland—they were not that crazy. It was one matter to ambush a small Osage hunting party and quite another to face a large Osage war party on their own ground.

It was not possible for the Spanish to realize the impossibility of getting a unified strike from Indians. Many Indian leaders from time to time have tried to unify Indian nations against Euro-Americans, and all have failed. In recorded history, Indian unification has always failed, and for one reason

Population of Louisiana, 1771						
District	Whites		Free Colored		Colored Slaves		Total
	M	F	M	F	M	F	
N. Orleans	1034	769	67	67	568	720	3190
Delta	229	200	26	32	838	773	2098
Alemanes	704	564	4	4	428	312	2016
Acadia	268	218	0	0	20	16	522
Cortada	284	264	0	0	0	0	548
Natchito-ches & Ra-pide	291	227	0	0	199	165	882
Atacapas & Opelusas	255	189	0	0	112	75	631
Iberville	154	123	0	0	0	0	277
Arkansas	32	30	0	0	9	7	78
St. Louis	251	122	0	0	74	50	497
Ste. Gene-vieve	212	120	0	0	166	107	605
Totals 11344	3714	2826	62	103	2414	2225	

*Colored persons include Negroes, Mulattos, and Indians.
NOTE: There was a loss of 250 people between the enumera-tion and the completion of the table above.
Source is the same as *fn* 55.

Fig. 20. This table shows how few non-Indians there were in Louisiana. The available men for an army would have been less than 1,000 able-bodied men.

above all others. Indians differ too greatly from nation to nation. Each nation has its own customs, its own goals, its own thought patterns, and its own experiences.[56]

The Spanish experience in trying to use Indian allies to exterminate the Osages follows a classical pattern: speeches are made that promise support against the despised enemy; some token raids are made; powder and ball are issued, and the support fades away. Each of the nations had their own motive for not warring on the Osages. We have merely listed a few to show why the Spanish were doomed to failure in a war with the Osage.

While population alone would defeat the Spanish, there were other factors against them. The terrain and vegetation would have insured the defeat of an army ten times larger than the Spanish dreamed about. If this were not enough, the supply line ratio, that is, an extended vulnerable supply line versus a compact defensible line of supply, would have made the Spanish invasion position untenable. All the advantages favored the Osage—the Spanish held only one remote advantage. They could have placed a Spanish army from Cuba or from all their American colonies in the field, but we fear such a Spanish army would have met Braddock's fate or destruction such as General St. Clair's army. Withdrawal of enough troops to decisively defeat the Osages would have left the Spanish colonies open to attack by the French or English. Spain could have poured enough troops into St. Louis to defeat the Osage, but it would have been the most expensive piece of real estate they ever acquired in terms of lost manpower, money, and territory.

Francisco Cruzat gives us some idea of what an Osage warrior could do.[57] La Balafre (The Scar), a Little Osage chief, was seized as a hostage while visiting St. Louis, supposedly under a flag of truce. A few days after his treacherous seizure, phrased as an arrest, The Scar tried to escape. It took the entire garrison to restrain him. Cruzat writes in awe of "the fury, wrath, and blind animosity with which he opposed his arrest."[58] Cruzat's awe grows as he relates that forty days after his imprisonment The Scar again tried to escape: "Various inhabitants bear witness to his furious delirium. It became impossible to lay hold of him without injuring him because he was like a mad dog foaming at the mouth. With the greatest barbarity he attacked anybody who came near to him, like a desperate person who looks not to his life. Finally it was possible to tie him, although he was a man of superior strength."[59] The Scar evidently killed himself in his cell or died of wounds he received in trying to escape. This is why it was impossible to enslave adult Osages—their liberty was so dear to them that they chose death over slavery.

Osages were famous for their fury and a complete disregard for their lives in combat. It was these traits as well as their size and strength that awed all who fought them. Speaking from our own observation, when angered, an Osage feels no pain and his strength is greatly magnified. Cruzat's account is the only known record of the Spaniard witnessing an Osage warrior in action. They were fortunate The Scar was unarmed. It had taken the entire St. Louis garrison to subdue one unarmed Osage warrior and the Spanish were preparing to go to war against 1,200–2,000 armed Osage warriors. There can be little doubt that the Spanish would have suffered a terrible defeat in an actual physical war with the Osages. As matters evolved, though, they did not emerge very well in the paper war either but maybe with a less evident defeat.

The Paper War

Indian Attacks Against the Osages

Between September of 1789 and April of 1792, the Spanish reported three attacks upon the Osages by other Indians. The first of these was in the fall of 1789 against a small Osage village at the Grand Saline east of Claremore, Oklahoma. It should be remembered that all able-bodied males and females were out on the Plains on the fall hunt. The outlying Osage village contained only the infirm and very young children.

Louis de Blanc of Natchitoches gleefully reported to Governor Miró the details of this victory over the Osages: "I must tell Your Lordship that the Comanche, Tawehash, Wichita, Yscanis, and Tawakoni formed an army of 700 warriors and went to fall upon the Osage, with all the success that might be expected. This advantage has encouraged them to such an extent that in the spring of the coming year they intend to collect many more to enter the Osage village itself."[60]

It is notable that even with an army of seven hundred able-bodied warriors, who knew they faced only the aged and infants, that they chose to attack a small outlying Osage village. These "great warriors" did not have the courage to face the one hundred aged and infirm Osage warriors in the main village. Another fact, never mentioned by the Spanish, is that they never tried another invasion. It is possible that the old Osages in the small outlying village inflicted heavy losses on the invading force. The "courageous warriors" certainly did not want to run into a small rearguard force of able-bodied Osage warriors who might be left as protectors the following hunting season.

Joseph Valliere at Arkansas Post reported another Indian attack on the Osages in April of 1790.[61] Seven Mascou (probably Muskogee) and two Euro-Americans managed to surprise six Osages. They killed five Osages in the surprise attack and later killed the Osage they had captured. Such raids were common on the fringes of Osage territory. In the overall picture, the Osages probably won more of these clashes than they lost, or the Spanish would have reported more victories.

In April of 1792, Manuel Perez at St. Louis reported a Sac raid on the Osages to Governor Miró:[62] "A party of Sauk [Sac] who went to fight the Osage succeeded in killing three men and taking two prisoners. Another party of the same nation of the Sauk has gone to war against the Osage. There is no doubt that, if the Sauk, Renard [Fox], and Kickapoo wish to continue making war on the Osage, they will succeed in terrorizing them and cause them to come to reason without any necessity for us to become implicated in a war with them which might be very prejudicial to the country on account of its present situation."

We doubt that the Osages were ever terrorized by the Sac or Fox, although they had a healthy respect for them. However, Perez was absolutely right in regard to the Sac, Fox, and Kickapoo ability to cause the Osages great concern. In 1792, the Osages stood in the greatest danger on their northeast border, and they knew it. Perez had evidently reached this same conclusion, but he had some doubts that the Sac and Fox would choose to push hard enough to effectively weaken the Osage. In the end, the north-eastern nations decided to make a stand against the Americans rather than push against the Osage.

The Osages may have looked upon the Caddos as an overawed people, the Quapaw as a kindred but weaker people, and the Southeastern nations with contempt, but they respected the northeastern people. One old Osage, in commenting on the fighting abilities of the short-legged Delaware, said, "Him fight like hell, him can't run." While the old warrior's eyes had a twinkle, one knew he said this as a tribute. Stories among the Osages clearly show they respected the fighting abilities of the Sac, Fox, Pottowatomie, Kickapoo, Delaware, and Illinois.

There was enough concern among the Osages about a possible invasion of Sac and Fox in 1792 that they took an unprecedented step. They asked the Kansas nation to help them stop what they thought was an impending invasion. Although it was also advantageous to the Kansas to halt the Sac and Fox advance, for reasons of their own they refused. From that time to the present, the Osages have applied the archaic Dhegiha word, Kaw, to the Kansas. At that time, the word meant coward. One must consider that in 1792, the oldest sister (*Me na,* the oldest sister was always the prize) of Claremore I and White Hair I had just married White Plume, who was the leading Kansas chief. Therefore, there was a supposed alliance between the Osage and Kaw because of this marriage.

Plans

In January of 1790, Louis de Blanc of Natchitoches proposed that the Governor commission him to lead a party against the Osages at his own expense.[63] During the spring of 1791 a meeting of the Chickasaw, Mascouten, Cherokee, Shawnee, Abenaki, and Saulk was to be held. This council of nations was to reach an agreement to make war on the Osages.[64] In March of 1792, Perez at St. Louis reported that the Big Osages had seized trade goods destined for the Kaws. He added that the traders were not harmed and that the Osages promised full value for the goods. The traders said the Osages would continue this practice unless traders were sent to them. Perez carefully points out that if all Missouri trade is cut off, the entire trade would be lost to the British.[65]

A new team of Spanish administrators appeared in the early 1790s. Governor Estevan Miró was replaced by Hector Carondelet, Lieutenant Governor Manuel Perez was replaced at St. Louis by Zenon Trudeau, and Ignacio Delino was installed at Arkansas Post. Trudeau, being French by birth, was probably more knowledgeable about the Osages than the other new administrators. These new officials followed the same pattern as their predecessors.

Thus a new round of embargoes and threats against the Osage followed the appointment of these Spanish leaders.

Carondelet wrote to Delino in June of 1792, advising him to press upon the Osages from all points. He had given the Quapaw thirty guns and three pounds of powder for each warrior.[66] As usual, the Quapaw were glad to accept these gifts and made suitable "big talk" about what they were going to do to the big bad Osages. Of course, this was for show. Trudeau shows astuteness and comprehension in a letter he sent to Carondelet in October of 1792.[67] He points out that the Osages were at war with the Iowa, Sac, and Fox and would not be likely to get goods from the British. However, Trudeau notes that this would lead the Osages to attack the Mississippi settlements. He assures Carondelet that if four or five inhabitants are killed the rest will move away. Trudeau makes an original suggestion to Carondelet that, if an embargo is to be implemented, traders with a two year supply of goods be sent up the Missouri before the embargo is announced.

In his reply to Trudeau in December of 1792, Carondelet approved of Trudeau's new suggestion.[68] He also ordered an embargo with heavy fines and penalties for violators. His declaration of war on the Osages is worth quoting.

> At the same time you will proclaim that any subject of His Majesty, or individual of the other nations, white or red, may overrun the Great and Little Osages, kill them and destroy their families, as they are disturbers of the prosperity of all the nations.
> It is extremely important to humiliate or destroy those barbarians which can only be done by using severity.[69]

Governor Carondelet probably believed he had taken a decisive step to eliminate the Osage problem once and for all. Over the following months, like the Governors before him, he was to learn that "big talk" rolled off the Osages like water off a duck's back. Like other Euro-Americans, he had to learn that the Osages were unlike any other Indians in his experience. They were too independent-minded to be controlled by mere threats. It was evident to the Osages that the Spanish could not make good on their threats.

Big Talk—No Do

Amid the flood of letters rushing in a torrent among the Spanish administrators, only one reflected the cold hard stamp of reality. On April 10, 1793, Zenon Trudeau in writing to Carondelet gave accurate reasons why he was delaying announcement of the embargo and of war on the Osages until

July.[70] He candidly notes that all the Indian nations are at war with the Osages, but that despite this none of them kill more than two Osages a year. Trudeau points out the strategic geographic location of the Osage homeland. Again, he notes the danger of losing the Mississippi settlements if the Osages become angered. This was a distinct possibility, and it must have taken extraordinary efforts on the part of the Little Old Men to prevent the Osages from fulfilling Trudeau's fears.

We must point out the basis for the conflicting viewpoints among the Osages. The Arkansas bands led by the Bear and Panther clans wanted to do away with the Euro-Americans. Many among the Little Osages living with the Big Osages and the Osage River Big Osages agreed with the Arkansas bands. The Little Osages of the Missouri and most of the Big and Little Osages on the Osage River favored trade over driving the Euro-Americans out. This argument set the stage for the splintering of the Arkansas bands about three years later, in 1796. The final conflict was the selection of White Hair I (Iron Hawk) as Grand *Tsi shu* Chief over Claremore II (Town Maker). These conflicts weakened the power and influence of the Society of Little Old Men because it weakened the bond of the gentile system. We will come back to this matter near the end of this chapter.

Apparently, Trudeau's realistic information only angered Carondelet who was guided by what he thought the situation should be. He noted his reply on the margin of Trudeau's letter. Carondelet's directions were explicit: he directed that the Indians be incited against the Osages to deliver a general blow. Significantly, he directed that these Indians be issued arms against the King's account in the amount of one thousand pesos. This is significant because it is the only recorded authorization to spend such a large sum against the Osages.

Delino at Arkansas Post informed Carondelet on April 12, 1793, that he would march against the Osages early in May. This force was to consist of fifty or sixty Euro-Americans and as many Indian allies.[71] On September 28, 1793, Trudeau informed Carondelet that only the Shawnees and Loups were ready to march against the Osages in July.[72] Since they only amounted to a total of one hundred men, the July campaign was abandoned. It is interesting that Trudeau mentions that the other tribes feared the Americans would march on their villages if they left to fight the Osages. Trudeau points out that possibly as many as two hundred Euro-Americans could be raised in the Illinois district, but not a single one volunteered. He suggests that the embargo would bring the Osages to their knees.

Trudeau was too well informed about the Osages to believe in the embargo. He was probably trying to delay a direct conflict with the Osages.

Clearly, very few if any in the Illinois district wanted to make war on the Osages. Equally evident is that the Illinois district was better-led than the residents of Arkansas and Red River districts.

Louis Lorimer was a special Indian agent and interpreter for Carondelet. He had been sent among the Indian nations to stir them up against the Osage. On September 17, 1793, he sent a report to Carondelet.[73] He reports the usual desire of these nations to strike against the Osages. When asked to set a time for the attack, the nations said it was up to Carondelet to do that and that they could be ready in ten days. Obviously, the time lapses involved in this "war," as well as trying to get the various elements to strike as a single force, contributed to the Spanish failure.

Without knowing the motives, culture, and backgrounds of the various Indian nations, it is impossible to determine how much of what they said was true and how much was false. It seems reasonable to assume that because they did not have the strength to oppose the Spanish, Americans, and Osages simultaneously, they did use a certain amount of diplomacy. That is, they would try to cozen the Spanish into believing that they and the Spanish shared the common goal of destroying the Osages. There was enough truth in this to make it believable to the Spanish. However, undoubtedly many counter motives existed that varied from nation to nation and that would override the desire for Osage territory. Since these were the real determining factors in the Indian decisions not to unite in war against the Osage, they are important in both Osage history and United States history. Because detailed histories about these nations are not available, we cannot determine what these factors were.

One of the greatest fallacies perpetuated in Indian wars is the role played by firearms. It is difficult to find all the reasons for this, but some facts do stand out. Up until the production of the repeating rifle, the firearm was inferior to the bow and arrow in Indian warfare. The Indians knew this, the mountain men knew, and those who fought Indians should have known it. Facts clearly show that until the repeating rifle appeared, the firearm was too slow against the bow and arrow. In other words, a fighter armed with a firearm would look like a pin cushion before he could reload.

The mountain men compensated for this weakness by withholding their fire. A certainty that the leader of an Indian charge would die discouraged most Indian attacks on mountain men. In groups of two or more mountain men, no two rifles were empty at the same time. Indians did use firearms for their psychological effect and for a first round of fire, but the bow and arrows were the weapons of death. For deer hunting and other woodland hunts, the firearm was superior to the bow. This is why the Indians wanted firearms. Osages rarely used firearms to hunt buffalo before the advent of metal cartridges. Not only were they dangerous to use from horse back, but the prime was often lost in the chase. The bow and lance were just as effective and they were safer and more reliable.

We wanted to mention these facts about firearms because Euro-Americans have always wanted to believe the firearm was essential in warfare. Indians knew Euro-Americans believed this, and, accordingly, used it as an excuse whenever the need arose. It was used as an excuse to avoid fighting an unwanted war and it was used to acquire munitions for the hunt. The Spanish were committed to the belief in firearms and based much of their policy on this belief.

Carondelet had more than the Osages to worry about. George Rogers Clark, who had led a successful expedition down the Ohio during the American Revolution, was heading a second expedition. Americans west of the Appalachians had no outlet for their products except down the Mississippi. Their products were bulky and heavy, making overland transport prohibitive in cost except for whiskey. Alexander Hamilton's Whiskey Tax and the resultant crushing of the Whiskey Rebellion led to an outcry in the West for an open port at New Orleans. The Spanish wished to curb American expansion to protect the Floridas, Texas, and New Mexico. For this reason, Carondelet closed the Port of New Orleans to American trade. Clark intended to float down the Mississippi and open the Port of New Orleans by force if necessary.

By 1794, Carondelet had been well educated in the Osage problem and was more than ready to drop the Osage war. Clark's expedition worried Carondelet, so he directed a halt to the Osage war to concentrate more on the American problem. For many years, a post to be constructed among the Arkansas bands had been proposed. Arkansas Post had consistently opposed this, offering the excuse of low waters creating supply problems. Probably, it was opposed because Arkansas Post wanted the trade. In any event, Carondelet was now ready to try the French post system as a means to controlling the Osages. Although it was the Arkansas bands that gave the Spanish the most trouble, they made the choice of placing the fort among the Osage River bands. Therefore, they began negotiations with Missouri River drainage Osages.

Fort Carondelet

The Beginnings

Manuel Perez proposed a fort among the Osages as early as October 1791.[74] He suggested a small wooden fort be erected overlooking the Osage villages on the Osage River. Perez argued that this would strengthen the hand of those Osages who did not approve of the raids by the Arkansas bands.

Governor Miró was replaced by Carondelet before he acted on these suggestions. Carondelet would not commit himself to this proposal until he had gone through the Osage educational process.

The time was ripe for someone to revive the idea of an Osage fort as suggested by Perez. Auguste Chouteau probably instigated the suggestion by Perez, but now he decided to present the idea himself. "[Auguste] Chouteau presented his petition to Carondelet on May 18 [1794] and the latter accepted it three days later. Carondelet eagerly seized upon the plan and authorized Chouteau to proceed while awaiting royal approval, as it was certain to come."[75] It appears that Chouteau went to New Orleans well prepared to make his point. Six Osage chiefs were in New Orleans to petition for just such a fort.

A tragedy was in the making with the presence of the Osage chiefs in New Orleans. Three of the six chiefs were slain on their way home. The deaths of these chiefs was tragic enough, but the effects of the deaths made it a much greater tragedy. Among the three slain chiefs was Jean Lafon (Tracks Far Away I), who was the Grand *Hun ka* Chief. The Grand Division Chiefs Jean Lafon and Claremore I (Arrow Going Home) were the right and left hands of the Little Old Men. Through these chiefs, they had managed to keep the gentile bonds intact and curb the excesses of the Arkansas bands.

With the death of Jean Lafon, the Grand *Hun ka* Chieftainship went to Tracks Far Away II (miscalled Big Track). This shifted the Grand *Hun ka* Chieftainship to the Arkansas bands and split the gentile divisions. For the first time, the Grand Chiefs lived in separate villages. Thus, one of the objectives of Fort Carondelet—to strengthen the Osage River Osages so as to better control the Arkansas bands—was destroyed at its inception. This was tragic for the Spanish because it ruined one of the most intelligent moves they had made during their tenure in the Mississippi Valley. It was tragic for the Osage people because it weakened their greatest cultural strength on the eve of their severest challenge—the coming of the Americans.

It was Governor Manuel Gayoso de Lemos of Natchez who unwittingly set up the murder of the three Osage chiefs. On May 22, 1794, he sent a letter to Ugulayacabe, a Chickasaw chief. As a casual note of interest he wrote, "There is now six Osages in New orleans [*sic*] that went there to entreat for peace. When I know the results I shall acquaint you with them."[76] On June 10, 1794, Carondelet wrote to Trudeau, "The great chief Lafond and two chiefs of the Little Osages were assassinated some twenty leagues from this fort [New Orleans] through the treachery of the Chickasaw chief Ouilabé, who, having lost his son in the beginning of the year in an encounter with the Osages, came down here in search of the latter with twenty-two warriors. Notwithstanding all the means I employed, the carelessness of the six Osages in coming to land without arms gave him the opportunity to kill three of them."[77]

Fearful that these murders under Spanish protection would cause a renewal of Osage animosities, Carondelet made the usual "big talk" against the Osages. The Chickasaw knew the Osages were coming and were waiting on the west bank. It seems evident that they acted on de Lemos's information. Carondelet reveals one facet of his character in his last statement of the quote.[78] He did not like to accept responsibility for his poor judgment.

The Fort

There was some latitude allowed in the specifications for what became Fort Carondelet. The blockhouse was to be two-storied, the lower section was to be of stone, and the upper story of horizontally laid logs. Both levels were to be thirty-two feet square. A diagonal setting of the top story was specified. That is, the sides of the upper section were centered over the corners of the lower floor. All buildings of the installation were to have tile, slate, or sod roofs.

One may find a reason to fault Carondelet in some matters, but clearly he understood fortifications. He specified that the blockhouse command an unobstructed view of the Big Osage village. This provided direct artillery fire into the village. With a stone lower floor, ten feet high, the tall Osages would have difficulty in firing the blockhouse. The offset in the upper story of the blockhouse provided covering fire in eight directions, with the upper-story corner overhangs protecting the center walls of the lower floor from above. Although Carondelet wanted tile or slate roofs he did agree to accept a sod roof. It is obvious that this was to frustrate any attempt to set the roof afire with fire arrows. Such arrows were not as effective against thick log sidewalls as they were against shake shingles.

Placed at the north edge of Halley's Bluff, this blockhouse had a full view of White Hair's village on the north side of the Osage River. It is worth observing that there are no known pictures of Fort Carondelet or maps to verify its location,[79] leading to a suspicion that the fine touch of Auguste Chouteau was at work. It is possible that Chouteau deviated more than a little from Carondelet's specifications and did not wish this to be known outside his sphere of control. However, a fort was constructed and archaeological evidences suggest it was on Halley's Bluff and that it did conform in many respects to Carondelet's specifications.

Chief Making

The Osages were vulnerable to flattery. Since symbolism played a large role in their lives, any symbolic article was held in awe and veneration. To be singled out, to receive a symbolic object was a very special honor. In a culture based on honors instead of material greed, this was taken as a token of the Great Creator's esteem. It mattered not what source the symbol came from, for the Great Creator often used unusual means to reward his favored ones. The desire for honors amounts to greed. White men had a greed for "things"; the Osages had a greed for honors.

By judicious selection of chiefs who promoted their interests, the Spanish could present medals to them and thus increase the chief's stature among the people. It is notable that in 1795, Iron Hawk or White Hair I received a large medal, but Town Maker (Claremore II) received only a commission for a large medal. Between 1795 and 1796, White Hair I became Grand *Tsi shu* Chief. We do not want to infer that these medals caused the selection of White Hair I over Town Maker. Medals could have played a minor role, but Osage laws governing the Council of *Ah Ke tas* would have been the decisive factor in selecting White Hair I.

Band chiefs were another matter since they did not lead by law, although they did lead by consent. If their people were sufficiently impressed by the medal gift, all other things being equal, the medalist had a better chance of becoming a band chief. Thus, the Spanish did have some influence in Osage government. Significantly, the band chiefs and the Grand *Tsi shu* Chief grew in power during the Spanish period, while the Little Old Men and the Grand *Hun ka* Chief lost power and influence. However, as in the example of White Hair I and Town Maker I, there were other overriding factors at work.

Shortly before the Euro-Americans came to the Osage country, it had become necessary to reorganize the Osage military government. The Grand War Party organization, controlled by the Little Old Men, had become so encumbered by ceremonies that a quick response to an attack could not be made. In effect, creation of this new organization for war divided the power to make war between the Little Old Men and the individual bands. Nowhere was the effect of this reorganization more evident than in the activities of the Arkansas bands. The erosion of power held by the Little Old Men was steady from 1700 to 1850. In the same period, the power of the band chiefs grew in proportion to that lost by the Little Old Men.

During the struggle of the Little Old Men to curb the raids of the Arkansas bands, the Grand Division Chiefs were also involved. Up to 1794, when Jean Lafon was killed, both Grand Division Chiefs stood equal to each other and both supported the views of the Little Old Men. With the ascension of Tracks Far Away II to the Grand *Hun ka* Chieftainship, the Grand Division Chiefs were divided. Tracks Far Away II was with the Arkansas bands and Claremore I was with the Osage River bands with most

of the Little Old Men. With the help of the Little Old Men, the Grand
Tsi shu Chief gained in power while the opposition of the Little Old Men
lessened the power of the Grand *Hun ka* Chief. As a note of interest, if
Claremore II had become Grand *Tsi shu* Chief, this would have placed both
Grand Chiefs in the Arkansas bands and most of the Little Old Men with
the Osage River bands. This was probably a factor in choosing White Hair
over young Town Maker.

The Spanish were certainly aware that some kind of internal conflict was
going on among the Osages. However, it is doubtful if they understood the
details of the conflict. They knew enough to improve their own position
but not enough to avoid canceling out the improvement they had tempo-
rarily gained. Although they improved their position with the Osage River
bands, they further weakened their position with the Arkansas bands. Their
strongest support came from the Little Old Men, but by strengthening the
band chiefs they weakened the Little Old Men and thus gave more strength
to the Arkansas bands.

THE TRANSITION PERIOD

There are many stories about why Spain was willing to transfer Louisiana
to France. Thomas Bailey gives three reasons for the transfer.[80] Louisiana was
a heavy liability to Spain and she had been willing to dispose of it since
1795. Thus, the cost of administration and defense of the colony was the
first listed. Next, the colony was an open invitation to invasion and the consequent cost of a war to defend it would be difficult to justify. Lastly, it had
always been considered as a buffer area for Texas and New Mexico, and
Spain was weary of trying to preserve that status.

One can see the Osage influence in each of these, but Bailey does not
mention the Osage influence. We cannot claim that the Osages were the
outstanding factor of administrative and defense costs in Spanish Louisiana.
However, they were certainly a major factor. Both in direct and indirect
costs, coping with the Osage problem was expensive for the Spanish. Nearly
a third of the letters published from the Bancroft Collection of the documents relating to the Spanish in the Mississippi Valley involve the Osage
problem. The carefully selected Spanish documents related to Tennessee,
which have been published in the East Tennessee Historical Society's Bulletin, show a much smaller percent of mention, but the fact that any mention is made indicates the far-reaching effect of the Osage problem. From
these facts alone, it is evident that a considerable amount of administrative
time was devoted to Osage matters, as well as direct defense expense.

The Osages hurt Spain indirectly by depriving her of income she would have had if they had not stood in the way. Spain used the other Indian nations and their territory in the Mississippi at will. She could use the Osages and their territory only on Osage terms. Thus, she was deprived of the richest part of Spanish Illinois and of access to the riches that lay west of the Osage domain.

In comparison with the areas north, south, and east of the Osage domain, the resources of the Osage territory were untouched. The Spanish knew this, the British knew it, and the Americans knew about the potential for development. This rich prize was tempting to eastern Indians and Euro-Americans alike. The effort of stemming the tidal surges of eastern Indians, American, and British intruders while also trying to get a portion of the Osage empire was a constant problem for the Spanish.

By 1795, it was evident that Spain would not be able to subjugate the Osages. Without control of the heartland of Louisiana, its value as a buffer was greatly reduced. Constant Osage pressure on Natchitoches and the compacting of defeated Indians as far south as San Antonio, Texas, was hurting the very areas Louisiana was supposed to buffer. Furthermore, Osage pressures on the Comanche and Lipan Apache prevented their movement away from the Rio Grande settlements and prolonged the Indian attacks there. No wonder Spain was weary of supporting Louisiana. Spain willingly transferred title of Louisiana to Napoleon and at Bonaparte's request kept the transfer secret.

Toussaint L'Ouverture is sometimes called the black Napoleon. Bonaparte sent his best general, Leclerc, and fifty thousand of his best troops to Haiti to establish an operational base. He needed this base because on the day he openly took over Louisiana, the British would cut his oceanic supply line. Toussaint and yellow fever destroyed Leclerc and his troops. If a group of poorly armed rebel slaves in the mountains of Haiti could do this to the finest army produced in Europe, we must ask a question: What would have happened to Bonaparte's army against well-armed Osages in the Ozark Mountains? Failing to establish a Haitian base, Napoleon abandoned his Louisiana ambitions and turned to the European wars. Thus, Louisiana was made available to the United States.

The Osages paid a heavy price for their resistance to intruders and their expansion, not because of any Spanish policy or intentional actions but from many indirect influences. The weakening of the Little Old Men and the gentile bonds greatly reduced the Osage ability to unite against intruders. Dispersal of what had been a compact force weakened their strategic advantage of striking from a core area. Spreading out from the compact core base in west central Missouri distributed the base over a wider area and made rapid communication difficult. The Little Osages had moved to the headwaters of the Neosho-Grand and the Arkansas bands had moved to the lower reaches of the same river. Given time, uninterrupted by outside forces, the Osages probably would have resolved these problems within a generation. However, time to adjust did not come to the Osages. They were facing a cataclysmic change that was totally alien to anything they had experienced before.

The coming of the Americans caught the Osages unprepared to repel the American type of intruders. They were torn by internal strife and were poorly located to effectively resist agricultural intruders such as the Americans. As a result, their dominant status in the heartland of Louisiana was coming to an end. Up to this time, 1803, they had met the French, Spanish, and British. Yet, their exposure had been largely to traders, hunters, and a few habitants. The traders and hunters wanted furs, which fit into the Osage way of life. Habitants typically lived in a few small cluster villages and farmed around the village, which caused little disturbance to game animals. These the Osages could tolerate with few adjustments.

A totally new type of intruder awaited the Osages. The coming of the Americans was to present situations that the Osages had never experienced before. They had very little information to guide them in how to respond to these new situations. While they had fought Americans on the Wabash River and helped defeat them, they were well aware of Anthony Wayne's decisive victory at Fallen Timbers in 1794. All too well they knew of the terrible treaties that followed.

Acting on what little information and experience they did have, in typical Osage fashion, they developed a few guidelines in advance. First, and foremost, they were determined to never make war on the United States, and they never did. Fallen Timbers had clearly demonstrated the futility and retaliation of such actions. This is the only clear and consistent guideline the Osages had. The others are cloudy because of lack of information and experience on the part of the Osages. They might have suspected that many eastern Indian nations would try to move into their territory. However, they could not have known of President Jefferson's plan to move these nations into their territory on a wholesale basis.

Osages did have some idea of the agricultural intruder problem and had formulated a policy of avoiding the settlers. They hoped that by avoiding contact they could prevent the conflicts. What the Osages did not know was that the United States government had completely lost control of the settlers when it came to Indian affairs. Thus, they were totally unprepared to cope with the intruder settler. There is an Osage distinction between a legal settler and an intruder settler: A legal settler settled on lands that had been cleared of Indian title, while an intruder settler was on lands to which the Osages still had title.

Over a span of years, the Osages had evolved ways to deal with other intruders. Indian and hunting Euro-American intruders were killed and beheaded and their heads were placed on stakes. Trader intruders were robbed and turned back. Intruder farmers were harassed and their horses were stolen. The American intruder settler presented a new situation. These intruder settlers were not the "noble pioneer" so often portrayed—this stereotype fits the legal settler much better. The intruder settlers were the dregs of American society, lawless misfits who sought the frontier to escape punishment within their own culture. They were the *Bohéme* of America with one inalienable right—they were citizens of the United States. Loudly and persistently they proclaimed that right and broke every law of the country that protected them.

The inconsistency inherent in these people completely baffled the Osages, who were an orderly people. While the Osages had *Bohéme,* these were cast outside the culture and were afforded no protection. French and Spanish practice had been to protest and frown on the slaying of their *Bohéme,* but they had let these actions pass as not worth the effort to retaliate. The Osages never really found a solution to the problem of the United States' failure to enforce intruder provisions in treaties while at the same time punishing the Osages for enforcing those provisions.

Governor Joe (Star Chief) came close to finding a solution. He was a huge Osage and better educated than the average Euro-American of his time. Chancing upon some intruders camped in Osage territory, he helped himself to their meal. As he ate, the man and wife discussed their possible fate at the hands of this wild Indian. When he finished, Joe gestured for them to hitch up and get out. Relieved, they did so and hurried toward the border, discussing their good fortune in escaping with their hair intact. As they neared the border Joe overtook them, and, in better English than they could command, told them if they came back they would be arrested and tried under Osage law. They never reappeared on Osage lands. Of course, Joe thoroughly terrorized them before they hitched up, and when he overtook them they were certain he had changed his mind and would lift their hair.

Baffled in their efforts to halt the deluge of intruder settlers the Osages were to turn their efforts to the emigrant nations. Osage experience told them that attacking other Indians caused less concern than attacking Euro-Americans. They could not have known that this would bring the wrath of the United States government down upon them. Osage attacks on emigrant

Indians caused those east of the Mississippi to be reluctant to move west of the great river. It would be more accurate to say it added to their reluctance. Thus, the voluntary removal envisioned by Jefferson ultimately became a mandatory removal by military force under Andrew Jackson. The Osages could not understand this aspect of their own warring on other Indians until many years later. No one has fully researched this facet of Indian removal.

It was these unknown factors combined with internal strife and dispersal of the bands that made the Osages so vulnerable as the Americans crossed the Mississippi. One cannot read the historical records without noticing an abrupt change in Osage conduct. No doubt this was partly because of the deep-seated desire to avoid war with the United States. Yet, the true causes lie buried deep in the passage of time. Maybe we will never know all the reasons for this abrupt change. Surely, the reasons we have discussed were factors in this change, but there were undoubtedly others. The Osages were not sorry to see the Spanish go, but they were not overjoyed to see the Americans come into their domain. Being realistic in their approach to life, they accepted the situation as it was and tried to save what they could of their culture and domain.

The Osages had lived with the French idealism tempered with a realism which was so much like their own approach to life. No doubt, the wonderful Spanish idealism both appealed to the Osages and at the same time repelled them, for it conflicted with their sense of realism. Americans tended to be pragmatic. This brusque approach to life offended the Osage love of pomp and deep idealistic symbolism. Yet, at the same time, it inspired the sense of realism in the Osage character. The observant Osage curiosity was continually piqued by the fact that whatever the Americans did, it worked, at least for the Americans.

They were amazed at the technological changes that appeared after 1803. Improved firearms quickly caught their attention. New trade goods led to rapid depletion of their game reserve, so great was their desire for the new items of trade. Boats that walked on their rivers brought hordes of Americans to their country. Wagons that were vastly superior to those of the French and Spanish brought more Americans. The changes were so sudden that the people could not adapt to them fast enough. It was a catastrophic force beyond their ability to adjust. They were overwhelmed.

PART TWO

Eroding the Osage Civilization, 1803–1850

4

Coming of the Americans

LEWIS AND CLARK

First Reaction

Although the Osages were aware that the Americans would ultimately occupy Louisiana and had made some plans to cope with these new people, the suddenness of its occurrence caught them by surprise. We are fortunate to have an account of the Osage reaction to the news of the Americans taking over Louisiana. On May 31, 1804, the Lewis and Clark Expedition met a canoe which had descended the Osage River.[1] A Frenchman with an Indian man and woman were the canoe's only passengers. The Frenchman gave the Expedition an account of the Osage reaction to Chouteau's letter to them in which he informed them of the American Occupation.

They burned the letter because they did not believe it spoke the truth. After some deliberation, Chouteau's agent among the Osages was told that if this was true, the Osages would no longer trade with St. Louis. The inference was that the Osages would trade with the British instead of with the Americans. Undoubtedly, this was an Osage bluff war thrust. It carried the threat of a shift in Osage trade and support from St. Louis to the British. We cannot be certain this was entirely a bluff tactic. However, it would be in keeping with the many times this ploy had been used against the Spanish with gratifying effect. Certainly, the Osages were realistic in diplomatic matters. They were undoubtedly aware of the many Americans along the Ohio River, which far outnumbered the British traders to the north. If this was a threat, it was probably a move to place the Americans in a more suitable frame of mind to make concessions to the Osages. Assuming it was a bit of bluff war, it would fit in very well with the next Osage move. Yet, the Osages were to be disillusioned if their intent was to gain concessions from the Americans.

FIRST OSAGE DELEGATION TO WASHINGTON

The Osages Meet Jefferson

If the Osages expected any significant concessions from the American father, President Jefferson, they were doomed to disappointment. Centuries of treating with the Indian nations would have taught them to expect few concessions in a first diplomatic encounter, so they likely had no early expectations. However, they were surely shaken by later events, for the Americans made few, if any, concessions to the Osages.

Yet, the American officials from Jefferson on down were well aware of the necessity of keeping the Osages friendly to the United States. Therefore, they planned the reception of the Osage delegation with care. By July of 1804, the delegation of twelve Osage chiefs and two boys, escorted by Auguste Chouteau, were near the Shenandoah Valley. On July 9, 1804, Henry Dearborn, Secretary of War, sent orders to hurry the party to Washington with a special military escort.[2] This effort was evidently effective, for on July 12, 1804, President Jefferson welcomed the delegation to Washington.[3]

Jefferson wrote of the meeting the next day in a letter to Robert Smith, Secretary of the Navy.[4] He describes the Osages as, "the most gigantic men we have ever seen." Jefferson also wrote, "They are the finest men we have ever seen." Being aware of the importance of these Osage visitors, the President wanted to impress them with American justice, liberality, and power. With this in mind, he encouraged them to sightsee in the Washington area.

Jefferson's statement about the Osage importance to the United States deserves repeating: "Jefferson then summed up the American attitude toward the stronger western tribes, revealing in a few words the justification for the expense; the anxiety; and the elaborate detail with which he and Dearborn had arranged for Lewis to send back these delegations. 'The truth is,' he said, 'they are the great nation South of the Missouri, their possession extending from thence to the Red river, as the Sioux are great North of that river. With these two powerful nations we must stand well, because in their quarter we are miserably weak.'"[5]

Clearly, the President differed from the Spanish in his dealings with the Osages. Possibly it was because of Jefferson's strange mixture of idealism and realism, which was shared by the Osages. Such mental outlooks cannot be turned on or off to suit special situations. The Osages sensed this mental trait in the French and they sensed it in Jefferson. While they liked the President, they also realized that he was nonetheless a great danger to them. Reading faces, gestures, and body movements was a highly developed art practiced among the Osages. These nonverbal clues, along with Jefferson's words, told them what to expect.

Jefferson's Formal Speech

In his formal address to the delegation (on July 16, 1804), Jefferson outlined his intentions.[6] He made eleven major points in his speech: (1) He expressed regrets and sorrow for the deaths of Osages at the hands of the Sac and Fox (A raiding party had killed these Osages as their delegation was leaving Missouri). While Jefferson presented this as a condolence, he also included a clear notice that warring under United States law would not be allowed; (2) In his second point, Jefferson tried to establish a bridge of common bond. He pointed out that Americans were born in America and came from the same soil as those in the Osage delegation; (3) He continued this theme into the third point and assured the delegation there would be no more changes in government. He noted that France and Spain were governed by a European government, but Americans were governed by an American one; (4) The President then entered into trade matters, which had been his main purpose in addressing the delegation. After pointing out the mutual advantage of trade, Jefferson hinted at a government-sponsored fur trading factory, with stress being placed on fair prices and fair treatment. Ultimately, this system was initiated by the establishment of Fort Clark, better known as Fort Osage; (5) Building on the basis of mutual benefit from a fair fur trade, Jefferson's speech turned to the need to expand trade, and he explained the American necessity to explore the Missouri River. In this way, Jefferson opened the subject of exploring Louisiana;

6) Since Jefferson realized the importance of the Osages in these explorations, he promoted his plans to explore the Red and Arkansas Rivers as an enhancement to the Osage trade. Furthermore, he asked for Osage assistance toward the expeditions that would visit them[7]; (7) Besides the Missouri and Arkansas expeditions, Jefferson also announced his intentions to explore Kansas and into the Republican Pawnee country;

8) The rift between the Missouri bands and the Arkansas bands were of great concern to Jefferson. He promised that he would do all in his power to help heal the rift and bring the people together again; (9) To keep peace between the Osages and the Americans, an agent was to be sent among them to settle disputes that arose between the two people; (10) Jefferson invited the Osages to explore and observe the area around Washington, likening it to the American desire to explore and observe in Louisiana; (11) The President concluded his address with a plea for peace among all the nations.

A copy of the reply by White Hair I and the Little Osage chief, Dog Soldier, does not exist. It certainly would have been interesting to know how they responded to the intentions outlined by Jefferson. Their response was probably cloaked in courtesy and probably contained notable omissions. Certainly, the President did not mention his plans to remove eastern nations to Osage territory.

Ample evidence shows that the Osages ignored Jefferson's first point, that warring among the nations would not be permitted. All through the 1804–1850 period the Osages warred on the other Indian nations. The President's sixth point, which involved the exploration of the Red River and the Arkansas River, shows the depth of Jefferson's information. He knew very well that the delegation represented only the Missouri bands. This is also evident in a letter from Dearborn to Pierre Chouteau dated July 12, 1804 (four days before Jefferson addressed the Osage delegation from Missouri): "You will take the necessary measures for obtaining permission of the Bigtrack [Tracks Far Away] and his party for the safe passage of any party which may be sent by the President of the United States to explore the sources of the Arkansas river and the interior country generally bordering on the waters of the Red River."[8]

One aspect leaps out at the reader of these early American documents, that is, the practice of asking permission in advance of an action. It is unlikely that this was overlooked by the Osages, since important Osage intruder laws hinged on prior permission. Jefferson apparently knew that the success of the explorations required prior permission. The Osages could not refuse assent under their law, but their cooperation was less than enthusiastic.

One cannot help noticing the contrast between the American approach to the Osages and that of the Spanish. The Americans were well led by one of the most brilliant minds in history. Jefferson's knowledge of the Osages attests to his ability to garner information and, more important, use the information to accomplish significant goals. The Spanish attempted to dictate Osage conduct and met failure. Possibly, their successes with the more docile Indians to the south had conditioned them to a dictatorial approach in Indian affairs. Jefferson and his countrymen had experienced terrible Indian wars and realized that, until they were in a position to dictate, they must respect Indian laws and customs. Once they had attained a majority, the Americans dictated terms as well.

The Return Trip

Great care was exercised in returning the Osage delegation to their homes. Henry Dearborn wrote to Moses Hooke at Pittsburgh, directing him to be ready for the delegation by August 20, 1804.[9] The delegation rode horseback from Washington to Pittsburgh, then took a boat down the Ohio River, accompanied by a military escort consisting of a noncommissioned officer and six men. They left the Ohio at Massac, Illinois, and traveled overland under military escort to Kaskaskia. One member of the delegation became ill in Washington and could not leave with the others. He was personally and carefully escorted back to St. Louis by the United States government.[10]

Some time had passed without any word from the Lewis and Clark Expedition. A rumor started that the Osage delegation was serving as hostages for the safety of the expedition. But even though a false report of the death of both Lewis and Clark reached the Capital during the time the delegation was still in Washington, they were not treated as hostages.[11] It is possible that the British initiated the false rumors in an effort to alienate the Osages and other Indians from the Americans.

On April 17, 1805, Captain Meriwether Lewis sent Jefferson a collection of flora and fauna he had collected, along with a catalog of the items.[12] Among the specimens were the skins and skeletons of a male and female antelope. These pronghorn samples were the first to be seen by the scientific world. Jefferson had heard about the pronghorn while visiting with the Osage delegation and was eager to learn more about the animal. In a letter to the naturalist William Bartram, dated April 7, 1805, he wrote, "The Osage Indians shewed me a specimen of its leather, superior to any thing of the kind I ever saw. Their manner of dressing the leather too receives enquiry, as it receives no injury from being wet. I count on special information as to this animal from Capt. Lewis, and that he will enrich us with other articles of Zoology, in which he is more skilled than in botany."[13] Note that Lewis was sending Jefferson, from Fort Mandan, the very thing he wrote about, on the same day, April 7, 1805.

SEARCH FOR PEACE

Jefferson, like the Spanish before him, tried to bring about peace among the Indian nations west of the Mississippi. He meant what he told the Osage delegation in Washington. The President was aware of the differences among the various Indian groups, but thought that, as an administrative matter, establishing a single uniform policy would make it easier and cheaper to administer Indian affairs. As history testifies, this decision was extremely expensive for both the United States and Indians in general. Before such a policy could be applied, the warfare growing out of the Indian differences must be abolished. Neither Jefferson nor the United States government ever solved this problem of Indian differences. As a result, there are more exceptions than uniformity in United States Indian Policy.

As usual, all peace efforts involving the Indian nations started with a general council, and so did the peace efforts of the United States. James Wilkinson, commanding at St. Louis, wrote to Secretary Dearborn on September 22, 1805,[14] pointing out that the two greatest expenses in Indian affairs are the visits to St. Louis and Washington by Indian delegations. Visiting was a strong custom among the Osages. It was a gesture of friendship to visit someone, and it was less than friendly to refuse to receive a visitor or to refuse a visitor food, drink, and gifts. The reception of a visitor was a way to distinguish friend from foe.

Wilkinson urged the rapid establishment of factors and agents among the nations in order to reduce the expenses of visiting St. Louis. Yet, at the same time he was suggesting that delegations to Washington be continued for two years so the nations would be impressed by the United States. At this time, 1805, Wilkinson was sending to Washington a western delegation composed of representatives from the Arikaree, Otoe-Missouri, Sioux (Dakota), Sac, Iowa, and Fox. As the delegation was about to leave, seven Republican Pawnees arrived in St. Louis and were also sent to Washington.

Wilkinson mentioned the coming conference of the hostile nations as a final note in his letter. Apparently, twenty Osage chiefs, led by White Hair I, were in St. Louis for the peace council. Little came of the council since so many hostile chiefs were in Washington. Surely, there would have been very little, if any, easing of warfare among the Indian nations. However, the trips to Washington apparently were effective in curbing attacks on Euro-Americans.

FEAR OF WAR

The Americans feared an Osage attack upon them. In a letter written August 18, 1809, Meriwether Lewis—who became governor of the Louisiana Territory after returning from his expedition—expresses a fear of an Osage war.[15] Pierre Chouteau was up the Missouri while the Osage Treaty of 1808 was waiting for Senate ratification (it was ratified April 28, 1810). Lewis feared Chouteau, who had negotiated the treaty with the Osages, might be replaced by another agent. He writes, "The reasons for wishing Mr. Chouteau not to be displaced is that if the event takes place before one or the other Osage treaties are ratified there will in my opinion be War with that nation."[16]

The plural of treaty is used in Lewis's comment because there were actually two treaties. The main treaty was negotiated by Pierre Chouteau on November 10, 1808, at Fire Prairie near Fort Osage, but this treaty was signed only by the White Hair and Little Osage bands. A second companion treaty was negotiated by Governor Lewis at St. Louis on August 31, 1809. Provisions of the second treaty were identical to the Fire Prairie Treaty, but it was signed only by the Arkansas bands.

FOLLOWING IN SPANISH FOOTSTEPS

Governor Lewis had reason to fear an Osage war. In a letter of July 26, 1808, he wrote, "I have in several late conferences with the Shawnee, Delawares, Kickapoos, Soos, Saues [Sac], Jaways [Iowa], &c. declared the Osage nation no longer under the protection of the United States, and set them at liberty to adjust their several differences with that abandoned nation in their own way, but have prohibited their attacking them except with a sufficient force to destroy or drive them from our neighborhood."[17] Lewis, in a fit of pique, had provided an opening for the British to expand into the Osage country. By declaring the Osages no longer under the protection of the United States, he inadvertently left the Osages free to seek protection under the British flag.

It is obvious that the Osages had not been cooperative in keeping the peace. Like the Spanish before him, Lewis became so frustrated that he let his feelings take control of his better judgment. But by November of the same year, he had regained his poise. Article Ten of the Treaty of 1808 specifically places the Osages under the protection of the United States. Thus, Lewis reversed himself. From the wording in Article Ten, clearly Lewis feared his rash action would drive the Osages into the British camp: "[A]nd the said nations, on their part, declare that they will consider themselves under the protection of no other power whatsoever; disclaiming all right to cede, sell or in any manner transfer their lands to any foreign power." [18]

One must bear in mind that the boundaries of Louisiana had not yet been determined in 1808. The French-Spanish claim, which the United States had acquired by purchase, conflicted with the British claim to the northern portion of what ultimately was included in the Louisiana Purchase. However, in 1808, the British claim, while weak, would have been materially strengthened if the Osages had placed themselves under British protection.

Another factor at work against Lewis was the growing war movement in the United States. The West wanted the British removal from the Old Northwest, as provided in the Treaty of Paris (1783), the treaty that ended the American Revolution. By 1812, the war movement had gained such momentum that it brought about the War of 1812. The United States could ill-afford to have the most powerful nation on the lower Missouri allied with the British while the shadow of a possible British–American war lay upon the land. The Treaty of Ghent in 1815 ended the War of 1812 and removed any possible Osage–British alliance. This possibility was further barred in the Osage Treaty of 1815.

While the Treaty of Ghent and the Osage Treaty of 1815 severed any possible Osage–British alliance, neither offered any immediate solution to the British problem. The British were in no hurry to vacate the territory they occupied in the Old Northwest and Northern Louisiana. They still exerted a considerable amount of influence among the Indian nations in these areas. Governor William Clark, in writing to Thomas Jefferson on October 10, 1816, from St. Louis,[19] mentioned that while he could keep the nations of Missouri at peace, the tribes east of the Mississippi, especially high up that river, were a problem. In at least one case, he allowed the Missouri nations to war on those nations east of the Mississippi. He gives his reasons for allowing this as prevention of British influence among the Missouri Indians and to prevent a confederation of Mississippi nations that could destroy the Louisiana settlements. This condition could not have existed much beyond 1820, for by that time the British were concentrating their efforts from the eastern Rockies to the Pacific in the Northwest, thus setting the stage for the struggle to establish the border at 54°40′.

In the same letter, Clark gives an estimate of population in upper Louisiana. He gives the non-Indian population as between 35,000 and 40,000 people. This would be over thirty times the non-Indian population in 1771, which was only 1,102. Virtually all this increase came between 1804 and 1816. The increase was so large between 1804 and November of 1808 that the Osages became alarmed enough to want space between the new settlers and themselves. Therefore, they were willing to cede three quarters of eastern Missouri and Arkansas. If only Euro-Americans had been involved, they would have been more reluctant to make these cessions. However, many northeastern and southeastern nations were also crossing the Mississippi and settling in Osage territory. The tidal wave of impacted Indian nations and land-hungry Americans were now engulfing the Osage People.

5

Treaties and Land Cessions

TREATIES

Introduction

Treaties are agreements between two or more sovereign nations. Sovereignty lies at the base of all treaties. To avoid any misunderstanding here, sovereignty must be clearly defined. *Sovereignty* is the power to make and enforce laws. This power is divided into two types: *internal sovereignty* and *external sovereignty.* Internal sovereignty is the power to make and enforce laws within a geographical area, and it is applied to the society within that area only. External sovereignty is the power to make and enforce laws outside one's own boundaries, which affects other areas and societies.

One indisputable fact stands out in the relationships between the American Indians and the nations of Western civilization. The American Indians had owned, occupied, and exercised sovereignty over the land for at least ten thousand years before Columbus stood on American soil. Euro-Americans had no alternate sane choice other than to recognize this fact, so they did recognize Indian sovereignty.

By applying the egocentric logic of assumed superiority, Western civilization rationalized the usurpation of Indian sovereignty and the seizing of Indian territory. This rationalized "justice" was cloaked in various terms, such as "we are saving heathen souls," "we can put the land to its highest use," and "we have a right to unused, unoccupied lands." But, no matter how one looks at these "justifications," they are all merely expressions of an assumed superiority.

No reasonable mind could deny that the technology or hardware of Western civilization was superior to that of the Indian civilizations. However, in matters of cultural intangibles, there are valid reasons to question the superiority of Western civilization over Indian civilizations.

In a very real sense, Indian governments were superior to those of Western civilization in many respects. If one accepts the premise that the government that provides the greatest benefit for the greatest number of its people and the greatest voice in its control is the best government, then one must admit that Indian governments *were* superior to those of Western civilization. There is no doubt that in 1500, a higher percentage of Indians enjoyed better housing, better nutrition, better clothing, and greater freedom than the conditions that prevailed in Western civilization. One may argue that this was because there were fewer resources per person in Europe than in America. The counter argument to this is that such imbalances in resource-population ratios are caused by flaws in a culture and not by flaws of the land. Since governments are a leading factor in a culture, then, in part, such imbalances reflect back to flaws in government.

We have digressed from our main discussion of treaties to show that the basis for the actions of Euro-Americans was not really valid. Thus, we have dealt with the academic aspects of our discussion. Reality consists of illogical acts instead of acts of reason.[1] Regardless of how one reasons, the fact stands that the European colonial powers recognized Indian sovereignty as a necessity to establish a foothold in the Americas. Once a foothold was established, Indian external sovereignty was restricted to agreements with the occupying European power. For example, the Indians in the areas claimed by the British could make treaties with the British but not with the French or Spanish.

The Proclamation of 1763

The Proclamation of 1763, issued by George III, was a significant event in the making of treaties with Indian nations.[2] As the French and Indian War was ending, Pontiac led an effort to oust British settlers from Indian territory. Realizing some order had to be established to avoid such clashes between the two cultures, the London government issued the Proclamation. The sections of this new colonial policy dealing with Indians set a pattern that was followed by the United States.

In the first provision, the individual colonial governments were forbidden to make Indian treaties. The second provision gave exclusive Indian treaty making powers to the central (London) government. The reasoning that no uniform Indian policy could emerge from thirteen sources lay behind these two provisions. Several gaping holes were present in this reasoning, however, not the least being the uniformity concept itself. It was thought in London, with some justification, that treaties made by the colonial governments led to exploitation of Indians by traders and land speculators. Although it was expected that centralized treaty-making would stop the exploitation, this expectation was not fulfilled, for those with influence in the central government also exploited the Indians. In effect, this policy only added another layer of exploitation.

The third and final Indian provision of the Proclamation of 1763 introduced the segregation concept into Anglo-American–Indian policy. This provision drew an imaginary line along the crest of the Appalachians. Euro-American settlement was permitted east of this line, but west of the line was reserved for Indians. It was hoped that by segregating the two cultures, incidents such as Pontiac's war could be avoided. Thus, two patterns in Indian relationships were established: The first was centralized treaty-making; the second established the impossibility of keeping settlers out of reservations. Thus segregation could not work.

From the English colonists' viewpoint, they were the ones who had fought and won the French and Indian War in America. Nowhere was this feeling stronger than on the frontier. With the French threat removed and a fortified belief in their ability to deal with the Indian menace, the frontier settlers developed a confidence in their self-sufficiency. Thus, they ignored the British efforts to keep them out of the Indian reservation west of the crest of the Appalachians. This practice of reservation "jumping" was so firmly ingrained in the frontier character that it remained a problem into the twentieth century.

As controversy with the mother country changed to conflict, the United States had no option except to follow the Indian policies that had already been established by the British. If the Confederation were to repudiate the policies, they would face a real possibility of a general Indian war all along the western frontier. Any increase in Indian hostility, however slight, would tip the balance for the British and invite a Spanish or French invasion from the south.

Articles of Confederation

Realizing the importance of Indians to their cause, the Continental Congress, in 1775, acted to deal with Indian problems. A commissioner was appointed for each of the departments, north, middle, and southern. These commissioners were more diplomat than administrator, with men such as Benjamin Franklin and Patrick Henry being appointed to the positions.[3] With the ratification of the Articles of Confederation in 1781, continuation of these policies was assured. Article Six has two provisions that bear on the policies and Article Nine contains another provision.

> ARTICLE SIX: "No state without the consent of the United States in Congress assembled shall send any embassy to, or receive any em-

bassy from, or enter into any conference, agreement, or alliance or treaty with any king, prince, or state;

No state shall engage in any war without the consent of the United States in Congress assembled, unless such state be actually invaded by enemies, or shall have received certain advice of a resolution being formed by some nation of Indians to invade such state, and the danger is so imminent as not to admit of a delay."

ARTICLE NINE: "The United States in Congress assembled shall also have the sole and exclusive right and power of . . . regulating the trade and managing all affairs of the Indians, not members of any of the states, provided that the legislative right of any state within its own limits be not infringed or violated."[4]

It is evident from these provisions that the central government was to not only have the sole right of making Indian treaties, but it also reserved the right to make all official contacts, including making war on Indians.

In its short eight years of existence, the Confederation accomplished more than most governments accomplish in a century. To call this government a failure is a gross abuse of the truth. The Confederation issued two ordinances that still stand as two of the greatest legislative acts in history. These were the Land Ordinance of 1785 and the Northwest Ordinance of 1787. Regretfully, we must confine our attention to the portions dealing with Indians. The Land Ordinance of 1785 opens with a statement of Indian policy that has rarely been violated: "Be it ordained by the United States in Congress assembled that the territory ceded by individual states to the United States, which has been purchased from the Indian inhabitants, shall be disposed of in the following manner."[5]

According to C. C. Royce and C. Thomas, the only exception to this policy was the "Sioux Indians in Minnesota, after the outbreak in 1862."[6] In this case another reservation was provided and the net proceeds from the land sale was credited to the Sioux.

Article Three of the Northwest Ordinance of 1787 also contains a provision involving Indians:

The utmost good faith shall always be observed toward the Indians; their lands and property shall never be taken from them without their consent; and in their property, rights, and liberty they shall never be invaded or disturbed unless in just and lawful wars authorized by Congress; but laws founded in justice and humanity shall from time to time be made for preventing wrongs being done to them, and for preserving peace and friendship with them.[7]

We believe this is a sincere, well intentioned, but wishful policy statement. Too much is left to interpretation depending upon which cultural yardstick the interpreter uses. No one in a right mind could ever believe these policy objectives were ever obtained.

The Constitution provided for a federal union instead of a confederated union like the Confederation. Although the proponents proposed a balancing of powers between the central government and the member commonwealths (called states), the central government emerged as stronger in practice. The only specific mention of Indians in the Constitution is in Article One, Section Eight: "To regulate commerce with foreign nations, and among the several states, and with the Indian tribes."[8] Since in 1789, Indian nations were still considered to possess full internal sovereignty and minimal external sovereignty, this clause placed them in a special quasi-foreign-nation class. Until after 1815, the reality in North America was that most Indian nations possessed full sovereignty. The "fiction" of sovereignty did not become a reality until after 1815. Abandoning the earlier use of *nation* and using the term *tribe* seems to indicate that the United States under the Constitution expected to reduce the Indian nations to subordinate units of government somewhere between foreign nations and commonwealths. Apparently, the Indian governments of today are somewhat below commonwealth status but above county government in several aspects. They exist as a unique form of government within the structure of American government yet apart from all other organized governmental units.

United States

Between 1778 and 1871, over 400 treaties were negotiated with Indian nations. Of these, 370 were ratified by the Senate.[9] The last negotiated treaty was the Drum Creek Treaty or the Osage Treaty of 1868. This treaty was so bad that even the settlers opposed it, and, therefore, it was never ratified. In the light of the storm engendered by this outrageous treaty and the increased use of treaties for the benefit of corporations, especially railroad land grants, Congress abolished the treaty-making process with Indian nations through the Act of March 3, 1871 (16 Stat. 566). The Osages were the first to come under this new process in the Act of July 15, 1870 (16 Stat. 362).

Although the actual Act eliminating the treaty-making process was not enacted until 1871, the 1870 Osage agreement was made under the authority of the pending Act of 1871. Actual purchase of the Osage reservation was not made until June 5, 1872 (17 Stat. 228). This Act of 1872 verified the agreement of 1870, as well as served its main purpose of authorizing purchase of the present reservation.

No Indian government of the United States possesses any external sovereignty today. Internal sovereignty is extremely limited by the veto powers of the Bureau of Indian Affairs. Yet, some inalienable sovereignty still exists, but it is only a whisper in the winds of the "fiction" of Indian sovereignty. This last thread with the past could be snapped asunder by a simple Act of Congress. If this thread is sheared, a significant part of this great nation will be cast adrift in a sea of uncertainties and a valuable part of the United States will be lost forever. The honor and integrity of this nation and the principles of natural rights upon which it was founded will also be lost, for a nation without honor and integrity cannot survive.

The Seven Treaties, 1808–1839

The Treaty of 1808

The land cessions within the seven Osage treaties made between 1808–1839 will be discussed later under a different heading. Here we will discuss the provisions in the seven treaties that covered other matters. The background involving the Treaty of 1808 has already been given in the preceding sections of this chapter.

The first two Articles of the Treaty of 1808 (7 Stat. 107) provide for the establishment of Fort Clark (Fort Osage) and a federal trading factory.[10] The wording of Article One—which stresses that the role of the fort is to provide protection for the Osages—is misleading. Over centuries of conflict, the Osages had capably protected themselves. No mention of protection from Euro-Americans is made, only protection from other Indians. Since the fort clearly was not built to protect the Osages, we must seek other motives for its construction.

While Jefferson did place the United States in debt through the Louisiana Purchase, he was one of the more frugal presidents and did not spend without reason. Therefore, it becomes evident that the expense of constructing Fort Osage was necessary from a viewpoint of national interest. If it was in any sense a gift or payment for the benefit of the Osage people, it was coincidental to the general welfare and national defense needs of the United States. Obviously, the fort was built to promote commerce and to curb British expansion on the Missouri.

All Indian treaties we have studied show this type of "placing the monkey on the Indian's back," that is, making the desires of the United States appear to be a desire for the benefit of the Indian. No doubt, the Indians often detected this device, but usually they were not in a position to effectively object. In other cases, the language barrier or deliberate cloaking of the real intent prevented Indians from detecting harmful and expensive provisions in treaties.

Article Two was a well thought out provision and fair to the Osages. Greed leads to terrible abuses of justice. The fur trade was profitable, but it was an open invitation to exploit Indians and fur-bearing animals. If the general population and the Indians were to reap the maximum benefit from the fur resources, the industry had to have established standards of regulation and ethics. The federal factory system introduced by Article Two did this. Osages could bring their furs to Fort Osage at any time of the year and trade for a wide range of fair-priced goods. Some measure of the success of this plan can be gained from the anguished complaints of the private traders. They could no longer pressure the Osages to trade for shoddy, limited, over-priced goods. The traders' complaints ultimately forced the closing of all government factories (see the Treaty of 1822).

Several provisions were contained in Article Three. A blacksmith was to be provided at Fort Osage, and either a horse- or water-operated mill was to be built. Plows were to be furnished and blockhouses were to be built at Fort Osage for the chiefs of the Missouri Big Osages and Little Osages.

The *Moh se Kah he* (Blacksmith) was an important person to the Osages. Since they had no experience or tools needed to work metals, any damage to a firearm often rendered the weapon useless. Without a blacksmith, a damaged firearm could only be discarded. Since this was true of all articles containing metals, an inordinate amount of replacement trading was necessary. Thus, a blacksmith was very important in Osage life by 1800.

American mills were designed to grind wheat, corn, and other small domestic grains. Since the traditional Osage hand-grinding tools processed all the corn they raised, plus nuts, dried meat, and dried fruits or roots, the power mill was of no benefit to them. In fact, both the mill and plows were totally useless to the Osages. Both were premature assumptions that the Osage hunting culture would become an agrarian culture in two or three years. For many years (to 1890), the Osages traded the plows for things they could use.

Block houses and cabins for influential chiefs were common features of Osage treaties. These operated as "a carrot on a stick" in order to gain support for acceptance of a treaty. Either unwittingly (or possibly knowingly) on the part of the Americans, these incentives struck a chord of pleasure in the honors-based Osage culture.[11] It was not a desire of the chiefs for material gain that made these structures so influential at this early date. In the Osage culture of 1808, all the people shared in this honor bestowed upon their leader. We can say with confidence that these structures remained unoccupied by Osages, for they had a deep mistrust, verging upon fear, of log structures. Their oval lodges were safer and more comfortable.[12]

Article Four touches upon a raw wound. A sum of five thousand dollars was set aside to pay American citizens for property taken by Osages. Nothing is said about stolen Osage horses, plundering of Osage graves, or killing of Osage game and fur animals. While these matters were sometimes caused by different cultural views of land ownership, it amounted, after all, to a two-way road in the acts and a one-way road in payment as the consequence of the acts. One must also consider which of the two parties was the intruder and which had prior claim to the area where the incidents occurred.

One of the most misunderstood Articles in the Treaty of 1808 was Article Eight. The Osages always understood this Article to mean that they still retained the hunting rights on all the lands they ceded in Missouri and Arkansas. Their agreement was that all areas not occupied by American citizens or *specifically* assigned to emigrant Indian nations were to be considered as Osage hunting territory.

Since no interpreter is named in the Fire Prairie version of the treaty, it is assumed that Pierre Chouteau acted as both the American negotiator and interpreter. Noel Mongrain should have been the Osage interpreter. Pierre Chouteau probably had a more limited Osage vocabulary and understanding of the Osages than Noel Mongrain.

Despite Pierre Chouteau's command of the language, the wording in Article Eight is complex and difficult to comprehend in English. Placing these concepts into the Osage language would be close to impossible. Thus, it is very probable that Chouteau and the Osages misunderstood each other's intent and agreement. Since the Arkansas band also went over this same Article, which was explained by Mongrain, and they arrived at the same understanding as the Missouri bands, apparently the misunderstanding was either a flaw in communication or a deliberate misconstruction.

In any event, the misunderstanding of Article Eight caused both the Osages and the United States serious problems. The most serious problem arose on the Arkansas between the Osage Arkansas bands and the emigrant Cherokee "Old Settlers." These "Old Settlers" moved west of the Mississippi and settled on selected lands that had been Osage territory. Problems arose when these Cherokees started hunting on unselected lands considered by the Osages, as they understood Article Eight, to be their hunting territory.[13]

It was the rigid enforcement of their hunting rights by the Osages that made the Cherokee "New Settlers" so reluctant to move west of the Mississippi. This reluctance was a real problem for the United States, since the Cherokee country to the east was filling rapidly with Anglo-American settlers. President Jackson finally forced the "New Settlers" to move west under military escort. This action has been so dramatized that other removals are forgotten.

Article Nine was a conglomeration of provisions meant to solve problems arising from cultural conflicts. However, like most treaties between the Osages and the United States, the solutions were one-way in favor of the United States at the expense of the Osage. All cases of controversy were to be settled by the United States. While showing a complete distrust and lack of confidence in Osage justice, the United States was asking the Osages to trust and accept American justice.

If a two-way approach had been instituted, many problems could have been avoided. For example, the more serious offenses could have been settled by American justice and minor offenses by Osage justice. In all but the most serious offenses, Osage justice had milder punishments than American justice, but they would have been enforced.

As the condition evolved under this Article, the Osages were always guilty and Euro-Americans or members of the emigrant nations were always ruled to be innocent, if they were ever indicted at all. No wonder the Osages refused to participate in such "justice." Only when they could no longer evade surrender of a wanted Osage would they participate.

Article Eleven is a companion to Article Nine in that it authorizes Osages to arrest intruders and turn them over to American authorities. If the Osages acted under this Article, they became embroiled in claims against themselves, and the intruders would be released with apologies. The intruder problem was never solved. The government either could not or would not keep intruders off the reservations. To make matters worse, the government would not cooperate with the Osages to oust intruders.

There were one hundred twenty Osage leaders listed as signers of the Fire Prairie version of the treaty and fifteen Osage signers of the Arkansas version. The phonics of the names in the Fire Prairie version are very poor and those in the Arkansas version are not much better. This indicates more than a minor communication problem. Pierre Chouteau must have been the interpreter of the former, because the person who inscribed the names on the document wrote ragged French. The French phonics of the names are bad.

Two factors suggest a poor comprehension of the Osage language in writing. First, the French sounds of the syllables rarely match the sounds in the Osage language, nor do they match with any known Osage names, which are centuries old and still used today. It is unlikely that some of them would not appear on a list of one hundred twenty names.

Second, no interpreted names follow the Osage name. In such long lists, it was customary to give interpreted names for the major chiefs and the position or band of the others. Only positions and bands are given in this list. It is evident from these names that whoever acted as interpreter was either less than fluent in Osage or they were more comfortable with English than with French. Thus, the difficult task of translating complex American legal concepts from English, through French, and then into Osage was accepted as legally understandable.

The Arkansas version shows a greater comprehension of Osage in the names. Since the two Osage interpreters, Noel Mongrain and Bazil Nassier (Naseur), signed by their marks, we assume they were illiterate. John P. Gates, the other interpreter, probably wrote the names on the document. The phonics are in English and the syllables match known Osage names. While the phonics are not good, the names are recognizable. The interpreted names and positions show an excellent knowledge of Osage.

Noel Mongrain was married to Marie Pahushan, who was White Hair's oldest daughter.[14] The son of Basil Naseur, John Basil Nasuer, married Seraphine Estis.[15] Their baptism and marriage records are in French and undoubtedly these people were more comfortable with French than with English. While the two Osage interpreters were fluent in French and Osage, their comprehension of English was probably not very extensive. Hence, John P. Gates probably acted as French-English interpreter. After filtering the provisions of the Treaty of 1808 through three languages, it is doubtful that a clear understanding of the treaty was obtained by the Arkansas bands. It would strain the imagination to believe mere coincidence could have placed almost every possible barrier in the way of both groups of Osages understanding the key provisions of the treaty.

The Treaty of 1815

The Treaty of 1815 (7 Stat. 133) was a very short, clear treaty. It consisted of a preamble and three short Articles. In essence, it simply reaffirmed the *status quo ante bellum* (situation before the War of 1812). That is, it reaffirmed loyalty between the Osages and the United States, as well as continued all existing treaties between the two nations. There were twenty-four Osages who "touched the feather" (signed) and three Euro-American Commissioners.

The phonics are good and are in English. Evidently, Auguste Chouteau acted as a Commissioner and Noel Mongrain as interpreter. Interpretation of the names are also given. Iron Hawk's name is especially significant because it shows a very good comprehension of the Osages. *Gra to Moh se* is usually interpreted as Iron Hawk but the name applies to a specific kind of hawk which in English is called KITE. Thus, when *Gra to Moh se* was interpreted as Iron Kite in the Treaty of 1815, it shows the interpreter had an excellent command of the Osage language and culture. Whoever recorded the name also had a good command of both languages because the phonics are clear and the interpretations accurately recorded.

It is either strange or possibly intentional that excellent comprehension was available for this simple treaty. It would seem that when a complex treaty full of concessions to the United States was involved, every possibility for misunderstanding was present. On the other hand, simple treaties with clear provisions are clearly communicated. This is indeed strange, if coincidental, but one must suspect that coincidence was given more than a little assistance when officials suspected the Osages would not accept some provisions.

The Treaty of 1818

Two of the vexing problems facing both the United States and the Osages brought about the Treaty of 1818. Both of these problems arose from intruders. In the first instance, it was Euro-American intruders, and in the second case it was emigrant Indian intruders. Under their understanding of the Treaty of 1808, the Arkansas bands attempted to deal with these intruders in their own way. While no Euro-Americans were killed for intruding into these Osage hunting areas, property of various kinds was taken.[16] The seizure of property was probably in retaliation for property stolen from the Osages. Since it was easier to recover claims from the less-experienced Osages than it was from the more-experienced emigrant Indians, many of these claims were actually due to emigrant Indian thefts.

The "claims game" was not practiced by the Osages until much later in time. However, the emigrant nations of the southeast had perfected their methods to the point where it had become an exact science. It was not unusual for Cherokee claims against Euro-Americans to exceed Euro-American claims against the Cherokee. Being considered as a "civilized tribe" by virtue of a long association with Americans, the so-called five civilized tribes took full advantage of their status. They filed claims against the Osages on the slightest pretext. If they could not find an excuse to file a claim, they created one. Part of the game was to cast the Osages into the role of wild uncivilized Indians.

Americans were more than willing to accept this characterization of the Osages because the five tribes were from the Americans' old homeland and the Osages were buffalo Indians. The Osage habit of solving their problems by themselves prevented a formal Euro-American type of response to thefts by Euro-Americans and the five tribes. Thus, the traditional Osage responses left them open to innumerable claims. Lack of Osage formal response not only tended to strengthen the validity of the claims against them, but it also heightened the stereotype of the Osages as a wild, stupid Indian nation.

The Osages had an excellent comprehension of trade goods and their value in terms of furs and hides. But they had no concept of money, its uses, or its value. Thus, the money paid to settle claims as provided in treaties had no meaning for them. They were aware that past claims were settled, but they did not realize what it had cost them until much later.

While the Treaty of 1808 had provided for a north-south line from Fort Osage due south to the Arkansas River (Fort Smith), the Osages misunderstood the function of the line. The fact that the Osages were not to hunt east of this line was hidden in complicated wording. The Osage understanding was that until the area to the east was settled or assigned to some other Indian nation, it was to remain Osage hunting territory. This misunderstanding was not corrected until 1825. Meanwhile, between 1808 and 1818, the Cherokee were increasingly crossing to the west side of the Osage line to hunt. While these actions were deliberate violations of the Treaty of 1808, the United States authorities ignored the Cherokee intrusions into Osage territory and punished the Osages for protecting their legal domain against the Cherokee intruders. The area west of the Osage line was not only legal Osage territory under Osage law, but by virtue of the Treaty of 1808 it was also legally Osage area under United States law.

Fort Smith was founded in 1817 not to keep the Cherokees east of the Osage line but to keep the Osages from driving the Cherokees out of the legal Osage territory.[17] In 1824, Fort Gibson was founded for much the same reason. Like the United States government, some writers have been more sympathetic to the Cherokee in this matter than to the Osage. Yet, in fairness, they do usually mention that the Cherokee was the intruder. The Osages had every justification for attacking the Cherokee and driving them out of an area that even by American law belonged to the Osages. This was an Osage area by prior occupation and by Indian law as well as by American law. How then can anyone make the Cherokee intruders and provokers of attacks the heroes and make the owners and defenders of their lands the villains? This nonconformity to the evidence is confusing and more than a little irrational.

The truth of the matter is that, since the last half of the 1700s, the Cherokee had longed for the choice parts of the Osage domain. They could not accomplish this by force of arms, although they outnumbered the Osages. First, they tried to get the Spanish to acquire Osage territory for them, but the Spanish were too weak to accomplish this. By 1816, the Cherokee had so aroused the government against the Osages that they could get almost anything they wanted. As an added inducement, the American government had promised the western Cherokee that they would receive an outlet so they could hunt buffalo on the Plains.[18]

Subsequent events clearly show that it was not only an outlet the Cherokee wanted. If it were only an outlet they desired, the most practical route for the Cherokee to reach the Plains was between the Red and Canadian Rivers. The next most logical route was along the Arkansas and Cimarron Rivers. Following the Neosho-Grand northward and then turning west to the Plains was the worst possible route to the Plains from the Cherokee area east of Fort Smith. Clearly the Cherokee wanted more than an outlet.

What the Cherokee wanted and ultimately acquired was the lush Neosho and Verdigris valleys. The United States obtained this for them at the expense of the Osages. What the Cherokee and Spaniards could not do, the United States accomplished. The Treaty of 1818 was the second step in the outlet scheme. Regardless of what one may think of the Cherokees, one must admit they were shrewd and well organized in achieving their purpose.

The first step in the outlet scheme was to oust the Osages from the Three Forks or lower Neosho-Grand and Verdigris area. Ina Gabler describes the first step very well:

> Early in July, 1816, at the mouth of the Verdigris River, Major William Lovely, Cherokee agent in Missouri Territory, presided over a conference between representatives of the Osage and Cherokee tribes. He proposed to the Osages, who had exhibited great hostility toward the Cherokees, that the federal government would pay all claims against them for depredations they had committed if they would cede to the United States their land lying between the falls of the Verdigris and the eastern Osage line of 1808. Lovely's idea was that Osage abandonment of this large area of country would leave it free for the Cherokees to hunt over in peace. The Osage chieftains agreed to this on July 9, and thereafter this immense tract of land, approximately three million acres in extent, became known as Lovely's Purchase.[19]

Lovely had no authority from the United States government to make this agreement. While Lovely's agreement was never officially recognized, the Treaty of 1818 followed the Lovely agreement, and thus, in essence, affirmed the earlier pact even though Lovely had nothing to do with making the treaty of 1818. It seems the United States saw an opportunity to utilize a concession already made. The difference was that it made the cession binding under the Constitution. Thus, the Osages were the victim of an illegal treaty made legal to benefit other Indians.

One very significant point must be noted, since it has never been mentioned in the literature about this treaty. Under the 1808 treaty, the Osages were guaranteed hunting rights on all unassigned lands west of the Osage line. The Cherokees did not buy the cession of 1818 from either the Osages or the United States, nor was the land assigned to them except as an outlet to the Plains. Secretary of War John C. Calhoun on October 8, 1821, notified the Cherokee that they did not own this land and had only the right of passage.[20] The Osages never disputed the Cherokee right of passage through this cession but they rightfully asserted their hunting rights when the Cherokee hunted in the cession. This is a clear case of the United States knowingly forcing the Osages to accept a treaty violation.

The Treaty of 1822

The Treaty of 1822 was a simple, short treaty. It closed Fort Osage as a government factory by abrogating the second Article of the Treaty of 1808. Thus, the first government factory west of the Mississippi was closed. For allowing the end of the federal factory at Fort Osage, the Osages were paid a total of $2,329.40 in merchandise. This was probably the total supply of merchandise on hand at Fort Osage.

All three of the Osage tribes were represented among the signatures. The main chiefs who signed were White Hair of the Missouri Big Hills, Traveling Rain of the Little Osages and Town Maker (Claremore II) of the Arkansas Big Hills. Evidently, Paul Baillio (Belieu) and Robert Dunlap were the interpreters while the Agent of Indian Affairs, Richard Graham, was in charge. A notable witness was Fr. Charles de la Croix. The Jesuits and priests had worked among the Osages for sometime so Fr. de la Croix was trusted by the Osages.

The First Treaty of 1825

Two Osage treaties were made in 1825. The first of these contained many far-reaching concessions by the Osage, and the second is commonly known as the Council Grove Treaty. We will refer to the first 1825 treaty as the Treaty of 1825 and the second as the Council Grove Treaty. Like the Treaty of 1818, the Treaty of 1825 was brought about because of intrusions by Euro-Americans and the southeastern emigrant nations. Although the land cessions of these treaties will be dealt with in a later section of this chapter, it is necessary to touch on two related matters here.

Our first land consideration is the Cherokee Outlet and that portion of the Outlet known as the Cherokee Strip. All Cherokee territory west of the Mississippi came to them through Osage land cessions to the United States. With the exception of that ceded in 1818, all Cherokee land claims in Oklahoma came from the Osage cession of 1825. The so-called Cherokee

Outlet, well known in general histories, was Osage territory ceded to the United States in 1825.

In 1872, the Osages bought back a portion of the Outlet lying between the 96th Meridian and the Arkansas River (17 Stat. 228). The north line was the 37th parallel (Kansas-Oklahoma state line) and the south line was formed by the Arkansas River plus the north line of the Creek nation. The extreme northwest corner of this tract was sold to the Kansas nation by the Osages (see Fig. 21).

A widespread misunderstanding of the term *Cherokee Strip* is evident in the way it is used. In popular usage, the term is applied to the Cherokee Outlet, which lies entirely within the bounds of the state of Oklahoma. But in actuality, the Cherokee Strip lies entirely within the bounds of the state of Kansas. Article Two of the Treaty of 1825 sets the east, west, and north-south lines of the Osage reservation from the location of White Hair's Village. In 1825, White Hair's Village was located on the Neosho and across that river from Shaw, Kansas. Location of all boundaries in the Treaty of 1825 are keyed to a point due east of this village and twenty-five miles west of Missouri's western boundary. The Osage southern boundary was forty miles south of this point.

Although it was thought that this southern Osage boundary would fall on the 37th parallel, it fell short by somewhat less than two miles. Also, because of a surveying error, the line between Kansas and Oklahoma is slightly less than one-half mile south of the actual 37th parallel. Therefore, the north boundary of the Cherokee Outlet and south boundary of the Osage reservation were a short two and one-half miles north of the Kansas-Oklahoma line. This somewhat less than two and one-half mile wide strip extended from twenty-five miles west of Missouri to the 100th Meridian. All of this strip lies in Kansas and is correctly called the Cherokee Strip. The area west of the Strip and Outlet (Oklahoma Panhandle) was called No Man's Land. This name is also sometimes applied to the portion of the Strip that lies east of the Arkansas River. That same area east of the Arkansas is often called Lap Land because of the overlapping one-half-mile strip.

One cannot help but see a great deal of irony in the Osage-Cherokee situation. The Cherokee used a favorable United States government and intruders to acquire Osage lands on the Neosho-Grand and Verdigris. Yet, after 1865, the United States became friendlier to the Osages, and intruders gained control of the Cherokee lands on the Neosho-Grand and Verdigris.[21] The Osages profited through the Cherokee experience with intruders.

An unusual feature of Article Two was the provision for a buffer zone between the Euro-Americans and the Osages. We may be in error, but we

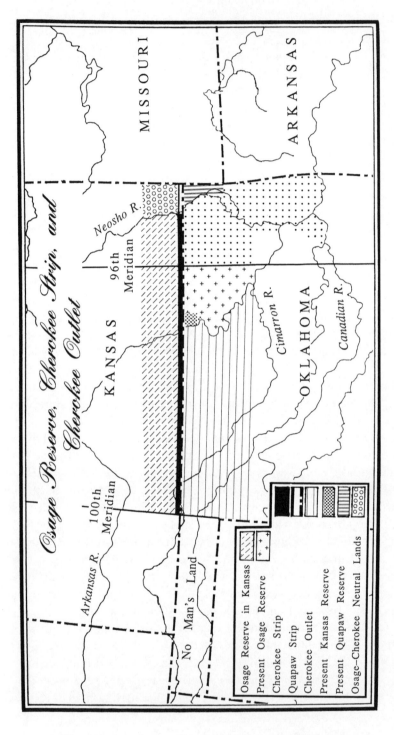

Fig. 21. Note the relative location of features on this map.

believe this is the only time the federal government tried this solution to the intruder problem. A strip twenty-five-miles wide, east and west, and fifty-miles long, north and south, was created between Missouri's west boundary and the Osages. Of course, the Osages donated the land for this buffer zone, and only Osage mixed-bloods could legally live in this zone. In 1835, these Osage Neutral Lands were assigned to the Cherokee by the federal government. From the entries in the Osage Mission Register, it is evident that many Euro-Americans, mixed-blood Osages, and mixed-blood Cherokees lived in these so-called Cherokee Neutral Lands, including a sizable band of Quapaw.[22]

This same Article Two contains an interesting version of "as long as the grass grows and the waters flow" idea. In this version, the concept, "so long as they may choose to occupy the same" is stated. But guess who chose to have the Osages cede the rich Neosho Valley in Kansas and a ten-mile strip off the north part of "the same"? We must admit that the Diminished Reserve (the remainder of "the same") was ceded by the choice of the Osages, although it was, of course, a choice between ceding the Diminished Reserve or being declared "an enemy of the United States."

While these satirical barbs are true enough, it would be unjust to let them stand without mitigation. The Neutral Lands idea was a failure from the outset. Euro-American intruders entered the zone without hindrance and spilled over into the Osage Reserve with equal ease. More area was needed for the "checker game" of moving the emigrant nations of the northeast from square to square. Thus, the Neosho and Ten Mile Strip cessions became necessary. We will go into more detail about these events later.

Article Four is a classic example of good intentions missing the mark. Clearly, the livestock and implements provided here were intended to start the Osages on the road to agriculture and "civilization." If either side understood the other's culture, it was not evident in this provision. From the American view, the Osages had to become farmers so they could fit into the American culture. The Osages could see no need to farm when they could trade one buffalo robe for a year's supply of corn. Furthermore, they had no inclination to merge with the American culture that they considered to be inferior to their own.

This same problem was also present in Article Six. Fifty-four square miles of the ceded lands were set aside to be sold to establish an Osage education fund. In later years this was called the Civilization Fund, although it was only one portion of the total fund. It is interesting that the President was to determine how the Osage children were to be educated. This meant that Osage education would be determined by American concepts of what they should be taught. While many aspects of cultural differences generate educational problems, none are more noticeable than the determination of relevancy. What is relevant to the President or to an American missionary is not necessarily relevant to an Osage. That is, the Osages had certain things they wanted their children to learn in the Euro-American schools, and these things were not always in agreement with what was taught.

It was a matter of cultural ethnocentrism for the Americans to assume the Osages would want to be totally educated in American culture. The Osages desired education in order to improve their existing culture; the American idea was to destroy Osage culture and replace it with American culture. The ability to see their own cultural weaknesses and to seek to improve their culture by borrowing from the Osages was never applied by the Americans toward the Osage culture in any formal way. Yet, there were American adaptations of Osage ways. These were so subtle that they passed unnoticed and unrecognized as being borrowed from the Osages. Except in education and official policy, the two cultures did merge and create a unique American character. It was not so much the meeting of Western civilization and wilderness that created the frontier spirit as it was the meeting of two vibrant cultures. It is a shame that the blending of the two has been so diluted with the passing influence of the Indian.

Articles Seven, Eight, and Nine are all part of the "claims game." In Article Seven, the United States government wanted full release from the Treaty of 1808 and so used traders' claims as the means of escape. The intruding Delaware and Euro-Americans got their benefits in Articles Eight and Nine. It would be interesting to examine these claims in detail, but space will not permit a detailed examination.

In many respects, Article Ten was a violation of trust responsibilities held by the government. Harmony Mission was to have two sections reserved to it and Union Mission one section. These were to be sold and reestablished in the reduced Osage reserve. While some minor missions were established, by 1837 all these missions were abandoned and the funds diverted to other missions. Thus, Osage Mission was poorly funded and was financed by the Osages and the Catholic Church. Funds that should have been available through Article Ten had been either diverted or dissipated.

The Council Grove Treaty

The Council Grove Treaty was one of a series of treaties to clear the way for the Santa Fe Trail. For the main part, it sought protection from Osage raids for travelers on the trail. At this time, 1825, Council Grove, near the headwaters of the Neosho River, was in Osage territory. The name of Council Grove originates from this treaty with the Osages.

We cannot identify any leaders of the Arkansas bands among the Osage signers. *Ki he ka Wa ti an ka* (Saucy Chief) is identified as Foolish Chief, but the other names are very clear, and they are all from either the Little Osage or White Hair bands.

The Treaty of 1839

Payments under the Treaty of 1839 were mainly in articles useless to the Osages but profitable to the suppliers. With a drastic reduction in their winter hunting grounds, the Osage living standard was greatly lowered. Closer associations with more Euro-Americans led to epidemics that eventually destroyed the Osage resistance to intruders. The Treaty of 1839 struck the Arkansas bands especially hard for it required their removal to Kansas and the cession of all Osage lands in Oklahoma. The present reservation was bought back from this cession in 1872.

Certainly, the annuity payments provided for some latitude in method of payment, so some benefit did devolve to the Osage people. It is also worth noting that funds that were not used to pay claims were returned to the Osages. However, one may look upon the return of the residual as an act of honesty, even if all the claims were not valid. The increasing special benefits to Osage leaders suggests a rising discontent among the rank and file Osages. Thus, the Americans were having to provide greater incentives for the leaders.

To give some idea of how Osage treaty benefits were perverted, we need only to look at the blacksmith and striker (blacksmith's helper) provisions in this treaty. R. A. Calloway, the Osage subagent, appointed John Mathews and Edward Lother as blacksmiths under this treaty. But, although they drew the pay, they rendered no service. To add insult to injury, Mathews's seven-year-old son and a small Negro slave were appointed to the striker positions.[23] Such practices were common, but more than anything else it shows how utterly absent the trust responsibility, so glibly proclaimed as a right by the government, became in practice.

LAND CESSIONS

Introduction

The entire question of Indian land cessions is an involved matter that has no academic solution and a debatable legal solution. In the actual legal practice, all American land titles ultimately rest on Euro-American concepts of justice, and no Indian concept is allowed to override Anglo-American law. The nearest combination of Indian and Euro-American land law is contained in the Osage Allotment Act of 1906 (34, pt 1, Stat, 539), in which the surface of the land was allotted under Euro-American law, but the minerals were held in common under Osage law.

One cannot claim the Indian land title was extinguished by any order of law. In a few rare cases some form of Western-style legal order was followed. These exceptions are noticeable because of their scarcity. With few exceptions, Indian land titles were usually obtained by chicanery of all kinds, coercion, flattery, bribery, false claims, and seldom by outright conquest. Many justifications were offered for seizing Indian lands, but the fact remains that Indian lands were taken without any real right and with compensations that were insulting in their insignificance.

With such a blunt statement, we can see little purpose in harping on the obvious. A wrong was committed that destroyed a way of life. Little choice remains but to rectify the wrongs as well as possible and to salvage as much as we can of a way of life that has joined the ages.

Our purpose in showing the land cessions is to show the process of destruction. Osage culture was a culture of the sky and earth. Loss of either meant the destruction of the culture. These cessions were more than mere yielding of territory. Along with the cessions went the sacred animals and the responsibility for protecting the land. Thus, each cession weakened the Osage spirit and limited their food base. Dispirited and undernourished, the Osages were increasingly vulnerable to assaults on their lands and culture.

There were four Osage land cessions between 1804 and 1850. These were the cessions of 1808 (see Fig. 22), 1818, 1825, and 1839. One often reads that the government gave a reservation to some Indian group. We have never attempted to verify these statements except where they were applied to the Osages. Invariably, such writers simply did not know any better or used such statements as a convenience to avoid explaining the facts. We will state clearly and with no limitations that the United States government did not *give* the Osages any reservation at any time. Every reservation the Osages occupied was their own territory long before the United States had any real or imagined claim to it. The present reservation was bought and paid for by the Osages. However, it had been Osage territory long before it was ceded to the United States.

The Land Cession of 1808

There were three basic tracts ceded by the Osages in 1808. The largest of these lay between the Missouri River on the north and the Arkansas River on the south. With the Mississippi River on the east and a line drawn from Fort Osage to Fort Smith as the western boundary, this was a sizable cession. The second tract was a two-league parcel for Fort Osage. A third tract dissolved any Osage claims north of the Missouri River to the Iowa state line.

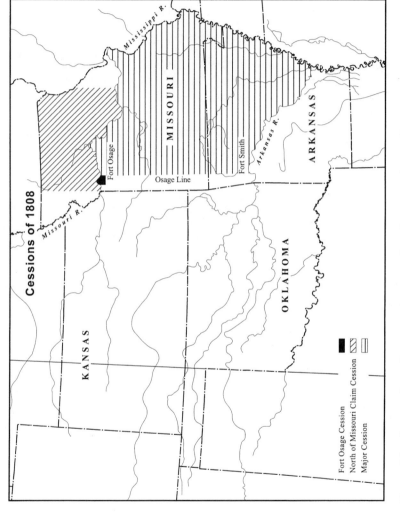

Fig. 22. The three cessions of 1808 are shown on this adaptation of Royce's maps.

Half of Arkansas, or 26,000 square miles (16,640,000 acres), was ceded. Seven-eighths of Missouri, or 56,000 square miles (35,840,000 acres) were ceded. The cession was at least 52,480,000 acres.[24] Considering that all forms of compensation for these lands totaled less than one-sixth of a cent per acre, it is reasonable to suspect that someone was cheated. One may argue good intentions and a thousand other justifications, but one fact still stands out, this cannot be called just compensation.

The Land Cession of 1818

The land cession of 1818 confirmed what had been called Lovely Purchase (see Fig. 23). Approximately 600,000 acres were mainly a clearing of claims that the Osages held to reservation areas claimed by other Indians. By contrast, in 1825, 20,000 square miles in Kansas, 18,000 square miles in Oklahoma, 6,000 square miles in Missouri, and 1,000 square miles in Arkansas were ceded to the government.

There were notable omissions in this cession, as well as that of 1839. First, the solid Osage claim south to the Red River is ignored, as is their claims south of the Arkansas to Natchitoches, Louisiana. Next, the Osage claims ceded in Arkansas and 1,200,000 acres in Oklahoma are omitted by this cession. As compensation for these 1,800,000 acres of land, the United States paid claims against the Osages up to $4,000. This would be about four and one-half cents per acre. Since these lands were immediately sold to the Cherokee for $2,000,000, one cannot help noticing a great discrepancy in this transaction. Such actions surely justify Osage doubts about the desire of the United States to look after their interests, their so-called "trust obligation."

The Land Cessions of 1825–1839

The cession of 1825 was the last big land cession the Osages made between 1804 and 1850 (see Fig. 24). The cession of 1839 west of the 100th Meridian is understandable because that area was in dispute with Spain and Mexico. Yet, the firm Osage claim to areas west of the 100th were never settled, even after the Mexican–American War cleared the United States claim to this area. William Clark's map of Osage territory and the Spanish records clearly establish a valid Osage claim to these areas.[25]

In this period, 1804–1850, the Osages ceded 96,800,000 acres of their territory to the United States. For this, they were paid in all forms of compensation $166,300 or approximately five and three-quarter cents per acre. While the monetary injustice inherent in these cessions is obvious, it was the spiritual and physical damage to the Osages that was so crucial. There is no way an assessment of spiritual damage can be made. We know the burden

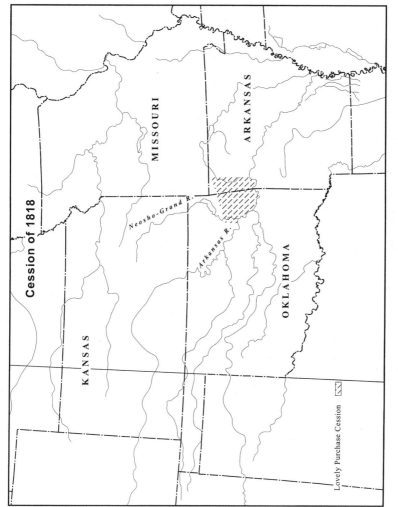

Fig. 23. The Lovely Purchase cession (adapted from Royce).

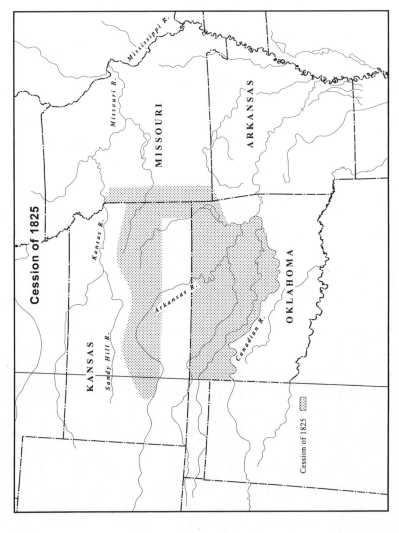

Fig. 24 After the cession of 1825 the Osages only had a shadow of their territory left (map by Royce).

of guilt carried by the Osages was great. They had betrayed *Wa kon ta*'s trust and given over the little brothers to a strange people. To what extent the retribution for this act affected the Osages we cannot know. We do have signs that new roads were being explored because the very base of Osage religion was shaken. The foundation of Osage civilization was crumbling. Hence, Osage resistance to the catastrophic flood of American people and emigrant Indians was weakened.

6

The Indian State and Removal

THE INDIAN STATE

Background

The origin of the idea of the Indian state is difficult to pinpoint. Certainly, the British had toyed with the idea of creating a province made up of self-governing Indian people. While the idea was not necessarily bad, it met considerable opposition from Indian and Euro-American alike. From the Indian viewpoint, no nation was willing to cede leadership to another nation. The situation would be the same as trying to get all the nations in the world to unify under a single potent government and to abandon their existing governments.

Euro-Americans were opposed to the idea for a variety of reasons. These ranged from fears of a truly unified Indian population to a firm belief in assimilation of Indians into the general population. There is some indication that Indian removal, the reservation system, and the Indian state were all interwoven in a random, varied, United States Indian policy.

Insofar as United States history is concerned, the Treaty of Fort Pitt with the Delaware in 1778 was the first provision for an Indian state.[1] Under this treaty, the Delaware could lead other nations into the formation of a state that Congress could admit to the Confederation. Since neither the Delaware nor the Euro-Americans pushed the matter, no steps were taken to implement the idea. Like so many schemes involving Indians, the Indian state idea was based on the very real fact of Indian sovereignty. While after the United States became a powerful nation Indian sovereignty was a legal fiction, through her early history such sovereignty was very real. Thus, the Indian state would have avoided special sovereignty status for Indians.

The acquisition of Louisiana opened several new possibilities to solving Indian problems. Colonization of Indians was not a new idea, since it had been practiced since the late–1600s. Louisiana presented the new idea of removal to areas out of the path of American expansion. Spain had used this to some extent, but Thomas Jefferson envisioned large scale removal. However, Indian reluctance to leave their traditional lands limited voluntary removal.

The "Indian Problem"

It may be prudent to look at the "Indian problem." First and foremost, one must bear in mind that Indian cultures of the woodlands and plains were primarily hunting cultures. So long as Euro-American contacts with Indians harmonized within the framework of hunting cultures, very little friction was generated. Failure to respect the laws of hunting cultures did cost some Euro-Americans their lives but only when those laws were violated. Great friction arose with the intrusion of agriculture into hunting territory. A hunting culture and an agrarian culture could not coexist in the same area simultaneously.

Thus, as settlers moved more and more into new plow areas, the game left the area. In hunting cultures, poaching and destruction of hunting grounds were extremely serious crimes. Therefore, the punishment for such intrusion was especially brutal and severe. The Osage practice of decapitation and placing the heads on stakes was typical. Free passage of the land was also a law of hunting cultures. Personal ownership of land and control of passage over the owned land was not understood by a hunting people.

These and other differences led to friction wherever a settler's clearing appeared in the Indian's hunting territory. From the Euro-American view these were unused, vacant lands and as such were available for settlement. We would add to Frederic Jackson Turner's description of the frontier line as the meeting place of the axe and the bow—one was the symbol of the clearing and the other the symbol of the hunt.

The Osages

As each successive wave of settlers moved west, they compacted the game and the Indians into a smaller and smaller area. This in turn set up a shock wave of pressure on the Indians west of those Indians impacted by the settlers. The expanding waves of contact shock were felt by the Osages long before they received the first shock of settlement. Thus, the Osages have had a long history of problems with emigrant Indian nations.

Their vast domain was an attraction to the voluntary emigrant Indians. Yet, the Osage defense of their lands discouraged many groups from emigrating. Since this ran counter to United States' policy, the Osage problem had to be dealt with even before settlers appeared in any numbers. The major source of Osage irritation to the Spanish was the warring on other nations that prevented the full use of resources and trade. For American authorities, the major Osage irritation was the warring on the eastern Indian nations that deterred them from voluntarily moving west of the Mississippi.

Such actions not only hampered the ideas of removal and reservation, but they also pointed to the difficulty of creating an Indian state. There were four solutions that evolved from the Indian question. One was to annihilate the Indians. Another was to confine them to reservations. A third was to create an Indian state, and a final solution was to incorporate Indians into the general population. Without a doubt, the Osages affected all four of these.

President Jefferson gave no hint that he ever intended to create an Indian state. However, his idea of the removal and concentration of Indians in the Osage territory could easily have led to organizing an Indian state. Jefferson left no clue as to whether this was his intent. His main interest seems to have been removing Indians from the path of westward expansion. Congress, on the other hand, made no secret of its interest in the Indian state idea.

House resolutions of December 17, 1824, and December 27, 1825, clearly stated the intention to create an Indian Territory that was to be governed like any other American Territory and subject to the same requirements for admission to statehood.[2] Senator Benton of Missouri introduced a bill into the Senate that set forth the creation of a territory, made up of Indians, that would ultimately become an Indian state. While the bill passed the Senate, it did not pass in the House.

The Cherokee fought every attempt to organize Indian Territory as a regular territory. Their great fear was the loss of sovereignty. As a territory made up of sovereign Indian nations, the territory was more accurately termed Indian Country. Under territorial organization, each Indian nation would necessarily have to cede their sovereignty to the territorial government. Yet, as the question of merging Indian Territory with Oklahoma Territory arose, some Cherokees opposed the merger because they had reached a point where they hoped for an Indian state.

At this point, the Osages entered the question. They had refused to join the so-called five civilized nations because the Cherokee controlled the confederation. Now, faced with a real possibility of being forced into a white man's state, an Indian state, even under Cherokee domination, became more appealing. In the meantime, the Cherokee returned to their earlier position of opposition to the Indian state, leaving the Osages as the last Indian nation to champion the cause of the Indian state. Failing to attain this goal, the Osages did the next best thing, from their viewpoint. To get the Osage assent to add the Osage reservation to the newly merged Oklahoma

Territory and Indian Territory, the entire reservation was to be created as one county.

INDIAN REMOVAL

Origin of the Idea

Removal as a policy or as an idea did not originate with Thomas Jefferson in 1803. President Jefferson introduced the concept into American practices with the Louisiana Purchase,[3] but the French had used voluntary removal as early as 1709.[4] Removal was also a regular feature of Spanish policy in the Mississippi Valley between 1765 and 1794.[5]

The term itself, *removal,* is a broad term that covers several objectives. It may be used to establish colonies of Indians; to clear the way for other peoples; to break up possible confederacies; or to consolidate a people into a compact area. The term also denotes any contrived migration. Thus, any action that alters natural migration may be considered to be a removal. Furthermore, a removal may be either voluntary or involuntary.

While American removal policies were at times all these things, we tend to associate the term with the consolidation of Indians into increasingly smaller areas. Correctly or incorrectly, we also tend to associate removal with coercion and trickery. Certainly, the Louisiana Purchase caused drastic changes in American Indian policy. For the first time, the federal government had a vast area without any territorial or state strings attached to it. It follows that some Indian policy would evolve from this situation.

As Annie Heloise Abel noted in 1906 that the Louisiana Purchase has been studied in almost all conceivable ways, yet no one has pointed out its relationship to Indian policy.[6] The majority culture and many ethnic groups have so overshadowed the American Indian cultures that Americans of the 1990s have difficulty realizing how strong the Indian influence has been. Yet the documents in American history show an Indian influence in every Euro-American event up to 1890. There are several reasons why the Indian influence is so widely ignored in the history of the United States.

In terms of proportionate population, Indians, as a whole, constitute a small minority group. This small proportionate share in the population causes a diluted political voice because the total Indian population is fragmented by differences among themselves. That is, each Indian nation has its own hatchet to grind and, thus, Indian unity is absent as a political bloc. An often overlooked factor in Indian influence is the rapid decline of full-blood stock or the gene pool of Indian blood.

At least two types of Osage full-bloods exist. A few Osages are actually full-blood Osage while others are full-blood Indian. The distinction here is that a person may be full-blood Indian and still be only a small fraction Osage. Mixed-bloods among the full-bloods and near full-bloods are almost as common among Indian nations as mixed-bloods between the New and Old World peoples. Instead of bringing unity among the merged peoples, a system of divided loyalties often evolves in the offspring. We will touch on this problem later, but it has to be mentioned here as a problem in Indian influence.

The United States is rapidly becoming a country in which the majority rules despite injustices to minorities. A minority with an effective voice can still attain justice, but the trend is to follow the majority interest where the minority does not have political clout. Thus, cultural influence and political clout go hand in hand. Without either, Indians stand impotent to defend themselves against the excesses of the majority. This is all too evident in the passing of the Indian influence on American culture.

Removal was a primary policy of eradicating Indian influence in American society. In some respects, the basic rationale for removal still exists today. That is, Indians are nomadic in nature and, thus, it would be of little consequence to remove them to another place.[7] While this rationale was based on observation, it must be noted that both the observation and conclusion drawn from the observation are flawed.

A hunting culture by its nature must follow the game and disperse as the group increases in population. The more dependent on hunting a culture becomes, the more accurate these facts become. Thus, a pure hunting culture would be more constantly on the move in small family groups than a hunting culture tempered by gathering and agriculture. Since none of the Woodland Indians, such as the Osages, were solely a hunting people, their nomadic tendency was limited. That is, they always had permanent villages where they returned after hunts. Varying degrees of agriculture were practiced around these villages. More important were the gathering-resources available around the villages.

Removal and the Osages

If the Osages, and other Indian nations like them, were nomadic, consider the Euro-Americans. Most had left their European homeland and voyaged over three thousand miles of sea and a thousand miles of land to reach the Osage territory. Native-born Euro-Americans were constantly on the move and rarely settled more than a few years in the same place. Surely, this was true of frontier Americans. One may argue that the New England merchant and Southern planter were sedentary. However, both often made protracted business trips both within North America and abroad. Saying these were mere business trips begs the question that the Osage hunting trips were also business trips. One may in candor ask, Who were the nomads, the Osages or the Euro-Americans?

Assuming the nomad and unused-lands argument was valid, another question must be asked. Why were the home villages or the most heavily used areas the first to be taken by Euro-Americans? These were occupied areas, even under the measurements of Western civilization. Osage removal was as devastating to them as the removal of any other Indian nation. While conclusive evidence of the effects of earlier removals are cloudy, we have clear evidence of the effects of the 1870 removal.

The Annuity Rolls of 1878 show few children survived the 1870–1875 period. This same trend is shown in the age groupings for 1822–1827. Between 1865–1870, both children and their mothers evidently died in vast numbers. Their absence on the Annuity Rolls bears testimony to the rigor of removal.[8] Yet, despite these facts, Indians, such as the Osage, were removed repeatedly (See Fig. 25).

Removal and Jefferson

While Jefferson introduced the removal idea into American government in 1803, it was some years before the idea became government policy. There were too many other problems demanding the attention of the young nation to allow an interest in Indian removal. Jefferson quite possibly turned to removal because of the Georgia Compact of 1802.

This compact between the United States and Georgia settled the western land claims of Georgia. Thus, title to what became Alabama and Mississippi passed to the United States. Our primary interest in this compact is the price the United States paid to Georgia. The United States promised that it would, at its own expense, extinguish the Indian title to all lands within the boundaries of Georgia as soon as possible.[9]

The significance of this agreement should not be overlooked when considering the United States' Indian land policy. Emerging from the Georgia Compact of 1802 is the basic Indian land policy followed by the United States. Out of the need to meet the obligations of the compact, Jefferson introduced the removal idea into American Indian Affairs.

Sectionalism was potentially involved in the compact and, consequently, in the resultant Indian policy formulation. As a section, the South had a heavy Indian population. The Northeast also had an Indian population, but it was evidently smaller than that of the South. More significant than the population size was the tendency of the Southern Indians to unify as an effective force. While the Northeastern Indians attempted several confederations, all these tended to disperse under conflict.[10]

Possibly, the Indians in the South could have had as much bearing on the

Osage Age Groups in 1878
TOTAL IN EACH AGE GROUP

Age		
1	◆◆◆◆◆◆◆◆◆◆◆◆◆◆◆◆◆◆◆◆◆	(1878)
2	◆◆◆◆◆◆◆◆◆◆◆◆◆◆◆◆	
3	◆◆◆◆◆◆◆◆◆◆◆◆◆◆◆◆◆◆◆◆◆◆◆◆◆	
4	◆◆◆◆◆◆◆◆◆◆◆◆◆◆◆◆◆◆◆◆◆	(1875)
5	◆◆◆◆◆◆◆◆◆◆◆◆◆◆◆◆◆◆	
6	◆◆◆◆◆◆◆◆◆◆◆◆◆◆◆	
7	◆◆◆◆◆◆◆◆◆◆◆◆◆◆◆	
8	◆◆◆◆◆◆◆◆◆◆◆	
9	◆◆◆◆◆◆◆◆◆◆◆◆◆◆◆◆◆◆◆◆◆	(1870)
10	◆◆◆◆◆◆◆	
11	◆◆◆◆◆◆◆◆◆◆◆◆◆◆◆◆◆◆◆◆◆◆◆◆◆	
12	◆◆◆◆◆	
13	◆◆◆◆◆◆◆◆◆◆◆◆◆◆	
14	◆◆◆◆◆◆◆◆◆◆◆	(1865)
15	◆◆◆◆◆◆◆◆◆◆	
16	◆◆◆◆◆◆◆◆◆◆◆◆◆◆◆◆◆◆	
17	◆◆◆◆◆◆◆◆◆◆◆◆◆◆◆◆	
18	◆◆◆◆◆◆◆	
19	◆◆◆◆◆◆◆◆◆◆◆◆◆	(1860)
20	◆◆◆◆◆◆◆◆◆	
No.	0 5 10 15 20 25 30 35 40 45 50 55 60 65 70 75 80 85 +	

Fig. 25. Adapted from Burns, *The Osage Annuity Rolls of 1878.*

slow population growth of the section as the presence of slavery. The prevailing view of the slow Southern growth is that slavery discouraged the small family farmer and thus kept the population small. We have no argument with this concept, except that the Southern border states were areas of small farmers and slavery. The difference with the Indians was in the size and nature of the Indian population.

It is doubtful that Jefferson tried to implement removal as a special benefit to this section. The nation had not yet reached the point where sectionalism colored its every act. Surely, the events leading to the War of 1812 clearly set the sections against each other. Yet, it was not until after the War of 1812–1815 that Jefferson's removal idea became a viable option to the American people.

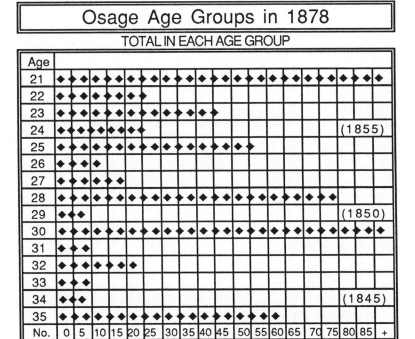

Fig. 25 (continued). Adapted from Burns, *The Osage Annuity Rolls of 1878*.

Jefferson drafted two constitutional amendments dealing with Indian removal and possibly the creation of an Indian state. In the first, an east–west line was to be established on the 32nd parallel. The second draft of an amendment placed this line at the mouth of the Arkansas River. Only Indians removed from the east and Indians native to the area were to be allowed to own lands north of these lines. As soon as the Louisiana Territorial Act passed in 1804, the President was empowered to exercise Indian removal. At this same time, plans were being made to negotiate a land cession treaty with the Osages. It was upon their territory that Jefferson hoped to settle the eastern Indians. Ultimately, these efforts culminated in the Osage Treaty of 1808.

The War of 1812 and Removal

Before 1812, any attempts to remove Eastern Indians by force would have been foolhardy. Certainly, the Southeastern nations were too powerful at this time. Judging by the effects of Tecumseh's protest, the Northeastern nations were also too powerful for removal by force. With the presence of the

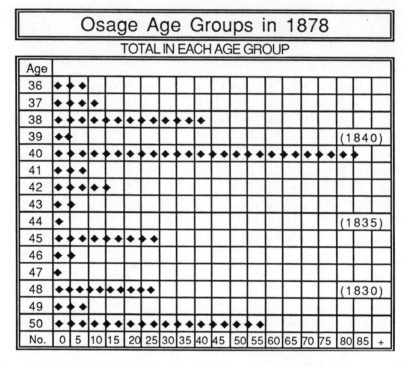

Fig. 25 (continued). Adapted from Burns, *The Osage Annuity Rolls of 1878*.

British threat, the American nation could not afford to generate further animosities among the Eastern Indians.

Indians of the east had every reason to harbor ill feelings toward the Americans. The widespread greed of land speculators kept the Indians agitated. Such activities ignored prior title and other Indian claims to the land. When they fought to defend their homes and rights, the Indians were placed in the role of the villain. These problems eventually led to the Treaty of Greenville in 1795. Such harsh treaty provisions as those found in the Treaty of Greenville only heightened the ill-feelings of the Northeastern Indians toward the Americans. These nations were frequently threatened with removal if they made British alliances. Thus, the idea of voluntary removal gradually moved to coercive removal.

Certainly, Tecumseh's argument of common ownership of all America by all Indian groups was never accepted by American law. He argued that no one Indian or group of Indians had the right to cede lands. Only all Indians had the right to cede lands; therefore, any treaties lacking assent of all Indians was invalid.

As the War of 1812 ground its way to an end, peace discussions at Ghent,

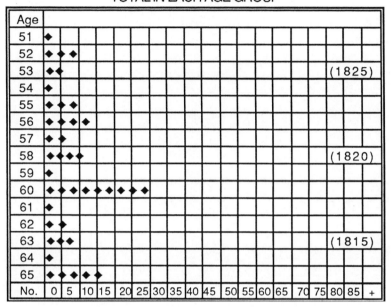

Fig. 25 (continued). Adapted from Burns, *The Osage Annuity Rolls of 1878.*

Belgium, were almost discontinued because of a British Indian proposal. Under pressure from the Canadians, the British introduced a proposal for an Indian state to act as a buffer between the United States and Canada. This proposal was the result of British Indian alliances during the war. They were determined that Indian interests would not be ignored at the peace conference.[11] It is sad that this proposal was rejected because of misunderstanding. Had the United States agreed to their own terms in the Greenville Treaty, an Indian nation, sovereign in all respects, would have been created in the Old Northwest and Canada. Thus, removal to Osage territory would not have been necessary.

Background on the Removal of the Northeastern Nations

In 1792, the Northeastern nations sent a letter to Zenon Trudeau, who was the Spanish Lieutenant Governor at St. Louis.[12] Two other earlier Lieutenant Governors are mentioned in the letter, Francisco Cruzat, who served from 1774 to 1776, and Manuel Perez, who served from 1787 to 1791. The Indians were complimentary in their remarks about Cruzat, who encouraged them to move across the Mississippi into Osage territory. Perez is treated poorly in the letter because of the many Osage attacks on the intruders. Members of the Loups (Wolf-Pawnee), Miamis, Ottawas, Potawatomis, Shawnees, and Peorias sent the letter.

The significance of this letter is that it shows the Northeastern nations had not only become familiar with removal by 1776 but that they had already experienced a partial removal by that year. Clearly, the problems of these early emigrants were mainly from Osage attacks. In the presence of this evidence, it is probable that some of the reluctance in removal that Jefferson met with was due to the experiences of these early emigrant nations. Removal was a new concept to Jefferson and the Americans but not to the Indians on either side of the Mississippi. The role played by the Osages must not be overlooked.

It is evident in Spanish letter after Spanish letter that the Osages were a deterrent to Indian emigration from the east. Caught between the Americans on the east and the Osages on the west, the Northeastern nations had little choice but to make a stand on their home ground. They knew their small disorganized war parties had little chance of success in the Osage homeland. In their own area, each group held the advantage of fighting on familiar ground.

Indian Wars of the Old Northwest

Large land speculation companies such as the Ohio Company and the Scioto Company greatly disturbed the Northeastern nations. Movement of Euro-Americans onto their lands surely put the nations in a bad mood. They were experienced enough to know that the first trickle of intruders would soon swell into a torrent.

As a sidelight to the Scioto Company importation of French settlers, we have some indication that one of these Scioto French married an Osage.[13] The Penn family is a well-known French-Osage family. Apparently, Antoine Penn was one of the Scioto settlers, although this may not be entirely true, because he could have been a French Canadian who acted as guide for the Scioto French.

Aside from the activities of the land companies, the British were also active among the Northeastern nations. Although the British had agreed to abandon the Old Northwest at the end of the Revolution, they still occupied the region. One must bear in mind that the new United States was barely surviving in the post–Revolutionary period. Thus, the British did not abandon the Old Northwest for fear it might fall into French or Spanish hands. While they desired the fur trade of the area, they also wished to create an Indian state as a buffer between themselves and whoever emerged in possession of the areas to the south.

With this goal in mind, the British attempted to unify the various Indian nations toward the common goal of an Indian state. However, as the French and Spanish discovered earlier, unification of the Northeastern people was impossible. There were too many small groups with goals of their own to bring unified action of the whole. Yet, for a short time, unification was achieved. This was enough to generate fear of the Indian south of the Ohio River.

In order to create disorder that would break up the new-found Indian unity, a series of raids was initiated in 1788 by the Kentucky settlers. These raids were the torch that lit the dry fuse of the Indian powder keg. Indian retaliation was swift and massive. Such hostilities could not be overlooked by the United States. Thus, a series of devastating Indian Wars was launched in the Old Northwest.

Between 1790 and 1793, three American generals tried to subdue the Northeastern Indians. The first of these was Josiah Harmer. Harmer moved so slowly that the Indians had no difficulty in avoiding him and fell upon his forces at will. Next to try his hand at Indian warfare was Arthur St. Clair. The Osages participated in the campaign of 1791, joining with their Illinois allies to fight the Americans. It was at the defeat of St. Clair that White Hair I is said to have acquired the White Hair name.

St. Clair had a force of three thousand but only two thousand of his men were fully effective. On November 3, 1791, his forces were encamped on a plateau of the Wabash River. Few guards were posted, so all through the night of November 3 the Indians infiltrated the camp. On the morning of November 4, they struck the Americans. Six hundred and thirty Americans were killed and 283 wounded. The defeat was so complete that the survivors retreated to Fort Jefferson in only twenty-four hours. By comparison, it took them ten days to make the same distance before the battle.

The effects of this defeat were far-reaching and were reflected in the Spanish letters. Lieutenant Governor Perez at St. Louis wrote to Governor Miró at New Orleans on March 31, 1792:

> The advantage which the savages obtained in the beginning of last November against the Americans when the latter were defeated, as I informed Your Lordship in my official letter No. 204, has caused many of the tribes to become extremely insolent. This is evident in their manner of speaking when they present themselves. At the same time they are secretly encouraged by the English, who support them vig-

EMIGRANT INDIAN GROUPS OF THE NORTHEAST AND OLD NORTHWEST AND THEIR RESPECTIVE POPULATIONS–1829[15]			
Tuscarora	250	Sac–Fox	6,600
Seneca	2,900	Shawnee	2,000
Onondaga	450	Piankashaw,Wea,	
Oneida	1,100	and Peoria	478
Stockbridge	300	Kickapoo	2,200
Brothertown	360	Winnebago	5,800
Cayuga	100	Pottawatomi	6,500
Miami	1,550	Chippewa	15,000
Wyandot	600	Ottawa	4,000

Fig. 26. These Indians were removed to Kansas and then most were removed to Oklahoma.

orously, and in the counsels which they give them, as some of the chiefs have told me, it is clear that they even try to persuade them to discontinue our friendship. All this is nothing else except the ambition of the English to obtain the commerce of the Missouri. If the tribes should succeed in holding an advantage over the Americans again, as they did before, this district would have no assurance against their attacks.[14]

Indians were not to gain such a victory again until many years later at the Little Big Horn. General Anthony Wayne was appointed in 1793. Unlike his two unsuccessful predecessors, Wayne was successful in defeating the Northeastern Indians at Fallen Timbers. While only about fifty Indians were killed in the battle, the effect was to break the Indian spirit. It was not so much the loss of warriors as the absence of British support that disheartened the Indians.

The Treaty of Fort Greenville in 1795 ended effective Indian Wars in the Old Northwest. Many individual Indian families migrated to Osage territory instead of fighting the Americans. Certainly, the Fort Greenville Treaty compacted the Northeastern nations into a much smaller area, which made Indian life there all but intolerable. Now the way was open for settlers to move into the southern part of the Old Northwest along the Ohio River. The stage had been set for the ultimate removal of the Northeastern nations. All that was needed was land to remove them to, and that was provided by the Louisiana Purchase and the Osage Treaty of 1808 (see Fig. 26).

Again efforts were made to confederate the Northeastern nations but these efforts were not fruitful. Tecumseh and the Prophet came close to an effective confederation, but they too failed. Some idea of the scope of their efforts can be gained from their visit to Claremore's Town. Black Dog and the other band chiefs were all impressed by Tecumseh and detested the Prophet. But they refused to join in the confederation. They were well aware of the loss at Fallen Timbers and the subsequent Fort Greenville Treaty.

7

The Effects of Removal

INDIAN TERRITORY

Creation

Indian Territory came into being because of the removal of the Northeastern nations. Missouri and Arkansas were quickly filled with emigrant Indians. As the population of Euro-Americans increased west of the Mississippi, pressure was applied to again remove these people from the path of "Manifest Destiny." Thus, the Osages were once more compelled to cede lands to the United States for the benefit of Euro-Americans and emigrant Indians.

While Osage lands in Missouri and Arkansas, ceded in 1808, were never organized as Indian Territory, large areas of the cession of 1825 were designated as Indian Territory. At one time or another, almost all the lands ceded by the Osages in 1825 were incorporated under the title of either Indian Territory or Oklahoma Territory. Originally, almost all of Indian Territory was in the eastern half of Kansas. That portion north of the Kansas River was ceded by the Kansas (Kaw) nation. South of the Kansas River, as far south as the Red River, was ceded by the Osages. The Osages still held a fifty-mile-wide strip from Missouri to the 100th Meridian in Kansas. A strip twenty-five miles wide and fifty miles long in the extreme southeast corner of Kansas was designated as Osage Neutral Lands. All the rest of their vast domain had been taken by trickery, threats, and force.

We must stress the unique nature of the Osage experience with removal. Whereas virtually all other Indian nations ceded their lands for the use of Euro-Americans, most of the Osage domain was dedicated to the use of other Indians. These lands eventually passed to Euro-Americans from other Indians rather than the Osages (see Fig. 27, Fig. 28, and Fig. 29).

However, the ultimate title to most lands in Missouri, Kansas, Arkansas,

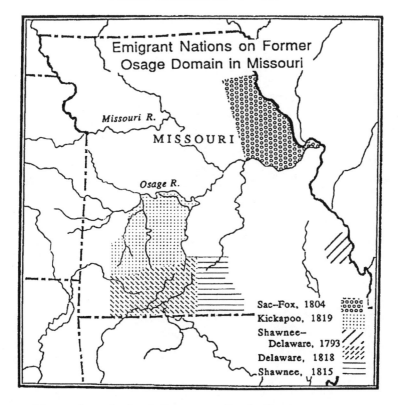

Emigrant Nations on Former
Osage Domain in Missouri

Missouri R.

MISSOURI

Osage R.

Sac–Fox, 1804
Kickapoo, 1819
Shawnee–
Delaware, 1793
Delaware, 1818
Shawnee, 1815

Fig. 27. This map shows the first Indian owners after the Osages.

and Oklahoma rests upon the authenticity of the Osage claim and not upon the claims of secondary Indian claimants or the United States. Disputed claim to these lands passed through France to Spain and back to France and then to the United States. All through these transfers of moot claims, only one people consistently ruled and occupied the area, and these people were Osages.

Osage Lands

We often read that the Osages were assigned or given a reservation. This may be partly correct from an Euro-American viewpoint, but "assigned" in the usual sense normally means an arbitrary designation. In connection with removal, it indicates removal by arbitrary decision to *different* lands and subsequent residence on that land without actual ownership. At no time could this meaning be applied to the Osages. They always resided on their own land. The present reservation is owned in fee simple and was never

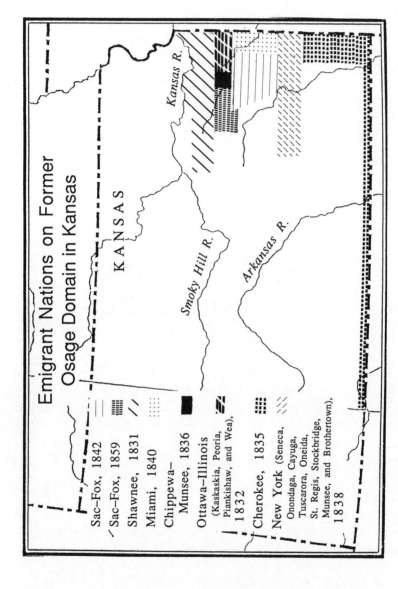

Emigrant Nations on Former Osage Domain in Kansas

KANSAS

Kansas R.

Smoky Hill R.

Arkansas R.

Sac–Fox, 1842
Sac–Fox, 1859
Shawnee, 1831
Miami, 1840
Chippewa–
Munsee, 1836
Ottawa–Illinois
(Kaskaskia, Peoria,
Piankishaw, and Wea),
1832
Cherokee, 1835
New York (Seneca,
Onondaga, Cayuga,
Tuscarora, Oneida,
St. Regis, Stockbridge,
Munsee, and Brothertown),
1838

Fig. 28. This map shows the first owners after the Osages. Not all the Shawnee reservation was in former Osage territory.

assigned or given to the Osages. They selected this part of their old domain and paid for it with their own money.

Confusion of these terms as applied to the Osages arises because of their unique position as contributors of land for the use of other Indians. Another pattern of confusion arises because the Osages purchased their present reservation. Some writers are so confused that they consider the Osages to be emigrants to Oklahoma. Apparently, they are unaware that the Osages are among the few Indian nations native to the state. Since Indian Territory and removal is so much a part of Osage history, the terms *assignment of land* and *removal* should be clarified.

REMOVAL BY EXCHANGE

Northeastern and Southeastern Nations

Removal was not a great problem for the American government in the Northeast. Most of the Indian nations there were small and could offer little effective resistance to removal. Yet, this did not lessen the trauma these nations experienced from removal. The larger Indian groups to the southeast presented a more difficult problem for the Americans. By virtue of the size of the groups and greater ability to confederate, the Southeastern nations were considered to be a greater threat to the United States.

This difference in possible resistance on the part of the Indians of the Northeast and those of the Southeast resulted in the Northeastern nations being the first to experience removal. The first removal by land exchange was with the Indiana Delawares, October 3, 1818.[1] Next to be removed were the Kickapoos on July 30, 1819.[2] So, in this way, a pattern of removal by land exchange was established. In almost all cases, the Indians being removed expressed fear of the Osages. We do not presume to judge if these expressions were true fear or fears expressed to avoid removal. In the light of the Spanish accounts, it would seem to be a little of both. Yet, there were surprisingly few clashes between the Northeastern emigrants and the Osages. The same cannot be said for the Southeastern emigrants.

While removal by exchange of lands dates from 1818, removal by inducement carries earlier dates. Certainly, the Spanish practiced inducement removal with the eastern Indians. This type of removal between the United States and the Cherokees dates from 1808. In May of that year, a Cherokee delegation visited Washington.[3] The Cherokees requested that all their people who wanted to live as hunters be allowed to emigrate west of the Mississippi. Jefferson promised to make the necessary arrangements. There is no doubt that this was a part of the reason for the Osage cessions in November of 1808.

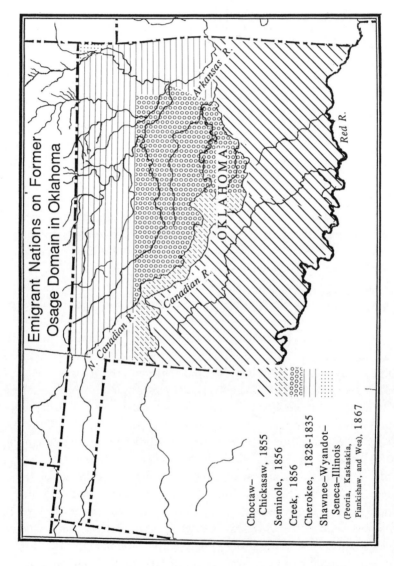

Fig. 29. A small part of the Choctaw-Chickasaw reserve was not in the old Osage domain.

Osage-Cherokee Wars

Background

After the Arkansas bands signed the Treaty of 1808 at St. Louis, Jefferson notified the Cherokees that the way was clear for removal. He specified the area along the lower White and Arkansas Rivers.[4] Nearly two thousand Cherokees left Georgia and Tennessee and moved to Arkansas. From this new base, Cherokee hunters intruded into Osage territory and, thus, a new series of Osage-Cherokee wars ensued.

While the exchange of land had been discussed with the Cherokee, no exchange had taken place. In the council of 1809, the Cherokee national council refused to exchange any land. Hence, the Cherokees in Arkansas were there as unassigned Indians. Under the Osage understanding of the Treaty of 1808, these unassigned Cherokees were intruders on Osage hunting territory. Therefore, even before the Cherokee crossed the Fire Prairie–Fort Smith Osage Line to hunt, they were intruders on Osage territory and as such they were subject to Osage law (see Fig. 30).

Grant Foreman states the following, without acknowledging the above background: "For many years the powerful Osage were probably more active than any other force in maintaining a state of warfare throughout Oklahoma and preventing its peaceful occupation by either red or white men. They challenged practically all tribes of Indians they encountered on the prairies and east to the Mississippi."[5]

In justice to the Osages, it must be said that they certainly made an epic effort to protect their homeland. Yet, even today, they are pictured as troublemakers because they defended their land. We do not believe it is bias to point out that it was their enemies that were reporting the Osages as troublemakers.

Possibly, the United States cast the Osages in the role of villains for the same reasons the Spanish had. That is, the Osages followed their own laws and simply did not conform to the plans made by Euro-Americans. The record clearly shows the Arkansas bands attacking Indians and Euro-Americans alike for invading their hunting territory. Such defense of their territory and rights upset the plans of the United States and the other Indian nations. In order to alleviate some of the violence inflicted by the Arkansas bands and, thus, to proceed with their own plans, Pierre Chouteau was instructed to influence these bands to reunite with those of the Missouri. These efforts not only failed, but they also alienated the relationship between the Claremore bands and Chouteau. Thus, what little influence the Americans had with the Arkansas Osages was lost. A. P. Chouteau finally reestablished some of the Chouteau influence in 1817.[6]

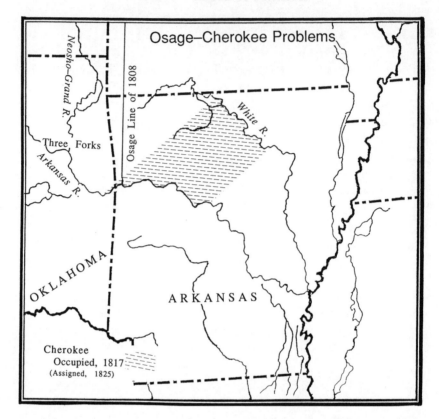

Fig. 30. Notice the date of occupation and the date of assignment. Hunting west of the Osage Line was a major cause of conflict between the Osages and Cherokee.

Osage Raids

An impressive list exists of Osage raids on Euro-Americans.[7] Hunting camps belonging to John Well were robbed in 1814, 1815, and 1818 by Osages. Peter and August Friend were deprived of their beaver traps, powder, and bullet molds in 1818 on the James River. Elijah and Abraham Eastwood were hunting on the Gasconade and were robbed in 1814. William and James McMurtry were robbed on the Arkansas in 1821. These were all filed as claims against the Osages. Yet, in all these cases, the people being robbed were illegal intruders in Osage territory.

The list continues in other localities. In 1815, four white men were killed on the Arkansas and another was killed on the Red River. Two men were killed near the mouth of the Canadian in 1816. During the same year a member of a hunting party was killed on the Kiamichi River. One man was killed and another wounded near the mouth of the Kiamichi in 1817. It should be noted that these killings took place west of the Osage Line. East of the line the parties were robbed but not killed. Perhaps it would be interesting to compile a list of lives lost in Indian encounters and thus have some comparison of the various nations. Our purpose here, however, is to acknowledge the Osage willingness to protect their lands.

On November 17, 1823 a hunting party of twenty Americans and Frenchmen were attacked by Mad Buffalo of the Claremore bands. Four of the party were beheaded, the traditional Osage treatment for unauthorized intruders who kill game. Because of this encounter, steps were taken to establish Fort Gibson. Nuttall gives us a fair assessment of the Osage situation on the Arkansas drainage. He offers a well-considered presentation of the Euro-American view and then gives this assessment of the Osage view: "And, on the other hand, we have surely no just reason to expect from the Indians an unstipulated license to rob their country of that game, which is necessary to their convenience and subsistence."[8]

Unfortunately for the Osages, not all Americans were as understanding and forgiving as Nuttall. William Clark had understanding but lacked some of the forgiving. He confessed to the hope that the Osage-Cherokee war then in progress (1817) might serve to subdue the Osages. This particular war came from a Cherokee raid into Osage territory on the Canadian in the fall of 1816, after the Osages had recovered some stolen horses and killed a Cherokee in the process.

"Fair-Haired" Cherokees

A large group of Cherokee volunteers had been halted as they crossed the Mississippi. But Clark was suggesting that maybe it would be beneficial to allow enough Cherokees to cross from the east so the Claremore bands could be defeated.[9] It is fortunate that this was not permitted, for despite their differences, the White Hair and Little Osage bands would hardly stand aside in such a war. No combination of Cherokees could have defeated a force of united Osages on their own land in 1817. And defeat of a large Cherokee force would have wrecked the American removal plans.

Clark, at least, had an understanding of the Osage view, and he was not entirely unforgiving. He absolutely refused to touch any further Osage land cession treaties after 1825 and felt a great sorrow for his part in earlier cessions. President Monroe and Secretary of War Calhoun had neither understanding nor forgiveness for the Osages. All they could see was that the Osages barred Cherokee access to the great buffalo herds to the west. Since they wanted to remove the Cherokee west of the Mississippi, they saw the Osages as a hindrance to their plans. From their viewpoint, the Osages should be willing to cede a part of their domain as an outlet for the Cherokee. To facilitate Cherokee removal, the wishes of the Arkansas Cherokees was to be granted, even if justice to the Osages was sacrificed.[10]

The Massacre at Claremore's Mound

Much has been made of a Cherokee victory over the Osages in what is sometimes styled the "Battle of Claremore's Mound." However, two points should be noted. First, this was not solely a Cherokee victory. Secondly, the Osage force consisted of very aged men, women, and young children amounting to less than a fourth of the number in the attacking force. There cannot be any doubt that even a "paper tiger" victory over the Osages was cause for celebration. Certainly, the Cherokee and American officials were jubilant. Yet, the Cherokee and their allies paid a terrible price for their victory during the following twenty years. The Osage thirst for vengeance was not easily satisfied. While their vengeance upon the Cherokee was complete, it was also severe on the other nations that participated in this massacre.

This victory over the Osages took place at Claremore's Village in the fall of 1817. The attacking force consisted of both eastern and western Cherokees, Choctaws, Shawnees, Delawares, Caddos, Tonkawas, Comanches, Coushattas, and a sizable body of white men,[11] altogether the invading army probably amounted to between six hundred and eight hundred persons.

The invaders knew full well that all able-bodied men, women, and older children were out on the Plains on the fall hunt. These great "victors" did not have the courage to face able-bodied Osages. Yet, even knowing they faced only feeble old Osages, they did not dare to strike without further treachery.

A runner was sent to the Osage village to tell the Osages that ten or fifteen Cherokees were waiting to discuss their differences. An old chief returned with the runner to tell the Cherokees that Claremore was away and a council could not be held until his return. As a matter of Indian courtesy and goodwill, the old chief accepted the Cherokee offer of food and drink. As he sat down, the Cherokees murdered him. We are not acquainted with Cherokee customs, but among the Plains Indians an offer and acceptance of food and drink was a guarantee of friendship. To violate this pledge of honor was the vilest act an Indian could commit. To our knowledge, this is the only example recorded west of the Mississippi of a violation of this pledge of friendship.

After slaying the old chief, the invaders fell upon the unsuspecting village. Fourteen old Osage men were killed defending the village. Sixty-nine old women, boys, and children were killed. Slightly more than one hundred young children were taken captive.[12] All of these Osage captives were taken to the eastern Cherokee villages. A few were eventually returned to the Osages, but many lived out their lives as Cherokees.

After killing and mutilating these feeble victims, the allied force looted and burned the village. They then turned to Black Dog's Village, which was nearby. However, Black Dog's people had concealed themselves in a cave that Black Dog had constructed for this purpose. Although the village, like Claremore's, was burned and looted, the Black Dog people were spared the fate of Claremore's people.[13] Although Cherokee claims against the Osages were paid by the Osages, this looting and killing in two Osage villages was never compensated by the Cherokee or allies involved.

One facet of this attack has never been addressed before. This is the effect of the attack on the Osages. Among the thirteen war honors held in esteem by the Osages, none stand higher than successfully defending the village from the attack of an enemy. This was also one of the most difficult war honors to attain, since an Osage village was rarely attacked. Only two incidents have been recorded, the one mentioned here and an earlier attack. Conversely, to allow one's village to be looted and its elderly men, women, and children to be slain or captured was a great dishonor to an Osage warrior. Over the ensuing twenty years, warriors of the Claremore band were especially diligent in their retaliation.

CONTRAST OF CULTURES

Removal and the Euro-American presence had many detrimental effects on the Osages and other Indians. Traditionally, any actions taken by the Osage were initiated only by unanimous consent of the people. Euro-American contact brought ideas of Western civilization to the Osages. Among these ideas was the concept of a leader who spoke for his people. This trend can be seen all through the early records.

By the time the Americans appeared on the Osage scene, the practice of Osage leaders making the decisions for all the people was well established. When consent by all was the rule, everyone acted in unison and disputes were rare. When decisions were made by the leaders alone, disputes often arose because of differing opinions. The practice of land cessions by Osage leaders generated great dissension. One must understand that from the former Osage view, action by consensus bound all to the course taken. Without consensus, only those who agreed with the action felt obligated to honor the course taken. Thus, many Osages did not feel bound by the concessions made by their leaders. It is this matter that Tecumseh based his speeches upon when he spoke to other nations. That is, the actions of Indian leaders held no more force than the power exerted by individual Indians.

Without a practice of universal consent, the only alternative is factional-ism or the formation of sects. As Tecumseh so remarkably observed, the ten-dency of the Indian groups to factionalize under Euro-American influence was destructive to Indian unification. This tendency, as we have indicated, was certainly not limited to the Osages. It is ironic that as Euro-Americans tried to bring Indians under one universal law and rule, they were simulta-neously making this impossible.

No social concept can be transmitted intact from one culture to another. For perfect transmission of concepts from one culture to another, both cul-tures must have shared the same experiences in exactly the same way. Since different cultures lack shared experiences, a concept of one culture would be viewed in a different way by another culture. It is this problem that forms the major difference between the Physical Sciences and the Social Sciences. In the Physical Sciences, an idea can be reproduced in a laboratory to test its validity. This is impossible in the Social Sciences because one can-not reproduce a culture identical to the original culture. So, a successful practice in one culture does not necessarily mean the same practice would be successful in another culture.

Thus, the Western civilization concept of decision by leaders did not function among Indians as it functioned in Western civilization. Herein lies a great and important distinction between Western civilization and Ameri-can Indian civilization. All through the history of Western civilization, heavy stress is placed on the leader who fights against the odds of nature and the men aligned against him. Osage myths place emphasis on people learning to live with nature and with other people. Their history has no great heroes, only stories of a heroic people. Rather than men against na-ture and other men, Osage literature seeks to place the Osage people in harmony with nature and with other people. There is no unity behind an individual—unity is seeking harmony with all.

With these opposing viewpoints, it is interesting to note the effects of the marriage of the two viewpoints upon the Euro-American community and the Osage community. As the Osages became more leader-oriented and Euro-Americans became more people-oriented, each experienced a grow-ing disunity. In Western civilization the long history of philosophy related to man's relation to the state had always stressed the strong leader. The leader may have acquired his position by divine right, the force of arms, wealth, or intrigue. Regardless of how a leader acquired his position he was the ruler. He made the decisions, or an elite group made the decisions. The people had very little if any real voice in their government. The introduction of the Indian-inspired natural rights philosophy was a revolution in Western thought. So long as the Indian influence existed, so did the dominance of natural rights philosophy. With the decline of Indian influence, Western civilization again returned to their old themes in philosophy.

The only Western government that approached the old Osage government in its people orientation was that of the Articles of Confederation of the United States of America. Yet, this government was abandoned in a few years as being unworkable. One cannot argue that the basic ideas of the Confederation were unworkable, because those ideas had been functioning for centuries in Indian cultures. One can argue that the ideas of the Confederation were unworkable in a government of Western civilization because the people of that culture did not have the background to make it work.

We cannot determine where the Indian idea of people-government will go in Western civilization. Hopefully, it will be a benefit to all people. We can determine that Western ideas of the strong leader have disunited the Osage people and Indians in general. Furthermore, this disunity is likely to continue for many generations. For the Osages, exposure to this idea was very harmful. Our fervent hope is that Osage concepts of people-orientation will not be as harmful to Western civilization.

8

Osage Culture and United States' Policy

UNITED STATES INDIAN POLICY

Introduction

In August of 1789 the new government of the United States created a war department. Among the duties assigned to this department were those "relative to Indian affairs." By an Act of Congress, July 9, 1832, the office of Commissioner of Indian Affairs was created. In June of 1834, an Act of Congress created the Department of Indian Affairs within the War Department.

With the creation of the Department of the Interior in 1849, the Department of Indian Affairs was attached to the new department as the Bureau of Indian Affairs. This new organization was comprehensive in Indian affairs, since it included everything connected with Indians.[1]

The date of 1849 is significant in Osage history because it brought a softer approach toward the Osages. While the effects of this change did not become evident until twenty years later, nevertheless, a change occurred. Possibly the change of view toward the Osages was as much the result of the War in Kansas and the Civil War as it was due to the change from the War Department to the Interior Department. Yet, even before the War in Kansas in the 1850s a softer attitude toward the Osages was noticeable. So, it seems safe to say that the change in organization brought a change in attitude toward the Osages.

Not only does 1849 mark the beginning of a softer approach to the Osages, but it also marks the high-water mark of the traditional Osage life. From this time onward, the Osages moved rapidly from their traditional life. The Osages were fortunate in having a rare agent at the Neosho Agency for part of these transitional years. We do not believe A. J. Dorn was a saint, but he surely was an improvement over his predecessors. At the least, his actions show he tried to protect the Osages, and, most unusual, he was the first Osage Agent who spoke in their defense.

Despite its faults, and there are many, the Bureau of Indian Affairs appeared on the scene in time to prevent the total extinction of the Osage people. The War Department had already set the stage for their destruction. Previous measures by the War Department had all but destroyed the Osage people. Three outstanding Bureau of Indian Affairs Agents were at least partly responsible for saving the Osage people. These were A. J. Dorn, Isaac Gibson, and Major Laban J. Miles. Their job was never easy, and they made mistakes, but they should be remembered by the Osage people.

Unfortunately, many practices established under the War Department were carried over into the Bureau of Indian Affairs. Many problems existed within the Indian Department apart from graft and corruption. An enlightened policy was beyond hope in an era marked by paternalistic greed for everything owned by the Indians. It would be difficult to assess which harmed Indians the most, paternalistic well-wishers or outright greed of corporate and settler interests. Some type of policy had to evolve in the midst of conflicting interests.

Elements of Indian Policy

There were three basic elements to Indian policy. Land is the first of these elements. The body of Indian land law is staggering in its complexities.[2] Most of the early relationships between the two cultures were commercial, but land soon replaced trade as the leading economic factor. The next element was cultural. Since Indians could not be allowed to occupy such vast tracts of land they must become Westernized, or as it was commonly expressed, "civilized." Finally, population and variety among Indians had to be dealt with in any policy for dealing with the Indian. Sadly, this latter element was too often overlooked in the opinions of reformers and in the greed for Indian land.

Each of these elements will be dealt with under their respective headings in this chapter. At the outset, it must be said that these three elements are interrelated and overlap in many respects. However, of the three elements, land is the most persistent thread running through the fabric of Indian Policy. This does not necessarily lessen the importance of the others at various times.

Indian Land Policies: The Basic Concepts

There were three basic concepts involved in Indian land policies. First, it was agreed among the European powers that only the discoverer of the area had the sole right to acquire Indian land title. Secondly, at no time was the right of occupancy by Indians ever denied. That is, the Indians' right to the lands they occupied was not denied. Lastly, in American policy, only the national government had the right to acquire Indian lands. The Indians could neither alienate nor transfer their title to any other entity.

There is little need to touch upon the ethics of the agreement by the European powers to recognize the discovering nation as sovereign over the area. The fact that Indians did not concede this right until Euro-Americans were capable of enforcing their claims serves a single purpose. It clearly shows that Indian lands were taken by force instead of by purchase. The situation is much like the school yard bully who offers a smaller child five cents for a ten dollar agate marble. If the smaller child refuses to sell his agate for a nickel, he gets thrashed by the bully and the bully takes the marble anyway.

It would be a mistake to assume that recognition of the right of occupancy was a clear concept. Occupancy is subject to a multitude of interpretations, and the use of the term *right* is more often used in a loose instead of restricted sense. What constitutes occupancy depends upon a variety of cultural factors. Occupancy in an agrarian culture would likely imply cultivation of the land. In an industrial culture, it would suggest utilization of the land to produce resources for industry. However, *use* as a vehicle to define occupation is only one facet of the definition. Certainly, occupation means a physical residence upon the land. Yet, here we encounter the problem of determining the limits of residence.

When one resides on, say, a one-fourth acre, does the person reside on the entire parcel or only a portion of the parcel? It is easy to see that when one starts examining occupancy a variety of problems arise. We will not go through the same process with the term *right,* but it is even more open to abuse in usage. The point to be made is that right of occupancy can be defined in almost any way our desires dictate. This is exactly what happened to Indian lands. That is, Euro-Americans wanted the Indian lands without the stigma of being labeled thieves. Thus, the convenient fiction of right of occupancy was created.

It would be pure speculation to try to determine how Indians would have fared under state and local governments or private control. Indian affairs would have been even more chaotic than they were under federal control, because the sheer numbers of state and local governmental units would have insured chaos. However, speculation is needless. The whole matter was fated to come under control of the central government because the Indians were sovereign nations. Since this involved external sovereignty, the central government was the only one who could deal with Indians.

In the beginning of the relationship between the two cultures, there was no question of whether Indian nations were sovereign or not. They possessed full sovereignty. Yet, while the fiction of control was lodged in the central government, actual contacts and agreements with Indians were made at the local or individual level. This did not change materially until the Articles of Confederation clearly placed Indian affairs in the hands of the central government. As the power to enforce the Euro-American will over Indians grew, the sovereignty of Indian nations was eroded. Finally, the point was reached where Indian sovereignty became more fiction than fact.

The continuation of the fiction of sovereignty made dealing with Indians a matter of dealing with a quasi-foreign power. Thus, treaties were necessary to legalize Indian policies. Following the Civil War, large corporate entities largely ran the United States by influencing the selection of Senators in Congress. Thus, the Indian treaties were heavily slanted to corporate interests. Eventually, the Populist Revolt changed the method of selecting Senators to a popular vote and, thus, diluted the corporate influence in American government and Indian affairs. We will come back to this matter in more detail later.

While corporate interests have always influenced Indian relationships, they did not dominate the formation of Indian policy until after 1850. Thus, the settlers, intruders, and reformers had the greatest influence in making Indian policy until 1850, at least insofar as the Osages are concerned. We must also be aware that a considerable amount of Indian policy was and still is made by government employees who administer Indian affairs. Thus, we find that Indian policy was primarily made by corporate interests, settlers, intruders, reformers, and government personnel.

Cultural Policy: Cultural Contrasts

In August of 1806, Jacob Bright made a trading expedition to the Arkansas bands and recorded a speech by Town Maker (Claremore II).[3]

> What is bad now, Nothing is bad, the water is good and the Road is good. . . . The Land is good and the Game is Plenty—you shall go back with a glad Heart—the Road is Wide for all the White People. . . . we find that you don't want to sell your goods too high you part with them with a good Heart. . . . I should be glad to go and see our American Father—You American Chiefs have more than one Soldier—they have plenty of them you see the Chiefs and soldiers here, they are sitting Round you. . . . When you come again we wish you to have Coats made of blue and red facings—we have thirty seven soldiers and five Chiefs—Your talks are very good, we and the white hairs are not

very good friends—him and his People are Americans, and some of them have been to see their great Father and received his good talks but I believe they have lost most all his words on their way home, we wish to be Americans too—

This speech reveals bits and pieces of Osage culture. It also shows some of the manipulation taking place between the Claremore bands and the White Hair bands.

For those who are not familiar with Osage ways, references to good water and a good road may not be clear in meaning. Good water had a special significance to all the Dhegiha peoples. It was symbolic of blood and kinship among persons. Thus, to be offered a drink of good water was to be treated as a blood relative. In the sense it is used here, the relationship with the animals has been good, and they have many furs to trade.

The Road, mentioned twice, is not a reference to a physical thoroughfare but the road of life. If the road of life is narrow, it is beset with a multitude of misfortunes. If the road is wide, one is at liberty to pick the easiest passage. A good road offers a person a good life and the achievement of old age. Other expressions seem clear as they stand.

We started this topic with Claremore II's speech in order to stress the existence of cultural differences. All humans tend to view the world around them from their own backgrounds. While all humans share much in common, enough differences exist between cultures to cause misunderstandings. If we assume that the majority of the Euro-American culture had some good intentions toward the Indians, we should expect these to appear in the Indian policies. Likewise, if these intentions do appear in the policies, they would fail to consider the Indian culture as a factor. That is, even well-meaning policies were often destructive to the Indian because the Indian culture was not considered in making the policy.

Cultural Policy: Misconceptions

"In the early years of the sixteenth century, educated whites, steeped in the theological teachings of Europe, argued learnedly about whether or not Indians were humans with souls, whether they, too, derived from Adam and Eve (and were therefore sinful like the rest of mankind) or whether they were a previously unknown subhuman species."[4] While this may seem insane to us today, we must realize that five hundred years from now, some of our cherished ideas may seem to verge on insanity. We must be aware of not only cultural smugness but also of a smugness bred of our own times.

Another source of misconceptions arose from the fact that North American Indians had no written language. Thus, all the early accounts about Indians were filtered through the backgrounds of Western civilization. The initial biases of the early writers still have a bad influence on what is written about Indians. When native writers write of their people, the most difficult task is to determine what is Indian and what is Western. Surely, Indian policy based on what had been written about Indians prior to 1880 was certain to border on fantasy. A purely Osage history with no Western influence would be incomprehensible to a modern Osage. By the same token, Western history without reference to Indians is incoherent.

For the historian of Indian life, the task becomes complicated. So far as we know, no Indian history has ever been written solely within the river of Indian civilization. Arnold Toynbee states this problem as "the misconception of the unity of history—involving the assumption that there is only one river of civilization, our own, and that all others are either tributary to it or else lost in the desert sands."[5] Thus, Indian histories we have read all hang on the course of Western civilization and are not independent in and of themselves—including this effort. Naturally, this same factor greatly affected the formation of Indian policy.

Your new-caught, sullen peoples
Half devil and half child.

Take up the White Man's burden
And reap his old reward:
The blame of those ye better,
The hate of those ye guard.[6]

Thus, Kipling expressed a not uncommon feeling in Western civilization. Although he was writing about the British Empire, his thoughts were common among Euro-Americans with respect to the American Indian. With very little reservation one can say that "the white man's burden" attitude was influential in shaping American Indian policy.

Closely related to Kipling's view is the feeling that Indians were an impediment to the development of the United States.[7] There was a widespread belief that Indians did not utilize the land as well as Americans did. Thus, the thinking was that the inferior use of the land deprived America of a higher use. No fair-minded economist could argue that the subsistence agriculture of the American frontier was a higher use of the land than the uses applied by Indians. Certainly, the agrarian revolution following the Civil War brought a higher use, at least in the sense of an immediate increase of production. Yet it also reduced the number of people who labored on the land to produce food. We must note that while the immediate farm toil necessary to feed the peoples of the United States has been reduced, the total hours of labor involved has been increased. This is counting factory workers, extractive industries, transportation, and on and on into the various labors needed to make farm machinery and to transport, process, and market the foodstuffs. Arguments notwithstanding, seeing Indians as an impediment was a major force in shaping Indian policy.

For some reason, the Indian population supported by a given area and, indeed, the total Indian population for the lower forty-eight states have been consistently understated. The usual total for mainland United States is placed at between 500,000 and 1,100,000. This is an unreasonable estimate, if one looks at the archaeological evidences and manipulated information. A more realistic estimate would have been between 7,000,000 and 8,000,000 in 1500. We have earlier noted the Spanish underestimation of the Osages at 1,200 warriors. Major George Sibley's estimate is only slightly larger. The Osages themselves estimated their population at 14,000 as late as 1850. This would indicate a warrior strength of 2,200–2,500 men at least. Excavated Osage village sites tend to support the Osage estimate of their own population.

An excellent discussion of this problem can be found in *The Invasion of America*. As the discussion in Francis Jennings's book concludes, Europeans did not find a wilderness here in North America: "With all their resources, and including both migration and natural increase, the English apparently required the full century [the seventeenth century] to duplicate the populations that Indians alone had maintained in New England prior to invasion." [8]

The matters of population, use of land, and stage of civilization are all interrelated. People assuming that the American Indian was at the so-called savagery stage of civilization cannot accept the truth of actual Indian populations. In spite of archaeological proofs of dense Indian populations discovered in the 1990s and early–2000s, the traditional Indian population estimates are still used. A savage culture could not support large Indian populations. It is probable that the population of Indians north of Mexico totaled somewhere around 10,000,000 in 1500. Therefore, the Indian population had attained a high order of civilization with the ability to support populations exceeding those of medieval Europe. Their use of the land was, in some respects, more advanced than that of sixteenth-century Europe. In some respects this is still true today, especially in terms of conservation and maintenance of an ecological balance.

By far, the most erroneous assumption about American Indians was that they must be assimilated into the majority or perish. [9] The Osages still cling to many of their customs. Although these have been somewhat altered, their culture still exists outside of the majority culture. Considering the fact of over three hundred years of contact and at least one hundred years of all-out effort to destroy Osage culture, it is remarkable that any shreds of the culture remain. While most Osages have accommodated themselves to the majority culture, they still retain a separate culture of their own. This would be an indication that despite all efforts to destroy the culture to achieve assimilation, assimilation is not necessarily inevitable. Other Indians also show this cultural persistence, which strongly suggests an error among those who thought Indians must assimilate or perish.

OSAGE CULTURE

Descriptions

"Powerful and well-organized, the Osages were respected by whites and Indian tribes alike as formidable foes."[10] Thus, the Bureau of Indian Affairs describes the Osages as fighters. However, Swanton gives a further comment on the Osages, as fighters noted for their social organization.

> During the eighteenth century and the first part of the nineteenth, the Osage were at war with practically all the other Indians of the Plains and a large number of the woodlands, to many of which their name was a synonym for enemy.
> As above stated, the Osage attained a high reputation as fighters among all the tribes of the southern Plains and many of those of the Gulf region. They are also remarkable for their social organization.[11]

While most writers stress the fame of the Osages as fighters, those who knew them best stress other traits. Among those who knew the Osages by living with them was Fr. J. J. Bax, S. J.: "According to my experience, there are few nations in this region as affable and as affectionate as the Osages. Indeed, it may be said that it is natural to them to wish to live in perfect friendship with all whom they know. Peace and harmony reign among them; no harsh words ever escape their tongues, unless when they are drunk to excess."[12]

Although Fr. Bax was obviously partial to the Osages, others, such as Dr. Francis La Flesche of the Smithsonian, also reflect this view of the Osage character. Perhaps the most detailed physical description of the Osages is given by George Catlin. Catlin spent some time at Fort Gibson. During his stay he sketched and painted several Osages. It is doubtful that Catlin visited the Osage village north of Fort Gibson, but probably met and sketched his Osage subjects at the Fort. Catlin never visited or sketched any of the White Hair or Little Osage people.[13] Catlin would have agreed with Washington Irving's physical description of the Osages:

> Near by these was a group of Osages: stately fellows; stern and simple in garb and aspect. They wore no ornaments; their dress consisted mainly of blankets, leggins, and moccosons. Their heads were bare; their hair was cropped close, excepting a bristling ridge on the top, like the crest of a helmet, with a long scalp lock hanging behind. They had fine Roman countenances, and broad deep chests; and, as they generally wore their blankets wrapped round their loins, so as to leave the bust and arms bare, they looked like so many noble bronze figures. The Osages are the finest looking Indians I have seen in the West. They have not yielded sufficiently, as yet, to the influence of civilization to lay by their simple Indian garb, or to lose the habits of the hunter and the warrior; and their poverty prevents their indulging in much luxury of apparel.[14]

A more modern view is stated by Bill Burchardt: "Father Marquette, Washington Irving, the French Trader Chouteau, were much impressed with the Osages. They were not wrong. If the Osages have a tribal characteristic, it is that they are philosophical, perhaps even mystical, an admirable people who underwent a fantastic ordeal on America's final frontier."[15]

We will touch upon the ordeal that is mentioned above in the next period, 1850–1865. Our purpose here is to show the Osages as they were in the first half of the nineteenth century.

Physical Feats

The Osages were remarkable walkers. Although there are many accounts of this fact, the following quote is possibly the best account:

> The pedestrian powers of these indians [Osages] is almost incredible. . . . To give you some idea of their speed in traveling—a young warrior was dispatched on foot, from Col. Chouteau's with an express to the Creek Agency, a distance of about forty miles; he started at 12 o'clock noon and returned with an answer, between 9 and 10 o'clock on the same evening; performing a walk of nearly eighty miles in less than ten hours. . . . it is indeed, very common for the men and women to proceed with their skins from Clairmont's village to Col. Chouteau's do their trading and return home, on the same day; the distance, going and coming, being not less, certainly, than seventy miles.[16]

Some accounts stress the fact that the Osages made better time afoot than they did on horseback. Yet, one must not be misled into thinking that the Osages were not excellent horsemen. "The Osages learn to ride from earliest infancy: they become surprisingly expert. . . . at war, they escape the arrows of their enemies by concealing themselves so adroitly behind the flanks of their beasts that they show only one foot. At play they gallop bareback with bridles hanging loose, and lean so far over that one would think they were going to lose their balance. They shoot their arrows with surprising accuracy from this awkward position."[17]

Victor Tixier went on a buffalo hunt with the Osages and had ample opportunity to observe Osage horsemanship. He also gives the best-known description of Osage riding equipment. While cooking is not usually considered to be a physical feat, anyone who has cooked over an open fire would dispute this common misconception. "Nearly every tribe on the Missouri had some interesting skill that set them off from other Indians. . . . The Osages had a class of men who served as chefs or cooks, devoting themselves to the culinary art, to preparing and presiding over formal feasts, and also acting as town criers."[18]

These unusual men were called marmitons by the French. In most instances, they were old warriors who had no other way of making a living. Undoubtedly, the Marmaton River in the old Osage country of Vernon County, Missouri, takes its name from these cooksheralds, although the spelling is slightly different.

In another place, Tixier describes a variant of the Osage ceremony of "Striking the Earth": "I returned to the camp; I could hear angry words in the distance; I was told that the warriors were striking the post. I came near and saw that a red post had been set in the ground. The braves came forward one after the other [and] struck it with their tomahawks; then, extending their hands toward it, they listed their acts of courage and the reasons for their hatred of the Pawnee."[19]

The Osage ceremony of Striking the Earth was very much like Tixier's description. An ancient war club was used instead of a tomahawk. First, a dent was struck into the ground, then a straight east-west line was drawn on each side of the dent. Wavy lines were drawn north and south of the dent. The dent represented the sun and the straight lines its path. Benefits of the sun's rays were represented by the wavy lines. As part of the ceremony, a respected warrior was asked to recite his war honors.

The purpose of this ceremony was to thank the Great Creator for bringing sky and earth together, and thus creating the unity of sky and earth so that life on earth was possible. In a broader sense, this ceremony expressed the unity of the Osage people and their promise to the Great Creator to protect the lands he had given them from transgressions of intruders. Striking the Post was a variation of the main ceremony. Here, the red post represented the lifeblood of the enemy who had intruded onto Osage lands. Each tomahawk stroke was a promise to strike the enemy. Recitation of war honors were humble pleas to the Great Creator to help them protect the "center of the earth," as they called the Osage territory. Like Striking the Earth, this also was a rite of unity, but it expressed their unity in striking the Pawnee.

Religion

If the Osages were not the most religious of all the Indian people, they were close to it. All who came into contact with them noted this facet of the Osage character. Perhaps the best statement about the Osages and religion was given in *Beacon on the Plain.* Speaking of the Osages, Isaac McCoy says: "No tribe with which I have come into contact has given more unequivocal evidence of their belief in God, his superintending providence, and the immortality of the soul."[20]

One often reads of the "mourning" at sunrise. The Osages had three prayer eagles. These were the Red Eagle, White Eagle, and Dark or Black Eagle. Each of these eagles symbolized a time of prayer. The red of sunrise made the eagle's wings seem to be red. At noon, an eagle's wings shimmered in the rays of the sun's zenith and seemed to be white. At sunset, the long shadows made the eagle's wings dark with the promise of night. Thus, the Osages were reminded to pray at sunrise, noon, and sunset.

No time of the day was more sacred than sunrise. The coming of the sun symbolized the beginning of life. This in turn reminded everyone of those who had departed from life, since the beginning and ending of life were associated with each other in Osage minds. Thus, mourning at sunrise, which was a happy occasion, also brought a sadness. Old Osages often said, "they walked the spirit path even as they lived." We have ample evidence of this sadness at sunrise and mourning on other occasions: "John Bradbury, in 1811, attributed this phenomenon of crying to sorrow for their dead, but he also recounts the Osage mourning for those they were about to rob. Twenty-five years later Josiah Gregg also noted this characteristic. He stated that the Osages were the most accomplished mourners of all the savages and could be prevailed upon to cry for the troubles of a total stranger."[21]

Bradbury was correct when he noted the Osages mourning for those they were about to rob. This was done before and after the fact. Robbing a fellow human was an act of disharmony. When the harmony of the world is disturbed, one must express sadness and regret for the act that upset the unity of nature. More difficult for an Osage warrior was to mourn the death of an enemy he had slain. To destroy a life is a serious unharmonious act. While this applied to all life, both animate and inanimate,[22] it was especially true of human life.

Osage Dress

Before trade goods became common among the Osages, the men wore breech clouts secured by a sash of finger-woven buffalo hair. In colder weather, hip-length buckskin leggins were worn as an addition to the breech clout. Moccasins were made from skins of deer, elk, or buffalo. On some days, a robe was worn. This might have been made of skins from buffalo, panther (puma), bear, or any number of smaller animals. Women wore deerskin wraparound skirts fastened on the right side. Another deerskin was fastened over one shoulder and fell below the opposite arm. The ladies also wore high-top moccasins and leggins.

Men wore their hair in a roach on top, and a long "tail" of hair grew on the back side of the roach. Women wore their hair shoulder length or longer. A part down the middle was dyed red to represent the sun's path. Normally, married women or ladies not interested in marriage wore their hair behind their ears and shoulders. When a lady wore her hair in front of her shoulders, it indicated she was interested in marriage.

Both men and women wore adornments—earrings, bracelets, pendants, and necklaces. These were made from a variety of materials such as seeds, copper, stone, bone, wood, and fossils. Painting the body was another form of adornment. Clay deposits of iron oxides (red), aluminum oxides (yellow), and copper oxides (blue and green), including vegetable dyes, were used. The four sacred colors were red, yellow, blue, and dark (usually black or navy). Besides the paint, wealthier Osages were often tattooed. The men were tattooed on the chest and over the shoulder with representations of the sacred red-handled knife and their war honors. The ladies were tattooed on the chest, backs, and arms. These were all symbols of peace and life, since adornment for women forbad symbols of taking life.

With the coming of trade goods, both clothing and adornment changed. Yet, it must be said that even today the Osages dress more somberly than other Indians. This is not to say bright colors are not used, but flashiness is tempered by more sedate colors and designs. Typically reds and yellows are toned down with blacks, blues, and greens. Designs tend to stand out on stark backgrounds instead of a massive splash of colorful designs.

Around 1812, a noticeable change took place in the styles of the ladies of the Claremore bands.[23] The skirts were shorter than those of the upper Neosho bands. Bare midriffs became common among the women of the lower Neosho or Grand River. Hairstyles were also shortened for a time, but the White Hair band women wore their hair long. Little differences existed in the styles of the men. Men still wore hip-length leggins, moccasins with deer skin uppers and buffalo hide soles, and the usual breech clout. The leggins tended to be made of broadcloth, which was sometimes called strouding, and the breechcloth was made of the same material. In colder weather, the traditional robes of skins were giving way to striped woolen blankets. However, the Osage word for robe, *me,* was used to describe these trade blankets.

Marriage and Divorce

By 1850, a new version of the marriage ceremony began to appear. Since it has many aspects in common with the French celebration following marriage, we assume it came from the Osage–French mixed-bloods. The young ladies who were friends of the bride would run a footrace from the groom's lodge to a tree and back. The winner got extra gifts while the others took all of the bride's clothing except her very poorest.

Dressed in these poor garments she would be escorted to the home of the groom. Customarily, if they liked each other, the bride and groom would eat together and show that they enjoyed each other's company. However, if they were not pleased by the arrangement, they would sit for hours in a sullen pout.[24]

If a man wished to divorce a woman, he took his hunting gear along with his clothing and moved out of the lodge. However, if a woman wished to divorce a man, she threw his clothing and hunting gear out of the lodge. The lodge and all in it, except the husband's clothing and hunting gear, belonged to the wife. The children remained with the mother, and her oldest brother continued as their mentor. If the mother remarried, the new husband was called *In ta che* (father) by the children and stepsons were called *We she ka* (my son) while stepdaughters were called *We shon ka* (my daughter) by the stepfather.

The Osage Calendar

A year in the majority culture is equal to two Osage years. One Osage year was the Autumn or Winter Year which started in September/October and ended in February/March. The Osage Summer or Spring Year started in March/April and ended in August/September. Each year is composed of six moons. Osages did not count by days; they counted by nights.[25] For example, if they were away for a time, they would say three nights (three sleeps) instead of three days.

We will start with the Summer Year, which had six moons. March was usually called the Idle Days Moon, but some called it Just Doing That Moon. April was called the Planting Moon by most of the Old Osages, but a few called it the Prepare Ground for Planting Moon. May also had two names. It was mainly called the Flower Killer Moon, but it was also called When the Roses Bloom Moon. The roses were the wild rose of the prairies. June was called the Buffalo Bull Fattening Moon, but it was also known as the Earth Pawing Moon. July was the Buffalo Breeding Moon. The Yellow Flower Moon of August finished the Summer Year.

Autumn Years started in September with the Deer Hiding Moon. Deer Breeding Moon coincided with October in the Western calendar. J. Joseph Mathews reports that November was called the Coon Breeding Moon,[26] but the name When the Deer Break (shed) Their Horns (antlers) Moon was more widely used for November. Black Bears Give Birth was the name for December. A difference of opinion exists over the names for January and February. Many believe that January was the Solitary Moon month and that it was followed by the Long Days Moon of February, but some say these are reversed.

The idea of weeks was probably not known before the advent of the white man. Surely, the days of the week that have come down to us from the Osages show the hand of Western civilization. Sunday was called the Great Mystery Day or God's Day. Monday was called the First Day; Tuesday, the Second Day; Wednesday, the Third Day; and Thursday, the Fourth Day. Friday shows the Catholic influence since it was called Not Eat Meat Day. Saturday, being the Sabbath, was called Nothing is Done Day.

Food

The Osages did not have milk or butter; however, bone marrow and buffalo fat were good substitutes for butter. Fry bread was cooked in boiling fat from the buffalo or bear. Marrow and fat was kept in doeskin sacks. Buffalo short ribs were flattened and sewn together with bark thread so as to make a large sheet, which was thrown over a rack to dry. Long strips of muscle were dried and sometimes braided together before the final drying over fires. Once dried, meat was saturated in fat then stored in parflesches.[27] With proper care, the meat preserved in this way would keep for two or three years.[28]

Two types of sausages were made by the Osages. The small intestine of the buffalo was washed and turned inside out. This placed the fat to the inside. Meat cut in thin strips was then enclosed in the intestine with water added. This sausage was then broiled on glowing charcoal embers.[29]

Another type of sausage is commonly called pemmican. A deer skin bag would be filled with a mixture of pulverized dried buffalo meat, berries, nuts, marrow, and suet. This mixture would be tamped tightly into the bag so as to leave no air spaces. Stored in this way, the mixture would keep for several years. It could be eaten as either an uncooked or cooked meal.

Stanica, made of wild persimmons, was another food that would keep for some time. Since this wild fruit tends to be attached to large seeds, the Osages developed a means to separate the fruit from the seeds. Finger-sized switches were placed side by side with some slight space between them. By pressing the persimmons back and forth over this frame, the soft fruit would pass between the switches into a container below. The seeds would remain on the top of the frame.

Once about a quart of fruit was accumulated, the pulp was spread thinly on a wooden paddle. By holding the paddle above a fire, the pulp was dried into a fruit "leather." For storage, stanica strips were braided and placed in parfleches.

Topeka means the same in Osage as it does in Kaw. That is, it means "place where we dug potatoes." The Kaw and Osage potatoes were not the same as the Irish potato. These were legumes that grew wild along streams. Pomme de Terre is French for ground apple or potato, which was abundant on a river by that name in Missouri. There is a large and varied collection of Osage foods, but these examples are enough to indicate they were a well-nourished people.

Some Osage Views

Ah ke tah Tun ka (Big Soldier) made a statement early in the 1800s. He was commenting on why he did not adopt the white man's ways.

I see, and admire your way of living, your good warm houses, your extensive cornfields, your gardens, your cows, oxen, work horses, wagons and a thousand machines that you know the use of; I see that you are able to clothe yourself, even from weeds and grass. In short, you can do almost what you choose. You whites possess the power of almost every animal you use. You are surrounded by slaves. Everything about you is in chains, and you are slaves yourselves. I fear if I should change my pursuit for yours, I, too, should become a slave. Talk to my sons; perhaps they may be persuaded to adopt your fashions, or at least recommend them to their sons; but for myself, I was born free, was raised free, and wish to die free. . . . I am perfectly contented with my condition.[30]

Two points stand out in Big Soldiers' statement. First, he praises the material culture of the white man and then he deplores the spiritual culture. He seems to be saying, "You have traded your freedom for material possessions. My freedom is dearer to me than material possessions." Maybe Henry David Thoreau at Walden Pond and Big Soldier on the Osage Prairies had a message that modern Americans should take to heart.

If Euro-Americans got mixed signals from the Osages, the same may be said in reverse. Nowhere is this better illustrated than in the matter of drinking. In a letter from Fr. John J. Bax to Fr. Peter J. De Smet dated June 1, 1850, Fr. Bax relates that he had lectured Little Beaver's band about the evils of drink. Beaver's response is worth noting: "Father, what thou sayest is true. We believe thy words. We have seen men buried because they loved and drank fire water. One thing astonishes us. We are ignorant; we are not acquainted with books; we never heard the words of the Great Spirit; but the whites who know books, who have understanding, and who have heard the commandments of the Great Spirit,—why do they drink this firewater? Why do they bring it to us, when they know God sees them?"[31]

Beaver was probably sincere in asking these questions. However, it would fit the Osage sense of humor to pose such questions. Two other observers had occasion to note the Osage humor in serious matters.

Henry Leavitt Ellsworth had been appointed Commissioner in order to bring about a peace between the Osage and Pawnee. Washington Irving's party had fallen in with the Ellsworth party and so Irving was present at Ellsworth's speeches. In one speech, Ellsworth addressed a group of aged Osage men and women. During a long oration about the blessings of peace and admonishments to keep the peace, the old Osages listened attentively. They then assured Ellsworth, to his great satisfaction, that they would keep the peace. Of course, they were well aware that because of their age they had no choice except to keep the peace.[32]

Count Portalés gives us another account of Osage humor. Again, this was generated by Ellsworth on the same mission of peace on the Plains. Osages find pompous characters like Ellsworth a good target for their humor. Such characters never grasp the fact that they are the butt of the joke and this pleases the Osage funny bone. It is like counting coup without the prey being aware that he had been touched by the coup stick. In this incident, Ellsworth again made an oration on the evils of warfare and the blessings of peace. He struck a pose and emphatically stated that the Great White Father was going to put an end to the war between the Osage and Pawnee. After a few remarks, the Osages left. The interpreter, Pierre Beyette, informed Portalés that the Osages had said, "If the Great White Father was going to end the Osage war against the Pawnee they had better make the most of the time left and kill as many Pawnee as they could."[33]

Captives

Most captives taken by the Osages were either traded as slaves or adopted into an Osage family. Many captives who had been adopted held the honored office of *Sho ka* (messenger). Observers usually called these adopted messengers slaves because they ran errands for the Osages. This was clearly either a misunderstanding or an intentional misstatement. Adopted persons were preferred as *Sho ka* because it was thought they would be more impartial in disputes and arrangements than a blood Osage. *Sho kas* not only ran errands and carried messages, but they also arranged marriages, mediated disputes, and acted as an impartial spokesman. Of course, for these services a *Sho ka* was rewarded with gifts. Even today, at the *I'n lon schscka* dances, the crier is not an Osage by blood. Each of the twenty-four clans had a sub-clan that acted as *Sho ka* for its clan.

Often, captives were traded by the nation that captured them. It was not unusual for a captive to be traded among three or more nations. The Osages had acquired by trade three boys captured by the Comanche in Texas during the early 1840s. Possession of these two boys involved the Osages in the diplomatic affairs between the United States and the Republic of Texas.

Much of the background of this incident is given in a letter from T. Hartley Crawford of the War Department, Office of Indian Affairs, dated January 12, 1843. This letter was sent to Major William Armstrong, acting Superintendent of the Choctaw Agency west of Arkansas.

Sir

Information having been communicated to the State Department by the Chargé d'Affaires of Texas [Isaac Van Zandt] that his Government had been informed by a gentleman residing among the Osage indians west of the State of Missouri that a youth some twelve years of age who had been captured by indians in the county of Fayette Texas named—Lyons is now among the Osage indians and within the limits of the United States, I am requested by the Secretary of War to instruct you to inquire for the captive lad above mentioned and to obtain his release, and when released to place him in charge of the commandant at Fort Gibson or Fort Towson, to be kept until called for by an agent of the Texian Government.

You will therefore please to give the necessary instructions to the subagent of the Osages, with as little delay as practicable and urge his immediate and diligent attention to the release of young Lyons and to the further instructions contained herein.

Very respectfully etc.[34]

Subsequent to this letter, it was determined that the Osages held two other boys in addition to Lyons. From this seemingly simple clear-cut beginning, this whole affair became a complicated diplomatic exchange between the United States and the Republic of Texas.

The Republic of Texas agreed to allow three hundred dollars for each of the boys. Two hundred dollars was spent on the purchase and one hundred dollars for transportation and subsistence. As a result of this final incident of a series of Indian problems between the United States and the Republic of Texas, a council was held at Waco, Texas. The treaty made at this council dealt with the problem of Indians raiding in one country and seeking sanctuary in the other. The practice of redemption was established in this Osage case. Both the United States and the Republic of Texas heretofore had refused to pay for the release of captives. The belief was that such payment would encourage the Indians to take captives as a business. Possibly, taking children captive for the ransom was used at times, yet Osages wanted children to adopt. We found no Osage record of taking captives for ransom.

Continuing Warfare

While much of the vigor of Osage warfare was lost in the smallpox epidemic of 1830–1831, they still carried on their warfare on the Plains. The Kiowa gave the second spot on their calendar to note an Osage attack in the summer of 1833. This was known as the "summer that they cut off their heads" among the Kiowa. It is depicted as a knife below a severed head on the Kiowa calendar. Omission of the Sundance symbol on the calendar for the summers of 1833–1834 were due to the Osages taking the portable shrines. By the summer of 1835, the Osages had returned the two shrines and would accept no more than one pony for them because of the peace then prevailing between themselves and the Kiowa. This is reflected in the calendar during the summer of 1835 because the sundance lodge is displayed with its open door (see Fig. 31).[35]

This killing of the Kiowa was a massacre since the Kiowa did not make much of a defensive stand. To make matters worse, it was an all black paint or no quarter affair from the Osage point of view. It is probable that the Little Osage chief Chetopa (*Tse To pa* or Four Lodges) acquired his name from this event.

The Kiowa were camped at the mouth of Rainy Mountain Creek, which

Fig. 31. This portion of the Kiowa calendar is read from the right to the left. The first summer depicted on the calendar refers to the massacre by the Osages (from *17th Annual Report*, BAE, Smithsonian).

is a tributary of the Washita River. Most of the warriors were away fighting the Utes. The alarm was given when an Osage arrow was found in a buffalo. The Kiowa broke camp and divided into four parties which fled in different directions.

One of the parties under Island Man stopped on Otter Creek about twenty-five miles northwest of Fort Sill. Thinking the Osages had abandoned pursuit, the Kiowa paused to rest. At first light the following morning, the Osages struck the sleeping Kiowa. They fled to the rocks on the mountainside nearby. Two children were captured and five men were killed. A large number of women and children were also killed. It should be noted, however, that the bodies of the slain were not mutilated other than by decapitation.

Each head complete with its scalp was placed in a brass pot or bucket. This is the only known account where the heads were not placed on stakes. In Osage logic, it made sense to not only warn the Kiowa not to hunt in Osage territory but also not to trade with the Pawnee. These brass pots were acquired by the Pawnee north of the Osage territory and traded to the Kiowa. The Osages wished to keep the southwestern trade for themselves. The Republican Pawnee often competed for the southwestern trade.

Two facets of this attack must be mentioned. The brass kettles and the fact that the Osages were afoot require some additional comment. Indians such as the Osages who had direct trade contacts with Euro-American goods had learned not to use brass and copper cookware. Such cookware often generated copper poison and caused death over a period of time. Cast-iron cookware was safer, but it was too heavy to carry as a secondary trade item. Thus, cookware made of sheet brass and copper was traded to the Indians who did not have direct trade contact with Euro-Americans.

Because the Osages were afoot, we have a clear indication that this was not a stray Osage hunting party that chanced upon the Kiowa. Clearly, this was an Osage war party that was seeking the Kiowa. In all probability, they were specifically after the Kiowa of Island Man's band. Evidently, this group had hunted in Osage territory. The Osages had a choice of four groups and chose this particular group for some reason. Tracks would identify those who violated Osage territory.[36]

As an outgrowth of this incident, the Dragoon Expedition of 1833–1834 was organized. This was a visit by the First Dragoons in 1834, and it was the first official relationship the Kiowa, Comanche, Wichita, and other Indians had with the United States. Some returned to Fort Gibson with the dragoons. There, a meeting of eastern and western Indians took place. As a result, the following year, 1835, a peace meeting was held at Camp Holmes (about five miles northeast of Purcell, Oklahoma). Finally, in the Treaty of 1837, the Osages, Kiowa, and others agreed to keep the peace.[37]

9

The Search for Comprehension

BEGINNINGS OF FORMAL EDUCATION

Introduction

The death of Claremore II (Town Maker) brought out the conflict between the desire to learn new things and the desire to retain the old culture. Claremore II was always friendly to the Protestant missionaries at Union, but he refused to send his own children to the mission school. This friendly noncooperation was never understood by the Protestant missionaries. They had a fixed idea as to how the education of Osage children should be conducted and made no effort to fit formal education into the Osage culture. All educational adjustments were made by the Osages and none by the missionaries.

Claremore's death shows that people of both cultures were searching for comprehension. It is one of humankind's curses that people cannot submerge their own ethnocentrism and accept that of another culture. The Osages considered their culture to be better than that of the Euro-Americans. Likewise, Euro-Americans considered their culture to be superior to the Osage culture. Under these conditions, neither the Osages nor the Protestant missionaries reached a comprehension of the others' viewpoints.

After eleven or twelve years of effort, the Protestant Missions were closed. Without a doubt, the missionaries felt they had failed. Certainly, they did not bring the Osages to the unrealistic heights of the missionary dreams. Yet, they accomplished a very difficult feat. They exposed the Osages to a part of the Euro-American culture that had never before been seen by the Osages. It is a shame that the missionaries were so self righteous and placed such strong stress on buildings and fields and not on humanity.

On September 27, 1819, a delegation of Claremore's bands went to Fort Smith and delivered the following message: "All of you fathers,—I shake hands with you, and the Great Spirit is witness that it is with a good heart. In shaking hands with you, I embrace all my white brethren."

Having, after this introduction, expressed their thanks to their great father in Washington for sending his white children to instruct them, and signified their desires that their young men might be initiated in the mechanic arts, their young women in domestic economy, and that all the young people might be taught to read and write, they concluded by saying: "I shall consider the house which our great father will build for the education of our children our home, as we do this place. I wish our great father would send us the teachers as soon as he can, with their necessary equipments. I shook hands with our great father at Washington and still hold it fast. We must all have one tongue."[1]

The Missouri bands could not let the Arkansas bands get the best of them, so they too asked for schools. They sent Sans Nerf (Without Sinew)[2] with his chief counselor and highest warrior to Washington to plead their case.[3] Because it suited the American policy of the moment, the delegation was well received, and they attained an immediate response to their request.

The Civilization Act of 1820 had just been enacted. No better timing could have been planned for the delegation. Their appeal, coming after a two hundred mile trip, touched the American heart. The United Foreign Missionary Society responded. While over one hundred persons volunteered to be missionaries to the Osage, only forty were selected. Although they left Pittsburgh on March 5, 1821, the first group did not arrive on the Neosho-Grand until November of 1821. Travel was difficult, but most of the delay was spent accumulating funds as they traveled. En route, people gave them food, money, and supplies to help with their expenses.[4] This event was one of those wonderful times when the American heart was touched without limit.

Two of the seven Protestant Osage Missions were founded by the United Foreign Missionary Society: Union and Harmony. Eventually, the three Hopefield Missions, Neosho Mission, and Boudinot Mission grew out of Union and Harmony.[5] However, by this time (1826) the United Foreign Missionary Society had merged with the American Board of Commissioners for Foreign Missions.

The Mission Schools

Christianity was the first consideration of the missionaries. Education was secondary to their goal of making all Osages Christian. It is ironic that the education of the Osages was about the only constructive, albeit small, achievement of the missions. They utterly failed to convert the Osages. Although they all but missed achievement in education, at least they did have a few modest successes.

Officially, the first pupils started school on August 27, 1821.[6] Most of these students were Osage–French mixed-bloods. Whether the children were mixed or full-blood, the most difficult problem was to keep them in school. Enrollment remained small for this reason. Children would enroll, stay a month or two, then leave, only to be replaced by a new wave of pupils.

Warfare between the Osage and Cherokee complicated the educational problems at Union. The Osages did not trust the missionaries to protect their children and were constantly taking them out of school in the face of Cherokee attacks. Throughout the history of the missions on the lower Neosho-Grand no solution was ever found for this problem.

The early years were especially happy years at Harmony Mission. Possibly this was because of the absence of the Cherokee threat. Yet, the enthusiasm and zeal of the missionaries were probably the more important reasons for the period of happiness. No one could ever accuse these missionaries of not trying to help the Osages. Their problem was their misdirected efforts and failure to see the world through Osage eyes. So, it was with happiness that Harmony opened its school in January of 1822.

A fragment of the Harmony school record of 1824–1825 has come down to us (see Fig. 32).[7] Three pupils listed on the record are given as full-blood Osage, but their names indicate they were mixed-bloods. One cannot help noticing the presence of other Indian children who were not Osage. It should be noted that, in part, these children were educated at the expense of the Osages. In later days, the total cost of educating children in Osage schools was paid by the Osages regardless of the child's tribal affiliation.

Another aspect of these mission schools was the teaching of agriculture. Right or wrong, the missionaries were convinced that the only hope for survival of the Osages, and their Christian conversion, was by following the plow and tilling the soil. Aside from producing the food needed to sustain the missions, the agricultural lessons tended to make the students more willing to listen to the sermonizing. Yet, although there were a few mixed-bloods enrolled in the agriculture classes, there were no full-bloods. The missionaries could not know that the Osages would never be farmers. Their affinity for animals led them into ranching instead of farming.

All three of the Hopefield Missions were devoted to teaching agriculture and the other useful arts. Two of these Hopefield Missions were in Oklahoma and the last one was in Kansas. No two of the Hopefield Missions existed at the same time. Boudinot Mission was almost entirely a religious mission and never attempted to be an educational mission. Neosho Mission was the first educational institution in Kansas. While it was an educational Mission, it never reached the achievements of the Hopefield Missions.

Location of Missions

Union was the oldest of the Protestant Missions. It was located in Mayes County, Oklahoma, five miles northeast of Mazie, Oklahoma. Hopefield

HARMONY SCHOOL 1824–1825			
Name	Admitted	Age	Descent
Catherine Strange	14 Jan 1822	3	Eng–Osage
Susan Larivive	12 Mar 1822	6	Sioux–Fr–Osage
Rebecca Williams	12 Mar 1822	9	Pawnee–Fr–Osage
Mary Ludlow	12 Mar 1822	4	Pawnee–Fr–Osage
Louisa Anna Bean	12 Mar 1822	7	Pawnee–Fr–Osage
Maria Seward	22 Apr 1822	6	Osage
Mary Williams	10 Oct 1823	8	Osage–Eng
John B. Mitchell	11 Jul 1823	10	Osage–Fr
James Chouteau	10 Oct 1823	10	Osage–Fr
Julia Michael	11 Jul 1823	9	Osage–Fr
Lewis Michael	23 Feb 1824	6	Osage–Fr
Gabriel Marlow	6 Nov 1823	16	Fr–Pawnee
Augustus Chouteau	28 Jan 1824	9	Fr–Osage
Wm. C. Brownlee	12 Jun 1824	18	Delaware
Wm. Rogers	26 Jul 1824	17	Pawnee
John B. Packett	23 Aug 1824	17	Mother Saik [Sac]
John McDowell	2 Sep 1824	9	Osage
Mary E. Sibley	24 Oct 1824	13	Osage
Jane Renick	10 Aug 1824	7	Osage–Fr

Fig. 32. Several well-known mixed-blood families are represented in this list.

number one was approximately four miles north of Union on the left bank of the Neosho–Grand. Hopefield number two was about one-half of a mile southwest of Pensecola, Oklahoma. Hopefield number three was in Labette County, Kansas. It was probably in the vicinity of Oswego, Kansas (see Fig. 33).[8]

Harmony Mission was located on the bank of the Marais des Cygnes about five miles above the junction of the Marais des Cygnes with the Little Osage–Marmaton. From this junction downstream, the combined streams are called the Osage River. Neosho Mission was on the right bank of the Neosho opposite of Shaw, Kansas. Boudinot Mission was in Neosho County, Kansas, on the south side of Four Mile Creek, a short distance from its mouth.[9]

Failure of the Missions

The Ministers

It is difficult to find all the factors which caused the failure of the first Osage missions. However, the ministers were of the wrong character to work among the Osages and, therefore, became an important factor in failure. Mathews relates a story that points out two characteristics of the ministers, that is, their unwillingness to take advice and their inability to admit merit in an opinion that differed from theirs.

Bill Williams had possibly been the first to act as a Protestant missionary

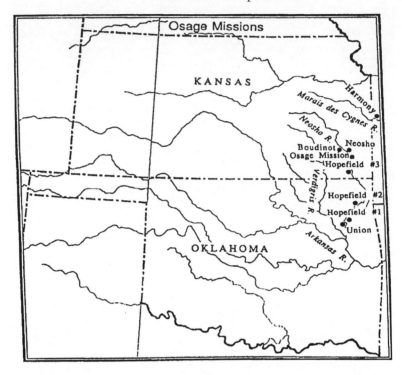

Fig. 33. Notice how these missions were clustered along the Neosho-Grand River.

to the Osages. He had married into the tribe, spoke the language, and respected Osage beliefs. He tried to help the Protestant missionaries as an interpreter and advisor. One Sunday he told the minister that the text selected for the sermon, which was the story of Jonah and the whale, was not suitable for the Osages. He explained that it would undermine the minister's credibility. However, the minister insisted on going ahead with the sermon as planned.

The results were as Williams had predicted. One of the headmen arose and said, " 'We know the Heavy Eyebrows will lie, but this is the biggest lie we ever heard;' and with this he drew his robe about him and walked swiftly away. The others stayed with their eyes closed and made no move, but they stayed only from courtesy."[10]

Reverend Benton Pixley

The case of Reverend Benton Pixley not only exposes the Puritan character of the missionaries, but it also bares some problems they faced. No one could doubt Reverend Pixley's devotion and good intentions toward the

Osages. His primary problems arose out of his character and his nearness to success.

Being a product of New England in his day and time, it was natural for Reverend Pixley to draw a distinct line between right and wrong as he saw it. Accustomed to attacking all wrongs without any reservations, which was laudable conduct in New England, Pixley attempted to apply the same conduct on the Osage frontier. Apparently, he never grasped the realities of life on the frontier, for he acted exactly as he would have acted if he had still been in New England.

That Pixley would soon find himself in "hot water" with the Osages, the fur traders, and the Osage Agent was predictable. He had hardly opened Neosho Mission before the "pot began to boil." Horse stealing, polygamy, and worship of *Wa kon ta* might have been time-honored practices among the Osages, but to Pixley they were contemptible evils.

His blunt, tactless assaults on these venerable Osage institutions not only appalled the Osages but also made them downright angry. An angry Osage is not desirable even today. In the 1820s and 1830s, it would have been a very dangerous situation. Reverend Pixley was fortunate in being able to retire to Missouri with his body and head intact. But if he rubbed the Osage fur the wrong way, he flayed the fur traders.

Accusing the fur traders of discouraging the Osages from being farmers was only the opening shot in a barrage of attacks. Pixley was right, of course. Traders did not want the Osages to abandon the hunt, for this was the source of the hides, tallow, and fur of their trade. If Pixley became successful in converting the Osages into agriculturists, the fur traders' livelihood would fade away. However, being right only made the sting of Pixley's attack smart more than if it had been false.

There were only five groups of people on the Osage frontier between 1820 and 1840: (1) Indians; (2) government employees, such as Agents, millers, and blacksmiths; (3) traders; (4) intruder settlers; and (5) missionaries. Pixley managed to antagonize all these groups, except the missionaries. However, we must mention that some Jesuit letters contain more than a few harsh words about him. Even his fellow missionaries had several less-than-kind remarks about him in their letters.

A deluge of letters to the government and to the Board of Commissioners followed each of Reverend Pixley's assaults. Neosho Mission was closed, and Pixley retired to Missouri to await reassignment. Without a doubt the problems with Reverend Pixley affected the ultimate decision by the Board of Commissioners to close all the Osage Missions in 1837. The Osage petition for their removal also had a bearing. It is a pity that so many good intentions were lost in a sea of problems and personality conflicts.

An Osage petition sets forth their feelings toward the missionaries. This petition is in the classical Osage style of address. *In ta che* (father) is still used today in formal Osage speeches. This letter was drafted at White Hair's Town, August 25, 1828.

Father, From the moment the missionaries came among us we gave them the hand of friendship.

Father, We gave them our land, we gave them our children.

Father, We moved our people toward the setting sun and left the missionaries two days march toward the rising sun.

Father, One of them followed us, and has been living on our land though we gave them enough land for all of them to live on.

Father, We do not wish him to live here.

Father, He has quarrelled with our men and women and we hear he has also quarrelled with the white men who our Great Father has sent here to do us good and to live among us.

Father, We have enough of the white people among us without him, even if he was good, but he is a bad man, is doing no good here, but a evil, is living on our land, quarrels with our men and women, forgets his black coat and fights them, finds faults with all, disturbs our peace, and many other things which you know and we have not time now to tell you.

Father, We hope you will make him leave our country.

Father, The missionaries at Harmony are near enough, we do not wish them to come to our land to live.

Father, We hope you may live long and be happy, and we sign ourselves to this paper.

(Signed)

Pa hu ska, White Hair

Chin ga wa sa, Fine Bird [*Shin ka Wa sa,* Pretty Bird]

First Counsellor *Ha ra tia,* War Eagle

[*Hu lah Ta ke*]

First war leader *Wa no pa she,* Fearless

Great warrior

[All above are signed by mark]

Signed in presence of

P. L. Chouteau, sub-agent

N. Pryor, sub-agent

B. Morgan, interpreter[11]

Other Factors of Failure

The closing of Fort Osage and the federal trading post in 1822 had a detrimental effect in the Osage fur trade. Despite its faults, the government post had acted as a brake on the excesses of the fur traders. With the closing of Fort Osage, anything that seemed a threat to the fur trade was crushed. Thus, the fur trade alone was enough to defeat the Protestant missionaries.

Yet, there were other factors working against the missionaries and their efforts to Christianize the Osages. The Treaty of 1825 removed the Osages from both Union and Harmony. That is, the Osages were relocated far north of Union and forty or fifty miles west of Harmony. This was a great distance in the 1820s, and it made ready contact between the Osage and the missionary schools difficult.

The federal policy of massing the Osages into a series of compact villages clustered near the Agency was not conducive to agricultural pursuits. Agriculture must of necessity spread out in order to have land to cultivate. Without a doubt, the agricultural-minded missionaries and the administrative-minded agents had good intentions. Yet, the two policies conflicted and the missionaries lost.

Ultimately, it was the Osages who paid the price of compaction into village clusters. We will deal with this problem in a later chapter. However, we would like to point out that the terrible epidemics experienced by the Osages grew out of this compaction practice. Also, the compaction placed a heavy burden on the available wild food plants. Combined with the slavery controversy in Kansas and the subsequent Civil War, this caused famine among the Osages.

By the end of 1837, the last Protestant Osage Mission was closed. For ten years, the people had no mission or school. Apparently, the Osages had mixed feelings about the missionaries and the schools. It was a gigantic step from the Osage culture to the Euro-American culture. While they knew that the change must be made, the habit of past generations kept calling them to the freedom of the clean Plains and the hunt. Like a confirmed smoker, they could put aside their habit for a time, but the memories of past pleasures lured them back to their old addiction.

Being torn by an awareness of the need for change only made the old free life of the past dearer in the Osage heart. Thus, their actions were confusing to the missionaries, who had never experienced such a conflict. How can anyone who has never stood in two worlds grasp the terrible dilemma goring them at every turn? William Shakespeare touches on a similar problem in *Hamlet*.

To be, or not to be—that is the question:
Whether 'tis nobler in the mind to suffer
The slings and arrows of outrageous fortune
Or to take arms against a sea of troubles,
And by opposing end them. To die—to sleep—
No more; and by a sleep to say we end
The heartache, and the thousand natural shocks
That flesh is heir to. 'Tis a consummation
Devoutly to be wish'd. To die—to sleep.
To sleep—perchance to dream: ay, there's the rub!
For in that sleep of death what dreams may come
When we have shuffled off this mortal coil,
Must give us pause. There's the respect
That makes calamity of so long life.[12]

Hamlet solved his dilemma by revenge; the Osages sought peace of mind on the Plains by drinking deeply the last draught of the past. Most people never miss what they have until it is gone. The Osages knew their way of life was passing, and they longed for it before it passed. It is not that the ways of the Osages were incomprehensible; it was that the Euro-Americans of the time were not capable of comprehending.

A new beginning was coming to the Osages. It was clear the Euro-Americans had at least some grasp of the Osage mind. Possibly, the ability to curb the self enabled the Jesuits to reach out and touch the Osage soul. Certainly, the surface resistance to change had been abraded away by the Protestant missionaries. In any event, the Osages had started the long, hard journey into the Euro-American world.

THE BLACK ROBES

Introduction

In a petition to President Tyler dated June 14, 1843, the Osages pointed out the Osage education fund created from the sale of lands under the Treaty of 1825.[13] Since it was their money, to be spent on education, the Osages specifically asked for Catholic missionaries. They also pointed out that their subagent, R. A. Calloway, was opposed to missionaries. Being well aware of the "spoils system" as practiced by Calloway, the Osages could only hope he would be removed. The opposition of their agent and the fur traders, including the failure of the Protestant Missions, tended to push the Osages to the Jesuits. Thus, the casual relationship between the Osages and the Catholic Church became more intense.

Despite the policies set in Washington for the "civilization" of the Indian, there were more effective forces working against assimilation into Western civilization. So long as the Osages were a prime source of furs and hides, the fur traders encouraged them to live by the hunt. Typical of this attitude is the story of the Osage who was asked why he did not become a farmer. His reply was, "I can buy all the grain I need for a year with one buffalo hide." Traders well knew that such arguments would find a wide acceptance among the Osages.

Too often agents were selected because of loyalty to the party in power. And, aside from the party controlling the government, they were selected to reflect the Euro-American views instead of the Indian view. Treaty provisions usually involved sizable sums of money for that day and time. These funds were large enough to be a major attraction to those with greedy ambitions. Very few agents were willing to kill "the goose that laid such golden eggs."

It was unfortunate that the intruders who settled on Osage lands were such poor examples of the Euro-American ideal. A casual look at their type of agriculture, their subculture, and their absolute poverty would be enough to discourage any emulation. Very few Osages ever became farmers. Possibly, these intruders created such an aversion to agriculture among the Osages that it is still being handed down to the present generations. Most Osages found the step to ranching more to their liking. It is probable that they instinctively took this important step instead of leaping directly into agriculture. We are assuming herding is a necessary prelude to agriculture. However, the Osages were naturally drawn to ranching because of their love of animals. They were shrewd observers of animal habits and, thus, were well qualified to be cattlemen.

Finally, the eastern nations were rapidly surrounding the Osages. The effects of the advancing American frontier affected more than the Indians on the frontier line. Like ripples spreading out from a stone thrown in water, the impact touched nation after nation until those on the remote shore of the Pacific felt the shock. We would estimate that somewhat more than ninety percent of the Eastern Indians who were removed west of the Mississippi were eventually settled on what had been Osage territory.

Being centrally located as they were, the Osages were accustomed to a diversity of Indian cultures. However, with so many varied cultures being added to the natural cultures, they were hard put to cope with them effectively. At the same time, the compaction into increasingly smaller areas also complicated the problem. Surely, the multitude of Indian experiences reflecting Euro-American failures in "civilization" experiments were no inducement for the Osages to become another failure.

These factors—the traders, the agents, the intruders, and the Indian refugees from "civilization"—were all forces working against Osage acceptance of Euro-American culture. When one adds the reluctance to give up their own culture—which had features superior to the Euro-American culture—one must wonder how the Osages changed as quickly as they did. These were the odds against the Jesuits as they undertook the task of bringing the people into the folds of Christianity and introducing them to the arts, sciences, and crafts of Western civilization.

Establishing Osage Mission

The Osages had been familiar with the Jesuits, whom they called Black Robes, almost from their first contact with Euro-Americans. While many marriages between the French traders and Osage women were performed under Osage law, some were performed by the Jesuits as early as 1750. It was natural for them to want the familiar Jesuits as their teachers.

They had invited Bishop Louis W. V. Du Bourg to visit their villages in 1820. Bishop Du Bourg made an attempt to secure Jesuits in 1821, but he was not successful until March of 1823.[14] Although Fr. Charles De La Croix started working among the Osages in 1820, his health broke in 1822. A group of Jesuits came from Whitemarsh, Maryland, under Fr. Charles Van Quickenborne, who led the group of Jesuits from Maryland to Missouri. He and Fr. Peter J. Timmermans guided seven novices in Missouri. These were: (1) Judocus Van Assche; (2) Peter John De Smet; (3) Peter John Verhaegen; (4) John Babtiste Smedts; (5) Francis De Maillet; (6) Felix Livinus Verreydt; and (7) John Anthony Elet. Also, there were three lay brothers: Peter De Meyer, Henry Reiselman, and Charles Strahan.[15] It is interesting to note that of these twelve Jesuits three served among the Osages.

Yet, from this small nucleus a total of eighty-four Jesuits eventually worked among the Osages. Fr. De Smet (called "the little flower of the prairie") is often mentioned in general histories of the United States, and he is always mentioned in the history of the American West. Thus, he is probably the best known of the Jesuits that worked with the Osages. The reason he is mentioned in the histories is probably because he worked among the nations of the Upper Missouri. Therefore, he stood in the path of the flow of migration to Oregon and California. By contrast, the Jesuits who worked among the Osages were in the shadow of the Osage blockade and their work went unnoticed by the general histories.

At first, it was thought that the Indian boys would come to Florissant, Missouri, to attend St. Regis Seminary.[16] Iron Hawk, the fourth White Hair chief, and Not Afraid of the Pawnee, father to Governor Joe, did attend St. Regis. The first Red Corn, sometimes called Bill Nix or Bill Mathis, also attended St. Regis. However, there were few Indians at the school, and even fewer Osages. St. Regis and the girl's school both operated without government funds and the expense per pupil was overwhelming.[17]

Fifty-four sections of land had been set aside for Osage education and training under the Treaty of 1825. Selling these lands was a condition required by the American government in return for the Treaty of 1839. It was the proceeds from the sale of these lands that supported the Protestant Missions. Under the agreement between the Osages and the United States, the funds derived from the sale of these lands were to be administered at the discretion of the President.

Between 1839 and 1847, the interest from these Education Funds was merely dissipated. That is, it was spent on farm equipment that the Osages could not use and programs that yielded no benefits to them. All benefits were in favor of the Americans. It seems this education fund of the Osages was used to pay political debts.

By the spring of 1843, the Osages were petitioning the Commissioner of Indian Affairs for Jesuit Missionaries. The Commissioner wanted no part of either the Osages or the Jesuits. Evidently, the commissioner was tired of both the Osages and the Jesuits. He informed the Osage agent to discourage a visit by the Osages but to construct a suitable schoolhouse. In addition, he stated his intention to hire a schoolmaster who was not the minister of any faith.[18]

Major Thomas H. Harvey, the new Superintendent, was among the Osages in May of 1844. The Osages used this event to push their desire for the Black Robes. They argued that the government was not living up to the promises made to them. Furthermore, they pointed out the benefits the Potawatomi were receiving. Hence, Major Harvey recommended granting the Osage request. An abrupt shift in policy was made, and the Jesuits were invited to establish a mission among the Osages.[19]

On August 8, 1845, the contract for the erection of two school buildings was granted. Fifty acres of plowing was also included. By January of 1846, this work was finished. However, the school did not officially open until May 10, 1847.[20]

The United States was reluctant to pay Osage education monies to the Jesuits. After examining the monies offered the Jesuits for an Osage school, the Jesuits refused to sign the contract. Shocked by the rejection, the Commissioner "found" more money and the Jesuits accepted the mission. At least fifty-five dollars per pupil was available, but only fifty dollars per pupil was paid to the Jesuits. Financial problems, government "red tape," and travel difficulties delayed the arrival of the missionaries until April 28, 1847.[21]

Believing that it would be a waste of funds and effort to educate an

Osage boy who could only marry an uneducated Osage girl, the Jesuits also instigated a girls' school. The Sisters of Loretto from Nerinckx (present-day Nerinx), Kentucky, established the girls' school. Mother Concordia and her assistants, Sister Mary Petronilla, Sister Bridget, and Sister Vincentia arrived at the mission on October 10, 1847.[22] Thus, Osage Mission and the Osage Indian School were established.[23]

The establishment of Osage Mission marks the end of an era in Osage history. With the coming of the Americans came a decline in Osage power and culture. Within forty years, the heart of America passed from Osage control. Simultaneously, many forces were altering Osage culture until by 1847 it bore little resemblance to what it had been in 1800.

Fortune placed Fr. Schonmakers and his Jesuits among the Osages at a critical point in their history. Without the Mission, it is doubtful if the Osages would have survived the span of time between 1850 and 1870. Decimated and weakened by devastating epidemics, swept up into the fratricidal slavery controversy, and torn by the loss of their way of life, only the Jesuits stood between the Osages and the Four Horsemen.[24]

PART THREE

Facing the Four Horsemen, 1850–1865

Pestilence Strikes the People

INTRODUCTION

Background

And behold a pale horse: and he that sat upon him, his name was death.
And hell followed him. And power was given to him over the four
parts of the earth, to kill with sword, with famine and with death and
with the beasts of the earth.

In the ordeal of the 1850s and 1860s the Osages were fortunate to have
three factors working for them. These were Andrew J. Dorn, their agent;
the Jesuits; and the school at Osage Mission. These three factors were the
counterbalance that saved the Osages from extinction in this period.

To the Old Osages, there were seven bends in the River of Life. Each of
these bends represented a crisis in one's own lifetime. In a larger sense, the
River of Life was also applied to the people as a whole. The myths tell us
of the first crisis of the Osages—when they met a strange warlike nation.
After a long series of wars with these people, the Osages emerged victorious.
Surely, the 1850s and 1860s were another bend in the River of Life for the
Osage people. However, we do not know which bend it represents.

Reservation policies of the United States government had a serious effect on the Osages. Bunching the people together in many small villages
clustered near the agency was a convenience to the government. It was,
however, an open invitation to epidemics. Aside from the ease of spreading
a disease, the compacting of villages concentrated human wastes into a
small area and overworked the supply of local wild food plants. Thus, not

The epigraph is from "The Apocalypse of St. John The Apostle" 6:1–8, Douay version.
The pale horse was a pale sickly green and while it had death as its rider, the horse
represented plagues or pestilence.

only was there an increase in population density, but there was also a growing sanitation and nutrition problem.

No other period in Osage history shows a greater fluctuation in population. Epidemic after epidemic struck the people. Each epidemic was followed by a surge in the birthrate. While the next epidemic took most of these newborns, a few survived to carry the Osage blood to the next generation. The people met pestilence, the pale horse of the Apocalypse, and survived.

The Neosho Agency

In 1849, Indian Affairs was transferred from the War Department to the newly created Department of the Interior. A reorganization of the old agencies took place in 1851. Hence, Neosho Agency was created by combining the former Neosho and Osage subagencies. Major Andrew J. Dorn began his duties as the Neosho agent in 1849 and served until 1861.[1]

Major Dorn was born in New York state, but he was residing in Missouri when he was appointed to the Neosho Agency. He was highly esteemed by the Osages, the missionaries, the traders, and the settlers. Everyone had such a high regard for him that the original combined Neosho and Labette Counties in Kansas was given Dorn as its name. However, after the Civil War, when the original county was broken up into two counties, neither Labette nor Neosho County would retain the Dorn County name. Possibly this was because Andrew J. Dorn served in the Confederate Indian Department. Rumors state that he was responsible for forming the Confederate Indian brigade and the invasions into Southeast Kansas.

Clearly, Major Dorn was the first Indian agent who was sympathetic to the Osage viewpoints. The BIA files are full of his letters on their behalf. In his decade or more of service to the Osages, there is not one letter against him from the Osages. He must be the only Osage agent to receive this unusual honor.

With the terrible decade ahead for the people, having such an agent as Dorn was crucial. He did his very best to see that they had the medical care that they desperately needed. Perhaps his greatest service was to fight for cash payment of the annuities so that all the goods did not go to the Osage leaders. In fact, he also had to fight to have the annuities paid in some semblance of an orderly schedule. Erratic payment, if they were made at all, characterized earlier payments. This threw the people into a terrible position and inflicted unusual hardships upon them.

Osage Mission

The Jesuits and Sisters of Osage Mission, probably more than any other outside factor, were responsible for the survival of the Osage people. It is no small wonder that eighty percent of the Osages are still Catholic today. These dedicated souls accomplished more than they lived to realize. Their influence on the souls and aspirations of the Osage people is still present today.

When the Osages established the oldest Catholic parish in Oklahoma, they had a little white church on Bird Creek. After the little white church was taken in a flood, they built a fine brick church, which recently witnessed the Centennial of the Parish. By special dispensation, the Osages were allowed to depict the coming of Fr. John Schonmakers in the stained glass windows of this church. These windows remind all Osages of the important role Osage Mission played in the lives of the people.

While Fr. Schonmakers had a special place in Osage hearts, it was Fr. John Bax who reached to the core of their being. They called him "Father Who is All Heart." Many Osages said he spoke Osage better than themselves. Fr. De Smet credited Fr. Bax with baptizing 2,000 Indian adults and children during his five years at Osage Mission.[2] A casual look at the Osage Mission Register more than verifies this assessment by Fr. De Smet.[3]

No one labored harder or nursed the stricken more tenderly in the epidemic of 1852 than Fr. Bax. Weakened by his efforts to aid the people, he too succumbed to the disease. His interment record states:

> On the 5th of August 1852 died at Fort Scott 1 1/2 A.M. Rev. J. J. Bax, S.J. on the 6th of the same month he was burried in the graveyard of St. Francis Mission on the Neosho. He was borne the 15 of Jan. 1817, received in the Society on the 19th of November 1840.
>
> J. B. Miege, S.J.[4]

That Bishop Miege officiated at Fr. Bax's interment is a significant fact. His see was at St. Mary's Mission of the Potawatomi, and it included all of Indian Territory.

Fr. Bax had dedicated his life to the Osages. As he lay dying, his last words to his assistant, Fr. Paul Ponziglione were, "Father, take care of my children."[5] He left "his children" in good hands. To most older Osages of our acquaintance, Fr. Ponziglione was a living saint.

Fr. Ponziglione left Osage Mission in 1889. He was at Marquette College for seven months, and then he was sent to St. Stephen's Mission among the Arapahoe in Wyoming. After nearly two years at St. Stephen's, he was sent to St. Ignatius College in Chicago. Fr. Ponziglione died in Chicago on March 28, 1900.[6]

The school at Osage Mission taught the usual academic subjects. In the manual labor division, the boys were taught agriculture and the girls were taught needlework. Like the Protestant missionaries before them, the Jesuits had to search hard for signs of progress. Yet, in time, they witnessed many of their former students well settled in life, a tribute to their success.

In a letter to A. J. Dorn, Fr. Schonmakers states his philosophy toward teaching agriculture to the Osages.[7]

28 August 1856

I do not think that to establish farms in the midst of our Osages could have a benefical effect upon their character, certainly not if they be carried out on a liberal scale; our Indians will be mere spectators, admire the industry and avarice of the farmers, which will not excite their partiality for agricultural pursuits; they will only study on the abuse made of their money, and devise means to rid themselves of their pretended benefactors, which will ultimately lead [them] to burn the improvements.

As an alternative to this demonstration farm idea, Fr. Schonmakers established small plots and paid the boys for the work they performed.

The effectiveness of this method was evident in the statistics. There were five Osage farms on the Neosho in 1847 when the Jesuits established Osage Mission. In 1855, this number had increased to twenty-five. While a twenty-farm increase in eight years may seem small, it does indicate a significant advancement.[8]

One must bear in mind two facts. First, it had taken over two hundred years to establish the first five farms. Second, it took a few years for the students to reach adulthood and to establish their own farms. However, even at this time, the Osage farmers were showing a greater preference for animal husbandry than for tillage of the soil.

As a result of frequent raids by Euro-Americans during the War in Kansas and the ensuing Civil War, several bands of Osages had moved to the Verdigris Valley. A flood of intruders quickly occupied the old village sites. The Jesuits could see the future of the Osages by observing this trend. The Treaty of 1865, or Canville Treaty, placed the Osage villages forty or fifty miles farther from Osage Mission. The Osage educational annuities were so diluted that by the time they reached the Jesuits it was only half enough. At least half the cost of Osage education was provided by the Jesuit order. Because of the trend toward more distant removal and lack of funds, the Jesuits were forced to abandon their position among the Osages.

The growing realization that the shrinking Osage population would no longer justify a mission possibly had a bearing on the abandonment. Then again, the Osages probably had reached a point where they had to make the step from the past to the future without guidance from the Jesuits. Fr. Schonmakers's statement in a letter to A. J. Dorn dated 28 August 1856 was more than a little prophetic: "Our Osages are well aware that their former mode of living is fast closing upon them; ten years ago they numbered 5,000 souls, at present they hardly exceed 3,500."[9]

Fr. Schonmakers's last visit among the Osages shows the high esteem they had for him. He visited the Osage villages on the present reservation during the last of July and the first half of August in 1875. In the night of August 11 he became very ill, and, although he was attended by the Agency doctor, his condition was critical.

Being uneasy about him, the Osages crowded around his bed. When the doctor asked them to leave, they threatened to scalp him if Fr. Schonmakers died. Finally, a compromise was reached. Two Osages at a time watched the doctor and Fr. Schonmakers until he had recovered enough to make the return trip to Osage Mission. Fr. Schonmakers died over a decade later at Osage Mission, on Saturday about four o'clock in the afternoon of July 28, 1883. Over 3,500 people attended his funeral.[10]

Fr. Ponziglione's last visit to the Osages was described as follows: "Father Paul M. Ponziglione passed thru Elgin [Kansas] on Tuesday on his way from Chicago, where he has been stationed for two years, to Pawhuska, the capital city of the Osages, which he has for years taken so lively an interest in. The good old gentleman carries his seventy-eight years lightly and looks no older than twenty-five years ago when we used to see him in his little covered wagon on his regular trips from Osage Mission to visit the tribes on their reservation south of us."[11]

THE EPIDEMICS

Introduction

If it be the present policy of the administration to confine the Osages to a small tract of country, it ought to be carried out with generous liberality. Our Indians know well that they are born free by nature, and will not easily submit to coercive systems."[12]

As Fr. Schonmakers feared in the quote above, the Osages were confined to increasingly smaller areas. Even in 1856 when he wrote these words, the problems of compaction were affecting the Osages.

As an administrative convenience, the Osages were bunched together in a number of small villages. Centuries of experience had taught the Osages to spread out for the sake of sanitation and that large villages should only be allowed for defense. Osage myths stressed the idea of sanitation, which was strictly followed until Western influence undermined the old customs.

Through custom, Osage villages were kept clean of debris and waste. This was accomplished by carrying such matter some distance from the village. In time, a mound of waste material, referred to as the outskirts of the village, grew around the village. All purification ceremonies were conducted beyond the outskirts of the village.

Osage women took special pride in keeping a clean, orderly lodge. Men, women, and children took frequent baths, even in the winter. Many older Osages broke the ice on a stream to take a bath. Compaction placed the village outskirts very close to overlapping each other and encouraged poor sanitation practices. Personal cleanness became less important as tolerance for human odors became more developed because of association with Euro-Americans. So a major cause of Osage epidemics was the compaction into a small area.

The settlers were possibly a major cause of Osage epidemics, but native nations also transmitted epidemics. Certainly, the emigrant Cherokee brought at least one epidemic to the Osages. With equal certainty, the Quapaw and Comanche each caused at least one epidemic. However, settlers and troops were almost surely the ultimate source of the epidemics.

Diseases that had only a mild effect on Euro-Americans because of their inherited immunity had devastating effects on the Osages, who had no immunity. At the same time, those diseases that were severe on Euro-Americans were even more severe among the Osages. Lacking resistance to the diseases of Western civilization, the Osages contracted these diseases with greater ease and frequency than Euro-Americans.

The conflicts of the white people had a terrible effect on the Osages. One could say with more than a little truth that the Indians generally, and the Osages specifically, paid a terrible price for the freedom of blacks. Their being on the doorsill of the first bloodshed by the Euro-Americans was unfortunate for the Osages.

In Kansas history, the first burst of this insanity is called the Wakarusa War. Most of the general histories refer to it as the War in Kansas. Stephen A. Douglas sponsored the Kansas–Nebraska Bill in the hopes of taking the slavery controversy out of Congress and placing it into the territories. While it did not remove the controversy from the halls of Congress, it certainly brought it into the territory of Kansas and, thus, laid it upon the backs of the Osages.

We will deal with this conflict later, but we must mention that between 1852 and 1870 (eighteen years) the Osages could not leave their villages unguarded. That is, they could not engage in the two grand hunts for the buffalo each year, and they were limited in the grand winter hunt. This is not to say they did not hunt buffalo, deer, and bear, but large-scale hunts

Known Osage Epidemics		
Year	Disease	Deaths
1829	influenza	total for
1831	influenza	1829 to
1834	cholera	1843
1837	smallpox	1,242
1852	scurvy	total for
1852	measles	1852
1852	typhoid	800
1855	smallpox	400
1856	scrofula	100

Fig. 34. Notice the cluster in 1852.

were impossible and there were no grand hunts. The impact on the people was immediate and devastating. Dietary deficiencies were severe and prolonged. Thus, we have another cause for the severe epidemics experienced by the Osages.

Early Epidemics

We have no extremely early accounts of epidemics among the Osages. Chances are that they had a few epidemics through most of the seventeenth and eighteenth centuries. Certainly, they were indirectly and directly exposed to Euro-American diseases by the mid–1600s (see Fig. 34).

The first mention of Osage epidemics to be found were mentioned by Grant Foreman, who reports: "During the years 1829 and 1831 the Osage had suffered much from a prevailing epidemic called by the people, 'the cold plague or influenza,' from which hundreds had died."[13] One of the most widely mentioned of the earlier epidemics was the cholera epidemic of 1834.

The year 1833 was one of extensive floods on the Great Plains and its eastern borders. The following year was marked by severe drought in the same areas. Such conditions tend to foster epidemics. When Jackson forced the removal of the eastern Cherokee to former Osage lands, they brought the cholera with them. By the summer of 1834, the Osages and other Plains nations were seized by a cholera epidemic.[14]

Foreman reported that in September of 1834 the Osages were dying by the hundreds from cholera. He later gave an estimate that between three and four hundred Osages died of cholera in this year.[15]

Tillie Karns Newman gives us an interesting, but confusing, account. She reports that "the population of the Osages in 1829 was estimated at five thousand. In 1843, when there was a recount, it was found that only thirty-seven hundred and fifty-eight were living. Smallpox had taken a big toll of the Osages and they were seeking health in other localities."[16] This statement is correct, but it may give the impression that 1,242 Osages died of smallpox between 1829 and 1843. The population estimates given would include the deaths from the influenza epidemic of 1829–1831 and the cholera epidemic of 1834, as well as the smallpox epidemic of ca. 1837. We might add that although the Osage population dropped somewhat in the 1840s, it was back to 5,000 by 1850, according to other sources.

Epidemics of the 1850s

On May 20, 1853, Fr. Schonmakers wrote to the Commissioner of Indian Affairs. He informed the Commissioner that upon the urgent request of the Quapaw leaders and the Neosho Agent, he had admitted twenty-four Quapaw children to the Osage Mission school. He informed the Commissioner that he could accept no more Quapaw pupils and would have to dismiss those now enrolled unless the school was paid fifty-five dollars per year for each Quapaw pupil.[17]

The presence of these Quapaw pupils at Osage Mission in 1852 was the immediate cause of the major epidemic of 1852. On about March 1, a Quapaw came to the Mission to visit his daughter. He seemed to be ill the next day, and upon examination it was determined that he had the black measles. Although he was moved far from the mission, by evening some pupils were showing symptoms of the disease. Possibly the coming of a warm early spring after a harsh winter encouraged the disease.[18]

By 1850, the number of Osage children had increased. The winter of 1851–1852 was severe, and shortly after the beginning of 1852 scurvy became widespread among the Osages. Then the measles epidemic broke out in the spring. As summer ripened, typhoid fever struck the people. Over half of the Osage children and many adults died in 1852 of at least one of these three afflictions. In total, over 800 Osages died in 1852.[19]

The Osages hardly had time to bury their dead before the next epidemic struck. Unlike typhoid fever in the terrible times of 1852, smallpox was a major epidemic in its own right in 1855. No one has described the circumstances behind this epidemic better than Sister Fitzgerald, who begins her account, "Late in November [1854] the Little Osage were returning from the fall hunt."[20] (Because the quote is long we will paraphrase the remainder.) Three of the braves spotted a small Comanche camp. The Little Osage, seeking revenge for an old insult, planned an attack at dawn. However, the Comanche had detected the Osages and baited a trap. Slipping away in the darkness of the night, they left an old man who was dying of smallpox. He was dressed in rich robes and had fine weapons about him. When the

Osages struck at dawn they killed the old man and stripped him. Carrying the plunder of the Comanche camp, they left the Cimarron and returned to their village. The following spring smallpox broke out in the Little Osage village and quickly spread to the other villages.

Major Dorn engaged "Dr. Edwin Griffith of Jasper County, Missouri, to vaccinate and care for the Osages." Although most Osages had been vaccinated in 1837, a whole generation had grown up without vaccination since that time. "In his report to Dorn Dr. Griffith said he travelled 450 miles (he had to overtake one band of Osages who had departed on their spring hunt) and altogether vaccinated over two thousand Osages. As the plague subsided he instructed the Chiefs how to vaccinate those tribesmen he had missed."[21] This epidemic of smallpox killed an estimated four hundred Osages.[22]

One would think the pale horse, pestilence, and his rider, death, had taken enough Osage lives. Yet, they still rode roughshod through the Osage villages. Pestilence dug deep into his bag of woe and brought forth scrofula, a tuberculous condition with enlargement and degeneration of the lymphatic glands, especially those of the neck. A common name for the disease is the king's evil.

On September 4, 1856, Major A. J. Dorn wrote to Charles W. Dean, who was his superintendent, saying, "I would speak of the very considerable sickness that has prevailed among the Osages, and by which I would suppose there had at least one hundred of them died. The disease that has prevailed among them was said to be scrofula, and I learn that it has almost entirely abated since they scattered on the spring hunt."[23] Scrofula lingered among the Osages until allotment in 1906. *Ho ta Moie* (Comes Roaring) (or "John Stink," as he was called), supposedly was buried because he was unconscious from a severe scrofula attack and was thought to have been dead. Actually, people avoided him because he had scrofula, which caused an offensive body odor. In time, he overcame the disease, but he chose to remain an outcast the rest of his life.

Tuberculosis in many forms became common among the Osages. Being crowded into compact areas and still trying to follow a way of life they had followed for centuries created an ideal environment for the disease to grow. The dirt floors of their lodges were covered with mats, but there were always dust motes in the air of the lodge. In happier times, this made little difference, since most of the day was spent in the open air and the tubercular germ did not exist in the Osage country until the coming of the white man.

With so many intruders around, the Osages were increasingly spending more time in their villages. As their time in the villages increased, time in the clean air of the hunt decreased. Thus, the increased time in foul air and growth of nearby waste and debris became a heaven on earth for the tubercle bacillus.

POPULATION

Closely related to the epidemics is the matter of population. When considering populations, both the overall numbers and fluctuations are significant. The major problem in any consideration of the Osage population is the availability of reliable figures. One would think the Osage Annuity Rolls, which start ca. 1834 and run to the turn of the century, would have accurate counts since they involved payment of treaty monies. However, this was not the case, since each annuity payment missed at least one hundred or more Osages. Furthermore, they sometimes included non-Osages. The census rolls, which started in 1885 and ran to 1940, are equally faulty, although after 1906 they are reasonably reliable.

One difficulty in obtaining accurate Osage population figures was the tendency of Euro-Americans to consistently underestimate Indian populations. This practice was not the result of any Osage action, but it was the refusal of Euro-Americans to believe that the Osage civilization could support a larger population than their estimates. Also, the Osages constantly patrolled their vast empire and had exploring parties out. Somewhere around one-fourth of its fighting force and families were always away from the villages. Thus, even the more reliable figures are probably off by one-fourth.

Some idea of the Osage population can be obtained from the earliest estimates before the practice of reducing Indian population estimates started. In 1680, Hennepin recorded that the Osages had seventeen villages, and Coxe, in 1770, places the number at seventeen to eighteen villages.[24] From archaeological studies and written records, we know the Osage villages varied in size from 500 to 3,000 people. It seems that an average of 1,000 people per village would not be an unreasonable assumption. Thus, a population of 17,000 to 18,000 is suggested to at least 1800 (see Fig. 35).

There was some "bleeding off" of individuals and groups of Osages who joined other nations. However, the additions from other nations to the Osages probably kept pace with this population loss. Recorded casualties of Osages killed in engagements with other Indian nations must be taken with a generous grain of salt. In one instance, the Sac and Fox reported they had killed over one hundred Osage warriors. However, in the same year, traders reported that the Sac and Fox had killed only two Osages for the entire year.

Despite their extensive expansion and many battles in defense of their

Estimates of Osage Population		
Year	Bands	Population
1680	totals only	17,000
1815	totals only	12,000
1820	Claremore	5,000
1820	White Hair's	
	Little Osage	2,083
	Big Osage	3,333
1820	Little Osage	2,000
1830	totals only	10,000
1850	totals only	8,000
1860	totals only	3,500

Fig. 35. Notice the steady decline in population.

territory, the Osage population apparently remained stable until about 1800. By 1815, the Osage population had probably dropped to around 12,000 to 14,000. Seemingly, it leveled off at 10,000 where it remained until the 1840s. At the beginning of the 1850s, the Osage population was probably around 8,000. Individuals who were in a position to know, however, placed the Osage population at 5,000 at the beginning of the 1850s. Yet, when one totals the reported deaths from the epidemics and subtracts that from 5,000, one gets much less than the reported 3,500 in 1860. Therefore, we must abide by our figure of 8,000 in 1850.

One of the most cited estimates is Major Sibley's in 1817. For example, he places the warrior strength of the Claremore bands at 600. If we allow five people per warrior, this would place the Claremore bands at 3,000. Yet, less than five years later, a Protestant missionary placed the population of Claremore's village alone at 3,000. Thus, either Sibley erred in his estimate or an Osage warrior supported more than five people.

We know from the written record that Black Dog's band numbered between five and six hundred in 1820. The Grosse Côte village was between Black Dog's and Claremore's in size, so we will count it as 1,000 people. We have no idea how many small villages clustered about these larger villages, but we believe a total estimate of five hundred persons is not unreasonably large. Thus, the Arkansas bands must have totaled around 5,000 Osages. This figures to be eight and one-third persons supported by each warrior. This seems to be an unreasonable number to be supported by one warrior, so we are inclined to believe that Sibley's report reflects the usual underestimation of Indian populations. However, we will apply the warrior/population ratio derived from Sibley's estimate and written accounts to the rest of Sibley's estimate.

If we take Sibley's estimate of two hundred fifty Little Osage warriors and multiply by eight and one-third, we get 2,083 Little Osages. Following the same process with the estimated four hundred White Hair Big Osages, gives a population of 3,333 White Hair Big Osages. This yields a total Osage population of 10,416 between 1817 and 1820. Sibley omitted the three independent Little Osage bands, which would have numbered at least as many as the White Hair Little Osages. This would place the population near to 12,500 between 1817 and 1820, as a very modest estimate.

We have labored our way through these mental gymnastics to show how we arrived at our population estimates. Another bit of information gives us a clue to Osage population from the Osage viewpoint. Thomas Nuttall notes that "Scarcely any nation of Indians have encountered more enemies than the Osages; still they flatter themselves, by saying, that they are seated in the middle of the world, and, although surrounded by so many enemies, they have maintained their usual population, and their country."[25]

To 1820 and perhaps a few years beyond, the Osages were largely correct in saying they had maintained their population. Yet, there had been a slow attrition upon the Osage population that went unnoticed. This condition prevailed up to 1850. That is, the Osages were saying they were maintaining their population but in fact, by slow attrition, they were losing population.

In 1839, Tixier made the following comment about the attrition upon the Osage population: "The Osage, who were formerly considered among the most powerful nations, have lost much of their numerical importance; internal quarrels, wars, epidemics, and smallpox in particular have decreased their numbers considerably."[26] It is impossible to accurately pinpoint the cause of the slow attrition in Osage population. Epidemics and wars are major causes, but these alone could not account for the steady and almost constant decline in population up to 1850. We would be inclined to include Tixier's "internal quarrels" as a major reason for the decline instead of epidemics and war, at least to 1850.

The internal quarrels would, and did, cause an unstable society. Such societies often experience a decline in birthrate. Sociologists have never found a satisfactory reason for the phenomenon. However, its existence is real, and it seems to have been at work among the Osages. Another possibility is that changes in diet, clothing, and especially cookware could have caused a decline. We know in the earlier periods cookware was made of copper and brass. It is possible that the copper caused a few to die each year. However, this would not account for a prolonged decline, because the Osages switched to cast-iron cookware as soon as the effect of brass and copper was detected.

Another effect of internal strife is the growth of population through voluntary realignment of loyalties. A society experiencing internal strife is not attractive to those who would immigrate to a stable society. The Osage myths clearly show that much of the Osage population growth came through merging with other peoples and through adoption. By 1800, the Missourias, the last group to do so, had merged with the Little Osages. At this same time, the number of Pawnee captives available for adoption was severely curtailed.

Apparently, a declining birthrate and a decline in immigrants were the major factors in the reduction of Osage population between 1800 and 1850. Earlier in this chapter we traced the disaster of the 1850s. While epidemics, war, and famine were the major causes of population decline between 1850 and 1880, the birthrate and immigration causes still persisted. We have, then, a nagging continual decline of population and dramatic, abrupt changes in population.

While pestilence and death never left the Osages, by 1860 they were moving more gently among them. As the pale horse and his rider became gentler with the Osages, the red horse and his rider rode among them. War swung his great sword to the left and right, and Osages melted away before the red charger. Thus, the Osages came face-to-face with the second horseman, war, riding his red horse.

11

The White Man's War Visits the Osages

INTRODUCTION

And there went out another horse that was red. And to him that sat thereon, it was given that he should take peace from the earth: and that they should kill one another. And a great sword was given to him.

The Wakarusa (Wah kuh' roo suh) River is a tributary of the Kansas or Kaw River. It enters the Kaw from the south, slightly east of Lawrence, Kansas. Specifically, the term Wakarusa War is applied to the opening part of the conflict in Kansas arising from the passage of the Kansas–Nebraska Act.[1] As a matter of fact, to be accurate, we should apply this name to only the first two weeks of this conflict. However, we may sometimes use Wakarusa War interchangeably with "The War in Kansas" and "The Border War."

Reforms

The reform movement in the United States began in the 1820s and continued into the 1860s, but its crest was reached in the mid–1840s. Among the issues brought forth were women's rights, human rights, prohibition, the abolition of wars, ideal communities, and educational reforms. However, we are especially interested in the abolition of slavery, Indian reforms, and the Gospel of Individualism, all of which lay behind many reforms.

Although Indians were involved in all these issues of reform, their influence was most evident in the creation of ideal communities, educational reform, and the Gospel of Individualism. Finding humans living in a state of natural freedom and possessing individual choice stimulated the minds of Western civilization. Such stimulation led to the creation of many kinds

The epigraph is from "The Apocalypse of St. John the Apostle" 6:1–8, Douay version. The red horse represented bloodshed and its rider represented war.

of ideal communities that sought to fit Indian practices into the industrial, religious, or political institutions of Western culture. Oneida Community, which produced silverware under the Indian communal organization, was one such adaptation.

The obvious need to educate the Indians in order to incorporate them into the Euro-American culture—as most reformers wanted—led to a serious look at education in general. In an earlier period Benjamin Franklin had quoted an Indian chief's views of Western education:

> We are convinc'd, therefore, that you mean to do us good by your proposal; and we thank you heartily. But you, who are wise, must know that different nations have different conceptions of things; and you will therefore, not take it amiss, if our ideas of this kind of education happen not to be the same with yours. We have had some experience of it; several of our young people were formerly brought up at the colleges of the Northern Provinces; they were instructed in all your sciences; but when they came back to us they were bad runners, ignorant of every means of living in the woods, unable to bear either cold or hunger, knew neither how to build a cabin, take a deer, or kill an enemy, spoke our language imperfectly, were totally good for nothing. We are however, not the less oblig'd by your kind offer, tho' we decline accepting it; and, to show our grateful sense of it, if the gentlemen of Virginia will send us a dozen of their sons, we will take great care of their education, instruct them in all we know, and make men of them.[2]

Franklin used this quote to make the point that education should be relevant to the society in which it exists.

Both Franklin and Thomas Jefferson argued that an education which stressed *only* the Liberal Arts was not relevant in the American society. Because of Jefferson's views, William and Mary stressed the practical and Applied Arts and Sciences as well as physical development and the Liberal Arts. Franklin's ideas were taken up by Eliphilet Knott at Union College in Pennsylvania and required every Union graduate to have both a classical education and a practical education. Thus, every Union graduate had a practical skill in some trade. George Tinker, who later married into the Osage nation, was a graduate of Union and worked as a blacksmith, although he was also trained in the professions.

It was in this era that Horace Mann revolutionized American education in Massachusetts. There, for the first time, compulsory free education was enacted into law. Universal literacy became an educational goal of America. It is sad that Indian education in the BIA schools was not patterned on Indian ideas of relevancy instead of those adopted by Western civilization.

While the Gospel of Individualism was applied to business and industry, it reached its greatest heights in literature. This came with the natural rights philosophy and the rise of nationalism in the United States. Natural rights philosophy and the rise of American nationalism are an outgrowth of Indian culture, both in origin and impetus. Three outstanding writers made individualism an American credo. These writers were Henry David Thoreau, Ralph Waldo Emerson, and Walt Whitman.

The slavery issue became an enormous emotional matter because of the reform movement. All programs and efforts to eliminate slavery by a gradual emancipation were lost in the heat of the abolition movement, which demanded the immediate emancipation of all slaves. Also lost in the rising tide of emotion was the conflict between an agrarian economic base and a rising industrial-commercial economic base. Politically, the States' Rights question was also overlooked. In fact, all issues, including the Indian question, were shoved into the background as the emotional tide of abolition swept over the American nation.

The Gathering Storm

The slavery issue colored every matter that came before Congress. As emotions became increasingly aroused, Congress became a battleground. With the end of the Mexican–American War in 1848, a railroad to the Pacific grew from a remote dream into a possibility. Both the Northeast and the South wanted the transcontinental railroad, which now appeared to be possible. The Gadsden Purchase of 1853 gave the South a feasible path by following the old Butterfield Route (Ox-Bow Route) to California. Not only did this route have forts along the way for protection, but it also passed through organized territory.

This organized territory argument was seized by the Northeastern railroad men, who demanded that Nebraska Territory be organized. Therefore, the Kansas–Nebraska Bill was introduced into Congress. This Bill proposed to divide Nebraska Territory into two territories. Kansas Territory was the southern part and Nebraska Territory became the northern part (see Fig. 36). A provision to let the people of the territory decide whether they were to be admitted as a slave or free-soil territory provoked a storm.

The proviso of "popular sovereignty" was added to gain Southern support for the bill, which was needed for passage because the bill primarily dealt with the interests of the Northeastern railroad. Yet, Northeastern congressmen fumed and argued that in allowing the possibility of slavery in

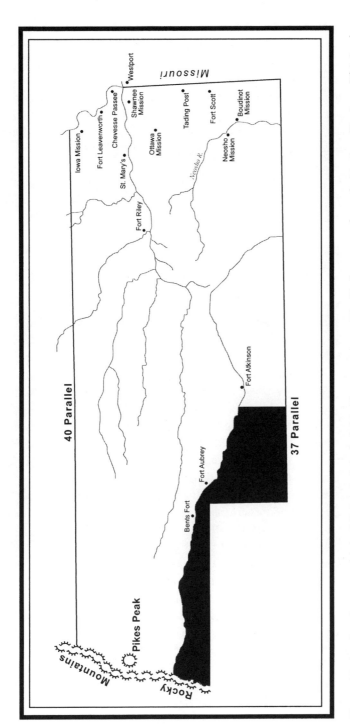

Fig. 36. Notice that about one-third of Colorado is included in Kansas territory. The black area was formerly Mexican Territory. This is why the Osage Reserve ended at the 100th meridian.

Kansas the bill violated the Missouri Compromise. At the outset Kansas was expected to become a slave state and Nebraska a free-soil state. Despite objections, the bill passed in 1854, and the Kansas–Nebraska Act became the law of the land.

Stephen A. Douglas wanted a northern transcontinental railroad with its eastern terminus at Chicago, where he had investments. He also hoped to take the slavery controversy out of Congress. As expected, he failed in this last objective, although he did bring the argument to Kansas Territory.

Prairie Storm

The immediate effect of the Kansas–Nebraska Act upon the Osages was a surge of intruders from Missouri who settled upon Osage lands. These first intruders, for the most part, were temporary, although later intruders tended to be permanent. They gathered for the first territorial election in November of 1854. Because of Missourians who became "Kansans for a day" and voted in this election, the election results were voided. A census was conducted in 1855, and a second territorial election was held in March of 1855. Over five thousand Missourians voted in this second election, and the Osages were deluged with intruders. These two elections and a re-vote in six of the districts still left the question of slavery in Kansas pending.

Violence first broke out on the Wakarusa, south of Lawrence, Kansas, when a free-soiler was killed. A pro-slavery party of 1,500 marched to the free-soil stronghold of Lawrence. Little came of this since the "army" did not take Lawrence. Kansas rapidly became an armed camp. Free-soil and pro-slavery "armies" were formed. These "armies" became little more than raiding parties who used the slavery issue to raid the Osages and other Indians, as well as those who opposed their pro-slavery stance.

At this point, John Brown decided to kill some pro-slavery men. With Brown on the loose at the northern side of the Osage Reserve, intruders who were armed to the teeth became common on Osage lands. To curb some of the violence, the United States government sent dragoons to Kansas. These were mounted troops who normally rode to battle but then dismounted and fought as infantry in combat. This same type of fighting was used by the Kansas "armies," such as Jim Montgomery's.

Montgomery roamed all over Southeast Kansas. He was active in Bourbon and Dorn (Neosho–Labette) counties. The Osages had reason to know him well because of his frequent forays into their territory. Montgomery has the distinction of being the only "border army" to fire upon federal troops, an engagement in which Montgomery killed one trooper and wounded two others. One of own his own men, John Denton, was wounded and later died from the wound.[3]

A situation developed much closer to the Osages in July of 1861. Besides the horde of illegal Euro-American settlers on the Osage Reserve, there were traders and government employees, as well as the Jesuits and Sisters of Osage Mission (see Fig. 37). These, like other Euro-Americans of this time, took positive positions for or against slavery in Kansas. Samuel Gilmore, who had a store near Osage Mission, was an outspoken free-soiler. Father Schonmakers seldom involved himself in political questions, but he was firmly against the institution of slavery and advised the Osages to remain neutral.

John Mathews was a trader at Oswego, Kansas, downstream from the Mission. He was a slaveholder and was ardently a pro-slavery adherent. Mathews was married to both half-blood daughters of Bill Williams, the Mountain Man. Another player in this drama was the stepson of Mathews, who was at various times called Bill Nix, Bill Nixon, Bill Mathes, or Red Corn.[4] Red Corn had attended the Jesuit schools at Florissant, Missouri, and at Osage Mission. He later became a Baptist Minister, but in the summer of 1861 he was a sincere Catholic and devoted to Fr. Schonmakers.

John Mathews had gathered a force of pro-slavery people who were determined to silence both Gilmore and Fr. Schonmakers. They left in a heavy rainstorm to carry out their purpose. Red Corn had started earlier and had crossed the Neosho before it had reached the flood stage. The "army" collected by Mathews had to wait for the water to subside. Meanwhile, Red Corn warned Fr. Schonmakers of the pending attack. Leaving the mission in the care of Fr. Ponziglione, Fr. Schonmakers and Gilmore fled to Humboldt, Kansas. After a brief rest at Humboldt, Fr. Schonmakers went on to St. Mary's Mission to the Potawatomi. Fr. Schonmakers stayed at St. Mary's Mission for eight months.

In justice to Mathews it should be mentioned that when his group reached the mission he made sure that neither the Sisters, the Mission, nor anyone in it was harmed. Hoping to capture Gilmore at Humboldt, Mathews took the town and then plundered and looted it. Horrified by this act, the free-soilers tracked Mathews down and killed him at Chetopa, Kansas. Thus, the free-soilers committed some of the same acts as Mathews. Neither side could claim to be free of similar or even worse acts of violence.

Such incidents as created by Montgomery and Mathews, and many others like them, greatly disturbed the Osages. Due to their location, their villages were to be vulnerable in the years ahead to invasion and looting. Thus, a high proportion of warriors had to remain in the villages to protect the women, children, and aged. This reduced the hunting force and, consequently, the meat supply. Others have noted the strategic location of the Osages, among them Sister Fitzgerald, who mentions the location factor in her great work,

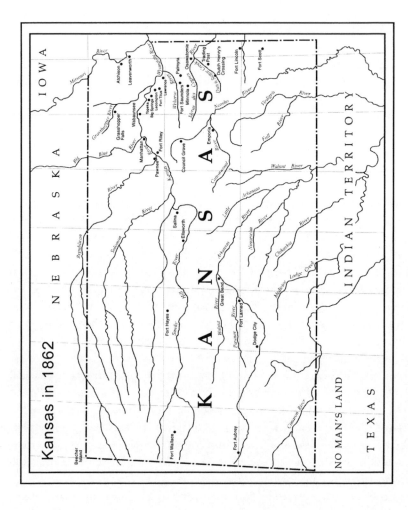

Fig. 37. Notice the heavy settlement along the Kansas River.

Beacon on the Plain: "Geographically, the Osage were so located that they could swing the balance of the western campaigns either in favor of the Union or the Confederacy."[5]

Their location made the ordeal of the Osages very severe between 1855 and 1865. There was no escape from the inroads made upon their lands by the contending forces. In a very real sense, the Osages paid a terrible price for the freedom of blacks.

THE CIVIL WAR

Euro-American Views of the Indian

Views held by Euro-Americans toward the Indian during the Civil War era greatly affected the sequence of Indian events. While this applied to some Indians in a general way, it applied very directly to the Osages. So we must examine these views.

It seems strange that those people who were willing to give their lives in opposition to slavery could be so racially biased. Yet, those who most ardently opposed slavery were as racially biased as those who defended slavery. The institution of slavery itself became the issue and not the question of racial equality.

Bias toward blacks was only slightly greater than the bias of most Euro-Americans toward the Indians. Ellsworth Huntington is considered to be the greatest geographer of the twentieth century. His cyclic theory of climates is a great contribution to scholarship. Yet, this great scholar, who was a product of the Civil War era, was terribly biased toward the Indian. His bias is summed up in his own words: "As to the Indian, his past achievements and present condition indicate that intellectually he stands between the white man and the Negro in about the position that would be expected from the capacity of his brain."[6]

We would not want to be guilty of counter bias, but Osage school children score slightly higher on intelligence tests than their non-Osage classmates.[7] This objective evidence strongly suggests that Huntington was in error because of both his bias and a faulty skull theory.

Euro-Americans clung tenaciously to the belief that Indians were savages. Since a savage could not be like a white man, who was civilized, Indians, being savages, were inferior to the white men. Therefore, it was the responsibility of the Euro-American to decide who and what was a savage.[8] The Euro-Americans used this circular reasoning to justify in their own minds their unethical behavior toward the Indians.

It was popular to point to the degradation of the Indian in order to support the belief of inferiority. No consideration was given to the fact that this inferior position was the result of Euro-American policies and not a fault of the Indians themselves. Surely, the American Indian fared better without the Euro-Americans than with them. In the light of observable facts, no one could consider the coming of Euro-Americans to this continent as a blessing for Indians.

The only distinction between Euro-American reformers and the majority was in their intentions. Reformers always meant well; their desire was to aid in a humanitarian crisis. Yet, most Euro-Americans were motivated by enlightened self-interest. Unfortunately for the Indian, the majority wanted what the Indian had, and the reformers unwittingly furnished the means to get it.

One must remember that reformers were products of their own culture, as is evident from their efforts to bleach the Indian and make him like themselves. The re-creation of the Indian in the Euro-American image was almost universal in the American culture. Statements such as the following were frequently made by both the reformer and non-reformer: "His whole nature must be changed. He must have a white man's ambition, to be like him. He must have the objects and aims of a white man."[9]

Euro-Americans of the Civil War Era could not see any value in the Indian culture. They could not recognize greed for material things as an evil because, in their minds, material greed was identified as ambition. The Indian's lack of greed for material objects led Euro-Americans to believe Indians had no ambition.

An image of the Indian as a lazy idler became popular in the Civil War era. Almost without exception, earlier accounts had pictured the hard lot of Indian women and the easy life of Indian men. While this was far from true, it was taken as truth by the culture that produced the accounts. From this evolved the belief that Indians, and especially the men, were lazy.

A vast difference exists between hunting for food and hunting as a sport. The labor involved in hunts to establish a meat supply is staggering. Securing a meat supply from a domestic herd is much easier than securing it from the hunt. That is why herding was established in the Old World. Lacking meat animals that could be domesticated was a great handicap to Indians, causing them to have to hunt for their meat supply. Thus, they had less leisure time to pursue higher needs. Euro-Americans were not hunters in the sense of securing the total meat supply from the hunt. Thus, they had no appreciation for the labor involved in such activities. They tended to view the hunt as a sport and, therefore, considered it to be a leisure-time activity.

Few Euro-Americans met situations where their lives depended on their ability to run for prolonged periods. Osage men and women often walked seventy to eighty miles in a day. Under emergency conditions, Osage men more than doubled this. Osage men often were required to run so hard and so long that they coughed up blood from their strained lungs. Few Euro-Americans ever worked this hard. Indian men rested when they were in their villages, a fact that gave Euro-American observers the impression that all the men did was loaf around and enjoy the sport of hunting or making war.

Facts have much less to do with human actions than beliefs. Thus, the faith in labor and the belief that Indians were idlers found reflection in Euro-American deeds and words. David Nichols argues, "Labor is a great civilizer. I do not believe that the efforts to civilize or convert to Christianity an idle race of Barbarians will ever succeed unless you first induce them to become industrious, prudent and thrifty."[10]

When one speaks of thrift the Melanesian tribesmen of the island of Efate in the South Pacific come to mind. These people would take castaway bottles and make diving goggles and many other products from them. American Indians also utilized things the "thrifty" Euro-Americans cast away.

Modern man has no concept of industry, prudence, and thrift until he has objectively observed primitive people. Either the Indian was so highly civilized that he had lost his prudence, industry, and thrift or the writer of the above quote was not correct. The Indian was certainly not as advanced in technology as Western civilization, but it is definitely untrue that Indian culture was inferior in other respects.

If the American Indian had not been hard working, prudent, industrious, and thrifty, he would not have survived the affliction of Western civilization. Western history records no such calamity striking their culture, so accurate comparisons cannot be made. When the experience of the American Indian is compared to what happened after the fall of Rome, the question of which culture recovered and adapted to the change in a shorter span of time arises.

Manifest Destiny

Farming evolved into the ideal of the American Utopia in the first half of the 1800s. This trend of glorifying the farming occupation continued into the twentieth century. Both the South and the West were heavily agrarian. Before 1860, the Northeast was a mixture of agricultural, commercial, and a growing industrial economic base. Because of the Civil War, the industrial base was greatly accelerated. Yet, even the industrial worker dreamed of someday being an independent farmer. By 1900, America had the largest group of middle-class farmers in history.

From this background, it was natural for reformers to suggest farming as a solution to the Indian problem. Thus, the concept of individual allotment was introduced into Indian affairs. Intentions were that the individual Indian would take pride in owning and tilling a piece of land of his own. Without any background of individual land ownership, the Indian was at a loss to determine what to do with the land. Land speculators and individuals seeking farms quickly taught the Indian to sell his allotment.

Indian policy makers who were determined to make farmers of Indians could not see that this was in direct conflict with "manifest destiny." Their intentions were to enable the Indian to survive as full members of the majority culture. The Indian people had no desire to become members of the Euro-American culture and the unwashed frontier settlers did not want them as neighbors.

Manifest destiny was a strange quasi-religious belief that the United States was destined to occupy all of North America. While this is related to the Protestant beliefs in predestination and predeterminism, many Catholic Americans and others who believed in free will also shared the belief in manifest destiny. Most Euro-Americans believed God had ordained that they would achieve the occupation of the entire North American Continent. Against this groundswell of belief, Indians had little opportunity to become successful farmers, even if they had ardently desired to do so. The Indian would have lost his land regardless of what policy was followed. This is assuming the government would continue to ignore its obligation to enforce treaty provisions.

This brings out a key problem in Indian affairs. No matter how well conceived a policy was, in the final appraisal it depended on the enforcement of treaty provisions. The provisions most frequently neglected were those of guaranteed reservation and prohibition of intruders. At the close of the Civil War, the United States had the largest, most experienced, modern military force in the world. Yet, it could not or would not, and surely did not, keep intruders out of Indian reservations. Nor did the government stand behind the guaranteed reservation as provided in treaty agreements. "As long as the grass grows and the water flows" has become a symbol of bad faith in a contract.

Manifest destiny led many Euro-Americans to predict the extinction of the Indian—a natural conclusion, given an understanding of manifest destiny. Yet, the Indians had descended from survivors of great disasters. As has been indicated in the preceding paragraphs, the settlers, being driven by manifest destiny, wanted the only valuable thing the Indian owned. The life of the Indian is not what was desired. Indian lives were taken when they stood in the "path of empire," but so long as the Indian stood aside, he survived.

A remarkable statement by Abraham Lincoln reveals his ethnic blindness:

"The pale-faced people are numerous and prosperous because they cultivate the earth, produce bread, and depend upon the products of the earth rather than wild game for subsistence. This is the chief reason of the difference; but there is another. Although we are now engaged in a great war between one another, we are not as a race, so much disposed to fight and kill one another as our red brethren."[11] This statement shows Lincoln's total ignorance about the Indian. We suspect what is true of the Osage is basically true of other Indians.

A comparison of Osage myths and legends with Western myths and legends shows a sharp contrast. In Osage literature, war and combat is rarely mentioned, and atonement is included in the killing of an animal or a human. By contrast, Western literature glorifies war, combat, and violence. To be sure, the American Civil War was an exceptionally bloody war. Yet one cannot help noticing that more has been written about this war than any other event in the history of the United States or the world.

How then could Lincoln accuse Indians of being more prone to kill their fellow men than the peoples of Western civilization? We believe the nature of two kinds of wars are involved. First, we are assuming warfare is a form of insanity which afflicts humanity. Basically, it is not a sane act to deliberately take a life, especially when one risks one's own life in the process. Among the Osage, life was spared if possible, except on rare occasions. It is true that lives were taken in the frequent wars of the Osages. The difference is that few lives were taken in many Indian wars while many lives were taken in fewer Western wars. It is much like comparing the two World Wars with the many post–World War II "Cold Wars" and the large number of "Brush Fire Wars."

This distinction of many wars versus few wars led Euro-Americans to believe Indians were more blood-thirsty than themselves. Yet, if one totaled the percent of deaths per combatant over a score of years, Western civilization would show a greater percent of loss. Lincoln could not have foreseen the great industrial-commercial revolution that followed the Civil War. Nor could he have foreseen the staggering population growth of the "pale-faced people." Even if he could have foreseen these facts, and the consequent contamination of the earth, he probably would still have argued that Western civilization was superior to the Indian civilization.

Every civilization carries the seed for its own destruction. In Western civilization, the seed of destruction lies in the race between advancing technology and population growth. It is customary to soothe alarm by observing that science will solve all problems. The faith in science and the technology it produces has replaced manifest destiny. Yet, more and more the contamination of the earth and the atmosphere and the depletion of resources are telling us that the race is nearing the finish line. In some ways, Western civilization stands where the Osage people stood in 1850, and it must face a basic law of survival—adapt your culture to reality or perish.

Lincoln's program for the West revolved around three things. These were the Homestead Act of 1862, the development of mineral resources, and the construction of a transcontinental railroad.[12] As one might suspect, the Homestead Act accelerated the demand for Indian lands. In their search for minerals, especially gold, Euro-Americans and the government ignored their own laws of Indian rights. Thus railroads, because of the land grant practices, were financed by Indians. These matters will be taken up in later chapters, but their roots were in the Civil War era.

Indian Influence in the Civil War

Lincoln found the Office of Indian Affairs to be a powerful bureaucracy with both political and economic aspects.[13] The money involved in Indian affairs was vast for Lincoln's time, although the amount would not seem so great today. Treaty annuities alone were enough to attract individuals who sought riches above all else. Yet, the greatest source of Indian monies came from the sale of their lands.

In each of these categories—treaty annuities and Indian land sales monies—special means were used to siphon off funds. Insofar as treaty annuities were concerned, the most common device was to provide the Indian with a product or service that was neither desired by him nor would give him little more than a token benefit. With the millions of dollars accumulated from Indian land sales, it was profitable to invest the money at a high interest rate and pay the Indian a low interest rate. Variations in the investment of Indian funds were so abundant that one must be impressed by the white man's ingenuity. Possibly, the investment in railroad bonds was the most ingenious. Indians not only furnished thousands of acres of land to the land grant railroads, at less than bargain basement prices, but they also loaned the funds necessary for railroad construction. Thus, the Indian was made to finance his own destruction.

We have not investigated very deeply the use of Indian funds to finance the Civil War. However, a surface exploration suggests that Indians may have, to a sizable degree, financed emancipation of blacks. Surely, the Osages financed the establishment of at least one Negro college.[14]

With the large sums being managed by the Indian Affairs Bureau, it is not surprising that positions within the bureau were political plums. Since these were the choice positions of political patronage, the Bureau of Indian Affairs became politically powerful. Its personnel were among the most influential political party members. Thus, they had considerable political clout.

More often than not this placed people with little interest in Indian welfare in charge of Indian affairs. Hence, the Union was badly disorganized and unprepared to utilize Indians in the Civil War. So, the Confederacy was first to gain the support of Indians.

One of the most vexing problems was the matter of claims. This was a one-way road in favor of the whites, since their claims were assumed to be valid as long as annuities were available to pay the claim. Yet there was no procedure available for an Indian to file a claim against a white person. It was politically expedient to approve the claim of a voter, but Indians did not have a vote. Some claims were so blatantly false, however, that even the BIA would not approve them. In these rare cases, a friendly congressman could easily be persuaded to introduce a private bill, and the claim would be paid. Here again, through bribes and election support using Indian money, the Indian financed the reelection of congressmen who were destroying them—in much the same way as the railroad financing was destroying the Indian nations.

For those involved in these various practices, there was an added bonus— it was perfectly legal. Only when someone dipped directly into the funds was there a public cry of corruption. Claims, loans, or sales of useless services and products were all legal forms of graft. In essence, as long as the graft affected only Indians, it was legal. It was upon this background that Lincoln took into consideration the role of Indians in the Civil War.

Indians were not so naive that they were unaware of some graft. The frustrating thing was that they did not have the means to defend themselves or to retaliate. One old Indian summed up the whole mess very graphically: "Dam rascal plenty here. He steal him horse. He steal him timber. He steal him everything. He make him good business. Many agents come here. Sometimes good. Sometimes bad. Most bad. The agent say, you must not do so. The next one come, he say you do very foolish. The Government not want you to do so. Agent much dam rascal. Indian much dam fool."[15]

The Osages and the Civil War

The Union

Lincoln and the Union were slow to recognize the potential of the Osages in the war and slower still in using Osage forces. The North was very much opposed to using Indians as soldiers, although their use as scouts and interpreters was accepted. Although some four hundred Osages did serve as soldiers in the Union Army, the actual issue of Osages serving as soldiers was not settled until World War I.[16]

Possibly, Lincoln was aware that the Union was vulnerable to a Southern Indian attack through Kansas. If Southeastern Kansas could have been occupied by Confederate Indian forces, it is possible that Missouri might have joined with the South. Aside from the course pursued by Missouri, it would have required diversion of needed troops to keep the land connection with the Far West intact. In essence, this was the service rendered to the Union by the Osages. They acted as buffer troops to prevent Stand Watie's forces from occupying Southeast Kansas. Osages not in the military acted as a homeguard to prevent surprise actions by the Confederacy.

Thus, in the service of the Union, the Osages were subjected to the see-saw actions in Southeast Kansas. Their villages stood between the Union forts to the north and the Confederate strongholds to the south. Being in such a position, their villages would be invaded by first one side and then the other, and at times their villages were the site of battles between the two factions. Naturally, any useful supplies or horses belonging to the Osages were seized by the invading forces of both sides.

Sister Fitzgerald summed up this type of action in *Beacon on the Plain:* "Passing troops never failed to leave their mark on the Indian country. With something akin to diabolic ruthlessness they plundered Indian cottages, destroyed fields and set fire to schools and churches."[17] With so many of their young men in the service of both sides and with hunting parties seeking food, the village force was not always large enough to repel these larger invasion forces. With their food reserves stolen, crops destroyed, and a restricted supply of meat, the Osages suffered almost constant famine.

The Confederacy

Following the advice of Fr. Schonmakers, the Osage, like other nations, tried to remain neutral. The Lincoln administration abandoned the Indians in the West. In desperation many joined with the Confederacy. The South was actively seeking Indian support. A. J. Dorn, the Indians' former United States Agent, was now working with Albert Pike, the Confederate Indian Commissioner. To a great extent, his influence upon the Osages canceled out the influence of Fr. Schonmakers. However, by August 20, 1864, Dorn had left the Osages ample room to do as they pleased. In a report to S. B. Maxey, who was then acting as Superintendent of Indian Affairs for the Confederacy, R. W. Lee, the Assistant Superintendent, addressed a problem with the Osage Agent A. J. Dorn: "The Agent for the Osages resides at Bonham, Texas, recent difficulties at the Osage camp might have been prevented by the presence of the Agent, and if it were not already obvious, this occurrence would serve to demonstrate the propriety of the law, requiring Agents to reside with or near the people of their charge."[18]

We could not determine the nature of this difficulty in the Osage camp. Since the two hundred forty-one Confederate Osages were camped on the left side of the Arkansas River west of present-day Tulsa, they were near the cutting edge of the fighting. Dorn was wise in setting his residence in Texas; it is also probable that he was not being paid.

In any event, early in the conflict, Dorn was busy among the Osages. Dorn and Augustus "Ogeese" Captain took advantage of Fr. Schonmakers's eight month exile from Osage Mission and persuaded them to attend a general council at Tahlequah, Oklahoma. The Cherokee leader, John Ross, was greatly respected by the Osage leadership, and they were led to believe that the great Cherokee chief supported the Confederacy. This was not true, since John Ross led the neutral Cherokees and Stand Watie led the Confederate Cherokee.

Confederate Treaty

Albert Pike, the Confederate Commissioner, chaired the council and managed to persuade the Big Osages to sign a treaty with the Confederacy at nearby Park Hill. The Little Osages led by Little Bear and Hard Rope refused to sign the treaty. Among those who "touched the feather" were: Big Chief; White Hair; Sacred Sky; Black Dog II; Little Beaver, who was leader of the White Hair Little Osages; Tallchief; Dry Plume; Saucy Chief; Little Chief; Yellow Horse; Horse Chief; Guesso Chouteau; Ogeese Captain; Louis J. Chouteau; and many others.[19] The treaty is very long, with a total of forty-five Articles. We will not attempt to discuss the entire treaty, but we will touch upon some Articles.

Article III gives the usual assurances of friendship and territorial guarantees. To our knowledge, the Treaty of 1861 is the only Osage Treaty to use the phrase, "as long as grass shall grow and water shall run."

Article VIII is of special interest because it shows a different trend in Indian affairs. In this Article, the Confederacy promises that no part of the Osage territory will ever become a part of any state or territory nor will any state or territory ever exercise sovereignty over them. This indicates that the Confederacy intended to create either a series of semi-independent nations or a special Indian state.

Article IX gives assurances of hunting rights west of the five nations' possessions. While this is an affirmation of what was then an existing right, it does show the Osages had some claim to lands in Oklahoma. However, the United States, although granting hunting rights, retained complete title of ownership. The Confederacy did not insert a clause of ownership.

Article XVI required the Osage Agent and interpreter to reside among the Osages. As we mentioned earlier, Major Dorn was in violation of this agreement since he resided in Texas.

Article XVII forbad the Osages to go on the warpath without the consent of the Agent. An exception to this is made in the case of an invasion by a hostile force. Significantly, the Osages were forbidden to hold a council without the Agent's permission. This was especially mentioned in connection with those at war with the Confederacy. Although this was an effort to solve a serious problem, there is no way it could have been enforced.

Article XXIV shows the effect of Dorn's experience with epidemics among the Osages: "The Confederate States will also furnish, at proper places, the Great and Little Osages with such medicines as may be necessary, and will employ a physician for each, who shall reside among them, during the pleasure of the President."[20]

Article XXVI is possibly the most unusual provision of any treaty in Osage history. We are not aware of any other document in Osage history, other than some features of the marriage laws, where the Euro-American government accepts as legal an existing Osage law. So, although it is lengthy, we will quote it in its entirety: "No State or Territory shall ever pass laws for the government of the Osage people; and except so far as the laws of the Confederate States are in force in their country, they shall be left free to govern themselves, and to punish offences committed by one of themselves against the person or property of another: *PROVIDED, that if one of them kills another, without good cause or justification, he shall suffer death, but only by the sentence of the Chiefs, and after a fair trial, all private revenge being strictly forbidden.*"[21]

The portion in italics is an excellent statement of a basic Osage law. With the exceptions that (1) payment must be offered in atonement for the act in lieu of execution, and (2) the Division Chief of the offender made the ruling and the *Ah ke ta* conducted the execution, if any. In Osage law, the death sentence was imposed only after all other avenues of atonement had been exhausted.

Article XXVII is of special interest because of its effect on a later law. Article IX of laws made under the Osage Constitution of 1881 provides that a Euro-American married to an Osage could become an Osage citizen by residing on the reservation and taking an oath of allegiance to the Osage nation.[22] This same idea first appears in the Confederate–Osage Treaty of 1851 in Article XXVII.

Article XXXII is interesting because it recognizes and condones an ancient Osage practice. Under this provision, persons of other Indian nations were allowed to settle among the Osages. This article was probably to legalize the Quapaw who resided with the Osages.

Article XXXIII allows free passage through Osage territory. It is especially interesting that the right to hunt while passing through Osage territory is not mentioned, but the right to graze livestock in passage is mentioned. In a way, this provision is foretelling what is to come. That is, the passing of the hunt and the coming of the "long drive" and ranching.

It is worth noting that the Lincoln administration made no effort to either prevent this treaty from being made or to seek a treaty canceling out the Confederate treaty. This fact tends to verify the abandonment of the Osages by the Lincoln administration. Yet, when the Lincoln administration reversed their neglect, they found the Osages willing to support the federal government.

While the Osages furnished at least four hundred men to the Union forces, the Little Osages who were not in the military made the greatest single contribution to the Union. Since this is a long story, we will present it under its own heading. It should be mentioned here, however, that for every Osage who supported the Confederacy there were at least five who supported the Union. Surely the Osages had abundant reason to dislike the United States government. Yet, to the Osages, the United States government was a known factor and one favored by Fr. Schonmakers. The respected Cherokee leader, John Ross, like Fr. Schonmakers, urged neutrality. Despite the choice made by individual Osages, the tribal bond overrode any animosities toward each other. They tried to avoid fighting any units containing Osage members. When they met in combat they would break off the contact.

Confederate Officers

On May 15, 1863, the Osages undoubtedly saved Kansas from a series of devastating Indian attacks. By this time, all three of the independent Little Osage bands had located their villages on the Verdigris drainage. The Claremore Big Hills were on Big Hill Creek downstream from Independence, Kansas. All the Little Osage villages were north of Independence. Both the Big Hills and Little Osage villages were on the east side of the Verdigris. Hard Rope and eight or ten of his men had left the Big Hill village after a visit. Their intention was to go to Osage Mission before returning to their village.

They had crossed Drum Creek southeast of Independence when they spotted a group of mounted white men. Approaching the party of about twenty-two men, Hard Rope asked them to identify themselves. The men replied that they were a detachment of Union irregulars stationed at Fort Humboldt. Hard Rope told them he knew the men stationed at Humboldt, and he did not see any familiar faces among their party.

The men ignored the request of the Osages to accompany them to Fort Humboldt for identification. As they started to move away, the Osages tried to restrain them. In the ensuing scuffle, one of the white men shot and killed an Osage. Being outnumbered, Hard Rope withdrew his men and sent a messenger to the nearby Big Hill village for help.

With the Big Hill reinforcements, the Osages struck the party of white men about five miles from a loop in the Verdigris. There was a running fight in which two white men and another Osage were killed. If the white men had stayed in the open, they might have been able to hold the Osages back. However, they made for the timber bordering the loop in the Verdigris. The Osages used the timber on the flanks of the white men for shelter and ultimately forced the white men out on a gravel bar. From the tree shelter, the Osages fired upon the doomed men.

A total of twenty bodies of white men were found. Signs indicated that two wounded men had escaped. All the heads were severed from the bodies, the age-old treatment for those who intruded into Osage territory without permission.

From the uniforms and recovered papers, it was determined that these men had been Confederate officers. Their mission was to disperse among the various northern Indian nations and to stir them into attacking northern settlements. Thus, the Osages saved Kansas from a series of devastating Indian raids.[23] Later in the war, five Osages tracked down and killed two Confederate officers on the same kind of mission in Southeastern Colorado.

Maybe it is needless to say, but the Osages were greatly relieved to discover they had not killed any Union people. They had been very careful not to kill United States citizens and thus provoke a war with the United States. This is not to say they never killed Americans—it is to point out that they had never engaged in such wholesale slaughter of United States citizens at one time. In the long run, it is probable that the Osages slew more Euro-Americans than any other Indian nation. This was surely true in the pre–American period and very probably true in the American period. Yet, to most Americans, the Osages are not known as fighting Indians. In a way, this is a tribute to the skill of the Little Old Men. They conducted warfare without arousing the United States to the point of using troops against the Osages.

As we have already indicated, far more Osages followed the Union than the Confederacy. An Osage battalion served under Stand Watie, yet far more served in Colonel John Retchie's Second Indian Regiment in Kansas. The Osages were proud of this fact and did not hesitate to remind the "great white father" of this service when the occasion required it.

Refugee Indians in Osage Territory

We must not assume the Osages were the only Indian nation divided by the Civil War. With the admission of Kansas as a state in January of 1861, the last vestige of the Kansas portion of Indian Territory ceased to exist.[24] On the whole, the Indians in Kansas remained loyal to the Union. The Osages and the Indians in what remained of Indian Territory in Oklahoma were almost all divided to varying degrees. This situation created a refugee Indian problem in Kansas.

The Indians who wished to remain with the Union but lived in Indian Territory were placed in a perilous position by Lincoln's indecision. It is understandable that Lincoln had met many serious decisions in a decisive manner, but the problem of the Western Indians was characterized by indecision. Without a doubt, this was due to a lack of knowledge about Indian Territory and Indians. Lincoln's delays and reversals in Indian Affairs forced many Indians, such as some Osages, to join with the Confederacy. It was this indecision of Lincoln and positive action by the Confederacy that forced so many Indian nations to split early in the Civil War.

We must clearly understand that a split within an Indian nation over the slavery issue did not have the same effect as it did among Euro-Americans. Generally, the mutual affection of the tribal bond and respect for each other remained unchanged even though the Indian nation was divided by different views of the slavery issue. We are speaking of Indians who followed the traditional life and not of mixed-bloods who did not follow the traditional life. The dictum of "there can be no neutral ground in a Civil War" was forced upon the Indian nations by external forces. In their relationships with the Union and Confederacy, the Indian nations did not seek neutral ground, but within their own tribal organization their position tended to be tolerant and somewhat neutral toward each other.

The danger to the refugee Indians did not come from within their own tribal system, but instead it came from the nontraditional members of their own nation who followed the Confederacy and other Confederate Indians. One must bear in mind that there could be no neutral ground among the Indian nations. Tolerance was an internal matter that did not extend to external matters. Thus, a northern sympathizer among southern Indians, other than within his own tribal system, was "fair game." The same thing was true in the north. Yet the problem was greater in Oklahoma because of the sheer number of splits or divisions involved.

As more and more pro-Union Indians moved into Kansas from Indian Territory the people of Kansas demanded action.[25] Thus, the Lincoln administration was forced into making a decision to take Indian Territory. Since this was easier said than done, it should not be surprising to discover that the Union was unable to take more than a small part of Indian Territory. Hence, thousands of Indian refugees sat out the Civil War by residing in Kansas, mainly in Osage territory.

| Kansas Population Growth |||
Year	Population	% of Increase*
1854	600–700	-----
1855	8,601	12.25
1860	107,206	12.50
1870	364,399	3.50
1880	996,096	2.50
*These % figures are rounded off.		

Fig. 38. Notice the rapid growth between 1854 and 1860.

These refugees were pawns in a political power play going on in Kansas. The Creeks were in a drastic condition, but they only asked for assistance to return to Indian Territory. In the two months they spent in Kansas, 240 of them died, and more than a hundred frozen limbs were amputated.[26] The Wichitas were also in a desperate condition. They asked the Osages if they could hunt and reside at the present site of Wichita, Kansas. The Osage consent enabled the Wichitas to survive the war, and they were not molested by the Osages.[27] The Wichitas remained in Osage territory from 1863 to 1867, when they were returned to the Washita, arriving there in the spring of 1868.

In reality, not all these refugees were Wichita. Of the 1,908 Indians sheltered by the Osages as Wichitas, 392 were Wichitas, 155 were Wacos, 151 were Tawakonies, 362 were Caddos, 520 were Shawnees, 114 were Delawares, 70 were Creeks-Cherokees, and 144 were Keechies.[28] Most of the refugees were Caddoean cousins of the Wichitas that the Osages had driven to the Red River in the 1700s.

Aside from the act of mercy by the Osages to the Caddoean peoples and Creeks, the refugee problem in Kansas brought an unexpected threat to the Osages. The slavery controversy had brought a deluge of both northern and southern settlers to Kansas (see Fig. 38). Many of these were only "voting day residents," but a majority truthfully became Kansas settlers. Although intruders on Indian reservations were an old story, it all changed with the new type of intrusion into the Osage reservation.

Foremost among the characteristics of this new type of intrusion was the volume and short time span of the intrusion. Never before had so many settlers intruded on an Indian reserve in such a short time span. One must also be aware that these intruders were not the usual "woodsy intruder." In contrast to the "woodsy," these new intruders were not easily bluffed or frightened off the reserve. Generally, they were a strong, vigorous, "get things done" type of people. They were more resourceful than the typical "woodsy" in devising ways to dispossess the Indian of the land that they wanted.

These settlers made no secret about their desires; they wanted all Indians out of Kansas. This included not only the refugee Indians but those who owned lands in Kansas as well. Senator James Lane of Kansas had ambitions that agreed with the settlers' desires. In 1864, he managed to pilot a bill through Congress to remove the refugee Indians from Kansas. Under the guise of removing refugee Indians, the bill included a provision to extinguish *all Indian land titles in Kansas.*[29] An insight into the settlers' conscience, or rather their lack of conscience, is their comment on removal as "an act of justice to the Indians and to the people of Kansas."[30]

INDIAN RECONSTRUCTION

Indian Reconstruction was different in some respects from Reconstruction in the Confederate and border states, although it did share the bitterness and vindictiveness. Fortunately for the Osages, they were spared the foul breath of Indian Reconstruction. After 1865, the Cherokee and the five tribes no longer were favored by treaties that took from the Osages to benefit the five nations. While this did not place the Osages in a favored position, it did place them in a position to receive some consideration as an outgrowth of their support of the Union.

Because of their participation in the Confederate Treaty, the Osages were represented at the Reconstruction Council held in September of 1865 at Fort Smith, Arkansas. Although the Council was primarily intended for the five nations, many other nations were also represented. Besides the Osages there were members of the Wichita, Caddo, Seneca, Shawnee, Quapaw, and Wyandot (Huron) attending.[31]

During the thirteen-day council, the concessions the five nations would have to make to resume relations with the United States were discussed. The four basic concessions had a considerable effect on both the Osages and the Indian Territory in the years between 1865 and 1907. These are as follows:

1) each tribe must enter into a treaty for permanent peace and amity among themselves and with the United States;
2) slavery must be abolished and steps taken to incorporate the freedmen into the tribes as citizens with rights guaranteed;
3) each tribe must agree to surrender a portion of its lands to the United States for colonizing tribes from Kansas and elsewhere; and
4) tribal leaders must agree to the policy of uniting all tribes of the Indian Territory into a single, consolidated government."[32]

Concessions three and four were the two that had the most effect on the Osages. It was the third requirement that made it possible for the Osages to buy their present reservation. The Osages clung to the fourth requirement, which was meant to create an Indian State, until 1907. They were the last Indians to give up the dream of the Indian state. In lieu of an Indian state, the Osages demanded that their reservation be kept intact as one governmental unit if they were to agree to become a part of the proposed state of Oklahoma. This is why Osage County and the Osage reservation have identical boundaries.

IN THE WAKE OF THE FOUR HORSEMEN

The Osages had met the four horsemen. They paid a terrible price as the horsemen rode roughshod among the people, but they survived. They emerged from this terrible period decimated and sapped of energy as well as resources. They were sick of the white man and only wanted to place distance between themselves and the Euro-Americans. The Osage people had now reached another bend in the River of Life. Was this to be the seventh bend that would spell the end of the people or was it merely the second or third bend?

What the Osages needed, more than anything else, was to be alone so they could be themselves again. These starved, punished, invaded, betrayed people who survived the charge of the four horsemen were hardly recognizable as the once proud and free Osages. Yet they had the undying spirit of a people seasoned by adversity that carried them into survival and to eventual conquest of the evils that beset them. This, above all else, saved the Osages—they believed in themselves. They could and would solve the problems they faced. They were a people with a hidden character trait of steel tempered by ages of survival.

PART FOUR

The Euro-American Affliction, 1865–1875

12

The Outcasts

COMMENTARY ON PART FOUR

Between 1865 and 1872, the great Osage people experienced fantastic indignities. An Osage scholar has pointed out: "Doubtless the discovery and narration of these facts will be disturbing to every Osage now living as they will be embarrassing to the living descendants of the old rugged, American pioneers. But Osage history is not for the sensitive soul who would avoid unpleasant facts."[1]

History always involves the pursuit and interpretation of truth. A person may take truth and, according to that person's own interpretation, use it to praise or condemn. Too often in the past, the facts have been used to condemn the Osages and to praise other peoples.

There seems, however, to be a consensus among historians that the Osages were terribly wronged in their last removal. The evidence is so conclusive that it is revolting to any perceptive mind. Thus, for the reader, Part Four of this history could be very disturbing.

BACKGROUNDS

Introduction

The Osage and Kansas Indians considered that they had owned and occupied the eastern one-third of Kansas since before 1700. That is, they had occupied this area in the Indian sense of occupation. In the Euro-American sense, the Osages had occupied this area since only shortly before 1825. After that date, Eastern Indians had been moved into the region. Thus, the eastern one-third of Kansas became a wall of Indian nations which stood in the way of the expansion-minded Euro-Americans who were stalled on Missouri's western border.

Thanks to Pike's label of The Great American Desert, most Euro-Americans were not interested in the Great Plains. But it was necessary to cross the Plains in order to reach the woodlands of the Far West. Generally, Indians were willing to grant passage to the Far Western emigrants. Such agreements were ancient Indian practices. Yet, Indian custom required a gift for passage and a conservation of wildlife while traversing the hunting grounds. Widespread abuse of these customs by Euro-Americans was a constant source of friction among the cultures.

For about one hundred twenty-five years, the Osages had acted as a barrier to Euro-Americans seeking to cross the Plains. Without a doubt, this Osage barrier shielded the Plains nations from the Euro-Americans. As the Osage shield became broken and shattered, the Plains nations felt the full impact of the Euro-American affliction.

Being relatively inexperienced in Indian and Euro-American relationships, the Plains Indians tried to repel the intruders by force. Thus, a series of Indian wars erupted upon the Plains after 1865. Unfortunately for the Plains people, they faced a battle-hardened military force armed with the most advanced weapons of Western civilization.

These Plains wars turned the frontier people against all Indians. Thus, defeat of the Plains nations created an atmosphere of contempt toward Indians in general. This was a prime factor in generating the disregard for Osage rights and brought about the demand for their removal. So, the Indian wars on the Plains are also an important part of Osage history.

Viewpoints

As humans, we see the world through a window of beliefs. While this gives us a sharp focus on what we want to see, it sometimes prevents us from seeing how wrong we are. Therefore, it is important that we understand how Euro-Americans saw the Indian during any given period.

Jefferson set the pattern for beliefs about Indians during his generation. He saw the Indian as a farmer who through intermarriage would become a Euro-American. By the end of the Civil War (1865), Euro-Americans had radically revised this Jeffersonian view. In this period, the Indian was regarded as one of the "damned." Thus, the "elect" was ordained by God to, "Be fruitful, and multiply, and replenish the earth, and subdue it."[2] Indians had rejected the Christian God and the Euro-American civilization. In doing this, they were damned and could not be saved. These actions were taken as a clear indication that God meant for the Euro-Americans to have the Indian lands.

These concepts became especially harsh after they had been filtered through the minds of the Civil War generals. The commander of the Military Division of the Missouri, Lt. Gen. P. H. Sheridan, had this to say in

1882: "the majority of the wasteful and hostile occupants of millions of acres of valuable agricultural, pasture, and mineral lands [had] been forced upon reservations under the supervision of the Government . . . and the vast section over which the wild and irresponsible tribes once wandered [were] redeemed from idle waste to become homes for millions of progressive people."[3]

Sheridan uses some words (i.e., "wasteful," "hostile," "wild," "irresponsible," and "wandered") that carry a heavy cargo. It would be interesting to carefully analyze these terms and compare them with truth. In contrast to the derogatory terms used against Indians, the sweet, heroic words used to describe the achievements of Western civilization stand out. We will have reason in this chapter and those following to examine the meaning of the words, "been forced upon reservations under the supervision of the government."

The United States' experience with the Plains Indians involves more than regional history. One must view the evolution of attitudes toward the Indian as a part of the worldwide expansion of the United States. As the Indian was treated, so were other people in the so-called third world treated. In a sense, Indians were placed in the same category as the peoples of any other subjugated nation. Yet Indians often hear of the fiction of sovereignty. The Euro-Americans illogically treat Indians as a conquered people, acknowledging that they had been sovereign yet, at the same time, denying that they had ever been sovereign.

Government Relationships

There can be no doubt that puppet rulers were created among the Indian nations. This was a natural outgrowth of the Euro-American concept of the strong-leader government.[4] That Indian peoples limited the power of their leaders and placed the real power in the hands of the people did not matter. Thus, to treat with the Euro-Americans, Indians were forced to restructure their political organization. As long as the Indian held the power over Euro-Americans, they went through the formalities of treating through a pseudo strong leader merely as a matter of courtesy to guests in their territory. It is interesting to note, however, that the United States created their own version of government in the later insular possessions.

Anatole France once remarked, "The law is enforced with fine impartiality, rich and poor alike are hung for sleeping under bridges." France was making a distinction between law and justice. Too many of us assume the two are one and the same. "Justice Holmes argues in *The Common Law* (1881) that law only reflects the standards of a majority, not the will of God or even more sensitive consciences."[5] When one fully considers the implication of these quotes a chilling thought enters the mind. What was done to the Osages and other Indians in Kansas was surely not just, but *it was done legally under United States law.*

As one reads the views of some government officials, an utter contempt toward Indians is revealed. Congressional Acts with Indian consent had been substituted for treaty-making in 1871, but even this did not satisfy some officials. Commissioner Edward P. Smith remarked in 1873: "We have in theory over sixty-five independent nations within our borders, with whom we have entered into treaty relations as being sovereign peoples; and at the same time the white agent is sent to control and supervise these foreign powers, and care for them as wards of the government. So far, and as rapidly as possible, all recognition of Indians in any other relation than strictly as subjects of the Government should cease."[6]

We can clearly see that the attitudes and views of the majority were also reflected by the United States government in its laws. It was in Kansas as a product of the Indian Wars and removal that these views solidified into an organized concept.

Manifest Destiny

As early as 1837, in a Phi Beta Kappa speech, Horace Bushnell stated: "there are too many prophetic signs admonishing us, that Almighty Providence is pre-engaged to make this a truly great nation. . . . This western world had not been preserved unknown through so many ages, for any purpose less than sublime, than to be opened, at a certain stage of history, to become the theater wherein better principles might have their action and free development. Out of all the inhabitants of the world, too, a select stock, the Saxon, and out of this the British family, the noblest of the stock, was chosen to people our country."[7] The egoism and absolute ethnocentrism so obvious in this speech was typical of Manifest Destiny.

We have often heard the adage, "As the twig is bent, so grows the tree." A parody of this is, "What a nation practices at home, it practices abroad." Indian policy, which was based upon Manifest Destiny, is a classic example of this rule. Treatment of the Indian set the pattern for treatment of third world people.

Manifest Destiny was clearly present in Commissioner Francis A. Walker's Annual Report in 1872:

> No one will rejoice more heartily than the present Commissioner when the Indians of this country cease to be in a position to dictate, in any form or degree, to the Government; when, in fact, the last hostile tribe becomes reduced to the condition of supplicants for charity.

This is, indeed, the only hope of salvation for the aborigines of the continent. If they stand up against the progress of civilization and industry, they must be relentlessly crushed. The westward course of population is neither to be denied nor delayed for the sake of all the Indians that ever called this country their home. They must yield or perish; and there is something that savors of providential mercy in the rapidity with which their fate advances upon them, leaving them scarcely the chance to resist before they shall be surrounded and disarmed.[8]

One may argue that the Commissioner was stating conditions as they were and were yet to be. However, a person in a position to influence the direction of events could also do more than reflect the *status quo*. This would be especially true when that person was charged with the responsibility of attending to the affairs of Indians as a trust requirement.

We would be generating a great injustice if we did not point out that efforts were made to stem the tide of Manifest Destiny. While these efforts did not materially aid the Indian, it is possible they eased the impact somewhat. It is more significant that there were individuals who did make a sincere effort to prevent a great wrong. Such people, who are present in all societies both great and small, lift humanity above the level of beasts.

The Indian Condition

Commissioner Walker, despite his weakness as a leader in Indian reform, was an excellent observer. His summation of the Indian condition and its cause is accurate and to the point:

> The freedom of expansion which is working these results is to us of incalculable value. To the Indian it is of incalculable cost. Every year's advance of our frontier takes in a territory as large as some kingdoms of Europe. We are richer by hundreds of millions; the Indian is poorer by a large part of the little that he has. This growth is bringing imperial greatness to the nation; to the Indian it brings wretchedness, destitution, beggary. Surely, there is obligation found in considerations like these, requiring us in some way, and in the best way, to make good to these original owners of the soil the loss by which we so greatly gain.[9]

The Commissioner did not stand alone in his observations of the Indian's condition. On November 23, 1869, the first Report of the Board of Indian Commissioners was made. While this report also reflected the same observations as the Commissioner's Report, it also contained a long list of suggested reforms.[10]

We do not want to saturate the reader with the wrongs wrought against Indians. Our purpose in touching upon these topics is to show what was done and why it was done. Wars are usually the result of real or imagined wrongs that have accumulated over time. As Jefferson expressed it in the Declaration of Independence, "a decent respect to the opinions of mankind requires that they should declare the causes which impel them to the separation." This is followed by a long list of real and imagined wrongs the colonists had suffered under George III.

The preceding topics give the reasons that drove the Plains Indians to go to war against the United States. We have seen how views shape policy. Now we will see the effect of these policies and views.

INDIAN WARS ON THE PLAINS

Sand Creek and the "Hancock War"

While many Indian nations went to war on the Plains, some did not. Black Kettle tried at first to keep his Cheyennes at peace. After requesting a peace council, Black Kettle camped on Sand Creek near Fort Lyon, Colorado. As a peace sign, he flew the United States flag on a tall pole.

In November of 1864, Colonel J. M. Chivington and the Third Colorado Cavalry fell upon Black Kettle's people. Without any warning or provocation, men, women, and children were killed without mercy. Chivington claimed they killed five hundred Indians. Black Kettle survived to later enter the fight against American troops, only to be killed in the Battle of the Washita.[11]

This wanton act of violence against the Cheyenne shocked the nation and brought some efforts toward reform. However, after 1864 most of the Plains people were distrustful of the United States military forces and the intent of the government. Thus, when General W. S. Hancock sought to bring peace to the Plains by a display of manpower supported by artillery, he found the Indian elusive, combative, and not the least terrorized. The so-called Hancock War was a total failure. Some argue that Custer was made the scapegoat for this failure. Certainly Custer was relieved of his duties for a year at the close of the Hancock War.[12]

Medicine Lodge

Because of Hancock's failure, a treaty commission came to the Plains in the summer of 1867. This commission held one of the largest known Indian councils at Medicine Lodge, Kansas, in the Osage reserve. Approximately five thousand Indians attended this council, and some estimates go much higher. The Osages were there as uninvited observers, since their traditional enemies the Comanches, Kiowas, Kiowa-Apache, Arapahoes, and Cheyennes were the main participants.[13] Also attending was *Isadawah*, the head Wichita chief who was later slain by an Osage mourning party. The Osages appeared only twice, each time either merely to observe or to insult the Euro-Americans. Among the Prairie/Plains tribes, to eat a person's food and then leave without a word or sign is the supreme insult. Since the Osages demanded food and the Euro-Americans supplied it, the direction of the insult was clear. The insult was not directed to the other Indians present, and they were well aware of this.

It was a nervous collection of Euro-Americans who camped on Medicine Lodge Creek in the fall of 1867. Recognizing that the few hundred troops, reporters, and commissioners could be easily overcome by the Indians made them nervous. They well knew the Indians had reason enough, and more, to destroy them all. One of the reporters who was then working for the *Missouri Democrat* was Henry M. Stanley, who later achieved fame as the discoverer of Dr. Livingstone in Africa.[14]

The Cheyenne were making medicine down on the Cimarron and thus would be late. On October 19, 1867, the Arapahoes, Apaches, Comanches, and Kiowas started the Council. While the Arapahoes were present, they decided to wait and council with the Cheyenne. Both sides spent considerable time airing their problems.

On October 21, a prepared treaty was laid on the table. By October 25, all but the Cheyenne and Arapaho had signed the treaty, which ceded thousands of acres to the United States. Of special interest to the Osages was an agreement to grant hunting privileges south of the Arkansas River to the nations signing the treaty.[15] One wonders where the United States acquired the authority to grant this privilege allowing these nations to hunt in recognized Osage territory.

After the Council, presents were brought out and placed in three great piles. The middle mound was for the Cheyenne, the eastern heap was for the Kiowa and Comanche, and the remaining pile to the west was for the Arapaho and Apache. Aside from these gifts, vast amounts of food, clothing, and ammunition were also distributed.[16]

The Treaty of Medicine Lodge brought an uneasy peace to the Plains for a time. However, hostilities began again in the fall of 1868. As another series of wars developed, the Osages entered the conflict as scouts for the troops.

The Battle of Arickaree Creek

General Sherman received reports of about two hundred Indians moving into northwest Kansas from Colorado. Sherman dispatched Colonel Forsythe and fifty experienced frontiersmen to check the movements of these Indians. This force camped on a branch of the Republican Fork called Arickaree Creek.[17]

At dawn on September 11, Indians were discovered. The command took a position on nearby Beecher's Island and repelled the first charge. A second charge was led by Roman Nose, the Cheyenne chief. Roman Nose was killed and the attack ceased. Dull Knife led the third charge, which was also turned back. A scout managed to reach Ft. Wallace with news of the continuing battle, and troops were immediately sent to relieve the besieged force.[18]

This battle of several days duration set off a series of engagements throughout the Central Plains. General Sheridan had been placed in command of the South Central Plains. He immediately prepared for a winter campaign against the Plains Indians. One of his first actions was to restore Custer as commander of the Seventh cavalry.[19]

The Battle of the Washita

The Osage Scouts

Most of the Central Plains Indians were wintering in Southwest Oklahoma during the winter of 1868–69. Sheridan was having a considerable amount of trouble locating the Indian camps and even more trouble in forcing a fight.

Custer sent an officer to White Hair's village to see if Osage scouts could be obtained. He knew the Osages had successfully fought the Plains Indians for over a hundred years. If he could obtain Osage scouts, their experience would be valuable to his forces. Little Beaver of the White Hair Little Osages and his counselor Hard Rope, with eleven warriors and an interpreter, agreed to scout for Custer. These fourteen Osage scouts were paid the regular soldier's pay, plus they were given weapons, clothing, and a mount.[20]

The last of the Osage scouts to die was Big Wild Cat. Custer was called *Paw hu Stet sy* (Long Hair) by the Osages. C. J. Phillips was one of the two editors of *The Osage Magazine* in 1910, but in 1892 he ran a trading post. Big Wild Cat came into the post one day and ordered a silk American flag. It was eight feet long, like the one Custer carried on the Washita. Big Wild Cat wanted it to fly over his grave so everyone would know a soldier was buried there.[21]

Hard Rope was another of Custer's scouts. He was one of the signers of the protest against the Sturgis or Drum Creek Treaty. As mentioned earlier, he was also one of the leaders in the fight against the Confederate officers near Independence, Kansas. On March 29, 1869, Custer gave Hard Rope the following citation: "Hard Rope, the bearer, is head war chief of the Osages. He was with me on all my marches and campaigns since Nov. 1, 1868, par–

ticipating in the battle of the Washita, and particularly distinguishing himself by his skill in discovering and following trails. He is a man of excellent judgement, and is a true friend of the white man."[22]

Eugene "Gene" Herard of Elgin, Kansas, loved to tell this tale about Hard Rope: "Some years ago delegations of Pawnees and Osages were conferring near Elgin, Kansas, trying to adjust a claim of the Pawnees for one of their members killed by the Osages. Hard Rope appeared late, after the conference had lasted all day without results. He stood for nearly an hour without saying a word. Then he held up his hand and said to the Pawnees: 'We give you fifty ponies and you go home. You can't kill any Osages. If you don't take horses and go home, we kill you.'"[23]

The only other member of this group of Osage scouts for whom accurate identification exists is Little Beaver. Little Beaver is *Shop pe Shin ka* in Osage. The Osage Mission Register gives his name as *Shabeskinga* and Biever. His second daughter was Marie *Me Gra to* or Hawk Woman.[24] This would indicate that Little Beaver was from the Mottled Eagle Clan. The Register also identifies Little Beaver's Town as Briar's Town. This was only three miles southeast of the Mission and very near the mixed-blood settlement on Flat Rock Creek. The Little Beaver who was among Custer's scouts and signed the Confederate treaty was John Beaver or Little Beaver II. In his old age he shared the chief's office with Sophia Chouteau, who was called Mother Chouteau.

The Battle

Sheridan's troops did a considerable amount of moving around. They finally arrived at Camp Supply, which is at the junction of Wolf and Beaver Creeks in Oklahoma. This was on the south side of the North Canadian River about thirty-five miles east of the 100th Meridian.[25]

Custer left Camp Supply early on the morning of November 23, 1868. The attack of Black Kettle's village was at dawn on November 27.[26] For once, the impatient Custer listened to good Osage advice and held back his attack until dawn. After a rest of about an hour, Custer visited among the various clusters of shivering men. It was very cold and sleep was all but impossible without fires.

The Osages did not tell Custer until after the battle that they did not entirely trust him. It was their belief that if the battle did not go well, Custer would betray them to the Cheyenne. Thinking that they could best protect themselves behind the standard bearer, they took this position in the attack. By virtue of this position, they were in the midst of the heaviest fighting.[27]

Custer had divided his command of eight hundred men into four nearly equal parts. Each section was to attack the village from a different direction.

Thus, the Cheyenne were caught in a trap with little chance of escape. Custer reported 103 warriors killed and sixteen women and a "few" children.[28]

An interesting sidelight to the Osage association with Custer is given in the Kansas Historical Collections. The citation states: "Some of these Osages [Washita Scouts] were killed in the massacre of Custer and his army on the Little Bighorn river in Montana."[29] We had heard a rumor in our youth that an Osage and Delaware were with Custer on the Little Bighorn and had escaped by mingling with the attacking Indians. In any event, no real proof of either story has been found.

REPUDIATION OF THE MEDICINE LODGE TREATY

The Peace Commission was outraged by the renewal of hostilities on the Plains in the summer of 1868. The blame was placed on the Indians, so the recommendation of the Commission to repudiate the treaty would seem to be justified. They suggested abrogating the right to hunt south of the Arkansas River to limit the hunting area. Also, the suggestion was made that these Indians should be confined to their reservations.[30] In time, some of these restrictions were also placed upon the Osages. An uneasy peace settled over the Plains after the Battle of the Washita. However, only the military force of the United States restrained the Plains people.

General Sherman had already abrogated the right to hunt anywhere south of the Arkansas River. Little effort was made to punish the Indians causing the outbreaks. Peaceful people were more easily located and punished. Ralph K. Andrist notes that "the Army subscribed to the genial theory that one Indian was as good as another for purposes of punishment, and neither Sherman nor Sheridan was going to change the system."[31]

It was this way of thinking that caused the Kansas intruders to treat the Osages as if they were blood-thirsty savages. There can be little doubt that the Indian wars on the Plains gave the intruders additional ammunition to use against the Osages. These wars provided the necessary emotions for actions that lay outside normality. Without this emotional stimuli, it is likely that the Osage removal would have been much easier.

In the physical sciences, we are told that nature abhors a vacuum. The same law seems to be present in human relationships. If government does not enforce its laws, lawless acts will fill the void and replace the order of law. High emotions and the failure of the United States to enforce its own Indian laws brought the Osages to their lowest stage of degradation.

13

Osage Land Cession of 1865

CANVILLE TREATY

The Unratified Treaty of 1863

In response to the intruders' desires for Osage lands in the rich Neosho Valley, an effort was made to extinguish the Osage title. A treaty was made in 1863 with this purpose in mind. 1,500 square miles of area was to be taken from the eastern part of the Osage reserve. The total price to be paid was $300,000.[1]

A second cession of a trust area twenty miles wide along the north side of the Osage reserve was also made. The Kansas school sections of sixteen and thirty-six were to be set aside in the trust area but not in the ceded lands along the Neosho River. A total of twenty-five cents an acre was to be paid to the Osages for these trust lands. However, when the treaty was again submitted to the Osages for amendment, they refused the terms and the treaty died.[2]

One important point that was omitted in the proposed treaty of 1863 was included in the treaty of 1865. No mention is made of the eventual removal of the Osages in the proposed treaty of 1863. This may seem surprising in light of the known Kansas policy of removing all Indians from the state.[3] Yet if one considers the need to keep the Osages friendly to the Union it made sense not to antagonize them during the Civil War.

Reasons for the Treaty of 1865

There can be no room for doubt that the basic reason for the Treaty of 1865 and eventual Osage removal was the desire for Osage lands. These reasons are stated by Superintendent Elijah Sells, who negotiated the Canville Treaty of 1865 with the Osages: "The Osage Reservation is within the geographical limits of the State of Kansas, and white settlements are crowding down upon Indian lands and in many instances within the Indian reservation. The imminent danger of conflict between the whites and the Indians as well as the demands for these lands for white settlement by the authorities of and settlers in Kansas furnishes satisfactory reasons why the Indian title to these lands should be extinguished at an early date."[4]

The Canville Treaty contained some unusual wording. While we will discuss this in the next section, we must point out that the intent of the treaty was not to provide benefits to the enemies of the Osages. In effect, this was clearly a nonreason for the treaty. Instructions to the Treaty Commissioners make it very clear "that no part of such ceded lands shall be appropriated to Indians not on friendly relations with the party making the cession."[5]

Through interpretation of the unusual wording, the BIA was enabled to create a "slush fund" for all Indians and some Negroes. The Osage ceded lands totaled 871,791.11 acres. From the sale of these lands, the cost of surveying the tract and $300,000 were subtracted. A balance of $776,931.58 was deposited in a "slush fund" which was called the "Civilization Fund." Money from this fund was spent for the benefit of Indians friendly and unfriendly to the Osages, which was a violation of the spirit of the treaty. The Osage and Kaw together received only $189.55 from this fund.[6]

CIVILIZATION FUND

The Problem

Article One of the Canville Treaty contains an excess of legal jargon. Over and above the usual "legalese," a key section of the article contains poor sentence structure. This section comes near the end of the Article, which is exceptionally long and complicated: "[T]he remaining proceeds of sales shall be placed in the Treasury of the United States to the credit of the 'Civilization fund' to be used under the direction of the Secretary of the Interior for the education and civilization of Indian tribes residing within the limits of the United States."[7]

Over one hundred tribes benefited from this fund. It was not the Osage intent to be the benefactor to all these Indians. Their great concern was that they did not want their money to be expended to aid the Osages who had gone to Mexico and Canada during the War of 1812 and the Civil War.[8] Thus, in an effort to exclude those who had abandoned the Osage people, an unintended wording was introduced into the treaty.

The bulk of the money placed in the Civilization Fund was used to establish and maintain certain "Indian" schools. Among these were Hampton School; Carlisle School; Forest Grove School, Oregon; Pacific University, Oregon; Octanah School; Freedman School; Albuquerque School; Salem

School; Genoa School; Fort Stevensen School, North Dakota; Howard University at Washington; and Haskell Institute at Lawrence, Kansas. None of these schools were for the exclusive benefit of the Osages. Most of them were of no benefit whatsoever to the Osages and at least Hampton School, Freedman School, and Howard University were not for Indians in a reconstruction legal sense.[9]

After years of protest and expense, the Osages were finally paid for this injustice, insofar as the money was concerned. However, there is no way to assess the suffering and deaths among the Osage people because of such a long delayed payment. The battle to claim what was theirs is a long, classic example of Indian Policy fumblings.

Reasons for Delaying Objections

The Osages voiced protest of the Civilization Fund provision at the council negotiating the Drum Creek Treaty in 1868. Article Eight of the Drum Creek Treaty states: "If the proceeds of the sale of the lands ceded to the United States by the first article of the treaty of January 21, 1867 [ratification date of Canville Treaty], shall exceed the amount of purchase money paid therefor by the United States and expenses incident to the survey and sale thereof then the remaining proceeds shall be invested by the Osages in United States registered stocks and the interest thereon applied semi-annually as other annuities."[10] Without a doubt the Osages thought the problem was corrected, although the Drum Creek Treaty was not ratified. By 1870, the failure of the treaty to pass in the Senate again stirred the Osages.

The United States had enacted legislation to make it easier for settlers to purchase land in the Osage ceded tract. This delayed the flow of money from land sales, so it did not become evident until after 1870 that surplus monies were being diverted into the Civilization Fund.[11]

One must bear in mind that in 1865 the Osages were in a terrible condition because of the controversy over slavery. The swarm of intruders upon their reserve between 1865 and 1870 only worsened their plight. They desperately needed the annuities from the sale of the ceded and trust lands. The removal in 1870–75 added to the troubles of the Osage, who could best be described at this time as being on the edge of extinction. Thus, this was not a simple matter of dollars that were eventually repaid but a matter of great suffering and loss of life because of governmental blunders.

All previous treaties made with the Osages had provided that the total benefits were to devolve upon the Osages. They had no reason to suspect that a new principle in treaty-making had been introduced in this last ratified Osage treaty. One claim notes that this is "the first and only time in the history of Indian treaties or agreements in which the United States had acquired the lands of one Indian Tribe and used the proceeds of its sale for the benefit of other Indians."[12]

Communication Problems

Surely a major problem of communication is evident in the time consumed in the negotiation. At Canville's Post, a total elapsed time of three hours was used in making the treaty.[13] The southern Osages at Ft. Smith were probably rushed through the process as well, but the record is silent on this point. A convention of Philadelphia lawyers could not fully understand this treaty in three hours.

All negotiations were conducted with the full-bloods. Few among them, if any, were fluent in English. The mixed-bloods, like the interpreters, spoke frontier English and limited Osage. English was a recently acquired language, and most of the mixed-bloods were more accustomed to French. In any event, none among the full-bloods or mixed-bloods were familiar with the legal language used in the treaty.[14]

Possibly the greatest communication problem was the Osage language itself. The language consists of a few hundred root words (estimated as 2,000) which are compounded to enlarge meanings. This is a language of a hunting culture. It is rich in terms of its own culture, but it is barren in terms of the legal language of Western civilization. For example when *Ne ka Shu tsy* (Red Man) is used, it signifies the Indians being addressed. When speaking of other Indian people, the name of the tribe is used. The word *U Ke te* means "others" or "foreign," but it is also an insult, so it would not be used in treaty negotiating.[15] Thus, the Osages would have a very different interpretation of Article One than its various meanings in English.

Comments on the Error

The United States and their representatives made two admissions of the error in creating the Civilization Fund. First, admission was made in Article Eight of the Drum Creek Treaty. Another admission was made by a 1941 Senate Committee on Indian Affairs: "These Indians who have been denied relief under a technical legal construction of the acts of Congress are morally and equitably entitled to the sum which the United States received and expended for the relief of other Indian Tribes."[16]

An inherent conflict exists in the strange relationship between the United States and the Indian nations. It is to avoid similar conflicts that the legislative, judicial, and executive powers of the United States government are separated. In the guardian-ward relationship, the conflict arises when the guardian also acts as an adversary in bargaining. Thus it is easy for abuses to enter the relationship.

In the Treaty of 1865, the United States, acting in its own interest, neglected the interests of its ward. In the language of Indian law this is termed overreachment, in view of the Osage naivety. Thus, while the United States acted honorably in its own right, it committed a dishonorable act toward its Osage wards. Recognizing the error in this conflict of interest and correcting it was an act of justice.

The Treaty of 1865 is especially notable because it precipitated a whole chain of events. One cannot discuss Osage removal from Kansas without including this treaty and the storm it generated among the Osages, the Kansas intruders, and settlers, as well as the railroad corporations. From 1865 to 1871, the history of Southeast Kansas was heavily influenced by this treaty. To some extent, it shaped and gave impetus to the Populist Revolt in Kansas.

THE OSAGE LANDS IN KANSAS

School Lands

Neosho and Labette counties in Kansas were what had been called the Osage Ceded Lands. The Treaty of 1865 did not provide for any school land grants in this cession. However, by a congressional Act of April 10, 1869, sections sixteen and thirty-six of both the Ceded and Trust Lands were set aside for schools. Thus, 22,408 acres were set aside in Labette County and 20,480 acres in Neosho County.[17]

Sections sixteen and thirty-six were not always available, since they were sometimes preempted. The Kansas state constitution provides for this eventuality in Section Three, Part One: "*First*—That sections numbered sixteen and thirty-six, in every township of public lands in said State, and where either of said sections or any part thereof has been sold or otherwise been disposed of, other lands, equivalent thereto, and as contiguous as may be, shall be granted to said State for the use of schools."[18] This insured that Kansas education would be financed. However, the special Act of April 10, 1869, was necessary because of school lands omission in the Treaty of 1865. The wording of the key part of the Act is interesting, "And provided, further, That the sixteenth and thirty-sixth sections in each township of said lands [Ceded and Trust Lands] shall be reserved for State school purposes In accordance with the act of admission of the State of Kansas: Provided, however, That nothing in this act shall be construed in any manner affecting any legal rights heretofore vested in any other party or parties."[19]

The last proviso of this act raises the question, Did the Osages still have a vested legal right in the Ceded Lands? They surely had a legal trust interest in the Trust Lands. However, the problem at hand is to determine if the Osages were ever paid for the school sections in the Ceded Lands.

Action on this question was not taken by Congress until the spring of 1880. Chapter 251 of the Act of June 16, 1880, deals with this question. Section One deals with the Trust Lands and provides payment for the Kansas school sections in the Trust Area. The last proviso of Section Two deals with the Ceded Lands: "Provided that a like settlement shall be made with the Indian-civilization fund for the sixteenth and thirty-sixth sections, given by the United States to the State of Kansas, within the limits of the Osage lands, ceded by the first article of the treaty aforsaid."[20] This act makes a clear point that, while the Osages were paid for the school sections in the Trust Lands, they were not paid for the school sections in the Ceded Lands until much later, and then only by indirect means.

Since the Civilization Fund received the school sections money for the Ceded Lands, ultimately, the Osages were paid for the land. As mentioned earlier through the Claims Cases, the Civilization Fund less the expenses (off-set) was paid to the Osages in recent years.

Ceded Lands

Railroad Land Sales

Many intruders had made illegal improvements within what later became the Osage Ceded Lands. This was, in part, done with the supposition that the Homestead and Preemption Act of 1862 would prevail in the Ceded Tract. Unfortunately for these intruders, the Treaty of 1865 specifically set aside the Act of 1862 insofar as the Ceded Lands were concerned. This was done so the railroads could take up all the Ceded Lands as their right of ways and land grants.

Frederic Jackson Turner, the original frontier historian, identified two types of pioneer farmers. The first was the "woodsy," people who went into the Indian lands and built their "half-face" camps or crude cabins. If possible, they took over Indian "old fields." If this was not possible, they made "girdled clearings." These were the improvements that they either sold to the second pioneer farmer or used as the basis for their preemption claim.

The second type of pioneer farmer was what Jackson called the equipment farmer. This settler was fairly well financed and had some personal property for collateral. The railroads had no more use for the first type of pioneer farmer than the Indians. It was the equipment farmer who bought the railroad lands and paid the woodsy for his improvements.

As Gates points out, the railroads used the improvements as a selling point: "To the wealthier and more conservative class of immigrants who follow in the wake of adventurous pioneers, who value railroad facilities and the advantages of a comparatively well settled country, and are willing to pay something for them, no better opportunity can be found than is here afforded to buy land on which a commencement has already been made."[21]

The Leavenworth, Lawrence, and Galveston Railroad Company was the main beneficiary from the Osage Ceded Lands. In probability, most of the land sold by the LL&G in 1871–72 was from the Ceded Lands. In this time span, 42,539 acres were sold. The average price was $8.15 an acre.[22] Originally, the Osages received about 35 cents an acre. Approximately three cents per acre was used to pay for the survey and selling costs to the United States. The LL&G acquired the land for $1.25 an acre.

No matter how you compute it, a minimum profit of over $29,000,000 is an amount that bewilders the mind. Something surely seems amiss when the Osage share was only about one thirty-fourth of the total price obtained. However, by 1878 the LL&G had lost the unsold Osage Ceded Lands. Since the Osages did not have the franchise, their complaints were not effective. But the settlers did have a vote and, hence, the Ceded Lands were placed in the public domain, though not without a bitter struggle.

The Ceded Lands Controversy

The Railroad Land Grant Act of March 1863[23] set the scene for a historic struggle that was not to end until about 1875. This act made the Leavenworth, Lawrence, and Galveston the beneficiary of land grants in Kansas. In 1866, a similar Act added the Missouri, Kansas, and Texas railroad to the same land grant provisions.[24] Without a doubt, the congressional intent was to encourage railway construction in sparsely settled Kansas. However, it soon became apparent that the land grants had become as important as operating a railroad. Railways, as land vendors, customarily sold land at a higher price than the government. This price was usually double or triple the standard price of $1.25 an acre charged by the government. It was this price differential and not solicitations about the welfare of the Osages that aroused controversy.

The debate centered around the status of the land immediately after and during the ending of the Osage title. No question was raised about the status of land already in the public domain. However, there was a very real question about Indian lands acquired by treaty.[25] The question was whether Osage lands could pass directly into private ownership without entering the public domain. If the answer was "no," the settler stood to gain land at a lower cost or to have the Homestead and Preemption laws applied to newly acquired Indian lands. As already noted, the railroads stood to gain a vast fortune if the newly acquired Indian lands could pass directly into private ownership. The Osages stood at the end of the line in this battle of the settlers versus the railroads.

More than land was involved in the Osage Ceded Lands controversy. This controversy spilled over into the Drum Creek Treaty ratification attempt. Both treaties, the Treaty of 1865 and Drum Creek, involved the new commercial–industrial favoritism that had emerged from the Civil War. Corporate businesses grew by leaps and bounds in the immediate post–war days. Leading this new unregulated corporate growth was the railroad corporations.

No ethical guide to corporate action was available, since developments on such a large scale were new to the American experience. In some respects, the fur trade had established a pattern for corporate growth and operation, but it was on a smaller scale. The Senate was a smaller body than the House by virtue of limiting each state to two senators. Since the lower house was selected by a popular vote, the House was more directly accountable to the electorate than the Senate. State legislators selected the two national senators for their state. This made the senators answerable to the state legislatures and not the voters. Therefore, whoever controlled the state legislature controlled the senators from that state.

This arrangement was an open invitation to the corporations. With their pooled finance, it was easy for a corporation to "buy an election." Also, a favorable loan or gift could frequently buy a senatorial vote. Senators were often supported by influential Indian Affairs officials who stood to profit handsomely if key treaties were ratified or special laws were enacted. Thus, Indian land cessions in Kansas were made by treaty as usual, but the land was ceded to the railroad corporations. Like the preeminence of the corporations, this was new to the American experience and a means to combat it did not evolve until the ratification of the Osage Treaty of 1865.

The railroads had practically won their battle for the Osage Ceded Lands when the settlers took their case to the courts. Although the Supreme Court was divided, the majority ruled for the settlers in 1875.[26] Thus, while on the brink of victory, the railroads fell into the chasm of defeat. By this time, the Osages were settled on their new and last reservation. They were deeply involved in trying to obtain their money from the Civilization Fund.

Osage Ceded Lands, Settler's Protective Association

The settlers' experiences with railroads and land speculators on the Delaware and Neutral Lands had proven the value of active, determined resistance. With these experiences still fresh on their minds, it was natural for the settlers to form a resistance organization on the Ceded Lands. In time, the Settler's Protective Association became "the government" on the Ceded Lands.[27]

In order to fight the issue of land ownership in the ceded lands, a special assessment was levied upon the Association members. This formed a fund for lawyer fees and court costs. After failure in the state courts, the case reached the Supreme Court in 1875, as mentioned earlier. The Association members signed a promissory note to pay a fee of twenty-five cents an acre if and when the lands were placed in the public domain.[28]

It is a commentary on the character of the settlers that very little of this modest fee was paid. In fairness to the settlers however, it should also be mentioned that the fight was long and expensive. Crop failures had further strained the meager resources of these squatters. Yet it is doubtful if these poor homeless drifters would have paid the fees if times had been flourishing. Repeatedly, these people had promised everything until they got what they wanted and then they delivered nothing.

The Osage Trust Lands

Description

So much has been made of the Osage Ceded Lands controversy that it is easy to forget that the Treaty of 1865 also created the Osage Trust Lands. While the Osage Ceded Lands amounted to 843,927 acres, the Osage Trust Lands included 3,200,000 acres. These Osage Trust Lands were a twenty-mile-wide tract along the north boundary of the remaining Osage Diminished Reserve. They lay between the Osage Ceded Lands and the 100th meridian.

By virtue of the fact that these lands were less desirable than the Osage Ceded Lands, there was little controversy over them. The eastern one-third of these Osage Trust Lands was originally known as the Grand Osage Prairies. However, today it is known as the Flint Hills. While a limited amount of tillable land is in the swales and valleys of the region, most of the area is covered with a thin layer of rocky soil.

As one moves west, the tall grasses of the Grand Osage Prairies give way to the short grasses of the Great Plains. The western one-third of the Osage Trust Lands was almost treeless and too dry for the agricultural practices of the 1860s. This left the middle one-third, which at best was marginal agricultural land in the 1860s. One must realize that it takes special methods in agriculture and special people to farm on the Great Plains.

Fort Dodge Reserve

The absence of publicity, which is usually associated with controversy, allowed an injustice to the Osages to pass unnoticed. So far as we could discover, this has never been corrected either by credit to Osage accounts or through the Claims Commission. As Ft. Dodge lost its usefulness, preparations were made to close it down. In 1879, Senator Ingalls of Kansas introduced a bill to open the northern two-thirds of the Ft. Dodge Military Reservation for homesteading. Believing the lands were available for homesteading, both Houses passed the bill.

As preparations were being made to transfer this tract to the Interior Department, a protest was voiced: "Henry Price, a commissioner with the department found that part of the reservation [Fr. Dodge Military Reservation] had been carved from former Osage Reserve lands [Osage Trust Lands] and that any funds accruing from their sale should be transferred to a trust fund for the tribe."[29] While this created what could have been a problem, it was solved by the simple expedient of ignoring the protest. Thus, the Osages were cheated out of part of their funds.

If a person were to draw upon Osage history for guidance into the future, a few object lessons are available. First and foremost, the Treaty of 1865 suggests that controversy forces facts into the open and tends to solidify arguments. The object lesson here is to fight for what you think is right and force the opposition to prove they are right. Publicize your position.

THE EFFECT OF THE BATTLE OVER OSAGE LANDS

As one looks at the role the Osages played in Southeast Kansas, there is a tendency to see only the immediate effects. There can be little doubt that this struggle had a modern nationwide effect. We must agree with others who state this same line of thought. "In the last battle, the boomer had acquired lands previously guaranteed to the Indians, and serviced by railroads —at the preemption price of unsurveyed wilderness. The states' populist tendencies were given a rousing lift."[30]

Kansas was noted for its populist leanings, and it was in the forefront of the Populist Revolt of the late–1880s and early–1890s. The usual treatment gives the Grange Movement credit for bringing the Populist Revolt into reality. This ignores the role played by Indians and especially the Osage. It was the struggle in Southeast Kansas that taught the agrarian people to fight and organize to reach their goals. Their actions for influencing government are reflected in the Populist Revolt.

Witness two of the most radical planks in the platform of 1891: (1) Government ownership of railroads, telegraphs, and telephones; and (2) The return to the government of all land held by railroads and other corporations in excess of their needs. These are not the only planks that reflect the controversy in Southeast Kansas. A heavily graduated income tax was proposed to prevent the accumulation of vast fortunes that could be used to "buy the government." Significantly, the platform also demanded the popular election of senators, the secret ballot, and the initiative, recall, and referendum.

It seems ironic that these agriculturists established the basic ideas of modern urban-industrial America while urban minds were creating the Communist Manifesto of 1887 for rural Russia. However, we can trace

Populist concepts through the Progressives, such as Theodore Roosevelt, who argued that a corporation was not entitled to a vote in American elections. Essentially, the New Deal was a process of adapting the Populist ideas to the realities of the twentieth century. The Populist Revolt was the last creative overhaul of the American government, and the Osage lands gave a gigantic shove to the infant revolution.

14

The End of Indian Treaty-Making

INTRODUCTION

The Osages are associated with some of the most remarkable legislation in the history of Western civilization. Abolition of Indian treaty-making did not make more than a ripple in the history of Western civilization. However, Congress enacted legislation in 1862 that thrust the United States into the position of leader of Western civilization and revolutionized agriculture throughout the world.

Two senators named Morrill were responsible for legislation affecting the Osages. Justin Smith Morrill of Vermont sponsored the Homestead and Preemption Act of 1862, as well as the Agriculture and Mechanical (A & M) College Land Grant Act of the same year. Associated with the latter act was the Hatch Act of 1887, which established agricultural experimental stations. Justin Smith Morrill also sponsored the Railroad Land Grant Act. Lot Myrick Morrill was a senator from Maine who stood up for the Osages. He argued that under the Treaty of 1865 the Osages were promised $1.25 an acre for their Kansas land should they agree to remove from Kansas. Thanks to Lot Morrill, the Osages received a better price for their lands, which insured their survival.

The Justin S. Morrill Acts encouraged the would-be agriculturists to invade the Osage Kansas lands. His actions also induced the railways to try to obtain the Osage lands as a part of their land grants. These efforts were successful in forcing the Osages to cede their Kansas lands and in ending the process of Indian treaty-making. As Congress debated the Osage removal, Lot M. Morrill argued the honor of the United States must be upheld and that the Osages should be paid what had been promised to them.

Contributions of the A & M Colleges and their associated experimental stations have brought new foods, larger agricultural production, and a greatly expanded pool of trained engineers in the mechanical arts. Thus, the tri-part expansion of the United States was generated (that is, the frontier of land expansion, the frontier of industrial expansion, and the frontier of unprecedented population growth).

This chapter will show how these events affected the decision to halt Indian treaty-making. Our primary concern is to discuss the Osages, but if we omitted showing how the Osages were involved in general history, we would be as guilty as others who leave the Osages out of general histories.

THE DRUM CREEK TREATY

There were other Indian treaties beside the Drum Creek Treaty being considered in 1868 and the two following years. However, due to the size of the Osage Diminished Reserve (8,000,000 acres plus 3,200,000 in the Osage Trust Lands, a round figure of 11,000,000 acres), the great treaty debate of the late–1860s centered on the Drum Creek Treaty.[1] Intruders and state government protest also pushed the Drum Creek Treaty to the center of the stage. Without a doubt, the controversy over the Osage Ceded Lands, which by 1868 had reached every corner of the nation, also tended to focus attention upon the Drum Creek Treaty.

Surely, the House of Representatives was in no mood to allow the sale of Indian lands by treaty to continue. A worse time could not have been found to submit an Indian treaty to the Senate for ratification. At the time, as David Parsons points out, "Congress had just finished a discussion of the southern homestead Bill in which the land policy of the United States had been ably reviewed and revitalized. Control of the public domain had just been redeclared to be a prerogative of Congress. The treaty sale system of disposing of Indian reservations had just been denounced by the House."[2]

On December 15, 1869, Representative Sidney Clarke of Kansas introduced a resolution which condemned the sale of Indian lands by treaty. This resolution passed the House by unanimous consent. A threat embodied in the resolution gave it sharp teeth that bit into the practice of land sales by treaty: "this House will refuse hereafter to make any appropriations to carry out the provisions of Indian treaties in which the terms of this resolution are not adhered to."[3]

Because all bills of revenue must originate in the House, this threat was especially significant. To phrase it differently, although the Senate had the treaty-making power, the House controlled the purse strings. It was actions such as this that ended treaty-making with Indians.

So far as the Osages were concerned at the time, they had no particular feeling either for or against treaty-making. In practice, agreements by treaty and agreements by congressional act seemed the same to the Osages. This was because almost all special Indian Bills provide a condition of approval by the Indians involved.

We would not want to engage in a debate on the question of constitutional hierarchy of laws. If we assume the Constitution and treaties made under the Constitution are the supreme law of the land, then the Osages lost an advantage with the ending of Indian treaty-making. But, if acts of Congress stand above or equal with Indian treaties, the Osages gained an advantage. In a partial answer it would appear that while treaties and the Constitution stand above Congress, the Supreme Court has placed Indian treaties in a special class, which lowers the status of such treaties in comparison with other treaties.

INDIAN TREATIES IN THE UNITED STATES GOVERNMENT

Introduction

No human action stands apart from its time and place. Thus, Indian treaty-making varied from place to place and from time to time. All history shows periods of great morality and periods of venality. Likewise, we find great swings from one extreme to its opposite. Like a pendulum swinging first to one side then to the other, history unfolds before our eyes. Thus, it is prudent to examine the path of Indian treaty-making.

Indian Treaty-Making

Characteristics

As a matter of some interest, insofar as we know, there is not a single instance where Indians asked to have a treaty made. Surely, the Osages never initiated a treaty. Euro-Americans were the ones who desired to have treaties made. Thus, we may assume, if our observations are correct, that it was the Euro-Americans who desired to obtain something.

Throughout the history of Indian treaty-making, the acquisition of land areas was the single most important motive for making Indian treaties. The other motives were to maintain peace, to retain loyalty, to secure right of passage, to adjust previous treaties, and to provide for payment of claims. All these were related in one way or another to the cession of lands. Thus, it is difficult to classify Indian treaties by motive alone.

A cursory survey of Indian treaties shows that most of them tend to have been made in clusters. Classical examples of this are shown by tracing the treaties made with the Osages. The first Osage treaty with Americans was in 1808. This was primarily a land cession treaty with secondary peace and loyalty provisions. Peace and loyalty were elements in a whole series of treaties with the nations west of the Mississippi made at this time due to the Louisiana Purchase. The Osage land cessions of 1808 had a direct bearing on a series of removal treaties made with the Northeastern and Southeastern nations.

The Osage Treaty of 1815 was only one of many treaties made because of the War of 1812. This was to reestablish the sovereignty of the United States over the nations involved. In 1819, we find a land cession combined with claims. A whole series of adjustments such as this were made with other nations at this same time. Apparently, a treaty with one of the nations affected other nations and necessitated a series of adjustment treaties.

Another series of treaties were generated by a change in governmental policy. This was the abandonment of the government trading factory system. Closing of Fort Osage would have violated the Treaty of 1808. Thus, the Osage Treaty of 1823 was necessary to adjust the abandonment of the Fort Osage factory.

Pressure from the advancing Euro-American frontier had generated a demand for the removal of the Northeastern nations. Thus, the ripple effect of the advancing frontier touched the Osages. The Treaty of 1825 was a major land cession treaty with all the other elements included. It was a part of the greatest cluster of treaties in the history of Indian treaty-making. A second Osage treaty of 1825 was necessary because of the opening of the Santa Fe Trail. This Council Grove Treaty was also one of a series negotiated with various Indian nations so the Santa Fe Trail could be protected. This brings us to the Treaty of 1839, which was another in a series of interim adjustment treaties.

The outbreak of the Civil War caused a series of treaties to be negotiated with the Confederacy. Among these was the Confederate Treaty made with the White Hair and Claremore bands. After the war, another series of peace and loyalty treaties were made. At Little Rock, Arkansas, the Osages signed such a treaty. This was followed by many reconstruction treaties among the five nations.

Osages

We have now returned to the Treaty of 1865. This and the unratified Drum Creek Treaty of 1868 were in a series of Indian removals from Kansas by treaty. For the first time, the Osages were in direct contact with the Euro-American frontier line. Thus, they were in this series removed from the white man's path for the first time.

From the above sketch, it becomes apparent that Indian treaty-making can be organized by events in the expansion of the United States. By the same token, it is evident that a close relationship between Indian compaction and Euro-American expansion existed. That is, as the Euro-American culture expanded into a larger and larger area, the American Indian cultures were squeezed into a smaller and smaller area.

Anna Abel mentions an excellent way of organizing land cession treaties: "[I]n practice, there have been several ways of extinguishing the reservation title—by direct cession in fee to the general government for a consideration, by cession in trust, by direct sales to individuals or to corporations, by conditional grants in severalty, by patents without restrictions, and by preemption of lands already occupied by settlers. All have, however, resulted in removal, and the departure of the Osages was a very fitting close to the story of Indian colonization west of the Missouri river."[4] We have pointed out the matter of organizing Indian treaties for two reasons. First, it provided a way to trace a subject that has received very little attention in Indian literature. Secondly, with fond hopes, we would like to see someone eventually pursue this subject of Indian treaties in its many aspects.

With this said, it is time to return to more direct Osage history. Some excellent information can frequently be found in congressional reports. The following is a summary of Osage–United States relationships.

> The Osage Indians have had congressional attention and executive and judicial attention as follows:
>
> Between 1808 and 1865 10 treaties were made between the Osage nations and the United States.
>
> Between 1824 and the present time [July 22, 1953] there have been 64 Acts of Congress enacted having to do with the Osage Indians.
>
> More than 175 court decisions, including many in the United States Supreme Court, have been given having to do with the rights of the tribe.[5]

We have not made an actual count, but it would be safe to assume the bulk of acts and Supreme Court decisions were made between 1900 and 1953. In any event, the testimony reveals an extensive relationship between the Osage nation and the United States.

This general thought has been expressed by writers in other contexts. Judge T. F. Morrison of southeast Kansas acknowledges, "It may be truthfully said that the Osage Indians have made more history and have done more for the material advancement of the West than any other tribe of Indians. They were a strong powerful war tribe and equally strong in peace."[6] Judge Morrison had reason to make such a sweeping statement about the Osages, for he knew them very well.

The Final Phases of Indian Treaty-Making

Ending of Osage Empire

After tracing what he called "bad faith treaties," another Kansan, C. E. Cory, made this statement: "Thus disappeared the last remnant of that splendid empire, originally the home of this powerful tribe [the Osages]."[7] Although Cory was speaking of the vast Osage empire that existed in 1800, it is interesting to note the end of that empire seventy years later. Therefore, the quote is fitting for the end of the Old Osage Empire and the beginning of a New Osage Domain.

The Cherokee Tobacco Case

We have now come to the immediate causes for the end of Indian treaty-making. Aside from the protests of those who had vested interests, a significant Supreme Court decision became involved in the question of Indian treaties. What is popularly called the *Cherokee Tobacco Case* became a shocking interpretation of the Constitution. Earlier we avoided a detailed examination of the hierarchy of United States law, that is, which class of law comes first, which is second, etc. It is precisely this matter that was decided by the *Cherokee Tobacco Case.*

By treaty, the Cherokee could market tobacco products in the United States tax free. However, Euro-American tobacco product producers argued that this created unfair competition. Specific tax laws were then enacted, taxing Cherokee tobacco products sold in the United States. Arguing that treaties made under the Constitution stood equal with the Constitution as the supreme law of the land, the Cherokees took their case to the Supreme Court.

Evidently, the court was placed in a quandary by the validity of the Cherokee argument. The Constitution is exceptionally clear and specific on this point. It is so clear that it leaves little room for special interpretation. Since the wording would not allow the desired interpretation, a special redefining of the term—foreign nations—was introduced. Thus, Indian nations—which had always been considered to be foreign nations as a convenience to the United States and other Euro-American nations—were declared to be a special class of domestic nations and, therefore, Indian treaties were different from other treaties. This argument conveniently enabled the Supreme Court to rule that Indian treaties stood below and not above acts of Congress. As this case points out, the Constitution is only what the Supreme Court says it is at any particular moment. In other words, we are not so much a nation of laws as we are a nation of Supreme Court interpretations.

Apparently, we are a nation with order and justice if our laws vary to suit the majority or an elite minority.

While the Supreme Court has no constitutional *right* to interpret the Constitution, its *power* to interpret the Constitution has made this an academic question since the Civil War.[8] Such abuse of the Supreme Court's power would not have been tolerated if the same decision had been made against the majority culture in the same way it was made against Indians. It has been said that the greatest danger of a democracy is in its treatment of minorities. So long as decisions such as the *Cherokee Tobacco Case* are tolerated by the majority, this nation cannot in truth and justice claim to be governed by laws. Laws have no meaning unless they are applied equally and with justice.

Surely, the elimination of Indian treaty-making stands as an indictment of the United States. Due to the *Cherokee Tobacco Decision,* the treaties already ratified were downgraded and stand as a blotch on the honor of the United States government. Yet some congressmen complain when Indians voice distrust, and nature groups wonder why Osages do not trust promises made in special acts. How can one trust a government that has shown such dishonor and repudiation of its sacred word? The answer to that question is that despite the past evils there has been a reasonable amount of fair treatment of the Osages since 1900. Like it or not, trust it or not, the United States government is what we have, and the alternatives are far worse.

Osage Reactions

The various Indian nations reacted to the end of Indian treaty-making and its companion, the *Cherokee Tobacco Case,* in different ways. Osage reactions ranged from anger to reluctant acceptance. However, such high-handed treatment caused the remaining shreds of Osage pride in their culture and accomplishments to solidify into a determination to save the remnants of the past. Thus, the Osages resisted with great determination the efforts to force them to abandon their ways and accept what the white man wanted them to be. This is probably why they have managed to save much of their past.

It is with pride that Osages can say, "We have saved some of our culture." An interesting facet of this struggle to save a people and a culture is the role that the Kansas land sales money, grass lease money, and oil money played. How strange the ways of Euro-Americans are. When the Osages were moneyless, they were dirty ignorant savages. After they got the land and grass lease money, they became the "richest pagans on earth." Yet it is difficult for the Euro-American mind to separate the possession of money from success. The possession of money brought the Osages a release from the constant pressure to become an Indian edition of a Euro-American. We will see this transformation in later chapters. We will also see the Osage person emerge as a unique member of American society.

The End of Indian Treaties

The end of Indian treaty-making was a shift to modern Indian policy and a separation of the past and present. It comes almost as a shock to read the short passage of the enactment of this turning point: "*Provided,* That hereafter no Indian nation or tribe within the territory of the United States shall be acknowledged or recognized as an independent nation, tribe, or power with whom the United States may contract by treaty: *Provided, further,* That nothing herein contained shall be construed to invalidate or impair the obligation of any treaty heretofore lawfully made and ratified with any such Indian nation or tribe."[9] This momentous act was attached to the Indian Appropriation Bill of March 3, 1871.

If the Osages were not the first Indian nation to come under the new changed policy, they were among the first. Certainly, the Act of July 15, 1869, by which Congress set aside a reserve for the Osages in Indian Territory, was a step in a new direction.[10] On July 15, 1870, $50,000 was appropriated as a loan to the Osages to assist them in the removal from Kansas.[11] In the same act that ended Indian treaty-making, March 3, 1871, Congress included a provision to allow Osage mixed-bloods to remain in Kansas.[12] The Executive order of March 27, 1871, which set aside a tract selected by the Osages as their new reserve, was also an action within the changed policy.[13] Then, on May 18, 1872, Congress reaffirmed the $50,000 loan for removal made in 1870.[14] Finally, on June 15, 1872, the present reservation was confirmed to the Osages.[15] Since these acts and actions were made and taken before, during, and shortly after the elimination of treaty-making, the Osages were among the first to come under the new policy.

15

The Drum Creek Treaty

INTRODUCTION

While we have discussed the end of Indian treaty-making, we have not carefully examined the treaty that caused it. The Drum Creek Treaty (also called the Sturges Treaty, or Treaty of 1868) was never ratified because of widespread vocal opposition to it. Those who wished to end Indian treaty-making were not the only people opposing the treaty.

In the fall of 1867, Thomas Murphy, who was Superintendent of Indian Affairs at Atchison, Kansas, suggested to the Commissioner of Indian Affairs that an Osage treaty was needed. He argued that intruders had already entered the reserve for several miles on the east side. Since these intruders ignored the Osage Agent, it would be necessary to either remove the intruders with troops or to remove the Osages. Furthermore, the state government of Kansas was supplying the intruders with arms and ammunition.[1] So if the Osages dared to oppose the stealing of their reserve, the settlers and the militia were prepared to battle with them.

This communication set the stage for negotiating the largest land sale in the history of the United States government, had the treaty been ratified. Not only would it have been the largest single tract sale in American history except for some waste lands, but it would have been the lowest price ever paid. There can be no doubt that twenty cents an acre for desirable, arable land was a real estate bargain without equal.[2]

A lot of maneuvering was taking place behind the scene. Certainly, neither the Osages, the general public, nor anyone outside the "railroad ring" was consulted.

Little White Hair (*Wa Sop pe* [Black Bear]), the last of the White Hair Chiefs, had become the principal Osage chief despite his poor health. He refused to participate in the Drum Creek Treaty at first saying, "I have no land to sell."[3] It may be that he was too ill to be effective, since he died shortly after the treaty council ended. Yet, in view of the position of other leaders, it is likely that he did not have any land he would willingly sell. It is probable that had Little White Hair been in good health, the Drum Creek Treaty would not have been negotiated. Without an acknowledged and effective leader, the headmen were disunited and unorganized. Under these conditions, the Osages were easy prey for the railroad vultures.

Later events clearly show Osage opposition to the Drum Creek Treaty. However, the intruder problem placed a great strain on the Osage determination not to war on Americans. Isaac T. Gibson, the Osage agent, noted in the winter of 1870 that there was danger of an Osage outbreak against the intruders.[4] By this time, the Society of the Little Old Men had all but disappeared. However, the counsel of the few remaining members still commanded respect. Thus, the chiefs held their brash young men in check, and the Osages sought only to place distance between themselves and the intruders.

The situation had become a mixture of agreement and cross purposes. Both the intruders/railroads on one side and the Osages on the other wanted the Osages out of Kansas. However, their motives for and the manner of removal conflicted. It was in these cross purposes that the Osage removal became especially interesting.

NEGOTIATION OF THE TREATY

Osage Reluctance

A key point has been determined through analysis of the speeches made by the Osages at the Drum Creek Council. The point is that the Osages opposed making any new treaty until the errors in the Treaty of 1865 were corrected.[5] These errors were in reference to the "civilization fund" interpretation derived from the Treaty of 1865. Forked Horn was the only Osage who spoke directly to this point, stating, "They do not wish their chiefs to make any such treaty as they have made, and when you hand out the pen he don't want them to touch it."[6] Thus, it is evident both from the discussion of the Treaty of 1865 and the sole direct speech to the Drum Creek proposals that the Osages did not intend to make a new treaty.

The Osage speakers are listed as, "Twelve o'clock, Chetopah (*Tze To pa* [Four Lodges]), Hard Rope, No-pa-wah-la (*No pa Walla* [Thunder Fear]), Big Elk (*O pon Tun ka*), Wah-ti-um-ka (probably *Wa ti An ka* [Dry Plume]), Kou-e-ce-gla (unidentified), Wah-ho-ta-she (probably Loud Clear Voice), Drum, White Hair, Forked Horn, No-kah-kah-he (unidentified), and one other."[7]

Threats and Bribes

The Commissioner of Indian Affairs led the negotiations for the United States—but for the benefit of the railroad and not the Osages. According to him, all the past wrongs could be corrected in this new treaty. Furthermore, this treaty would provide the necessities for many years and would give them a new reserve for only fifteen cents an acre. Seeing that the milk and honey promises were not appealing to the Osages, the Commissioner shifted to threats. These ranged from threats to cut off provisions to threats to unleash the Plains nations and allow them to make unrestricted warfare against the Osages.

Surely, the Commissioner was not well acquainted with the Osages. They had no fear of the Plains nations; however, they would have missed the provisions, which they desperately needed. These provisions enabled the Osages to successfully combat the other Plains nations. The loss of provisions would have been a serious handicap for the Osages.

As the time to end the Drum Creek Council neared, it became evident that the Osages were not going to sign the treaty. To prevent certain defeat, a further consideration of the treaty was obtained by a variant of the "divide and conquer" maxim. Although it was an exceptional revolution in Osage government, a committee of twelve Osage councillors and braves was created. The Osages were induced to allow this committee to either reject or accept the treaty.[8] But even this ploy failed, since the Committee of Twelve only offered to sell another strip from the Diminished Reserve.

At this point, Joe *Pawnee No Pa she* (Not Afraid of the Pawnee) drove home some significant points about Osage treaties and Indian treaties in general. He pointed out the futility of these treaties. Among the reasons for this were that provisions for protection were canceled by threats to leave them unprotected and that instead of removing intruders as promised in treaties, they came for more land.[9] The records support Joe's speech; he spoke the truth.

Chicanery

Why the Osages eventually signed the treaty is difficult to determine. While there are many irregularities in the X-mark signatures, most Osage leaders evidently signed the treaty. We must look for the extraordinary instead of the mundane for the reason they signed, because the Osages would not have signed under ordinary conditions.

We can only suspect that an unusual pressure was placed upon the Osages to obtain their assent to the Drum Creek Treaty. Surely, such an opportunity was present at an opportune moment. Bribes had been offered to key chiefs and even to Fr. Schonmakers. However, these were either refused or did not obtain the desired results. It is a fact of human existence that when all else does not bring people to a desired action, rumors have a way of getting the job done.

In looking back, it seems evident that rumors of an Osage massacre were influential in obtaining their assent to the treaty. It seems that two brothers had been hunting on the Walnut River near present-day Arkansas City, Kansas. The Osages reportedly killed one brother. Arriving at the stalemated Drum Creek Council, the other brother gave a dramatic tearful report of the alleged murder to the Commissioner.

If it was a fabrication, and it probably was, it was concocted by someone who knew the Osages very well. The Osages present had no way of knowing if the story was true or false. However, they were fully aware that anyone hunting without permission on Osage lands that far from Euro-American settlements were very likely to be killed by the *Moh Shon Ah ke ta* (Protectors of the Land). With this possibility in mind, the Osages assumed the rumor was true.

Surely, the Commissioner made full use of the rumor, for he declared the Osage councillors and chiefs to be his prisoners. Declaring their lands to be forfeited, he graciously offered them a way out. They could sign the treaty and turn the murderer over to him and the incident would be closed. If they refused, they would remain in arrest and the mob of intruders would likely kill them.[10] Faced with these choices, the Osages signed the treaty on May 27, 1868. The Osage who was given as hostage for this alleged crime escaped. In retrospect it is apparent that if such a murder had occurred, the incident would not have been dropped so abruptly.

OPPOSITION GROUPS

The State of Kansas

Kansas experienced one of the longest and hottest land contests in American history over the Osage Ceded Lands. The contest had fully aroused the people of the state by 1869. Thus, when news of the provisions in the Drum Creek Treaty became known, a groundswell of protest caused the Kansas government to launch a campaign of protest to the national government.

The Governor, the legislature, and other state officers protested the treaty. However, the most effective protest in the state government came from the Superintendent of Public Instruction. Having been excluded from sections 16 and 36 in the Ceded Lands, the Superintendent wanted to be sure the school land grant was not omitted in the Drum Creek Treaty. However, he was horrified to discover while at Drum Creek that the treaty contained no grants for the Kansas schools.[11]

Loss of sections 16 and 36 was more than the loss of land area. It meant that the total burden for school support would fall on the taxpayer. Since unsold railroad lands in Kansas were customarily kept off the tax rolls, this placed the full burden of school support on the shoulders of the individual property owners.

One can fully appreciate the storm of protest this generated among Kansas citizens once they understood what was involved. They understood the matter quickly, for the Superintendent soon got the word to the people by way of each County Superintendent of Public Schools. Senators were quickly buried in an avalanche of protest from Kansas citizens.

Both the Republican and Democratic parties in Kansas adopted resolutions of protest to the Drum Creek Treaty at their state conventions.[12] Thus there was a unified wall of protest from voters, political leaders, state officials, and state legislators. While all these were important, the latter was especially important since they elected the Kansas senators. There was no way the Kansas senators could avoid answering the demands of the state legislature. While they still supported the Drum Creek Treaty, they did get it amended to include school land grants, which removed much of the state pressure on the senators.

In this protest by the state of Kansas, no concern is shown for the Osages. All of the Euro-Americans were protesting out of greed for Osage lands. During the early stages of protest, the Osages had no effective voice speaking on their behalf to insure justice.

Osage Opposition

The terrible disunity of the Osage people is evident in the on and off support of the Drum Creek Treaty. Like most of the Indian nations, the Osages became more disunified as their associations with Euro-Americans became closer and more frequent. In some respects, the degree of Westernization bore a direct relationship to the amount of disunity. Early in 1869, one of these changes in support of the Drum Creek Treaty was reported.

Demonstrating a change of mind, the Osages asked that the treaty be ratified. Their reason for changing their minds was the fear of being dispossessed and, thus, having no home. The intruders were swarming into the reserve in such numbers that this fear was not without some justification. At the same time, the Osages asked that those intruders occupying the village sites be removed.[13]

By June, the Osages made another switch back to opposing ratification of the Drum Creek Treaty. This protest was signed at Alexander Beyett's post on the Elk River about eight miles north of Independence, Kansas. While there were not many signatures, those signing were the main leaders of the Osages. Among the ten signers were Little White Hair, Hard Rope, Nopawalla, Chetopa, and Little Beaver.[14] Their reasons for protest were that the treaty did not represent the wishes of the majority of the Osage people. Furthermore, they pointed out that the treaty was obtained by threats and false promises. One of the obvious false promises was that the Osages could remain in Kansas for four or five years. Another promise was that the "Civilization Fund" error would be corrected. The concluding argument was that the lawful interpreter was replaced by an irresponsible interpreter. In conclusion, the Osages stated, "We are sorry we did it. We do not want you to ratify it."[15]

Opposition in the House of Representatives

House Versus Senate

Over a period of time, the Congress had evolved a public land policy that had originated in the Northwest Ordinance of 1785 and had been liberalized in 1862. Between 1864 and 1870, the Bureau of Indian Affairs, with the help of railroad interests, had developed a way to bypass the congressional land policies that had been so carefully crafted. This involved sale of Indian lands by treaty. Since senators were not elected by a popular vote, as Representatives were, they were easier to bribe. Thus, money became the power to control Indian land sales.

Customarily, the Office of Indian Affairs did not release information about pending treaties. The Senate always conducted treaty ratification debates in a closed session. Therefore, most treaties with Indians did not become public knowledge until after the treaty was ratified.[16] In fairness to the American citizens, it should be noted that they had no opportunity to protest these treaties until they had been ratified. Thus, an Euro-American protest that could have been favorable to the Indian was lost "like a whistle into the wind."

Such practices did not escape the attention of the House of Representatives. A joint resolution was introduced into the House which noted that the Drum Creek Treaty was "in contravention of the laws and policy of the United States affecting the public domain."[17] Another resolution requested the executive department to send copies of all documents relating to the Drum Creek Treaty to the House. This action upset the timetable of the pro-treaty forces by forcing exposure of the treaty to public scrutiny before the Senate could ratify it.[18]

Some sense of the House's feeling about the Drum Creek Treaty can be gained from a House address by Representative Sidney Clarke of Kansas: "It is clearly within our power to enter a protest against ratification of this treaty on behalf of the United States; and to say to the Senate that if this remarkable treaty is ratified by that body we will not make the appropriation to carry it out, and will not recognize its validity."[19]

This address may lead one to believe that the Drum Creek Treaty was the sole basis for challenging the treaty-making power of the Senate. This was not the case, as is shown by the report of the House Investigating Committee: "Sir, for myself I intend never to give my consent to allowing the treaty-making power to add to or diminish the domain of this country. It has no power either to cede away the state of Maine to Great Britain or to acquire new territory on the Northwest, or to exercise exclusive control of the House of Representatives over the limits of this country either to contract or enlarge them."[20]

The allusion to ceding the state of Maine to the British is probably a reference to the Webster–Ashburton Treaty of 1842. After some years of dispute over the Maine-Canadian boundary, it was settled by compromise. Great Britain was ceded 5,000 of the 12,000 square miles in dispute. Around 1865, maps were found which supported the American claim to all 12,000 square miles of the disputed area, hence the remark about ceding away Maine.

Mention of the new territory on the Northwest was a definite reference to the Alaska Purchase Treaty of 1867. There was heavy opposition to the Alaska purchase among American citizens. While these objections were primarily due to ignorance and were overcome by education about Alaska, the House was opposed for other reasons. For a time, the entire purchase was endangered because the Senate had obligated the nation to pay $7,200,000 without consulting the House. The House concurred in the treaty only to preserve the honor of the United States and to preserve relations with Russia.[21] Thus the Osage Drum Creek Treaty was the first real opportunity for the House to limit the Senate's treaty-making power.

Osages: The Ignored Factor

Representative Sidney Clarke was responsible for again suggesting that the House control treaty-making by refusing to provide the necessary funds. However, it is doubtful this was his purpose in opposing the Drum Creek Treaty. Clarke met with representatives of the White Hair, Little Osage, and Big Hill bands. Black Dog and Claremore had not yet brought their bands in from the spring hunt of 1869. Two reasons for his opposition to the Drum Creek Treaty were given to this council. First, Clarke said he thought the Osages were being cheated. Secondly, he said if they wanted to sell their land, they should sell to the government so it could be sold directly to the settlers.[22]

The Osages had absolutely no interest in who ultimately bought their lands. But selling to the government made sense to them. Clarke was evidently being candid with them, because he must have known that the Osages had good reason not to accommodate settlers. By the same token, he must have known that the Osages needed the intruders to defeat the treaty. Surely, Clarke's support of later amendments to the treaty clearly shows he was more interested in fairness to the settlers and the state of Kansas than he was about the effect on the Osages.

With a few notable exceptions, objections to the Drum Creek Treaty in the House, state of Kansas, or among American citizens were made without any consideration of the Osages. The House was opposed primarily because the treaty usurped power the House felt belonged to them. Kansas government was mainly opposed to the treaty because it did not include a grant of school lands. Most citizens were opposed to the treaty because it made the land too expensive for the settler. No effective group was opposed to the treaty because it was unfair to the Osages. Certainly, the Office of Indian Affairs did not honor their trust position and defend the Osages since they were backing the railroad position.

The battle in the House over the Drum Creek Treaty ended on March 3, 1871. In an obscure rider to the Indian appropriation bill, treaty-making with Indians was ended. "*Provided,* That hereafter no Indian nation or tribe within the territory of the United States shall be acknowledged or recognized as an independent nation, tribe, or power with whom the United States may contract by treaty: *Provided, further,* That nothing herein contained shall be construed to invalidate or impair the obligation of any treaty heretofore lawfully made and ratified with any such Indian nation or tribe."[23]

Any Indian reading the last proviso would have some cause for concern, in view of Indian history. On the surface, this seems to affirm all preceding Indian treaties. However, one must wonder how "lawfully made and ratified" would be interpreted when an old treaty stands in the way of a government project or the desires of the majority. Would it be interpreted as a rule of law or as a rule of men?

Intruder Opposition

The Kansas intruder problem is said to have originated on the Delaware reserve. In succession, the intruders evolved new techniques on the New York, Iowa, Cherokee, Shawnee, and Potawatomi reserves. By the time a severe intruder problem reached the Osage reserves, the intruders had become especially effective at ousting the Indian from their reserves.[24] This is not to say that the Osages did not have any problems with intruders before 1865. It is to say that the intruders did not make any serious effort to oust the Osages from the Kansas reserves until 1865.

As a matter of fact, there were three waves of intruders into the Kansas reserve of the Osages. The first of these were motivated by the slavery controversy in Kansas. A second invasion consisted of Union veterans of the Civil War. They went to war as boys and entered the reservation as battle-hardened, poor men. Some of the third invasion came as the Osages were leaving Kansas. Nearly all these were settlers who bought their land and by virtue of this fact were not intruders. However, the first of these had responded to news of the imminent departure of the Osages and had intruded to preempt choice lands.[25]

Each of these waves had different types of people. Mingled with the first two waves were the typical woodsys of the earlier frontiers. This fact alone indicates that the Kansas frontier was different from the earlier frontiers. It was not only the Osages, Kaw, and emigrant Indians compacted athwart the path of the western movement that made the Kansas frontier so different. The Kansas–Nebraska Bill and the ensuing conflict in Kansas was positively something new in frontier history. A pent up demand for land had built up during the Civil War. Young men who would have moved west in the normal sequence were at war. In the turmoil of the post-war period, there were a vast number of displaced persons. Thus, as never before in frontier history, a large body of poor, battle-hardened young men was available to advance the American frontier.

It would seem obvious that the character of the people in these three waves was different from that of the earlier frontiers. The first wave consisted of highly opinionated, intolerant, and idealistic people. These traits were unusual on earlier frontiers. Men of the second wave had not been able to accumulate any worldly goods, as previous generations had been able to do. Yet they had their war experiences and were accustomed to settling differences with violence, if peaceful means did not produce immediate results. In my childhood, they were called "sudden men." While the third wave was comparable to Turner's equipment farmer, it differed in the character of the people involved.[26] Like the two preceding waves, these people were products of the Civil War era. Because of their strong sense of defending their government, they did not hesitate to demand support from that government even if their demands were contrary to the rule of law and justice.

The rapidity of intrusion was enough to alarm anyone. In three years, between 1867 and 1870, over a thousand intruders moved into the eastern part of the Osage Diminished Reserve.[27] Many more had entered the northern part as far west as Wichita, Kansas. Montgomery County on the east had a population of 8,000 intruders by March of 1870.[28] In 1867, the spring wave of intruders was so alarming that the Osage agent requested a military force to turn them back.[29] Certainly, one group of intruders was a special embarrassment to Agent Isaac Gibson. These were Quakers who settled southwest of Independence, Kansas. This same area was the setting for Laura Ingalls Wilder's *Little House on the Prairie.*

GROWING POWER OF THE INTRUDERS

Power of Organizations

Mark Twain once commented, "Wherever two Americans meet, one of them is sure to get a gavel and call the other one to order." This was surely true of the intruders on the Osage Diminished Reserve. They were well organized into active, effective organizations. Supported by these local organizations and the Kansas state government, the intruders became increasingly bold.

Isaac Gibson, the Osage agent, feared the intruders were trying to provoke the Osages into an attack. In their combined strength, it was possible that given the excuse of an Osage attack no matter how justified, the intruders could have destroyed the Osage people. Their boldness and disregard for national laws are well illustrated by the fact that a village belonging to 900 Osages was destroyed by plundering intruders.[30] The intruders preferred these village sites because the fields were cleared, the underbrush was cut away, and the locations were well supplied with water.

Some idea of the intruders' organizations can be gained if we realize they held meetings both within and outside the Diminished Reserve. These meetings, wherever they were held, featured a speaker who might have been their Washington delegate, a Kansas official, or a congressman. In every case, the speaker managed to inflame the intruders to commit greater atrocities. Goaded by each other, intruders appropriated the Osage cornfields for their use and even forbad the Osages the right to cut wood on the stolen claims.[31]

Independence, Kansas, traces its origins to early 1869 when forty families settled there. At first, the community was called Hay Town because the houses were made of grass. Even the Osages called the settlement *Pa she To wan* or Hay Town. Certainly, Independence and Montgomery County were illegal, since they were both organized and recognized by the state of Kansas before the Osage title was extinguished.

State Government Support

It appears that more than enough intruders were upon the Diminished Reserve. However, Governor Crawford, speaking for Kansas, declared: "Kansas cannot afford to remain idle while other states are using every honorable means in their power to encourage immigrants to settle within their borders. The immigration for 1867 was fifty thousand, and it should have been one hundred thousand."[32] These were words backed by action. In addition to advertising Kansas land opportunities in every conceivable way, Crawford also took steps to "protect" the intruders.

He organized four companies of militia around the eastern and northern boundaries of the Diminished Reserve. Although it was reported that the Osages were preparing for war, this was a false rumor. The intruders were not the threatened people. In a very real sense, however, the Osages were truly threatened. Faced with the fact that they were caught between the horns of the dilemma, the Osages spent as much time as possible out on the Plains and kept the peace.[33] Fortunately for the Osages, federal troops arrived in time to aid their determination to keep the peace and real threats did not again arise until 1870. Yet, more of the Osage property was still being taken.

Most of the mixed-bloods, as well as the very old and very young Osages, remained on their claims or in their villages when the Osages went to the Plains for the hunt. These, in their helpless position, were powerless to stop the intruder thefts and depredations. They were also the ones who suffered the insults and atrocities inflicted by the intruders. It was a wry turn of history that made the Osages, who had made the greatest progress toward accepting the Euro-American culture, bear the brunt of that culture's malice.

Sections Twelve and Thirteen

While the battle for ratification of the Drum Creek Treaty was on its deathbed, $50,000 for removal expenses was appropriated as a loan to the Osages. However, to receive the loan the Osages had to agree to accept Sections Twelve and Thirteen of the Appropriation Act. Aside from the donation of school lands and other gifts, these sections also set the "across the board" price of $1.25 an acre for the Osage lands.

This requirement especially upset the mixed-bloods. Most of the mixed-bloods had lost the fruits of their labor when they were forced to cede their "improvements" on the Neosho River by the Treaty of 1865. Now, five years later, after building new cabins, barns, and fences, plus again clearing and breaking out new land on the Verdigris River, they were again being required to walk away from their hard labor without adequate compensation. Their lands were modestly estimated to be worth eleven or twelve dollars an acre, but this did not include the value of their improvements.

To get support for Sections Twelve and Thirteen of the Act of July 15, 1870, the Commissioners agreed to do "everything within their power," to force the intruders to honor the following agreement: "The community of settlers agreed to guarantee to the mixed-bloods full protection in their rights to enter their claims as white settlers, should they desire to remain upon them, and if not of selling them, and extending to the purchaser of such Indian claims the same protection in their rights to enter."[34]

This agreement was a premeditated hoax. The ink was not dry on Osage signatures affixed to the acceptance of the Indian Appropriation Act before the "community agreement" was violated. Property of the mixed-bloods was destroyed or stolen. Barns, corn cribs, fence rails, and standing crops were burned; livestock was either run off or stolen. The Commissioners made a few token gestures to stop the damage and harassment, but their pledges of good faith had the force of a dying wind.[35]

THE VANN-ADAIR AFFAIR

The Beginning

It might be supposed that the defeat of the Drum Creek Treaty and final removal of the Osages from Kansas would be the end of the Osage involvement with the treaty. Such a supposition would be far from the truth. For almost fifty years after the defeat of the Drum Creek Treaty, it caused the Osages a great deal of trouble. The problem started innocently enough, but as so often happens, innocence can quickly become a harsh taskmaster.

According to W. P. Mathes,[36] in November of 1869, six Osages asked him to act as interpreter with the Cherokee. These Osages were from Big Chief's and Black Dog's bands and represented only these two bands. The announced purpose of the discussion was to purchase a new reservation from the Cherokee. However, the Osages were escorted to a room for a conference with Clement N. Vann, William P. Adair, and Cornelius Boudinot, who were Cherokee mixed-bloods.

The gist of the discussion was that these three offered to try to get the Osages more money for their Kansas lands than the eighteen cents an acre offered in the Drum Creek Treaty. Their fee was to be half of everything over ten cents an acre above the Drum Creek Treaty offer. Since the three were going to Washington, they would need a power of attorney to act on behalf of the Osages.[37]

While some documents of this arrangement had existed before February 8, 1873, it was a written contract of that date which became the basis of the Vann-Adair claim. This document set the total fee due Vann and Adair at $330,000 for services rendered. It should be noted that Boudinot had dropped out of the affair. He stated that when the three arrived in Washington, the Drum Creek Treaty was already all but dead. Thus, there could be no fee since no service had been performed. It must have taken a great exertion of their egos for Vann and Adair to persist in their claim.

Fateful Annuity Payment

The June Annuity Payment of 1873 had several interesting events associated with it. The Wichita chief Isadawah was very popular among the Plains nations. An Osage mourning party had slain the Wichita chief and the Plains nations were bent on revenging his death unless the Osages paid a suitable atonement for the murder. The council with the Wichitas was being held during this payment. If this was not enough to put the Osages in hot water, another mourning party supplied additional fuel. A white man had been killed on the Plains and two U.S. Marshals were at the Agency to arrest the guilty Osages.[38]

This situation was tailor-made for Vann and Adair. Feeding upon the fears from these threats to the Osages, they managed to get the Osage Council to approve the February 1873 contract. In return, they promised to save the Osages who might be punished for the two murders. Bribes were offered to Council members, but it is doubtful if any of the Osage leaders knowingly took the bribes. It seems more likely that the Council misunderstood the amount of the claim, thinking it was $3,300 or $33,000 instead of $330,000.[39] The Osage language does not lend itself to accurate comprehension of amounts over 1,000.

We are not sure the Osages were unduly disturbed by either of the murders. There was certainly concern about the Wichita refusal to accept the atonement offers of the Osages. However, Joe *Pawnee No Pa she* settled this matter rather curtly as a Council officer:

> There have been many words. Wichitas have sent many words from their tongues; they have said little. Osages have talked like blackbirds in spring; nothing has come from their hearts. When Osages talk this way, Wichitas believe they are talkers like blackbird. I have listened long time to this talk of blackbirds, and I said when my people talk like blackbirds, Wichitas think they are women. I want to say few words, then Wichitas can go to their lodges and mourn for their chief. I want Wichitas to know this thing. I want them to know that Osage are great warriors. Today they have talked like women but they are warriors. They have those things which Wah' Kon-Tah gave to men, so that he could tell them from women. They know how to die in battle. I want Wichitas to know this thing. We will give ponies to Wichitas for this Chief, then they can go home to their lodges. I have spoken.[40]

An Authorized Payment of Fee

Considering the known facts, it is somewhat difficult to explain how the Commissioner of Indian Affairs could justify payment of any amount to Vann and Adair. Surely, Osage Agent Isaac Gibson and Superintendent Enoch Hoag were opposed to any payment. The Board of Indian Commissioners was also against any payment to them. Yet, despite this opposition from those in the best position to judge the evidence in the Vann–Adair case, $50,000 of Osage money was given to Vann and Adair by the Indian Office.[41]

The Commissioner's Report of 1873 contains Gibson's account of the Vann–Adair affair. In this report, Gibson accurately identifies the real supporters of the Osages: "The act referred to was a part of the Indian appropriation Bill, passed July 15, 1870, having the approval of the President, his board of Indian commissioners, Secretary of the Interior, Commissioner of Indian Affairs, the chairmen of the Senate and House Committees on Indian Affairs, and all of the leading men in Congress, and all the philanthropic and earnest friends of the Indians, because it was an act of justice, plain and uncovered, requiring no corrupting influence to make for it hopeful and constant supporters."[42]

Gibson was referring to the defeat of the Drum Creek Treaty. He goes on to report that when he ordered Vann and Adair to cease bothering the Osage chiefs, they threatened him. Yet, the Indian Office made a donation of $50,000 of Osage money to Vann and Adair.

One would be inclined to believe that having received $50,000 as payment in full for any possible service would have settled the Vann–Adair claim for all time. Like this whole affair, reason would prove to be a poor guide to what actually happened. For example, no miracle of a reasoning mind could ever conceive that Samuel J. Crawford, the ex-governor of Kansas who so bitterly oppressed them in Kansas, would defend the Osages in the later Vann–Adair case.[43]

On May 2, 1910, the long drawn-out Vann–Adair Affair and the aftermath of the Drum Creek Treaty was all but ended. The Supreme Court ruled against the Vann–Adair heirs. The Osages for the first time in over thirty years were free from the Vann–Adair claim. In more recent years, the Osage nation entered a claim against the United States to recover attorney fees incurred in an effort to defeat the Drum Creek Treaty. Thus, this infamous treaty has clung to the Osage people into the 1980s.

16

The Osage Removal

INTRODUCTION

Removals

Without a doubt, the best-known removal in United States history is Jackson's removal of the Cherokee. While the Cherokee removal was a great injustice that caused suffering and loss of life, the Osage removal from Kansas was equally unjust, equally full of suffering, and, on a percentage basis, equally costly in lives. However, so little has been written about these aspects of the Osage removal that David Parsons, in his dissertation about the removal, referred to the removal as a simple move with little loss of life or suffering. Subsequent to Parsons reaching that conclusion, new evidence has surfaced.[1]

The Osage removal was not an isolated event. It was a result of a shift in Indian policy. This change became evident after the enactment of the Kansas–Nebraska Bill and the ensuing war in Kansas. Basically, the changed policy was to remove all Indians from Kansas. While the Civil War delayed the actual removal, it also provided a solution to the problem of where to settle the Indian nations that were in Kansas reserves. By requiring the Confederate Indian nations to sell portions of their Indian Territory reserves in what is now Oklahoma, space was available to colonize the nations from the Kansas reserves. Therefore, from 1864 to 1871 all but a few token groups of Indians were removed from Kansas to Oklahoma.

The last Indians to be removed from Kansas were the Osages and Kaw. The Osage removal was especially prolonged and full of hardships because of the large size of the Osage reserve and because they were the last to be removed. For this reason, among others, we have written about this period in some detail.

It would be interesting to study generations by the degree of control they have over their emotions. Surely, the Civil War generations had very little emotional control. They tended to move from one emotional issue to another and rarely submitted their choices to reason or compromise. Thus, they were easily aroused to violent action as a means of problem solving. The frontier, being on the fringes of Western civilization, was probably more inclined to violence than the more settled areas.

Earlier generations of Osages would have gone to war over the intruders and the many abuses associated with their removal. The removal generation of Osages was directed by the certainty of annihilation if they resisted with violence. Thus, there was reason and compromise induced by necessity. This great cultural difference was, to a considerable extent, a factor in the Osage removal being especially harsh in both overt and covert abuses.

The Neosho Agency

Isaac Gibson

Changes in the Neosho Agency reflect shifts in Indian policy. In 1851, the Neosho Agency was under the Southern Superintendency, having been changed from the Western Superintendency. Besides the Osages, this Agency included the Seneca-Shawnee, Seneca, Quapaw, and what was loosely called the New York Indians. Although the Neosho Agency was supposedly changed to the Central Superintendency in 1867, it was still listed under the Southern Superintendency until the 1869–1871 report. In the spring of 1870, all nations but the Osages were dropped from the Neosho Agency. Four years later, the name was changed to the Osage Agency.[2]

Isaac Gibson was the first agent of the new Neosho Agency organization that included only the Osages. He was also the first of the Quaker agents. Gibson had been appointed in 1869, which was a crucial time in the life of the people. Under Gibson's administration, the Osages slowly moved away from the brink of extinction. With only minor reservations we can say with justice that Gibson was both loved and hated by the Osages.

Governmental Changes

While the people appreciated and loved Gibson for his efforts on their behalf, they hated him for destroying much of their culture and institutions. Gibson set out to destroy the two tribal chieftainships. These were the two division chiefs who presided over the gentile or tribal system. Although earlier efforts to get the Osages to accept *Me ka Ki he ka* (Star Chief; better known as Joe *Pawnee No Pah she,* or Governor Joe) as governor had failed, upon the death of Little White Hair (*Wa Sop pe* or Black Bear) in 1869, Gibson's choice prevailed.

The Council of *Ah ke ta* could not agree on who should succeed to the White Hair Chieftainship. To complicate matters, the *Ne ke A Shin ka* or

Society of Little Old Men had become weak and disorganized. In effect, the tribal system with its twenty-four clans had slowly passed away as a unifying force. Thus, Gibson was able to gain acceptance for Governor Joe.

It must be explained, however, that Joe's acceptance was not entirely because of Gibson, disunity, or the failure of the tribal system. One must remember there were two division chiefs. The White Hair line was recognized by all Osages as head of the Sky Division. However, only about one-third of the Osages recognized the White Hairs as the head chief of all Osages. This designation is a Euro-American creation and not a creation of all the Osages. Star Chief or Governor Joe was the head chief of the Earth Division and was so recognized by all the Osages. His acceptance as Governor largely was due to this fact. To the Osage mind, failure of the Council of *Ah ke ta* to select a White Hair successor from the many aspirants threw the decision upon the people, since the Little Old Men could not act in this selection. Thus, for the first time in Osage history a head chief was selected by the people. While this was a notable modification of Osage law, it must be remembered that the people selected a division chief for the new office.

As we have shown in the matter of an appointive governor, in the final analysis, it was the Osage people who selected the governor. This same process was at work in selecting the first appointive council. In effect, Gibson nominated and the people, while holding a veto power, accepted the council. The selection of a governor and council in this manner broke forever the power of the *Ne ke A Shin ka* and the *Ah ke ta* (Chief Protectors). Never again would the Osages select their leaders in the traditional way, nor would they ever again govern themselves free from outside interference. They now possessed only a token sovereignty.

From the Euro-American view, the Osages had taken a giant step toward becoming Westernized. Without a doubt, this was Gibson's intent. However, many of Gibson's actions seemed to indicate that he was also grooming the Osages for a leadership role in what was then a possible Indian State. It is significant that the Osages were the last Indians to give up on the creation of an Indian State. In any event, Gibson brought the Osage people from the brink of extinction into "clear, cloudless days."[3]

Senator Lot Morrill

Another friend of the Osages was Lot Morrill of Maine. It was this Senator Morrill that reminded the Senate of Articles Two and Sixteen of the Treaty of 1865. Article Two fixed the price of the Osage Trust Lands at $1.25 an acre. All subsequent removal actions including the Trust Lands had reduced this price drastically. Article Sixteen guaranteed the Osages the same price,

$1.25 an acre, for their remaining Kansas lands should they agree to remove from Kansas. Yet, all removal proposals had included a greatly reduced price per acre for these lands also. Morrill argued for justice to the Osages and for the honor of the Senate. Shamed into honoring their treaty obligations, the Senate removal bill not only included the agreed upon price of $1.25 an acre, but it also included a payment of $30,000 due from unfulfilled provisions of the Treaty of 1839.[4]

PROLONGED REMOVAL OF OSAGES

The slow progress of a removal act for the Osages was a source of irritation to the intruders in the Osage Diminished Reserve. These intruders met in the illegal city of Winfield, which was in the illegal County of Cowley, Kansas. They passed a resolution that they sent to Congress urging passage of either the House or Senate version of the Osage Removal Bill. They expressed the need to remove the Indian title so the actual dweller upon the land could buy the land.[5]

We have ample evidence that the intruders had become so motivated by greed that they had become emotionally unstable and a threat to the Osage. The Lieutenant Governor of Kansas well illustrates this in a statement: "When Congress fails to do justice it 'broke the law, and the people have a right, in justice to take possession of the reservation.'"[6] We do not believe a person in control of his or her emotions could be so remote from reason and respect for the order of law.

THE REMOVAL COUNCIL

The Removal Act

The Osage Removal Act was so important to the future of the Osages that Gibson went to Washington to exert as much influence as he could. Gibson must be included on a list of those who aided the Osages to get as many benefits as possible incorporated into the removal act. This bill was enacted on July 15, 1870.[7] Gibson was delighted with the act, but he was especially pleased with assurances that the new reservation would not cost more than fifty cents an acre. He left Washington with this final good news from the Secretary of the Interior.[8]

Gibson was instructed to return to the Neosho Agency and to do all he could to induce the Osages to agree to the recently enacted removal act. He was also directed to select a place in the proposed new reserve to hold a council for discussing and signing the act. The first instruction was reinforced on August 11, when the Central Superintendency was told the act would not be valid unless the Osages approved it. Pressure was to be applied to get their approval if all else failed.[9]

Insofar as the second instruction was concerned, it was the outgrowth of the Osage failure to select a delegation to Washington. Before Gibson had left for Washington, the Osages had requested permission for a delegation to go to the capital to arrange for their removal. This had been approved, but the people's feelings of opposition to treaties made it impossible to find any Osage delegates willing to take the unpopular step. Thus, they had requested a commission to hold council with them on the proposed new reserve in August. They proposed to make a short spring hunt and return to the new reserve instead of to the old Kansas reserve.[10] So, a council was arranged to be held in the new reserve on August 20, 1870. However, it should be observed that a meeting in the new reserve did not occur until 1871.

Convening the Council

Change in Plans

Gibson selected a site near Louis Chouteau's post on the Big Caney for the council. The site was sometimes called Gillstrap's crossing and it was located between Silver Lake and the mouth of Sand Creek. A Cherokee delegation was also to meet with the Osages at this site to discuss a price for the new Osage reserve. All the arrangements were made on the assumption that the Osages would accept the recent removal act. To alleviate this apparent pressure, the site was left to the Osages, and they selected the Drum Creek site in Kansas for the 1870 council.

While everyone except the Osages were assembled and ready to hold a council on the appointed date of August 20, the date was reset for August 29. Gibson had sent runners to call the hunting parties in, but they had not returned by the new date of August 29. By August 31, Governor Joe and the Big Hills had returned from the hunt. Apparently, the mixed-bloods had arrived earlier, and the Little Osages had arrived immediately after the Big Hills.[11] The delayed arrival and order of arrival strongly suggest the Osages were deliberately delaying the council.

Delayed Hunts

Prolonging the spring hunt into late August would have been unusual before 1860. Corn usually entered the "milk stage" by the third week in July. Thus, it was necessary to end the spring hunt in time to harvest "roasting ears" to make dried corn. Most Osage corn was harvested in the "milk stage" instead of as mature corn. However, some was harvested as mature corn to be processed into parched corn and hominy. Due to the destruction of Osage cornfields during the Civil War and by intruders, the Osages often missed having a corn crop. Thus, there was no need to return from the spring hunt in July.

Aside from a deliberate intent to delay the council or the loss of a corn crop, there were other reasons for prolonged hunts. More and more, other nations were invading Osage hunting territory. With so many additional hunters present it not only required more time to find, kill, and process buffalo, but more time was required to protect the hunters and the camps. Between 1865 and 1870, the Osages were killing as many as ten thousand buffalo on each of the two hunts, or at least they were trading this many buffalo hides. Trade with other Indian nations may account for some of these hides. However, we are referring to the total bison killed on the Southern Plains per year. If we assume other nations were killing a like number between the Salt Plains and the Arkansas River in Kansas, hunting would indeed be slowed by the small size of the herds.

Possibly, the last reason was the most significant. It is noticeable that as contact problems increased, the Osages spent more and more time on the Plains. Out in the great openness of the Plains, the people were again free. The worries and disturbing influences of Western civilization were forgotten as the people savored the ages-old life of their ancestors. These moments of the past became dearer to the people as it became evident that they would not have this last refuge from the white man for very many years. They wanted to enjoy the last shred of the past, for they knew these days must sustain them forever.

By September 8, the mixed bloods, Governor Joe's Big Hills, *Nopawalla,* and *Chetopa* of the Little Osages, including Claremore and Tally with their bands, had arrived. We assume the White Hair bands were also present, since Black Dog the Younger and *Wa ti An Ka* with the two Black Dog bands were the only Osages absent.[12] Thus, the council opened on September 9, 1870.

The Council

Questions

The Osages had prepared a list of four questions, and these were answered by Superintendent Enoch Hoag as soon as the opening prayers were completed. These questions were: (1) Would the Osages be protected in their new home? (2) Would their money be paid to them annually, or as they wanted it? (3) Would the Osages be permitted to have their own regulations in their new home? and (4) Could the Osages have some money appropriated for their removal expenses paid to them immediately? These questions seem well considered and are directed to critical points. The questions were probably formulated out on the Plains and prepared by Governor Joe.[13]

Evidently, these questions caught Superintendent Hoag by surprise, because his answers were evasive and provided little satisfaction to the Osages. His answer to the first question—Would the Osages be protected in their new home—was answered by quoting the Cherokee Treaty of 1866, Article Twenty-seven.[14] He also read a telegram stating that troops were in the process of removing intruders. It is probable that the telegram gave the Osages some assurance, since for them actions were more influential than words.

In answer to the second question about the payment of their money, the Superintendent gave a round-about refusal to give them a voice in how their payments would be made. This was not a satisfactory answer for the Osages. For many years the problem of payment, both in kind and time, was a source of friction between the Osages and the Bureau of Indian Affairs. Evidently, Hoag did not want to commit the Indian service to a limitation of their intrusion into Osage government. To avoid this he waved the "red herring" of the right to participate in the Grand Council. This council was probably in preparation for the creation of an Indian State. Possibly Hoag was aware of Osage interest in such a state. In fact, Gibson seemed to be grooming them for a leadership role in such an organization.

The fourth question was also hedged, since Hoag could not determine when the appropriated money could be paid. Even with a set time, the Osages would only get about one-fourth of the money. However, this could have increased to one-half with Gibson's approval. Hoag answered that the fall annuity and gifts would be distributed at the conclusion of the council.[15]

Requested Changes

The Osages presented a written petition with what they considered to be requested changes. Since the removal act was signed without incorporation of the Osage requests, very few of the changes were made. This petition had five requests: (1) A larger reservation than the 160 acres per person was requested. It was the Osage hope that the reservation could be extended to include the Salt Plains. However, they also feared to be too closely confined in a small area. (2) Having seen the evil effects of allotment on other Indian people, the Osages wished to avoid forced allotment. Therefore, they asked that they would not be forced to allot without their consent. This provision was included in the removal act, which enabled the Osages to be the last Indian nation in either Indian Territory or Oklahoma Territory to allot.

Of the remaining three requests, only number three was granted: (3)

This request asked that they be allowed to hunt in the Diminished Reserve and other public lands as long as the buffalo was available. Generally, the United States upheld this right of the Osages. Only during the Cheyenne "War" of the 1870s were the Osages forbidden to hunt on the Plains. In the events leading to the Cheyenne outbreak, Medicine Lodge settlers killed some Osage buffalo hunters and the United States paid the Osages compensation for the act. (4) Intruders were on Osage minds. They did not want a repeat of the intruder invasion following the Treaty of 1865. Seeking the strongest possible guarantee of backing by the United States government, they asked for a special treaty dealing with this problem. One of the reasons they resisted Gibson's efforts to acquire tillable lands for them was to obtain a reservation intruders could not farm. Thus, they hoped to remove their reservation from the greed of intruders.

The final request was avoided, but some compensation was made: (5) An amount of land equal to the amount of school lands donated to Kansas was requested.[16] This request made too much sense to be accepted by Congress. A cash payment was made instead of an equal land area swap. In fairness to Congress, it must be said that they were limited by the Cherokee Treaty of 1866 in the amount of land they could allow one Indian nation to acquire. However, the Cherokee overreached themselves by demanding $1.25 an acre for the Osage Reserve. The ultimate price of seventy cents an acre violated both the Osage Treaty of 1865 and the Removal Act of 1870 which fixed the price at no more than fifty cents an acre. To compensate for these violations, and to justify a higher price to the Cherokee, the Osages were allowed to acquire nearly 1,500,000 acres.

Approving the Removal Act

The Removal Act of 1870 was approved by all the Osage leaders except *Wa ti An ka* on September 10, 1870. *Wa ti An ka* (Dry Plume or Dry Feather) was the leader of that part of the Black Dog band that had earlier followed Wolf. Dry Plume claimed he did not know about the council in time to get there before the signing. It seems this was a device to emphasize a point of importance to the Osages. In his speech at the extra session, Dry Plume again asked that the Osages be allowed to buy land as far as the Salt Plains.[17] The fact that the various bands were so close together in their requests clearly indicate they had held council on the Plains before they came in for the Removal council.

The Osages often used the late arrival to emphasize a point they ardently wished to make. As a matter of fact, this device was incorporated into the Osage ceremonies. One clan was always late for the ceremonies. The officials and other twenty-three clans would be assembled for the procession to the

House of Mystery. Yet, all would have to wait on the slow clan, since the ceremony could not begin without all twenty-four clans. This little drama was played out to stress both the unity and completeness of the tribal organization.

THE REMOVAL FUND

An Effective Weapon

The Removal Fund was in the removal act as a part of Section Twelve. A stated purpose was to make the removal easier for the Osage people. However, the Osages were in dire need of money because of the intruders and the misdirection of their funds from the Ceded Lands. Thus, the $50,000 loan that was a part of Section Twelve was an effective weapon to encourage the Osages to approve the Removal Act of 1870.

As it worked out, the $50,000 was a great convenience for the Bureau of Indian Affairs. Custom dictated that gifts be given to Indians after a council. This was especially true when one party to a council was asking for special concessions. Indian tradition demanded payment of a gift for any concession.

Gifts

The entire practice of gift giving was poorly understood by Euro-Americans, since it was foreign to Western civilization. Usually, this custom at councils was considered to be a bribe. In the early contact times, it was considered to be a tribute. Among the Osages, gifts were tokens of thanks, a seal of high esteem, or a gesture of respect to someone who had bestowed something upon you. Anyone who had received a story or service from an Osage who held proprietary rights to the story or service owed that Osage a gift. To an Osage, the greatest indignity is to be thought of as a stingy person. Withholding a gift is proof of the ultimate in stinginess. Even the Euro-Americans could sense the scorn, contempt, and ill-feeling when they omitted gifts after councils in which concessions had been given to them.

The gifts given after the Removal Council were very poor in quality. Courtesy forbad protest or holding hard feelings toward the giver of poor gifts when it appears they are the best he can afford. However, for a person to give poor gifts when he obviously can afford to give much better gifts is a serious insult. Yet the Osages needed these gifts so desperately that they were accepted with a gratitude far greater than the spirit of the giving and the quality merited. One cannot help wondering what the reaction would have been if the Osages had known these "gifts" had been bought with their money. To the minds of Americans today, it not only seems bizarre to buy "gifts" for Indians with their own money but equally strange to use Osage money to pay the expenses of the host Commissioners. One does not need to be Osage to realize that something was terribly wrong with the financial arrangements of the Removal Council.

Gibson did not discover the misuse of the $50,000 loan until March 9, 1871. He was horrified to discover that the "gifts," expenses of the Removal Council, and the cost of surveying the ninety-sixth Meridian had been paid from the Removal Fund. His report of the expenditure gave the figure as $11,419.43 but he was $100 over the actual costs.[18]

The reason given for using the Removal Fund for these governmental functions was that there was no other fund available for these purposes. Despite careful audits, no record of the Osages being reimbursed for these expenditures has been found. However, it might have been included in a general settlement of claims during the 1970s.[19]

THE SCHOOL LANDS

Special Provisions

Through an interpretation by the General Land Office, Indian reserves did not constitute public domain when the Indian title was extinguished. Because of this interpretation, Kansas was especially concerned about the school land grants in the Osage Reserves. So, specific school land grants were included in the Removal Act of 1870. Kansas requested that three provisions regarding the school land be a part of the act. These were: (1) To reserve sections sixteen and thirty-six to Kansas for public school purposes; (2) To secure equivalents in lieu thereof if these sections had been previously committed; and (3) To secure said equivalents within the bounds of the Osage Reserve.[20]

The act did not include all the state of Kansas had requested, but it did include a school lands grant. This grant was stated in the act in these words, "excepting the sixteenth and thirty-sixth section, which shall be reserved to the state of Kansas for school purposes. . . . "[21] We assume that the other requests were handled administratively instead of encumbering the act with unnecessary verbiage.

It should be noticed that no mention of compensation for the Osages is made. Chapter 251 of 21 Stat. L. 291 provides payment for the school lands in the Osage Trust Lands and to the Civilization Fund in the Osage Ceded Lands. Yet, no mention is made of payment for school lands in the Diminished Reserve.[22] It seems strange that specific mention of the Trust Lands and Ceded Lands is made but no mention of the larger Diminished Reserve is made. Since both the Diminished Reserve and Trust Lands were included

324 / Osage Removal

in the Removal Agreement of 1870, it is possible that the term Trust Lands in the 1880 Act applies to both areas. However, this omission and the Ceded Lands provision do raise some questions.

We have not found any source that indicates either payment or nonpayment for school lands in the Diminished Reserve. The question here is: Were the Osages ever paid for the school lands in the Diminished Reserve? A second question arises from the Ceded Lands and the Civilization Fund. In settling old claims, was the school lands money included in the total indemnity payment?

Amounts Involved

Parsons commented on the amount of land and money involved in these school lands: "The total amount of Osage land sold under the removal act of July 15, 1870, was 8,000,000 acres. Of this amount the act reserved to Kansas one-eighteenth, or 14,444, acres for public purposes. At one dollar and twenty-five cents an acre, this amount would have brought $555,555."[23] It seems there are some mathematical errors in this comment. One-eighteenth of 8,000,000 acres would be 444,444 acres instead of 14,444 acres. $1.25 times 14,444 would be $18,055 rather than $555,555. We multiplied 444,444 acres by $1.25 and got the figure of $555,555. In any event, apparently well over one-half million dollars were involved. Somewhere around this amount should appear to the credit of the Osages for school lands, if the Diminished Reserve was included.

The case for the Trust Lands and Diminished Reserve seems clear enough. However, the school lands problem in the Ceded Lands is muddied by other complications. By 1869–1880, most of the Ceded Lands had been committed, thus the Act of 1880 had little effect there. However, due to this fact, the state of Kansas was awarded in lieu lands plus five percent in cash for all Indian land sold for cash.[24] The in lieu lands and 5 percent cash on cash sales seem to include the Trust Land and Diminished Reserve as well as the Ceded Lands. This again raises the question of Osage compensation, since all expenses were deducted from the Osage share of the sales.

The whole problem of the compensation for the school lands needs more careful investigation than we are prepared to undertake for this history. Another unexplored area is compensation for Osage property stolen or destroyed by citizens of the United States. The Osages were required to pay for property they took or destroyed. One must wonder if the American laws work only in one direction (i.e., the Osages paid for their wrongs but neither United States citizens nor the United States ever paid for Osage property stolen and destroyed by American citizens).

THE MIXED-BLOODS
Leaders

Amazing as it may seem, very little has been written about the mixed-bloods.[25] In a general work such as this, it is impossible to deal with this large subject in detail. However, one small detail should be mentioned. There were only two known mixed-bloods who served in a leadership capacity before the Osage removal from Kansas. These were Jean Baptiste Mongrain (Mogrey) and Sophia Captain Chouteau. Jean Baptiste was chief of the Neosho village, Reaches the Sky. Mrs. Chouteau was called Woman Chief[26] and served as second chief and subsequently as chief of the Beaver band on Flat Rock Creek near the Osage Mission in Kansas. Yet it is important to remember that these mixed-bloods lived the traditional life and were considered to be full-bloods by the Osage full-bloods themselves.

Mixed Marriages

The earliest mixed marriages with Euro-Americans grew out of the fur trade. Three portage routes brought the early French fur traders to the Middle Waters and the Osages. These were the Georgian Bay–Green Bay–Mississippi River route, the Georgian Bay–Des Plaines River–Illinois River–Mississippi route, and the Georgian Bay–Detroit–Toledo–Maumee River–Wabash River–Ohio River–Mississippi River route. While some traders came to the Middle Waters from New Orleans, most of them used the portage routes out of Montreal.

Before 1763, these traders who intermarried with the Osages lived at Vincennes, Indiana; Kaskaskia, Illinois; Cahokia, Illinois; Ste. Genevieve, Missouri; and Cape Girardeau, Missouri. With the founding of St. Louis and St. Charles in Missouri, most of the Osage-French families settled in these two communities. During the War of 1812, the majority of the Osage-French families lived at Côte Sans Dessein, located opposite the mouth of the Osage River in Missouri. This situation changed in 1820 with the founding of Westport Landing, which later became Kansas City. At this date, and until a few years after 1847, practically all the Osage-French mixed-bloods lived either at Westport or Papinsville, Missouri, near the major Osage villages in Bates and Vernon County.

A small number of French-Osage mixed-bloods were with the Astorians and settled on French Prairie in Oregon. So far as we know, none of these ever rejoined the Osages. Several families of French-Osage mixed-bloods settled near Tumwater, Washington, at a place called Cowlitz Prairie. Most of these returned to the Osages in 1870–1872. A few of the French-Osage participated in the California gold rush, but apparently all these returned to the Osages.[27]

Many mixed-bloods were intermarried with both the Osage and Kaw. At allotment, this caused a considerable amount of hard feeling. Some mixed-bloods were enrolled on the Kaw rolls and some on the Osage rolls. Therefore, the Osages did not want to accept any of the French-Osage-Kaw mixed-bloods. It was not a question of Osage blood since many of these mixed-bloods were known to be Osage related. The big question was where the mixed-blood resided or where they were enrolled. The feeling was that if one did not reside with the Osages, he or she should not be considered as Osage. United States laws also recognized only the enrollment in one tribe.

It was advantageous to the fur traders to have an Osage wife and a white wife. From the Osage view, this carried no stigma unless the marriage was a non-Osage marriage. While the Osages accepted the validity of a Christian marriage between two Euro-Americans, they did not recognize such marriages when an Osage spouse was involved. Children of such marriages could not be named and carried the stigma of the marriage all their lives. No honors could devolve on the partners of such a marriage. Since a white man had no Osage clan, if he married an Osage woman the children could not be named without adoption by a male member of an Osage clan. In a reverse marriage, however (that is, if the husband was Osage and the wife a white woman), the children could be named without adoption because the Osage father had an Osage clan.

Most of the early Osage mixed-blood marriages with Euro-Americans were between a white man and Osage woman. Some estimation of the esteem held for a trader by the Osages was revealed by the daughter that was allowed to marry the trader. Osage sons and daughters have pet names that are given in the order of birth. That is, the first son born is called *E gro,* the second was called *Ka shon,* the third was called *Ka shin ka,* and so on. The daughters were called *Me na* for first daughter, *We ha* for second daughter, and *Ah sen ka* for the third daughter. In most families, *Me na* was the favored daughter. Thus, a white man who married a first daughter was indeed held in high esteem. If the white man was allowed to marry the second daughter, it was also a great honor but somewhat less than that of a first daughter marriage. The third daughter on down to the last daughter were considered to be equal but less desirable than the first two daughters. Most mixed marriages with Euro-Americans were with third daughters.

Two Groups of Mixed-Bloods

There were two distinct groups of Osage–Euro-American mixed bloods. One of these groups tended to live apart from the traditional Osages. They were very much like any French habitant in their lifestyle. The other group tended to live with the full-bloods, and they followed the traditional Osage lifestyle. All mixed-bloods of the latter group were counted as full-bloods in population reports, and they were considered to be full-bloods by the true full-bloods. Only the first group was enumerated as mixed-bloods in the pre-removal reports. At the time of the Kansas removal, this first group was called the Half-Breed Band for the first time.

Some research based on the early practice of enumerating mixed-bloods living the traditional life as full-bloods show an unrealistic growth of mixed-bloods in the early–1880s. In some studies, it is assumed this growth was the result of Euro-Americans or other mixed-blood Indians being added to the Osage rolls. Certainly, to some extent this is true. However, many families that were contested were not excluded by virtue of not having Osage blood, but because they had not resided on Osage lands in 1881. In part, this was to exclude Osages who had foresworn Osage citizenship for some other Indian nation or for United States citizenship.

As mixed-bloods increased and full-bloods declined, the mixed-bloods exerted an increasing influence in Osage affairs. The increase in mixed-bloods was due to several factors. By 1868, it was increasingly evident that the Osage annuities would provide a sizable cash income for the times. Therefore, several persons with some Osage blood either returned to the Osages or changed to Osage citizenship. Some full-blood Indians on the Osage rolls are only a small fraction Osage, but elected to be enrolled as Osages. For some reason, these mixed-bloods caused no demand for proof of Osage blood as was required of Osage–Euro-American mixed-bloods.

By far, the single greatest factor creating the shifting ratios, was the relative birthrates. Both the Osage-French and the Osage-Irish mixed-bloods had very large families of ten to fifteen children. By contrast, full-blood families show only two to four children on the annuity rolls.[28] Related to the birthrate is the death rate. While both full-bloods and mixed-bloods show an abnormal death rate following removal, the death rate of the full-bloods was easily twice that of the mixed-bloods.

This was possibly due to living conditions and diet. A lodge becomes unhealthy when less time is spent on the hunt and more time is spent indoors. Since the full-bloods were relying less on the hunt and more on issued rations, they were not as active outdoors and especially not on the healthful Great Plains. Rations were a poor substitute for the rich, varied diet of earlier Osage generations. The mixed-bloods had adopted ranching and subsistence farming so they had a much better and more reliable diet.

As full-blood and mixed-blood numbers reached equality and then the mixed-bloods grew more numerous than the full-bloods, friction grew between the two groups. Tribal power was passing from the full-bloods to the mixed-bloods. For the first time, the mixed-bloods experienced the humility of discrimination from their full-blood relatives. To be shunned by Euro-Americans was an experience that was not novel. Such actions carried a sting that made the Osage blood especially dear to the mixed-bloods, for they were treated well by their Osage brethren. Now that which had healed many wounds inflicted by the white culture was inflicting wounds of its own.

Such actions turned the mixed-bloods inward upon themselves and in effect created a separate Osage culture. Thus, when one spoke of Osages, two groups were included. These were the full-blood and mixed-blood Osages, which included two separate cultures. They shared a common ancestry and tradition, but they were almost as different as the British and Americans. Fortunately, the two groups are drawing closer and hopefully the Osages will be one people again in another generation.

"Hopefully" is used advisably, for new alignments are beginning to emerge. Currently, the mixed-blood distinction is all but gone. Yet, a growing division is evident, based on those within commuting distance of Pawhuska and those who live far away. It is sad that the Osages have been their own worst enemy. The rift of 1800[29] weakened the people and contributed to a rapid decline. With the removal came a growing rift between full-blood and mixed-blood. This rift of 1880 brought an end to the great Osage tribal organization. Even the term *tribe* was replaced by the name, Osage nation. Now we risk disunity and failure to create a form of government that is *of* the Osage people and *for* the Osage people. Petty factionalism weakens a people by diverting energies against each other. These same energies could be better used in restoring the Osage people to their rightful position in the world.

The foregoing essay about the mixed-bloods was to provide background and direction for the mixed-blood role in the removal from Kansas and the aftermath. We are ready to enter the story of that role.

Mixed-Blood Objections to Removal

Without a doubt, the conference the Removal Committee held with the Osage mixed-bloods was the first time they had been consulted about Osage affairs. It is also the first time the records mention opinions of the mixed-bloods. Apparently, it was the mixed-bloods who first objected to the intruders on the new proposed reserve in Indian Territory. Having twice been dispossessed by intruders in the past five years, the mixed-bloods did not want to repeat the experience a third time. One can understand, in the light of past experiences, why oral or written promises carried little assurance with the mixed-bloods. With them, "seeing was believing." When the intruders were removed, they would believe it, but not before a physical removal had been effected.

The mixed-bloods also had other concerns. The lands they occupied were worth much more than $1.25 an acre. New improvements had barely been completed since the 1865 removal from the Neosho Valley. Understandably, the mixed-bloods felt they should be paid for these improvements. Insofar as possible, they felt some payment should be made for their property destroyed or stolen by the intruders. Finally, several of the mixed-bloods had a desire to remain on their claims, to take American citizenship, and to become a part of the Euro-American community.

The intruders, seeing that these reasonable objections of the mixed-bloods could well delay the acceptance of removal, sought to ease the mixed-blood's concerns. Meetings were held throughout southern and southeastern Kansas to deal with the mixed-blood problem. In every case, promises were made to the mixed-bloods that they would be supported in every way. Climaxing these meetings was a mass meeting in Montgomery County that drafted a "guarantee of community support" for the mixed-bloods. Naively, the Removal Commission accepted this statement in good faith and pledged to do all in their power to enforce the community pledge. After the mixed-bloods signed the Removal Act, the settlers commented, "The Osages have signed the bill, and we have got the land; let the half-breeds go to H—l."[30]

Filing for United States Citizenship

Following the signing of the "community compact," nineteen mixed-bloods filed their first papers for United States citizenship.[31] Their names and ages were as follows: (1) Joseph Mosier [Monjeon], 28; (2) Francis Mitchell [Mikles], 45; (3) Alexander Beyett, 33; (4) Heweh ha ka Toby, 30; (5) Wild Cat, 30; (6) Martin Redman, 25; (7) Wooster Bigheart, 28; (8) Peter Chouteau, 40; (9) John Fitz-Gerald, 25; (10) George Redeagle, 35; (11) Cyprian Tayrian, 34; (12) Joseph Mitchell [Mikles], 30; (13) Dodridge Boonby [Barnaby], 48; (14) Jack Eatsataneka, 28; (15) Peter O'Carter, 35; (16) Mad Chief, 35; (17) Te ka ah ka pa na, 26; (18) Gesso Chouteau, 48; and (19) William Tinker, 30.[32]

Harassment by the intruders who had promised to support the mixed-bloods soon reduced this list of nineteen to only twelve—thirty had originally expressed a desire to remain in Kansas, but only nineteen took out first papers. The twelve remaining by Christmas of 1870 were: (1) Alexander Beyett; (2) Gesso Chouteau; (3) Peter Chouteau; (4) Joseph Mosier [Monjeon]; (5) Frank Mitchell [Mikles]; (6) [?]; (7) Martin Redman; (8) Tobey

Mogrey [Mongrain]; (9) Red Eagle; (10) Mad Chief; (11) Little Wildcat; and (12) Hlah se jack.[33]

The mixed-blood situation in Kansas grew worse as time passed. All of the mixed-bloods were harassed, and, eventually, they returned to the Osages. Certainly, the case of Joseph Mosier (Monjeon) illustrates the terrible things done to these mixed-bloods. Joseph Mosier had served honorably as a Union soldier during the Civil War. He was forcibly removed from his home at night and of necessity had to wade through the snow to find help. His home and granary were burned. Joseph died from the exposure. He had committed no crime except being part Osage and owning land that white men wanted.[34]

We will not dwell on these wrongs. However, as a people, the Osages must remember that these experiences were bought at a terrible price. They must remember not to trust even written promises that lack an absolute means of enforcement. All agreements should have a guaranteed right of redress for violation of agreements. Lastly, beware of greed and excessive emotions, for they are the traits of an unstable mind.

SEARCHING FOR THE THIRTY-SEVENTH PARALLEL

A Matter of Errors

Thirty-seven degrees north latitude is the boundary line between Kansas and Oklahoma. One would suppose that if Columbus could locate and sail a course along the 25th parallel in 1492, a surveyor could locate a parallel and survey a straight line in 1870. Between Ennisville[35] and Elgin, Kansas, the distance is about twenty miles east and west. The surveyed line of 1856 was approximately one-quarter mile off in this twenty miles. Apparently, there was a magnetic deflection in Sprague's Valley or Elgin, Kansas. Captain Poland, who had been sent to clear intruders from the new Osage reserve in 1870, met surveyor Max Fawcell who said that because of a compass problem he had set the line a quarter mile north as a supplementary line.[36]

There are one-quarter-mile errors all along the thirty-seventh parallel between the two states.[37] We cannot account for the errors along the panhandle of Oklahoma, but we do have the reason for the offset at Elgin. Having walked and traveled horseback over the thirty-seventh on either side of Elgin, I can state it has no offset today. It is a straight east-west line between Chautauqua Springs and Cedar Vale, Kansas. In a high school Physical Geography course, a class project was to survey the line along the south edge of Elgin. Then, we noticed no special magnetic deflection on the transit compass. This entire area was carefully resurveyed in the 1940s and 1950s for the Hulah Dam on the Caney. The topographic maps all show the

37th as a straight line. Evidently, the supplementary line formed a base line in the Elgin area in 1870. By measuring with the chain a quarter mile south from this line one could accurately locate the true line.

Elgin, Kansas

Elgin originated one-quarter mile south of the thirty-seventh. It was then called Jim Town after the Jimson Weeds that were growing there.[38] The town was on the site of an Osage hunting camp called *Gra to Me Shin ka* or Little Hawk Woman. The name was changed to Elgin to satisfy the Postal Department, which established an office in the town when it was moved north of the thirty-seventh.[39]

Captain Poland, who arrived in Elgin after it had been moved, always in his journal calls the town Elgin and never Jim Town. And he states that the supplementary line was north one-quarter mile. This would be about where the quarantine line of the cattle shipping days was located or north of the present line about one-quarter mile. It was probably the survey of Max Fawcell in 1870 that caused the town to remove one-quarter mile north.

The southern boundary of Kansas has caused concern by other historians. In 1910, George W. Martin, Secretary of the Kansas State Historical Society, wrote to John Francis Jr., then acting chief of the Federal Land Division. Martin was attempting to clarify the locating of the thirty-seventh. In his reply, Mr. Francis gives a comprehensive survey of the history of the southern boundary.[40]

INTRUDERS ON THE NEW RESERVE

Responsibility

According to the agreement of 1870, all intruders were to be removed from the new reserve before the Osages left Kansas. In trying to meet this agreement, the United States government encountered unexpected problems. Hence, the removal of intruders was not effective. The basic problem was a matter of determining which department of the government would accept responsibility for the removal of the intruders.

It was no small matter to offer one's self to be the target for all the expansion-minded American citizens. Politically, it was a very dangerous move. Surely, the army did not want to endanger the popularity it was enjoying in the post–Civil War days. While the Indian Office was in no way experiencing popularity, it was at least out of the public eye. Few of the people holding Indian Office positions wanted their activities exposed to public view. Another aspect of the situation was the behind-the-scene efforts of the War Department to reclaim the Bureau of Indian Affairs. Accepting responsibility for using troops to remove intruders could tip the balance against the War Department.

The matter of removing these intruders from the new Osage reserve was the subject of a Cabinet meeting on August 5, 1870. At this meeting, the Cabinet was definite in a decision that these intruders must be removed. On August 5, General Sherman sent orders to General John Pope to remove the intruders.[41] Pope was in command of the district involved. He sent orders to Captain John Scroggs Poland, who commanded in southeast Kansas, to meet Captain Craig, who was the Cherokee agent, at Baxter Springs, Kansas.

A classic example of "passing the buck" on an unpopular action can be seen in Captain Poland's orders from General Pope. General Pope was very careful to stress the importance of not originating any plan or accepting any responsibility for removing intruders. Pope reasoned that since Indian reservations were the exclusive jurisdiction of the Indian Office, then that office should be responsible. Captain Poland was further ordered to act only under the direction of an Indian agent.[42] Generally, Poland followed these orders, but he did take minor individual action without consulting the Cherokee agent.

Remember that in 1870 the army was trying to regain control of Indian Affairs. There is no way to determine how much of this "buck passing" was due to this factor and how much was due to the desire to stay politically popular. In all probability, some of the reluctance to expedite the removal of intruders was an effort to cast the Office of Indian Affairs in a bad light.

Apparently, the Cherokee agent had few misgivings about removing the intruders. He firmly requested Captain Poland to "remove as promptly as possible all intruders in this territory."[43] The only remaining problem for Captain Poland was to determine where the southern line of Kansas was located. Although the line was dimly marked by a survey, a great deal of uncertainty about its location existed. Captain Poland and the Cherokee agent agreed to leave the doubtful settlers alone until another survey could be made. Yet, the greater problem of settlers far to the south was also practically ignored.

Captain Poland's Actions

From Ennisville, located a few yards below the Kansas-Oklahoma line on the Little Caney, Captain Poland went to the mouth of the Little Caney. It was thought in 1870 that Ennisville was in Kansas. This was subsequently proven wrong.[44] However, assuming the settlers were on legal ground Captain Poland did not disturb them. No intruders were found between Ennisville and the mouth of the Little Caney. Their cabins were vacant, and it was assumed they had returned to Kansas.

On the next day, Captain Poland went south to Bird Creek, which he called Dog Creek. By September 27, 1870, Captain Poland was camped near Elgin, Kansas. What intruders he had found willingly moved back across the thirty-seventh as Captain Poland defined the location of the line. Traders in the area were not disturbed as long as they had trading licenses. Poland went as far west as Arkansas City, Kansas, and then returned to Elgin. From there he went east to Chetopa, Kansas, and then back to his headquarters.[45]

Captain Poland was not overly concerned about removing intruders. His movements suggest more of an exploration operation than a removal action. According to his reports, he did little more than let the intruders know of his presence. It has been estimated that there were between 2,500 to 3,000 intruders in the Caney Valley watershed at the time of Captain Poland's visit.[46] Nothing in his reports indicate this many intruders.

It is evident that the Captain did not explore many valleys of the Caney drainage. Neither Buck Creek of the northwest, Pond Creek, Turkey Creek, Mission Creek, Elm Creek, Beaver Creek, nor Salt Creek was mentioned in his reports. These streams were also omitted on his map. Settlements on these tributary streams were often as heavy as along the Big Caney.

Both the intruders and Captain Poland followed the well-worn Osage buffalo trails, which has been described and shown on maps in an earlier chapter. It may be worth the effort to review these, because the intruders used the well-traveled trails to invade the area.

Conflicts between Captain Poland's Reports and the Views of the Intruders

Captain Poland reported his activities to his superiors. Without exception, he reported that the intruders had returned either by request or by rumor. He had granted a delay for the intruders of the Donelson settlement. If one were to accept Poland's reports at their face value, it would be easy to believe the intruder problem in the new Osage reserve was solved.

However, the intruders themselves tell a different story. The evidence of our own day and time tend to support the intruder view instead of the reports of Captain Poland. These intruder families admitted that some of them did go back to Kansas but returned to their "stands" after the army left. However, the majority bluntly admitted that they remained where they were and ignored the orders to leave the area.[47]

Uncle John Buckmaster (sometimes given as Buckston) was one of the intruders of the Donelson settlement. He influenced several families from the St. Paul, Kansas, area to settle there. The Donelson settlement was at the White Swan ford on the Caney. That is, it centered on the left bank at that site, but it was strung out upriver and downriver on both banks. Two ceme-

334 / Osage Removal

teries were used by these people. One of these is the Canville Cemetery, which was moved with the Boulanger Cemetery one-half mile north of Boulanger, Oklahoma, when Hulah Dam was built. The other is between Highway 99 and White Swan ford, on the last hill between Pond Creek and the Caney. A. B. Canville built his second trading post at White Swan ford. This post was on the left bank and formed the center of the settlement.

In later days, the Bureau of Indian Affairs required these intruders to pay a rental fee to the Osage people. The Agency kept record books of the fees and whomever paid for the permit. These books are presently at the Fort Worth, Texas, Records Center.[48] The many evidences of the failure of Captain Poland's mission provide direct contradiction of his reports. When one looks at violations of agreements, it is interesting to seek out the reasons for the violation. Nevertheless, the fact that this agreement was violated stands as another crime against the Osage people.

17

The Final Move

When Isaac T. Gibson became agent to the Osage people in 1869, they were in danger of extinction. No better introduction to the final move of the Osages and their survival could be found than the relationship between Gibson and the Osage people. Roughly, this period would be between 1870 and 1875.

The 96° west longitude line, which is the eastern boundary of the Osage reservation, has been surveyed at least three times. A second survey was made upon the insistence of Gibson. This survey placed the 96th several miles east of the original survey line. Gibson was elated with the report of the second survey, but the Cherokee insisted the first survey was correct.

Agent Gibson was determined to make farmers of the Osages. However, the Osages were equally determined not to be farmers. To Gibson, the Caney River Valley was the only good farmland in the proposed Osage reservation. Yet, the Osages felt that good farmland would attract white intruder farmers. They possibly also realized that the absence of good tillage lands would prevent Gibson from converting them into farmers. These conflicting viewpoints had an important bearing on the acquisition of the present reservation.

Originally, the proposed reservation was divided in half by the present 96th west longitude line. This proposal comprised only about one-third as many acres as the present reservation, or nearly 500,000 acres. Gibson was delighted with this proposal since it included the better sections of the Caney Valley. He located the new agency near the center of this proposed reservation, which was on Rice Creek near Silver Lake, south of Bartlesville, Oklahoma. The Cherokee opposed this proposed reservation for two reasons. They argued that the original survey was the correct location of the 96th and that the offered price of fifty cents per acre should be one dollar twenty-five cents an acre. The Osages made "bluff gestures" toward the Caney Valley area east of the 96th, but their real goal was a larger reservation that extended west to the Salt Plains.

To resolve these differences, a commission was sent to evaluate the proposed reservation and a third survey was made to locate the 96° west longitude line. After a brief tour of the better parts of the proposed reservation, the commission recommended a price of one dollar twenty-five cents per acre. To make matters worse, the new survey located the 96th a few feet *west* of the original survey line. Gibson was furious and more than a little bitter, but he removed the agency west to Deep Ford on Bird Creek, now Pawhuska, Oklahoma. He then supported the Osage demand for a larger area and fought to lower the price per acre below fifty cents.

President Grant ultimately decided the price issue as provided in the Cherokee Treaty of 1866. Since the price was set at seventy cents per acre, neither the Osages nor Cherokees were satisfied. In both the Treaty of 1865 and the removal act of 1870, the government had promised that the new reservation would not cost more than fifty cents an acre. To compensate the Osages for reneging on the guaranteed ceiling of fifty cents an acre agreement and to give the Cherokee more money, the United States consented to enlarging the reservation by two-thirds. The Osages now had a home and it consisted of almost one and one-half million acres.

Several points should be observed in connection with the acquisition of the present Osage reservation. While Gibson and the Osages held conflicting cultural viewpoints, they shared the same sense of justice. Both parties sought the best possible terms for the people. Although we have not previously stressed it, the Osages bought their reservation. So far as we know, the Osages and Kaws were the only Indian nations in Oklahoma to acquire their reservation in this manner. As later events will show, this was an extremely important fact. Finally, with the acquisition of their last home, the mold of the future Osages was cast. They tended to become ranchers instead of farmers. The vast reaches of bluestem grass were an open invitation to grazing. Furthermore, the grass sprung from a thin layer of rich soil covering beds of plow-defying limestone.

While these facts alone would have made the Osage reservation a great grazing region, location and the developing history of the United States thrust the Osages into the mainstream of the cattle industry. Isaac T. Gibson and the Osage leadership had now assured the Osage presence as a people and had aided them in securing an economic future.[1]

It has been estimated that there were 3,150 members of the Osage people who made the move from Kansas. Ninety-two percent of these were full-blood Osages.[2] Today, the total for those with Osage blood numbers more than eighteen thousand. Unfortunately, the percentage of full-blood Osages has reversed. Most Osages of the present are Osage–Euro-American mixture with Osage–Other Indian mixture making up the second most numerous group.

SELECTING THE NEW RESERVE

The Selection Committee

Things were progressing well in the removal process, aside from the treatment forced upon the Osages by the intruders. A new Council had been created, and for the first time it included several mixed-bloods. This Council was comprised of *Ah ke ta Ki he ka* (Soldier Chief), Gus Strike Axe, Governor Joe, Little Lame Doctor, *Hu lah Tsah, Ki he ka Stet sy* (Tall Chief), *O la ho Walla* (Beautiful Voice), Cyprian Tayrien, *Mah shon ka Tal* (Black Dog), William H. Tinker, and Augustus Chouteau (interpreter).

The new Council appointed a fourteen-member committee to select the new reservation. It is interesting to observe that while the appointive Council was a creation of Gibson's, the Council named traditional leaders to this committee. The members were Governor Joe, *No pa Walla* (Thunder Fear), *Ki he ka Shin ka* (Little Chief), No Heart (Possibly Big Heart), Alexander Beyett, Augustus Captain, Sam Bienvineu, *Mon shou Ka shi, Ea hoh ka,* Hard Rope, *Che To pa (Tsi To pa,* or Four Lodges), *Wa ti An Ka* (Dry Plume), Old Claremore, and Black Dog.[3]

The Size of the Proposed Reserve and Population

Upon the findings of the selection committee and Isaac Gibson, the Council selected a tract for the new reserve on October 26, 1870. This area was equally divided by the 96th meridian, as was determined by a second survey of this line. The reserve was to be sixty miles long, north and south, and sixteen and two-thirds miles wide, east and west. It was to contain 640,000 acres.[4]

While it is almost entirely surmise, it seems that the traditional Osages were intentionally cooperating with Gibson to achieve their own purpose. We base this surmise on four factors: (1) The Osages were hunters who desperately wanted to avoid any further contacts with intruders; (2) They did not want to be farmers nor did they want to own lands that would be attractive to intruders; (3) The Osages knew these lands better than the Cherokee or anyone else. It is extremely unlikely that they were not aware of the location of the 96th (the Cherokee pointed out this fact); and (4) It would have been entirely in keeping with the Osage character to have made a thrust in one direction to make a gain in another direction. By contrast, meek acceptance of the desires of the Indian Office was not the Osage way.

Subsequent events tend to support these basic observations. One must keep in mind what the Osages wanted and not what the Bureau of Indian Affairs wanted for them. At every opportunity, the Osages pushed for more land and the extension of the reserve west to the Salt Plains. These requests were opposite to what Gibson was trying to get for them, and the Osage knew this. Yet, they also knew they could not get what they wanted without Gibson's blessing. Therefore, they convinced Gibson that they were terribly disappointed when they did not get the rich Caney Valley east of the 96th. A people who could mourn the death of an enemy they had killed would find this act of deception mere child's play.

The 640,000 acres of the first choice reserve further supports our surmise. Gibson had taken a census of the Osages and had arrived at a population of 3,150. However, the Osages had convinced him there were 850 absentees.[5] This brought the total to 4,000. Thus, 640,000 acres would provide 160 acres for each of 4,000 persons. This population "boost" clearly shows the Osages desired quantity instead of quality in land.

Silver Lake

Many mixed-bloods started making improvements around Silver Lake. This was east of the true 96° west longitude line, but about on the second, or false, line. Most of the buildings were on the east side of the lake, including the Agency, while Louis Chouteau's post was south of the little settlement.[6] As a sidelight to this community, Julia Roy Lessert Papin—the step-grandmother of Charles Curtis, Vice President under Herbert Hoover—is buried at Silver Lake. Curtis lost his parents at a young age and was raised by his grandfather, Joe Papin, and step-grandmother, Julia Papin. Julia Papin was born Julia Roy and married first Clement Lessert.

Throwing the Osages "Into the Bluffs"

Because of a third survey, it was determined that Silver Lake was indeed east of the 96th. Along with the survey of 1871 came a decision by Secretary of the Interior Columbus Delano that the Osages were not "civilized" Indians.[7] This fact barred the Osages from taking up lands east of the 96th. If the Osages were not "civilized" in 1871, it is a little difficult to explain how they became "civilized" within a decade. When the so-called five civilized tribes were forming their merger, the Osages were invited to join them. Fearing the loss of their autonomy, the Osages refused the invitation.

Superintendent Enoch Hoag bitterly declared that the Osage were being "thrown into the bluffs."[8] This was an expression of Gibson's low esteem for the bulk of the Osage reserve. However, beauty lies in the eye of the beholder. To the Osage eye, the cross timbers of the east and the rolling Osage prairies to the west were more beautiful than the Caney bottoms. Based on the Euro-American economy of the 1870s, the Osages were "thrown into the bluffs." Such land had little economic value in the post–Civil War period. Less than two percent of the present reserve is tillable land.

Without a doubt, the Osages were aware of the white man's greed, and they were aware that the Cherokee was infected with the same malady. They knew that a few years earlier the Cherokees had been eager to sell their restricted interest in the entire outlet for twenty-five cents per acre. Suddenly, when it was discovered that the Osages were to get one dollar twenty-five cents an acre for their Kansas lands and that the Osages were to be settled in the outlet, the price went to one dollar twenty-five cents.

Apparently, the Osages were being tapped to make the Cherokee richer. Surely, the fears of an Osage uprising expressed by American officials would lead one to suspect a clouded conscience. Note that these fears were much like the fear of the Osages expressed by the Spanish a century earlier. It was these fears generated by troubled consciences and possibly fed by Osage planted rumors that led to a meeting.

Many Osages had camped on Pond Creek in the present reserve. These were primarily the three independent Little Osage bands under Strike Axe. The campsite is one-half mile upstream from the Highway 99 bridge across Pond Creek. Strike Axe remained here for some years, but the other two independent Little Osage bands eventually settled on Mission Creek near Bowring, Oklahoma.

Isaac Gibson, Mahlon Stubbs (the Kaw agent), and George Howland (one of the three commissioners sent to settle the Osage problems) met with the Osages encamped on Pond Creek. They arranged for a general Osage meeting to be held at the Silver Lake Agency. Thus, the stage was set for the final scene in the drama of selecting a final home for the Osages.

Reaching Agreement on the Final Reserve

Seventy-five Osage leaders met with the three commissioners from Washington in the afternoon of March 1, 1871. The commissioners read their instructions, and the Osages retired to consider the alternatives given by the Indian Office. On the evening of March 4, the Osages requested a convening of the council. Once assembled, Governor Joe presented the commissioners with a document the Osages had prepared.[9]

In this document containing the Osage proposal we find the real Osage intention. In our opinion, this was the climax of the Osage maneuvers. The

Osages agreed to accept lands west of the 96th. However, they included an increase in size as compensation for the *loss* of lands east of that line. Boundaries were described as the Kansas line on the north and running sixty miles south to the Creek north line. Taking the 96th as the east line and the channel of the Arkansas River as the west line completed the bounds. These boundaries may seem clear at first glance, but the south line, in part, follows the Arkansas River and not the Creek line. Added to this requirement of acceptance was a request for a small tract west of the Arkansas.

A major purpose of this request was to provide an outlet to the buffalo hunting grounds. Although this request was not granted, the purpose was achieved. In the final act, the Osages were given the right of passage and the right to hunt buffalo as long as there were buffalo to hunt. Agreement was reached the next day and the Osages had their new reserve assured. The price remained to be set by the President, but the reserve had finally been selected. Nearly a square mile for each Osage had been included in the agreement.

A QUESTION OF SIZE AND PRICE

Setting the Size

While we have mentioned that the final size of the new reserve was much larger than originally intended, we did not go into any detail as to how it became so large. To discuss the size of the new reservation, we must go back to the agreement to removal. The Osages had petitioned for six things as a part of the agreement. These were: (1) They asked that the government should pay them $300,000 for damages caused by intruders; (2) They requested permission to buy more land than 160 acres per person; (3) They asked that they be permitted to hold their lands in common until they requested individual allotment; (4) They asked for the right to hunt buffalo as long as they were plentiful; (5) They asked for protection from intruders; and (6) They requested that they be allowed to purchase as additional lands the acreage of Kansas school lands in their purchase of a reservation.[10]

One does not need to be blessed with much insight to realize the Osages were deeply concerned about the size of their new reservation. They were not merely hunters—they were buffalo hunters. It was a matter of serious consequence to them if they should be blocked from the buffalo hunt. They allowed the $300,000 indemnity claim to lapse in preference to a larger reserve which, in turn, meant access to the buffalo.

By asking and getting the right to hold their land in common until they requested individual allotment, the Osages gained an important right. Neither the Dawes Act (General Allotment Act) nor the later Curtis Act could be applied to them. Thus, on the eve of Oklahoma statehood, the Osages, by holding their lands in common, were in a strong bargaining position. Among other things, which we will discuss in due course, this position enabled them to retain mineral rights in common.

A serious barrier to enlarging the new Osage reserve was the Cherokee Treaty of 1866. By this treaty, all reservations carved from the outlet were limited to 160 acres per capita. However, since the Osage Treaty of 1865 had been bent and twisted to accommodate the Cherokee, it was felt that a violation of the Cherokee Treaty would balance things out. The Cherokee were interested in the total amount of money and not necessarily the amount of land.

There was a concern within the United States government about the amount of land involved in settling the Osages on their new reservation. Commissioner Francis A. Walker raised this question in his comments about the Osage request for more land.

> Without apprehending that there will be any considerable difficulty in obtaining future further cessions of territory from tribes within the Indian country as the government shall desire, it would still be my belief that it was decidedly injudicious to exceed in any case the amount contemplated in that treaty, *viz.,* 160 acres to each member of a friendly tribe so settled upon the ceded lands, were it not that the Osages have suffered great hardship and wrong in the country from which they came, and have now encountered a grievous disappointment in their expected home in the Indian country, solely through the failure of the government to properly determine their location. If the injuries which the Osages have suffered in the past, their disappointment now through the fault of the Government, and the manifest and urgent importance of adjusting the difficulty without delay, are held to constitute a sufficient reason for allowing these Indians to purchase more land than was contemplated in the treaty of 1866, I know of no reason why this agreement should not be pronounced expedient, so far as the United States is concerned. . . . [11]

Walker clearly states the reasons for granting the additional lands to the Osages. The fact that he urges the acceptance of the Osage wishes suggests more than usual motivation. We believe the Osages were successful in their efforts to acquire more land because they employed their traditional strategy.

Fixing the Price

In discussing the price the Osages paid for their present reservation, it is necessary to examine an unratified Cherokee Treaty of 1868 and the Cherokee Treaty of 1866. Our first consideration is Article Sixteen of the 1866 treaty: "the boundaries of each said district to be distinctly marked, and the land conveyed in fee simple to each of said tribes. . . . "[12] We must tread carefully through the maze of terms and treaties to determine the validity of title. *Black's Law Dictionary* defines "fee simple" as follows: "An absolute or fee simple estate is one in which the owner is entitled to the entire property, with unconditional power of disposition during his life, and descending to his heirs and legal representatives upon his death intestate."[13] A final point must be added to the two above. The Cherokee patent of 1838 required the Cherokee to occupy the Outlet or it would revert to the United States.[14]

There is a legitimate reason to question the Cherokee title to the Outlet in 1870. We must first point out that in 1838 the United States did not have a clear title to the Outlet. The Osage title was not entirely extinguished until ratification of the Treaty of 1839. Without reaffirmation after 1839, the Cherokee patent of 1838 was clouded.

While the United States elected to recognize the validity of Cherokee ownership of the Outlet in 1868, there is ample reason to question this recognition. Terms of the Cherokee patent required occupation of the Outlet. The Cherokee did not occupy the Outlet in either the Western civilization sense or in the Indian sense of occupation. For a time they occupied it in the Indian sense in going to and from buffalo hunts. However, this had been discontinued sometime before 1868. Cherokees never occupied the Outlet in the Western civilization sense and, therefore, had forfeited the right of ownership under the Treaty of 1838. However, since the Cherokee title was recognized by the United States in the unratified treaty of 1868 and to the sale to the Osages, we must assume the title was legitimate.

Insofar as the Osage title to the present reservation is concerned, it is as sound as the United States and over a century of occupation can make it. The Osages hold possession in fee simple from the United States' support of the Cherokee title. This fee simple document is held in trust by the United States government.

By far, a more debatable question is how the Outlet lands could increase in value from twenty-one cents an acre in 1868 to seventy cents an acre in 1873. In the intervening five years, positively no improvements were made upon the land. It was still totally "wild land." One can only assume the rise in cost was politically or socially inspired. Surely, it could not be economically justified.

The early price negotiation was concerned with only the Caney Bottoms on either side of the 96th. However, by early 1870, it was decided not to allow the Osages east of the 96th. Acting under the assumption that the second survey of the 96th was correct, a second reservation was laid out and the search for price continued. Since this involved some of the best farmland in the Outlet, a larger price than twenty-one cents an acre would seem to be justified. In the spring of 1870, the Cherokee representative would not reach a price agreement with the Osages. However, he suggested a meeting with the Cherokee National Council to fix the price.[15]

Acting upon this suggestion, the Osage Council appointed a committee to negotiate with the Cherokee National Council. While the Osages had dealt with the Cherokee before and knew there would be delays, they were not prepared for the long drawn out wait imposed by the Cherokee. After a two-week delay and the prearranged meeting with the Cherokee still did not materialize, the Osages returned home in disgust.[16]

Upon the return to the Drum Creek Agency, Gibson wrote to his superiors recommending that the price issue be submitted to the President, as provided in the Cherokee Treaty of 1866. On May 27, 1871, the President set the price of this land at fifty cents an acre.[17] Since this was within the promises made to the Osages as a condition of removal, the Osages were content with the Presidential decision. However, the Cherokee were vocal in their discontent with the decision. These Cherokee protests were undoubtedly influential in raising the final price to seventy cents per acre.

By the fall of 1871, the third survey of the 96° west longitude line had been completed. The news that the Osage would have to select a *third* reservation exploded like a bomb amid the Bureau of Indian Affairs officials. Not only was the Agency and improvements at Silver Lake lost, but all the negotiations had to be undertaken for a third time.[18] Judging from the Euro-American histories of the Osages, the officials braced themselves for a full-scale Osage war. Yet, the Osage apparently accepted this setback with a calm demand for more land.

In the final negotiation of price, much the same pattern of delay and final referral to the President was followed. On February 4, 1873, President Grant fixed the price of the final Osage reservation at seventy cents an acre.[19] Since the Osage portion of this purchase was 1,470,059 acres, they paid $1,029,041.30 for their reservation. Actually, they bought and paid for the Kaw portion too, but the Kaw eventually paid the Osages for their portion.

Both the Osages and the Cherokee objected to this price of seventy cents. The Osages objected because it exceeded the fifty cents an acre promised in the Treaty of 1865 and the Removal Act of 1870. Feeling the Outlet was as valuable as the Kansas lands the Osages sold for $1.25 an acre, the

Cherokee complained also. It should be noted that this Osage price could have set the price for the entire Outlet.

The end of all the negotiations and payments and also the significance of how the Osage reservation was acquired are well summed up in the following quote: "The Osage Indians bought their reservation from the Cherokee Tribe of Indians, and paid thereof a stipulated amount. With reference to their lands and minerals, they are in a different position from most Indian tribes in the United States, in that they bought and paid for their lands, while the greater part of the other Indian tribes were settled upon their lands by the United States government, and given the right of occupancy and to said lands. A deed from the Cherokee nation to the United States of America, in trust for the use and benefit of the Osage Indians, was given on the 14th day of June, 1883."[20]

LEAVING THE OLD HOME

The Osages Leave Kansas

For the Osages, leaving Kansas was a difficult task. So long as they lived, those involved in the removal often found it necessary to go to Kansas on business. Many of the new generation born in Oklahoma moved to Independence or Arkansas City, Kansas, as soon as they acquired United States citizenship. While many boys of the new generation attended military academies in Missouri, a sizable number of the girls attended Catholic Academies in Kansas.

The Act of 1870, providing for the Osage removal from Kansas, was barely signed before the demonstrations of sadness commenced. As the Board of Indian Commissioners described it, "At dawn on the day after the treaty had been signed the air was filled with cries of the old people, especially the women, who lamented over the graves of their children, which they were about to leave forever. . . . "[21]

It is not without reason that Miner and Unrau selected the Osages as a prod to the American conscience. Their book, *The End of Indian Kansas*, touches on the Osage plight under the sub-heading, *And Then There Were None*.[22] Surely the Osages had every reason to detest the Euro-American intruders of Kansas. After the removal and well into the 1870s, incidents almost provoked retaliation by the Osages. Only the presence of troops enforcing martial law upon the Osages saved the Kansas border settlements from Osage war parties.

Yet, there were memories of better days in Kansas. There were those who dealt fairly with the Osages and most of all there were the Jesuits. It was this connection of hearts between the Osages and the Jesuits that pushed the evils aside. In time, the bond of sharing the love of the land healed old hurts.

The actual physical removal of the Osages was accomplished in bits and pieces due to the fumbling of the government. Certainly, the necessary buffalo hunts also contributed to the irregular removal. Somewhat less than 3,000 Osages left on the fall hunt of 1870–71 after agreement to the Act of 1870 had been reached in late September. Gibson led the remaining 300, who were mostly those unable to hunt buffalo, to Silver Lake, where they wintered.[23]

Most of the buffalo hunters returned from an exceptionally long hunt in March of 1871. They left from their Kansas villages and returned to Silver Lake. In their return from the hunt, the Caney was crossed near where Hickory Station was later established. Today, it would be near to the Hulah dam. The three independent Little Osage bands under Strike Axe crossed the Caney at the Little Hawk Woman crossing one-half mile south of Elgin, Kansas. They did not go to Silver Lake, but settled on the Pond Creek campsite. The others returned to Kansas to salvage what they could of their possessions, but the three independent Little Osage bands never returned to their old Kansas villages. While a few mixed-bloods came to the new reservation in 1872, most of the Osage people came in 1871.

In a heavily edited version of an Osage farewell speech, we find a fitting closing for this topic. A group of Osage men gave a war dance for the people of Independence, Kansas. After the dance *Kon sa Ka ho la,* counselor for the Big Hills, gave this reported speech:

> Brothers of the pale faces: I want to make a talk with you. We have danced for you our last war dance and sung you our last war song. Many moons ago the Osages were a great nation. Our warriors and women and children were as many as the stars of the sky, the leaves of the trees, and the sands of the seashore; now they are merely a handful.
> . . .
> Over these beautiful hunting grounds we have chased the deer, the bear and buffalo. By the sides of these green groves we have built our wigwans [*sic*], danced our war dances and lighted up our council fires. We love the lands which the Great Spirit gave us long before the pale faces came across the great water. . . . Now we go away.[24]

The New Reservation

The Beginning

Finny sums up the acquisition of the Osage reserve in the following: "The land the Osages now occupy and own, was purchased from the Cherokee at 70 cents per acre, and was confirmed by Act of Congress July 5th [it actually was confirmed in June], 1872. Their Reservation is held not simply by suffrage nor a donation by the government as a hunting ground, but by title in fee simple by purchase."[25] There were, however, some strings attached. First, the confirmation required that the conditions of acquisition conform as nearly as possible to Article Sixteen of the Cherokee Treaty of 1866. Secondly, the lands were to be confined to the area described. These bounds were the Kansas line on the north, the 96th meridian on the east, the Creek nation and Arkansas River on the south, and the Arkansas River on the west.[26] The third requirement altered these bounds slightly. This requirement was that the Kaw be allowed to select their lands from the northwest corner of this reserve.

Note that although the Osages bought and paid for their reservation with their own money, the government holds the deed in trust for the Osages. In 1882, 1890, and 1891 the Osages requested their deed.[27] Other times they hired attorneys to get possession of their deed. Yet, to this day, the people are not allowed to hold the deed to their own property.

All the individuals who have tried to reach an accurate count of the Osages up to 1875 have commented on the difficulty of getting an accurate count. Isaac Gibson was no exception. In 1873, Gibson reported the population as 3,906. Yet he qualifies the 1873 figure by stating that he believes the actual figure is closer to 3,500.[28]

We may assume the Osage population declined by somewhere between 400 and 1,000 persons in the first year on the new reservation. This would mean a loss of at least one out of ten persons. Such a loss demands a greater explanation than the usual comments about the difficulty of taking an Osage census. The Annuity Rolls of 1878 suggest strongly that the true loss the first year was closer to the higher figure of 1,083 persons. It would not be unreasonable to state that one out of four Osages who removed from Kansas died in the first year.

As we noted earlier, the fall hunt of 1870–71 was an exceptionally long hunt. That is, it lasted from September of 1870 to March of 1871. This fall hunt was followed by another exceptionally long hunt that had, in effect, become the winter hunt. Without a doubt, these earlier hunts were caused by an extreme food shortage. Intruders had destroyed or stolen the crops of 1870 and 1871. The first crop planted in Indian Territory was planted at Silver Lake.

We have an account of the fate of that crop: "Having been to much expense and trouble in procuring a good machine for thrashing and cleaning the crop of wheat harvested by the Osages, from the fifty acres sown in their former reservation [Silver Lake], I was nonplussed to find that a Cherokee named Joseph Bennett had taken possession of the crop and was threshing and wasting it."[29] Thus, the crop for 1871–72 was lost, and due to the move there was no other crop. Therefore, the only food available was from the hunt and what could be gathered from wild plants. Game of all kinds was scarce because of over-killing by both Euro-Americans and American Indians. The same was true of the available wild plants.

Much is made of the government-issued "rations." However, almost without fail, these were too little too late. A common assumption is that these "rations" were gifts of the government. We wish to correct this misconception and point out that not only did the Osages pay for these rations but they had to work at white man's work to get them. Thus, they paid for the rations twice.

Aside from a food shortage and the consequent malnutrition, there was a housing problem. The wickiup is easily made but it is small, so it was usually used on the hunt. Intruders had stolen or destroyed the "furnishings" of the village lodges. Thus, proper lodges were not built until the fall of 1873. Gibson was forcing many full-bloods into cabins.

The traditional Osage did not know how to live in a cabin. A white man would think a cabin was superior to a wickiup or a lodge, but cabins presented many faults. Osages found the white man's dwelling extremely hazardous to their health as well as being inconvenient. While most of the mixed-bloods were accustomed to cabins, the need for haste in construction produced poorly constructed cabins. This, in turn, caused deaths among the newborn.

Added to poor nutrition and inadequate housing was growing conflicts on the Plains. The skirmishes were with other Indians and with Indian-hating white men. While the losses were not great to the other combatants, even a slight loss was dramatic among the Osage people. Their margin of survival was strained already and so each loss aggravated a situation that was extremely dangerous. Thus, pressures from the expanding Euro-Americans were eroding away the margin of survival.

Finally, added to the malnutrition, faulty housing, and pressures of expansion were the fumbling, graft, and corruption of the government. The preference given to Euro-Americans lay at the base of the entire Osage problem. This preference pervaded every aspect of Osage life and their survival. All the fumbling, graft, and corruption in Indian Affairs came from this preference or priority. The Osages and other Indians stood at the end of the line and got only the leavings. It was a simple case of, I will take all you have and give you back what I don't want.

Troubles: Gibson and the Osages

It is not difficult to perceive that the Osages had an abundance of reasons to be discontented. Even without a ghost from the Drum Creek Treaty to haunt their harmony, it was predictable that they would exhibit some form of rebellion. Gibson was a sincere and, we believe, honest agent to the Osage people. The Osages' situation was desperate and severe even with Gibson, but it could have been much worse without him. Isaac Gibson stood by the Osages and fought for their rights.

To say the Osages resented the delays, the wasting of their funds, and the pressure to become "civilized" would be an understatement. In the minds of the Osages, these and other frustrations could be laid at the door of the United States government. Since Gibson was the nearest representative of that government, it was natural that he would become prey to their anger.

The discontent became so great that by June of 1873 the Osages petitioned for a change back to the Jesuits. In their petition, they give us clues as to some of their worries: "If we can judge from what we hear in our private and public councils, our present officers and missionaries are suspected of seeking self interest and keeping us in the dark. Our large annuities are partly wasted; they build schoolhouses and other buildings, make large farms, raise grain, etc.—(For whom?). All this for the benefit of the Friends, and without consulting our Chiefs."[30] Almost identical words of complaint were used against the Board of Commissioner's Missionaries in the early 1800s.

One must bear in mind that to the Osage mind houses, barns, shops, mills, schools, and tilled fields were symbols of an enslaved people. The Old Osages thought of the white man as a slave to his possessions. All these things symbolized the efforts to force the Osages into the same pattern of enslavement. In effect, what frightened the Osages was that they knew that the old life they loved so well would soon pass away. They wanted to preserve the old life as long as possible. They had removed to a new area to escape the very things Gibson was establishing in their midst.

Mixed in with the restlessness encouraged by the passing of their old life was the Vann-Adair claim. In his efforts to protect the Osages from these two Cherokee opportunists, Gibson angered the two Cherokees and irked some Osages. Vann and Adair used the Osage discontent and restlessness to discredit Gibson, which worked to some degree.[31]

Nothing came of the Osage petitions against Gibson, so a delegation of Osages presented their case against Gibson in Washington on March 31, 1874. A whole series of petitions and counter-petitions followed. Ultimately, an investigation of Gibson was made to see if he was guilty of a long list of charges. These charges were: (1) interfering in tribal affairs, laws, and customs; (2) partiality in distributing rations and money; (3) discharging employees for signing petitions for his removal and in favor of Catholic schools and missionaries; (4) employing white men when Indians and half-breeds could do the work equally as well; (5) interference with the religious predilections of the people and endeavoring to proselytize them to his own beliefs; and, finally, (6) misappropriating funds.

Although the investigating committee found no evidence of wrongdoing on Gibson's part, there was ample evidence that all was not well between the Osages and their agent. It was probably this factor that caused the change to a new agent, for any agent without the support of the people he is leading generates more problems than he solves.

Osage Depredations

Driven by the necessity to obtain food to survive, the Osages no doubt committed illegal acts. Possibly, some of these depredations were due to cultural differences, which certainly affected how the acts were viewed. Surely, in some few cases, they were deliberately committed by resentful young Osages. Typical of these depredations was the theft of cattle and horses from drovers on the Chisholm Trail. The drovers were also sometimes victimized by Osage "tax collectors." This consisted of a tax on each animal allowed to continue the northern drive. Usually, one steer was enough to pay the total "tax." United States troopers put a stop to this practice, killing an old nearsighted Osage man in the process.[32]

Throughout the fall and winter of 1874–75, the Osages apparently made use of a cattle herd that had been scattered by a storm. In one of the very early grass lease arrangements in the reservation, Gibson had leased grass to the owners of a thousand steers in the late summer of 1874. On November 20, 1874, a severe blizzard scattered this herd, which had been wintering nine miles south of the Kansas line. It has been estimated that the Osages took between two and three hundred head of these cattle.[33]

While the situation above was an exceptional situation, it does show the desperate need of the Osages for food. Gibson always placed a man with the Osages when they left the reservation to hunt on the Plains. This tended to curb some of their depredations, but they sometimes escaped his scrutiny and could steal some food anyway. Gibson insisted that his spy see that the victims were paid immediately and that the sum was deducted from the violators' annuity.[34]

Gibson's report on the first Osage delegation to Lawrence, Kansas, has a slightly amusing aspect:

> Thy invitation to the governor and chiefs to visit thee at Lawrence, was regarded by those who had participated in depredations on persons and properly [sic property] on the plains as a trap to get them into prison. The governor and some other leading men could not be induced to go; fifteen chiefs and head-men consented. This their first

ride on the cars [railroads], three days' stay in the city of Lawrence, visiting the schools, shops, and other places of interest, the plain and emphatic talk they had from their superintendent in reference to depredations on the plains, the encouragement they received for good conduct, made so deep an impression upon their minds that they are now the principal leaders in their bands in favor of civilization.[35]

The second delegation to Lawrence in 1874 was well represented by major men among the Osage people.

A primary cause for the Osages killing another human on the Plains was an odd funeral custom. This originated outside the ceremonies conducted by the *Ne ka a Shin Ka* (Little Old Men). Believing that the journey to *O Ke sa* (Mid-Way), which was the middle of the upper worlds, was a long lonesome journey, the Osages believed that the presence of another soul would make the journey easier.[36]

It was such a quest that led some young men to kill *Es ad da ua,* the prominent Wichita chief. After the killing, the Osages gathered to repel an expected counter attack from the Wichita. A delegation of thirty-eight Wichitas came to Pawhuska to seek a settlement for the act.[37] After a great deal of bickering, the matter was settled for a total of $1,500 worth of gifts. Such incidents worked both ways since the Arapahoes wounded an Osage and killed his horse at this same time. Like the Wichitas, the Osages settled the matter peacefully with the Arapahoes.

The Medicine Lodge Massacre

In his report for 1875, Isaac T. Gibson reported that, in view of the provocations, the Osages had behaved very well during the past year: "No satisfaction has yet been obtained by them for the four men killed at Medicine Lodge, Kansas, over one year ago, nor for the sixty head of ponies and other properly [*sic property*] taken at that time."[38] On August 7, 1874 a group of settlers from Medicine Lodge in Barber County had killed these Osages, who were peacefully returning from a hunt. It was with great difficulty that Gibson had been able to keep young vengeance-seeking Osages from striking the settlers in Barber County, Kansas.[39]

The federal government made every effort to hold the state of Kansas and its citizens accountable for this act of outright murder. However, the Governor of Kansas protected the murders by mustering them into the militia and back-dating their papers. In a long exchange of letters between the governor and the United States government, the governor maintained that the murders were militia acting in defense of their area.[40] This was surely not the finest hour in Kansas history.

Ultimately, the United States government paid an indemnity to the Osages in lieu of a payment from the state of Kansas: "The Secretary of the Interior is authorized and directed to pay to the heirs of certain Osage Indians killed while on a hunt on Medicine Lodge Creek, in eighteen hundred and seventy-three [actually 1874], the balance on hand of the sum of five thousand dollars appropriated by act approved March third, eighteen hundred and seventy-seven, 'to reimburse the Osages for losses sustained, and in accordance with pledges by their agent,' amounting to two thousand four hundred and fifty-one dollars and fifty cents, which is hereby reappropriated for this purpose" (Approved, March 3, 1885).[41] Thus, the Medicine Lodge Massacre ended, but a curious sequence of events grew out of this incident in Osage history.

Restlessness among the Plains Indians was not confined to the Osages. The Cheyenne and other nations were becoming increasingly active on the Plains. In fact, Gibson had became concerned in 1874 and had sent runners ordering the Osage hunting parties to return immediately to the reservation. It was thought that by removing them from the Plains, the Osages would not be blamed for the depredations of other Indians. Unfortunately, the runners had not been able to contact Hard Rope's party and, thus, they were caught in the massacre at Medicine Lodge.

Following the Medicine Lodge incident, all Indians in Indian Territory were confined to their reservations. Thus, in the fall of 1874, the northern Cheyenne "jumped" the Fort Sill reservation and started on that great trek so aptly titled Cheyenne Autumn. In their crossing of Kansas, the Cheyenne threw enough of a scare into Kansans to ease the "big talk" about what they would do to Indians.

Causes of the Long Hunts

Beside the obvious need for food, there were five basic reasons for the long hunts of 1870–75. The Medicine Lodge Massacre and the subsequent restriction to the reservation would surely be one reason. Changes in Indian Office policies, such as making the Osages work for rations bought with their own money, served to generate both hard feelings and a desire to escape the reservation problems. Possibly, one of the most upsetting reasons for spending more time on the hunt was the erection of many buildings. Very noticeable was the horde of white men and their families who soon appeared on the reservation. Some of these were authorized employees of the Agency and licensed traders. However, many were unauthorized farmers and free-booters drawn by Osage land and annuity payments. Finally, Vann and Adair, the Cherokee mixed-bloods, were constantly using the Osage discontent to generate more discontent with Gibson.

The Osages could clearly see that the days of the buffalo were numbered. They were keenly aware that the way of life they had been heir to was doomed. It was only a matter of a few years before they could no longer lose themselves in the labor and excitement of the hunt. Thus, the activities of Gibson in erecting schools, churches, barns, mills, blacksmith shops, and agency houses served as reminders of a coming revolution in culture. The swarms of white men coming into the reservation only served to make life a bitter experience. Only out on the Plains doing what they did best could the Osages be happy and contented. Thus, they remained on the hunt beyond the necessity to collect food. They were reluctant to return to the rapidly changing world that had become their new home.

Most human actions are set off by some particular cause, but like the final straw on a camel's back, the real causes for actions are often both varied and numerous. In this case, the Osages were facing a catastrophic change that they did not want to make. While the reasons for the long hunt given above are immediate manifestations of their reluctance to change, their entire history to this point is the real cause for their resistance. But without the some two hundred years of contact with Western civilization, it is possible that even the alert, adaptive Osages could not have survived the catastrophe that struck them. Yet because of the long contact, within a generation the Osages stepped into the twentieth century as members of Western civilization. For most twentieth century Americans, it had taken over 3,000 years to become Westernized. The Osages became Westernized in only two hundred years.

Social and Economic Conditions

For purposes of administration, Gibson divided the reservation into five districts. He called these: (1) The Agency District; (2) The Bird Creek District; (3) Hominy District; (4) Salt Creek District; and (5) Little Osage District. Today, these areas would be comparable to the (1) Pawhuska, (2) Barnsdall, (3) Hominy, (4) Gray Horse-Fairfax, and (5) Boulanger-Bowring areas. It is interesting to consider the close comparison with various Osage groups that these divisions include. Using the same numbering order, we find: (1) The Heart Stays and Thorny Bush people at Pawhuska; (2) Some White Hair Little Osages at Barnsdall; (3) The Upland Forest people at Hominy; (4) The Big Hills at Gray Horse-Fairfax; and (5) The three independent Little Osage bands at Boulanger-Bowring. We must hasten to mention that these areas and peoples held true only in the 1870s. In less than a decade, the various groups became so mixed that most of the old distinctions vanished.

In his report of 1875, Gibson was enthusiastic about the progress the Osages appeared to be making toward his idea of "civilization."[42] Evidently, his view of the progress was somewhat enlarged from the facts. Hints of troubles appear in his complaints about corruption among some Osage leaders.[43]

We would not want to leave an impression that the Osages had made no steps toward acceptance of Western civilization. What we are trying to suggest is that the production of food, even if it is produced by Western methods, is a poor measure of cultural change. Most of Gibson's report is based on technological changes,[44] which is understandable, since these are things easily measured. However, it is the intangible aspects of a culture that are the heart and soul of the culture. These aspects are not easily measured, but this neither denies their presence nor importance. Thus, we maintain that Gibson's "gains" with the Osages were surface "gains" that did not reach the heart and soul of Osage culture.

Yet Gibson made a start and set the Osages on a firm basis for survival. The Jesuit approach was gentle and touched the core of Osage culture. Gibson's approach was harsh and touched on the physical needs of the people. We must realize that this dual aspect of cultures is vital to comprehending how the Osages adapted to Western civilization. They clung to the shreds of their culture that had been brutally abused by the majority culture. Only unavoidable aspects of Western civilization were accepted, so this left some nooks and crannies for the Old Osage culture.

PART FIVE

The Road to Accommodation, 1875–1906

18

Farewell to the Past

INTRODUCTION

Isaac T. Gibson was replaced by a new Osage agent, Cyrus Beede, early in 1876. At this time, the Osages were extremely restless and uncooperative. Beede reported that "most of them [the Osages] are wild blanket Indians far from civilized, many of them hardly ready to give up the war dance and the scalping knife."[1] During the winter of 1875–76, Gibson became so concerned about the growing discontent of the Osages that he called for military aid. A detachment of the Fifth Cavalry from Fort Sill spent the winter in Pawhuska to prevent an outbreak of Osage hostilities.[2]

Obviously, Beede looked at the Osages through a different window from Gibson. The negative descriptions of Beede contrast sharply with Gibson's positive descriptions. However, on the subject of "civilization," Beede's description of the Osage change to "civilization" is more realistic than Gibson's vision.

As explained in the previous chapter, the unrest, rebellion, and vengeance were brought on by several causes. Beede was witnessing a people who had reached the limits of their traditional survival methods. A period of synthesis followed the dissatisfactions of the mid–1870s. That is, between 1875 and 1906, the Osage people managed to blend their culture with Western civilization. New methods of survival were developed to replace those no longer useful. Through this and the next two chapters the reader will see the Osage people changing to the new while still clutching the old culture.

Frank Finney Sr., who knew the Osages well, describes this process differently from the way we have. He touches upon a striking aspect of the Osage adjustment to Western civilization: "In the time of Agent Beede, the Osages retained their inborn sense of superiority, were proud to be Indians and had no desire to model their lives after the white or any other people. Most of them were satisfied with their way of life and suspicious of any attempts to change it, yet there were a few full bloods who saw changes were unavoidable and with the mixed bloods were willing to co-operate with the Government."[3]

No other Indian nation shows such great diversity in adjustment as the Osage people. To this day, the people range from highly educated professionals to individuals who have been lightly touched by the West. This diversity was probably brought about because of money, which gave the people a freedom of choice. Thus, the manner of adjustment was left to the individual Osage. Yet, the bond among the people remains. In a manner of speaking, the Osages are a series of subcultures united by the common bond of being Osage.

THREADS OF THE PAST

Laban J. Miles

Cyrus Beede did not last very long as the Osage agent because he was too far away from them in feelings. He was replaced by a much-admired agent, Laban J. Miles.[4] In his second report, Miles describes the Osages with his characteristic gentleness of spirit: "The full bloods are almost all blanket Indians; although quite a number have in years past been educated to speak English, read, and write, yet we find them with the garb and habits of the uneducated, and a stranger could scarcely detect them; they all cling tenaciously to their Indian customs and religion, and pride themselves in their nationality, although they have entirely given up their old hunts, and are making quite an effort at self-support."[5] Miles gave an accurate report about the Osages with the possible exception of the hunting habits. The last big hunt was the fall hunt of 1876, when over 10,000 buffalo were taken. During the following six years, the hunts were much smaller. However, in 1880, which was the year of Miles's report of no hunting, the Osages took enough buffalo to satisfy most of their need for meat. After 1880, they made two or three virtually unsuccessful hunts and never again hunted buffalo.

Money

During the 1880s and up till 1906, the Osages had a better income than the average in the American society. This income came primarily from two sources. The first source was from interest on money obtained from the sale of their lands in Kansas. A second source was money obtained from farming and grass leases on their reservation. As the tempo of Kansas land sales increased, the Osage trust fund grew to $8,295,079.69 in 1891, which was $6,000,000 larger than any other Indian nation trust fund.[6] Grass leasing grew rapidly all through the 1880s and 1890s. Thus, the Osages were in the position of receiving larger and larger annuity payments as time for allotment approached. Envy by many Euro-Americans in the area caused them to watch the Osages carefully to see how they used this money. The tendency was to seek out and stress the wasteful uses and avoid mention of the constructive uses. The Bureau of Indian Affairs officials were outraged that these "wild blanket Indians" were economically secure and independent. This economic status enabled the Osages to avoid most of the Bureau's efforts to "civilize" them.

Most people in Osage County, including the young Osages, believe that the "richest people on earth" description came from the oil annuities. This description originated with William J. Pollock, who was the Osage agent in 1898. "The Osage Indians are probably the wealthiest people per capita on earth, owning as they do over 800 acres of land for each man, woman, and child, and each receiving an annual annuity of over $200 in cash. To illustrate: If an Indian and his wife have eight children, the annual cash income of the family is over $2,000. They are aristocrats and like all wealthy people, scorn to perform manual labor."[7] These sums are almost laughable in terms of money today. However, one must remember that this was a substantial income in 1898.

Despite the reckless use of their money, the Osages were not totally careless. They were human and reacted to sudden wealth much as any human would in a similar situation. Miles wrote in his Commissioner's Report for 1890, "Much has been written and published the past year about the profligacy of the Osages. Having known them for many years, and having a personal acquaintance with every member of the tribe, I believe they are as frugal as the average white man would be under similar circumstances, and they are far more easily controlled, and submit more cheerfully to the laws that govern them than any other community of my acquaintance. Could the government but protect them successfully from the evil consequent upon too close contact with degraded whites their prosperity would greatly increase."[8] Miles knew and appreciated the Osage People.

The Osage sense of humor and flair for the dramatic surely generated many enjoyable tales that gained in extravagance at each telling. One cannot deny that a basis for the tales existed, and some were as "wild" as the exaggerations. Yet, there was a tender, wholesome side to the use the Osages made of their money. Powwows were frequently given to honor other Indians, and the guests received lavish gifts. Thus, the Osages helped many Indian people less fortunate than themselves. White men sometimes do not understand this Indian trait of generosity.

Osage Marriages and Reformers

A matter of great concern to Osage missionaries and agents has been the Osage marriage customs. There were three facets of Osage marriages that

Western civilization disliked. These were marriages of the very young, po-lygamy, and multiple divorces. All of these were well established Osage cus-toms. However, not all Osages participated in young marriage, polygamy, or divorce. Others may have practiced one or two of these customs, but it would have been rare for a single Osage to engage in all three of the practices.

It is possible that marriage of the very young was harmful to the people as a whole. Yet, if one understands these "young" marriages as the Osages practiced them, there seems to be no harm to either individuals or the people. By the yardstick of Western civilization's morals, one might say such mar-riages were morally wrong. However, Osage practice and that of Western civilization differed where a female child and a male adult were involved. In Western civilization sex was usually involved, but in the Osage culture sex was rarely involved.

The very young Osage female was connected with marriage in two situa-tions. One was when a man married all the sisters in a family. Almost surely, the younger sisters would be under sixteen years of age. The other situation arose when a man married his current brother-in-law's daughter, that is, the daughter of the wife's brother. As a man and his wife or wives matured, a young wife became desirable to help with the household tasks. Thus, an old man may have a twelve-year-old wife. In these cases, sex was not necessarily an object of the marriage. In a few instances a male child and a female child were married at a very young age, but they each lived with their parents until they became "newly grown," that is, in their midteens.

Agent Laban J. Miles commented on a change in the child marriages in 1891: "During the past year among others they have passed a law, with a heavy penalty, prohibiting the marriage of any citizen under the age of 16, thus practically breaking up the practice of young marriages, which has existed for generations."[9] Miles was speaking about the Osage Council cre-ated under the Constitution of 1881. On the twenty-seventh of November 1890, the Council enacted the law Agent Miles was writing about. "Article IV, Section 34. BE IT ENACTED BY THE NATIONAL COUNCIL OF THE OSAGE NATION: That every person a citizen of the Osage nation who shall take away any female child a citizen of the Osage nation, under the age of sixteen years, from her father, mother, guardian or other person having legal charge of her person, either for the purpose of prostitution, concubinage or marriage, shall upon conviction thereof, be punished by imprisonment not exceeding three (3) years, or by a fine not exceeding one thousand ($1,000) dollars, or both."[10]

Since this government was suspended, the enforcement lapsed. After the turn of the century, the BIA took firm action and issued a directive to all agencies. The problem of polygamy plagued the Osage agents for some time, although it surely presented no problem to the Osages. Yet, Agent Dorn attributed the Osage decline in population to polygamy: "polygamy only exists among the Osages to any extent, and I have noticed that they are declining more rapidly in proportion to their number, than the other tribes within this agency; and my conclusion is, that [it] is mainly attributable to their living in a state of polygamy."[11]

Surprisingly, several later Osage agents echoed this same argument against Osage polygamy. That is, polygamy causes loss of population. No proof other than that offered by Dorn is given to support this argument. We are not defending the practice of polygamy, but this argument against it is flimsy. Osage population loss is directly attributable to white man's diseases and a radical decrease in the nutrition levels of the Osage people. These facts are easily verified.

Without a doubt, the order to require a license for Indian marriage surely ended the three Osage practices (child marriage, polygamy, and easy divorce) causing so much stress in the white community. Osage Agent O. A. Mitscher commented on the effect of the license order upon the Osages in 1901.

> The order recently issued by the Indian Office, effective July 1, 1901, requiring the issuance of a marriage license by the agent to those contemplating matrimony is an innovation productive of the best results. Heretofore a laxity has existed in the marriage relations among the Indians, for the reason that engagements were made and marriages contracted without the knowledge of the agent in charge, and often after the first quarrel husband and wife separated, each going to their own teepee, after a lapse of a short time (very short in some instances) to reappear on the eligible list of some Indian match maker. We have full-blood Osage young men and young women who are not over 25 years old that have been married as many as five times. By giving the matter attention and impressing them that they could not marry again without first having obtained a legal separation from their former spouse, I have succeeded in reuniting several disaffected families during the past year.[12]

SIGNS OF CHANGE

Passing of the Buffalo

Between 1875 and 1880, the buffalo rapidly became more difficult to find. After a half-hearted hunt in 1881, the Osages gave up their traditional grand hunts, although small hunts continued for a few more years. No stronger indication of change for the Osages existed than the passing of the buffalo.

They had been aware of this disaster approaching and were now reluctantly ready to adjust to the catastrophe that had been waiting for them.

Clearly everyone was aware of the significance of the buffalo when the time of their passing came. Laban J. Miles wrote in 1879 about this event. "The Osage number 2,135, of which 263 are mixed-bloods. All are peaceably located on their present reservation, and have apparently given up the idea of living by the 'hunt.' This change of life has manifested the need of a material change in the management of their political and civil affairs . . . I trust that in the near future they may be encouraged and assisted to make for themselves some simple laws for their individual protection in holding property, and thus, secure to those that labor, the fruits of their labor."[13] The very thing the Osages had feared would happen was now happening. For two hundred years, the Osages had refused to become Westernized. They argued that Euro-Americans were slaves to their possessions, especially lands and other real estate. Now Major Miles was urging that the Osages make laws to restrict freedom, to protect the possessions of those who were becoming "civilized."

It is possible that Charles de Montesquieu heard the Osage argument in 1725. In any event, a statement of his mentions what the Osage feared about "civilization" and what in a dozen years would happen to them. Montesquieu wrote, "The division of lands is what principally increases the civil code. Among nations where they have not made this division there are very few civil laws."[14] In essence, the Osages argued that land and possessions held in surplus of survival need generated restrictive laws. These laws then became so numerous that the owner of surplus possessions became a slave to his possessions. Thus, their greatest fear was the enslavement to civil laws and the possessions they protected.

It is sometimes said, with a large lump of truth, that the mountain men were the last free men in the majority culture of the United States. We fault the statement only because they were not members of the majority culture. They stood in a culture of their own that tolerated only basic possessions and basic laws. Each mountain man was a law unto himself and, therefore, a free man. No Osage was this free, but all Osages were free from possession enslavement.

The passing of the buffalo imposed severe conditions upon many Osages, for some time was needed to accept the harsh facts once calamity struck them. There was a great diversity among the Osage people as the buffalo faded from their lives. This is brought out in the following contemporary news item: "Father Ponziglione arrived home Wednesday from a long trip of 350 miles in Indian Territory. He visited the Osages at their agency at Pawhuska and found the half-breeds thriving and prosperous, with considerable stock and cultivated lands; but the full-bloods, since the buffalo were driven further away, have had a hard time in obtaining enough to live on and are really suffering. 'Lo, the poor Indian.' "[15]

Dreams

Like many other Indians, the Osages were seeking firm religious ground to stand upon. *Wa Kon ta* (The Sovereign Being of the Universe) seemed to have abandoned them. The great "Messiah Craze" of the early–1890s reached the Osages in the fall of 1890. During the summer and fall of 1890, rumors of an Indian Messiah or Christ spread across the West. Although the version and ceremony varied from tribe to tribe, they all held close to a fundamental belief.

Basically, the story runs that a northern medicine man had met the Christian Christ. His face and wrists were scarred, and he spoke of his crucifixion. Christ explained to the medicine man that the white people had forgotten all he had taught them. He then taught the medicine man the dance that white men called the Ghost Dance. Counseling love and kindness to each other, he promised that the Indian dead would be resurrected to aid them in ridding their lands of the white man. Youth would be restored to the "Good Men" and "Good Women."[16] A dance was required for six successive days each moon. If Wah Kon ta was pleased, the buffalo and other game would return. When the day of miracles comes, supposedly the spring of 1891, the white man would be unable to make gunpowder. The gunpowder they have would not be able to throw a bullet hard enough to penetrate the skin of an Indian. New soil and forests would cover the land and bury the white man and all his possessions.[17]

We have always heard that the Osages only danced the Ghost Dance once at the junction of Salt and Elm Creeks. Mathews gives the location as the headwaters of Sycamore Creek southeast of Gray Horse. This is undoubtedly the correct location.[18] In any event, the Osages only completed four days of the six-day dance. Thus, they did not complete the first and only Ghost Dance they started to dance.

The dance on Sycamore Creek was probably the Osage farewell to the old life they loved so well. John Wilson was a Caddo medicine man who championed the Messiah movement. From the movement, he created a new Indian religion. His Quapaw disciple, Victor Griffin, worked with the Osages. Wilson, or "Moonhead" as the Osages called him, established two fireplaces at Hominy. Thus, the American Indian Peyote Church was established among the Osages.

In 1899, William J. Pollock commented on the Peyote: "During the past year a few of the Osages have acquired the habit of eating the mescal bean, which produces delirium, visions, etc. They acquired this pernicious habit from western Indians, and it has not become a general habit and I do not think it will."[19] Pollock apparently either did not know the religious aspects of peyote use or he elected not to mention it.

Round houses sprung up throughout the reservation and the Native American Church became well established among the Osages. A general charter for the incorporation of the Native American Church was granted by the state of Oklahoma in 1911.[20] The Native American Church still exists among the Osages, but many old round houses have vanished. One facet of the Native American Church is rarely mentioned, that is, the benefits derived from participation in it. No one knows how many Osages were saved from the use of whiskey, but there were many. One cannot remain a member of the Native American Church and drink whiskey. Dr. M. R. Harrington, Curator of Southwest Museum, Los Angeles, stresses the great role of peyote in Indian life: "I think the use of peyote and the rites and teachings accompanying such use have been of great benefit to the Indians with whom I came in contact during my Oklahoma work. This is especially true of tribes whose organization and native life was breaking down with the consequent loss of morale and pride in their racial heritage."[21] Dr. Harrington spent a great deal of time among the Osages and knew them well.

Fred Lookout also made a significant statement in the same report: "I cannot see why so-called reformers should attempt to interfere in the religious practice of Indians who do not interfere with the white man's religion, and I feel that the Congress of the United States should encourage Indians to practice the religion that seems to do them most good and has the proper influences on the younger generation."[22]

Intruders

A Continuing Problem

Intruders continued to be a problem to the Osages until the reservation was finally opened by allotment. However, in the years following 1875, the American frontier was drawing to a close. The continuous frontier line had disappeared and only frontier pockets remained after 1892. Included in the most significant of these pockets was the Osage nation. To the west of the reservation lay the last unrestricted free land in United States history.

Here, all the characters of the American West gathered for a final race for land. Thus, on a day (September 16) in 1893, the land frontier ended. The good settled in the Outlet, building homes and cities while the bad collected in the Osage nation. These intruders, especially the outlaw variety, did not cause the Osages as much trouble as the petty-thieving, poor, white variety. The outlaws were less of a problem because they used the Osage nation as a hideout to escape the law officers in the states. Therefore, they tried to keep on good terms with the Osages, who often hid them from federal marshals. Judge Parker at Fort Smith, Arkansas, became known as the "hanging judge" because so many of these outlaws were executed after they were captured.

However, it would be a mistake to assume the Osages were the only Indians experiencing intruder problems from poor whites and others. The Commissioner's Report for 1879 records that "Intruders have been equally troublesome on other Indian lands. There is hardly an Indian reservation within the limits of the United States which has not been subject to their encroachments. They resort to all kinds of devices and schemes to obtain a foothold on Indian soil, and offer ready and varied excuses for their continued unlawful occupancy of the same."[23]

The Final Gathering

As the end of the frontier neared, the failures and misfits tended to cluster on Indian reservations in hopes of having one last chance to acquire free or cheap land. It was unfortunate that the Osage reservation attracted not only these failures and misfits but also a more dangerous type. These were opportunists, that is, gamblers, con men, free-booters, and do-anything-for-money types.

Some of these characters married Osage citizens and profited handsomely. Carroll H. Potter reports, "It has lately come to my notice that a large quantity of walnut timber on the reservation has been cut and sold to parties in the States. This has been allowed by members of the Osage nation. Steps have been taken to try and stop the evil, but it is very doubtful if it can be accomplished, so many inducements are offered by outside parties for this valuable property."[24] In an old bunkhouse built in this period, the inside walls of the common room were found to be sheeted inside with rough sawn, one-inch thick walnut boards. These boards were two feet wide and twenty-four feet long, and all of it was core wood. That is, there was no outer layer white wood on the boards. It would take a tree at least three feet through twenty-four feet above the falling cut to scale out to two feet of core wood.

As one can readily see, the final intruders were a varied lot. However, the typical poor white woodsy intruder of the American frontier remained as a gadfly to the Osages. Miles reports, "The presence of numerous vagabond white people on the reservation is a detriment to the welfare of the Indian. Many of them prove to be gamblers or whisky-peddlers, who succeed in evading the officers until an opportunity offers itself for them to steal a horse or rob an Indian; and from all I can learn this class greatly increased during the past few years. More stringent measures should be used to rid the Indian country of this class, and to control those who come in here as farmers and laborers."[25]

Indian Intruders

It is easy to forget that Indians could be intruders as well as white men. But Indians were an entirely different type of intruder. From a full-blood viewpoint, these Quapaw, Potawatomi, and other Indians were not intruders. However, from an Osage-French mixed-blood viewpoint they were intruders as much as the white intruders. We must hasten to say that strictly speaking, these Quapaw were invited by the full-bloods to reside with the Osages and, thus, they were not intruders. Yet, the mixed-bloods did not invite them and in this sense they were intruders.

In any event, the Quapaw were present on the Osage reservation and apparently they caused no problems. Miles writes, "The Quapaws now on the reservation, about 70 in number, belong to the Quapaw Agency. They came to this agency many years ago a number of them having married with the Osages, and are loath to return to their own reservation. They live in huts they have built for themselves, subsisting by working for their more fortunate Osage brothers."[26] Major Miles was familiar with the Quapaw presence and had reported them much earlier and in greater detail: "The Quapaws, having many of them connections among the Osages, and in accordance with agreement made between the two tribes by which they should be incorporated with the Osages, came here in the spring of 1879 in number about 150, leaving, as I learn from them, about 30 on their old reservation."[27] It is noticeable that the number of Quapaw was greatly reduced between the two reports.

The Bureau of Indian Affairs refused to allow a merger of the Quapaw and Osages. So, all but a few families returned to the Quapaw Agency before Osage allotment. The Quapaws remaining with the Osages settled on Quapaw Creek west of Skiatook.

CONCLUSIONS

Evidently, the Osages were aware of the need to radically change their culture. Yet, they made only a few slight adjustments to this change before 1880. In other words, the tempo of change in Osage culture was slow and gradual to 1880. After this date, the tempo of change became almost unbearably rapid.

To escape the rapid pace of change after the passing of the buffalo, many Osages sought relief in alcohol. Others used a more constructive relief in a new religious practice. Although this religion used a drug to ease the impact of change, it also taught desirable principles for living properly. Regardless of what one may think of the Native American Church, it did preserve many fine principles of Osage culture.

Intruders continued to plague the Osages as again they stood in the main stream of United States' history. The dramatic closing of the American land frontier and the end of the "long drive" placed the Osages in the direct path of the developing West. While they were still trying desperately to cope with the rapid developments, the Osages entered the twentieth century standing more in the Osage world of the past than in the two worlds that were half Osage and half twentieth-century Western civilization.

19

Bluestem and Cattle

THE LONG DRIVE

New Developments

The American Civil War affected every aspect of life in the United States during the latter half of the 1800s. Along with other industries, the cattle industry was deeply affected. Prior to the Civil War, pork was the first choice of American meat consumers. However, due to wartime shortages, pork was seldom available. Beef became the most common substitute. After almost five years of forced beef consumption and the high post-war price for pork, beef became the meat of first choice by the American consumer.

A serious problem existed in the cattle industry. This was due to two factors: the great distance between the supply and the demand, and the expensive transportation cost of live weight. The latter was solved by Gustavus F. Swift. He was the first to move west to Chicago with his meat-packing business. At first, he could only ship meat during the winter months, because the meat spoiled during the warm months. However, Swift hit upon the idea of cutting ice on Lake Michigan during the winter and using it in railway cars to preserve the meat in transit during warm weather. Therefore, he eliminated the shipping of live weight between Chicago and the east. In doing this, he materially reduced the cost of western beef on eastern tables.

Yet, the problem of distance between source and demand remained. No distance is economically impossible to overcome provided cheap transportation can be found. It was natural that Texas ranchers would first try the economical river transportation. Thus, for a time, New Orleans and other Mississippi ports became shipping points for Texas cattle. However, this did not prove to be practical because it was far too slow and the cattle lost too much weight. Because of rancor in the wake of the war, the early post-war railroads were passing to the north of Texas. Kansas was about as far south as the new railroads were coming to Texas. However, the earliest and nearest railroad terminal was at Sedalia, Missouri.

The Sedalia Trail was the earliest of the long drive trails to be used. From the Red River north to Sedalia, it followed the old Osage trails. Memories are short, so this and the next oldest cattle trail to Baxter Springs were called the East Shawnee Trail instead of the Osage Trail. This trail branched at Fort Gibson with one fork going to Baxter Springs and the other following the old Osage trail on the left side of the Arkansas to Caldwell, Kansas, and crossing the Arkansas near Kaw City, Oklahoma. A West Shawnee Trail followed another Osage trail north from Boggy Depot to Caldwell, touching the right bank of the Arkansas at the Salt Fork. The famous Chisholm Trail ran a few miles to the west of the West Shawnee Trail at the Salt Fork.

The developments by Swift, the railroads, and the long drive solved both marketing problems of live weight shipping costs and great distance. The long drive involved a practice that is usually overlooked, yet this practice was the key to the entire early western cattle industry, including marketing. Drovers did not drive their herds to the rail heads as depicted in the movies. They grazed them on the so-called long drive, which should be more accurately termed the long-graze. That is, they started from Texas with lean hungry cattle and arrived at the railhead with contented grass-fat market beef.

Most frontier historians correctly give the opening of the Outlet to homesteading as a cause for ending the long drive. A few historians attribute it to the fencing of the trails. This is a misconception, for cattle could be driven from Fort Worth to Caldwell today despite the fences. It was, and still is, illegal to close a public road with fencing or any other barrier. In fact, in 1935 a trail herd was driven from the Fort Worth area across the Osage and into the Flint Hills near Eureka, Kansas.[1] Generally, this herd followed Highway 99. As a child we often mentally used bad language because of the many gates we had to open between our ranch and town. The road meandered through open pastures, but gates were placed where the road crossed a fence line. The point is that the trails were not closed by fencing, but the grass was fenced by homesteaders and, thus, it was no longer economically feasible to make the long drive because of the lack of cheap grass.

Origin of Osage Ranching
Taxing Trail Herds

It was during these long grazing drives that the outstanding qualities of the Osage bluestem was discovered. Cattle not only fattened rapidly on green bluestem but they also wintered well on the cured bluestem. Thus, by an accident of geographic location between supply and market as well as an exceptional grass, the Osages were in the forefront of the developing western cattle industry.

Surprisingly, the Osage entry into the cattle industry was not as the lessor of grass. A report by Isaac T. Gibson in September of 1875 shows how the Osages sought to profit from the cattle drives.

> During the past year several herds of cattle were pastured on unoccupied lands west of and contiguous to the Osage reservation, where the Osages habitually herd their ponies. I have no doubt it is true, as alleged that, the Osages have killed several head of these cattle. Drovers having authority to herd them should be well paid for such losses. Five horses were also stolen from a rancher on the cattle-trail, which was returned to the owners. This summer three families of thriftless, indigent Osages left the reservation without permission, and located on the Chisholm cattle-trail, to gain a living by collecting tax of the drovers.[2]

The matter of taxing trail herds caused the Bureau of Indian Affairs a considerable problem. As we have shown above, the Osage problem was small. Yet, the Cherokee trail herd tax became such a problem that a court ruling was made. The Senate Committee on Indian Affairs ruled that the Cherokee were justified in a tax of ten cents a head for cattle crossing the Cherokee reservation. The courts, on the other hand, ruled otherwise: "The United States court in the western district of Arkansas (Judge I. C. Parker), however, takes a different view of the subject, and holds that a tax imposed by the Creek nation on cattle passing through their country is a burden laid upon commerce between the States, the regulation of which belongs to Congress alone."[3]

Ending the Long Drive

Without a doubt, settlers in the Outlet were the primary cause for ending the long drive. However, there were two other significant reasons why the long drive ended. The first of these was the quarantine which prohibited the driving of southern cattle on Kansas or Missouri soil during the warm months. Texas cattle were immune to Texas fever, but they carried ticks to northern cattle that were not immune. Thus, movement of southern cattle was limited to the cool months when the ticks were inactive.

A second additional cause for the cessation of the long drive was the construction of southern railways. Two of these, the Southern Kansas Railway and the Gulf, Colorado, and Santa Fe Railway were especially effective in ending the long drive. For a time, these railroads carried southern cattle to a point immediately south of the Kansas state line. They were off-loaded and trailed on the Elgin branch of the Chisholm Trail into the Osage reservation.

It was, largely, the railroads and the boomers to the west that caused ranching to be established on the Osage reservation. Robert M. Burrell notes, "Thus, aided by the railroads, a new pattern of cattle movement developed. Cattle were loaded in Texas and started on their way to market. Along the way, wherever grazing land was available, and somewhere south of the then existing quarantine line, the cattle were unloaded and allowed to spend several months fattening themselves on grass. Once the cattle had been fattened, the problem of the quarantine was no longer important, since Kansas did not prevent the rail passage of cattle going directly to slaughter."[4]

Quarantine

It must be explained that the quarantine did present a problem to the traditional Kansas trail towns. This was the problem of trailing cattle on Kansas soil. While the laws permitted rail passage, they prohibited trailing southern cattle across the Kansas line during normal marketing months. Thus, Elgin, Kansas, became the largest Kansas trail town in the 1880s and up to 1907.

Elgin's southern city limits also served as the northern line of the Osage nation. A viaduct was constructed over the state line and a dip pit was dug on the Kansas side of the overpass. One old-timer quipped, "We drove 'em *to* the viaduct, they went *over* the line not *across* it; we made 'em *swim* to Kansas, just to be sure they were not *driven across*." Actually, these measures were legal. The viaduct facilitated the dipping of the reluctant longhorns. This dipping kept the ticks at an acceptable level under the quarantine law of 1884. To further comply with the law, a semicircular, stone "quarantine fence" was constructed around Elgin to prevent fugitive cattle from entering any other part of Kansas. The open ends of the semicircle joined with the Osage nation quarantine fence.[5]

All the ingredients for an Osage cattle industry had come together by 1885, and the great Osage grazing region took its place in the history of cattle ranching in the United States. The time had come for the Osages to make another contribution to the development of this country. Like most significant events, this started as a collection of seemingly insignificant factors.

MADE FOR GRAZING

Ranch Country

At present you can travel for miles and not see a house or an animal of any kind. An excellent grade of grass grows luxuriantly, doomed to be consumed by the fall fires. We have here 1,570,196 acres [including the Kaw lands] of fine grazing land. It is estimated that to take all the land together, four acres is a fair estimate needed per head per annum for horses or cattle. From the best information I can get, there is not more than 14,000 head of cattle, horses, and mules in the Territory. It can be easily seen that a very large number of acres of grazing land is not utilized. There are about 550 farms opened in this nation. They have under fence for farming (aside from cattle leases) each from 10 to 100 acres. According to the Indian laws each farm is entitled to one-fourth mile on all sides of that enclosed for cultivation, which is 12,000 acres; the grass utilized in the nation for 14,000 head cattle, horses, and mules, say 5,600 acres; leaving over 1,000,000 acres of fine grass that should be leased, which would bring a net income of over $300,000 per year."[6]

We can see from the foregoing report that the Osage reservation was a great grazing region and that its potential was recognized. In a later report, the grazing feature is noted along with the development of good homes by the Osages: "This country is largely a grazing one, and must continue so for all time. While the Indians are averse to taking their lands in severalty, yet they have pride in building up good homes for themselves, and a number of them have got orchards started."[7]

It must be pointed out that a typical Osage Country ranch has a comfortable headquarters. Usually, these ranches have several small fields available, and often orchards are a part of the grounds. While such an arrangement is locally called a farm, in truth, they are more often the headquarters for a ranching operation.

Green Grass and Fresh Water

The tempo of grass leasing was not very fast in 1886, but the promise of more to come was present: "There are but few leases in this nation [the Osage]. There is a very large territory that could be leased with great profit to this people, and in my judgement they would thereby be benefited much. An Indian improves by having intelligent and industrious neighbors; he sees others have cattle, and the benefits and profits thereon; watches the methods and is improved thereby. An Indian is a very close observer."[8] Clearly, Osage Agent David was trying to make ranchers of the Osages instead of farmers. Unfortunately, the Indian Office officials in Washington had a mind set on making farmers of all Indians despite the circumstances. Thus, a series of restrictive policies were introduced.

These policies made as much sense as trying to make a road runner (chaparral bird) out of a duck and a duck out of a road runner. They were surely not built for the others' role in life. The Osages were not built to be farmers, but ranching was something they could easily adapt to. Long after the Osages had become adept at ranching, the officials were lamenting that the Osage income was so high that they could not be induced to become farmers. It is amazing that bad ideas die harder than a good idea.

Osage Agent David had more to say about the Osages and ranching: "The Indians [Osages] have advanced sufficiently to receive encouragement in stock raising. This is certainly a stock raising country. Large numbers of the Indians have ponies and some few have cattle. A great drawback, but not so great as formerly, to cattle raising is the 'Order of the Dove.' Many have promised if they could be started again in cattle they would not allow them [to be] taken or used by the order."[9] The Order of the Dove refers to the Mourning Ceremony. After three days of preparation and great feasts, a special party leaves for the west. This is, symbolically, the direction of war and death. Having as their mission the taking of a scalp, the dance of this special party has often been called a war dance. Agent Miles, with the assistance of Black Dog, had managed to get the Osages to take only a snip of hair instead of the entire scalp. This worked well, but occasionally the knife cutting the snip of hair inadvertently cut into the scalp and a thin strip of scalp came off with the snip of hair. There was again a feasting after the "hair" was brought back. It was these feasts that consumed all the available Osage cattle.

Four years later (1890) a new agent, O. A. Mitscher reported that a total of 819,934 acres of the reservation was available for grass leases.

Pastures–Under the direction of Special United States Indian Agent Gilbert B. Pray, the lands of this reservation have been largely thrown into cattle pastures, each pasture having been carefully surveyed by competent engineers, and an excellent map of the Kaw and Osage reservations made, showing the location of 14 pastures on the Kaw Reservation, with a net acreage of 71,966 acres, and 184 pastures on the Osage Reservation, with a net acreage of 819,934 acres. These pastures, on account of their nearness to the cattle markets, their richness in grass and abundance of clear, clean water, find a ready rental, and are eagerly sought by the cattlemen of Texas and the West. They are especially valuable for Texas stock, as they break the long haul from that State to the markets.[10]

It appears from the closing statements that all or almost all the 819,934 acres of Osage land was under grass lease in 1890. Details of this leasing will be given in the next topic.

GRASS LEASES

Beginnings

"Sneak Grazing"

The Osages got into the business of grass leasing as a self-protection measure. Stockmen on the Osage boundaries were lax about keeping their stock
off the reservation. Thus, they could acquire free grass since the Osages
could rarely get any money for grass consumed by these accidental strays.

A few earlier leases had been made, but in 1883, the leases were put on
long-term and at a fixed rate. In order to erect a barrier to the sneak grazing,
six leases were laid out adjacent to the Osage boundaries. Three of these
were on the north side where the Kansas cattlemen flourished. The other
three were distributed on the south, east, and west boundaries of the reservation.[11]

Altogether, about 350,000 acres were leased for five years at three to
three-and-one-half cents an acre per year. These leases were fenced by the
lessees. With Indian Office approval, the leases were connected with enough
fencing to fence in the reservation. This perimeter fence was patrolled by
the Indian Police to keep the fence in repair and to keep "strays" out.[12]

The first of these leases was with Edwin "Ed" Hewins, who was to pay
three-and-one-half cents an acre. The Hewins ranch headquarters was about
six-and-one-half miles west and slightly north of Elgin, Kansas. Eventually,
it was incorporated as the city of Hewins, Kansas. Only a handful of people
live there today but it was a sizable place in its heyday.

These leases might have been fenced, as Major Miles states in his report,
but both the Hewins and Carpenter riders say they were line riders.[13] It is
possible that their job was to keep the cattle spread evenly over the lease, yet
the riders always said their job was to keep the herds separated. However, it
is more likely that Major Miles meant that these fences were erected along
the Osage boundary and not that they entirely enclosed the lease. In subsequent reports, this seems to be what he meant. In my own memory, fences
and those eternal gates were everywhere.

Renewal

The first leases and most of the subsequent leases carried an option for renewal. Most of the original lessees renewed, but some had been subjected to
great losses in the winter of 1885–1886. Ed Hewins was one of these, but
he partially recouped his losses and again resumed leasing from the Osage.

Losses in winter were mainly due to a practice that has been discontinued. The old-time cattlemen let the animals winter on their own and tried
to supply them with hay only when the stem-cured grass was snow or ice

LEASES OF 1893[16]		
Lessee	Acres	Annual Rent
W. E. Stich (K)	25,120	$879.20
George M. Carpenter (K)	92,400	1,029.00
D. S. Green	64,000	2,240.00
Edwin M. Hewins (K)	30,700	1,075.20
Jessee M. Pugh (K)	46,000	1,610.00
John Lee (K)	9,000	336.00
Adams, Shafer & Broderick	30,720	1,075.20
Denoya & Pearson	11,520	403.20
J. H. Carney	4,800	168.00
Edward T. Comer (K)	16,320	575.20
Thomas J. Rogers	7,680	268.80
Thomas Leahy	15,360	537.60
John Pappin	5,760	201.60
Virgile Herrard	48,280	1,689.80
G. J. Yeargin	1,600	56.00
S. J. Soldani	25,000	875.00
W. T. Mosier	15,000	525.00
W. H. Connor	16,000	560.00
Frank Lessert	9,600	336.00
Totals	474,860	$14,440.80

Fig. 39. Notice that the lessees are about one-half Osage related and about one-half are Kansas stockmen.

covered. As the quality of the herds improved, it became the practice to supplement the stem-cured grass with high protein feed. Thus, the cattle wintered much better. In the winter of 1885–1886, Hewins saved only sixty-two head out of a herd of 15,000 cattle.[14]

The growth of leases and acreage was rapid. By 1895, the Commissioner of Indian Affairs could report: "Osage Reservation, Okla.—The last annual report mentions the existence of thirty-four grazing leases on this reservation, each for the period of three years from April 1, 1893, at the uniform rate of 3 cents per acre per annum, containing a total estimated area of about 831,188 acres, at an annual rental of $20,091.58. No additional leases have been executed during the past year."[15]

Growth of Grass Leasing

If we use 1893 as our base year and compare this with the leases in 1898, we see some interesting differences (see Fig. 39 and Fig. 40). Some of the names are set in italics to indicate those known to be an Osage mixed-blood or a white man married to an Osage citizen. Some have probably been overlooked for lack of information. Those known to be Kansas stock-

LEASES OF 1898[17]		
Lessee Annual Rent	Acres	
Thomas J. Moore	46,000	$4,600.00
George M. Carpenter (K)	28,000	2,800.00
Virgile Herard	25,280	2,528.00
William R. Whitesedes	28,400	2,840.00
Thomas Leahy	15,000	1,500.00
Adolph C. Stich (K)	20,000	2.000.00
Albert J. Adam (K)	30,720	3,070.00
John Lee (K)	9,000	900.00
Joseph R. Pearson	10,000	1,000.00
Edward T. Comer (K)	16,320	1,632.00
Lorrin B. Moreledge (K) and Edgar A. Allen	9,600	960.00
Adolph C. Stich (K)	25,120	2,512.00
Green J. Yeargain	2,000	200.00
Thomas Leahy	14,360	1,436.00
Maggie Lawrence (K)	12,000	1,200.00
Mortimer L. Mertz and **George J. Bird**	60,000	6,000.00
Mortimer L. Mertz	25,000	2,500.00
James H. Carney	4,800	480.00
Sylvester J. Soldani	20,000	2,000.00
Phillip Beard	7,000	700.00
William J. Leahy	4,000	400.00
Charles N. Prudom	4,000	400.00
Thomas B. Jones	15,040	1,504.00
Totals	431,640	$43,162.00

Fig. 40. The per-acre price has gone up considerably higher than reported in 1893.

men are marked with a (K). Although both lessees and acreage are fewer in 1898 than they were in 1893, clearly grass leases are bringing three times the income. That is, the income from grass leases was $28,721.20 more in 1898 than it had been in 1893. From this, it is clear that we must make our growth comparisons in dollars instead of in acres or number of lessees.

In 1900, the number of lessees increased to a total of forty (see Fig. 41). It is very noticeable that more Osage mixed-bloods were leasing these grass lands than in an earlier period. The presence of many unknown names indicates that more Texas cattlemen were leasing direct from the agency instead of subleasing from mixed-bloods and Kansas stockmen. If true, this would mean the Texas ranchers were hiring their own cowpunchers to care for the cattle on Osage grass. In a subleasing arrangement, the person who subleases out the grass tends to the cattle.

There is a dramatic dip in both the acreage and income between 1898 and 1900. This is partly because the three-year leases made in 1898 had another year to run. A closer estimate of acreage under lease and annual

LEASES OF 1900[18]		
Lessee	Acres	Annual Rent
Ben F. Avant	1,600	$160.00
E.L. Barber	2,000	200.00
Elizabeth Baylis	1,860	136.00
G.S. Chambers	1,420	142.00
Geo. R. Carter	1,200	120.00
Jno. Collins	5,500	550.00
L.L. Denoya	9,390	939.00
Jno. L. Ely	2,120	212.00
Do	3,290	329.00
Honea & Ferguson	4,500	450.00
J.H. Gilliland	2,681	268.10
Virgil Herard	2,500	250.00
A.W. Hoots	970	97.00
Eugene Hayes (K)	4,000	400.00
E. Hooper	5,000	500.00
Chas. Jennings	8,137	313.70
B.M. Kennedy	2,000	200.00
Wm. Leahy	3,000	300.00
Wm. T. Leahy	3,000	300.00
Do	5,790	579.00
Leahy & Mosier	10,321	103.21
Morphis & Price (K)	4,000	400.00
Prudom, Denoya & McGuire	1,480	148.00
R.H. Rowland	6,880	688.00
F.N. Revard	2,000	200.00
Alex. Revard	4,135	413.50
S.J. Riddle	9,000	900.00
Louis Rogers	7,000	700.00
J.C. Stribling, Jr.	9,500	950.00
D.C. Sager	2,500	250.00
S.J. Soldani	6,840	684.00
J.C. Stribling, Jr.	5,170	517.00
C.N. Sloan	5,053	505.30
Short & Brown	1,780	178.00
Chas. M. Vadney	4,000	400.00
N.O. Watkins	3,347	334.70
William W. Irons (K)	8,000	800.00
D.N. Wheeler	1,968	196.80
L. Appleby (K)	1,300	130.00
L. Appleby (two years) (K)	1,000	100.00
Totals	164,732	$14,844.31

Fig. 41. Most of the unidentified names are undoubtedly from Texas.

grass income would be to add the two years together. Thus, in 1900, there would have been approximately 596,372 acres under grass lease and this would have yielded around $58,006 annually. Actually, both figures would have been larger than this indicates because of overlapping leases from years for which we do not have the figures.

LEASES OF 1901[19]		
Lessee	Acres	Annual Rent
Mertz & Bird	12,777	$4,503.99
Wm. S. Fitzpatrick (K)	15,023	2,398.62
Lewis C. Adam (K)	13,100	2,450.25
Wm. T. Leahy	780	117.00
Benj. F. Avant	1,596	159.60
James B. George	800	135.00
James H. Clapp	12,980	8,247.50
Atkin & Brook	6,472	1,978.30
Elizabeth Baylis	1,343	342.46
Woodley & Vance	17,349	4,886.79
Thos. J. Webb	9,740	2,359.80
James H. Carney	4,090	715.75
Irve Ellis	15,200	2,366.60
Prentis Price (K)	920	92.00
Adam & Sharon	15,380	4,078.85
Howard M. Stonebreaker	27,992	7,697.80
Russell & Bevans	31,495	10,096.87
John Pappin	3,774	377.40
Geo. M. Carpenter (K)	53,347	15,128.95
Chas. N. Prudom	9,720	647.00
Thos. Leahy	8,578	880.05
Hargis & Everett	11,652	2,543.82
Thos. P. Kyger	10,580	1,588
Lorin B. Morledge (K)	7,208	1,160.49
James H. Gilliland	2,896	600.05
Robert Thomas	10,599	1,749.94
Solomon Mayer	2,694	484.92
Samuel J. Riddle	11,334	1,233.40
Morphis & Price (K)	3,420	513.00
Virgile Herard	23,767.	1,765.95
James C. Stribling	18,900	3,767.95
Charles Jennings	67,977	9,214.30
Eugene Hayes (K)	12,420	2,424.80

The Beginning of the End

Certainly, the totals for 1901 show an incredible gain in grass lease income (see Fig. 42). $225,951.28 is a sizable sum even in our own inflated times. However, the annual income was probably nearer to $300,000 a year from grass leases alone. The Foster Oil Lease was in effect at this time, but it added very little to the total annual Osage income. If we consider the interest on Osage trust funds, the annual Osage income must have been almost $600,000 in 1901. The original leases were huge tracts, but as time passed and the price per acre for grass increased, the size of the leases became smaller.

LEASES OF 1901 (cont.)		
Lessee	Acres	Annual Rent
Virgile Herard	4,687	468.70
Rosa M. Hoots	4,745	664..85
Sylvester J. Soldani	19,570	19,570
O.T. Word and Ira W. Word	36,072	10,317.33
William F. Smith	5,324	1,357.62
John Collins	12,492	1,591.95
Collins & Wallace	9,492	949.20
Albert Lombard	1,431	157.41
Wm. Watson	1950	292.50
Kate Gorman	2,190	372.80
Timothy J. Leahy	1,240	93.00
Wm. Johnstone	6,956	695.60
Walter Lombard	3,788	568.20
Don C. Sagers	1,922	192.20
Lenora Stewart	2,969	445.35
Wm. T. Mosier	530	79.50
Thos. P. Flanagan	910	191.10
Luther Appleby (K)	4,860	729.00
Joel McGuire	5,747	675.35
John E. Campbell	19,207	2,003.20
Stephen Lessert	319	47.85
Green Yeargain	3,396	509.40
Charles R. Keeler	6,366	477.45
Norris Watkins	5,012	902.16
Thomas L. Rogers	4,933	493.30
Edward S. Brown	3,180	495.96
Antwine Rogers	7,889	1,183.35
Mary J. Clawson	1,865	186.50
Lasater & Noble	17,590	5,013.45
Harris H. Brenner (K)	1,636	163.60
Frank De Noya	3,650	547.50
Walter Russell (K)	4,649	1,441.19
Lee L. Russell (K)	31,438	9,403.68
Arthur Rogers	1,439	143.90
Dwight N. Wheeler	5,121	796.11
Totals	727,260	$225,951.28

Fig. 42. Notice the large size of some of these leases. While many of these leases were large, a trend toward smaller leases than had been made earlier is evident.

Statehood for Oklahoma Territory and Indian Territory had become a definite possibility by 1900. Hence, the Osage Agency tended to enter one year leases instead of longer term leases. The Cherokee Commission had already indicated that Osage allotment prior to statehood was necessary and, therefore, many cattlemen became nervous about making grass leases in the Osage. This and the fact that Osage national laws permitted fencing of 640 acres by each of its citizens caused a decline of leases through the agency.

LEASES OF 1904[20]		
Lessee	Acres	Annual Rent
Harris H. Brenner	6,243	$639
Thomas P. Kyger	8,567	910
Charles N. Prudom	4,348	434
Thomas Leahy	1,110	111
Jonathan B. Clawson	9,192	1,919
Virgile Herard	36,188	4,095
William Watson	10,146	558
Luther Appleby	15,684	1,664
Oscar E. Swanson	2,252	675
Robert H. Rowland	7,190	3,774
Solomon Mayer	5,709	2,624
Jas. E. Henderson, Jr.	8,939	4,737
Charles Jennings	5,767	1,158
Frank De Noya	3,350	837
Higginbothan Bros.	10,508	1,811
John M. Hooton	3,468	346
Samuel G. Kennedy	2,699	337
Frank Thompson	633	80
James J. Quarles	17,772	7,742
John D. Atkin	3,732	1,224
Russel & Vasbinder (K)	9,272	4,166
James M. Slator (K)	8,620	4,810
William K. Hale (K)	9,200	4,830
Vandruff & Townsend	7,354	2,279
Sherman Dudley	886	221
Ottomer G. Hugo	1,727	358
Albert Lombard	1,431	228
Kyger & Brown	5,181	518
Louis E. Hogan	800	120
W. Ralph Morledge	973	121
James C. Stribling	8,246	2,473
Eugene Hayes (K)	19,827	2,401
Earl D. Bailey	1,860	250
James E. Martin	1,696	169
Leslie Claypool	1,348	423
James G. Gilliland	1,216	425
Clement Denoya	1,750	542
George T. Vance	72,519	34,763
John M. Shannon	4,850	2,858
Irve W. Ellis	4,650	799
Ralph H. Harris	10,217	6,845
Leander G. Bishop	8,894	4,096

LEASES OF 1904 (cont.)		
Lessee	Acres	Annual Rent
Wm. H. Kuykendall	7,014	2,191
George M. Carpenter (K)	11,257	4,716
Wm. E. Halsell	5,097	764
Jas. L. Borroum	19,348	8,103
Don C. Sagers	4,798	479
Joel D. Sugg	9,743	3,118
Bayley M. Collyns	4,428	1,328
John Collins	4,956	1,239
Andes H. Murchison	2,919	1,109
Thomas Leahy	3,390	1,017
Samuel C. Tucker	4,468	2,010
Edward S. Brown	830	332
Howard M. Stonebraker	14,735	11,158
Sylvester J. Soldani	24,117	2,357
John E. Campbell	18,967	1,896
Adam & Shaver	26,027	12,431
Timothy J. Leahy	2,570	257
Alfred W. Hoots	883	88
Totals	513,627	$159,013

Fig. 43. There were a total of sixty lessees in 1904.

By the early–1900s, the Kansas Flint Hills section had developed well enough within the quarantine restrictions to cut in heavily on Osage grass leasing.

It is evident from these tables of 1904 and 1905 (figs. 43 and 44) that the fencing laws of the Osage nation were making it attractive for the Osage mixed-bloods to fence in and avoid renting grass from the agency. This is shown in the smaller numbers of Osage lessees. There must have been as many or more cattle in the Osage after 1901 as there had been before that date. The peak year for shipping cattle from the Elgin loading pens was 1907, and the bulk of these cattle came from the Osage pastures.

Apparently, the peak year for grass lease income was in 1901. After this year, the income from grass leases decreased significantly. This could be misleading, because the tables show only the grass leases made through the Osage Agency. They do not show the number of acres nor the annual rent of leases made for areas under fence by Osages. Thus, the decline between 1901 and 1907 was largely due to direct leasing by independent Osage ranchers. What these tables show so dramatically is the rising trend of leasing and then the decrease in grass leasing through the Osage Agency. The Osage ranches have carried between 150,000 and 200,000 cattle annually since the late–1880s. While the tables from the Commissioner's Reports give us the basic information, the Elgin, Kansas, Brand Register gives us confirming and additional information.

LEASES OF 1905[21]		
Lessee	Acres	Annual Rent
Louis Adam, Jr. (K)	5,080	$2,044.70
Louis C. Adam (K)	4,850	2,206.75
Adam & Shaver (K)	1,644	990.50
Charles R. Allen	4,393	1,449.69
Frank Baker	3,110	1,959.30
Brown & Boren	3,390	1,525.50
J.H. Gilliland	1,216	425.60
W.H. Kuykendall	7,014	2,402.30
Thos. Leahy	2,500	625.00
George W. Lewis	633	63.30
J.E. Martin	1,696	186.56
A.N. Shaver	12,830	5,164.08
J.C. Stribling	19,254	4,024.80
Don C. Sagers	4,798	479.80
G.R. White	10,899	5,948.87
E.W. Wallace	12,433	6,245.63
Jane Appleby	10,877	1,087.70
J.H. Bond	5,181	518.10
L.G. Bishop	8,213	5,112.20
H.H.. Brenner	1,687	168.70
J.E. Campbell	8,090	809.00
Eugene Hayes (K)	3,200	820.00
Ewing Halsell	9,955	2,495.05
C.N. Prudom	6,013	601.30
G.T. Vance	8,971	2,422.17
Stonebraker	15,590	9,599.71
G.T. Vance	10,217	3,269.44
C.W.B. Collyns	4,428	1,107.00
W.T. Leahy	11,637	1,192.79
A. Lombard	1,431	286.20
Joe Price	4,111	431
Prentiss Price	3,874	426.14
R.R. Russell	75,264	40,275.22
Higginbotham Land & Cattle Co.	7,387	2,839.66
Maher Bros.	1,420	142.00
S.J. Riddle	2,057.00	226.27
Frank J. Wootan	1,120	148.40
R.L. Boog Scott	8,057	1,849.49
B.F. Avant	1,596.00	159.60
A.W. Hoots	883	93.80
Totals	310,488	$113,125.24

Fig. 44. The table above shows a drastic reduction in grass lease income.

The Santa Fe Railroad kept loading pens at Elgin, Kansas. They hired a man to keep track of the cattle shipped. This was done with "tally sticks" while standing at the loading chute. The cattle would be counted by twenties. A notch was cut in a stick for every twenty. When one lot had been loaded out, the notches would be counted to determine the total for the lot. The stick would then be discarded. We are told that piles of these sticks sometimes accumulated to a depth of one and one-half to two feet deep during July through September. While not all shippers registered their brands with the railroad, quite a number did register all brands in their herds. Isaac Phillips kept the brand register from 1887 to 1897. Keno Vasbinder kept it from 1897 to 1907.[22]

A check through the 126 individual names on the foregoing tables, excluding companies, yields information about many of these lessees.[23] Without a doubt, the largest identifiable group of lessees were Osage mixed-bloods or white men with Osage wives. We could not identify with an acceptable degree of accuracy the Texas cattlemen. However, approximately one-half of the unidentified names were probably Texas lessees. The remaining one-half were either Osage reservation cattlemen living on lease ranches or Kansas cattlemen.

LEGAL PROBLEMS

The Fenlon Decision

Secretary of the Interior Teller ruled in 1883 that Indian grass leases were illegal because Congress had not specifically authorized such leases. This policy was summed up in a letter to Edward Fenlon, who held an Indian grass lease. This so-called Fenlon Decision did not prevent grass leases from being made. However, it did remove the United States government and the Indian governments from any liability arising from the illegal grass leases.[24]

Under these conditions, the fees for grazing had to be kept low because of the open risks involved for the lessee. While the cattlemen did not object to these low prices, they were vocal against this policy because of the very real risks inherent in the practice of illegal leasing. The Osages objected to the policy because they owned their reservation in fee simple and, therefore, had the legal right to lease their property.

The Dawes Act of 1887

In a well-intentioned effort to hasten the "civilization" of the Indian, Congress enacted the Dawes Act. Under this act, Indians were compelled to allot their reservations. The only exceptions were those nations that had treaty provisions allowing them to decide when they were ready to allot. This included the five nations and the Osages. Thus, practically all of Oklahoma Territory and most of Indian Territory were opened to homesteading on surplus Indian lands after allotment.

This action was severely limiting the grasslands available for even illegal leasing. Homesteaders quickly fenced in the land and plowed the grass under. Therefore, the Osage reservation and Cherokee reservations were about the only available grass between Texas and the packing plants at Kansas City and Chicago. While Kansas had excellent grass in the Flint Hills, the quarantine regulations limited their use. At this point, about the only difference between grazing in the Osage and grazing on Cherokee lands was the higher quality grass in the Osage.

The whole matter of illegal leasing was brought to a climax by a proclamation of the President made on February 17, 1890:

> Now, therefore, I Benjamin Harrison President of the United States, do hereby proclaim and give notice:
> First. That no cattle or live stock shall hereafter be brought upon said lands for herding or grazing thereon:
> Second. That no cattle and other live stock now on said Outlet must be removed therefrom not later than October 1, 1890, and so much sooner as said lands or any part of them may be or become lawfully open to settlement by citizens of the United States. . . . [25]

From such actions, it can be seen that the homesteaders had more votes and political power than the cattlemen, and the Indians had no votes. Since the Outlet included the lands bought by the Osages for their reservation, this proclamation affected them also. However, the Osages took their argument of fee simple ownership to Congress. Hence, they were successful in getting special legislation enacted which legalized grass leases in the Osage.

> Chap. 383. Sec. 3. Provided, That where lands are occupied by Indians who have bought and paid for the same, and which lands are not needed for farming or agricultural purposes, and are not desired for individual allotments, the same may be leased by authority of Council speaking for such Indians, for a period not to exceed five years for grazing, or 10 years for mining purposes, in such quantities and upon such terms and conditions as the agent in charge of such reservation may recommend, subject to the approval of the Secretary of the Interior.[26]

This legislation was added as an amendment to the Dawes Act on February 28, 1891.

Thus, the Osages were probably the only Indians that could legally enter into grass leases. Please note that the Osages were learning to fight with some of the tricks used by white men—that is, fighting by using the law and legislation to achieve victory. While the Osages were jubilant over their victory, they had no realization of how far-reaching this legislation was to be. Who could have anticipated that this act would make the Osage far wealthier than the grass leases that brought about the enactment? Five years later, in 1896, the Osages entered into the ten-year Foster lease for gas and petroleum under this amendment to the Dawes Act. By virtue of fee simple ownership, the Osages are the legal owners of all minerals in Osage County.

It seems the Secretary of the Interior was determined to deprive the Osages of their victory. He ruled that no cattle could enter the reservation from below the quarantine line. This circular was issued February 5, 1891, shortly before final approval of the special Osage legislation. Burrell notes that "[a]gain the Osage Council sent a delegation to Washington, and this time they were able to get the restriction . . . removed."[27] Many lessees subleased the grass to Texas ranchers. Others restocked from Texas, so the cattle from below the quarantine line was vital to Osage grass leasing and ranching.

Probably, an agreement to bolster the quarantine fence and other measures to protect the Kansas herds was at the base of this second victory. A strong wire fence one-quarter mile south of the Kansas line was constructed, replacing earlier, weaker fences. This fence ran from the 96th meridian to the Kaw reservation. A stonewall quarantine fence was built around Elgin and joins with this wire quarantine fence. All cattle coming into Elgin from the Osage or direct from Texas were dipped to kill the ticks.

The single essential fact to emerge from the Osage experience with grass leasing was the establishment of the fee simple rights of the people. If the viewpoint of Attorney General Garland's ruling of July 21, 1885, had stood, the Osages would not have had either the grass leases or the oil leases. This ruling states that "whether such title be a fee simple, or a right to occupancy merely, it is not material; in either case the statute applies. Whatever the right or title may be, each Indian tribe or nation is precluded, by the force and effect of the statute from either alienating or leasing any part of its reservation or importing any interest or claim in and to the same without the consent of the Government of the United States."[28] By eliminating the fee simple title from this ruling, Congress affirmed the right of the Osages to lease grass and minerals.

TRENDS

Ingredients of Success

History frequently has a sequence of events showing the development of a particular thing. One of these sequences shows the creation of the Osage reservation and its relationship to the development of the cattle industry. We touched upon this matter earlier in this chapter; however, we did not point out the inter-relationship between the creation of the Osage reserve and its legal aspects regarding other ingredients in the development of the beef industry.

The two major forces at work in any historic event are man and nature. Too often man, in his conceit, looks only at man's role in history and misses the effects of nature. Man's contributions to the development of the cattle industry were the economic, technological, and political facets. Of these three, technological and political aspects are the most remote from nature. Surely, the relationship between the Osages and the government of the United States has no direct relationship to nature, since it was created by man. However, the cultural aversion of the Osages to agriculture does carry more than a hint of natural influence in selecting their reservation.

The geographic location of the Osage reservation between the supply of beef and the demand for beef was a fact of nature. Likewise, the desirable grass was a natural product. Technological developments, such as the railroad, were created by man because of the necessity to overcome the nature of space and distance. Temperature and its effect on slaughtered beef led to the technological development of the refrigerated rail car.

Thus, from the man-made taste for beef arising from the American Civil War, we find a sequence of events that revolves around the cattle industry. Step by step, the necessary ingredients fell into place. Thus, the Osage grass leasing period became an important step in the development of a major American industry.

Osage Politics

Associated with the role of the Osages in the development of the cattle industry was the changing population of the Osages. Generally speaking, the mixed-bloods favored allotment and the full-bloods opposed it. Thus, so long as the full-bloods constituted the controlling majority, the grass leases would be available to the Texas ranchers.[29] We phrased this as a general rule because we believe this argument is somewhat over stressed. It overlooks forces that were at work outside the Osage culture.

It is our opinion that a majority of either full-bloods or mixed-bloods would have had less effect on allotment than the demands of the predominant culture. As a fact of Osage history, control of the Osage government passed to the mixed-bloods as the last unrestricted free land vanished from American history. For 286 years (1607 to 1893), the Euro-American people had free or cheap land available. Now it was gone. The only possible, desirable cheap land remaining was surplus Indian reservation land. Since the Osage reservation was so large, it was apparent that even after each Osage was allotted 160 acres, over 500 acres of surplus land per capita would remain.

With this tempting prize in front of the land-hungry, hopeful homesteader, the pressure on the Osage Council to allot was tremendous. Added to this were the statehood movement and the possibility of becoming an isolated unrepresented annex to the new state. The mixed-bloods had not forgotten their bitter experience during the Kansas removal. They were no more willing than the full-bloods to allot. However, they saw that it would be forced upon the people and that it was necessary to agree to allotment in order to have some say in the terms.

Thus, we would attribute the term of the grass lease period as being dependent on available free land instead of the conflict between full-blood and mixed-blood. Ultimately, it would not have mattered what the full-bloods, mixed-bloods, or cattlemen wanted. Facts support the concept that the homesteaders' demand for land and pending statehood would have ended the old-style grass leasing by about 1906, regardless of who controlled Osage government.

Apart from the term of the grass lease period, the conflict over control of the Osage government did lead to a change in grass leasing. Article V, Section 5, was passed by the Osage National Council on April 5, 1892, and it states: "That each family citizen of the Osage Nation is entitled to fence in one mile square (640 acres) for grazing purposes, and that not more than three families be allowed to fence together."[30]

In effect, this law created a dual system of grass leases in the Osage nation. If a man, wife, and three children were all Osage citizens, they could fence in five sections or 3,100 acres. This could be subleased to a Texas rancher. At the same time, the agency was leasing grass. Therefore, the individual Osages could lease grass and the agency could lease grass. An increase in these family leases after 1892 caused a reduction in agency leases.[31]

An unfairness was inherent in this mixed-blood-sponsored law. Money paid for grass in the family fenced leases was paid directly to the family. To this point, the law was only slightly unfair in that it gave family fencers a quick lump sum payment. The law became grossly unfair when money from the agency leases was paid in quarterly payments to all Osages, family fencers and non-fencers alike. Thus, the mixed-blood family fencers collected grass lease money twice and non-fencers collected only once in quarterly payments.

Summary of Trends

Between 1890 and 1900, the Osages obtained the legal right to enter into lawful leases of their reservation and its resources. During this same time span, a rapid increase in grass leases is reflected in the records. Four other developments should be mentioned that are associated with this decade. There was a noticeable increase in leasing by mixed-bloods and their spouses. Secondly, the Osage enclosure law caused a shift from agency leases to individual leases. Another trend was a shift to outside lessees, that is, a shift from subleasing from Kansas ranchers to direct leasing by Texas ranchers. Finally, the large pasture units originally leased tended to become smaller throughout the 1890s.[32]

These trends indicate an Osage contribution to the development of the American cattle industry. However, this alone would not justify placing the Osages in a position of importance in the development of the industry. The single most important factor giving the Osages a place in the history of the cattle industry is well stated by Burrell: "Because of the quarantine line north of the reservation, these pastures [Osage Reservation] were also the northernmost ones open to cattle from the Southwest. Their continued use helped establish the transient-cattle industry on bluestem prairies."[33]

SEQUEL TO THE PIONEER OSAGE GRAZING INDUSTRY: THE OSAGE, 1906–1945

Allotment of the Osage surface rights in 1906 virtually ended large-scale grass leasing. However, the smaller area leases that had developed in Kansas continued in the Osage. A great difficulty arose from the method of allotment. First, unlike most Indian nations, the Osages allotted their entire reservation. This was a departure from the customary 160 acres per capita and the designating of the remainder as surplus land. Only random, undesirable shreds of surplus lands became available, and even these lands were in very small amounts after Osage allotment.

Secondly, Osage surface allotment was allotted in three draws and the assignment of a fourth tract by uncontested preference. In nearly every individual case, the four 160 acre allotments were not adjacent to each other. Given time, some Osages managed to put their land into one area under one fence. A few Osages went further and by trading and purchase put together sizable ranches. Thus, economically sized grazing units were created.

In the late–1950s, an Oklahoma guidebook could still describe grazing in the Osage: "In the hills near the city [Pawhuska] are widespread grazing lands on which as many as 250,000 cattle are pastured in one season. Approximately two-thirds of the herds are owned by Osage ranchers. The remaining third is shipped in from Texas and other states, during March and April, to be fattened for July and August markets."[34] The best Osage grazing region is the southern tip of the Grand Osage Prairies, which is called the Flint Hills in the terminology of today. While the Kansas Flint Hills graze more cattle than the Osage section, it is probable that Osage County, Oklahoma, grazes more cattle than any single county in Kansas.

It would be debatable which state has the largest single ranch, but the Barnard-Chapman in the Osage, is a sizable ranch. "The Barnard-Chapman Ranch . . . , which covers 11,000 acres of rolling, prairie hills on which more than sixteen thousand head of Hereford cattle graze. . . . It is said that there are more grass-fattened cattle shipped from here annually than from any other point in the United States. Of Osage County's 1,465,520 total acres, 1,218,000 acres are in permanent grasslands."[35] Despite state lines, the Flint Hills constitute an important factor in producing American beef.

No better conclusion to grazing on the Grand Osage Prairies could be found than the following:

> Pasture leasing, transient cattle grazing, and pasturemen survived the hard times of the 1930s, resurged during the 1940s, made the transition to truck transport in the 1950s and early 1960s, and remain important parts of land use in the Flint Hills today. The Crop and Livestock Reporting Service still issues a 'Bluestem Pasture Report' reporting on rates and progress of leasing pastures in the Flint Hills. The relative importance of this activity had declined, however. With consumer tastes having abandoned grass finished beef, and with the cost-price squeeze having made it simply uneconomical to mature cattle several years, the function of leased pastures has become to provide feeders for the lot.[36]

Constitutional Government and Allotment

CONSTITUTION

Two Constitutions

Upon two different occasions, the Osages tried constitutional government. The first attempt was on August 31, 1861: "a convention of the Osage people 'assembled at Council Village on the north side of the Neosho river in the Osage Nation. . . . ' "[1]

Apparently, at least two forces worked against this first attempt at constitutional government. The most obvious of these two forces was the outbreak of the Civil War and the consequent turmoil in southeast Kansas. The white man's war left the Osages with little opportunity to conduct a new experiment in government.

While the second of the two forces may have been less obvious, it surely was equally potent in destroying the first attempt at constitutional government. In 1861, the tribal system, gentile system, or clan organization—or whichever term one prefers to use—was still intact. That is, the Little Old Men and the Division Chiefs still exerted an effective power among the people. Without a doubt, the Little Old Men and the Division Chiefs would seek to destroy this threat to their power.

In simple truth, the Osages were not ready for constitutional government in 1861. Their tribal government and band governments were functioning very well, and a switch to a Western-style government could not have been acceptable by the people. Therefore, some reason outside of the Osage people must have been responsible for the creation of the 1861 Constitution.

Because the Indian's traditional governments often prevented the white man from controlling their leaders, it was customary to force a reorganization of the Indian government. Of course, there were some well-intentioned Euro-Americans who really believed these reorganizations were beneficial to the Indians and that they would aid them to become "civilized."

Although the Civil War prevented the plans of the Kansas government from being immediately implemented, the movement to oust the Osage from Kansas had been under way since 1854. The strong Osage government made it obvious that the Osages would be a "hard nut to crack." Therefore, it would be convenient to set up a constitutional government and, in the conflict between the traditional government and the new government, it would be easier to oust them from Kansas. After the Civil War, this was not as necessary because that conflict had so weakened all aspects of Osage life that they were somewhat easier to manage. Yet a new reorganization *was* introduced by Isaac Gibson, who appointed a governor and council as the official Osage government.

A second attempt at constitutional government was launched December 31, 1881. Agent Miles describes the formation of this government in his report of 1882.

> In this connection I will speak of the agency government that was instituted during the winter and spring. At a general council a large committee was appointed to draft a constitution and some simple laws for the governing of the nation, they generally taking the Cherokee law as a guide, which was formally submitted and adopted by the tribe by ballot, and under its provision they elected a council composed of members from five districts, a principal and second chief, four sheriffs, three judges, and other officers were appointed by the chief and approved by the council. The council has, since its election, been recognized by the tribe as having authority to act for the tribe as far as their laws provide . . . I believe the move a good one, and think they should be encouraged, as it will gradually but surely destroy the old chieftainship and Indian forms of government.[2]

An important distinction between the 1861 Constitution and the Constitution of 1881 can be found in their origins. In 1861, the origin lay *outside* the Osage people and in 1881 it arose from *within* the Osage people. A generation lay between the two constitutions. During the twenty years which had lapsed between them, many Osage institutions had passed away. Among these institutions were the Society of Little Old Men and the Division Chiefs. By 1881, the pressure to remove the Osages from Kansas was no longer a force against the people. The greatest force against the Osages in 1881 was the desire to "civilize" them. Agent Miles was concerned about the band chiefs and their influence among the people. His motive for desiring the demise of these last shreds of traditional Osage government was to hasten "civilization" of the people.

It is sometimes difficult to determine the relationship the Osage government had with the United States. Finney mentions one odd aspect of the relationship: "There were no laws of the United States to apply to Indians for their behavior among themselves, and one Indian could kill another with complete immunity from any punishment by the Federal Government. The law in force in Indian Country explicitly did not extend to crime committed by one Indian against the person or property of another Indian, and was consistent with the treaties which included pledges that Indians would have the right to govern themselves without interference from the white man."[3]

It was situations such as this that provided the motive for creating a constitutional government. With the passing of the Society of Little Old Men and the Division Chiefs, the band chiefs could not provide the traditional protections that had always been an Osage birthright. Traditional Osage law had never included any property protection and dealt only with crimes against one's person. With the growing trend in acquiring farming and grazing claims, property protection was becoming a necessity. Thus, the Constitution of 1881 was created out of a need and not because of ulterior motives of Euro-Americans.

One final motive for adopting a constitutional government should be noted, that is the problems that were arising with other Indian nations. While the United States frowned upon and sought to prevent citizens of one Indian nation from killing citizens of other Indian governments, they did not claim any enforcement power. The only concern of the United States government—and one in which they did claim enforcement power —was to prevent disruption of the peace among the Indian nations. Since this impaired traditional Osage burial practice and revenge actions, a system of constitutional law to apply to these problems became desirable.

Crisis in Constitutional Government

Big Brother

A little government pamphlet contains the following gross understatement of fact: "The history of the Indian Bureau in the latter part of the 19th century is largely characterized by paternalistic policies."[4] By 1900, the BIA was not only the "great father" but also "big brother," to the Osages. The truth of this is evident in the suspension of the constitutional government of the Osage people.

The rise of this paternalism and big brotherism toward the Indian permeated American imperialism abroad. It is still this ingrained attitude that makes the third world nations of today so distrustful of the United States. The presence of this sense of superiority and of the conviction that the

American culture is better than any other culture is the seed that will probably prevent the United States from becoming a leader among third world nations. Euro-Americans cannot set it aside today any more than they could in 1900. This attitude probably had its origins in the evolution of Indian policy, but it was given added impetus because of insular possessions acquired in the Spanish–American War.

At any rate, the "great father" decided to set aside the Osage constitutional government. This was an arbitrary decision made within the BIA with a very questionable authority. The Commissioner's reasons for *abolishing,* as he termed it, the Osage government was given in his report of 1900: "The principal causes . . . were: (1) Acrimonious disputes between the two factions over elections; (2) entire absence of harmony between the Osage tribal officers and the Indian agent in administration of tribal affairs; (3) the selection of ignorant men as officeholders; and (4) the profligate use of moneys received from permit taxes."[5]

If we were to apply the same criteria to recent administrations of the United States government, it too would be abolished. Surely, the Democratic and Republican parties do not run around complimenting each other. Harmony is a rarity between the United Nations or the Organization of American States and the United States. Anyone who thinks the recent and present United States Officers are not ignorant, must be smoking a poppy-pipe. However, the capping climax is reached when it comes to the expenditure of tax money. At least the Osage government did not spend $300 for $3.00 ashtrays or spend in four years more than all previous administrations. When one considers that the Osages did not spend their future generations into a vast debt, one has a right to question the suspension of their government.[6]

Seeking Justification

An additional bit of rationalization was added by Osage agent O. A. Mitscher in the same report: "The Osage tribal government at present consists of a chief and assistant chief. By order of the Interior Department the Osage council of fifteen members and other tribal offices were abolished during April and May of this year, it appearing to the Department that the business of the tribe could be more economically and satisfactorily handled through the agency office."[7]

If economy and efficiency were the primary objective of government, the traditional Osage government was far superior to governments of the Western civilization because it cost nothing. A dictatorship is not only cheaper than a democracy but it is more efficient. The BIA was making

itself the dictator of the Osage people in the name of economy and efficiency. One must ask, Who derived satisfaction from the new arrangement,
the Osages or the BIA?

Upon examination, the reasons given for the suspension of Osage constitutional government are flimsy, to say the least. This Osage government
would not have been suspended if such large sums of money had not been
involved. Furthermore, the constitutional government kept the BIA from
having a free hand in managing these funds. Possibly, the Osage exemption
from the Dawes Act and its amendments lay behind the suspension. It was
known that the National Council was opposed to allotment. Allotment was
a necessity from the Euro-American viewpoint, especially with the possibility of statehood in the near future. Thus, it would be easier to deal with
a government of leaders selected by the BIA. In view of the difficulty encountered with these leaders over allotment, it is a foregone conclusion that
dealing with the Osage National Council would have been more difficult.

INTERIM GOVERNMENTS

Three governments followed the suspension of the Osage national government under the Constitution of 1881. The first of these consisted of a chief
and assistant chief appointed by the agent. As allotment approached, it became evident to the BIA that some cloak of representative government
must be created for appearance sake. Thus, a second government was created.
An election was held and carefully supervised to see that the right candidates won. This government, which in effect was created by the BIA, consisted of a chief, assistant chief, and a council. It was this government that
wrote the Allotment Act of 1906. The third interim government was created by the Act of 1906 to administer the mineral estate. This government
consists of a chief, assistant chief, and an eight member council. It can be
favorably compared with a corporation board of directors.

Since at the time this third government was created all Osages were represented, the government was representative, although it was not created by
the Osage people. However, as time passed, more and more Osages were
born and reached maturity without acquiring a vote in Osage government.
Thus, somewhat over two-thirds of the adult Osages have no share in the
only government recognized by the BIA.

In these supposedly enlightened times, it may be shocking to find that
the BIA still will not recognize any Osage government other than that
created by Congress in the Act of 1906. Thus, the Osage people are denied
the right to live under a government of their own creation despite treaty

guarantees. The fine speeches and stated policies of self-determination touted by administrations since the end of World War II are so much "hot air" as far as most Osage people are concerned. It is still more "economical and satisfactory" to operate through the federally created government than through a government of the Osage people.

In 1988, an effort was made to reinstate the old constitutional government. At first this too sought to limit the franchise to local Osages and a specified blood quantum. After a time it became clear that such limitations could not get enough support to achieve anything. The federal court finally ruled that the Osage People should be represented by a true people's government. Thus, an Osage national government was established by a democratic process that was supervised by the court. Unfortunately, the 1906 government appealed the decision on the grounds that under the Act of 1906 they were sovereign. The appellate court ruled against the Osage national government, and it was disbanded.

Today the 1906 government is the only recognized Osage government. Many fear that when the last allottee dies, the recognized government will die with them. While this is possible, some form of BIA government will probably continue. The big problem is what will happen to the mineral trust? There is no question that there will be serious litigation in the courts. Historically, Indians have faced many more losses in the courts than wins. Where money is involved, the Osages have been fortunate since 1870. Hopefully, that luck will hold into the future.

ESTABLISHING A ROLL
Mixed-Bloods
Shifting Views

An earlier chapter gave a brief sketch of the Osage mixed-bloods. However, it did not deal with the shifting views held by the majority culture toward these children of two cultures. These views have been summed up by one of the few people to write about the mixed-bloods. The first viewpoint appeared in the late–1700s. "With the European presence in America, there came into existence a people that claimed their descent from both the Indian and the European. By the late eighteenth century, this population served both as inspiration to philanthropists seeking new approaches for 'civilizing' the Indian, and a pawn in the debate between monogenists and polygenists."[8]

Acting upon the belief that mixed-bloods would act as a bridge between the two cultures, intermarriage was encouraged. "The American Board of Commissioners for Foreign Missions encouraged its missionaries to take Indian wives in order to establish closer ties with the tribe and to promote the cause of Christianity. The Board also found that mixed-bloods were vital to its missions, where they often acted as interpreters and sometimes even took over the service in the absence of the missionary."[9] This action by the Board of Commissioners was based on a belief that the mixed-blood was as much European as Indian. It is this idea that has caused so many problems for mixed-bloods. Congressmen of today are still heavily influenced by this line of thinking. The confusion arises because of the equation of blood quantum with culture traits.

Blood quantum is a matter of natural inheritance, while cultural traits are a matter of acquired tendencies. Thus a full-blood Indian child raised in the Western civilization would be more "civilized" than a white child raised in the Osage culture. This becomes especially noticeable among Osage mixed-bloods when the mother is Osage. In the Osage culture, the mother is the child's teacher for the first five to six years of life. The training of an Osage child is more intensive than preschool training in Western civilization. Thus, mixed-bloods with Osage mothers may be only one-quarter Osage by blood quantum but almost full-blood by training. This is the reason why measuring Indian-ness by blood quantum is so meaningless.

For this same reason, the progress in "civilizing" the Indian advanced at a snail's pace. No one likes to admit their "pet ideas" are incorrect. Thus, the missionaries blamed the Indian for their failure to become "civilized" within a generation or two: "The decline in Indian population and the Indians' intransigence in the face of change, despite attempts by missionaries and philanthropists on their behalf, led even the 'friends of the Indian' to question the assumption that Indians could be 'civilized.'"[10] This same idea was summed up more directly by the same source. "Attention to the Indian and the mixed-blood increased after the American Revolution. From then until the period of Indian removal in the late 1820s and early 1830s, attitudes towards the Indian and the mixed-blood shifted from a positive belief in their capabilities and potential for civilization to one of reservation and finally to discouragement over their lack of progress."[11]

The removal period caused a feeling among those east of the Mississippi that the Indian was a vanishing race. This was not true, since the Indians had merely been concentrated west of the Mississippi, primarily on what had been Osage lands. With the Indians now out of sight, they soon were also out of mind. Thus, attention was focused upon the slavery issue.[12]

It was evident that by the outbreak of the Civil War, the attitude toward the mixed-bloods was summed up in the hackneyed saying that "half-breeds adopted the evils of both races and none of the good." Acting on the spirit of this thought, the mixed-bloods disappeared from the plans of the

Indian reformers. In their minds, the mixed-bloods ceased to exist as partly European and became one and the same as full-bloods.

"We Threw Them Away"

For the Osage mixed-bloods, this condition ended with the removal from Kansas from 1870–1872. The excessive abuse of these people in the removal forced the American public to recognize the existence of the Osage mixed-bloods. The majority culture gradually became aware of some of the special problems faced by mixed-bloods. It is sad that as Euro-Americans moved to acceptance of these children of two worlds the Osage people moved away from them. The Osage expression for this action is, "we threw them away."

With this background, it is easy to see that a variety of legal problems could also arise for mixed-bloods. This subject of legal rights was especially significant among the Osages in the 1890s. The basic question involved the right to share in the tribal estate. Thus, several considerations must be included. A basic problem was to first determine the rights of the father, mother, or both parents. By using the logic of the child's rights following the father or the child's rights following the mother, a large number of mixed-bloods could be denied a share in the tribal estate.

The matter of residence also had to be taken into account. Osage full-bloods argued, with a great deal of merit, that only those who lived among them and maintained their tribal relationship were entitled to share in the tribal estate. A nation has a common boundary, shares in a common culture, and speaks a common language. Thus, citizenship is ordinarily determined by sharing in these common traits. The common soil argument cannot prevail in determining Osage citizenship today because the amount of common soil is too limited. The language has largely been replaced by American English, so it too could not prevail as a citizenship requirement. This leaves only a common sharing of culture and blood as determining factors of Osage citizenship.

Surely, Section Four of the Dawes Act defined the right of nonresident mixed-bloods to allotment. Section Six of the same act made such an allottee a United States citizen. Yet, for an Osage mixed-blood these provisions are debatable because the Osages were not included in the Dawes Act of 1887.

A third consideration is the admixture of blood. The question revolves around the point where the Indian blood becomes so minute that the person ceases to be Indian by blood. Closely related to this is the problem of citizenship mentioned above.

Adoptions were a very necessary consideration since they were common among most Indians and among the Osages in particular. Finally, the problem of unilaterally dropping a person from the tribal rolls had to be dealt with. That is, should the Osages be permitted to drop a person already on the roll?

From these brief descriptions of the considerations, one can see that establishing an Osage roll was no easy matter. The Osage allotment roll was probably the most contested roll in Indian history. Reasons for this are not difficult to find, but the predominant reason was pure greed. Nowhere in Osage history does greed for material wealth so dominate Osage actions.

One may argue that the full-bloods were motivated more by revenge than by greed—that is, revenge in the sense of depriving whites and mixed-blood whites of any benefit from Osage allotment. A case could possibly be made on the basis of political motive. By reducing the roll, the full-bloods could regain control of the Osage government. However, investigation of these alternate motives reveal that they too arose from greed for material gain. Certainly, the Osages had become Westernized to the extent that greed for material gain had become a part of Osage culture. However, one must point out that greed was evident in all persons associated with establishing an Osage roll.

Roll Qualifications

One of the problems of Osage allotment was the establishment of an accurate roll. Thus, the question of qualifications for inclusion on the roll became extremely important. White-Osage mixed-bloods were singled out and required to prove the right to Osage citizenship. Indian-Osage mixed-bloods were not required to prove a right to Osage citizenship, although they could not legally enter the allotment rolls of more than one tribe.

In August of 1888, Congress enacted a law prohibiting an intermarried white man from sharing in the annuities or allotment of his wife's tribe. However, this did not prevent the wife of such marriage from sharing in the benefits. By the Secretary's ruling, this would prevent a child with a white father and an Osage mother from being placed on the roll.[13] Two later acts set this ruling aside. The first of these was an act of 1897: "That all children born of a marriage heretofore solemnized between a white man and an Indian woman by blood and not by adoption, where said Indian woman is at this time, or was at the time of her death, recognized by the tribe shall have the same rights and privileges to the property of the tribe to which the mother belongs, or belonged at the time of her death, by blood, as any other member of the tribe, and no prior Act of Congress shall be construed as to debar such child of such right."[14]

Many contested families were placed on the rolls because of this act. Yet the traditional Osages continued to believe they were admitted fraudulently. Legally, the sex of a parent could not be used to disqualify a person for enrollment and, therefore, it was not a qualification. The Allotment Act of 1906 also set aside any distinction on the basis of sex of the parent.

Surely, there was an Osage blood qualification. While there were undoubtedly debates on blood quantum, no fixed degree of Osage blood was set. In some contested cases, the question of any Osage blood became an issue. In one case, a contested person claimed the right to be placed on the Osage roll because he claimed descent from Pocahontas. While this is an extreme case, there were people admitted to the roll with even less claim to Osage blood.

Apparently, a residence or affiliation qualification was required. This undoubtedly was based on a provision in the Constitution of 1881 that said, "whenever any [Osage] citizen shall remove with his effects out of the limits of this Nation, and become a citizen of any other government, all his rights and privileges as a citizen of this Nation shall cease: *Provided, Nevertheless,* That the National Council shall have power to readmit by law, to all the rights of citizenship any such persons who may at any time desire to return to the Nation, on memorializing the National Council for such readmission."[15] This qualification raised a great deal of controversy. The department disallowed the removal from the roll of such people. However, generally, if the person had enrolled in some other Indian nation, they were purged from the Osage roll by the department. Yet, several of these ultimately tried to have their names added to the Osage roll by a special Act of Congress.[16]

Another ruling of the Indian Office permitted some non-Osage persons to be placed on the rolls. If a person could prove they were on the Osage rolls on December 31, 1881, it was forbidden to remove them. This date marks the beginning of the Osage nation under the Constitution of 1881. Prior to this date, the roll had been purged, but the investigation was not as searching as it was in 1898–1908.

The Osage Allotment Act of 1906 added a final qualification for admission to the final roll. A special provision in the act provides for minors born after 1906. "That all children born to members of said tribe on and after the first day of January, nineteen hundred and seven, and before the first day of July, nineteen hundred and seven, the proof of birth of such children to be made to the United States Indian Agent for the Osages."[17] This would mean that the youngest living Osage allottees would be eighty-two years old in 1989.

In summary, we find four qualifications for admission to the final Osage roll. These are: (1) proof of Osage blood in any quantum; (2) either residence upon the reservation or some other evidence of continuing citizenship and affiliation with the Osage tribe; (3) proof of being on the roll prior to December 31, 1881; and (4) proof of birth prior to July 1, 1907.

Maybe we should add the information that most of the Osage people were known to each other. By virtue of this fact, only those who were doubtful Osages were challenged. In other cases, enough people accepted an all-Indian mixed-blood to enable them to be placed on the roll without challenge. Apparently, adopted white persons were barred from the roll and adopted Indians were admitted. There were probably no more than 300 challenges and of these about half were admitted to the roll. When the total value of Osage assets, diverted to those with debatable right to be on the roll, is considered, several million dollars are involved.

This struggle over the roll drove a wedge between two factions of Osages, the full-bloods and the mixed-bloods. However, these terms are more than a little deceptive since neither faction was made up entirely of full-bloods or of mixed-bloods. For the ten years between 1898 and 1908, this was the single greatest factor against allotment. It all ended in 1908 with the official acceptance of the final roll. "On April 11, 1908, the Secretary of the Interior approved the tribal roll which contains the names of 2,230 persons, of whom all but one are entitled to allotments. A white woman [Jane Appleby] who had resided with the tribe during; most of her life was enrolled for annuities only. A resolution introduced at the last session of Congress providing for the enrollment of some 37 other persons failed of passage, and unless other names are added by Congress the roll will remain as now constituted."[18]

ALLOTMENT PROBLEMS

Opposition

For many years the Osages, who were themselves exempt from the Dawes Act, watched the effects of allotment on other Indians. What they observed verified their own insistence as a condition of removal from Kansas the right to determine when they were ready to allot. Possibly, no other tribe in the United States had a greater spread in adjustment to Western civilization than the Osages. The range was from highly educated Osages to those who spoke no English.

This great spread in the accommodation range, among other causes, made the Osage allotment unique in Indian history. The need to merge the desires of those who were well accommodated and those who were still traditional Osages led to a new concept in American Indian law. Never before had American law allowed Indian allotment on the basis of separating the surface ownership from mineral ownership. The separation concept had evolved in the great worldwide gold rushes that started in California. To a great degree, this idea combined the Western concept of land ownership in severalty and the Indian concept of communal land ownership. It was a sincere effort to reconcile the diverse needs of the two major Osage factions. However, the unusual reservation of three Indian Camp areas was closer to the Indian communal land ownership idea.

Chapman gives seven reasons for Osage opposition to allotment.[19] The first of these reasons was the large number of dispossessed Potawatomis who had sold their Dawes Act allotments. Their plight made a deep impression on the Osages, who had memories of similar cases from their days in Kansas. Three of the reasons come under the heading of unsettled treaties. These were: irregularities in payment of interest on trust funds; the use of Osage money in a civilization fund growing out of the Treaty of 1865; and payment for lands in western Kansas.

The purging of the rolls was covered in the preceding section of this chapter. We cannot agree with Chapman's sixth reason, which claims the Osages wanted to join the five tribes by becoming the sixth tribe. All our lives, we have heard old Osages say they were invited to join the five tribes, but they refused because they feared the loss of their identity as Osages. In consideration of the Osage view toward the Cherokees, who dominated the five tribes, we believe what the old Osages said was correct. There can be no doubt that Chapman's final point is true. The Osages did want to form an Indian state instead of becoming a part of Oklahoma Territory.

It is customary to explain the pressure to allot by attributing it to the mixed-bloods. Bill Burchardt points out that "[as] more and more whites married into the tribe pressure from mixed-bloods and whites became strong enough to force allotment of the land."[20] We have no argument with such typical statements, except they seem to infer that this was the *only* source of pressure. That is, it is convenient to attribute the pressure to the mixed-bloods, but this is a surface answer that does not get down to the true source of pressure.

One must bear in mind that both the full-bloods and the mixed-bloods were motivated by enlightened self-interest. The mixed-bloods were well aware that allotment would destroy their profitable grass leasing business. However, they could also see that the United States government, under pressure from prospective homesteaders and "friends of the Indian," was determined to force Osage allotment. This was clearly evident in the actions of the so-called Cherokee Commission that was pressuring the Osages even as they were forcing the Cherokee to allot in direct violation of Cherokee treaties.

A distinction must be made to prevent further misunderstanding. By

1898, there were three distinct groups of Osage-white mixed-bloods. First, there were those who were traditional Osages, such as James Big Heart who led the full-blood faction although he was a mixed-blood. Secondly, there were the old French mixed-blood families that had evolved as an Osage band. Finally, there were the recent American mixed-bloods (after 1865), who were rapidly increasing.

Since this latter group married with full-bloods and mixed-bloods alike, it is difficult to determine exactly where the loyalty of the Osage spouses was directed. However, the white spouses obviously had more to gain from allotment than without it. Fortunately, the two mixed-blood groups and the full-blood element were able to retain some influence in directing Osage affairs. The old mixed-bloods eventually came to support allotment because they felt it was better to show support for it and thus gain some say in the terms. Otherwise, they felt that allotment would be forced upon them, as was done with the Cherokee, and they would have little voice in the terms.

In this way, a coalition of old mixed-bloods and new mixed-bloods aligned against traditional mixed-bloods and full-bloods. As it became increasingly evident that the government was determined to have an Osage allotment, a working group of full-bloods and the two older mixed-blood groups evolved. Thus, this group drafted what became the Osage Allotment Act of 1906.

The Survey Question

The problem of payment for surveys has always been a thorn in the side of the Osages. While the costs of these surveys have been comparatively moderate, usually they were made for some other reasons than for the Osage. By 1906, the Osages were well aware that the BIA was generous in authorizing expenditures from the Osage Trust Fund since there was so much money in the account. The Osages argued that they had already paid to have their reservation surveyed and that another survey in 1907–08 was an unjustified expenditure of their money for the benefit of the newly created Osage County, Oklahoma. Also, the Osages pointed out that the government paid for surveys made on other reservations.

In 1871–72, the J. C. Darling survey had laid out quarter sections but had placed markers only on the section corners. Thus, the reservation was marked by square mile or 640 acres.[21] For allotment purposes, it was easy enough for an allottee to locate his 160 acre or quarter sections. Therefore, it seems evident that the new survey of 1907–08 was not for allotment purposes but for some other reason. This is especially true since "the necessary surveys within section lines were left to surveyors of the Allotting Commission."[22]

Despite the Osage protest, the BIA proceeded to authorize the survey:

"*Resurveys.*—On October 10, 1907, the department directed a retracement of the exterior township lines and the relocation of section corners along these lines, and on March 14, 1908, a retracement of the original subdivisional lines of survey, at an approximate cost of $61,289.50. The survey is now progressing in the field under the direction of F. A. Dunnington, topographer in charge."[23] From this description, it seems obvious that this survey was done for the benefit of the government of Osage County and not for the benefit of the Osages, although they paid the bill. The Indian Office betrayed their trust responsibility in not defending the interest of the Osages but also in encouraging the survey. Governmental units, whether they be national, state, or local units of government, should pay for their administrative conveniences in Indian affairs. No single ethnic group should pay general welfare expenses for the benefit of the general population.

Out of seventeen treaties reported for 1865 in Kappler's *Indian Affairs, Laws and Treaties,* only the Osages paid for surveys.[24] Since this was the year of the last Osage treaty, this should be indicative of the BIA practices. The current Kappler edition does not go beyond 1904, so we assume this policy was continued. It would be a safe surmise that the policy was continued and that the Osages were the only Indians required to pay for both the survey of ceded lands and lands they purchased. The Osages could well have pointed out that they had already paid for two surveys of this same area.

Areas Withheld from Allotment

Basically, there were four types of areas within the reservation that were not allotted. These were: (1) camp and agency reserves; (2) gifts; (3) railroad right of ways; and (4) townsites. Three camps, which are called Indian Villages today, were reserved. These are at Gray Horse, Hominy, and Pawhuska. The Agency Reserve of today contains three reserves. The Agent's residence and the buildings around it (two acres) are the first of these. Second is the Osage Boarding School Reserve, which includes the site of the new office building and museum and former golf course (87+ acres). The last reserve is called the Reservoir Reserve, which lies west of the Cemetery Reserve and contains seventeen plus acres.

Some gifts were more in the nature of a priority of choice than a direct gift of monetary value. The first of these was a forty-acre tract at Gray Horse, which gave John N. Florer first choice on the tract. The second and third such "first choices" were extended to the chief and interpreter for the purchase of their houses in Pawhuska.

The Sisters of St. Francis received two gifts of land. One of these was sixty acres at the site of St. Johns Boy's School between Pawhuska and Gray Horse on Hominy Creek. Another was for 160 acres at the site of the St.

Louis Girl's School. Two cemetery gifts were made, one at Pawhuska (20 acres) and the other at Fairfax (10 acres).

Railroad right of way reserves were two rods (33 feet) wide with depot areas as large as needed. There were three railroad reserves. The first of these was 1,367.50 acres reserved to the Midland Valley Railroad Company. A second reserve of 1,114.09 acres was made for the Missouri, Kansas, and Texas Railway Company. Finally, the Atchison, Topeka, and Santa Fe Railway Company was given a reserve of 619.49 acres. It should be noted that each of these companies, especially the Santa Fe, could have later received additional gifts of land. These land reserves were given to the railroads "for their use and benefit in the construction, *operation,* and maintenance of their railroads."[25] The reason we have placed "operation" in italics will become apparent in the next paragraph.

Failure to include an abandonment clause with this gift has caused some difficulty. In the early–1980s, the council brought suit to recover these railroad lands. The court of origin ruled against the council recovering these lands. So far as we know now, the case has not been appealed. The absence of an abandonment clause possibly threw the court into the necessity of ruling on the basis of common practice instead of allowing reversion to the Osage people. In common practice, such abandoned areas usually revert to the adjacent landowners. It appears that among other things, the right of way grant was given under a condition of *operation* and since the operation has ceased, the land should revert to the Osage people as the party making the grant. This appears to be a violation of the contract of grant. An abandonment clause was in the Osage draft of the act. One of the few changes Congress made in the Osage version was to drop this clause as not needed.

There were five town sites reserved from allotment. These were Fairfax, Foraker, Hominy, Pawhuska, and Bigheart (now Barnsdall). Fairfax, Foraker, Hominy, and Barnsdall each consisted of 160 acres. Pawhuska was approximately 195 acres in area. Each town site was surveyed and laid out in lots, which were appraised and sold at auction at or above their appraised value.

Under the act of March 3, 1905 (33 Stat. L. 1061), an Osage town site commission of three members was created. The first member was the Osage agent who acted as chairman of the commission. A second member was appointed by the chief of the Osage nation, and the third member was appointed by the Secretary of the Interior.

A minor problem arose before the commission began its work. Frank Frantz, the Osage agent, was a close, personal friend of President Theodore Roosevelt. Franz had served as Captain in Roosevelt's Rough Rider regiment. Roosevelt appointed Franz as Governor of Oklahoma Territory, and Franz served two years as the last territorial governor of Oklahoma Territory. It was thought at the time that Oklahoma Territory would control the Constitutional Convention and Oklahoma would enter as a Republican state. However, the two Osage reservation votes and fifteen Indian territory votes wrecked this idea, and Oklahoma was Democratic when it entered the Union.

A special agent, William L. Miller, was appointed to look after the Osage Agency until a regular agent could be appointed. In February of 1906, Ret Millard, the new agent, assumed his duties. Special agent William L. Miller was then appointed to the town site commission by the Secretary of the Interior. Millard was chairman of the commission and Julian Trumbly was the Osage member of the commission. It is interesting to observe that two members of the commission were BIA men and only one represented the Osages. Apparently, the BIA wanted to insure their interest in the town sites.

ALLOTMENT

Method of Allotting

The Allotment Act of 1906 was drafted by the Osages. This alone would make the act unusual in Indian history and United States history. Congress made very few changes in the draft the Osages submitted for its consideration. The act provided for an equal division of the lands owned by the Osage people. As a first principle, there were to be no unallocated lands left over after allotment except small fragments of undesirable lands. In effect, this indicated that each person on the approved roll would receive somewhat over 650 acres of land or slightly more than one square mile of area.

However, since land varies greatly in desirability, the first three rounds were to be in 160 acre parcels. This, at least in theory, gave everyone a fair chance to acquire the best land on the first selection. Thus, this selection was called the homestead selection, although any of the three selections could be chosen as the homestead. The homestead could be neither sold nor taxed without an act of Congress. All remaining lands could be taxed after three years and could be sold after twenty-five years had elapsed. Yet, any adult could petition for a certificate of competency which would permit him to sell all his lands except the homestead if the certificate was issued by the BIA.[26]

One can readily see that the Osages had given a great deal of thought to the evils of a Dawes Act type of allotment. They built into their allotment many devices to protect the people from losing their lands. Despite this, the Osages, like many other Indians, became to some extent a landless people. It took longer and required new techniques to make an Osage landless, but eventually, "emergency" after "emergency" or agency mismanagement parted land and Osage.

The Allotment Commission was much like the earlier Townsite Commission, which was organized on August 14, 1906. Only one of the three members was an Osage. Black Dog had been picked by the government council, and its duties were to conduct each round of the selection and to arbitrate disputes.

Prior to passage of the Allotment Act, 1,350 first or homestead selections had been filed. These were confirmed with passage of the act. Between June 28 and September 28, 1906, five hundred more persons filed their first choices. By July 6, 1907, the remaining 380 allottees had filed their first selection. This first round generated many disputes, since it involved the choice land, and it was on a first-filed basis. Thus, the best land went to those who filed early. Those who filed later had to substitute their second or third choice when their first choice was taken by an earlier filer. To avoid this on the second and third selection, the commission introduced what they called "the wheel plan."

March 11, 1907, was set as the day to start on the second round selections. This allowed ample time to discuss the merits of a lottery type of selection and, thus, to limit the arguments about who filed first. The idea was to draw names from a wheel or drum and the number of the drawing became the order of selection. There were many objections to this plan, which was submitted by the interpreter, Harry *Koh pay*. Among these objections was the question of whether this plan was within the provisions of the Allotment Act. By an opinion of the Assistant Attorney General, the wheel plan was ruled to be within the authority of the Allotment Act.

The way was now cleared for the remaining selections to be made by a modified wheel plan. A number wheel and a name wheel were established. In one wheel were 2,229 name cards, and numbers from one to 2,229 were in the other wheel (the wheels were actually barrel churns). A blindfolded person stood at each wheel and simultaneously drew a number and a name. Thus the order for selection was determined for the person named on the name card.

Fifty drawings a day were made until the second and third selections were completed. These drawings were started on July 8, 1907, at 9:00 A.M. and the final drawing was completed by June 29, 1908. The fourth round was by assignment. That is, the commission assigned 160 acres to each allottee. This left the final or fourth round, which as nearly as possible was equalized in value by the Allotment Commission. The fifth and final round was completed by July, 1909. The first selection totaled 354,654.90 acres; the second totaled 355,078.65 acres; and the third came to 355,400.76 acres. These first three selections amounted to a total of 1,065,134.31 acres. Including the 179.50 acres of the final round, this gave each allottee approximately 659.51 acres. Apparently, this last selection figure of 179.50 is an average instead of an actual per capita figure. It seems that approximately 1,470,047.79 acres were allotted.[27]

An interesting sidelight of the Osage allotment is the presence of "locaters" on the reservation. Supposedly, these locaters could assist an Osage to make the best selection. They claimed to be well informed about which selections were still available and the relative value of these selections. Particularly active in this business was the Osage Land Company. The Allotment Commission was ultimately given orders to inform each allottee that more reliable information was available from the Commission at no charge.[28] One should never be surprised at the ways devised to part the Osages from their money and possessions.

THE DOMAIN IN COMMON

Introduction

The topic above described how the Osage allotment in severalty was done. Unlike other allotments of Indian assets, the Osages still retained a great deal of their assets in common after allotment. Allotment in severalty involved two types of assets. The first of these was the land and surface rights, which were discussed above. The second type of asset allotted was the monies held in trust by the United States government. These funds were accumulated from treaties and Kansas land sales. Thus, allotment placed all assets, except the mineral estate, into private ownership by each individual Osage.

This mineral estate was reserved from allotment, and for that reason it is sometimes called the mineral reservation. While it is customary to think of the mineral estate in terms of petroleum and natural gas, it is well to remember that it applies to all forms of minerals. A small income is derived from limestone quarried within the reservation. Lead, zinc, and coal deposits are known to exist on the reservation, but today's prices do not make these deposits economically worth mining. Possibly, in time, the view of water as a mineral, so commonly held in the Far West, will be accepted for application on the reservation.

To administer this mineral estate, which is held in trust by the United States government, a special Osage minerals government was created. We must review the background for the Allotment Act of 1906 in order to understand the position of this government. The constitutional Osage government created by the Osage people had been suspended (probably illegally) by the BIA before allotment. A chief and assistant chief were appointed by the BIA and a few years later a council was elected under guidance from the BIA. In effect, the election was merely a rubber stamp of what the BIA wanted. It was this BIA-created council that drafted the Allotment Act. Included in the act were provisions to create a minerals council. Evidently, the intent was to create a means to administer the mineral estate and not necessarily to replace the constitutional government.

Thus we find a situation where the legally constituted Osage government was quite possibly illegally suspended. While it was still suspended, a government that could not have been created by the Osage people provided for allotment and the creation of a government to administer the mineral estate. At the time of its initiation, every living Osage had one share in the mineral estate and, thus, had one vote in the election of the mineral council. At this point one could argue with some truth that the mineral council represented the Osage people since each Osage had a share or headright.

A problem arose with the passage of time. More and more Osages were born who possessed no portion of a headright. By virtue of this fact they had no vote in selection of the mineral council and, therefore, had no Osage government that represented them. As the numbers of these disenfranchised Osages grew, the injustices involved became increasingly obvious. Some recent legislation does give the minerals council a general Osage government role. However, this violates not only the spirit of policies stated by all recent administrations but it also violates the spirit of the individual's relationship to the state as envisioned by the Constitution of the United States. In effect, a small minority of Osages are recognized by the United States government while most Osages have been terminated under conditions of questionable legality as set forth in United States law and by general policies applied to other Indian groups.

The Minerals Council

The basic outline for the creation of the Minerals Council is in the Act of 1906. Since that time, some changes have been made by Acts of Congress. The section dealing with the Minerals Council is a long section of the Allotment Act, but because of its importance we will quote the entire section with its court and amendment citations to 1929.

> Sec. 9. That there shall be a biennial election of officers for the Osage tribe as follows: a principal chief, an assistant principal chief, and eight members of the Osage tribal council, to succeed the officers elected in the year nineteen hundred and six, said officers to be elected at a general election to be held in the town of Pawhuska, Oklahoma Ter-

ritory, on the first Monday in June; and the first election for said officers shall be held on the first Monday in June, nineteen hundred and
eight, in the manner to be prescribed by the Commissioner of Indian
Affairs, and said officers shall be elected for a period of two years,
commencing on the first day of July following said election, and in
case of a vacancy in the office of principal chief, by death, resignation,
or otherwise, the assistant principal chief shall succeed to said office,
and all vacancies in the Osage tribal council shall be filled in a manner
to be prescribed by the Osage tribal council, and the Secretary of the
Interior is hereby authorized to remove from the council any member
or members thereof for good cause, to be by him determined.

U.S.—*U.S. ex rel Brown V. Lane,* 232 U.S. 598, 58 L.Ed. 748, 34 S.C.
449. (1914.) *McCurdy V. U.S.,* 246 U.S. 263, 62 L.Ed. 706, 38 S.C. 289.
(1918.)
Fed.—*U.S. V. Aaron,* 183 F. 347. (1910.) *U.S. V. Board Commr's Osage
Co.,* 193. 485. (1911.) *Mosier V. U.S.,* 198 F. 54, 117 c.C.A. 162. (1912.)
Amended, Act March 2, 1929, 45 Stat. L. 1478.[29]

As noted in the quoted citations, these provisions were amended March 2,
1929 (45 Stat. L. 1478). The elections were changed from every two years
to every four years. In 1947, the council was given a special power: "and the
Osage tribal council may determine the bonus value of any tract offered for
lease for oil, gas, and other mining purposes on any unleased portion of said
land, and such determination shall be final."[30]

Three years later (1950), the council was given the power to determine
the royalties to be paid on minerals produced. Originally, this power had
been vested in the President of the United States.[31] In 1978, extensive re-
vision of congressional acts relating to the Osages took place, and some
changes were made in the tribal council.

A quorum of five council members was required. The Secretary of the
Interior was authorized to appoint new members of the council when an
unexpired term was vacated. Such an appointee served until the next election. The Secretary of the Interior retained the dismissal power, but he could
use this only after the accused had advance notice and was allowed a defense
hearing.

The final change in 1978 is so important that it must be quoted. "The
tribal government so constituted shall continue in force and effect until
January 1, 1984, and thereafter until otherwise provided by Act of Congress."[32] In the same act, the mineral estate was changed from "and there-

after until otherwise provided by Act of Congress," to "in perpetuity." Two other paragraphs about supervision of the trust by the United States government were changed to read the same as the quoted sentence above. From this, we are inclined to deduce that it is the intent of Congress to continue the mineral *estate* into perpetuity but not necessarily the mineral *trust* and the Osage government established to administer it.

The distinction between mineral *estate* and mineral *trust* must clearly be understood in order to comprehend the significance of this deduction. The mineral estate is the Osage ownership of all minerals in the present Osage County, Oklahoma. Mineral trust refers to the supervision and administration of the Osage mineral estate as provided in the Allotment Act of 1906 and its amendments. With this distinction before us, the deduction will be reworded. Congress has agreed to continue the Osage mineral estate forever, but it has reserved the right to discontinue or alter the supervision and administration of the mineral estate by the United States government. Thus, Congress has preserved a flexibility that could permit the reestablishment of a representative constitutional government for all the Osage people. Such a government could and should be established without affecting the mineral trust.

LOOKING BACK

In looking back at the Osages since 1906, some interesting trivia can be noted. There were thirteen Indian reservations in what is now the state of Oklahoma. The last of these to be allotted was the Osage reservation.[33] Although the state of Oklahoma does not recognize Osage County as a reservation, by virtue of the mineral reservation the federal government recognizes it as a reservation. This makes the Osage reservation the only existing Indian reservation in the state of Oklahoma.

Since the allotment to individual Osages, 425,000 acres have passed into the hands of white men or to some other Indians.[34] A significant statement was once made by Osage Agent Hall:

> Probably nowhere in the Indian country is there to be found a broader or more varied range in the degree of biological assimilation than can be found in Osage county.
>
> The cultural pattern closely parallels the biological pattern in range and variety—from the nonEnglish speaking full-blood to the refined cultured university graduate—with practically all the professions, trades, industries, and vocations represented among members of the tribe.[35]

INDIAN CITIZENSHIP

Osage Citizenship

Most people of Osage blood who have been born since the closing of the final roll have always assumed they were citizens of the Osage nation. However, some doubt about Osage citizenship exists. Current rulings of the Solicitor's Office make Osage citizens of the descendants of persons on the final roll. These rulings are based on references in the 1906 act and its amendments, which refer to descendants and children of allottees. Yet, to date we know of no specific court ruling on the status of Osage descendants of the allottees or on the Solicitor's opinion.

Hence, the only Osages with undisputed Osage citizenship are the allottees. In a showdown case, the courts or Congress would undoubtedly see that the status of the living Osages would be that of an Osage citizen. However, at the present time the status of unallotted Osages remains debatable. Identification cards issued to unallotted Osages *do not state they are Osage citizens.* These cards give a census roll number by year and the alleged degree of blood in the Osage tribe. Nowhere on the card is there the identification of the bearer as an Osage citizen. If the assumption of citizenship by *jus sanguine* (by blood) is made, then this violates the Osage concept of *jus solis* (by under the sun) or, as this is commonly stated, citizenship by soil. As was discussed earlier, the Osages required both blood and residence to establish citizenship. Therefore, one must question the blood identification as proof of Osage citizenship. Until a clear statement of Osage citizenship is established by a clear court decision or a clear act of congress, Osage citizenship remains a debatable subject.

United States Citizenship

No better review of United States citizenship for Indians could be found than six paragraphs in a BIA pamphlet, which we quote in its entirety.

Although Indians today have the same rights as other Americans, acquiring their citizenship was a long and involved process.

The 14th Amendment (1868) to the federal Constitution provided that all persons born in the United States and subject to its jurisdiction were citizens of the United States and of the State in which they resided. Tribal Indians were excluded, however, from the effect of the 14th Amendment on the ground that, by being born into a tribe (which was considered a domestic, dependent nation) they were not born in the United States and therefore, not subject to its jurisdiction (*McKay V. Campbell,* 1871).

The question of Indian civil rights first became a political issue at the close of the 19th century when the incongruity of the Indians' status was brought to public attention through the press.

In 1924, the Indian Citizenship Act was passed. But, even before that time, about two-thirds of the Indians of the United States had become citizens either through treaty agreement, special naturalization status naming tribes or individuals, general statutes naturalizing those who took land allotments, or other special legislation.

The 1924 act stipulated that 'all non-citizen Indians born within the territorial limits of the United States were to be declared citizens,' and provided further that 'that granting of such citizenship shall not in any manner impair or otherwise affect the right of any Indian to tribal or other property.'

Even with the citizenship act, Indians did not in all cases attain the franchise easily. Various State laws enacted from the beginning of the 19th to the early 20th century disenfranchised them, usually on grounds of their high degree of tribal sovereignty or because they were not required to assume the same burdens of citizenships as other Americans (Indian trust lands being exempt from real property and income taxes). By 1947, however, the number of States refusing to permit voting by reservation Indians had declined to two (Arizona and New Mexico), both of which withdrew their prohibition the following year.[36]

An interesting section can be found in the Dawes Act of 1887. Apparently while the Osages were exempt from the other sections of the Dawes Act, they were included in the citizenship provisions. "The effect of this section, however, is not to exclude from citizenship any member of the tribes named who may take up his residence in the United States, separate and apart from his tribe, and adopt the habits of civilized life, but only to exempt the lands occupied by said tribes, from allotment in severalty under the act."[37] Possibly, there were a few Osages that acquired United States citizenship under this provision, between 1887 and 1921.

However, there were too many stipulations in the citizenship section of the Dawes Act to allow granting of United States citizenship with Osage allotment in 1906. Thus, the Osages entered World War I without the majority being United States citizens. Because of this war, however, those Osages who were honorably discharged from the armed services were granted United States citizenship.

Section Three of an act amending the Allotment Act of 1906 has the citizenship law that made all Osages citizens of the United States. This was enacted March 3, 1921. Since the wording of this act is significantly different from other Indian citizenship laws before and after passage of the 1921 act, it will be quoted directly: "Sec. 3. That all members of the Osage Tribe of Indians are hereby declared to be citizens of the United States, but this shall not affect their interest in tribal property or the control of the United States over such property as is now or may hereafter be provided by law. . . . "[38] While other citizenship authorizations for Indians have wording to protect their interests in tribal property, they do not have the inclusion of the trust role of the United States government included.

PART SIX

Standing in Two Worlds,
1906–1989

Black Gold

THE BEGINNING

Discovery

The name black gold came from the Osage. Mrs. Rosa Hoots, an Osage mixed-blood who married a Texas cattleman, was trying to decide on a name for her new foal and saw a nearby oil well pumping. So the colt was named Black Gold. Later he won the 1927 Kentucky Derby against unfavorable odds. Black Gold gave a new term to the American language, combined the Osage love of the horse with ranching, and tied them to the oil industry.

The early oil fields were not discovered by the use of scientific instruments or extensive geological knowledge. In southeastern Kansas and northeastern Oklahoma, surface seeps of petroleum were the clues that led to discovery. Both the Osages and the Indians that followed them in Kansas were aware of the petroleum on the surface of the water at a spring near Iola, Kansas. Other springs in southeast Kansas also gave off petroleum.

Modern uses of petroleum were not known to either the Osages or the Euro-Americans prior to the nineteenth century. The Osages used it for frostbite, cuts, sprains, burns, and horse liniment.[1] Euro-Americans first sought petroleum commercially as a source of lighting oil. Kerosene was a product of petroleum that was obtained by a simple distillation. Coal oil, which was derived from coal, had replaced whale oil as a source of lamp oil. However, the price for both whale oil and coal oil was so high that few could afford it. Thus petroleum was in demand as a cheap source of lamp oil.

The invention and large-scale sale of the automobile in the late nineteenth and early twentieth centuries created a rapidly growing demand for petroleum and its products. Thus, as the grass leasing income of the Osages began to fade away, the income from petroleum and natural gas increased. As technology created more uses for these hydrocarbons, the demand also increased. Thus, the minerals under the Osage grass returned even greater sums of money than the grass.

Pipe lines, supply businesses, offices, refineries, and oil field crews collected in southeast Kansas as the Mid–Continent field opened. Many of these businesses and people came from the Pennsylvania oil producing area. The strike of black gold in the old Osage domain was to become the last great frontier mineral rush in the United States.[2] Possibly the biggest discovery of all was in the Osage reserve, but by this time the oil business was well established in southeast Kansas.

Lease ranchers in the Osage disliked the thin scum of oil that often appeared at springs and coated the stream waters. In the words of Jasper Exendine, a Delaware cowboy, "Oil no good. Make water bad."[3] Having a limited use of no commercial value, petroleum seeps were a nuisance instead of an asset. Yet, George B. Keeler, who rode with Exendine on the day the comment was made, remembered the incident.

Keeler joined with Johnstone, Frank Overlees, and others in an oil well drilling venture. These men joined with the Cudahy Oil Company and hired an Independence, Kansas, drilling company to drill a well in the bend of the Caney at Bartlesville, Oklahoma. On April 15, 1897, at 1,303 feet they hit oil in the Bartlesville Sand. This was the Nellie Johnstone, the first commercial oil well in Indian Territory, now the state of Oklahoma.[4] The site of this well is in present-day Johnstone Park and is well marked. In the fall of October 28, 1897, a well two miles to the west on Butler Creek was brought in on the Foster lease in the Osage reserve.[5] This was the first successful commercial well discovered in the Osage reserve.

The impact of this well was not as immediate as the effects of the Nellie Johnstone. Yet it was enough to affect Osage allotment. As a condition of agreement to allotment, the Osages reserved all mineral rights within the reservation. This was known as the Osage agreement and the Osages themselves wrote the act. The following testimony by John H. Palmer mentions this fact: "In 1905 a committee of the Osage People met here in this town [Pawhuska], and after a session lasting three months, off and on . . . not continually—but nearly all the time—what was known as the Osage Agreement was determined upon. I wrote that Osage Agreement out in longhand."[6] Thus, the Osages protected the future income that was to be derived from the mineral wealth of their reservation.

The Foster Leases

Edwin Bragg Foster is usually named as the holder of the Foster lease. In truth, there were three Fosters involved. The family came from Rhode Island to Independence, Kansas. Henry Foster, who was an eastern banker, joined with his brother Edwin and acquired a bank at Independence. They bought ranches, built railroads, and dabbled in the Kansas oil industry.[7]

Through the efforts of John N. Florer and the Osage National Council, a ten-year lease with the Fosters was signed. James Big Heart and Saucy Calf signed for the Osages.[8] Henry Foster went to New York City to raise money but died before the lease was approved by the Secretary of the Interior.[9]

Henry's youngest son, Henry Vernon Foster, became the treasurer of the newly created Phoenix Oil Company, which had been created to operate in the Osage. After two slightly successful wells, a series of "dry holes" discouraged further exploration. The Fosters turned to the marketing problem. This was eased by a two-inch pipeline to Bartlesville, where it was loaded in railroad tank cars and sold to the refinery at Neodesha, Kansas. A total of 6,212 barrels were shipped in 1900 and 10,536 in 1901.[10]

Edwin Foster died shortly after the Phoenix Oil Company and the Osage Oil Company merged to become the Indian Territory Illuminating Oil Company (ITIO). H. V. Foster then took over the company. Under his leadership, a much-opposed second ten-year lease was obtained in the Osage. It was H. V. Foster that started subleasing. Hence the Osage grew rapidly in oil production as the resultant increase in exploration.[11] Between 1906 and 1926, the Osage produced more money than all the combined gold rushes in American history.[12]

By an act of Congress on March 3, 1905, the Foster Lease was extended for a second ten-year period. At the first of the year in 1909, there were 867 oil wells and 74 gas wells. In six months, the last of June, there were 961 oil wells and still 74 gas wells. During the same fiscal year, 4,816,462.64 barrels of oil were produced.[13]

This volume of production could never have been marketed by tank cars alone. Freight charges would have eaten all the profit. On November 16, 1903, the Prairie Oil and Gas Company filed a pipeline application with the Commissioner of Indian Affairs. Congress enacted special legislation to allow a pipeline to be laid in the Osage and other Indian Territory areas.[14]

Eventually, this line ran from Tulsa and the Southern Osage up through Bartlesville and Independence, where it linked with other lines. In this way, Osage oil could reach the East Coast markets by pipeline. The Tulsa-Independence section was a six-inch line. At the present time, Osage oil can be pipelined to the gulf coast, west coast, and east coast.

LEASE SALES

Early Auctions

We knew Mr. and Mrs. (Marie) H. V. Foster as a boy, since our home was only one block away from the Foster home. Mr. Foster disliked being called the "richest man west of the Mississippi." The Fosters were not showy or flashy people. Mrs. Foster often took us for a ride in her electric automobile. We never left the paved alley, but it was a great experience. Because of their many kindnesses, we find it difficult to believe or write evil about these people.

With the end of the second Foster lease, a new system for awarding leases evolved. Available 160-acre tracts were put up for lease at an auction. These lease auctions are still held quarterly on the Osage Agency Campus. But the beautiful "Million Dollar" elm tree will never again shade the bidders. Disease took the venerable old tree a few years ago and it had to be removed.

At first, the leases were sold by sealed bids. However, it was decided that selling leases at public auction would be more profitable. Thus, for the Osages and oil men the lease auctions became a way of life.[15] "Colonel" Ellsworth E. Walters, the auctioneer, was from Skedee, Oklahoma, in Pawnee County. Apparently, Walters was a master showman and a shrewd judge of human character. Everyone should attend at least one Osage lease auction. In the 1920s, Walters and the boom added to the normal excitement. It is with some shock that one discovers that with the mere wink of the eye or twitch of a finger a million dollars could be spent.[16]

The early oil men spent money casually. When oil man Doheny was asked by a senator during the Teapot Dome investigation if remitting large sums in a satchel was not unusual, Doheny replied, "Senator, in the past year I have remitted several million dollars that way. You must remember Senator that, the $50,000 I loaned to my old friend, Albert Fall, was no more than five or ten dollars to the ordinary man." Oil men who attended the Osage lease auctions were accustomed to dealing in large sums. In a way, they seemed to be casual, but one could sense in them the same excitement one would find in a hunter about to make his first big game kill.

Money to be Made

There was money to be made in the Osage reserve. This fact is evident from the figures available. As of January 1, 1953, 16,962 wells had been drilled in Osage County. At this same date, there were 6,794 producing oil wells and 216 gas wells. Since the discovery of Osage oil, 640,000,000 barrels have been produced, which is approximately 2 percent of all the oil produced in the United States.[17] In 1924, the commissioner of Indian Affairs made an interesting report: "In the Osage Reservation alone 120,000 acres were offered for oil mining lease, 62,448 acres selling for a grand total of $16,457,000. The outstanding feature in these sales was the recordbreaking prices received for tracts in the famous Burbank pool, one 160 acre tract bringing $1,990,000, another $1,995,000 and each of several others selling for more than $1,000,000. The total revenue to the Osage Indians from oil and gas leases was $24,670,483."[18]

Famous Men and Companies

Many oil companies started in the Osage, and most of the early oil men have at some time sat under the million dollar elm and bid their way to a fortune. The Osage was surrounded by oil cities. Independence in Kansas, Bartlesville, Ponca City, and Tulsa in Oklahoma sat on the fringes of the Osage. However, no great oil town developed within the reservation. Barnsdall (originally Big Heart) once came near to greatness, but time and fate passed it by.

H. V. Foster was one of the few oil men who was born rich. Most of the others became rich by that odd mixture of "guts and luck." There was William G. Skelly, the teamster who founded Skelly Oil Company. Harry Sinclair of Sinclair Oil Company shot his foot off while hunting south of Bartlesville. With the $5,000 insurance money, he started his oil fortune. T. N. Barnsdall grew up in the Pennsylvania oil business and set up his B Square company at Big Heart, which was renamed Barnsdall. George and Jean Paul Getty made their share of money in the Osage. Profits from Osage oil lay at the base of the Getty fortune.[19]

While most of these oil men eventually clustered in Tulsa, three of the early Osage operators headquartered elsewhere. Frank Phillips, the barber turned oil man, settled at Bartlesville along with H. V. Foster. Marland, the Pennsylvania oil man who opened the Burbank pool, settled at Ponca City, where he established the Continental Oil Company (Conoco).

One sometimes reads or hears reference to "lots" in the Osage. The best explanation we have seen for these is quoted below.

> To come up with a system for designating the subleases ITIO divided the eastern portion of its blanket lease into three tiers, called "Lots" or "blocks." There were 348 of these Lots, each one a half mile wide north to south and about three and 3/4 miles long east to west, reaching from the Kansas border on the north to the chocolate-colored Arkansas River on the south. Lot 1 lay along the Kansas line and the rest of the blocks were numbered consecutively southward, so that Lots 33, 34, 35, and 36 fell on the western edge of Bartlesville and Lot 116 extended another forty miles south.[20]

It was Lot 50 that was so important to the Gettys. This lot netted $426,000 for them in production and another $120,000 when they sold it. Frank Phillips on Lot 185 hit his 1,000 barrel a day well within a half mile of the Getty well. This Phillips well was sometimes declared to be a 3,500 barrel a day well.[21]

UPS AND DOWNS

Production

Introduction

Between 1906 and 1920, the price per barrel of oil rose from a range of 39¢–52¢ to a high of $3.00 early in 1920. Natural gas was yielding about $1,000,000 a year to the Osages. As a matter of some interest and real significance, in 1920, oil wells in the Osage had a life expectancy of over twenty years. Osage gas wells lasted three times longer than gas wells elsewhere in the Mid–Continent field.[22]

The advantages of oil and gas production in the Osage was increasingly obvious by 1920. Nowhere else in the United States could be found such a large producing area under one ownership. This meant the leasing in the Osage was a simple, economical process as compared to other producing areas. It also meant that a uniform code of conservation could be applied over a large producing area. Although geological factors made the Osage an area of low production per well, long-lived wells and conservation practices prolonged the life of the wells. Thus, the Osages, the producers, and the nation benefited from the single ownership.

A scarcity of casing pipe and other materials acted as a brake to the drilling of new wells in the Osage. But in view of the drilling in the Burbank pool of thirty-five wells in less than six months, the brake of scarce supplies had only a slight effect. Westside leases (Burbank)[23] ran an average of $504.67 per acre in 1921, while the east side ran $43.29 and acre.[24]

Two changes in laws affecting the Osage mineral estate were enacted in 1921. First, a change was made in the number of acres any one entity could lease. 4,800 acres was the old limit. This was raised to 20,000 acres on the east-side, but all acreage limits were set aside on the westside. Secondly, on March 3, 1921, Congress extended the Osage Mineral Trust period to 1946. The price for this extension was to allow the state of Oklahoma to levy a 5 percent gross production tax and an additional county tax of 1 percent for roads and bridges.[25]

Like any mining venture, the production of oil is sensitive to changes in the economy. However, many other factors are also at work affecting production and profits. Manmade problems such as government regulations and competition among the producing areas surely affect profit and production. The Osage producing area is especially vulnerable to government regulations. Aside from federal and state regulations, the Osage is also affected by

BIA regulations. Fortunately, these three layers of regulatory agencies can usually resolve conflicts in regulations. Yet the time required to bring mutual agreement often allows a great deal of damage to be inflicted. Thus, we find cycles of ups and downs in profits and production.

Superimposed over the smaller cycles are the larger recession cycles of the general economy. Osage annuity checks were so small during the 1930s that they would have been laughable if it had not been so serious. Osages were not eligible for the New Deal recovery programs and the oil annuity checks were all they had. However, many Osages did not have even this, and they were also excluded from any government aid.

The Burbank Field

We humans have a tendency to stress the dramatic because it touches our imagination. The discovery of the Burbank pool was a classic in the American drama of a poor boy making his fortune. All the ingredients of the American ideal of individualism are present, with confidence in one's own beliefs leading the way.

"On May 14, 1920, at 2,965 feet, the crew struck an oil sand and produced 680 barrels of oil the first twenty-four hours."[26] Thus, the bringing in of the Burbank pool's discovery well has been described. E. W. Marland had assigned the drilling of this well to his Kay County Gas Company because he expected to strike gas at this site. Since his gas company had no oil lease, it turned the well over to his Marland Refining Company.

The Burbank soon became one of the top producing areas in the United States. Oil men came from all over the world to mine the "black gold" of the pool. In time, the flow pressure dropped throughout the pool and production declined rapidly. It was evident that the Burbank was dying.

Waterflood

On August 5, 1947, fifteen oil companies submitted a proposal to the Osage Council: "In re: Proposal to Unitize Leasehold Interests in that Part of the North Burbank Field Lying in Osage County Except the Stanley Stringer, and to Develop the Unitized Area by Water Flooding Involving a Request for Royalty Reduction under Unitized Operation."[27] Thus the largest secondary petroleum recovery program in the history of the oil industry was initiated.

We will quote freely from this proposal because of its significance to the Osage People and to the history of the oil industry. "The North Burbank Field is about 25 years old. A total of 161 million barrels of oil has been produced to January 1, 1946, from that part of the field lying within the proposed unitized area. The field had been subjected to secondary recovery operations since about 1932 in the form of a gas repressuring program which has been diligently conducted by the Operators over the past fifteen years."[28] It is obvious that the gas repressuring was only moderately successful. The Burbank was doomed to continue its decline unless a more effective secondary recovery was introduced. Marginal wells had increased and these would be plugged unless some means to revive them was developed.

The operators then stated their projections: "we are of the opinion that the future recovery from the lands herein proposed to be unitized will be somewhere between 150 and 175 million barrels. . . . will increase . . . production . . . from 24,000 to 32,000 barrels per day, a three to four-fold increase."[29] Since we are in a position to speak from hindsight, we can say these projections were reasonably accurate.

As a final quote from the proposal, the cost should be mentioned. "Water flooding operations of the size to be engaged in North Burbank are of such character that once the project is started, it must be continued to the end without interruption so that, the Operators must commit themselves to an investment annually of from 4 to 5 million dollars over the period of the next ten to fifteen years."[30]

It may be of interest to the curious to know who the fifteen operators were who made such a foresighted proposal. Their names as they appear on the proposal are as follows:

1. Royal Oil and Gas Company
2. Phillips Petroleum Company
3. Continental Oil Company
4. Magnolia Petroleum Company
5. Cities Service Oil Company
6. Mid–Continent Petroleum Company
7. Ohio Oil Company
8. The Texas Company
9. Gulf Oil Corporation
10. Moore Oil Company
11. Skelly Oil Company
12. Devonian Oil Company
13. N. Appleman Oil Company
14. Sinclair Prairie Oil Company
15. Kewanee Oil Company

Some of these companies are better known than others. Yet all the companies are substantial producers in the oil industry.

Petroleum reserves in the Osage fall into the following four types:

1. Proven developed and partially developed pools that are operated as primarily recovery pools;
2. Proven developed and partially developed pools that are operated as secondary recovery projects, by gas injection in a few instances or by water flood in the large majority of such projects;
3. Presently undeveloped by proven secondary recovery reserves; and
4. Undiscovered commercial deposits of oil and/or gas.[31]

These reserves have been estimated to be 647 million barrels. This estimate was based on the technology of the early–1960s and does not include the factor of improved technology. In plain English, this means that the Osage had enough oil to last beyond the year 2020.

Extensions

The First Extension

There have been four extensions of the Osage Mineral Trust plus one attempt to terminate both the trust and the tribe. The fourth extension was into perpetuity. Fortunately, the council has been able to cope with all threats to the mineral trust. However, these extensions to the mineral trust have not been obtained without paying a price. The two most significant prices paid have been the Gross Production Tax and paying all the expenses of operating the Osage Agency.

The Allotment Act of 1906 fixed the term of the mineral trust at twenty-five years. That is, both the mineral trust and the mineral estate were to end in 1931. At that time, the mineral estate was to pass to the property owner. Since it was obvious that only a small fraction of the oil could be removed by 1931, there was a great deal of concern among the Osages in the late–1920s. Beyond the loss of communal domain lay another very real problem. Wording in the 1906 act does not define "property owner." If it meant the property owner of record in 1931, then the mineral rights would pass to many white people. But if it meant the allottee who first held individual ownership to the land, then the mineral rights would remain in the hands of individual Osages. However, this would mean some allottees or their heirs would have mineral rights and others would not.

The operators as well as the Osages were very concerned about this problem. It is much easier and economical for an oil operator to lease from one owner instead of several. Also, a contract to drill obtained from the United States government is less subject to disputes and court litigation. Thus, the operators had ample reason to support extending the Osage Mineral Trust.

However, in and around Pawhuska, there were banks and Osage guardians who had acquired lands in Osage County. These persons formed what they were pleased to call the Home Owners Association. This association was doing everything possible to defeat the extension of the Osage Mineral Trust. They were thinking that if they could defeat the extension they might be able to acquire for a few dollars the mineral rights to the lands they had obtained.

On January 22, 1920, the Osage Tribal Council clearly demonstrated that they could adapt Osage wiles to the white man's world. The resolution they adopted is a masterpiece of Osage logic and a classic example of "bluff war."

WHEREAS, the most vital question that now confronts the Osage Tribe is the question of the extension of the mineral period; and;

WHEREAS, it has come to the knowledge of the Council that some of the officers and directors of certain banks are using their efforts to defeat legislation by Congress providing for the extension of the mineral period; and

WHEREAS, there are a number of persons acting as guardians of estates of members of the Osage Tribe of Indians, who are also endeavoring to defeat legislation by Congress to extend said mineral period; and

WHEREAS, said banks have large deposits of Osage Tribal funds and said guardians are receiving great benefits from handling the estates of members of the tribe, and in opposing the extension of the mineral period, are working to the detriment of the Osage Tribe of Indians and to the detriment of their wards, respectively; and

WHEREAS, the Osage Tribal Council feels that banks and persons who are receiving benefits from the Osage Tribe of Indians and from members thereof, ought not in any way interfere with or bring any influence to bear against the granting of said extension, and that if they continue to do so, said banks ought not to be permitted to have deposits of money belonging to the Osage Tribe, and such persons ought not to be permitted to longer act as guardians of estates of members of the Tribe;

THEREFORE, be it Resolved by the Osage Tribal Council, duly in session in the City of Washington on the 22nd day of Jan., 1920, and is so resolved; That the Council hereby requests the Honorable Secretary of the Interior and the Commissioner of Indian Affairs, to withdraw from any bank, whose officers or directors use any influence to prevent the granting of an extension of the mineral period, all funds of the Osage Tribe deposited therein, and that they use their influence and efforts to cause to be removed any guardian of the estate of an

Osage Indian who is using his influence to prevent the granting of the extension of the mineral period.[32]

This resolution was sent to eighty-four guardians and seven banks. Acting on the principal that "a bird in the hand is worth two in the bush," the banks and guardians withdrew their opposition. The Osages had used "a velvet glove over a mailed fist" and had won a victory. As in the past, when the Osages fought a "bluff war" they usually had the power to back it up. In this case, the BIA and Department of the Interior supported extending the mineral trust.

The Osages had won a battle but not the war. On the brink of passage, the entire proposal was brought to a standstill. Almost without warning, the entire Oklahoma delegation to Congress refused to support the extension bill. Without their endorsement, the bill would not have a chance to pass. Demanding that the bill be amended to require a 5 percent Gross Production Tax, the Oklahoma delegation blocked the extension. Having no alternative, the council agreed to the tax amendment to get the extension. After passage, it was discovered that an additional 1 percent roads and bridges tax had also been added to the amendment. This additional 1 percent tax had never been discussed with the delegation and was added to the bill without informing the Osages, who had agreed only to a 5 percent Gross Production Tax. The Osages filed a claim for this portion of the tax but the claims courts ruled against them.[33] After thirty years of paying this one percent to Osage County, the roads show very little relationship to the amount of money paid.

Second and Third Extensions

The second extension was accomplished without any problems. On March 2, 1929, Congress extended the Osage Mineral Trust to January 22, 1958. However, a clause to limit the extension was included, stating, "unless otherwise provided by Act of Congress." No concession was made to secure this second extension. Like the second extension, the third extension had no opposition and required no special concession. The wording remained the same, except the terminal date was changed to April 8, 1983.

Fourth Extension

To ease the recurring renewals, the council in 1963 proposed extending the Mineral Trust in perpetuity. Congress apparently liked the idea and without opposition enacted a fourth extension. The difference in this extension was that it had no specific term, but extended in perpetuity. Yet it also allowed the council to dispose of the mineral estate with a two-third majority vote of the headrights and approval of the Secretary of the Interior. Apparently, this provision was to allow the council to devise a means of termination that would insure the mineral benefits, if any remained, to devolve upon the heirs of the allottees.

Threat of Termination

What Would Happen to the Minerals?

As mentioned earlier, the first renewal involved the question of who would own the mineral rights if the trust was not extended and the communal rights were abandoned. The best answer to that question is summed up in two points.

1. Congress could not have given the minerals to the secondary surface owners because the Osages bought the lands and the minerals, thus, the Osages could not have been deprived of the minerals except by due process of the law and due compensation.
2. By virtue of the Allotment Act of 1906, Sec. 1, Sec. 2, Sub-Sec. 7, and Sec. 5, all mineral ownership, if the trust is discontinued, must revert to the individual allotees or their heirs.[34]

One could have argued that the 425,000 acres that had passed from Osage hands by 1920 was sold at a lower price to compensate for the lack of mineral rights to go with the land. Between June 30, 1915, and June of 1916, 13,123 acres had been sold at an average price of $6.31 per acre. In the fiscal year ending in June of 1917, 10,346 acres were sold at $9.51 per acre. No lands were sold in 1917–1918 but those sold in 1919 brought $18.44 per acre. From this, it is obvious that Osage lands were selling at a very low price.[35]

Agency Costs

Some confusion exists as to who has paid for the agency expenses in the past and who pays these costs today. Apparently, the Osages have paid for the costs of administrating the mineral trust since 1906. Possibly, this would include some nonmineral trust costs. In 1953, the Osages were facing termination in the form of House Concurrent Resolution 108. The testimony of the Osages in the hearings on this bill was heard July 22, 1953. The answer to who has been paying the costs of the agency and who is now paying the costs was brought out in the testimony.

MR. HARRISON. You are willing to pay every bit of the expenses?
MR. LABADIE [GEORGE V.]. Yes, sir.

MR. HARRISON. That will include not only the $40,000, which is the difference between the $300,000 cost of operation and the $260,000 you pay, but also the cost of administration by the Department of the Interior.

MR. LABADIE. Correct, and the area directors.

MR. HARRISON. I understand then you will take immediate steps to work out with the Department of the Interior representatives the plans to take care of the payment on a fair and equitable basis?

MR. LABADIE. Certainly.

MR. HARRISON. I might say I can find no fault with an agreement of that kind nor can I find any fault with the continuation of the trust provided you are willing to pay for the additional cost.

I must say just as frankly that I feel that a tribe that is as wealthy as your tribe is and people as competent as you are, making the record that you and other people have in business, certainly should not expect the federal government to continue payment of all the extra costs. If the continuation of [the] trust is going to be beneficial to you, then you should be willing to pay for it.

MR. LABADIE. That is correct. And we will do that.[36]

The Klamath Tribe

In essence, this bill proposed specifically to terminate the Flathead Tribe of Montana, the Klamath Tribe of Oregon, the Menominee Tribe of Wisconsin, the Osage Tribe of Oklahoma, the Potawatomi Tribe of Kansas and Nebraska, and some Chippewa. The Klamath and Osage tribes were the only two tribes who paid any part of their agency expenses. Since the passage of this bill, the Osages are the only tribe paying their agency expenses and the only tribe to pay all their agency costs.

Shrinking the Mineral Estate

Big Reservoirs

There were other troubles causing concern among the Osage people, aside from the gross production tax and termination. Surely, the problem of shrinking the mineral estate is of great concern. At first glimpse, a reservoir here and another there does not seem to involve much area. However, when one adds up the total areas that are removed from production, it translates into a considerable sum of money. Of course, one could point out that compensation was made for the lost production. While this meets the requirement of "due process of law," it nevertheless reduces the mineral domain. Experience has shown that these sums paid are far below the value of the lost production, as later events clearly support. As John Donne wrote, "If a clod be washed away by the sea, Europe is the less, as well as if a promontory were, as well as if a manor of thy friend's or of thine own were. . . ."[37]

The truth is that although some almost token payment is made, thousands of acres are effectively taken out of production because possible leakage discourages lessees. Dams such as Hulah, Birch, Candy, Kaw, Skiatook, Sand Creek, and Shidler have very large flood or maximum holding basins. While some of these are still in the proposal stage, the last six will eventually cover 39,500 acres. We would estimate that the Hulah reservoir would be approximately 8,000 acres. If this is true, 47,500 acres of the mineral estate would either be lost or for all practical purposes put out of production. Only an operator with an exceptional taste and purse for litigation would attempt to produce oil in these basins.

Small Reservoirs

A lesser problem arises from municipal and private lakes. While our list of thirty-nine lakes of ten acres or more does not include all such lakes in the county, their total acreage is surprising. These thirty-nine lakes cover 2,881 acres. The Osages, through the Attorney General's Office, sued the City of Pawhuska to recover lost revenues due to Blue Stem Lake (Civil Action No. 4057). As a result, the Osages received some compensation and established the legal precedent to collect from smaller reservoirs.

Parks and Preserves

A greater threat to reducing the mineral domain came in the cloak of a park. In 1980, the National Park Service fired its opening guns by seeking to acquire 97,000 acres for a tall grass preserve or park. Although this was subsequently scaled down to 50,000 acres of owned land and 50,000 acres of partial lease land, it did not pass through Congress. The problem is not dead, but it lies dormant and could erupt again at anytime. In these days of growing population in the urban areas, there is a corresponding demand for recreation areas. Osage County is one of the few sizable areas that have not been polluted by an excess of population. The future will bring increasing pressure for more reservoirs and more parks in the Osage country. It is a jewel that the urban dweller cannot resist.

THE MINERALS COUNCIL

Introduction

An interesting aspect of Osage government under the minerals council has been noted: "Those who served on the council were faced with a perplexingly diverse constituency. As they tried to balance their duties as a corporate board of directors with a humanistic solicitude for the tribe's welfare, the incompatibility of the two concerns seemed painfully irresolvable."[38] There can be no doubt that the minerals council has functioned extremely well as a corporate body. However, when one looks to the human aspects of government, the council has bumbled, delayed, and plainly fell far short of meeting the needs of the Osage people as a whole.

Largely, this is a legacy of that terrible conflict over establishing the roll. The greed which spurred that conflict still affects those in power. While the mineral estate is secure, other monies such as grants and claims would likely have to be shared with more Osages if things were changed. However, more than this inherited greed, the fear of creating more Osages from non-Osages sits in the back of Osage minds when a radical change in government is proposed.

It took the minerals government a full decade to realize there was a growing number of unallotted Osages. It bothered some of the old full-bloods that Osage children born after July, 1907, were not sharing in the mineral domain. This was not the traditional Osage way of conducting their affairs. From their view, all Osages shared and shared alike in common property. Chief Fred Lookout reflected another traditional characteristic on this question: "some will be in favor, and a good many will be opposed . . . [we should] unite and act as one and not argue this very serious question."[39] The proposal to include more Osages as full citizens of the tribe was dropped because the council could not unite and act as one.

While the problem of the unallotted "outcasts" remained unsolved, the council did come to grips with three other voting problems. These were: (1) the vote for female allottees; (2) absentee voting; and (3) votes for unallotted Osages who had inherited headrights or portions of headrights. All three of these were implemented.[40] However, a fourth problem is rarely mentioned and is not generally known among the Osage people.

Lost Votes

As it often happens, one heir, usually a white spouse, is left a life interest in a headright. At the same time, another heir or heirs are left title to the headright. In such situations the headright cannot be voted. That is, until the person with the life interest dies, and all monies legally go to the headright owners, no one can vote for that headright. So, a sizable number of headrights cannot be voted. In a "good" election, around 800 votes are cast. Some of these absent votes are owned by white persons or institutions. A few are probably nonvoters but out of the total votes possible, probably three hundred or more nonvotes are life interest headrights.

While considering the third extension of the Mineral Trust in 1957,

Congress had written the Bill with a requirement of district representation nationwide (United States), better procedures for absentee ballots, and a vote for all adult Osages. However, all these provisions were deleted from the bill before it was enacted.[41]

Unallotted "Outcasts"

Logan vs. Andrus

The problem of the unallotted "outcasts" kept festering. A group calling themselves the Osage National Organization (ONO) was formed and sought to change the governmental organization. Therefore, some investigation was made by a federal commission. Possibly the greatest impact was made as the result of the case of *Logan, et al. v. Andrus, et al.* In a decision dated October 5, 1978, three points were brought out, but the first point is of special interest: "Secretary of the Interior was attempting to exercise legislative power when he purportedly abolished government of Osage Nation in 1900, and thus such action was beyond scope of his authority and of no legal effect."[42]

Naturally, this decision was a bombshell in the BIA and Osage Agency. In a memorandum, Scott Keep, Assistant Solicitor for Tribal Government and Alaska, discusses the implications of the Logan case.[43] Among other matters the confused status of Osage citizenship as a result of the decision was discussed. Although the field solicitor cites references to unallotted Osages and minor members of the tribe in 1938 as making descendants of the allottees members of the tribe, the assistant solicitor expressed doubts about this "evidence:" "I am not confident, however, that either of these acts [cites acts mentioned above] resolves my dilemma which is to determine who are the members of the governmental entity, known as the Osage Tribe, as opposed to who are those Osage Indians or persons of Osage Indian descent who are entitled to share in certain property interests. Membership in an Indian tribe is a bilateral, governmental relationship as I have already mentioned. It is a relationship that clearly contemplates something more than mere descendency."[44]

Questionable Citizenship

If this problem of Osage citizenship was not enough to shake the administration on *Ki he ka* Hill (location of the agency offices), another statement by the Assistant Solicitor must have at least caused a slight quiver. "The membership situation is further confused by the court's recognition of the 1881 constitution as the law of the Osage Tribe." This latter point was to some degree put into limbo by the Appellate Court. Yet, the question of Osage citizenship still remains today. Subsequent court cases never touched on this point. After a long series of suits the status of citizenship and voting in a representative tribal government is absent for over 10,000 Osages.

While the trial court brought the matters above into the case, it ruled against the plaintiffs on the matter of suit. That is, it sought a judgment declaring that the Osage Tribal Council was limited in its powers to administration of the Osage mineral estate and did not have authority to participate in or represent the Osage tribe in the various federal programs made available to entities such as the tribe. Thus, the court ruled that the minerals council also had general governmental powers. So, the plaintiffs appealed.

The appellate court not only affirmed the lower court's decision, but it refused to consider either the citizenship question or the question of the 1881 Constitution. Its grounds for this refusal were that the plaintiffs all had headrights and the right to vote. As such, they were not entitled to seek relief from a condition which they were not a party. Thus, the question of the 1881 Constitution was placed in limbo; its validity as the Osage government had not been determined. The citizenship question remains, but it would possibly include descendants of the allottees as citizens.

FORTUNES AND MISFORTUNES

Income

Boom

By 1906, the trust and diminished reserve lands in Kansas had been sold, and the funds derived from their sale were drawing 5 percent interest. Grass lease money was also adding to the Osage income, but it was no longer paid after 1907. As was pointed out in an earlier chapter, the Osages were considered to be well off by 1890, and by 1900 they were described as the wealthiest people in the world.

However, the 1920s ushered in an era of high income for the Osages that far exceeded the above-average prosperity in the majority culture. Apparently, the income from oil and gas peaked in 1925 at $29,584,739. But from 1925 to 1931, oil and gas income shows a sharp decline.[45] This was largely due to the economic crash of 1929. A slight recession in 1925 did not stall the overall economy, but the agricultural sector of the economy did not recover from the 1925 recession until the Great Depression ended. This recession of 1925 partially reduced the demand for oil and gas and so reduced Osage income.

Bust

The unstable economy after 1925 made exploring for new pools of oil in the Osage a riskier business than normal. Hence, wildcatters could not get financing to drill exploratory wells. The lack of new production also cut into Osage income. A final factor in declining oil and gas income was an increasing number of aging wells. By 1930, over one-half of the wells in the Osage had become "stripper" wells. That is, they produced less than ten barrels a day. They were marginal wells that required favorable market conditions to operate at a profit.

As the economy staggered in 1925 and then collapsed in 1929, these marginal wells were the first to shut down. An oil well is not like a water tap in homes. One cannot turn a well on and off like a water tap. An idle well begins to seal off the pores in the oil-bearing layer around the well's collection basin. The lighter elements that keep the petroleum fluid evaporate, leaving an excess of paraffin and greases that act as barriers to any future flow.

Reactivating such wells is expensive and the return on the investment can often be a disappointment. In limestone layers, hydrochloric acid (commercial forms are called muriatic acid) can be pumped into the hole. Enough limestone is eaten away to allow the oil to flow again if all goes as planned. This will not work in layers that do not contain lime. Another technique called "fracking" is used in such layers. In fracturing, sand is forced between the rock layers around the well's collecting basin by hydraulic pressure. Thus, new channels of flow are opened. Only the demands of World War II could justify the expense of reactivating such wells, but usually these inactive wells had been "pulled" and "capped" by that time.

Credit

One of the more troublesome income problems was the use of credit. This was a lingering legacy of the fur trade. In a barter system such as was used in the fur trade, credit was necessary. However, in a monetary system, it was an expensive practice when used to supply daily needs. Yet, extensive use of credit in lieu of money was still utilized by the Osages long after the fur trade ended. Although the Great Depression all but ended the practice, it is still used today.

As in the fur trade, credit was customarily used to pad the accounts of Osages. This was a widespread practice by merchants, auto dealers, and those rendering professional services. Because of easily obtained credit, Osages often tended to overspend. As a result, they rarely had ready cash and did not develop a "feel" for the value of money.

In 1901, traders on the Osage reservation were still required to be licensed to trade. Credit to 60 percent of the last quarterly payment was placed as a maximum that the BIA would recognize for any individual Osage debt. Yet, this plan was flawed, for provisions to withhold as many quarterly payments as necessary to pay off an individual's debt were also provided.[46]

As part of the picture of credit available to the Osage, some idea of shopping areas and availability of goods should be given. "There are now 9 trading points on the reservation and 140 licenses are in force, representing nearly every line of business. There are also 4 banks. . . . There are 23 general stores, 4 lumber yards, 4 meat markets, 2 drug stores, 1 flour mill, 2 newspapers, 5 blacksmith shops, 6 hotels, 5 bakeries, 5 dressmaking and millinery establishments, 7 livery stables, 6 contractors; and a large number of other occupations are represented by from one to five persons or firms."[47] A system of trading cards had been devised to more easily keep track of individual debt. Amounts of each transaction were entered on the card, and, thus, the total indebtedness could be easily obtained at the time of purchase. When the individual card holder reached sixty percent of payment, he was to receive no more credit.

In 1901, the total claims for trading debts amounted to $429,596.32. At the end of June, 1903, the debt had been reduced to $142,265.98. By the end of June, 1904, the total debt was paid off. Each individual incurring the debt paid his or her share by repaying the tribal funds from their annuity payments.[48]

Shenanigans

Fun

During the Great Depression we often heard Osage allottees say ruefully, "If the money ever starts coming in again, I will be a little wiser in how I use it." This would usually be followed by a grin and a twinkle of the eye. Sometimes, the allottee would add, "Boy! We sure had a hellva' time while it lasted." After World War II, when the payments again became fairly large, very few Osages "blew their bundle." They were less trusting of their merchants, bankers, and other "friends." When they felt something was worthwhile, the checkbook was used but their spending was on the conservative side.

Stories of the wild Osage fantasies are endless. Here were a fun loving people of limited means who had acquired the economic means to fulfill their sense of humor and fantasies. A few of these stories will give a cross-sectional insight into Osage character and life in the 1920s.

The Tuxedo

One Osage man had to make a trip to Washington, D.C. He got on the train at Pawhuska wearing his blanket and moccasins. When he got back to the Pawhuska depot, he was all dressed up in a tuxedo and patent leather shoes.

He explained that when he got to St. Louis he thought he should get some citizen clothes. So he bought the shoes and tuxedo, including a lot of high collars. He claimed the collars were so high that all he could see was the sky. Anyway, he looked prosperous, so everybody in Washington respected him for his clothes and especially his collars.

Later, it was discovered that he had worn his blanket and moccasins all the time he was away. On his way home he had bought the tux and collars to make a joke. Osage humor always cuts at dignity.[49] The white men who wore their silly high collars were extremely funny to the Osages. To them, it seemed ridiculous that anyone who wore high collars and, thus, had their nose in the air continually could amount to anything because all they could see was the sky.

The Graduate

An Indian boy, a graduate of an Eastern university, came home from school with his diploma. His proud old father made him a present of a dozen of the gayest and most expensive blankets he could find and added several pairs of exquisitely beaded moccasins. On top of this he gave his son a huge new car. To the honor of the boy—and the honor of his university, too—the young man put aside his store clothes and his nifty college shoes, and whenever he rode in that car he wore a blanket and moccasins.

"It's my university outfit from dad," he used to explain.[50]

This story shows two other facets of Osage character—generosity and respect for one's elders.

The Bear

We would not want to embarrass anyone, so real names are not used in this story. Old Bill was a drinker; when he got his payment he vanished. The young men would make up a betting pool on how Bill would reappear. Everyone missed the bet when Bill came back less than sober, driving a motorcycle with a sidecar. A glance at his passenger made us all speechless. Sitting up in the sidecar was a bear cub.

Bill lost the motorcycle to pay off debts, but he kept the cub. The two often boxed and wrestled when Bill was sober. However, the day came when the bear reached a good size. Bill and the bear were boxing around one day when the bear gave Bill a swat that caused Bill to trade ends. That was the last of the bear—he vanished and he never came back. There is no particular point to the story. It was merely an episode in Osage life during the 1920s.

We worked with Bill for two months in the Indian Division of the CCC

(CCC-ID). At that time, we were digging wings and footings for wall dams. This required that one be down in a gully where no breeze could help cool the body. Although we were in our late teens, the heat was still almost unbearable. Bill's whisky-soft body must have shrieked in protest. Yet, he never complained and swung his mattock and wielded his shovel on the dry clay with the best of us young men. Bill swore that when his payment came he would not go away on a drunk—but he did.

Divorce

A cousin loves to relate his experience with his first wife, who was a white woman. In the divorce settlement, he was left with virtually nothing. This was common in the 1920s when young Osages were enticed into marriage with white spouses who were after Osage money.

One would expect the young man to be bitter about the divorce, and probably he was. But like the good Osage he is, he made a joke of the bitter experience. His description of the divorce decree is graphic, "Hell, I thought the judge said alimony, I didn't know he said *all the money.*"

Fleecing the Osages

The Guardians

"Bad! Man, they're crazy! Money-crazy! They started about five years ago cheatin' rich Indians, and now they've got to cheatin' themselves and no one knows where it'll end. They certainly need a revival up Pawhuska way."[51] Possibly, the description above is an exaggeration. Many non-Osages would choose to believe it is an inflated version of the situation, but Osages would tend to think it was a conservative description. There is enough evidence available to strongly support the Osage view.

The cheating by merchants was a terrible practice, but it was petty theft when compared to the guardianship larceny. According to G. Edward Tinker, "The blackest chapter in the history of the State will be the Indian guardianship over these estates. . . . Men made a profession of it. Sometimes as many as 15 guardianships have been under 1 man. . . . Why should any Indian, any Osage Indian . . . have a guardian? This Department is there for the purpose of taking care of them, though I understand they are trying to shirk their duty by getting them under guardianship; but, nevertheless, it is their duty to take care of them; and not the courts of the county."[52]

Tinker was challenged on his testimony by a Pawhuska attorney who argued that any wrongs detected in the guardianship system were quickly corrected by the courts. Ten years later (1953) an investigation by the BIA fully supported Tinker's rather temperate testimony.

We would like to cite three of the guardianship findings reported in the investigation. "At the time of the 1929 hearing, this Indian was in debt approximately $20,000 for mortgages held by his attorney despite the fact that he had, within the year, inherited an estate of more than $90,000 and had been drawing substantial quarterly payments averaging $7,000 to $12,000 annually since 1924. He was unable to account for $55,000 of his income."[53] Apparently, the attorney-guardian had taken an income that averaged $30,000 a year for five years and converted it into a $20,000 debt and $55,000 profit for himself. Since the debt was to the attorney also, this guardianship yielded the attorney at least $75,000 profit over and above his legal guardianship fees for five years. The truly terrifying aspect of this is that the county courts supported this attorney and, thus, legalized the corruption. "Not publicised, but matters of record, are numerous other cases of exploitation the Osages have experienced. One such case is that of an attorney who, on September 20, 1923, was found guilty in the Court of Osage County of defrauding his ward, an incompetent Osage Indian, in an automobile transaction. The guardian had purchased an automobile for $250 from another guardian, who had purchased it new for $1,145, and then arranged for its sale to his ward for $1,250."[54] This conviction of a mere $1,000 fraud (grand larceny) was indeed rare. The evidence and circumstance must have been overwhelming to render the court unable to avoid a conviction. Atonement for the conviction was apparently made by the court, however, since the attorney was subsequently made guardian over several other Osages.

The attitude of the guardian in another case is enlightening. The transcript in this case shows that Mr. ★★★, a 37-year old Osage of !!/16 blood, had received between July 1, 1916, and September 30, 1925, a sum of $100,200 and owed $14,000. His only property was valued at $19,630, and the testimony developed the fact that the ward had bought property from his guardian prior to the guardianship arrangement and at the time of the hearing was paying $1,200 a year on it and interest at 10 per cent.

The guardian strenuously protested revocation of his ward's certificate of competency, arguing that his ward "is entirely competent so long as I have charge of his affairs."[55]

We do not wish to dwell only upon the guardianship crooks. The courts were responsible for most of these problems.

The Courts

Probate courts opened the door for much of the crimes against Osages. The council finally enacted a formal resolution against the courts. This, of course, touches on other forms of exploitation. "[E]xperience had conclusively proved that welfare of those members of our Tribe who do not have certificates of competency cannot be entrusted to certain courts of the State of Oklahoma, as shown by the following incidents which are matters of public record:"[56] We will include only one of the many incidents in the report. "The County Judge frankly admits he approved these claims knowing they were barred by the statute of limitations. This matter was discussed . . . with the administrator as to why he approved these claims, knowing . . . they [were] not lawful charges against the decedent's estate. The administrator admitted it was a mistake . . . but said to get the creditors off his shoulders he approved the claims, relying on the Department to deny payment from estate funds."[57] One would think that these attitudes, practices, and crimes committed by the cheating merchants would have been the end of gouging the Osages, but this would be far from true. The county government had to get into the looting game too. One of its practices involved overcharging on recording fees.

However, the attitude that honest people could honorably cheat the Osages prevailed throughout the county. This permeated the business and professional community as well as the government and law enforcement. Unarmed Osages were shot down for minor offenses or jailed for no reason other than that they were Osages.

One of the worst such incidents was the killing of Roy Tinker, which occurred on April 6, 1919. Being a Sunday, it was quiet in Pawhuska. The quiet was disturbed by Roy Tinker, who was drunk. He had been stopped for a traffic violation and after signing the citation started to walk home. Hiram Stevens, the new chief of police, came up as Roy started to walk across the street. Hiram called out for Roy to stop. Roy either did not hear the command or decided to ignore it. Stephens then shot Roy twice in the back. Stephens started to the police station with him, but seeing he was dying loaded him in a taxi. Taking him to the Johnson funeral parlor, Stephens dumped the dying youth partly in the doorway and left. Of course, Stephens was tried for the cold-blooded murder, but he was not convicted because all he had killed was an Osage.[58] This was not an unusual occurrence. While police officers did not usually run around killing Osages, it was fairly common among private citizens.

Reign of Terror

Introduction

Probably no other aspect of Osage history has received as much attention as the series of Osage murders in the 1920s. An excellent account of a special facet of these murders was written by Bill Burchardt: "It is a mistake to view these crimes in a different light because the criminals were white, and the victims Indian. This was no race war. Criminals did not prey on the Osages because they were Indians, but because they had money. Vultures quickly descended on every western boomtown from California to Kansas, from Montana to Texas. The murderers, cardsharps, dope doctors, thieves, and shyster lawyers in the Osage would have schemed just as malevolently had their wealthy victims been white, and they would have succeeded equally as well."[59] This point was probably correct where the motive was purely to secure money. But some Osage murders did involve bias and attitudes toward the Osages and Indians.

It was murder because of greed for money and possessions that aroused the great American public. There was a vast difference in the violence and corruption in the Osage and that found in boom areas in the past. Burchardt notes that "The difference was that the Osage was viewed in the limelight of mass communications. Other western boom violence had been viewed in retrospect. . . . but the blood and thunder in the Osage was happening *now.* The nation was astonished, shocked, and secretly delighted, to find a last outpost of the Old West still alive, 'raising hell and putting a chunk under it.' It made for avid reading. . . . and brought forth howls of condemnation from the righteous."[60]

Most Americans thought the Old West was gone along with the nineteenth century. Yet, it was somewhat of a thrill to discover that it still existed in the Osage. However, few frontier historians would concede that the western frontier continued into the twentieth century. All over the West there were frontier pockets which were mostly boom areas. Nevertheless, the Osage Old West was unusual in another way. It was structured around Indians who stood at *O Ke sa* or midway. The Osages were truly the "Middle People" *(Ni U Kon scah)* for they stood midway between the past and the present. Standing in two cultures as they did, they were the Travelers in the Mists[61] of the new Indian of the twentieth century.

The Murders

The bodies of Charles Whitehorn and Anna Brown were found near the end of May in 1921. Whitehorn's body was found in the timber upon Dial Hill on the north side of Pawhuska. Anna's body was found in a pasture near Gray Horse. Although both had been shot to death and they were both Osage, this appeared to be the only connection between the two murders. The Sheriff made an effort to locate the murderers, but he never found the criminals. The case lay dormant in the local law enforcement files with other unsolved incidents involving Osage deaths.

On a cold Tuesday afternoon of early February, 1923, the frozen body of Henry Roan Horse was found. His body was sitting in his car slumped over the steering wheel. Henry had been shot in the head with a forty-five. The car was parked off the old Burbank road about six miles north of Fairfax.

While the murder of Henry Roan Horse was still being discussed, an event at Fairfax shook the city in a very literal sense. A terrific explosion early in the morning of March 13, 1923, completely demolished the Bill Smith home. Three people died because of the explosion. Mr. and Mrs. Smith and their maid were all killed. Mr. Smith and the maid were white persons. Mrs. Reta Smith was daughter to Lizzie Que and a sister of Anna Brown, who had been found shot to death over a year earlier. The Osage council appealed to the federal government for assistance since the local officers seemed to be unable to solve Osage murder cases.

The newly created Federal Bureau of Investigation (FBI) was sent to investigate these murders. These were the first murder cases the FBI ever worked on. It should be noted that these murder cases almost immediately began to open up. Widespread coverage of the murders had placed all governmental units under very heavy pressure to find the guilty persons and to prosecute them.

Some connections among the various murders and mysterious deaths began to emerge. Lizzie Que emerged as the center around which the murders revolved. Two months after Anna Brown's body was found, her mother Lizzie Que died from drinking bad whisky, probably deliberately poisoned. Mollie Kyle was sister to Anna Brown and Reta Smith. Lizzie, their mother, had three full headrights, and each of the daughters each had their own full headright plus a fractional headright inherited from a deceased relative. Now that all these headrights would come to Mollie, she became a suspect.

Mollie did not remain a suspect very long because her husband, Ernest Burkhart, emerged as a prime suspect. William K. Hale, a wealthy rancher in the Osage, was uncle to Ernest Burkhart. Hale came to the Osage from Texas. After he became established in the Osage, he encouraged other members of his family to join him. In this way, Burkhart came to the Osage and married Mollie Kyle. Thus, Hale became a suspect through his connection with his nephew.

The Trials

Hale's money and influence drug the case through three trials in almost four years. Not all these were county and state trials. The federal courts were the ones which ultimately achieved convictions. Osage County officers and courts could be affected by wealthy, influential white men, especially where Osages were involved. Thus, much of the difficulty was brought on by jurisdictional disputes between local and federal agencies. The first grand jury indictments were mysteriously quashed. This was only one of the many procedural delays in the proceedings. The federal grand jury led to indictment of fifteen persons involved in the murders. Although Hale, Burkhart, and several others received life sentences, over a dozen murders connected with the case remained unsolved.

The Osage tribe financed about one-third of the costs of bringing the guilty to trial and prosecuting them. "Osage murder trials, Oklahoma: For expenses in connection with the prosecution of the person or persons implicated in the crimes resulting in the murder of Osage citizens, for witness fees and expenses, records, additional investigations, and all other purposes, $10,000, or so much as may be necessary, to be paid from funds on deposit in the United States Treasury to the credit of the Osage Tribe, and to remain available until June 30, 1929: *Provided,* that no part of this sum shall be expended for the compensation of attorneys."[62] Despite the last proviso, the Osages hired T. J. Leahy to represent them at the trial. They contributed $20,000 to defray the costs exclusive of attorney fees.[63]

Curse of Wealth

In 1884, Laban J. Miles wrote: "During the month of June I personally visited almost every Osage camp while taking the census, . . . I was often made to exclaim, as I went from lodge to lodge and saw many with scrofulous sores, undressed, naked, and dirty-faced children, women broken down with carrying heavy burdens, homes without any evidence of comfort or refinement, 'Rich, yet how poor!' and wondered if even the hoarded millions that these people possess in common would ever be appreciated by them, or they use it to really better their condition."[64] Miles was writing of another time in Osage life when they were rich but lived poor. Possibly they were happier in these times of living poor because they understood poverty. Economic condition is a state of mind; happiness is a condition of the soul.

As the money increased, Osage souls shrunk for want of happiness. They found no happiness in possessing money; they enjoyed the passing pleasure of buying new "things." However, the "things" brought no lasting happiness because they had no meaning. Thus, Osage life had lost its purpose, and their souls suffered for direction. It was a case of being set adrift in a strange world. There was nothing familiar to clutch and stay afloat in the world of white man's wealth. Yet, one by one the Osages rediscovered old friends and gradually made new friends in the strange, new white man's culture. They clung to their old ways, although they were forced to adapt them to the new world. With more than a little fear cloaked in a haughty exterior, they reached for the new world and often got burnt or crushed. However, they persevered, they learned, and they adjusted until the strange sea became their sea. Through all these terrible experiences, they were unhappy. Yet, the task was made easier because of the money, although the money was also making things more difficult.

This is to say the Osages followed a different road to accommodation than other Indians. The problems of other Indians were largely caused by a shortage of money. The Osage problems were primarily caused by too much money.

It is this mixed blessing of money that is so often reflected in Osage remarks. John Goodskin's comment is well worth quoting: "I have a diploma from Lawrence and they put a guardian over me. I fought in France for this country, and yet I am not allowed even to sign my own checks. I don't know what chicanery he [the guardian] used to get control of me, but here I am, his ward."[65] Money made his education possible, but, nonetheless, it also attracted vultures to prey upon him and to prevent him from using his education.

Sophie Captain Chouteau was a very wise person. She is one of the few women to become an Osage chief. A reporter for *Harper's Magazine* interviewed her at the Pawhuska Indian Camp.

> "But your Osage tribe was very poor once," you say to Aunt Sophie.
> "Yes, yes!" she exclaims. "But we were better off then. My heart is crying for our young people, for our girls. Too much money is very bad." And then she adds, "It hurts the old folks, too, even the wise; men."[66]

There was this longing to go back to the old life they loved so well. Yet, there was an understanding that it was the young Osages who were carrying the real burden of the transition. Possibly, it was this knowledge that caused them to relax the stern discipline of excellence traditionally instilled into young Osages. Some think it was caused by spoiling the young with lavish gifts, but this cannot be true because the Osages had always done this. No, it was a lack of the firm hand of direction that cast the young Osage adrift in a strange sea.

As the *Harper's* reporter commented in another place, not all the problems came from within the Osages. The terrible spell cast upon the Osage reservation still lingers in milder forms today, as was also noted by the *Harper's* writer:

> There are 265,000 Indians in the United States; their race is not dying out. But, of them all, it is not improbable that these Osage In-

dians, with their wealth, are the unhappiest. You have that impression as you leave Pawhuska; it is not a happy town.

A blight of gold and oil and greed is on it, as heavy a curse as Indians have ever had from their wickedest medicine men.[67]

One day our grandfather stopped us as we were trying to kill a dragonfly with a clod. Horrified at what we were trying to do, he explained that this was one of the guardians.

There were at least seven guardians who looked after the honor of an Osage. For those who dishonored their people, strange penalties were assigned. Some laugh at these old Osage beliefs, but they are not mere superstition. Modern psychologists are finding that the state of the mind affects more than we once thought. The Old Osages, in their wisdom, knew this long ago. It was this condition or state of the mind that was called the punishment of the guardians.

The question here is, was it the guardians that placed the curse of wealth upon the people? Did they lift the penalty of unhappiness when the Osages again became an honorable people? Part of the penalty assigned by the guardians is that we will never know.

This we do know—the Osages passed another bend in the river of life. The people survived and became stronger because of the ordeal. Yet, some of the anguish lingers. Possibly, when it has all been said and time has healed the hurt, the following words of John Goodskin will no longer bring to the mind such terrible pictures: "In the old days, before we had money, it was easy enough. All you had to do was not get drunk. But, now your good behavior has nothing at all to do with it. Your money draws 'em and you're absolutely helpless. They have all the law and all the machinery on their side. Tell everybody, when you write your story, that they're scalping our souls out here."[68]

Indian Influences and the Modern Indian

THE MISSING HISTORY

Introduction

Perception and Reality

In 1887, James Bryce described the influence of the American Indian as he saw it. Bryce, reflecting what was then a popular opinion of the American people, wrote that they have: "done no more than give a touch of romance or a spice of danger to the exploration of some regions . . . while over the rest of the country the unhappy aborigines have slunk silently away, scarcely even complaining of the robbery of lands and the violation of plighted faith." [1] This is all too often the perception of the Indian in American history even today.

Arrell Morgan Gibson is better tuned to the beat of the true pulse of American history. He points out that the American public has been saturated with a stereotyped Indian that bears little relationship to reality. He concludes by saying that "with an intellectually inert public, it is less what a thing or person is, and more the perception panderers of popular culture are able to plant in their constituency." [2]

We see little fault in believing that people, land, and cultures are the main ingredients of the frontier. However, these are broad terms and when we start defining the terms in detail we may be faulty in our concept. It seems that land would also include resources both animate and inanimate. People would include Euro-Americans, Indian Americans, African Americans, and to some extent Asian Americans. Primarily, cultures would include Western civilization and Indian civilization.

Walter Prescott Webb set forth a "boom hypothesis," which seems to have a great deal of merit: "The major premise is that the sudden acquisition of land and other forms of wealth by the people of Europe precipitated a boom on Western civilization, and that the boom lasted as long as the frontier was open, a period of four centuries. A corollary of the major premise is that our modern institutions, as distinguished from medieval, were differentiated and matured during a boom, and are therefore, adapted to boom conditions."[3] We must point out that Webb completely omitted mention of the Indian. Possibly, this was because he was advancing an economic instead of a political or social hypothesis. Yet Indians did, in fact, affect the economic institutions formed between 1500 and 1900. We will deal with these contributions later.

Part of the difficulty with including Indians in general histories is the diversity or fragmentation of the Indian people—that is, the difficulty of generalizing Indian history. It was this diversity that enabled Euro-Americans to so easily part the Indian from the land. When we use the term "Indian," we are speaking of about 200 different groups or nations. While these nations undoubtedly shared many customs, practices, and characteristics in common, they differed as often as they agreed. William Brandon, among others, has addressed this problem: "A principal difficulty in treating Indian history in depth is its fragmentation. The task of examining each tribal group and each time-phase of each group and of conducting this investigation partly in such other languages as anthropology is forbidding. The Indian reality was of an astonishing diversity, a diversity that presents a constant problem in any wide-angle view of the American Indian."[4]

Indian Influence

Governor William Bradford of Plymouth Colony wrote in 1621: "And sure it was God's good providence that we found this corne, for else we know not how we should have done."[5] What a shame that from the very first, Euro-Americans chose to ignore the role of the Indian in their colonial ventures. Bradford and the Pilgrims did not "find" the corn—Indians gave the corn to them. Possibly God moved the Indians to do this. However, if this is true, he also made Indians generous in other situations.

Bernard De Voto, who is often quoted in Indian histories, says, "A dismaying amount of our history has been written without regard to Indians, and of what is written with regard to them much treats their diverse and always changing societies as uniform and static. . . . Most American history has been written as if history were a function of white culture in spite of the fact that well into the nineteenth century the Indians were one of the principal determinants of historical events. . . . American historians have made shockingly little effort to understand how all these affected white men and their societies."[6]

While the statements of authorities do not make anything true or false, respect requires recognition of their remarks. In dealing with this problem, one often encounters extreme statements that obviously have very little basis in fact. Possibly this is done in an effort to free one's mind from Bacon's Idols of the Mind.[7] Surely, this is admitted in some cases.[8]

Followers of Fredric Jackson Turner tend to present the frontier as a new, uninhabited area. The basic concept of the Turner thesis is that the frontier blended the various European groups and made of them a new type of man —an American. The thesis has a flaw in the premise that the frontier was new and uninhabited. It had been occupied by Indians for thousands of years and it was still occupied by them as the frontier advanced.

This image of a savage, new, virtually uninhabited frontier is a fallacy with only a spot or two of truth. Turner also neglects to account for four hundred years of intermarriage between Indians and Euro-Americans. Children of these marriages are the only new people created by the frontier.[9] If Turner was arguing that the blending of Euro-Americans on the frontier made a new man, he was mistaken. It was the blending of two cultures totally alien to each other that generated a spirit of being American instead of being European.

Our early historians, such as Francis Parkman, generated many Indian fallacies. Two of these were that Indians won battles and lost wars because they neglected to follow up on their victories. A second fallacy was that Indians could not maintain a prolonged siege. Both fallacies were based on the fact that Indians did not have supply trains and reserve forces.

A review of the conquest of the Southern Central Plains by the Osages would show a consistent follow-up of battles won. During a fifty-year period the Osages conquered an area about the same size as that conquered by Bonaparte in roughly the same amount of time. As for siege, the Osage blockade of the Missouri and Arkansas Rivers denied Europeans any significant access to the heart of North America for one hundred fifty years. However, if one thinks in terms of more conventional sieges, we find the Indian against Indian siege at Detroit in 1714. Also, there is the Pontiac siege of Ft. Pitt and Red Cloud's blockade of the Powder River road.[10]

Stress is always placed on how savage Indians were on the frontier. Rarely is any mention made of the fact that the "brave pioneers" were invading the "savage" Indian's territory and stealing their food, the wild game. The inconsistency of the stereotyped "savage Indian" is a falsification, as can be seen in the following quote. "Between 1783 and 1840 the Americans corrupted and dispossessed a new set of tribes between the Appalachians and the plains country. As they became more dependent upon him [the trader] for a wide range of commodities—guns and ammunition, kettles, blankets, hoes, knives, and mirrors, to name only a few—their native crafts were forgotten." [11]

These two frontiers, from the Atlantic to the Appalachians and from the Appalachians to the eastern fringes of the Plains, dominated the American thought during their existence. Connecting these two frontiers by rails certainly affected the ties between the Northeast and the West. [12]

Possibly the greatest fallacy is one of omission. That is, by omitting significant mention of the Indian role in American history one creates the impression that only the Euro-Americans were significant. Aside from the ethnic bias in presenting "evidence," there is the more important misrepresentation of historic fact. This prevents detection of important facts such as two frontier lines coexisting at the same time. The line of contact between Indians and Euro-Americans set up a shock wave. Like ripples from a stone thrown into a pool of water, the shock of the meeting of cultures radiated to the west. Thus, an Indian to Indian frontier was created from the effects of the Indian to Euro-American frontier. [13] The parallel to this concept would be that there must have been "ripples" of Indian concepts radiating from the Euro-American side of the frontier line, just as there were "ripples" of Euro-American concepts on the Indian side of the line.

There has been a persistent effort to make some connection between prehistoric Indian civilization and the Old World. Apparently, this effort is partly motivated by a fear that establishing independent development and maturity of the Indian civilization will undermine some "pet" theories. Surely, a basic foundation of capitalism would be destroyed, namely, the belief that motivation by the desire for material gain is a universal of human nature. More simply, this is expressed as the profit motive.

Thus, the question of independent development becomes a basic question in economics, since Indians did not meet this "universal" concept. However, the fact of independent development touches all areas of human learning. The old idea of the various developmental stages of mankind from savagery to barbarism and then to civilization does not hold water anymore. The Indian civilization was as mature as Western civilization, but it was mature in a different way. William Brandon points out, "It is not easy to feel that Shakespeare was more primitive than Edgar A. Guest because he did not have a typewriter . . . " [14] Likewise, the Osages were no less culturally mature than the English because they did not possess English hardware.

When people presume to argue for a place in history on behalf of any ethnic group, it behooves them to justify their contention. With this in mind, I would like to give an overview of contributions made by American Indians. Others have made justification statements, among them, Alvin M.

Josephy: "All aspects of Indian existence—agriculture, government, religion, trade, mythology, and arts and crafts—influenced white men at one time or another and helped to shape the destiny of each of the countries of the Western Hemisphere."[15]

Any time two strangers meet, the stage is set for a mutual friendship or a clash of personalities. We have all heard this old cliché and are aware that a meeting of aliens would create a greater variation. So it is when two cultures meet. With a surprising regularity, chronicle after chronicle throughout the Americas mention that Indians at first greeted the European with friendliness. One cannot help wondering what history would have recorded if the Europeans had been greeted with spears, arrows, lances, and clubs instead of the gifts of hospitality.[16] In any event, we have ample proof that the first contribution of the Indian was assistance in establishing colonies.

A second contribution was more of a "back door" gift. That is, Indian defense of their lands forced the colonists to seek means of uniting for mutual defense. Thus, when the Revolution came, they were accustomed to uniting for combat. Associated with this is the Albany Plan of Union proposed by Franklin. Franklin himself admits he acquired the plan from the Iroquois.[17]

One very important contribution of the Osages was of special value to the United States. Desiring to keep the Southern portion of the Central Plains trade for themselves and to prevent their enemies to the southwest from securing fire arms, the Osages blockaded the area. Thus, the French and then the Spanish were denied any real access to the three routes to the interior of North America west of the Mississippi. These routes were the Missouri and Arkansas River routes and the Overland Route across the Central Plains, which later became the road to Santa Fe. This factor was a consideration in the decision to sell Louisiana to the United States.[18]

In more recent years, a growing appreciation for the American Indian's views toward nature has come from the greater awareness of the need for preserving the environment.[19] A universal rule among Indians is to leave no sign of your use of the environment. This is a rule that should be adopted by every citizen.

The clearest contribution made by Indians is in the arena of botany and agriculture. Although to a great extent this also includes medicine and raw material for manufacture, these may not stand out as clearly. Such items as canoes, snowshoes, and signaling systems were also contributed by Indians, but these too are not as clear cut.[20] We will take up the Indian contribution to agriculture next, and it will be clearly evident there that the Indian merits a larger role in American history than he has been allotted. He merits this on agriculture alone, but when one examines his contributions in economics, literature, and political thought, the great wrong in omitting the Indian from history is all the more evident.

Agriculture

Background

One-half or more of the world's food crops are derived from the Indian civilization. Corn (maize) and potatoes (white potatoes) rank with rice and wheat as the four most important food staples in the world. Manioc and sweet potatoes (especially the yams variety) are close runners-up to the big four.

Other leading food crops that came from Indians are peanuts, squashes, red peppers, tomatoes, pumpkins, pineapples, avocados, cacao (a source of chocolate), chicle (chewing gum), a large variety of beans, and other fruits and vegetables. It is difficult to place an accurate number on the plants contributed by Indians.[21] Estimates run from eighty to over 200. Aside from the food plants contributed by Indians, there are many medicinal and industrial plants.

Industrial plants produce raw materials for manufacture. These plants are not always food plants like peanuts and potatoes, which are also used as raw material in manufacturing. Among the more important industrial plants are long-staple cotton plants such as the Sea Island, Egyptian, and Upland varieties. Tobacco may also be included as an industrial plant, but it is also a medicinal plant. Mauguary is a fiber plant used to make cordage of all kinds. These are the best-known industrial plants of Indian origin, but there are many more.

Medical plants introduced by Indians more than doubled the available drugs of Western civilization. Some of these valuable plants are coco (a source of cocaine), curare, cinchona bark, cascara sagrada, datura, and ephedra.[22] No matter how many Indian plants we list, one stands out above all others and it has a clear Indian origin.

Corn or maize is the most domesticated of all the plants used by man, and it is entirely dependent upon humans for its survival. Sometimes it is difficult for Euro-Americans to realize that Indians were much better farmers in 1500 than the farmers of the Old World. Not only did they produce more food in less space than European farmers, but they cultivated and used a much greater variety of plants. But corn stood out as a universal crop among Indians. Thus, it was extremely influential in Indian culture.

Land Tenure and Corn

Most important of the cultural influence of corn upon Indians was the system of land tenure that evolved from it. First of all, due to the Indian hunting tradition, the ultimate control of how the land was to be used was in the hands of the tribe.[23] Among the Osages, women were assigned land areas for agriculture. The area was the woman's to use for raising any crop she wished. There was no unified system of land tenure among the Indians of the United States. However, the different groups always had a logical well-developed land system, and the ultimate control of its use rested upon a group basis.[24]

The uniqueness of corn has generated awe among those who appreciate plants: "In its own way, and perhaps more beautifully, corn is a monument to Man. Look at it the next time you have corn on the cob or are surprised by one of those tiny ears of corn in your hors d'oeuvres at a cocktail party. The ear is the ultimate in efficient food packaging, a highly specialized flower cluster with hundreds of naked, energy-crammed seeds, compactly arranged on a rigid cob enclosed in husks. Remarkable!"[25] One can well understand the awe and respect generated by corn. In the 450 years Euro-Americans have been in the Americas, they have not developed from its wild growth a single major agricultural product.[26]

Amazing as it may seem, each grain of corn can produce three to four hundred kernels. Even more amazing than this high productivity is the range of conditions under which corn can be raised. Indians raised corn in hot, wet lowlands and cool, dry highlands.[27] It grew from the Gulf of Mexico to Canada and from the Atlantic to the Pacific. What was called Osage corn grew a very tall stalk and usually had six ears to a stalk. These ears were usually about nine-inches long with twenty-six or more rows.

Indian Agriculture Today

One would hardly believe that Indians, who were the world's best agriculturists in 1500, resisted being made into Euro-American-style farmers. The difference was in the purpose and methods of farming. No matter how one looks at Indians as farmers in the European sense, one must be aware that domestic animals were unknown to the Indian of the United States. A minor exception to this would be the dog, which had no agricultural use.

Human diet, despite fads, should include meat as well as vegetable foods. This may be disputed on statistical grounds, but the facts are that man has always sought nourishment from both sources. The absence of domestic animals meant the Indian had to supply his meat wants by the hunt and had to farm by human muscle alone. Thus, their farming methods differed greatly from Old World farmers. The enslavement of animals was as repulsive to Indians as the thought of a human owning the land. It took almost a complete destruction of Indian culture over a period of six or seven generations to make indifferent Western-style farmers of Indians.

Today, many Indians are farmers, especially in the drier regions of the American West. Thus, Indians and water rights are an issue today. "With 75 percent of the reservation population and 55 percent of Indian lands located in a region that receives less than twenty inches of precipitation annually, water holds the key to economic development, including agriculture."[28] Water is becoming increasingly in demand for household use, industrial use, and recreational use. Indian lands offer the largest relatively undeveloped areas available and, as such, offer the greatest potential for expansion of water and water-related facilities.

Indians are still one of the country's largest land-owning groups. In 1980, Indians still controlled 52 million acres. Forty-two million acres of this was still under tribal ownership but ten million acres of the total were under individual management.[29] Indians have always been better at group activities than at individual efforts. This is true of agriculture as well as their ceremonies and business ventures.

The Osage success as grass lessor to the evolving beef industry was self evident. While allotment in severalty destroyed this group business, some Osages still engage in the grass business on an individual basis. Operation of the mineral trust is a group venture, and it has worked well. One may say the BIA managed both of these, but it is necessary to include Osage assent, ideas, and participation, all of which contributed to their success. Our point is that Indians should try to utilize their greatest strength. In agriculture, Indians should evolve their own methods and not those borrowed from the white man, for Indians are the experts, not the white man.

Gifts to the Old World

Three broad types of crops were used by Indians. One type was that of wild plants, such as corn, that were altered to better fit the needs of man. A second type was those taken from the wild and simply cultivated in their natural state. Avocados are an example of this type. The final type was taken and used directly from the wild condition. Leaves, bark, roots, fiber, seeds, gums, and saps were commonly gathered from wild plants.[30] Pecans and walnuts are also typical of this type.

Aside from corn, which is the world's leading crop, the white potato is possibly the next Indian crop in importance. All one needs to do in order to appreciate the importance of the potato is to read about the potato famines in Ireland. The potato is produced in 130 of the 167 independent countries of the world. One yearly crop is worth more in monetary terms than all the gold and silver the Spanish took from the New World. Of over 5,000 potato varieties, at least 3,000 are still cultivated by Andean Indian farmers.[31]

Three of the crops raised by North American Indians are being developed for commercial agriculture. Johoba is now being cultivated in large Arizona fields to be mainly used in lotions and other cosmetics. We first saw guayle being grown during World War II. The latex from this shrub makes an excellent rubber. It is still being cultivated for this purpose in the American Southwest. Tepary beans are also being raised in the Southwest and they show great promise for the dry land areas of the earth.[32]

Many plants used by the prehistoric Osages are left off lists of Indian plants. Those frequently omitted are anise, buckbrush, buckeye, cattail, dogwood, Indian turnip, milkweed, poppy mallow, and wild onion. Anise was treasured for its flavor. Buckbrush and cattail were used to make baskets and mats. Buckeye was used ceremonially as a purgative, but the old people used it as a pain killer as well. Most people are familiar with snake root or giant cone flower. The Osage Little Yellow Flower is the little cone flower and its roots make an excellent pain killer. Wild beans are usually listed as groundnuts. Osages normally called this plant *to* or *toe* which means potato. French traders called this plant "earth apple" or *pomme de terre* for the name of the Pomme de Terre River in Missouri where the Osages dug the roots of this plant. The capital of Kansas—Topeka—is a Kaw-Osage word meaning Place Where We Dug Potatoes. However, this same plant also produced the so-called Osage beans or peas. Thus, both the seeds and roots were used.

We have never encountered any mention of the Osages using the amaranth plant. However, it would be unusual for their time and place if they did not use it. In a detailed study, it was determined that the prehistoric peoples of the Ohio Valley made little apparent use of the amaranth species (pigweed) growing in that region. The most productive species are *Amaranth Retroflexus* and *Amaranth Hypochondriacus.*[33]

"Amaranth has become one of the most important cereals in the diets of highland peoples in India, China, Pakistan, Tibet, and Nepal. Cultivation has spread so widely in the past century that Asia now cultivates and consumes more amaranth than the Americas."[34] We do not want to mislead the reader into believing all Asian amaranth is Native American in origin. Amaranth is also an East Indian plant, although some amaranth raised in Asia is Native American in origin.

Economics

Land

Land is not as easily defined as it may first appear. As long as one restricts the defining to the physical aspects of land, such as its acreage, the number of trees, or tons of coal produced from the land, it is fairly easily defined. However, when one crosses the hazy line between what is tangible and what is intangible, land becomes difficult to define.

Defining land as a homeland for a people is difficult to do. Measuring the effect of a land upon the people which spring from it is not possible. While we cannot place a measure on the effect of land, we know it plays a part in shaping lifestyles. Without their homeland, a people lose their lifestyle and become dislocated. For Indians, the loss of their homeland has meant the loss of sustenance and a loss of place, but in a legal sense it has meant the extinguishment of title to a continent.[35]

Somewhere in the zone dividing the tangible and the intangible is the effect of the extinguishment of the Indian title upon United States property laws. The condition that prevailed in Europe during the fifteenth century was totally changed—that is, changed from a society of limited lands in the hands of a few people to a society of abundant land in the hands of many. Such a revolutionary change in the nature of land holdings and its effect upon the economy, politics, and social life of a civilization cannot be ignored by historians who seek the truth.

Walter Prescott Webb describes the effects this change in the nature of land holding had upon American property laws: "The flow of property from hand to hand was a legal matter with legal ramifications too vast to be explored here. All matters pertaining to titles, deeds, abstracts, conveyances, inheritances, dowries, bequests, and wills came in ever-increasing volume into the hands of lawyers and advocates and before judges and juries; and these last two, however reluctantly, had in the long run no choice but to bend the law to the will and convenience of the new owners. Of course, all of these changes tie in closely with the gradual emancipation of the people. . . ."[36] The reference to emancipation of the people is an allusion to the feudal system with its monarchies and limited freedom for the majority. An abundance of cheap land completely destroyed the power of monarchies and gave a greater freedom to the majority of people.

While most people in the Western civilization were gaining more freedom, greater economic wealth, and a body of protective laws, the Osages and other Indians were losing ground in these same areas. Thus, with more than a grain of truth, it can be said that the rise of democracy in Western civilization was bought at the expense of the Indian. A lesson for historians and all others emerges from this: "It is quite likely that when we locate the owners of the property in any society we shall not be far from those who exercise the political authority—those who govern, and they govern regardless of any theory to the contrary."[37]

The Osages made a distinction between the land and the earth. Land is the top layer of the earth. The Siouan Crow say, "as deep as the roots go." Truly, he who holds the land rules the earth.

The Frontier and Economic Theory

Adam Smith is sometimes called the father of capitalism. His *Wealth of Nations* became the basis for the great colonial empires of history. Ultimately, his economic theories were valid, in the sense of workability, because of the continuing frontier areas of the world. Among these was the land/cultural frontier of the United States. Smith's concept of no regulation upon an individual's pursuit of wealth still has wide acceptance among some American groups. However, this principle of "hands off" can only work when the proportionate wealth per capita exceeds abundance. This overabundance was a frontier situation generated by appropriation of the Indian estate.

The Osage experience with the "dog eat dog" aspects of "hands off" capitalism made the council very cautious. Being aware that they were an Indian-style communal organization, the council had to be especially alert. The twentieth-century capitalistic world they functioned in made caution especially necessary. Considering the hazards they faced, the council functioned admirably.[38] Thus, they proved that governments based on purely Indian concepts can still function economically. It is in the area of human relationships that this government has had its greatest failings, that is, in serving the needs of the people in areas other than the economic.

Literature

The Indian and Literature

Without a doubt, the Indian was a romantic character in the European mind. Discovery of the Americas and Indians stimulated the imagination of European writers. Thus, the great Romantic period of European literature and art was created. It is an old adage that writers reflect the society of their time. Certainly this was true to some extent of the Indian frontier. Here was an abundance of nourishment for the imagination to create thousands of novel situations. All of Western civilization was stimulated in all fields of learning and the arts.

To some extent, the Western civilization also stimulated the Indian. Although Indians already had a strong romantic thread woven into the fabric of their culture, the white man's world added new themes. Their contact with Western people generated a comparison of the two cultures and produced a new body of humor. One must remember that the Indian had no written language, so his humor was acted out as he spoke. Indians already had the romantic trait of wandering in strange worlds, and they never adopted the impossible man-against-nature trait of Western Romanticism. Indian romantic themes were sometimes tragic, but more often they ended with an amusing "twist" or an all is well ending so characteristic of Western Romantic literature.

Indian humor always cut away at dignity and pretense to greatness. Westerners were vulnerable targets for Indian humor. A keen sense of observation and a mental pattern of seeing things as paired opposites created a large body of Indian humor about the white man. Innate courtesy spared Western man from exposure to this humor to any great extent. A classic example of Indian humor that became popular in the United States was the humor of Will Rogers. However, Euro-Americans never realized they were witnessing a humor foreign to their culture. Peoples of Western civilization do not normally laugh at themselves, for this requires a humility that is too often absent in Western man.

Blending Two Worlds

Over a period of three hundred years, Western literature has more and more blended Indian thoughts into their literature. This has become so thorough that many will doubt what we wrote about the Will Rogers type of humor. Where in the world could one find such tall tales as Paul Bunyon, Pecos Bill, and Wind Wagon Smith except in a partly Indian culture. Even Voltaire's *Candide* shows an identifiable Indian humor. Such humor *was* new to Western civilization in Voltaire's day, but *now* it is a part of Western civilization.

The blending of cultures and literature was a two-way road. Nowhere is this more evident than in the growing vocabularies. For example, the Osages had no name for the horse, so they called him a *Shon ke C Tun ka* or Big Yellow Dog. Later exposure to the Spanish brought them the Spanish word, *caballo* or cah buy yo. Thus, the Osage word *Ka wa* for horse was derived from the Spanish word. Since the Osages did not originally have churches in the Euro-American sense, they called a church *Wa kon ta Tse* or God's House.

Another group of new Osage words were caused by new goods from Western civilization. The Osage words for the flintlock musket and guns generally are examples of these words. *Wah Ho tun Le Moh ka She ka* (which means Skunk Leg That Makes Them Cry Out) is the name of the first flintlocks the Osages saw. *Wah Ho tun Le* is the general name for any gun, and it means Makes Them Cry Out. To the Western mind, this may seem to be incomprehensible. Yet, the name fits the product, for when an animal is shot it cries out. Early muskets had hammers shaped like a skunk's hind leg. This is hardly more incomprehensible than the American political term mugwump, which was borrowed from the Iroquois. Americans interpret this as meaning a politician with his mug on one side of the fence and his wump on the other side. More simply put, a mugwump is a politician who speaks in favor of one party but votes with the opposite party.

Frontier Literary Themes

The Indian influence can clearly be seen in the themes of Romanticism. These themes are:

1) Primitive man and nature;
2) Eldorado;
3) Utopia;
4) Civilized man in isolation;
5) Man in conflict with nature.[39]

It seems obvious that the Indian led writers to imagine themselves as a primitive man. This led to tales about primitive conditions that bore little relationship to Indian life. Few themes can equal the romance of Eldorado. The possibility of discovering a place of incredible wealth captured the imaginations of Western minds. Such wild stories led Cortez to Mexico; Pizzaro to Peru; and Coronado in quest of the Seven Cities of Cibola and Quivera. A variant of the Eldorado theme was Ponce de Leon's search for the Fountain of Youth, but then de Leon was an old man; old men dream of youth and young men dream of riches.

If the Eldorado theme brought out stories well fertilized with imagination, the Utopia theme was a product of greater fertility. Here were found a grand assortment of schemes for a perfect government with a perfect society. Long after the Indian and his culture had ceased to exert any great influence, Hilton found his *Lost Horizon* in Tibet, which was his Utopia.

Surely, Daniel Defoe placed his Robinson Crusoe in isolation. This theme, like all the frontier themes, goes back to the Indians who lived in isolation from the Old World. Such themes stir the imagination in "what if" situations. Some science fiction writers take up these themes and apply them to the frontiers of space. I have forgotten the author, but as a boy I read a story entitled *Minimum Man*. It was the Crusoe theme with a special "twist." Here was a true fumble-fingered failure who was sent to live alone on a small planet. The thought was, if he could survive, anyone could. Of course, his robot, Friday, was there to protect him from any real harm. However, Friday was also programmed to create problems.

When we speak of man in conflict with nature, we are not speaking about Indians. Surely, the idea of humans living in nature is Indian. While Indians probably inspired the theme, it was Western writers that supplied the application. Later we find the fabulous tales of the wild by Jack London. While we always enjoyed such tales, it was a little horrifying to see a puny human throwing himself against nature. The sheer audacity was enough to shock the reader into pursuing the story to the end.

What, then, does all this mean? Now that the frontier is gone and only tatters of Indian culture remain, where has man's imagination gone? Possibly Webb has the answer: "Man again has been turned back on himself to find his romance and adventure. If we may judge by current manifestations, literature is no longer concerned with man caught between an old world that is curious and a new one that is excitingly strange. It becomes more and more subjective, and seems to be concerned mainly with whether man is all sex or all psychology."[40]

Political Thought

Indian Political Influence

"Indian social and political concepts and structures profoundly influenced settlers and Old World philosophers alike and played a significant role in the evolution of many modern institutions of government and daily life."[41] This statement of Indian political influence includes not only the United States and the democratic nations of the world, but it also includes the Communistic bloc of nations.

Lewis Henry Morgan wrote several influential pieces of literature. Possibly the most significant was his *Ancient Society.* His argument that primitive societies were family-oriented while modern societies were property-based appealed to Karl Marx. To Marx, this seemed to confirm his dialectal, materialistic view of history. Since Marxism is based on this view of history, it is natural that Morgan would be viewed as one of the basic creators of modern communism.[42]

Morgan's massive *Systems of Consanguinity and Affinity of the Human Family* has thousands of different kinship terms from hundreds of the world's societies. Among these are 167 Osage kinship terms collected in the mid–1800s.[43] Morgan spent a large portion of his life among Indians and based much of his writing on what he knew of Indian life. This Indian influence upon modern communism is often overlooked.

It is more common to find the Indian influence upon natural rights mentioned than the influence on communism. Montesquieu, Locke, and Rousseau all wrote about the "noble savage" or "natural man." To what degree the Indian influenced their thinking and the downfall of monarchies is debatable. However, the fact of Indian influence is undeniably present.[44] Donald Grinde points out that "Paradoxically, the whites who came to America sought to subdue, enslave, or exterminate this free and natural society, primarily for economic gain."[45]

Philosophic Contributions

> The deductions of the philosophers about the Indians were not entirely wrong. Belief in the freedom and dignity of the individual was deeply ingrained in many Indian societies. . . . Among many tribes, also, councils decided on courses of action by unanimous, rather than majority, agreement; the feelings and opinions of each person were considered too important to override. Such influences, reflecting the equality of individuals and respect for their rights, made their mark on the European philosophers.[46]

The slogans of the American Revolution (1775) and the French Revolution (1789) reflect the Indian influence. For the Americans, the cry of Life, Liberty, and Happiness became the objective of revolution. In France, the goal became Liberty, Equality, and Brotherhood. While it would be interesting to pursue the difference of intentions, the common purpose demands our attention. Liberty was a dead lifeless word before Indians gave it life and vitality.

Search the philosophies prior to 1500 for the modern meaning of liberty and your labor would be in vain. The concept of universal "bosslessness" for all (that is, freedom to pursue one's desires without hindrance for one's self and all others alike) came from the Indians. Association of life with liberty goes back to such principles as the Osage practiced. No life could be taken without adequate reason. This applied to humans, animals, and plants. Within the tribe no person could be deprived of his life until after all other alternatives had failed, assuming, of course, there was just cause for execution.

The French associated liberty with equality. However, as Anatole France once noted, "rich and poor alike are hung for sleeping under bridges." His point was, although laws may be applied equally, they could still be unjust. Only the poor would have a need to sleep under bridges. For this reason, all laws must be tempered by justice. The Osage example also serves here, for even when a person had violated a law every effort was made to find some form of restitution rather than taking his life.

Fraternity or the brotherhood of man is purely Indian in practice. Only societies "bonded" together can rule without coercion and still allow its members free choice. The tribal bond is rooted in a mutual kinship that has tied even unrelated members together. It is akin to *E Pluribus Unum* or the old Roman fasces, but it is more of a social unity that dictates political choices. This is in contrast to political unity that dictates social choices. The unanimity rule is a social dictate and, thus, it is the ultimate in governmental equality.

Like the tribal bond, happiness is a social state or condition. Thus, the economic condition has little to do with happiness. Possibly, happiness is a wrong choice of terms for contentment.

> But, as he makes clear in the notes to the *Discourse on Inequality,* Rousseau believed two points of view were in conflict here, rather than contradictory ethnographical evidence: Yes, the savages were "poor" in a material sense in comparison to Europeans, but not a single savage had yet been persuaded to take up European "civilization" as a way of life, while thousands of Frenchmen and other Europeans had sought "voluntary refuge among these Nations, there to spend their entire lives. . . . The recognition of happiness," concluded Rousseau, setting the birth of the Romantic movement in one short line, "is less the business of reason than of feeling.[47]

Thus, life, liberty, happiness, equality, and unanimity which set the thrones of the world aside were all political concepts derived from the American Indian.

Forming the United States

> Felix Cohen, late international authority on Indian law and polity, has stated that "American democracy, freedom and tolerance are more American than European and have deep aboriginal roots in our land." The Indian example of self-determinism and local sovereignty "undoubtedly played a strong role in helping to give the colonists new sets of values that contributed to turning them from Europeans into freedom loving Americans." And it is out of a rich Indian democratic tradition that the distinctive political ideals of American life emerged, including the practice of treating leaders "as servants of the people instead of as their masters," and the "insistence that the community must respect the diversity of men and the diversity of their dreams."[48]

One of the unexplained mysteries of the American Revolution was how the ordinary, illiterate colonist became so well informed about the natural rights of men. Anyone who has labored through Plato, Aristotle, John Locke, and the natural rights philosophers can appreciate the difficulty of comprehending their arguments. Yet, here were illiterate people with an extraordinary comprehension of complex philosophic discourse. Since they could not read or write, nor had extensive contact with scholars familiar with philosophic discourse, one naturally has reason to ask where and how they acquired such knowledge.

The answer should be obvious. Colonists had constant contact with Indians. Through sheer necessity, they copied many Indian techniques of living in the American back country. It is equally obvious that they also adopted many Indian concepts of government and treatment of each other. The philosophies of natural rights as derived from the Indian were *theory,* but the ordinary colonist was *living* under these principles as they drifted to revolution.

Thomas Jefferson was a keen observer of the Indian and his ways, as well as a natural rights scholar. His views are well represented in the following quote: "As for France and England, with all their preeminence in science, the one is a den of robbers, and the other of pirates, as if science produces no better fruits than tyranny, murder, rapine and destitution of national morality, I would rather wish our country to be ignorant, honest, and estimable as our neighboring savages are."[49]

As one proceeds through American history up to 1900, the Indian influence is always present. In the colonial period, it was the Indian that forced the colonists to unite for mutual defense. Certainly, the Iroquois furnished the model for the Albany Plan of Union and even addressed the delegates on the benefits of union. While this plan was not adopted, many Iroquois methods found their way into Euro-American legislatures—congressional compromises on bills, for example.

The whole key to American government was summed up in a statement by Thomas Jefferson and it is pure Indian in principle: "The fool has as great a right to express his opinion by vote as the wise, because he is free and equally master of himself."[50] Populists in the Agrarian Revolt of the late–1800s also took concepts from the Indian. Populists believed in direct democracy as opposed to representative democracy. This was reflected in the demand for the initiative, referendum, and recall. They had a slogan which was related to Jefferson's comment. "We pay for governmental mistakes, so let us make our own mistakes."

Profusion and Confusion

Chief Justice John Marshall set the stage in 1831 for the ultimate assumption of Indian sovereignty by the United States. In this decision, the court held that the Indian governments were "domestic dependent nations." While this admitted the Indian nations had a status above the individual states, it opened the door for a drain of sovereignty by Supreme Court edict.

In the process of reducing sovereignty and increasing the dependency of the Indian nations, a body of highly specialized Indian laws was created. Indian law is an entirely different arena from the criminal and civil codes of our federal and state governments. It is an arena where the Constitution was twisted and distorted by what the majority wanted from the Indian. It is an arena where if the concepts of the Bill of Rights are applied at all they are hardly recognizable.

We do not have the space to become enmeshed in the great profusion and confusion of Indian law. In lieu of this, we will close this topic with a quote. "This bureaucratic paternalism hems the Indian in with an incomprehensible maze of procedures and regulations, never allowing him to know quite where he stands or what he can demand and how. Over 5000 laws, statutes and court decisions apply to the Indians alone. As one Indian student says, 'our people have to go to law school just to live a daily life.'"[51]

THE OLD AND THE NEW MEET
Indians and Western Civilization
The Different Minority

Secretary of the Interior Stewart Udall created a task force on Indian affairs in 1961.[52] In a report of this task force, it was noted that Indians differed from other minorities in three ways. The first of these was a very special trait of culture and identity preservation. This extends beyond the normal cultural preservation of other minorities. Secondly, Indians are a quasi-sovereign people. They had rights guaranteed by treaty and often had lands set aside for their exclusive use. Also, there is a body of special federal laws that apply only to Indians. Lastly, Indians have a partially dependent relationship with the federal government.

While discrimination against Indians is seldom as intense as that against African Americans, there are some situations and places where it becomes very intense. Frequently, this discrimination shows some economic cause. However, surprising as it may seem, some discrimination comes from people who once considered themselves friends of the Indian.

Most of these are former reformers who had sought to bring the Indian into the American society by assimilation. Indian resistance to their efforts eventually discouraged and then disillusioned these "do-gooders." In reaction to their rejection, these people reversed their feelings and became Indian haters.

It is this very thing that seemingly makes the Indian so incomprehensible to the non-Indian. How can a person who considers his own lifestyle, his own government, and his own society to be far above any other comprehend that not all Americans agree with him? If the present majority culture in America expects to survive the twenty-first century, it must realize that other cultures are entitled to be as proud of their heritage as the majority culture is of theirs. We, in this great nation of ours, must accept the right of others to be different in their own way.

Willingness to accept differences in other people was a characteristic of the Osage people. When they merged with smaller groups, which often happened, the majority adjusted to the minority so the new people would feel comfortable and welcome. That is, they adopted many minority ways of doing things. Western civilization has much to learn about living with others.

Possibly, there is a hidden guilt feeling mixed in with the desire to assimilate the Indian. Resistance to the efforts to assimilate him has produced frustration, because the Indian is still here and is still a different people. They are separate and apart from all others in the nation. Their presence is a goad which keeps the American conscience in a state of penance. No one enjoys such a role, and so the feelings of discrimination arise. Is it not possible for the Indian to reach accommodation without assimilation?

Certainly, this is what is happening; the Indian is accommodating himself to the majority culture. That is, he is adapting and blending elements of both cultures rather than becoming identical with the majority culture. It is possible that all Americans will eventually follow this same course. If that should happen, it would be a great source of new ideas. New ideas are products of diversity and not of uniformity.

Indian Traits

Nowhere are Indian traits more evident than at a social gathering among strangers. In such situations, a person from an Indian culture will be very quiet and almost seem to blend into the background. People from the majority culture act entirely differently. They move from group to group exchanging small talk until they find a place in which they are at ease. Meanwhile, the person from the Indian culture is studying each group and individual. When he is satisfied and has determined where he would be compatible, he immediately attaches himself to that group and soon becomes a contributing member.

These approaches to strange situations are symptomatic of two utterly different cultures. The Indian has a deliberate approach to life. He plans each major change with care, collecting all available information. If he determines that success is not probable he will not pursue that direction in life, but he will pursue with all his abilities a promising direction. Western people, however, are inclined to enter a situation and to try various directions until eventually they discover one that works for them. The difference here is "exploring with the mind," as the Old Osages called it, and exploring with physical action. Western man is a pragmatist; Indians are realists with a strong dose of idealism.

People from the majority culture tend to form opinions about new acquaintances upon first contact. This places a person raised in an Indian culture at a disadvantage. In job interviews, the Indian seems overly shy, withdrawn, and somewhat restricted in intelligence. However, once he is employed, he far exceeds the expectations of the personnel officer who hired him.

Unfortunately, these hidden beneficial talents, which so often please employers, have another side. Generally, Indians do not give any outward sign when they are slighted or wronged. After a variable time and with repeated occurrence, the Indian will sometimes erupt into a violent reaction. To the Western mind, it seems the Indian has reacted violently to a minor provocation and, thus, the Indian gets a reputation for being "touchy" and "hard to get along with."

The old majority ways of shaking hands and looking a person "square in the eye" are as out of place among Indians as the "slap on the back" for a job well done. Most Indians consider staring into another's eyes extremely bad manners. It is a disrespectful invasion of one's body, as is the slap on the back. Thus, when an Indian evades meeting another's eyes it is a sign of respect and good manners.

School teachers of Indian children must *not* judge their Indian pupils by Western standards. Indian children are taught not to ask questions; they are expected to observe and learn, not to interrupt the ongoing process with questions. It is very bad manners for a younger person to interrupt an older person with a question or comment. Often, an older person will shame a younger person who interrupts them. To be shamed is a severe punishment.

Special Osage traits

We must state at the outset that other Indians have at least some of these traits. However, these are the special traits by which the Osages are known. Generosity is a general Indian trait, as is the acceptance of generosity. The Osages are known for this trait because, by good fortune, they have had the means to be generous. As Osage wealth increased, so did their generosity. Other, less fortunate, Indian people were invited to lavish ceremonies in which needed gifts were bestowed upon them. Great care was taken not to shame those who received gifts. In fact, this is the hallmark of true generosity, that is, to bestow a gift in honor and not in shame.

Possibly, the Osage trait of aloofness is the most persistent Osage trait. Apparently this aloofness ran stronger in the Osage than in other Indian people. The French, Spanish, and early American explorers all made a special association of this trait with the Osages. It is as if the Osages knew they were a people apart from all other people. Throughout their recorded history, they have been a people apart. Although they have shared to some extent the same pattern as other Indians, they have also developed a pattern of differences. One does not need to look very far for evidence of this. There are more federal laws and regulations applying only to the Osages than for any other Indian nation or American minority group.

The Cherokees sometimes claim the Osages were not invited to join the so-called Five Civilized Tribes. Yet, the Osages claim they were invited to join but did not accept the invitation because they wanted to maintain their identity as Osages. Because of the Osage aloofness and their long history of avoiding Indian alliances, we must say the Osage view has a ring of truth.

It was a matter of some anguish and a bitter draught to the Osage agents in the late–1800s that the Osages could afford to stand aloof from the efforts to "civilize" them. The agency office force contained all white persons at that time. How it must have galled them when a "dirty Indian" apparently looked down upon them as servants. The Osages did not look upon the office force as servants, but they did treat them with haughtiness and aloofness. New employees soon learned that they could not treat the Osages as Indians were treated at other agencies. Anyone who has never witnessed a "tongue lashing" by an Osage woman or a haughty, aloof "freeze" by an Osage man may have difficulty understanding why the Osage agency was different.

Osage dancing displays other Osage traits. Around the year 1885, members of the *Kon sa* (Kaw or Kansas) nation visited with the Osages. They stayed throughout the winter teaching the Osages a dance. Fearful that their people were dying out and their dance would be lost, the Kaw were passing their drum and dance to the kindred Osage people. Since that time, the Osages have danced that dance every year. The dress of 1885 is still worn with very minor if any changes. The dance too is still the same.

The *E lon schscah* (Playground of the Eldest Son) is danced each spring. One should not expect to see elaborate fanciful costumes at these dances, although it should be noted that some dancers from other tribes do wear such clothing and do subdued fancy dances. Fancy headdresses and enormous bustles are notable by their absence. Wild body gyrations, strangely called "fancy dancing," is likewise prohibited. What one sees at these dances are fully clothed dancers, in a combination of somber and bright colors. All Osage dancers move erect in a counterclockwise direction, with the men to the inside and the women to the outside. The counterclockwise direction is to commemorate the rotation of the earth. The dancers stand erect, not crouched, keeping time with the "voice of thunder" (the ancient Kaw drum), the singers, and the clash of "panther teeth" (bells).[53] Men dance toe to heel on alternate feet and women from heel to toe on alternate feet.

At these dances, at least three Osage traits are evident. One is their love of tradition and the acceptance of the responsibility to keep the gift, given by the Kaw, alive and vital. Another is their seriousness, devotion, and absence of flashiness. A final trait that is revealed is their deep reverence, even to the old religion which they have mainly abandoned except for this dance and some adaptations in the Peyote Church.

Indian Ways

Living and Getting

A part of "the great conversation" deals with the question of, What is the purpose of life? Associated with this profound question is: How should man live? Like most of "the great conversation," man has not found any absolute answers to these questions. However, it would seem logical that man was not given life to destroy life and the earth. To reason otherwise would seem to cancel out the purpose of creating life.

In comparing the approaches to living as it was practiced in the Indian civilizations with living in Western civilization, it would seem the Indian was more logical than the Westerner. The Oriental civilization discovered that if they placed a mixture of saltpeter, sulphur, and charcoal in a restricted space and ignited it, an explosion would occur. Western man took the firecracker and parleyed it into an explosive that could destroy humanity. How logical is it to create a destructive force capable of destroying all life?

It seems obvious that some force impels Western people toward destruction. We sometimes wonder if the obsession to acquire "things" becomes a substitute for living. We wonder if Westerners worship idols of their own creation instead of the creations in the natural world around them. We believe the purpose of life lies in the sound of living water seeking the sea. It is in the voices of the newborn and in the passing of life. It is beneath our feet and above our head; we have the purpose of life around us. It is to live—to be!

This is a basic difference between Indians and Euro-Americans—the Indian made "living" the basis of his culture; the white man made "getting" the basis of his culture. Competition, one human vying with another, human against nonhuman, human conquest of nature, and human victorious over the Gods are popular themes in the literature of Western civilization. With the Indian, competition is a sport, an entertainment but not a way of life. Like most things in life, competition is neither good nor bad. The Stoics would have said competition is evil only in excess. It is the excess of competition in Western life that causes the greatest threat to the survival of Western civilization.

This is certainly evident in education. Stress is placed on *getting* an education to *get* ahead in the world by enabling a person to *get* more pay so he or she can *get* more of the things the culture has to offer. In the majority educative system one often hears the warning that one is in competition with other young people. The getting and competition themes worry young people, but they do not seem to motivate youths to strive for excellence.

To most Indians, Western education is a horrible experience. Yet it does not seem to be as extreme as some writers phrase it. "Our education seems [to the Indian] to consist in knowing how most effectually to cheat them; our civilization in knowing how to pander to the worst propensities of nature, and then beholding the criminal and inhuman results with a cold indifference—a worse than heathen apathy; while our religion is readily summed up in the consideration of dollars and cents."[54]

Possibly, the clearest distinction between the Indian "living" and the European "getting" is in hunting. The Indian hunted as a way to live; the European hunted to get trophies or to see how many animal lives could be taken. The Duke of Henneberg in 1581 killed 1,003 red deer in one season. Three years later, the Elector of Saxony slew 1,532 wild boars during November.[55] One may call this sport if they wish, but it is the wholesale taking of life with no other purpose than to acquire a record for the number of animals slain.

The Land

The Indian veneration for the land sprung from an acute awareness of the importance of the land. Traditionally, the Indians' love of the land and the Europeans' love of the land were based on separate reasons. Indians loved the land because it supported all life. Europeans loved the land because it represented position and power. Significantly, the Indian love of the land led to preserving it as near to a natural condition as possible, but the Europeans' love pushed the land to the limits of its potential.

Because of the background of Western civilization, Euro-Americans viewed the pristine condition of the land under Indian tenure as evidence of their backwardness and savagery. Using the argument that the land should belong to those who could and would bring it to the highest use, the Indian lands were seized. Like a terrible epidemic, Euro-Americans spread over the land destroying all they touched.

It has been truly noted that all living things depend on the first six inches of the earth's surface. In this sense, mankind is only six inches from annihilation. We learned in conservation courses that enough silt is carried by the Missouri River each year to cover its drainage basin with four inches of soil. Most of this silt comes from the Euro-American practice of open tillage agriculture. The Indian used closed tillage. That is, they only culti-vated the area immediately around the plant they were raising, leaving an area between the plants in native vegetation. By contrast, Euro-Americans plow every square inch and cultivate the entire area. The difference un-doubtedly grew out of the availability of animal power. With animal power and mechanical power, it is easier to cultivate the whole area devoted to a crop than selected areas. The reverse is true without animal or mechanical power.

Three things happen to precipitation that comes to the earth. These are fly off, cut off, and run off. Fly off is the moisture that evaporates. Cut off is the moisture that sinks into the ground and either moistens the earth or forms the water table. Run off is the moisture that searches for the sea and in doing so forms the continental drainage system. Open tillage increases the run off percentage, and in doing so it throws the mechanics of nature out of harmony and, thus, creates gigantic destruction to the six inches of survival soil.

We must question the validity of the highest-use argument, whether it be in the economic, social, or political sense. The most efficient is rarely the best of choices. Instead of basing decisions on efficiency and profit, Western-ers must come around to the Indian practice of making decisions on the basis of dislocation of natural forces. This would require the development of a new field of learning. Possibly it would be the study of harmony in nature, that is, the balances in nature and in societies interacting upon each other.

Resistance to Change

Indians and the American Dream

What has been called the American dream is a hazy concept. We will try to capture at least the spirit of the dream. As a first requirement, the great American "melting pot" must create from its diverse peoples a single united nation of a new race—Americans. A second requirement of the dream is that there shall be liberty and justice for all. The final requirement is that all shall be equally and fairly represented and have an equal and fair voice in government. It is a simple dream and it will possibly remain a dream. Re-ality reveals that of all governments in Western civilization, this govern-ment has come the nearest to fulfilling the dream. Possibly, it is because it is rooted in soil that once saw humans living the American dream.

While the "melting pot" evolved in Indian Country, the Indian has been the most difficult ingredient to accommodate and assimilate into the common Euro-American culture. This presents an embarrassment to the United States. If, after two hundred years of effort, the United States cannot honorably "get out of the Indian business," why not? More to the point is why, despite two hundred years of effort, is the Indian neither accommodated nor assimilated into the general mass of Americans?

The answer is so obvious that it is embarrassing to point it out. Indians simply do not want to be assimilated into the oblivion of becoming lost souls in the general mass of Americans. They are the first Americans and they have every intention of remaining not only the first Americans but also the last Americans. Indians have always welcomed new people and at times even adopted the ways of the new people to make them feel comfortable. However, there are limits and among these is an unwillingness to become the same as the new people. Above all else, an Indian must remain himself. Diogenes was looking in the wrong place for his authentic (honest?) man; he should have looked in the wickiups of America.

Change and Constancy

Goethe touched on the core of change: "Whate'er you have, bequeathed you by your father, earn it in order to possess it." The essence of change is the past, for all change is based on past experience. However, as Goethe has noted, one must earn what one inherits in order to possess it. That is, people may inherit a culture but unless they live the culture it cannot be theirs. Likewise, a solution to a problem can never be fully understood unless a person makes the solution his or her very own through living it. If the solution is not lived, it becomes "cultural baggage" that is carried without purpose or reason except that it is there. Thus, when the problem arises again in later generations a solution is recreated and the solution becomes a vital living force. However, the recreation can never be the same as the original since no one living fully comprehends the original.

If this concept were applied to ordinary life sequence, it would explain many cultural changes. Insofar as changes within a culture are concerned, the need for change, by inference, arises from within as well. We cannot fault the concept that faulty transmission of a culture from generation to generation is a powerful motivation for cultural revolution from within. However, this leads us to consider the nature of change from without the culture, that is, changes imposed by outside forces.

In a culture such as the Osage culture of the 1700s, the transmission of solutions from generation to generation was extremely efficient. While internal revolt did take place, these events were rare. In most cases it was probably the food supply problems that forced the revolts within the culture. Yet, the stress placed upon having respect for elders suggests a strong exchange of concepts from the older generation to a younger generation. Under these conditions, each new generation lives and comprehends the ideas of the older generation so well that they too possess the old culture.

A beautiful expression of the general idea we are trying to convey has been written by Fey and McNickle: "In this matter of change, people are like the grass. They toss and sway and even seem to flow before the forces that make for change, as grass bows to the wind. But when the rude forces move on, people are found still rooted in the soil of the past. Again, like grass, people produce seed; and the seed will fly with the wind and, finding a friendly soil and climate, start a new generation. To change, yet to remain steadfast—that would seem to be the need of all living things."[56]

Few peoples have experienced the forces of change as severely as that forced upon the Indian. All Indian history must deal with this overwhelming fact of forced change by an alien people. An interesting comment on this facet of living is made by Ortega: "Imitation of alien political institutions betrays a pathological state of society. A people cannot take its institutions from the manifest surface of foreign nations; it must discover them in its own innermost being if it wants to lead a life in freedom. Freedom cannot be achieved by proclaiming a few random liberties. Life in liberty presupposes a perfect continuity of circulation throughout the collective body, from the heart of its common belief to the skin which is the state, and back from the skin to the bowels of faith."[57]

Faith is the instinctive acceptance of tradition. This enables people to escape the terrible task of rethinking their inherited past and, thus, making it their own. So long as we live by faith, only minor change can take place. When man is forced to a loss of faith he becomes isolated and torn from his past. He has only himself and his own efforts to find and create a new security in a culture of his own making. Thus, the Osages and many other Indians are a new culture of two worlds.

Osages in Two World Wars

World War I

Osages are sometimes critical of the United States, as are most Indians. Yet, only a person with a limited gift of comprehension could mistake this as evidence of a lack of loyalty or love of this country. For such persons who mistake criticism for treason we have included this section.

In a Fourth of July, 1924, speech, Thomas J. Leahy described the role of Osages in the First World War. Some points he presented are brought out here. One must realize that in 1918 when the United States went to war in

Europe, the Osages were not citizens of the United States. They were not citizens during the Civil War and the Spanish American War either, but they still served the United States government. Draft notices were sent out to male Osage citizens even though they were not United States citizens and were under no legal or moral obligation to accept the draft. There is not a single case on the record of any Osage failing to respond to the draft in any American war.

Leahy mentioned this in his address. He added the further bit of information that one in four Indian males of fighting age either responded to the draft or volunteered for service in World War I. Leahy further noted that the Osage ratio itself, which was given as one in three, exceeded the national ratio. This fact does not have the ring of disloyalty, nor can it be considered as a lack of love for the country.

With all due respect to the Navajo Marines I served with in World War II, it must be mentioned that the "code talkers" of that second worldwide conflict did not originate in that war. The Oklahoma tribes, including the Osage, were the original "code talkers" in World War I. They did not have radio but used field telephones. German technicians who tapped into the lines could not crack the Native American code.

Osages not only placed their lives on the line for this country but they also put valuable property at the disposal of the government at no charge. No one could predict which direction combat would come from. In America's previous war experience, the Spanish American War, combat had primarily been upon the seas. With this in mind, the Osage people took what was then the most productive oil pool they possessed and gave it to the United States government as a Naval Reserve. This was probably the largest economic donation to the war effort made during World War I.

As things turned out, the United States was not involved in any extensive naval combat in World War I, so the reserve was not needed. In 1927, the Navy Department returned the Naval Reserve to the Osage people. The United States never used the reserve during the ten years they had it. In the ten years after its return to the Osages, the Naval Reserve produced 18,000,000 barrels of oil. During the ten years the Reserve was owned by the United States, oil averaged $2.15 a barrel. After making all allowances, this would be a gift of over $20,000,000 to the United States.[58]

World War II

Their war service and United States citizenship notwithstanding, Osages who served in World War II could not obtain loans under the Servicemen's Readjustment Act of 1944. A special Act of Congress (61 Stat. 747) was enacted to enable Osage veterans of World War II to receive this benefit. I was one of the first Osages to benefit from this Act of August 4, 1947. One who is neither Indian nor Osage cannot realize how often the tangle of laws affect an Osage's life.

The Osage record in World War II, as given in a BIA report, is, with much pride, reproduced below:

Agency records indicate that 519 members of the Osage Tribe served in the armed forces during World War II, and of that number 26 were either killed in action or while in training, one is still missing in action, and nine were awarded decorations for meritorious service, as follows: Air Medal, one; Air Medal and Oak Leaf Clusters, one; Distinguished Service Medal, one; Good Conduct Medal, one [many more were later reported]; Distinguished Flying Cross, two; Silver Star, three; and Purple Heart, 15. Of the total number serving, 261 were in the Army; 11 in the Navy, 26 in the Marines, one in the Coast Guard, 97 in Army Air Force, two in Merchant Marine; one was a Navy Nurse, two were Army Nurses, 12 were in the WAC, four in the WAVES, and two were in the U.S. Women's Marines. Commissioned officers included one major general (lost in action), one major (lost in action), seven captains, 27 lieutenants, seven ensigns, four lieutenants (j.g.), two army nurse lieutenants, and one navy nurse lieutenant—a total of 50. Noncommissioned officers included 23 sergeants and 24 corporals.[59]

By far, the best known Osage to serve in World War II was Major General C. L. Tinker: "On June 7, 1942 the General and his crew of ten were lost in action while leading a group of LB-30 bombers on a mission against the Japanese retreating toward Wake Island."[60]

Mixed-Bloods

Cultural Blending

It was natural that when the two cultures met there would be children born of both cultures. Since most of the first contacts Indians had with the Euro-Americans were with men, all the early mixed-bloods had Euro-American fathers and Indian mothers. Even after Euro-American women came into contact with Indians, there were few mixed-blood children with white mothers. Most of those who existed by 1850 were primarily born of white captive mothers who had been adopted into the tribe.

This factor of parental sex is often overlooked in studies of Indian accommodation. In nearly all cultures, the mothers are the most powerful force of tradition. Possibly, this is because they need safe and secure "nests" in which to bear children. Hence, it is quite possible that women favor tradition over the turmoil of change.

In any event, in the Osage society, women are the greatest influence on a new human's life. During the first five years, the mother is practically the only major force shaping the child's life. Whatever follows this first five years would of necessity need to be a potent force to overthrow the culture ingrained by the mother. If our conception has any validity, mixed-bloods with Indian mothers would have stronger ties to Indian culture than those with white mothers. However, we must also point out that among mixed-bloods, many white wives who had courage and love enough to marry a mixed-blood man often became the strongest champions of Indian ways.

Alexis de Tocqueville comments on mixed-bloods in his *Democracy in America* (1835): "Unhappily, the mixed race has been less numerous and less influential in North America than in any other country. The American continent was peopled by two great nations of Europe, the French and the English. The former were not slow in connecting themselves with the daughters of the natives, but there was an unfortunate affinity between the Indian character and their own: instead of giving the tastes and habits of civilized life to the savages, the French too often grew passionately fond of Indian life."[61] While we agree with de Tocqueville, we must point out that although most mixed-bloods followed the Indian culture they still retained some French culture. This became overshadowed by their predominant Indianness. Among the Osages, the French-Osages tended to congregate together in a half-breed band. Approximately one-fourth of the French-Osages lived with the full-blood bands. Although the half-breed band was predominantly Osage in culture, it still incorporated many French social activities. Virtually all of this band were bilingual (Osage and French), but French was the language of preference among the mixed-bloods.

With the coming of the Americans in 1803, a need to speak American English grew greater. Thus, by 1850, most Osage-French mixed-bloods were trilingual (Osage, French, and American English). Between 1850 and 1870, an increasing number of marriages with Americans lessened the attraction of both French and Osage language and customs. By the twentieth century, only a few older mixed-bloods spoke French. All younger mixed-bloods spoke American English. Only rarely did one speak French, and equally rare was an Osage-speaking mixed-blood. Thus, the blending of cultures was spread over a two hundred year period.

The Non-People

The métis (French-Indian mixed-blood) of Canada and the métis among the Osages share much the same history until 1800. As de Tocqueville so aptly noted, the métis of North America did not occupy the same position of the mestizo (Spanish-Indian mixed-blood) in Latin America. That is, they did not exert the influence that mixed-bloods did in other lands.

Possibly, this is because the predominant stock of Latin America *is* the mestizo. In North America, the métis and English-Indian mixed-bloods are a minority of a minority. "As late as 1980, one such group in Canada could refer to themselves, not without irony, as North America's 'non-people.' "[62]

The basic distinction between the Canadian métis and the métis of mid–United States hinges on the Louisiana Purchase. That is, with the coming of the alien Americans the Osage métis lost contact with the French influence. This threw them more to an Osage identification since the American culture was totally alien to them. Thus, in mid–America the mixed-bloods tended to lose their métis identity and to increase their Osage identity. Although both the Canadian métis and the Osage métis have become a "non-people," they have reached this status in a different context.

Osage Tribal Composition

"The membership of the Osage Tribe presently numbers about 5,307[63] persons. Osage members are located in 295 communities in 35 different States. The largest single group away from the State of Oklahoma is located in southern California. Only 9 percent of the tribal members are full bloods. Three-fourths of the tribal members are less than one-half Indian blood. A continuing trend of biologic assimilation is apparently well established."[64] This information was read into the record by Representative Harrison. In 1953, efforts were being made to terminate the Osages. It took the entire Oklahoma delegation to Congress and the complete funding of the Osage Agency by the Osages to prevent termination.

The Osage case is a landmark case for the argument against termination. On the surface the people seem well assimilated and certainly accommodated, yet, the complications of tribal affairs make continued supervision mandatory. The defense of the tribe by the council illustrates the sophistication of the Osages more than the figures.

WHITE MAN'S PROBLEM
The Great Depression
Indians and the Depression

Most Americans who lived through the 1930s are aware of the effects of economic depression on people, especially rural Americans. It was a difficult time for white citizens and much worse than that for black Americans. However, the Indian was hit the hardest. The Osages were fortunate in having a few dollars coming into the family from oil money. However, two things should be noted: not all Osage families had this income; and those few dollars kept all Osages from participation in government relief and recovery programs.

Purposes of the CCC-ID

After a great deal of effort, the Osages were allowed to participate in the Indian Division of the Civilian Conservation Corps. Fortunately, this was the most successful program applied to Indians during the New Deal. All work was performed on restricted Osage lands. I worked on a crew where no mechanical help was allowed. Rock was quarried without explosive or mechanical aids, then loaded in wagons by hand and carried to the construction site by teams of horses or mules.

Three types of erosion control dams were built. Apron dams were built on open flow ways; wall dams were built in gullies that were then plowed full of soil again; and filter dams were built in open downcutting gullies. Sheet erosion in tilled fields was checked by terraces.

Standard pay was thirty-five cents an hour with a maximum of forty hours a week allowed. Two dollars and eighty cents a day does not seem like much money by the standards of today, but it was riches beyond imagination in a time when farm and ranch labor only received one dollar a day for a ten-hour day.

Shelterbelts were also set out by the CCC-ID but my group was in the Cross Timbers area and did not plant shelterbelts. Another CCC-ID project was the range program, which was done by a crew different from mine. My group's contribution to the range program was the construction of filter dams on range lands.[65]

Settlement of Claims

The Claims Commission

In the post–World War II era, efforts were made to clear up old governmental business and to make a new start with a clean slate. Without a doubt, the matter of Indian claims was not only one of the oldest persistent problems but one that continued to goad the American sense of fair play. With these factors as the motivation, the United States created the Indian Claims Commission in 1946. "This was a quasi-judicial branch of Congress created . . . to deal *finally* with the longstanding claims of Native Americans against the Federal Government."[66]

Acknowledgement of these claims was a clear recognition of Indian sovereignty. The Indian Claims Commission gave notice to Indian land, water, and mineral rights. Furthermore, it asserted the rights of Indians to be different and to live apart if they wished.

Osage Claims and Settlement

The first Osage claim filed with the Commission was docket number 9, which was filed July 16, 1947. $3,480,627 was claimed and the award was set at $864,107.55 on March 1, 1955. Docket numbers 105, 106, 107, and 108 were filed on May 14, 1951. Two additional claims were filed June 20, 1951 and were assigned document numbers 126 and 127.[67] These were claims arising from associations with the United States. Namely, they were the Treaties of 1808, 1815, 1819, 1823, 1825, 1839, 1865 and costs arising from the unratified Drum Creek Treaty of 1868. Arguing that the Commission's awards were too generous, the Justice Department threatened to tie the awards up with counter offset suits (that is, claims of the government against the Osages). Along with this threat was a compromise offer of $13,250,000. The Osages were required to either accept this compromise offer or face a long, drawn-out legal battle with the Justice Department.

Basically, this money award was based on docket numbers 105, 106, 107, and 108.[68] The decision to either accept or reject the compromise offer of $13,250,000 was submitted to a vote of headright owners in a letter of March 28, 1970. This letter included a fair and detailed summary of the situation to be voted upon. Also included was a ballot with the question, "Shall the qualified electors of the Osage Tribe of Indians as defined by the Act of June 28, 1906 (34 Stat. 539), and Title 25—Indians, Code of Federal Regulations, Part 73, accept a proposed settlement of $13,250,000 in full payment of the Osage Claims, Dockets 105, 106, 107, and 108?"

The following comments are offered in fairness to those Osages who do not have headrights: Possibly, you have wondered why you did not share in the claims settlement since it was not money derived from the mineral estate. In theory, at least, being a descendant of either the Big or Little Osage people should have entitled you to an equal share in the award. However, you have no vote or recognition as an Osage citizen. You should know that the minerals council sought to obtain special legislation as early as 1969 to limit distribution of any awards to headright holders. This proposal was introduced by Mr. Edmondson on November 18, 1969. Although this was proposed in 1969, it seems that it was not enacted into law until early in 1971. The Act provided that only headright owners could share in any awards arising from any claims. Thus, it adds income to the tribe from sources other than mineral to the present mineral trust income of headright holders. It is a blight on the honor of the United States of America to allow and even to conspire to deprive Osage descendants of what is justly theirs. Not only does the United States deprive the majority of the Osage of their monetary inheritance, but it also deprives them of self-government by refusing to recognize any Osage government except the minerals government.

A million dollars was set aside to establish a tribal education fund. At least Congress had the grace to provide some benefit for young Osages from their heritage. Attorney fees of $1,300,442 were also paid from the award money. Thus ended the Osage claims cases placed before the Federal Indian Claims Commission.

The Threat of Termination

Introduction

There are those who viewed the termination efforts of the 1950s either as a consensus of ignorance or a conspiracy of Congress to get out of the responsibilities associated with Indians. While there is more than a little truth in such beliefs, the actual causes are not so clear. Surely, the failure of the New Deal Indian programs must be included in the causes.[69] Another cause was the failure of the Claims Commission to settle for all time the matter of Indian claims. For these and any number of undetermined reasons, Congress had reached a point where it felt the Indian would be better off without federal supervision.

No matter how one views the termination spasm, one fact stands out: Neither the Reformers nor those who favored termination had abandoned the practice of deciding what was best for the Indians in general and then trying to impose their ideas upon all Indians alike. Essentially, there are three flaws in this practice that guarantee the failure of such programs and policies. These are: (1) The ideas were not Indian ideas, nor did they include any significant Indian input; (2) Enforcement and implementation was not Indian-led; and (3) No universal program or policy for all Indians can work, because Indians differ so greatly.

While the Osages were effectively arguing against termination, the two Klamath delegates that were present had a firm mandate from the Klamath people to fight in favor of termination. The Osage arguments convinced the junior Klamath delegate (Boyd Jackson) that termination was a bad thing and, to the disgust of the senior delegate (Wade Crawford), his associate switched his stand and argued against termination.[70]

As the matter turned out, H. Con. Res. 108 was enacted into law with the Osage tribe omitted from the termination provision. The Klamath was terminated according to the mandate of the Klamath people. Their lands were sold and each Klamath received $40,000 as their share. A few years later many were on relief. "As one member of the tribe said, 'My grandchildren won't have anything, not even the right to call themselves Indian.'"[71]

Osage Termination

Through the excellent efforts of the council and especially of George V. Labadie, the Osages were able to convince Congress not to terminate them. Eleven very concrete reasons were given to show why the Osages should not be terminated. Most of these were associated with the mineral trust. It was the foresight of these reasons that is so noticeable. For example: "Any change from the tribe's present status could lead to corruption and dissipate the vast natural reserves owned by the Osage Indians." One can appreciate with gratitude the foresight of this statement in light of what happened to the Klamath forest reserves after termination.

Quite probably, the first reason given was the most compelling reason to continue federal supervision: "The Osage Tribe is self-sustaining and will pay all expenses for Federal supervision during the continuance of the mineral period."[72] In relation to this particular argument against termination, the testimony of Senator Mike Monroney is revealing.

SENATOR MONRONEY: My dear sir, there has been that ratification and there has been that protection of the best scientists and administrators that the Government can have.

MR. ENGLE: How much has that cost the taxpayers of the Nation for this?

SENATOR MONRONEY: I will say to the gentleman that out of the $300,000 a year which is a cost to run this the tribe itself pays $260,000 out of tribal funds. If it is necessary and the Government is so anxious to relieve itself of any burden, the Osage Tribe, although they pay many times that much in taxes on their lands and properties, I am sure probably pay more. I am sure you could get these conscientious members of the tribe to pay the other $40,000.

MR. HARRISON: Would the Senator yield? Did I understand you to mean that the tribe is willing to pay all of the costs of the tribal operation?

SENATOR MONRONEY: That is my understanding of the conversation with tribal members. It can be brought out when they are on the stand.

MR. HARRISON: That not only means the $40,000 additional, when you talk about the $300,000 cost and the $260,000 that the tribe pays for operation; but it means they will also pay the cost of supervision and review from the area and Washington offices of the Bureau of Indian Affairs, the Office of Audit, and Inspection by the General Accounting Office, and the costs involved in reviewing Osage tribal budgets and the appropriation of tribal funds and also the cost of the liaison staff and the cost of local hospitals and everything? I understand you to say the Osages are willing to pay all of those costs?

SENATOR MONRONEY: I do not know about these intangible costs. They are part of the United States. Maybe the gentleman would like to have them pay the cost of the Internal Revenue Office, because they have to collect taxes from them, and other things. But, I do not believe that is the policy of Congress.[73]

From the extreme interest shown by the committee in Senator Monroney's testimony, at least one motive for termination of Indians seems evident. The cost of administering Indian Affairs *is* expensive. Certainly, some members of Congress in the 1950s and some today would like to renege on the earlier treaties made in order to justify taking Indian lands. Possibly, Congress was like Benjamin Franklin, who as a lad paid too much for a whistle. However, the deal was struck and the debt must be paid. Alternatives, such as termination of the Klamaths, are *not* cheaper than maintaining Indian supervision. It would be interesting to make a study of how much tax money is now being spent to educate, house, feed, clothe, and furnish health care to terminated Indians. Gambling odds would favor the cost being much higher than using the previous agency system.

THE PRESENT AND WHAT IS YET TO COME

Indian Population

Population at Contact

Contrary to most population estimates of the American Indian in 1490, demographic studies have placed the total population in the Americas of 1490 at 100,000,000. Mexico alone had a population of 30,000,000. The United States and Canada had a combined population of 10,000,000. This is about ten times the usual estimates of Indian population at the time of contact in the United States. Efforts to disguise the terrible mortality brought by Europeans and to justify the unused, savage lands argument account for the consistent underestimates.[74]

One can hardly maintain the stereotype of uncivilized savages in the face of the actual population figures. As a matter of numerical fact, there were more Indians than Europeans. Indian nutrition was better than that of Europe, thanks to Indian agriculture. Generally, Indians were healthier than Europeans, if for no other reason than the absence of the epidemic diseases that afflicted Europe. These diseases were bred in the accumulated foulness so common in Western civilization. The Indian lived in more sanitary villages and cities.

It would be a surprise for most Americans to discover that the island of Hispaniola (Haiti and Santo Domingo) had a population of from seven to eight million. This is a larger population than the combined population of Europe's ten largest cities in 1500. How dismal the unused land argument or the greatest good argument is in the face of such populations! This, in turn, throws the justification for taking Indian lands "out the window." There was not then, nor is there now, any justification for taking Indian land except plain outright greed and theft.

Population Today

The term "vanishing American" was never valid outside its special context. It is true that Indians were vanishing from east of the Mississippi in the 1830s and 1840s. However, they were not a dying race as was believed at this time of reforms (1830s and 1840s). Eastern Indians were removed to re- serves west of the Mississippi. While many Indian nations, such as the Osages, were severely decimated, they eventually recovered.

We have ample evidence that Indians are still here and exhibiting great vigor. As a matter of fact, Indian populations are increasing more rapidly than the general population. BIA population reports clearly show an increase in Indian population.

A 20 percent increase had been reported from the 1940 to the 1950 Census, another increase of over 40 percent for the 1960 Census, and still another 50 percent increase for the decade from 1960 to 1970. New methods of identification and of gathering Census data, and re- cently a new pride in Indianness are given as partial explanation for these tremendous leaps foreword [sic forward]. Whatever the reason, the preliminary 1970 count for Indians, Aleuts, and Eskimos stood at 827,091 compared to 551,669 for the 1960 count.

Almost half of the Native Americans now live in five States: Okla- homa, Indian population, 97,731; Arizona, 95,812; California, 91,018; New Mexico, 72,788; and Alaska, 51,528; for a combined total of 408,877.[75]

The U.S. Census Bureau publishes a report of American Indian and Alaska Native Population. The report for 2000 gives the Osage population as 15,897. More recent estimates (June 2002) place the Osage population at slightly over 18,000.

Trends

Introduction

One fact about Indians has stood the test of time and badly formulated policy. That one unchanging fact is the diversity of the Indian groups. This diversity has been one of the consistent factors behind the failure of policy after policy.

As in most human problems, there are paradoxes—seeming contradictions. The relationship between the Indian and the BIA is one of the contradictions. By all measures of causes of human attitudes, the Indian should detest the BIA and wish to free himself from its clutches. Yet, many Indian groups fight desperately to remain under the BIA.

Surely, the BIA has badly mismanaged Indian estates. Yet, at the same time it has salvaged some Indian estate from the ravages of greed. From an Indian view, without the BIA there would be no estate to mismanage. At the least, with the BIA the Indian still has something of economic value. More than the economic factor, the BIA, by extending recognition to an Indian people, places them in a special position in the American society—they are Indian.

A healthy trend within the Indian culture is the rise of well-educated Indians. They are bringing Indian ideas to bear upon policy making. Possibly, this will give a ring of validity to Indian policy. In time, it is possible that the common denominators of the diverse Indian groups can be identified and, thus, a valid general Indian history can be written.

Another desirable trend is a movement away from policies formed for the benefit of the majority culture. Removal, allotment, and termination were deceptions of reform that benefited the majority at the expense of the Indian. Hopefully, a greater sincerity is woven into the fabric of today's Indian policy. It is in the best interest of Indians and the American nation to make it possible for Indians to contribute effectively to the nation's welfare.

Other trends suggest that Indians are again on "the move." It is somewhat of a shock to us to discover that the majority are seeking answers in the Indian culture. Such was the case with three thousand theologians who in 1972 said the American Indian religion "provided in its concept of the wholeness of man with nature a forgotten key to a viable theology for modern man."[76]

The growing tendency for Indian nations to publish newspapers reflecting their interests is a sign of the growing vitality of Indians. This has been of special importance to the urban Indian since it provides a touch with the people at "home." Other trends are: the application of Indian designs and clothing to modern styles; the increase in self determinism; and the increase of Indian political action.

Passing of the Land

No factor in Indian life is more significant than the land in which it was rooted. Now it is increasingly evident that most Indians are either landless or they soon will be. This presents an extraordinary challenge to adapt Indian ways to a landless existence. The implication of landlessness is especially important to Indians. There is one immutable law operating against the progressive expansion of Western civilization—there is no more land than what exists now. There is no prospect of creating or discovering any more new lands here on earth. For this reason, owners of land will experience a growth in power and importance in the years ahead. Make no mistake about this—land and power always go together when the people-to-land ratio increases.

In any Indian land discussion, the claims settlement must be considered. First, the Claims Commission was not a great success in settling claims disputes. Some Indians refused to accept money, for this would have left them no land to claim. Most Indians dislike the adversary nature of the American legal process. Thus, the Claims Commission left a "bad taste." Possibly, the Claims Commission's best contribution will prove to be the idea of a forum to settle differences.

The Modern Indian

While the modern Indian is so recent that we cannot comment extensively on his characteristics, possibly a few are evident even at this early date. The modern Indian has one trait in common: they have accommodated themselves to the majority culture. That is, they have adapted themselves to live, work, and compete in the white man's world while at the same time remaining Indian. To put it succinctly, the modern Indian successfully stands in two worlds.

There can be little doubt that a new group of Indian leaders are appearing. For the most part, they are well educated and not inclined to be "put off," as was commonly practiced with the older leaders. Associated with these new leaders is the "red progressive" movement. Possibly, World War II was responsible for turning the trend in Indian leadership.

Odd as it may seem, the movement of Indians from the rural reservations to the urban areas has created a trend toward a stronger Indian identity. In some respects, this has lessened the tribal associations and increased the general Indian association. However, the urbanization of Indians has lessened the public's view of them as "real Indians." Only recently has the urban Indian come to be considered to be more than transitional.

The greatest worry of an urban Indian is the possible loss of their rights to tribal membership and their Indian-ness. This is certainly true of urban Osages who treasure their Osage heritage. "Back home" movements commonly require physical presence for membership and participation. "Urban life presented a new environment, with new problems but also new solutions. As Indians residing away from reservations, urban Indians risked losing their ethnic identity. Legally, they risked being removed from tribal rolls, and emotionally, they risked losing the security and fellowship of their communities."[77]

The mixed-bloods represent a long-standing problem. Merged with this problem is where to draw the line between Indian and white blood, that is, where to draw the blood quantum line, or should there be a blood quantum cutoff line? It is a vitally important question for both a tribe and the mixed-bloods who have always identified with the tribe. It is a psychological factor with the individual and the economic factor of a growing roll for the tribe.[78]

Indian education is hampered by low income and remoteness from facilities. Most Indians have been "sent away" from home for a part of their elementary or secondary education. As expected, no educational system exists that is tailored for Indians in general, and even those schools dealing with only one group are far afield from Indian needs. Most of all, we include the BIA schools in this indictment. Of all schools in the nation, these should be most responsive to Indian needs.

A tender spot among any group of Indians is the textbooks their children are forced to use. There is not one textbook in American history that gives a fair and unbiased account of the American Indian. We are not speaking here of ignoring the Indian's role in making this a great nation, but, instead we are referring to the outright bias and misrepresentation. Typically, when studying about the frontier, the *brave* pioneers faced the *wilderness* and the *savage* Indian. Indians have no problem with the Europeans puffing up their egos with self praise, but we do object to their self worship at the expense of the Indian.

The Osage Museum

Archaeology in the United States is primarily based on Indians. America's only claim to antiquity is the Indian past. A growing body of information seems to indicate the possibility that the first *homo sapiens sapiens* or Cro–Magnon Man quite possibly originated in the Americas (although I do not agree with this idea). Since Cro–Magnon Man is currently held to be modern man, the implications are indeed interesting. Around thirty to thirty-five thousand years ago, the ancestral Indian quite possibly crossed the "land bridge" to the Old World. It is increasingly likely that the first Indians appeared in Europe as Cro–Magnon Man and replaced Neanderthal Man. If this proves to be true, all mankind originated with the American Indian. Thus, the indications discovered by American archaeology could be a revolution in human origin theory. All theories notwithstanding, Indians are still the oldest identifiable race on the face of the earth.

If for no other reason, this fact is enough to justify protection of archaeological sites and the establishment of Indian museums. The modern trend toward the establishment and operation of tribal museums started in 1934. John Joseph Mathews, a mixed-blood Osage, was the guiding force behind the first tribal museum, which was the Osage tribal museum established on the Osage Agency Campus at Pawhuska, Oklahoma. The museum started with the John Bird collection and mostly borrowed items from the Osage people; it now owns several outstanding collections. The first curator of the museum was Miss Lillian Mathews, sister to John Joseph. Under the leadership of the late Maud Blackbird Cheshewalla,[79] curator, the museum held classes in Osage Arts and Crafts. Currently, Catherine Red Corn is the curator.

Opening as it did in 1938, the museum faced some trying times. World War II brought gasoline shortages and many Osages advocated closing the museum as an unnecessary expense. Yet, the museum survived and led the way for other tribes to preserve their heritage. It was reported in a congressional report in 1943 that "The guest register (from July 1, 1942 to June 30, 1943) was signed by 2,994 persons, the names of which represented residents of every State in the Union, Austria, Wales, and England."[80]

Tomorrow

The Present Crisis

Like all other peoples of the United States and Western civilization, Indians are standing at the crossroads of today and tomorrow. Yesterday's past four hundred years were years of unprecedented expansion for Western civilization. They were years that saw the all but total destruction of Indian civilization. However, today the Indian feels the currents of change in the air and earth. Being carried in the current of Western civilization in which they are trapped, Indians may still leave an even firmer imprint on the direction of Western civilization than they did in the past four centuries. Western men and Indians alike are seeking and probing for a new life in a world without the great frontier areas of yesterday.

Possibilities

It is possible that tribal identities and a corporate governmental form, such as the Osages now have, will become a pattern of the future. Surely, business structures seem to continue the corporate pattern. It seems likely that land ownership will tend to the corporate ownership idea in the next century. This is much closer to the Indian idea of land ownership than the Euro-American concept brought to these shores. It does not seem very probable that this corporate land ownership will assume the stewardship role that prevailed in the Indian pattern. Unfortunately, Western civilization seems to be set in a pattern of exploiting the earth instead of protecting it.

No matter what direction and solutions emerge in the twenty-first century, the past will be viewed wistfully, with a profound sense of loss. The Indian will become dearer to the American people. His art, morals, and philosophy will be sought and treasured.

Two great Indian concepts may receive a considerable amount of examination. One of these is the absence of greed for material things. A greed-motivated society cannot prevail in the face of ever-increasing shortages of raw materials. Secondly, the Indian view of unity and harmony, such as the Osage concept of the unity of sky and earth, must be given serious consideration. Western man cannot continue to strip the earth and poison the atmosphere.

If ever mortal humans needed to be alone in a natural setting for a time of reflection, modern humans are prime candidates. Hopefully, humans will not destroy all of the natural environment, its plants, its animals, and its wonders. Without this, they will become less than human, for humans are of the earth. To become lost in an artificial manmade environment is to become as artificial as the world we create and move about in. Humans must learn to walk in harmony with the earth or cease being human.

23

Epilogue

SURVIVAL FACTORS
Nature of Change
Abrupt Changes

Change is a constant threat to survival. Abrupt changes such as floods, earth tremors, volcanic eruptions, and tornadoes leave no time for adjustment. While survival from these abrupt changes depends upon skill to a limited extent, survival under these conditions is more a matter of chance than it is of skill. Our story of the Osages shows very few examples of the abrupt type of change. Possibly, the advent of the horse is the best example of an abrupt change in Osage history, or possibly the legendary sudden flood.

Osages adapted to the horse with an ease that revealed an understanding of the uses of the horse. Possibly, it was the horse that led the Osages to the southwest across the Plains in a remarkable conquest. The coming of horses to the Osages is an example of a constructive change as opposed to a destructive change. The cultural adjustments were immediate—less than a generation. However, it should be noted that the Osages rarely used the horse in warfare. They preferred to fight on foot even on the Plains.

Gradual Change

It is the gradual change that is the most difficult to cope with. The devices created to live with these changes are called "culture." As time passes, people learn to identify the usual and mainly predictable changes even though they are gradual. However, the American Indian generally, and the Osages specifically, experienced a type of change unique in human experience. Their contact with a completely alien culture and the manner in which alien ways were imposed upon them were unique. Indian experiences with the Euro-American stand as the only such event in the totality of human knowledge.

While some small localized areas may have had a similar experience, nothing like the American experience had happened before. For this reason alone, it should be well understood for the good of all humanity.

The sign that a change was taking place was first seen in the adjustments in the survival base. (A survival base is the means used to supply the basic needs, such as food, clothing, and shelter.) Possibly, the Osages were aware that their survival was endangered at this point in the change process. They accepted the horse, the gun, the steel knife, and the hand axe as an improvement over their traditional tools used to provide food, clothing, and shelter. These and other trade items gradually changed the Osage culture from self sufficiency to a culture dependent on trade. Therefore, the basic survival institutions of the culture were altered to cope with the new dependency.

Some adjustments in their religious activities were necessary since religion was an integral part of their survival institutions, such as the hunt, gathering, and tillage. Possibly the most difficult adjustment was the necessary apology to the "little brothers" for killing them and trading their pelts for the new "necessities." Although they hunted the "little brothers" nearly to extinction, we doubt that a full justification was ever reached in Osage minds. The old religion has long since been abandoned, but many of its features exist in the Osage practice of Christianity. The "little brothers" are still honored in Osage ceremonies.

Changes in the Osage government were noticeable all through the historic period. The central government, which was based upon the gentile system, was characterized by two Grand Division Chiefs and the Society of Little Old Men. At the local level, the bands were led by minor leaders who held their positions by mutual consent of the people in the band.

The Grand Earth Division Chief was the first part of this government to fade away from the Euro-American records. The position was still a functioning part of Osage government, but the position was not mentioned in the chronicles. An identical fate was delegated to the Society of the Little Old Men. They existed as a potent power among the Osage people to 1870, but they were all but unknown to Euro-Americans until after their power was gone. Band leaders were the last to go, and they were the last to be chosen by traditional Osage practice.

To bring the Osages into conformity with Euro-American wishes, their institutions had to be replaced by Western versions of what they should be. At first, this was done by recognizing cooperative Osage leaders and snubbing those who did not cooperate. This practice weakened the gentile system, broke the power of the Little Old Men, and destroyed the common bond of Osage unity. By 1869, the Osage government had been weakened enough so that Euro-Americans could create an Osage government to fit the white man's needs and desires.

Margin of Survival

Zenith

Of the four stages of Osage survival, the zenith or peak in the margin of survival came early in the Contact period. Although the actual rise of Osage power predates 1750, we set this year as the beginning of a time when the Osages enjoyed a maximum margin of survival. This period lasted through the fifty years between 1750 and 1800. However, throughout the French and Spanish periods, the Osages experienced a great surge in survival capability. Through conquest, they were adding a greater variety of climates to their territory, and with this came a greater variety of useful plants and animals.

These plus the greater variety of minerals that became available provided security in nutrition, shelter, and manufacture of tools. Their hunting and trapping area was significantly increased and, thus, they had an increase in the all important raw material of the fur trade. These factors materially increased their margin of survival. More than this, their conquests honed their skills in diplomacy and war, and they thus became a potent force in mid–America.

Faced with both Indian and Euro-American foes, the Osages stood firmly entrenched in the Ozarks. Although the Osages faced more enemies at one time than any other Indian nation, they held firm to their lands. No available military force of Indian or Euro-American origin could dislodge the Osages from their position of preeminence. Again, they were secure from an attack of annihilation and thus had a wide margin of survival. Yet, their defenses from within were vulnerable and open to attack. All Indians suffered from one form or another of an inner vulnerability.

Decline

It was the inner vulnerability inherent in the Osage culture that brought a decline in the margin of survival. The white man had a greed for material gain; the Osage had a greed for what is loosely interpreted as honors. More accurately, this was a thirst for recognition and appreciation of one's deeds and good will to all men. Between 1800 and 1852, the Osages allowed their greed for honors to override their innate caution.

By 1852, the Osages were weakened in spirit and in body. Their country was occupied by intruders who had been welcomed at first, as Osage culture dictated. Dilution of their culture had taken place and, although it was far from a saturation of Western culture, it had passed a point of no return.

Nadir

The nadir or low point of the Osage margin of survival was reached between 1852 and 1885. Weakened by a cultural invasion with a consequent loss of spirit and health, the Osages were a target for disaster. Without mercy, successive epidemics of Old World diseases struck the Osages. Reeling from the impact of this blow, the Osages were struck by first the sectional strife in Kansas and then the plague of the American Civil War.

Decimated by causes not of their making, and sick with the "white man disease," yet another calamity fell upon the tattered remnants of the once great Osage people. Greed-driven intruders demanded the ouster of these few survivors from their lands because the intruders wanted them. Sick of the white man and wishing to be once again alone, the Osages bought a reserve in Indian Territory that was "plow proof." At this point, the Osage margin of survival was a thin, ragged, fragile thread.

Resurrection

By 1885, money from the sale of Kansas lands was easing the crushing results of the "four horsemen" riding among the Osages. Added to this was the growing income from grass leases. *Wah kon ta* had punished his people, but he had not abandoned them. Rapid adaptations were being made within the remains of the Osage culture. By 1906, the Osages were ready to step into the twentieth century. Their spirit was restored, their health was improving, and they now possessed the white man's power—money.

Possibly some Osages were money-foolish but they were not money-driven like the white men who swarmed to the money. Like vultures descending on prized carrion, the white men descended on the living remains of the Osage people. Oil brought riches to the Osages and a contradiction in power. It gave the Osages a growing margin of survival through tribal power in the halls of Congress, but it brought a restriction of personal power in the halls of the county courts. The Osages fought through legal battles, murders, threats to the mineral estate, and termination. Their margin of survival is now secure again, but only as a diluted people of mixed-bloods as they stand at the edge of another new century.

Recognition of Change

Contact

Unlike Indians of the coastal areas, the Osages felt the effects of Euro-Americans before they actually made contact with them. It is probable that the Osages might have observed segments of the Coronado party without making any contact. Surely, they had horses before the recorded contacts.

They also had eye witness accounts as well as indirect information about the white men. Being aware of the white man before contact gave the Osages an advantage when the contact was made, for they were neither awed nor surprised.

Yet, the Osages remained unaware that even before they met Euro-Americans, the changes brought by the meeting of two alien cultures were already at work among them. Both the horses and stories they heard placed the forces of change in motion. Changes related to the horse were rapid and evident. However, changes in thinking due to the stories preceding the presence of Euro-Americans were subtle and difficult to detect.

Probably, the most direct evidence of the effect on Osage thinking was the less than enthusiastic reception given to the earliest contacts. Sometimes, the customary friendliness of the Osages was replaced by cautious courtesy, but usually they displayed a firm determination not to allow passage to the west. This strongly indicates a preplanned reception based on prior information. It is both possible and probable that the Osage "aloofness" trait evolved in this early contact period. Aloofness is the best single-word description of the Osage approach to contact with the white man.

Evidence of Change

For most of the people on both sides who were involved in the contact of cultures, change was far from their level of awareness. It seems likely that other Indians had experiences similar to the Osage experience. The incidence of disagreement among the Osage after contact increased rapidly. Unanimity of action had always been the Osage practice. If this universal approval of an action was not obtained, no action was taken. After contact, there were few Osage actions that had the universal approval of the Osage people. As the bicultural contact grew, disagreements increased. Therefore, the size of action groups decreased, since it was impossible to get unanimous approval for a larger action group.

This became a first characteristic of change among the Osage. A static culture has few disagreements. Likewise, a united culture undergoing rapid changes has few disagreements. It is a third condition that brings disagreement. A disunified culture experiencing rapid changes is certain to have many disagreements. Acting under this third condition, the Osages became fragmented. The problem of disagreement probably arose from the varied strangeness of an alien culture. One must realize that, where Western civilization was concerned, the Osages had no experience to base their thinking upon. Therefore, their opinions varied greatly, which made unanimous response impossible.

The Euro-American had an advantage here, since they were accustomed to meeting somewhat alien cultures and, therefore, had some experience to guide them. However, while the fact has not been stressed, the preceding chapters show quite clearly that Euro-Americans were also feeling their way in a new situation. In addition, they were accustomed to action ordered by arbitrary decisions of their leaders; they were not yet acquainted with the democratic practice of actions based upon mutual agreement of all the people or at least a majority.

A second characteristic of change among the Osage was the shifting structure and powers of their government. While the powers common to all the Osages resided within the Society of Little Old Men, their powers were so eroded that on the eve of Osage removal from Kansas only the power of respect remained. Thus, the power of the unifying clan system was replaced by a rise in the power of the local band leaders. This too was a trend of disunity symptomatic of the changes wrought by the meeting of the two cultures.

The most telling characteristic of change was in the Osage diet. Without a doubt, the Osage were well aware of the changes taking place by the late Spanish period or 1790s. This deeply affected their shift in policy toward Euro-Americans in the early–1800s, which coincided with the coming of the Americans. The decision to cooperate was far from unanimous, but generally, no large-scale violent opposition to Euro-Americans was ever taken by the Osages after 1800.

This lack of opposition resulted in a curtailed diet brought on by land cessions, which consistently shrunk the food base availability. More severe limitations were imposed by the Kansas–Nebraska Act and the subsequent Civil War. Further dietary constrictions grew from land-hungry Indian haters who seized the Osage cornfields and hampered their hunts.

The effect of change among the Osages was terrible because the few beneficial changes were overwhelmed by destructive changes. Almost every destructive force imaginable was turned against the Osage people. Yet they survived still intact as a distinct people. We doubt that Western civilization could do as well if the same forces were to strike it for the next four hundred years.

Despair

It would be difficult to argue effectively that despair overtook the Osage people in the 1870s. Many survivors who later lived in the "lap of luxury," so to speak, looked back with wistfulness on the poverty and desperation of the 1870s when compared to the unhappiness their wealth and life of ease brought them. In the midst of their crushing poverty and desperation, the Osages still found happiness and not despair. This possibly contributed to their survival.

Geographic Aspects

Climate

Climate had a varying role in the rise and fall of the Osage people. Their expansion from the Missouri base added an increase in climates to the Osage domain, which, in turn, gave a greater variety of useful plants to the people. With the increase in food and industrial plants came a higher living standard that enabled the Osages to become very large in person and powerful as a people.

However, because of cultural aspects that made them vulnerable to Western men and the effects of cultural change, the Osages gradually lost their climatic advantage. We have already noted the effects of this reduction in area that reduced the climatic variety. Yet, the core climate of the Osage homeland remained the same. We can only conclude, therefore, that whatever changes were wrought among the Osages were not brought about because of climate.

Cyclonic Storms

Like climate, the path of cyclonic storms has remained a constant in the Osage homeland. The same physical and mental stimulation that launched the Osages into an expansion from the Missouri Ozarks still exists in the Osage Hills of Oklahoma today. So, we may not place the rise and fall of the Osage people upon the doorstep of cyclonic storms.

Relative Location

While the Osages still reside within the bounds of their old domain, the conditions of their relative location have been radically changed. That is, they still reside within less than a hundred miles of their old villages in almost identical terrain. Yet, the cultural and technological changes have rendered their former advantage in relative location completely useless. They are still a continental people with a continental culture, but even their continental location advantage is lost amid automobiles, airplanes, and railroads.

Cultural Aspects

Cultural Exposure

Indian-to-Indian exposure was a common experience to the Osages. Their central location in mid–America caused them to be surrounded by other

Indian groups. This, in itself, was not unusual, but their location on the Middle Waters and at the transition of the short grass and woodland regions was especially significant. Likewise, their location between the two great rivers to the West—the Missouri and Arkansas Rivers—was of great importance.

The Indian cultures of the northeast and southeast differed between themselves as well as from those to the southwest and northwest of the Osages. Cultures to the north and south of the Osages also differed. While other Indian nations were surrounded by other Indians, none were surrounded by such diversity of Indian cultures as the Osages.

It was this exposure to virtually all the North American continental Indian cultures that helped make the Osages so unusual. They probably reflect the broadest spectrum of continental Indian culture existent. In both prehistoric and historic times, the Osages were among the more cosmopolitan of the Indian nations.

Such an extensive exposure to diverse cultures should have enabled the Osages to easily adapt to the Euro-American culture. However, the Osages had developed, to some degree, a cultural trait of Western civilization. Western civilization's outstanding trait is the ability to borrow selected parts of other cultures and to adapt these parts to their own culture. This is not to say that they throw their culture away and replace it with another culture. It is to say that both Western civilization and the Osage civilization are composed of cultural aspects that have been borrowed from many cultures.

This habit of selecting specific parts of other cultures tended to develop a strong rejection of cultural aspects that were not desired. When the European and Osage met there were cultural exchanges both ways. However, there was also strong cultural rejection both ways. This same process was at work in contact with other Indians. With the Osages the acceptance and rejection of Euro-American cultural traits was probably stronger than with other Indian groups and followed a slightly different course.

Western Civilization and Cultural Borrowing

Few Indian peoples accepted Euro-American cultural hardware as rapidly or adapted it so well to their culture as did the Osage. Conversely, few Indian cultures rejected Euro-American social institutions as firmly as the Osage. It was this factor that made the Osage people such a strong example of adaptation to both the Western world and the Indian world. In simple terms, the Osage people stand firmly in two American worlds because of their cultural borrowing and rejection trait.

The significance to this idea from Osage history is that the same trait exists in the American majority culture in a more intensive form. In part, this could explain why Americans have such terrible relationships with many non-Western nations. The "Ugly American" did not appear from nowhere. He had roots in cultural borrowing and rejection practices. That is, he feels that what he keeps is superior to what he rejects. This feeling of superiority of one's own "rubs fur the wrong way."

Domestic Animals

Surely, the presence or absence of animals capable of domestication has been of vital importance to the Osage. We have ample evidence that the domestication of animals was not a new idea to Indians. The dog clearly demonstrates the validity of this statement. Llamas, alpacas, vicunas, and guinea pigs are further proofs. Modern efforts to domesticate the American bison, deer, and bear show only a small success with great effort. In short, other than the dog, it was not practical to domesticate the animals that were available to the Osages.

This absence of animals capable of practical domestication was a decisive factor in the development of Old World and New World civilizations. A civilization based on the power of human muscle must find solutions that differ from those based on power from animal muscle. Aside from the difference in basic power source, the presence or absence of domestic animals also affects the food supply. Supplying meat protein in the diet seems to be a historic necessity. Possession of domesticated meat sources and the lack of such a source require different solutions for survival. Thus, in these two cultural aspects, power and food supply, domestic animals are a determining factor.

However, the role of domestic animals goes far beyond these two obvious factors. Everyday use of animal power generates a mind-set toward power sources beyond the power of human muscle. This, in turn, directs the mind to other power sources and applications. The two go together and reinforce each other; that is, outside power and application is associated with animal power and application. Without domestic animal power, the concept of using any power other than that of humans would rely on accidental discovery. In this chain of discovery tied to the presence of domestic animals, the Old World had an unequal advantage over the New World, which led to the substitution of mechanical power for muscle power.

Yet, this factor was not all advantage, because this same idea has a bearing on the widespread practice of human bondage. Some Indian groups had used Western-style slavery in historic times. However, prehistoric Indians never engaged in this form of slavery. Milder forms were present, but even these were rare. The esne, serf, peon, and other land-bondage type of slavery were unknown to prehistoric Indians. There were classes of laborers, but they were not in bondage. Personal slavery or bondage of individuals was also alien to Indians. Indentured servitude is as near to the form of slavery practiced by some prehistoric Indians as one can find in Western civilization.

It is possible that the sense of mastering nature so typical of Western civilization also arises to some extent from possession of domestic animals. In any event, the Indian either could not or did not have the inspiration to either master nature or the animals around him. Among the Osages, the idea of one human owning another was repulsive. If the Indian rejected these traits of Western civilization, and he did, then we must turn to what took their place in the Indian culture.

Western civilization tended to progress from possession of domestic animals to mechanical power and its application. Such a course leads to a concentration on the development of technology or cultural hardware. The American Indian lacked domestic animals and, therefore, progressed upon a different course of development. He devoted much of his time in observing the world around him. From this, he evolved a concept of rhythm in the world. The world was alive, not in the sense of animism but in the sense of purpose. The Osage preoccupation with attaining old age differed from merely growing old. One should reach old age by living in step with the earth and all upon it. If this required one's death, that was a part of living and would continue to live through his or her descendants who did reach old age. The value in life was the journey of life and the quality of the journey. One can see that Osage thought was directed to living instead of to technology. All else in Osage culture followed this line of thought, which in its essence was to follow the natural pattern of life, not to conquer it.

Religion

Some aspects of Christianity are much like the old Osage religion. This is especially true of those aspects of Christianity that survived the revisions imposed by Germanic influence. The self-righteous, stern, militant approaches to religion were rejected immediately by the Osages. Hellfire and brimstone held no terror for an Osage, since he had no concept of eternal damnation. Kindness, gentleness, and understanding were religious concepts easily accepted.

Stern, sober services or ceremonies were not acceptable to a people who enjoyed living. Yet, symbolism and devout ceremonies were a part of their life. There is little doubt that the Catholic Church, of all Christian churches, appealed to the Osages. There were conflicts in doctrine between Catholicism and the Osages. The main conflict was in the marriage concepts. Osage Mission records clearly show this. There are very few, in fact, almost no full-blood marriages recorded by the Mission.

Among the thousands of baptisms recorded are hundreds of interment records. It seems evident in the Mission records that the Osages firmly believed in baptism. Why not? They had a ceremony that was almost identical in their own religion. Burial was somewhat different. Some minor differences, plus the absence of a priest, often caused the Christian interment to be omitted. Today, the Church permits Osage burial practices within Catholic interment.

The Catholic Church has shown an understanding of the Osages and has accepted many Osage practices in the local parishes. In return, the Osages have responded to the Church. The Pawhuska parish, for example, is eighty percent Indian, the highest percentage of Indians in any Catholic parish. While the Catholics and other denominations have adopted some Osage ways, the American Indian Peyote Church in Osage County incorporates an even higher percentage of the old Osage religion.

CONCLUSION

After all has been said, what remains is to state that the Osages have lived through a severe challenge to their survival. If a prehistoric Osage were to again trod upon the sand rock and move among the blackjacks, he would hardly recognize the Osage Hills. Furthermore, he would not recognize a modern Osage as a member of the Osage people any more than a modern Osage would be able to recognize him as sharing the same blood. Neither could converse with the other. They would represent two alien cultures meeting again.

To believe that the Osages survived intact from their ordeal is a delusion of the mind. What has been possible to salvage has been saved and is dearer to our hearts because it survived. What is gone is treasured because it was what we once were. We gather our past and present into the depths of our being and face tomorrow. We are still Osage. We live and we reach old age for our forefathers.

Notes

CHAPTER 1

1. Chapman casts doubts on the Osage legends and Dorsey's conclusions. He argues the Osages could have migrated from the southwest. See W. J. McGee, "The Siouan Indians: A Preliminary Sketch," *15th Annual Report,* BAE, Smithsonian Institution (Washington: U.S. GPO, 1897), pp. 187–188, and Carl H. Chapman, *The Origin of the Osage Indian Tribe,* (New York: Garland, 1974), p. 159.

2. John T. Terrell, *American Indian Almanac* (New York: World, 1971); also see Terrell, *Sioux Trail* (New York: McGraw-Hill, 1974).

3. Ibid.; also see Kenneth C. Carstens and Patty Jo Watson, *Of Caves and Shell Mounds* (Tuscaloosa: Univ. of Alabama Press, 1996).

4. Ibid., pp. 89–90.

5. Burns, pp. 27–38; also see the subsection "Forming the Confederation" in this chapter for discussion.

6. Alvin M. Josephy, *The Indian Heritage of America* (New York: Alfred A. Knopf, 1968), p. 103.

7. Ibid.

8. Louis F. Burns, *Osage Indian Bands and Clans* (Fallbrook, Calif.: Ciga Press, 1984), pp. 29–42.

9. John Joseph Mathews, *The Osages: Children of the Middle Waters* (Norman: Univ. of Oklahoma Press, 1961), p. 128.

10. Gibson, pp. 31–34.

11. Josephy, *Indian Heritage,* pp. 103–104.

12. Gibson, pp. 31–34; Josephy, *Indian Heritage,* p. 103.

13. Josephy, *Indian Heritage,* p. 103.

14. Black Dog I always led his people out on the Plains at the first sign of an epidemic. His idea was to avoid Osage population centers until the epidemic was over.

15. Josephy, *Indian Heritage,* pp. 103–106.

16. Elmo Ingenthron, *Indians of the Ozark Plateau* (Point Lookout, Mo.: School of the Ozarks Press, 1981), p. 56.

17. Chapman, *Origin of the Osage,* pp. 186–188; Brewton Berry, Carl Chapman, and John Mack, "Archaeological Remains of the Osage," *American Antiquity,* 10 (July 1944).

18. Preston Holder, *The Hoe and the Horse on the Plains* (Lincoln: Univ. of Nebraska Press, 1970), pp. 74–76.

19. Houck, *History of Missouri,* p. 50.

20. Burns, *Customs and Myths,* p. 15.

21. The Red Eagle subclan of the *Tsi shu* Peacemaker clan led the Osage dawn prayers. Its myths were never recorded. Hints of the contents of these prayers are in Bureau of American Ethnology Annual Reports. See: 36th, p. 51; 39th, pp. 120–123; and 45th, pp. 566–571.

22. William Brandon, *Last Americans* (New York: McGraw-Hill, 1974), p. 52.

23. Heart Stays comes from the Osage flood legends. These were Osages who survived the sudden flood by staying on small hummocks upon the flood plain. Thus, those who stayed were called Heart Stays and always established their villages on low ground near a river bench.

24. Phillip E. Chappell, "River Navigation: A History of the Missouri River," *Transactions,* Kansas State Historical Society, 1905–1906, 9: 241.

25. T. C. Pease, ed., "French Foundations, 1680–1693," *Collections of the Illinois State Historical Library,* French Series, vol. 1, 23: 389–391.

26. Thomas Nuttall, *A Journal of Travels into Arkansas Territory During the Year 1819,* ed. S. Lottenville (Norman: Univ. of Oklahoma Press, 1980), p. 280n.

27. Houck, *History of Missouri,* pp. 104–118.

28. Louis F. Burns, ed., *Osage Mission Baptisms, Marriages, and Interments, 1820–1886* (Fallbrook, Calif.: Ciga Press, 1986).

29. Houck, *History of Missouri.*

30. Lawrence Kinnaird, ed., "Spain in the Mississippi Valley, 1765–1794," *Annual Report of the American Historical Association, 1945,* vols. 2, 3, and 4.

31. In the *Tsi shu* version, these were red oak trees. In the Black Bear version, they alit on seven boulders. A fragment tells us that the red bird (morning prayer eagle or Red Eagle) gave the people bodies.

32. These and all other stories given in this chapter are from Burns, *Customs and Myths,* unless otherwise footnoted.

33. The earliest Osage term for the horse was *Shon ka Cee Tun ka* or Big Yellow Dog. A horse would certainly be an extraordinarily large dog. Under Spanish influence, the Spanish word for horse, *caballo,* became *Ka wa* in Osage.

34. Even in these early times the Osages buried their dead. They kept their villages clean; all waste was carried some distance from the village. In time, a midden ring developed around the village, and the midden ring was called the outskirts of the village. Cleansing rites for returning war parties were always conducted outside this ring.

35. To distinguish between the old shrine of the Grand War Party, which remained in the village, and the new portable shrines, suffixes were added—that is, *Wa ho pe Tun ka* and *Wa ho pe Shin ka* or Big Shrine and Little Shrine.

36. Man of Mystery was thunder, the life symbol of the *Ne ke Wa kon ta Ke* or Men of Mystery clan. This and the *Lo ha* or Buffalo Bull clan made up the *Tsi ha she*. *Lo ha* is archaic Osage for *Tsa To ka* (Buffalo Bull).

37. This Osage expression meant "pay attention." Much the same meaning is contained in William Shakespeare's *Julius Caesar:* "lend me your ears," 3.2.79.

38. Owner or keeper in the Osage sense means that all new Little Shrines had to be made under the direction of the Osages and payment had to be made to them. Many individuals of other clans owned and kept Little Shrines in the European sense of owner and keeper.

39. There were usually two Grand Buffalo Hunts a year. Going to and from the hunts each year entailed over 1,200 miles of travel.

40. Flint forms as irregular masses of silica in limestone beds.

41. McGee, "Siouan Indians"; Chapman, *Origin of the Osage.*

CHAPTER 2

1. John Hodgdon Bradley, *World Geography* (Boston: Ginn, 1951), pp. 106, 125, 135; This reference is based on the Glenn T. Trewartha classifications.

2. Ellsworth Huntington, *Principles of Human Geography* (New York: John Wiley and Sons, 1947), pp. 3–7.

3. Ellen Churchill Semple, "Geographical Location as a Factor in History," *Annual Report of the American Historical Association for 1907, 1908,* 1: 45; Full text in *Bulletin of the American Geographical Society,* 40: 1–17.

4. Roger Ward Babson was an economic statistician who predicted accurately the 1929 economic crash. He founded Webber College and Babson Institute of Business Administration. In addition, he wrote thirty-five books on economics and other subjects.

5. Noel M. Loomis and Abraham P. Nasatir, *Pedro Vial and the Roads to Santa Fe* (Norman: Univ. of Oklahoma Press, 1967), p. 23ff, 101n.

6. Finger talk is the Osage name for what Euro-Americans call sign language.

7. This founding date is taken from a brochure published by the Ponca City, Oklahoma, Cultural Center.

8. Arrell M. Gibson, *The American Indian: Prehistory to the Present* (Lexington, Mass.: D. C. Heath, 1980), pp. 130–132.

9. Ibid.

10. Kinnaird, "Spain in the Mississippi Valley," Vol. II: 125–126, 133.

11. George A. Custer, *My Life on the Plains,* ed. M. M. Quaife (Chicago: Lakeside Press, 1952), pp. 321–352.

12. Charles De Montesquieu, "The Spirit of Laws," ed. R. M. Hutchins, *Great Books of the Western World,* vol. 38 (Chicago: Encyclopedia Britannica, 1952), pp. ix–x, 3, 18, 124n, 127–128.

13. The foregoing discussion is based on Burns, *Indian Bands* and *Customs and Myths*

14. Burns, loc. cit.

15. The Osage had two years in each Euro-American year. Fall and Winter were called Winter Year while Spring and Summer were called Summer Year. Thus, the fall hunt was sometimes called the winter hunt and the spring hunt was sometimes called the summer hunt.

16. The Oneota aspect was strongly represented between the Des Moines River and Missouri River mouths. South of the Ohio, however, it was all but nonexistent.

17. Ingenthron, *Indians of the Ozark Plateau,* p. 63.

18. Ibid., pp. 59–60.

19. Waldo R. Wedel, *An Introduction to Kansas Archeology,* Bureau of American Ethnology, Bulletin 174, Smithsonian Institution, 1959, p. 56.

20. Black Dog I became a band chief about 1785. His father had moved the band to Baxter Springs, Kansas, some years before his death and while Black Dog I was still a young boy.

21. Col. Wallace Talbot of Gravois Mills, Missouri, has verbally assured us that he found this village on a map held by the Missouri State Library at Jefferson City. It is also shown on a map at Fort Osage.

22. M. F. Ashley Montagu, "An Indian Tradition Relating to the Mastodon," *American Anthropologist,* 46 (October–December 1944): 568–591.

23. Waldo R. Wedel, "Prehistory and the Missouri Valley Development Program," *Smithsonian Miscellaneous Collections,* 3: 40, 1948.

24. Ibid.

25. John R. Swanton, *The Indian Tribes of North America,* Bureau of American Ethnology, Bulletin 145, 1952, p. 271.

26. This Grand River is a tributary to the Osage River, and it should not be confused with the Grand River that comes into the bend of the Missouri River from the north.

27. Houck, *History of Missouri,* pp. 225–226.

28. Brewton Berry and Carl Chapman, "An Oneota Site in Missouri," *American Antiquity,* 7 (March 1942): 291.

29. Gilbert C. Din and Abraham P. Nasatir, *The Imperial Osages* (Norman: Univ. of Oklahoma Press, 1983), p. 268.

30. Ibid.

31. W. W. Graves, *Life and Letters of Father Ponziglione* (St. Paul, Kans.: W. W. Graves, 1916), p. 131; see also, Kinnaird, "Spain in the Mississippi Valley," Pt. II: 164.

32. Hereafter, we shall use the same terms to distinguish between these two groups of Little Osages. See Burns, *Baptisms.*

33. Berry, Chapman, and Mack, "Archaeological Remains," 10: 1–11.

34. Loc. cit.

35. Kinnaird, "Spain in the Mississippi Valley," Pt. II: 164; In a letter dated 12 December 1785, Gov. Estevan Miró states, "The village of the Little Osages, of which those who have settled upon the upper waters of the Arkansas are a part . . . "

36. W. W. Graves, *The First Protestant Osage Missions: 1820–1837* (Oswego, Kans.: Carpenter Press, 1949), pp. 179–180.

37. Loc. cit.

38. Loc. cit.

39. Tillie Karns Newman, *The Black Dog Trail* (Boston: Christopher Publishing House, 1957), p. 36.

40. W. W. Graves, *History of Neosho Count* (St. Paul, Kans: Journal Press, 1949, reprint, Osage Mission Historical Society, 1986), pp. 103–104.

41. Ibid., p. 114.

42. Din and Nasatir, *Imperial Osages*, p. 260.

43. Carl H. Chapman, "The Indomitable Osage in Spanish Illinois, 1763–1804," *The Spanish in the Mississippi Valley, 1762–1804*, ed. John Francis McDermott (Chicago: Univ. of Illinois Press, 1974), p. 299.

44. Din and Nasatir, *Imperial Osages.*

45. Francis La Flesche, *A Dictionary of the Osage Language,* Bureau of American Ethnology, Bulletin 109, p. 125.

46. Burns, *Baptisms,* p. 137.

47. John Francis McDermott, ed., *Tixier's Travels on the Osage Prairies* (Norman: Univ. of Oklahoma Press, 1968), p. 128n.

48. *Tsi shu Wa ti an ka* is a second name of *Moh se Num pa* or Iron Necklace; both of these names are traditional *Tsi shu* Peace Maker names. See M. P. Fitzgerald, *Beacon on the Plains* (St. Paul: Osage Mission Historical Society, 1985), p. 85.

49. Loc. cit.

50. Kinnaird, "Spain in the Mississippi Valley," Pt. III: 299.

51. Burns, *Baptisms,* p. 541.

52. Loc. cit.

53. Graves, *History of Neosho County,* pp. 18–26.

54. Burns, *Baptisms,* p. 375.

55. Graves, *Life of Father Ponziglione,* p. 131.

56. It should be noted that Osages are named in the clan of their father. Since Baptiste's father had no Osage clan, even though he was half Osage and married to White Hair's daughter, Baptiste had to be adopted before he could be named. The Isolated Earth clan presided over all naming ceremonies, so Baptiste was apparently adopted by this clan. He had to be named before he could become a chief.

57. McDermott, *Tixier's,* pp. 126–129.

58. A. T. Andreas, *History of the State of Kansas* (Atchison, Kans.: Atchison County Historical Society, 1976), p. 1466; Burns, *Baptisms.*

59. Burns, *Baptisms.*

60. McDermott, *Tixier's.*

61. Fitzgerald, *Beacon.*

62. Burns, *Baptisms.*

63. McDermott, *Tixier's.*

64. James R. Mead, "The Little Arkansas," *Transactions,* Kansas State Historical Society, 1907–1908, ed. George W. Martin, 10: 9.

65. Newman, *Black Dog Trail,* pp. 25–26.

66. George C. Sibley, "Extracts from the Diary of Major Sibley," *Chronicles of Oklahoma,* 5 (June 1927): 196–209.

67. Andreas, *History of the State of Kansas,* p. 1521.

68. Graves, *Life of Father Ponziglione,* p. 54.

69. Andreas, *History of the State of Kansas,* p. 1587.

70. James R. Christianson, "The Kansas-Osage Border War of 1874," *Chronicles of Oklahoma,* 63 (Fall 1985): 292–311.

71. Newman, *Black Dog Trail,* pp. 127–131.

72. Thomas Nuttall, *Travels into the Arkansas Territory,* p. 191n.

73. Grant Foreman, *Indians and Pioneers* (Norman: Univ. of Oklahoma Press, 1967), p. 91.

74. Ibid., p. 122.

75. Burns, *Indian Bands.*

76. Newman, *Black Dog Trail,* p. 36.

77. Grant Foreman, *Advancing the Frontier* (Norman: Univ. of Oklahoma Press, 1968), p. 119.

78. Ibid., p. 120.

79. Orel Busby, "Buffalo Valley: An Osage Hunting Ground," *Chronicles of Oklahoma,* 40 (Spring 1962): 22–23.

80. Nuttall, *Travels into Arkansas Territory,* p. 231n.

81. Foreman, *Indians and Pioneers,* p. 23n.

82. Sibley, *Diary of Major Sibley,* pp. 209–218.

83. Foreman, *Advancing the Frontier,* p. 116n.

84. La Flesche, *Dictionary of the Osage Language.*

CHAPTER 3

1. C. C. Royce and C. Thomas, "Indian Land Policy of the United States," *18th Annual Report, 1896–1897,* Bureau of American Ethnology, Smithsonian.

2. Loc. cit.

3. Loc. cit.

4. The distinction between *Crown* and *Royal* is that *Crown* denotes public ownership and *Royal* denotes ownership by a monarch. In the American system of government we do not have a monarch; therefore, *Royal* ownership does not appear. However, *Crown* ownership appears as *public domain* in our system of government.

5. T. J. Morgan, *Fifty-Eighth Annual Report of the Commissioner of Indian Affairs, 1889,* pp. 3–4.

6. J. Eric S. Thompson, *Maya Archaeologist* (Norman: Univ. of Oklahoma Press, 1971), p. 211.

7. Walter Prescott Webb, *The Great Frontier* (Boston: Houghton Mifflin, 1952), pp. 18–24.

8. Houck, *History of Missouri,* p. 133.

9. Yves F. Zoltvany, "New France and the West, 1701–1713," *Canadian Historical Review,* 46 (December 1965): 317–319.

10. Mathews, *Children of the Middle Waters,* p. 168.

11. W. David Baird, *The Osage People* (Phoenix: Indian Tribal Series, 1972), pp. 18–19.

12. Wedel, *Kansas Archaeology,* pp. 26–32.

13. Baird, *Osage People.*

14. Abraham P. Nasatir, *Before Lewis and Clark,* vol. 1 (St. Louis: St. Louis Historical Documents Foundation, 1952), pp. 12–27 (author's proof copy).

15. Baird, *Osage People,* p. 20.

16. Nasatir, *Lewis and Clark.*

17. Webb, *Great Frontier,* p. 223.

18. Houck, *History of Missouri,* p. 180.

19. Mathews, p. 227.

20. Din and Nasatir, *Imperial Osages,* p. 54.

21. Louis Francis Burns, *Turn of the Wheel* (San Marcos, Calif.: A. M. Graphics, 1980), pp. 209–210, 189–194.

22. Gibson, *American Indian,* pp. 95–96.

23. Miguel de Cervantes, *Don Quixote de la Mancha,* ed. Robert M. Hutchins, *Great Books of the Western World,* vol. 28 (Chicago: Encyclopedia Britannica, 1952); José Ortega y Gasset, *Meditations on Quixote,* ed. Julián Marías (New York: W. W. Norton, 1963).

24. Chapman, "Indomitable Osages," p. 287; Dr. Chapman was killed in an auto accident in the spring of 1987. His death was a great loss to all who study the Osage Indians.

25. Gibson, p. 111.

26. Din and Nasatir, *Imperial Osages,* p. 58.

27. Abraham P. Nasatir, *Borderland in Retreat* (Albuquerque: Univ. of New Mexico, 1976), pp. 18–19; see also Kinnaird, "Spain in the Mississippi Valley," Pt. I, Vol. II: 214–218.

28. Ibid., p. 228.

29. Loc. cit.

30. Kinnaird, "Spain in the Mississippi Valley," pp. 219–220.

31. Ibid., pp. 195–107.

32. Ibid., Pt. II, Vol. III: 230–231.

33. Ibid., Pt. III, Vol. IV: XVII–XX.

34. Ibid., Pt. I, Vol. II: 204–205.

35. Ibid, Pt. II, Vol. III: XXXI–XXXII.

36. Ibid., XXXI–XXXII, 171–173.

37. Loc. cit.

38. Din and Nasatir, *Imperial Osages,* p. 150.

39. Kinnaird, "Spain in the Mississippi Valley," Pt. II, Vol. III: 187–188.

40. Foreman, *Indians and Pioneers,* p. 15.

41. Kinnaird, "Spain in the Mississippi Valley," Pt. II, Vol. III: 312.

42. Ibid., pp. 316–317.

43. Ibid., p. 256.

44. Ibid., p. 203.

45. Foreman, p. 14.

46. Kinnaird, "Spain in the Mississippi Valley," Pt. II, Vol. III: 200.

47. Foreman, p. 18n.

48. Kinnaird, "Spain in the Mississippi Valley," pp. 335–336.

49. Kinnaird, ibid., p. 246–247.

50. Ibid., pp. 315–316.

51. Ibid., pp. 273–274.

52. Ibid., pp. 284–285.

53. Some Osage mixed-bloods may be interested in knowing that Sylvester La-badie was trading among the Osages at this time. Perez had him present his de-mands to the Osages. The Labadies are a well-known mixed-blood family.

54. Kinnaird, "Spain in the Mississippi Valley," Pt. II, Vol. IV: 312.

55. Ibid., p. 196.

56. See Wilcomb Washburn, "The Writing of American History: A Status Re-port," *Pacific Historical Review*, 40 (August 1971): 261–281. In this otherwise excel-lent article, there is a point made of the fact that a good general history of the American Indian has not been written. This seems to be a contradiction of reality. One cannot lump the varied Indian nations into one generalized mold and have an American Indian history. It would be the old "all Indians are alike" theme disguised as history.

57. Kinnaird, "Spain in the Mississippi Valley," Pt. I, Vol. II: 393.

58. Ibid.

59. Ibid.

60. Ibid., Pt. II, Vol. III: 281.

61. Ibid., pp. 331–332.

62. Ibid., p. 35.

63. Ibid., pp. 295–296.

64. Ibid., p. 406.

65. Ibid., p. 23.

66. Ibid., Pt. III, Vol. IV: 56.

67. Ibid., p. 94.

68. Ibid., p. 107.

69. Loc. cit.

70. Kinnaird, "Spain in the Mississippi Valley," p. 148.

71. Ibid., pp. 149–150.

72. Ibid., pp. 206–207.

73. Ibid., pp. 204–205.

74. Ibid., Pt. II, Vol. II: 414–417.

75. Din and Nasatir, *Imperial Osages,* p. 258.

76. Kinnaird, "Spain in Mississippi Valley," Pt. III, Vol. IV: 290.

77. Ibid., pp. 299–300.

78. Loc. cit.

79. Chapman, pp. 287–313. This is an excellent source of information about Ft. Carondelet.

80. Thomas Bailey, *A Diplomatic History of the American People* (New York: F. S. Crofts, 1947), p. 93.

CHAPTER 4

1. Ernest Staples Osgood, ed., *The Field Notes of Captain William Clark, 1803–1805* (New Haven: Yale Univ. Press, 1964), p. 48n.

2. Donald Jackson, ed., *Letters of the Lewis and Clark Expedition with Related Documents, 1783–1854,* 2nd ed., 2 vols. (Chicago: Univ, of Illinois Press, 1978), p. 198, #125.

3. Ibid., p. 199, #126.

4. Ibid., pp. 199–200 n

5. Jackson, *Lewis and Clark.*

6. Jackson, *Lewis and Clark,* pp. 200–203, #127n

7. While this request may seem innocent on the surface, it shows how well Jefferson had prepared to meet the Osages. He certainly knew the Osage law with regard to intruders. By making this request, he protected Pike and Marcy on their expeditions into Osage territory.

8. Jackson, *Lewis and Clark,* p. 203n.

9. Ibid., p. 203, #128.

10. Ibid., p. 308, #201.

11. Ibid., p. 66n.

12. Ibid., p. 234, #149.

13. Ibid., p. 238n.

14. Ibid., pp. 259–260, #170.

15. Ibid., p. 461.

16. Ibid.

17. Ibid., p. 626n.

18. Louis Francis Burns, *Treaties, Constitution and Laws of the Osage Nation* (Santa Ana, Calif.: Louis F. Burns, 1967), p. 5.

19. Jackson, *Lewis and Clark,* pp. 623–625, #390.

CHAPTER 5

1. Miguel de Cervantes deals with this aspect of life in his immortal *Don Quixote.*

2. Almost any standard United States history textbook contains information about this proclamation.

3. United States Department of the Interior, Bureau of Indian Affairs, *American Indian and the Federal Government,* n.d. (ca. 1965), p. 1.

4. Isidore Starr, Lewis Paul Todd, and Merle Curti, eds., "The Articles of Confederation," in *Living American Documents,* (New York: Harcourt, Brace & World, 1961), pp. 60–62.

5. Ibid., p. 65.

6. C. C. Royce and C. Thomas, "Indian Land Policy in the United States," *Eighteenth Annual Report, 1896–1897,* Bureau of American Ethnology, Smithsonian, p. 640.

7. Starr, Todd, and Curti, *Living American Documents,* p. 72.

8. Ibid., p. 78.

9. BIA, loc. cit.

10. The Jackson County, Missouri, Park System has been restoring Ft. Osage for many years, and the project is almost completed.

11. Greed for honors among the Osages was comparable to greed for material gain among the Americans.

12. One must keep in mind that the Osages had survived several severe earthquakes, such as the New Madrid earthquake, December 15, 1811.

13. These lands were selected by the United States, but they were not assigned, and the title remained with the American government. The plan was to later move the Cherokee to assigned lands.

14. Burns, *Baptisms,* p. 137.

15. Ibid., p. 135.

16. These Osage hunting areas were the areas ceded by the Treaty of 1808. Under the Osage understanding of the agreement, these unoccupied and unassigned areas were still Osage hunting territory.

17. Edwin C. Bearss and A. M. Gibson, *Fort Smith: Little Gibraltar on the Arkansas* (Norman: Univ. of Oklahoma Press, 1969).

18. When the Cherokee finally ventured out on the Plains to hunt buffalo, they were beyond the safety of the forts. The buffalo tribes, including the Osages, fell upon them at every turn. After a few hunts, the Cherokee abandoned hunting on the Plains.

19. Ina Gabler, "Lovely's Purchase and Lovely County," *Arkansas Historical Quarterly,* 19 (Spring 1960): 31.

20. Ibid., p. 33.

21. Donald R. Englund, "Indians, Intruders, and the Federal Government," *Journal of the West,* 13 (April 1974): 97–105.

22. Burns, *Baptisms.*

23. Fitzgerald, *Beacon,* p. 67.

24. George V. Labadie, *Osage Case for Federal Supervision,* 15 February 1954, pp. 27–33 (Osage Tribal Council information booklet).

25. Jackson, *Lewis and Clark,* vol. 1, p. 137 map; Kinnaird, "Spain in the Mississippi Valley."

CHAPTER 6

1. Annie Heloise Abel, "Proposals for an Indian State, 1778–1878," *Annual Report of the American Historical Association for 1907,* vol. 1, p. 89.

2. Ibid., p. 92.

3. Annie Heloise Abel, "The History of Events Resulting in Indian Consolidation West of the Mississippi River," *Annual Report of the American Historical Association for the Year 1906,* vol. 1, p. 241.

4. Zoltvany, "New France."

5. Kinnaird, "Spain in the Mississippi Valley," Pt. II: 254–255, 269, Pt. III: 106, 127.

6. Abel, *History,* p. 241.

7. Ibid.

8. Louis Francis Burns, *The Osage Annuity Rolls of 1878,* vol. 1 (Fallbrook, Calif.: Ciga Press, 1980), p. 4.

9. Abel, *History,* p. 245.

10. Ibid.

11. Ibid., p. 270.

12. Kinnaird, "Spain in the Mississippi Valley," Pt. III: 110–111.

13. Mary Lou Drew, Letter dated 29 July 1985. Mrs. Drew is a descendant of Antoine Penn.

14. Kinnaird, "Spain in the Mississippi Valley," Pt. III: 22–23.

15. Joseph T. Manzo, "Emigrant Indian Objections to Kansas Residence," *Kansas History, A Journal of the Central Plains,* 4 (Winter 1981): 249.

CHAPTER 7

1. Abel, "History," vol. 1, p. 290.

2. Ibid.

3. Edwin C. Bearss, "In Quest of Peace on the Indian Border: The Establishment of Fort Smith," *Arkansas Historical Quarterly,* 23 (Summer 1964): 123.

4. Bearss and Gibson, *Fort Smith,* p. 9.

5. Foreman, *Indians and Pioneers,* p. 7.

6. Wayne Morris, "Traders and Factories on the Arkansas Frontier, 1805–1822," *Arkansas Historical Quarterly,* 28 (Spring 1969): 38.

7. Foreman, *Indians and Pioneers,* pp. 47n, 161–164.

8. Nuttall, *Travels into Arkansas Territory,* p. 197.

9. Bearss and Gibson, *Fort Smith,* p. 13.

10. Ibid., pp. 22–23.

11. Bearss, "In Quest," pp. 149–152.

12. Ibid.

13. Newman, *Black Dog Trail,* pp. 53–54.

CHAPTER 8

1. Report of the Commissioner of Indian Affairs, 1924, p. ii.

2. House. Senator A. S. Mike Monroney speaking on the Osage Indians of Oklahoma to the Committee on Interior and Insular Affairs. H. Con. Res. 108, 83rd Cong., 1st. sess., 22 July 1953, p. 12.

3. Harold W. Ryan, ed., "Jacob Bright's Journal, of a Trip to the Osage Indians," *The Journal of Southern History*, 15 (November 1949): 519.

4. Josephy, *Indian Heritage*, pp. 4–5.

5. D'Arcy McNickle, "American Indians Who Never Were," in *The American Indian Reader—Anthropology*, ed. Jeannette Henry (San Francisco: Indian Historian Press, 1972), p. 30.

6. Rudyard Kipling, *The White Man's Burden*.

7. Donald A. Grinde, Jr., *The Iroquois and the Founding of the American Nation* (San Francisco: Indian Historian Press, 1977), p. ix.

8. Francis Jennings, *The Invasion of America* (New York: W. W. Norton, 1975), pp. 15–31.

9. McNickle, *American Indians*, pp. 34–35.

10. Bureau of Indian Affairs, *Indians of the Central Plains*, n.d., p. 6.

11. Swanton, *Indian Tribes of North America*.

12. This was a letter from Fr. Bax to Fr. De Smet, 1 June 1850. Graves, *Life of Fr. Ponziglione*, p. 229.

13. Two sources for Catlin's descriptions and sketches of Osages are: George Catlin, *Letters, Notes on Manners, Customs, and Conditions of the North American Indians*, vol. 2 (New York: Dover Publications, 1973); and Royal B. Hassrick, ed., *The George Catlin Book of American Indians* (New York: Promontory Press, post-1977).

14. Washington Irving, *A Tour on the Prairies*, ed. John Francis McDermott (Norman: Univ. of Oklahoma Press, 1962), pp. 21–22.

15. Bill Burchardt, "Osage Oil," *Chronicles of Oklahoma*, 41 (Fall 1963): 266.

16. Foreman comments, "Clairmont's village" was near the present Claremore, Oklahoma, Chouteau's at Salina, and the Creek Agency near the mouth of the Verdigris River. *Advancing the Frontier*, p. 119;

17. McDermott, *Tixier's*, pp. 167–168.

18. Stanley Vestal, *The Missouri* (Lincoln: Univ. of Nebraska Press, 1967), p. 214.

19. McDermott, *Tixier's*, p. 211; Long's expedition reported a similar ceremony among the Otto. Strict truth was always spoken at these rites. This was especially true of recitation of war honors.

20. Fitzgerald, *Beacon*, p. 25n.

21. Ryan, "Jacob Bright's Journal," pp. 509, 516n.

22. In English and to the Western mind, an inanimate object could not represent life. In Osage and in the Osage mind, there is no conflict in expression in this statement. The earth and all upon it were alive.

23. Newman, *The Black Dog Trail*, p. 40.

24. Ibid., p. 105.

25. McDermott, *Tixier's*, pp. 140, 149.

26. J. Joseph Mathews, *Talking to the Moon* (Chicago: Univ. of Chicago Press, 1945), p. 174.

27. A parflesche was a rawhide storage container. These were adorned with a repeat geometric design on the cover. Each design was as distinctive as a person's signature.

28. McDermott, *Tixier's*, pp. 195–196.

29. Ibid., p. 195.

30. Houck, *History of Missouri,* vol. 1, p. 183.

31. Graves, *Life of Father Ponziglione,* p. 230.

32. Irving, *A Tour on the Prairies,* p. 42.

33. George F. Spaulding, ed., "Count Albert-Alexandre de Pourtalés," *On the Western Tour with Washington Irving* (Norman: Univ. of Oklahoma Press, 1968), p. 46n.

34. Annual Report of the American Historical Association, 1908, vol. 2, part 2, pp. 107–108.

35. James Mooney, "Calendar History of the Kiowa Indians," Seventeenth Annual Report, Bureau of American Ethnology, Smithsonian Institution, 1895–1896, p. 259.

36. Ibid., pp. 258–260.

37. Ibid., pp. 168–171.

CHAPTER 9

1. Graves, *First Protestant Osage Missions,* p. 28.

2. This name refers to the bear, and it is a traditional name.

3. Graves, *First Protestant Osage Missions,* p. 87.

4. Everett Dick, *Vanguards of the Frontier* (Lincoln: Univ. of Nebraska Press, 1941), pp. 123–125.

5. Graves, *First Protestant Osage Missions,* pp. 6–7.

6. Ibid., pp. 77–78.

7. Ibid., pp. 77–78.

8. Ibid., pp. 219–220.

9. Ibid., pp. 212–220.

10. Mathews, *Children of the Middle Waters,* p. 527.

11. Graves, *History of Neosho County,* pp. 58–59.

12. Shakespeare, *Hamlet,* 3.1.57–69.

13. Fitzgerald, *Beacon,* pp. 66–67.

14. Ibid., pp. 32–41.

15. Ibid.

16. St. Regis was the second Catholic Indian school to be established in the United States.

17. Fitzgerald, *Beacon,* pp. 32–41.

18. Ibid., pp. 67–68.

19. Ibid.

20. Ibid., p. 71n, 77.

21. Ibid., p. 75.

22. Ibid., pp. 79, 102–103.

23. The official name of Osage Mission was Mission of St. Francis de Hieronymo (Jerome).

24. The Four Horsemen were death, famine, pestilence, and war. In the Catho-

lic Bible (Douay) the Four Horsemen are found in the Apocalypse of St. John the Apostle of the New Testament (6:1–8). Christ rode the white horse, which was the symbol of his gospel conquering the world. The other three horsemen represented the judgments and punishment for those opposed to Christianity. War rode the red horse, famine rode the black horse, and death rode the pale horse, which spread pestilence. We use this symbolism because the Osages did not live up to the responsibility *Wa kon ta* had placed upon them, which was to protect "the center of the earth." Thus, they turned to the faith of the black robes since *Wa kon ta* was angry with them. Therefore, the four horsemen were sent to judge and punish them for being unfaithful to their trust and faith.

CHAPTER 10

1. Dorn was absent because of illness from 1851 to 1853; W. S. S. Morrow served at the Neosho Agency during Dorn's illness.

2. Fitzgerald, *Beacon,* pp. 165–166.

3. Burns, *Baptisms.*

4. Ibid., p. 407.

5. Fitzgerald, *Beacon,* p. 165.

6. Ibid., pp. 187–188.

7. Report of the Commissioner of Indian Affairs, 1856, Letter No. 45, pp. 135–137.

8. Fitzgerald, *Beacon,* p. 97.

9. Report of the Commissioner of Indian Affairs, 1856.

10. Fitzgerald, *Beacon,* pp. 162–164.

11. Graves, *Life of Fr. Ponziglione,* pp. 56–57.

12. Report of the Commissioner of Indian Affairs, 1856.

13. Foreman, *Advancing the Frontier,* p. 121.

14. Mathews, *Children of the Middle Waters,* pp. 568–569.

15. Foreman, *Advancing the Frontier,* p. 133.

16. Newman, *Black Dog Trail,* p. 80.

17. Graves, *Life of Father Ponziglione,* pp. 187–188.

18. Fitzgerald, *Beacon,* p. 86; see also, Graves, *Life of Father Ponziglione,* p. 147.

19. Burns, *Baptisms,* pp. 239–270, 375–379; see also, Graves, *Life of Father Ponziglione,* pp. 131–132.

20. Fitzgerald, *Beacon,* pp. 93–94.

21. Valerie Tracey, "The Indian in Transition: The Neosho Agency 1850–1861," *Chronicles of Oklahoma,* 48 (Summer 1970): 164–182.

22. Newman, *Black Dog Trail,* p. 102.

23. Report of the Commissioner of Indian Affairs, 1856, Letter No. 44, pp. 134–135.

24. Houck, *History of Missouri,* p. 181.

25. Nuttall, *Travels into the Arkansas Territory,* p. 193.

26. McDermott, *Tixier's,* p. 125.

CHAPTER 11

1. Noble L. Prentis, *A History of Kansas* (Topeka, Kans.: Caroline Prentis, 1909), p. 90; see also, Bliss Isely and W. M. Richards, *Four Centuries in Kansas* (Topeka: State of Kansas, 1944), p. 132.

2. Benjamin Franklin, "Remarks Concerning the Indians of North America," *Real West,* January 1975, p. 23.

3. John Denton's son was born after his death. This son, John Denton II, became a U.S. Marshal in Indian Territory and was killed in a gunfight at Pawhuska, I.T., in 1892.

4. Garrick Mallery, "Pictographs of the North American Indians," *Fourth Annual Report,* Smithsonian Institution, Bureau of American Ethnology, 1882–1883, p. 84.

5. Fitzgerald, *Beacon,* p. 107.

6. Ellsworth Huntington, "The Red Man's Continent," in *The Chronicles of America Series,* ed. Allen Johnson (New Haven, Conn.: Yale Univ. Press, 1919), p. 6.

7. John H. Rohrer, "The Test Intelligence of Osage Indians," *Journal of Social Psychology,* 16 (August 1942): 99–105.

8. David A. Nichols, *Lincoln and the Indians: Civil War Policies and Politics* (Columbia: Univ. of Missouri Press, 1978), p. 175.

9. Ibid., p. 180.

10. Ibid., pp. 181–182.

11. Ibid., p. 187.

12. Ibid., pp. 193–195.

13. Ibid., p. 8.

14. Before the Indian Claims Commission, The Osage Nation of Indians, *Petitioner vs. The United States of America,* Defendant, July, 1947; this is the introductory brief. The case was later assigned No. 9., p. 30.

15. Nichols, *Lincoln and the Indians,* p. 24.

16. Michael L. Tate, "From Scout to Doughboy: The National Debate over Integrating American Indians into the Military, 1891–1918," *Western Historical Quarterly,* 17 (October 1986): 417–437.

17. Fitzgerald, *Beacon,* p. 114.

18. Allan C. Ashcraft, "Confederate Indian Department Conditions in August, 1864," *Chronicles of Oklahoma,* 41 (Autumn 1963): 283.

19. W. W. Graves, *The Broken Treaty* (St. Paul, Kans.: Journal, 1935), pp. 134–142.

20. Ibid., p. 211.

21. Ibid., p. 212.

22. Burns, *Treaties.*

23. William Lewis Bartles, "Massacre of Confederates by Osage Indians in 1863," *Transactions,* Kansas State Historical Society, 1903–1904, vol. 8, p. 62ff; George E. Tinker and C. J. Phillips, eds., "Massacre of Confederate Officers by Osages," *Osage Magazine,* February 1910, pp. 49–52.

24. It would be more accurate to say the creation of Kansas Territory in May of

1854 ended Indian Territory in Kansas. However, with statehood, Kansas ended the last Indian Territory connections and set about the task of removing all the Indians from the state.

25. Nichols, *Lincoln and the Indians,* p. 39.

26. Ibid., p. 48.

27. James R. Mead, "The Wichita Indians in Kansas," *Transactions,* Kansas State Historical Society, 1903–1904, vol. 8, p. 175.

28. Stan Hoig, "War for Survival," *Chronicles of Oklahoma,* 62 (Fall 1984): 273.

29. Nichols, *Lincoln and the Indians,* p. 62.

30. Nichols, *Lincoln and the Indians.*

31. Gibson, *American Indian,* pp. 384–386.

32. Ibid.

CHAPTER 12

1. David Parson, "The Removal of the Osages from Kansas" (Ph.D. diss., Univ. of Oklahoma, 1940), p. v.

2. Reginald Horsman, "American Indian Policy and the Origins of Manifest Destiny," in *The Indian in American History,* ed. Francis Paul Prucha (New York: Holt, Rinehart and Winston, 1971), p. 22, 21.

3. Frederic L. Paxson, "The Pacific Railroads and the Disappearance of the Frontier in America," in *Annual Report of the American Historical Association, 1907,* vol. 1, p. 111.

4. H. Craig Miner and William E. Unrau, *The End of Indian Kansas* (Lawrence: Regents Press of Kansas, 1978), p. 82.

5. Ibid., p. 39.

6. S. Lyman Tyler, *A History of Indian Policy,* Department of the Interior, Bureau of Indian Affairs (Washington, D.C.: GPO, 1973), pp. 84–85.

7. Klaus J. Hansen, "The Millennium, the West and Race in the Antebellum American Mind," *Western Historical Quarterly,* 3 (October 1972): 376.

8. Francis Paul Prucha, ed., *Documents of United States Indian Policy* (Lincoln: Univ. of Nebraska Press, 1975), p. 140.

9. Ibid., pp. 140–141.

10. Ibid., pp. 131–132.

11. Nellie Snyder Yost, *Medicine Lodge: The Story of a Kansas Frontier Town* (Chicago: Swallow Press, 1970), p. 23.

12. William E. Connelley, "The Treaty Held at Medicine Lodge," *Collections,* Kansas State Historical Society, 1926–1928, 17: 601–603.

13. Ibid., p. 603.

14. Yost, *Medicine Lodge,* p. 27.

15. Ibid., p. 32.

16. Connelley, *Treaty,* p. 603.

17. Prentis, *History of Kansas,* p. 179.

18. Ibid.

19. Connelley, *Treaty,* p. 605.

20. Custer, *Life,* p. 272.

21. Tinker and Phillips, "Massacre."

22. Graves, *History of Neosho County,* pp. 174–176.

23. I knew Mr. Herard very well. He taught me how to make rawhide quirts and twine ropes. I have heard him tell this story many times. See Graves, ibid.

24. Burns, *Baptisms,* p. 145.

25. John W. Morris, Charles R. Goins, and Edwin C. McReynolds, *Historical Atlas of Oklahoma,* 3rd ed. (Norman: Univ. of Oklahoma Press, 1986), p. 27.

26. Connelley, *Treaty,* p. 606.

27. Custer, *Life,* pp. 325–326.

28. Morris, "Traders."

29. Donald Lockhart, "Early History of Elk Falls," *Collections,* Kansas State Historical Society, 1928, 17: 842–43.

30. Prucha, *Indian Policy,* pp. 116–117.

31. Ralph K. Andrist, *The Long Death: The Last Days of the Plains Indians* (New York: Macmillan, 1964), p. 159.

CHAPTER 13

1. Paul Wallace Gates, *Fifty Million Acres: Conflicts over Kansas Land Policy, 1854–1890* (New York: Atherton Press, 1966), pp. 195–196.

2. Ibid.

3. Parson, "Removal," pp. 11–12.

4. Before the Indian Claims Commission, No. 9, The Osage Nation of Indians, *Petitioner vs. The United States of America,* Defendant, Request for Findings of Fact, p. 6.

5. Ibid., p. 5.

6. Ibid., p. 16.

7. Burns, *Treaties;* see also Charles J. Kappler, *Indian Affairs, Laws and Treaties,* vol. 1 (Washington: GPO, 1904) pp. 878–883.

8. Two of these families had the surnames of Dias and Garcia. See Burns, *Baptisms,* pp. 306, 344.

9. These three schools were Negro schools. Some Southern slave-holding nations were required to grant citizenship to their former slaves. This was part of Indian Reconstruction after the Civil War, thus, in a citizenship sense, these Negroes were "Indian." Before the Indian Claims Commission, The Osage Nation of Indians, No number, *Petitioner vs. The United States of America,* Defendant, July 1947, p. 30.

10. Burns, *Treaties,* p. 35.

11. Claims, Findings, p. 11.

12. Ibid., p. 10.

13. Ibid., p. 7.

14. Ibid., p. 8.

15. Ibid., pp. 8–9.

16. Ibid., pp. 25–26.

17. Graves, *History of Neosho County,* p. 401.

18. Prentis, *History of Kansas,* p. 353.

19. Ralph A. Barney, *Laws Relating to the Osage Tribe of Indians* (Pawhuska, Okla.: Osage Printery, 1929), p. 11; 16 Stat. L. 55.

20. Ibid., p. 25; 21 Stat. L. 291; Commissioner's Report for 1880, p. 199.

21. Gates, *Conflicts,* p. 214.

22. Ibid., p. 216.

23. 12 Stat. 772–774.

24. 14 Stat. 289–291.

25. Anna Heloise Abel, "Indian Reservations in Kansas and the Extinguishment of their Title," *Transactions,* Kansas State Historical Society, 1903–1904, 8: 107–108.

26. Miner and Unrau, *End of Indian Kansas,* p. 130.

27. Gates, *Conflicts,* p. 218.

28. C. E. Cory, "The Osage Ceded Lands," *Transactions,* Kansas State Historical Society, 1903–1904, 8: 191–192.

29. David Kay Strate, *Sentinel to the Cimarron: The Frontier Experience of Fort Dodge, Kansas* (Dodge City, Kans.: Cultural Heritage and Arts Center, 1970), p. 108; House Reports, 46th Cong., 2nd sess., Bill Number 3191, No. 723, pp. 1–3; and U.S. House Executive Documents, 47th Cong., 1st sess., Number 195 (Serial 2031), pp. 1–5.

30. Miner and Unrau, *End of Indian Kansas,* p. 132.

CHAPTER 14

1. This was the total acreage of the Trust Lands. Possibly as much as 200,000 acres were under sales contract. Many of these contracts defaulted because of hard times. It was after 1872 before the Osages received any money from the Trust Lands.

2. Parson, "Removal," pp. 135–136.

3. Ibid., p. 92.

4. Abel, "Indian Reservations," 3: 109.

5. Committee on Interior and Insular Affairs, Subcommittee on Indian Affairs, *Hearing on H. Con. Res. 108,* 83rd Cong., 1st sess., 22 July 1953, p. 15.

6. T. F. Morrison, "The Osage Treaty of 1865," *Collections,* Kansas State Historical Society, 1926–1928, 17: 696.

7. Cory, "Ceded Lands," p. 190.

8. This question of the constitutionality of the Court interpreting the Constitution was the basic states rights argument leading to the Civil War. Thus, by force of arms, the Court has assumed the power to interpret the Constitution. In effect, this decision was the first to be made without regional protest after the Civil War.

9. 16 Stat. L. 495.

10. Stat. L. XVI, 362.

11. 17 Stat. 228.

12. 16 Stat. L. 544.

13. Royce and Thomas, "Indian Land Policy," p. 853.

14. 17 Stat. L, 122.

15. 17 Stat. 228.

CHAPTER 15

1. Parson, "Removal," pp. 13–14.

2. Gates, *Conflicts,* p. 200.

3. Parson, "Removal," p. 17.

4. Berlin B. Chapman, "Removal of the Osages from Kansas," *Kansas Historical Quarterly,* 7 (August/September 1938): 290.

5. Parson, "Removal," p. 29.

6. Ibid.

7. Ibid.

8. Ibid., p. 31.

9. Ibid., p. 32.

10. Ibid., pp. 38–41.

11. Gates, *Conflicts,* pp. 203–204.

12. Ibid., pp. 204–205.

13. Parson, "Removal," p. 81.

14. Ibid., pp. 71–72.

15. Ibid.

16. Gates, *Conflicts,* pp. 200–201.

17. Ibid.

18. Ibid., pp. 202–203.

19. Prucha, *Indian Policy,* p. 115.

20. Ibid., p. 116.

21. Thomas A. Bailey, *A Diplomatic History of the American People* (New York: F. S. Crofts, 1947), pp. 401–403.

22. Parson, "Removal," p. 86.

23. Prucha, *Indian Policy,* p. 136; 16 Stat. 566.

24. Miner and Unrau, *End of Indian Kansas,* p. 108.

25. Cory, "Ceded Lands," pp. 187–188.

26. Frederic Jackson Turner's frontier sequence is discussed in George Rogers Taylor, ed., *The Turner Thesis,* Problems in American Civilization Series (Boston: D. C. Heath, 1956), p. 6.

27. Gates, *Conflicts,* pp. 221–222.

28. Parson, "Removal," p. 158.

29. Ibid., pp. 139–140.

30. Ibid., pp. 152–153.

31. Ibid., p. 146.

32. Ibid., p. 141.

33. In Greek mythology, the dilemma was a gigantic bull. When a person was

caught between his horns, they were gored no matter which way they turned. The Osages could fight and get "gored" with extinction or they could keep the peace and hope they would not be "gored" by the mobs of intruders.

34. Louis Francis Burns, "Osage History: Part Seven," *Osage Nation News,* February 1986; This is from a series of feature articles on Osage history.

35. Ibid. All the preceding mixed-blood paragraphs are taken from this source.

36. William P. Mathes was stepson to John Mathews and was probably a Southern sympathizer. He remained among the Cherokees, like many other Osages, after the Civil War. Mathes used a variety of names, such as Bill Nix, Bill Nixon, and Bill Mathews, as well as Bill Mathes. However, his Osage name was *Ha pa Shu tsy* or Red Corn. He was a Baptist minister.

37. Parson, "Removal," pp. 101–103.

38. Augustus Tinker was a likely candidate for one of the guilty ones. He fled the Osage nation leaving a wife and son who died a year later. Records show he collected his annuity until the June 1873 payment, which he did not collect. It is believed he fled to Georgia. In any event, he never returned to the Osages.

39. Parson, "Removal," pp. 108–109.

40. W. C. Vanderwerth, ed, *Indian Oratory* (Norman: Univ. of Oklahoma Press, 1979), p. 224.

41. Parson, "Removal," pp. 112–113.

42. Annual Report, Commissioner of Indian Affairs, 1873, p. 218.

43. Parson, "Removal," pp. 121–122.

CHAPTER 16

1. Four sources now show that the move was not simple and that it entailed a great amount in lost lives and suffering. These sources are: 1) The tombstones along the Caney River watershed; 2) The Osage Annuity Rolls; 3) Eye witness accounts of mixed-bloods who made the move; and 4) An indexed, cross-referenced version of the Osage Mission Register.

2. Tracey, "Indian in Transition," pp. 164–183; "Official Kansas Roster: United States Indian Agencies Affecting Kansas," *Collections,* Kansas State Historical Society, 1923–1925, 16: 722–745; Parson, "Removal," p. 10 n. 24.

3. In the Osage idiom a clear, cloudless day meant a long, peaceful life. The foregoing discussion of Gibson is taken from Burns, "Osage History: Part Nine" (March 1986).

4. Parson, "Removal," pp. 178–179.

5. Ibid., p. 173.

6. Ibid., p. 175.

7. Barney, *Laws,* pp. 12–13; 16 Stat. L. 335.

8. Parson, "Removal," pp. 201–202.

9. Ibid.

10. Chapman, "Removal," pp. 290–292.

11. Parson, "Removal," p. 210.

12. Ibid., pp. 215–216.

13. Ibid., pp. 241–242.

14. "[I]t is the duty of the United States Indian agent for the Cherokees to have such persons, not lawfully residing or sojourning therein, removed from the nation, as they now are, or hereafter may be, required by the Indian intercourse laws of the United States." Kappler, *Indian Affairs,* p. 950; 14 Stat. 799.

15. Parson, "Removal," pp. 241–243.

16. Chapman, "Removal," pp. 296–297; The foregoing requests are included.

17. Parson, "Removal," pp. 247–248.

18. Ibid., p. 261.

19. Ibid., pp. 261–264.

20. Ibid., p. 181.

21. Barney, *Laws,* p. 12.

22. Ibid., pp. 24–25.

23. Parson, "Removal," p. 251.

24. Abel, "Indian Reservations," 8: 109.

25. A notable exception to this is the doctoral dissertation of Dr. Tanis Thorne, "People of the River: Mixed-Blood Families on the Lower Missouri," (Ph.D. diss., Univ. of California, 1987).

26. This title, *Wa co Ki he ka* or Woman Chief, was usually bestowed on the wife of a chief. Sophia was given this title for actually being a chief.

27. For details about these families see Burns, *Turn of the Wheel.*

28. Burns, *Annuity Rolls.*

29. This was the split between White Hair's people and Claremore's people.

30. Chapman, "Removal," p. 295.

31. It was customary to include any full-bloods who lived with the mixed-bloods in the half-breed term. Likewise, mixed-bloods living with the full-bloods were called full-bloods.

32. Parson, "Removal," pp. 266–267.

33. Ibid., pp. 267–268; the sixth name cannot be read because the original document has an ink blot over it.

34. Ibid., pp. 270–271.

35. Ruby Cranor, *Caney Valley Ghost Towns and Settlements* (Bartlesville, Okla.: Blackman Printing, 1985), p. 54.

36. Parson, "Removal," pp. 234–236.

37. Morris, Goins, and McReynolds, *Atlas,* p. 2.

38. The jimson weed was named after Jamestown, Virginia, by the first English settlers in 1607. This weed flourishes on the sites of abandoned human habitation. The particular site had been used sporadically by humans for at least two thousand years.

39. The Elgin Post Office was established February 27, 1871; Robert W. Baughman, *Kansas Post Office* (Topeka: Kansas State Historical Society, 1961), p. 38.

40. George W. Martin, "The Boundary Lines of Kansas," *Collections,* Kansas State Historical Society, 1909–1910, 11: 55–56, 60–61.

41. Parson, "Removal," p. 219.

42. Ibid., pp. 220–221.

43. Ibid., p. 229.

44. Ruby Cranor (*Ghost Towns*) interviewed Caney, Kansas, residents who remembered the competition between Caney and Ennisville. One gentleman showed her the remaining ruins of Ennisville. It was definitely south of the state line.

45. Parson, "Removal," pp. 232–236.

46. Cranor, *Ghost Towns,* pp. 44–45.

47. Ibid.

48. Federal Archives and Records Center, Fort Worth, Texas, Region 7, Records of the Osage Agency, Bureau of Indian Affairs (Record Group 75), Records 195–197.

CHAPTER 17

1. The foregoing topic on Isaac T. Gibson was taken from Burns, "Osage History: Part 10," *Osage Nation News,* April 1986.

2. Frank F. Finney, "The Osage and their Agency during the Term of Isaac T. Gibson, Quaker Agent," *Chronicles of Oklahoma,* 36 (Winter 1958–59): 419.

3. Parson, "Removal," p. 277.

4. Chapman, "Removal."

5. Parson, "Removal," p. 278.

6. "Silver Lake Early Trade Center," *Oklahoma Rural News,* October 1978, p. 10.

7. Chapman, "Removal," p. 399.

8. Ibid., p. 402.

9. Ibid., p. 404.

10. Ibid., pp. 296–297.

11. Ibid., p. 405.

12. Kappler, *Indian Affairs,* vol. 2, p. 947.

13. Henry Campbell Black, *Black's Law Dictionary* (St. Paul, Minn.: West Publishing, 1951), p. 742.

14. Chapman, "Removal," p. 289.

15. Parson, "Removal," p. 254.

16. Chapman, "Removal," pp. 299–300.

17. Ibid., p. 400.

18. Ibid., p. 403.

19. Ibid., p. 409.

20. Brief and Argument on Right of Osage Allottees and Purchasers—Mineral Trust (Tulsa, Okla.: Osage Oil and Gas Lessees Association, December, 1920), p. 2.

21. Parson, "Removal," p. 283.

22. Miner and Unrau, *End of Indian Kansas,* p. 137.

23. Parson, "Removal," p. 280.

24. Ibid., p. 284.

25. *Wahshouwahgaley* or Frank F. Finny, *Pioneer Days with the Osage Indians West of '96* (Private Printing, 1972), p. 10.

26. Osage Council Information Letter: Development of the Osage Reservation and Summary of Special Laws Governing the Osage Tribe, pp. 1–2.

27. Laban J. Miles, Report to the Commissioner, 1882, p. 72; 1890, p. 189; and 1891, p. 353.

28. Isaac T. Gibson to Enoch Hoag, Report to the Commissioner, September 1873, p. 215.

29. Ibid., pp. 215–216.

30. Fitzgerald, *Beacon,* pp. 245–249.

31. Annual Report, 1873, p. 218; 1875, pp. 37, 74, and 277.

32. Ibid., p. 218.

33. Statement of Facts, In the Matter of the Claim of Kingsbery and Holmsley for Relief, On Account of the Wrongful Appropriation by the Osage Nation of Indians of 238 Head of Cattle belonging to said Kingsbery and Holmsley, in the Years 1874–75.

34. Annual Report, 1873, p. 217.

35. Ibid., p. 216.

36. Louis Francis Burns, *Osage Indian Customs and Myths* (Fallbrook, Calif.: Ciga Press, 1984), pp. 143–144.

37. Annual Report, 1873, p. 217.

38. Annual Report, 1875, p. 280.

39. James R. Christianson, "The Kansas-Osage Border War of 1874," *Chronicles of Oklahoma,* 63: 300.

40. George W. Martin, comp., *Osage Troubles in Barber County, Kansas 1874* (Topeka, Kans., 1875).

41. 23 Stat. L. 446, 464; 19 Stat. L. 292.

42. Annual Report, 1875, pp. 276–277.

43. Ibid.

44. Ibid., p. 74.

CHAPTER 18

1. Cyrus Beede, Annual Report, Commissioner of Indian Affairs, 1876, p. 54.

2. Ibid.

3. Frank F. Finney, Sr., "Progress in the Civilization of the Osage," *Chronicles of Oklahoma* 40 (Spring 1962): 3.

4. For incidents in Miles's life as Osage agent, see J. Joseph Mathews, *Wah' Kon-Tah* (Norman: Univ. of Oklahoma Press, 1932).

5. Laban J. Miles, Annual Report, Commissioner of Indian Affairs, 1880, p. 76.

6. Commissioner's Report, 1891, p. 122.

7. Annual Report, Department of the Interior, Indian Affairs, 1898, p. 241.

8. Miles, 1890, vol. 1, p. 193.

9. Miles, 1891, p. 353.

10. Burns, *Treaties,* pp. 75–76.

11. Andrew J. Dorn, Annual Report, Commissioner of Indian Affairs, 1856, pp. 134–135.

12. Annual Report, Department of the Interior, 1901, p. 327.

13. Laban J. Miles, Annual Report, Commissioner of Indian Affairs, 1879, p. 69.

14. Montesquieu, *Spirit of Laws,* p. 127.

15. Graves, *Life of Fr. Ponziglione.*

16. These are titles of honor among the Osages, that is, *Ne ka Log ny,* or Good Man, and *Wa co Log ny,* or Good Woman. The titles were bestowed only upon those who had lived their lives in the highest ideals of Osage culture.

17. This description is based on the Annual Report, Commissioner of Indian Affairs, 1891, pp. 123–127.

18. Mathews, *Children of the Middle Waters,* p. 742.

19. Annual Report, Department of the Interior, 1899, p. 297.

20. Kent Ruth, et al., *Oklahoma: A Guide to the Sooner State* (Norman: Univ. of Oklahoma Press, 1958), p. 333.

21. M. R. Harrington, U.S. Senate *Documents on Peyote,* Part I, Senate Bill 1399, Part 1, 8 February 1937.

22. Fred Lookout, ibid.

23. Commissioner's Report, 1879, p. XLIV.

24. Carroll H. Potter, Annual Report, Commissioner of Indian Affairs, 1888, p. 102.

25. Laban J. Miles, Annual Report, Commissioner of Indian Affairs, 1889, vol. 2, p. 193.

26. Ibid., 1890, 190.

27. Ibid., 1879, p. 70.

CHAPTER 19

1. This is a matter of personal memory. Our father rented a "trap" pasture to a thousand head of these cattle for an overnight stay.

2. Annual Report, 1875, pp. 276–281.

3. Annual Report, Commissioner of Indian Affairs, 1884, p. xxxix.

4. Robert M. Burrill, "The Establishment of Ranching on the Osage Reservation," *Geographic Review,* 62 (October 1972): 532.

5. This paragraph was taken from Louis Francis Burns, "Jim Town: Elgin, Kansas," *The History of Chautauqua County, Kansas* (Dallas: Curtis Media Corporation, 1987), p. 48.

6. Annual Report, Commissioner of Indian Affairs, 1886, p. 134.

7. Miles, 1889, p. 192.

8. Annual Report, 1886, p. 133.

9. Ibid.

10. Annual Report, Department of the Interior, 1900, p. 337.

11. Miles, Commissioner's, p. 83.

12. Ibid.

13. I knew these men very well as a boy and often listened to the stories they told about the big ranches.

14. Burrill, "Establishment," p. 536.

15. Annual Report, Commissioner of Indian Affairs, 1895, p. 37.

16. Commissioner's Report, 1896, p. 38.

17. Annual Report, Department of the Interior, Indian Affairs, 1898, p. 58.

18. Mitscher, Annual Report, Department of the Interior, p. 80.

19. Annual Report, Department of the Interior, Indian Affairs, Part 1, 1901, pp. 77–79.

20. Annual Report, Department of the Interior, Indian Affairs, Part 1, 1904, pp. 79–81.

21. Annual Report, Department of the Interior, Indian Affairs, Part 1, 1905, pp. 87–88.

22. Louis Francis Burns, ed., "The Elgin Brand Register, 1887–1907" (Kansas State Historical Society, Oklahoma State Historical Society, Oklahoma City, 1981).

23. Sources checked were: Burns, "Brand Register"; *Osage County Profiles* (Oklahoma City: Barc and Curtis, 1978); *The History of Chautauqua County, Kansas* (Dallas: Curtis Media Corporation, 1987); J. G. Sanders, *Who's Who Among Oklahoma Indians* (Oklahoma City: Trave Company, 1928); Burns, *Annuity Rolls;* Burns, *Baptisms, Turn of the Wheel;* and Sylvester J. Tinker, *Authentic Osage Indian Roll Book* (Pawhuska, Okla.: Sam McClain, 1957).

24. Commissioner's Report, 1884, pp. xiii–xiv.

25. Commissioner's Report, 1890, pp. lxxi–lxxiii.

26. 26 Stat. L. 794.

27. Burrill, "Establishment," p. 539.

28. Commissioner's Report, 1890, p. 539.

29. Burrill, "Establishment," pp. 534–535.

30. Burns, *Treaties,* 1896, p. 84.

31. Burrell, "Establishment."

32. Burrell, "Establishment," pp. 542–543.

33. Burrell, "Establishment."

34. Ruth, et al., *Sooner State,* p. 335.

35. Not even the Osage grass could carry 16,000 head of cattle on 11,000 acres. Today, the Chapman-Barnard headquarter ranch of 50,000 acres is a Nature Conservancy Tall Grass Preserve. Ibid.

36. Thomas D. Isern, "Farmers, Ranchers, and Stockmen of the Flint Hills," *Western Historical Quarterly,* 16 (July 1985): 263.

CHAPTER 20

1. Finney, "Civilization of the Osage," p. 2n; since the Neosho flows mainly southward with only a slight easterly course, we can only assume the left or east side

was indicated. However, this would seem to conflict with the Council Village, which would probably be White Hair's Village. If this is true, the convention was held on the right or west bank, since this was where White Hair's Village was located in 1861. Yet, Beaver, as chief counselor to White Hair, may well have hosted the convention in his village, which was on the left bank near Osage Mission.

2. Laban J. Miles, 1882, p. 731

3. Finney, "Civilization of the Osage," p. 3.

4. *American Indians and the Federal Government,* United States Department of the Interior, Bureau of Indian Affairs, US Printing Office, n.d., p. 3.

5. Annual Report, Department of the Interior, Indian Affairs, Part 1, 1900, pp. 173–174.

6. The administration of Ronald Reagan is marked by all these characteristics as time will verify. Partisan feelings are too strong now to remove the blinders from our eyes so we can have a full field of vision.

7. Annual Report, 1900, p. 339.

8. Monogenists argued that Indians were of the same species as the rest of mankind and polygenists believed the Indian was a new species of man; see Robert E. Bieder, "Scientific Attitudes Toward Indian Mixed-Bloods in Early Nineteenth Century America," *Journal of Ethnic Studies,* 8 (Summer 1980): 17–30.

9. Ibid.

10. Ibid.

11. Ibid.

12. Ibid.

13. Chapman, "Dissolution," p. 246n.

14. 30 Stat. 90.

15. Burns, *Treaties,* p. 52.

16. See *Opening of Rolls,* Senate Hearing on Joint Resolution No. 70, March, 1908.

17. Barney, *Laws,* p. 42.

18. Annual Report, Commissioner of Indian Affairs, 1908, p. 115.

19. Chapman, "Dissolution," pp. 244–245.

20. Burchardt, "Osage Oil," p. 256.

21. Chapman, "Dissolution," p. 384.

22. Ibid.

23. Annual Report, Commissioner of Indian Affairs, 1908, p. 116.

24. Kappler, *Indian Affairs;* In 1865, treaties were made with the Omaha; Winnebago; Ponca; Snake; Osage; Mini-Conjou Sioux; Lower Brulé Sioux; Cheyenne-Arapaho; Apache, Cheyenne and Arapaho; Comanche-Kiowa; Blackfeet Sioux; Sans Arcs Sioux; Hunkpapa Sioux; Yanktonai Sioux; Upper Yanktonai Sioux; Oglala Sioux; and Middle Oregon Tribes. Land cessions were either stated or inferred in all these treaties but the Osage treaty is the only one that mentioned payment for a survey.

25. Annual Report, Commissioner of Indian Affairs, 1908, pp. 115–116.

26. Annual Report, Department of the Interior, Indian Affairs, 1906, p. 160.

27. The foregoing topic was based on information in the Commissioner's Reports, 1898–1910.

28. Chapman, "Dissolution," p. 386.

29. Barney, *Laws,* p. 53; 34 Stat. 459.

30. 61 Stat. 459.

31. 64 Stat. 215.

32. 92 Stat. 1660.

33. Chapman, "Dissolution," p. 244.

34. Statement and Argument by the Osage Tribal Council on Behalf of the Osage Tribe of Indians in Support of Legislation to Extend the Osage Mineral Trust, ca. 1931, pp. 1–2.

35. Senate Committee on Indian Affairs, Subcommittee, *Survey of Conditions of Indians in the United States: Hearings on S. Res. 79,* 78th Cong., 1st. Sess., Part 41, 2 August 1943, p. 22770.

36. *American Indians,* pp. 5–6.

37. Commissioner's Report, 1891, pp. 18–22.

38. 41 Stat. L. 1249.

CHAPTER 21

1. Richard L. Douglas, "History of Manufactures in Kansas," *Collections,* Kansas State Historical Society, 1909–1910, 11: 135–140.

2. Michael Wallis, *Oil Man* (New York: Doubleday, 1988), p. 92.

3. Ibid., p. 60.

4. Ibid., p. 65.

5. Ibid., p. 86.

6. Before the Indian Claims Commission, No. 126, The Osage Nation of Indians, *Petitioner vs. The United States of America,* Respondent, Petitioner's Request for Findings of Fact and Brief, Finding #8.

7. Wallis, *Oil Man,* p. 85.

8. Burchardt, "Osage Oil," p. 255.

9. Wallis, *Oil Man,* p. 86.

10. Ibid., p. 87.

11. Ibid., pp. 87–89.

12. Burchardt, "Osage Oil," p. 256.

13. Annual Report, Department of the Interior, Indian Affairs, Part 1, 1909, p. 51.

14. Annual Report, Department of the Interior, Indian Affairs, Part 1, 1904, pp. 88–89.

15. Wallis, *Oil Man,* pp. 145–146.

16. Burchardt, "Osage Oil," p. 258; Wallis, *Oil Man,* pp. 147–148.

17. Labadie, *Osage Case,* pp. 60–61.

18. Annual Report, Commissioner of Indian Affairs, 1924, p. 14.

19. Wallis, *Oil Man,* pp. 92–96.

20. Ibid., pp. 89–90.

21. Ibid., pp. 130–132.

22. Statement and Argument by the Osage Tribal Council on Behalf of the Osage Tribe of Indians in Support of Legislation to Extend the Osage Mineral Trust [first renewal], pp. 6–8.

23. Ibid., pp. 8–9. East-side and west-side are often used in the Osage. The dividing line between the two is the line between ranges 7E and 8E.

24. Annual Report, Commissioner of Indian Affairs, 1921, pp. 17–18.

25. Ibid.

26. J. Joseph Mathews, *Life and Death of an Oilman* (Norman: Univ. of Oklahoma Press, 1985), p. 116.

27. Proposal of Fifteen Oil Companies to Council, August 5, 1947, Waterflood.

28. Ibid.

29. Ibid.

30. Ibid.

31. Justification, Brief and Argument of the Osage Tribal Council for Extension of the Osage Mineral Trust Period, November 18, 1963, Exhibit 3, pp. 1–6.

32. Labadie, *Osage Case,* pp. 10–12.

33. Before the Indian Claims Commission, No. 126, *Osage Nation vs. The United States of America;* Before the Indian Claims Commission, No. 127, *Osage Nation vs. The United States of America.*

34. T. J. Leahy, *Brief and Argument on Right of Osage Allotees and Purchasers—Mineral Trust* (Tulsa, Okla.: Osage Oil and Gas Lessees Association), December, 1920, pp. 3–9.

35. Statement [first renewal], pp. 3–6.

36. Committee on Interior and Insular Affairs, Subcommittee on Indian Affairs, *Hearing on H. Con. Res. 108,* 83rd Cong., 1st sess., 22 July 1953, p. 58.

37. John Donne, "Meditation XVII," *Devotions upon Emergent Occasions.*

38. Terry P. Wilson, *The Underground Reservation: Osage Oil* (Lincoln: Univ. of Nebraska Press, 1985), p. 174.

39. Ibid.

40. Ibid., p. 174.

41. Ibid., pp. 178–185.

42. *Logan vs. Andrus,* 77-C-363-C U.S. Dist. Ct. (1978).

43. Memorandum from Scott Keep to Field Solicitor, Pawhuska, September 27, 1979; Copy to Regional Solicitor, Tulsa.

44. Ibid.

45. "Osage Oil Wealth Fading," *Literary Digest,* 113 (14 May 1932): 43.

46. Annual Report, Department of the Interior, Indian Affairs, Part 1, 1901, pp. 612–613.

47. Annual Report, Department of the Interior, Indian Affairs, Part 1, 1904, p. 301.

48. Ibid., p. 297.

49. William G. Shepherd, "Lo the Rich Indian," *Harper's Magazine,* November 1920, p. 723.

50. Ibid.

51. Ibid.

52. G. Edward Tinker, testimony, Senate Committee on Indian Affairs, Subcommittee, *Survey of Conditions of Indians in the United States: Hearings on S. Res. 79,* 78th Cong., 1st. Sess., 2 and 3 August 1943, Part 41, pp. 23018–23020.

53. Bureau of Indian Affairs, *The Osage People and Their Trust Property,* Field Report prepared by Jessie Bloodworth, Osage Agency, Anadarko Area Office, April 30, 1953, p. 51.

54. Ibid., p. 50.

55. Ibid., p. 57.

56. Ibid., p. 68.

57. Ibid., p. 72.

58. This is a family account. A slightly different version of this murder is in Arthur H. Lamb, *Tragedies of the Osage Hills* (Pawhuska, Okla.; Osage Printery, ca. 1930), pp. 97–98.

59. Burchardt, "Osage Oil," p. 264.

60. Ibid., p. 263.

61. Travelers in the Mists was a clan of the *Wa sha she* subdivision; traditionally, they led the way whenever the Osage people were on the move or changing. The reference to the middle people refers to the ancient Osage name, *Ni U Kon ska* or People of the Middle Waters.

62. 45 Stat. 899–1928.

63. This section was compiled from the following sources: Wilson, *Underground,* pp. 145–146; Wallis, *Oil Man,* pp. 151–152; Lamb, *Tragedies,* pp. 151–201.

64. Laban J. Miles, Annual Report, Commissioner of Indian Affairs, 1884, p. 83.

65. Shepherd, "Lo the Rich Indian," p. 723.

66. Ibid., p. 731.

67. Ibid., p. 734.

68. Ibid.

CHAPTER 22

1. William Brandon, "American Indians and History," *American West* 2 (Spring 1965): 14.

2. Arrell Morgan Gibson, ed., *Between Two Worlds: The Survival of Twentieth Century Indians* (Oklahoma Historical Society, 1986).

3. Webb, *Great Frontier,* p. 43.

4. William Brandon, *Last Americans,* p. 20.

5. Alan Linn, "Corn, the New World's Secret Weapon and the Builder of its Civilizations," *Smithsonian,* August 1973, p. 59.

6. "The Native American: A Changing Perspective," *The American West* 10 (July 1973): 48; Brandon, *Last Americans,* p. 2.

7. See Francis Bacon, *Novum Organum,* #39. Bacon gives the Idols of the Mind as the idols of the tribe; idols of the den; idols of the market; and idols of the theatre.

That is, as we grow, our family and relations as well as our business associates and entertainment shape our thinking. Thus, the Idols of the Mind get in the way when we seek truth.

8. Grinde, *Founding of the American Nation,* p. X.

9. Jacqueline Peterson and Jennifer S. H. Brown, *The New Peoples: Being and Becoming Métis in North America* (Winnipeg: Univ. of Manitoba Press, 1985), p. 3.

10. Brandon, *Last Americans,* p. 21.

11. William T. Hagan, *The Indian in American History,* (Baltimore: Waverly Press, 1968).

12. Paxson, "Disappearance," p. 107.

13. Brandon, *Last Americans,* p. 19.

14. William Brandon, *New Worlds for Old: Reports from the New World and their Effect on the Development of Social Thought in Europe, 1500–1800* (Athens: Ohio Univ. Press, 1986), p. 164.

15. Josephy, *Indian Heritage,* p. 31.

16. Brandon, *Last Americans,* p. 10.

17. Hagan, *Indian in American History,* p. 6.

18. For some idea of the Osage effect, see Foreman, *Indians and Pioneers,* p. 9; and Paxson, "Disappearance," pp. 108, 111.

19. Gibson, *American Indian,* pp. 587–588.

20. Brandon, *Last Americans,* pp. 3–4.

21. Josephy, *Indian Heritage,* p. 32.

22. Ibid.

23. Note that Indians never claimed to own the land. They controlled its use by humans but this is different from the Western concept of owning the land. The Indian viewpoint upon first meeting the white man was that owning the land was a terrible shocking conceit of man.

24. R. Douglas Hurt, *Indian Agriculture in America: Prehistory to the Present* (Lawrence: Univ. Press of Kansas, 1987), p. 229.

25. Linn, "Corn," p. 59.

26. Edwin F. Walker, *World Crops Derived from the Indians,* 1953, 17: 2.

27. Hurt, *Indian Agriculture,* pp. 228–229.

28. Ibid., p. 24.

29. Ibid., p. 226.

30. Walker, *World.*

31. Robert E. Rhoades, "The Incredible Potato," *National Geographic,* May 1982, pp. 668, 676.

32. Noel D. Vietmeyer, "America's Forgotten Crops," *National Geographic,* May 1981, pp. 704–708.

33. Patrick J. Munson, ed., *Experiments and Observations of Aboriginal Wild Plant Utilization in Eastern North America,* Prehistory Research Series (Indianapolis: Indiana Historical Society, 1984), 6: 459–462.

34. Jack Weatherford, *Indian Givers: How the Indians of the Americas Transformed the World* (New York: Crown Publishers, 1988), p. 76.

35. Imre Sutton, ed., *Irredeemable America: The Indians' Estate and Land Claims,* Native American Studies (Univ. of New Mexico, 1985), pp. 4–5.

36. Webb, *Great Frontier,* p. 335.

37. Webb, *Great Frontier,* p. 337.

38. Wilson, *Underground,* p. 120.

39. Webb, *Great Frontier,* p. 357.

40. Webb, *Great Frontier,* p. 373.

41. Josephy, *Indian Heritage,* p. 32.

42. Brandon, *Last Americans,* p. 7.

43. Lewis H. Morgan, *Systems of Consanguinity and Affinity of the Human Family* (Oosterhout: Anthropological Publ., 1970), pp. 292–382.

44. Brandon, *Last Americans,* p. 5.

45. Grinde, *Founding of the American Nation,* p. IX.

46. Josephy, *Indian Heritage,* p. 35.

47. Brandon, *New Worlds,* pp. 110–111.

48. Gibson, *American Indian,* p. 581.

49. Grinde, *Founding of the American Nation,* p. 130.

50. Ibid., pp. 60–61.

51. Howard M. Bahr, Bruce A. Chadurich, and Robert C. Day, eds., *Native Americans Today: Sociological Perspectives* (New York: Harper & Row, 1972), p. 67.

52. Annual Report, Commissioner of Indian Affairs, 1961.

53. Originally the Osages used small tortoise shells with panther (mountain lion) teeth in them where bells are used today. Trade with Euro-Americans brought the metal bells of today, but the symbolism of the turtle and panther remains (the voices of the turtle and panther are still heard).

54. Hagan, *Indian in American History,* p. 11.

55. Brandon, *New Worlds,* p. 76.

56. Harold E. Fey and D'Arcy McNickle, *Indians and other Americans: Two Ways of Life Meet* (New York: Harper & Brothers, 1959), p. 13.

57. José Ortega Y Gasset, *Concord and Liberty* (New York: W. W. Norton, 1963), p. 47.

58. Labadie, *Osage Case,* pp. 39–41.

59. Bloodworth, *Osage People,* p. 34.

60. Thomas M. Brewer, *Maj. Gen. Clarence Tinker: A Photographic Tribute* (Oklahoma City: Office of History), Oklahoma City Air Logistics Center, Tinker Air Force Base, 1986.

61. Alexis de Tocqueville, *Democracy in America* (New York: Vintage Books, 1954), vol. 1, p. 359n.

62. Peterson, *New Peoples,* p. 4.

63. Many Osage parents do not report their children to the agency. Hence, the total Osage population is regularly under-reported. The most reliable estimates cluster around a population of 18,000 in 2002.

64. Committee on Interior and Insular Affairs, Subcommittee on Indian Affairs, *Hearing on H. Con. Res. 108,* 83rd Cong., 1st sess., 22 July 1953, pp. 28–29.

65. Donald L. Parman, "The Indian and the Civilian Conservation Corps," *Pacific Historical Review,* 40 (February 1971): 45.

66. Sutton, *Irredeemable,* p. 35.

67. John L. Taylor, House Committee on Interior and Insular Affairs, *Present Relations of the Federal Government to the American Indian,* 84th Cong., 2nd sess., January 1958, pp. 44–65.

68. Paul M. Niebell to D. E. Martin, March 6, 1970. This is the first announcement the Council had confirming the claims settlement compromise.

69. Kenneth R. Philp, "Termination: A Legacy of the Indian New Deal," *Western Historical Quarterly,* 14 (April 1983): 180.

70. Osage Indian, pp. 77–81.

71. Bahr, Chadurich, and Day, *Native Americans,* p. 68.

72. Labadie, *Osage Case,* pp. 15–16.

73. Osage Indian, pp. 17–18.

74. Henry F. Dobyns, *Native American Historical Demography: A Critical Bibliography* (Bloomington: Indiana Univ. Press, 1976), p. 1.

75. Tyler, *History,* p. 235.

76. Gibson, *American Indian,* p. 587.

77. Nancy Shoemaker, "Urban Indians and Ethnic Choices: American Indian Organizations in Minneapolis, 1920–1950," *Western Historical Quarterly,* 19 (November 1988): 446.

78. William T. Hagan, "Full Blood, Mixed Blood, Generic, and Ersatz, The Problem of Indian Identity," *Arizona and the West* 27 (Winter 1985): 326.

79. Maud Blackbird Cheshewalla, our dear friend and resource person, was murdered with her husband in February of 1989.

80. Senate Committee on Indian Affairs, Subcommittee of the Committee on Indian Affairs, *Survey of Conditions of the Indians in the United States: Hearings on S. Res. 79,* 78th. Cong., 1st. Sess., Part 41, 2 and 3 August 1943, pp. 23026–23027.

Bibliography

BOOKS

Agogino, George A. "Man's Antiquity in the Western Hemisphere." In *The American Indian Reader,* edited by Jeannette Henry. Series in Educational Perspectives 1. San Francisco: Indian Historian Press, 1972.

Agogino, George A., and Michael L. Kunz, "The Paleo Indians: Fact and Theory of Early Migrations to the New World." In *The American Indian Reader,* edited by Jeanette Henry. Series in Educational Perspectives 1. San Francisco: Indian Historian Press, 1972.

Andreas, A. T. *History of the State of Kansas.* 1883. Reprint, Chicago: A. T. Andreas, 1976.

Andrist, Ralph K. *The Long Death: The Last Days of the Plains Indians.* New York: Macmillan, 1964.

Bahr, Howard M., Bruce A. Chadurich, and Robert C. Day, eds. *Native Americans Today: Sociological Perspectives.* New York: Harper & Row, 1972.

Bailey, Thomas A. *A Diplomatic History of the American People.* New York: F. S. Crofts and Co., 1947.

Baird, W. David. *The Osage People.* Phoenix: Indian Tribal Series, 1972.

Barney, Ralph A. *Laws Relating to Osage Tribe of Indians.* Pawhuska, Okla.: Osage Printery, 1929.

Baughman, Robert W. *Kansas Post Offices.* Topeka: Kansas State Historical Society, 1961.

Beals, Ralph L., and Harry Hoijer. *An Introduction to Anthropology.* New York: Macmillan, 1965.

Bearss, Edwin C., and A.[rrell] M.[organ] Gibson. *Fort Smith: Little Gibraltar on the Arkansas.* Norman: Univ. of Oklahoma Press, 1969.

Black, Henry Campbell. *Black's Law Dictionary.* St. Paul: West Publishing, 1951.

Bradley, John Hodgdon. *World Geography.* Boston: Ginn and Company, 1951.

Brandon, William. *The Last Americans.* New York: McGraw-Hill, 1974.

———. *New Worlds for Old: Reports from the New World and Their Effect on the Development of Social Thought in Europe, 1500–1800.* Athens: Ohio Univ. Press, 1986.

Burns, Louis Francis. "Jim Town: Elgin, Kansas." *The History of Chautauqua County, Kansas.* Dallas: Curtis Media, 1987.

——, ed. *The Osage Annuity Rolls of 1878.* 6 vols. Fallbrook, Calif.: Ciga Press, 1980–81.

——. *Osage Indian Bands and Clans.* Fallbrook, Calif.: Ciga Press, 1984.

——. *Osage Indian Customs and Myths.* Fallbrook, Calif.: Ciga Press, 1984.

——, ed. *Osage Mission Baptisms, Marriages, and Interments, 1820–1886.* Fallbrook, Calif.: Ciga Press, 1986.

——, ed. *Treaties Constitution and Laws of the Osage Nation.* 1895. Reprint, Santa Ana: Private Printing, 1967, reprint of W. S. Fitzpatrick, 1895.

——. *Turn of the Wheel.* San Marcos, Calif.: A. M. Graphics, 1980.

Carstens, Kenneth C., and Patty Jo Watson. *Of Caves and Shell Mounds.* Tuscaloosa: Univ. of Alabama Press, 1996.

Catlin, George. *Letters, Notes on Manners, Customs, and Conditions of the North American Indians.* Vol. 2. New York: Dover Publications, 1973.

Cervantes, Miguel de. *Don Quixote de la Mancha.* Edited by Robert M. Hutchins. *Great Books of the Western World,* vol. 29. Chicago: Encyclopedia Britannica, 1952.

Chapman, Carl H. "The Indomitable Osage in Spanish Illinois, 1763–1804." In *The Spanish in the Mississippi Valley, 1762–1804,* edited by John Francis McDermott. Chicago: Univ. of Illinois Press, 1974.

——. *The Origin of the Osage Indian Tribe.* New York: Garland, 1974.

Chitwood, Oliver Perry, and Frank Lawrence Owsley. *A Short History of the American People.* New York: D. Van Nostrand and Company, 1946.

Cranor, Ruby. *Caney Valley Ghost Towns and Settlements.* Bartlesville, Okla.: Blackman, 1985.

Custer, George A. *My Life on the Plains.* Edited by M. M. Quaife. Chicago: Lakeside Press, 1952.

Cutler, Jervis. *A Topographical Description of the State of Ohio, Indiana Territory, and Louisiana.* 1812. Reprint, New York: Garland, 1975.

Diaz-Granados, Carol, and James R. Duncan. *The Petroglyphs and Petrographs of Missouri.* Tuscaloosa: Univ. of Alabama Press, 2000.

Dick, Everett. *Vanguards of the Frontier.* Lincoln: Univ. of Nebraska Press, 1941.

Din, Gilbert C., and Abraham P. Nasatir. *The Imperial Osages.* Norman: Univ. of Oklahoma Press, 1983.

Dobyns, Henry F. *Native American Historical Demography: A Critical Bibliography.* Bloomington: Indiana Univ. Press, 1976.

Fey, Harold E., and D'Arcy McNickle. *Indians and Other Americans: Two Ways of Life Meet.* New York: Harper & Brothers, 1959.

Finney, Frank F. *Wahshouwahgaley, Pioneer Days with the Osage Indians West of '96.* Private Printing, 1972.

Fitzgerald, Mary Paul, Sister. *Beacon on the Plain.* 1939. Reprint, St. Paul: Osage Mission Historical Society, 1985.

Foreman, Grant. *Advancing the Frontier, 1830–1860.* Norman: Univ. of Oklahoma Press, 1961.

———. *Indians and Pioneers.* Norman: Univ. of Oklahoma Press, 1967.

Gates, Paul Wallace. *Fifty Million Acres: Conflicts over Kansas Land Policy, 1854–1890.* New York: Atherton Press, 1966.

Gibson, Arrell Morgan. *The American Indian: Prehistory to the Present.* Lexington, Mass.: Heath and Co., 1980.

———, ed. *Between Two Worlds: The Survival of Twentieth Century Indians.* Oklahoma Historical Society, 1986.

Graves, W. W. *The Broken Treaty.* St. Paul: Journal Publisher, 1935.

———. *The First Protestant Osage Missions 1820–1837.* Oswego, Kans.: Carpenter Press, 1949.

———. *History of Neosho County.* Vol. 1. 1949. Reprint, Osage Mission Historical Society, 1986.

———. *Life and Letters of Father Ponziglione.* St. Paul, Kans.: W. W. Graves, 1916.

———. 1916 citing. *Osage Mission Journal,* April, 1884.

Grinde, Donald A., Jr. *The Iroquois and the Founding of the American Nation.* San Francisco: Indian Historian Press, 1977.

Hagan, William T. *The Indian in American History.* American Historical Association, 1963. Reprint, Baltimore: Waverly Press, 1968.

Hassrick, Royal B. *The George Catlin Book of American Indians.* New York: Promontory Press, 1977.

The History of Chauauqua County, Kansas. Dallas: Curtis Media, 1987.

Holder, Preston. *The Hoe and the Horse on the Plains.* Lincoln: Univ. of Nebraska Press, 1970.

Horsman, Reginald. "American Indian Policy and the Origins of Manifest Destiny." In *The Indian in American History,* edited by Francis Paul Prucha. New York: Holt, Rinehart and Winston, 1971.

Houck, Louis. *A History of Missouri.* New York: Arno Press and the *New York Times,* reprint 1971.

Huntington, Ellsworth. *Civilization and Climate.* New Haven: Yale Univ. Press, 1924.

———. *Mainsprings of Civilization.* New York: Mentor Books, 1945.

———. *Principles of Human Geography.* New York: John Wiley and Sons, 1947.

———. "The Red Man's Continent." In *The Chronicles of America Series,* edited by Allen Johnson. New Haven: Yale Univ. Press, 1919.

Hurt, R. Douglas. *Indian Agriculture in America: Prehistory to the Present.* Lawrence: Univ. Press of Kansas, 1987.

Ingenthron, Elmo. *Indians of the Ozark Plateau.* Point Lookout, Mo.: School of the Ozarks Press, 1981.

Irving, Washington. *A Tour on the Prairies.* Norman: Univ. of Oklahoma Press, 1962.

Isely, Bliss, and W. M. Richards. *Four Centuries in Kansas.* Topeka: State of Kansas, 1944.

Jackson, Donald, ed. *Letters of the Lewis and Clark Expedition with Related Documents, 1783–1854.* 2nd. ed. 2 vols. Chicago: Univ. of Illinois Press, 1978.

Jennings, Francis. *The Invasion of America.* New York: W. W. Norton, 1975.

Josephy, Alvin M., Jr. *The Indian Heritage of America.* New York: Alfred A. Knopf, 1968.

Kappler, Charles J. *Indian Affairs: Laws and Treaties.* 2 vols. Washington: GPO, 1904.

Lamb, Arthur H. *Tragedies of the Osage Hills.* Pawhuska, Okla.: Osage Printery, ca. 1930.

Loomis, Noel M., and Abraham P. Nasatir. *Pedro Vial and the Roads to Santa Fe.* Norman: Univ. of Oklahoma Press, 1967.

Mathews, J. Joseph. *Life and Death of an Oilman.* Norman: Univ. of Oklahoma Press, 1985.

——. *The Osages: Children of the Middle Waters.* Norman: Univ. of Oklahoma Press, 1961.

——. *Talking to the Moon.* Chicago: Univ. of Chicago Press, 1945.

——. *Wah'Kon-Tah.* Norman: Univ. of Oklahoma Press, 1932.

McDermott, John Francis, ed. *Tixier's Travels on the Osage Prairies.* Norman: Univ. of Oklahoma Press, 1968.

——, ed. *A Tour on the Prairies,* by Washington Irving. Norman: Univ. of Oklahoma Press, 1962.

McNickle D'Arcy. "American Indians Who Never Were." In *The American Indian Reader,* edited by Jeannette Henry. Series in Educational Perspectives 1. San Francisco: Indian Historian Press, 1972.

Miller, William J. *An Introduction to Physical Geology.* New York: D. Van Nostrand, 1956.

Miner, H. Craig, and William E. Unrau. *The End of Indian Kansas.* Lawrence: Regents Press of Kansas, 1978.

Montesquieu, Charles de. "The Spirit of Laws." In *Great Books of the Western World,* edited by R. M. Hutchins. Vol. 38. Chicago: Encyclopedia Britannica, 1952.

Morgan, Lewis H. *Systems of Consanguinity and Affinity of the Human Family.* Oosterhout: Anthropological Publ., 1970.

Morris, John W., Charles R. Goins, and Edwin C. McReynolds. *Historical Atlas of Oklahoma.* 3rd ed. Norman: Univ. of Oklahoma Press, 1986.

Munson, Patrick J., ed. *Experiments and Observations of Aboriginal Wild Plant Utilization in Eastern North America.* Indianapolis: Indiana Historical Society, 1984, 6: 459–462.

Nasatir, Abraham P. *Before Lewis and Clark.* 2 vols. St. Louis: St. Louis Historical Documents Foundation, 1952 (author's proof copy).

——. *Borderland in Retreat.* Albuquerque: Univ. of New Mexico, 1976.

Newman, Tillie Karns. *The Black Dog Trail.* Boston: Christopher Publishing House, 1957.

Nichols, David A. *Lincoln and the Indians: Civil War Policies and Politics.* Columbia: Univ. of Missouri Press, 1978.

Nuttall, Thomas. *A Journal of Travels into Arkansas Territory During the Year 1819.* Edited by Savoie Lottenville. Norman: Univ. of Oklahoma Press, 1980.

Ortega y Gasset, José. *Concord and Liberty.* New York: W. W. Norton, 1963.

——. *Man and Crisis.* New York: W. W. Norton, 1962.

——. *Meditations on Quixote.* Edited by Julián Marías. New York: W. W. Norton, 1963.

Osage County Profiles. Oklahoma City: Barc and Curtis, 1978.

Osgood, Ernest Staples, ed. *The Field Notes of Captain William Clark, 1803–1805.* New Haven: Yale Univ. Press, 1964.

Peterson, Jacqueline, and Jennifer S. H. Brown. *The New Peoples: Being and Becoming Métis in North America.* Winnipeg: Univ. of Manitoba Press, 1985.

Prentis, Noble L. *A History of Kansas.* Topeka: Caroline Prentis, 1909.

Prucha, Francis Paul, ed. *Documents of United States Indian Policy.* Lincoln: Univ. of Nebraska Press, 1975.

Ruth, Kent, et al. *Oklahoma: A Guide to the Sooner State.* Norman: Univ. of Oklahoma Press, 1958.

Sanders, J. G. *Who's Who Among Oklahoma Indians.* Oklahoma City: Travé Company, 1928.

Spaulding, George F., ed. "Count Albert-Alexandre de Pourtalés." In *On the Western Tour with Washington Irving.* Norman: Univ. of Oklahoma Press, 1968.

Starr, Isidore, Lewis Paul Todd, and Merle Curti, eds. *Living American Documents.* New York: Harcourt, Brace & World, 1961.

Sutton, Imre, ed. *Irredeemable America: The Indian Estate and Land Claims.* Native American Studies. Albuquerque: Univ. of New Mexico, 1985.

Terrell, John T. *American Indian Almanac.* New York: World, 1971.

——. *Sioux Trail.* New York: McGraw-Hill, 1974.

Thompson, J. Eric S. *Maya Archaeologist.* Norman: Univ. of Oklahoma Press, 1971.

Tinker, Sylvester J. *Authentic Osage Indian Roll Book.* Pawhuska, Okla.: Sam McClain, 1957.

Tocqueville, Alexis de. *Democracy in America.* Vol. 1. New York: Vintage Books, 1954.

Vanderwerth, W. C., ed. *Indian Oratory.* Norman: Univ. of Oklahoma Press, 1979.

Vestal, Stanley. *The Missouri.* Lincoln: Univ. of Nebraska Press, 1967.

Wallis, Michael. *Oil Man.* New York: Doubleday, 1988.

Weatherford, Jack. *Indian Givers: How the Indians of the Americas Transformed the World.* New York: Crown, 1988.

Webb, Walter Prescott. *The Great Frontier.* Boston: Houghton Mifflin, 1952.

Wilson, Terry P. *The Underground Reservation: Osage Oil.* Lincoln: Univ. of Nebraska Press, 1985.

Worcester, Philip G. *A Textbook of Geomorphology.* New York: D. Van Nostrand, 1949.

Yost, Nellie Snyder. *Medicine Lodge: The Story of a Kansas Frontier Town.* Chicago: Swallow Press, 1970.

PERIODICAL ARTICLES

Allen, Peter S. Review of *The Ancient Americans. Archaeology* 42 (January/February, 1989): 94–95.

Bearss, Edwin C. "In Quest of Peace on the Indian Border: The Establishment of Fort Smith." *Arkansas Historical Quarterly* 23 (Summer 1964).

Berry, Brewton, and Carl Chapman. "An Oneota Site in Missouri." *American Antiquity* 7 (March 1942): 1–11.

Berry Brewton, Carl Chapman, and John Mack. "Archaeological Remains of the Osage." *American Antiquity* 10 (July 1944): 1–11.

Bieder, Robert E. "Scientific Attitudes Toward Indian Mixed-Bloods in Early Nineteenth Century America." *Journal of Ethnic Studies* 8 (Summer 1980).

Brandon, William. "American Indians and History." *American West* 2 (Spring 1965).

Burns, Louis Francis. "Osage History." *Osage Nation News,* February–April, 1986.

Burrill, Robert M. "The Establishment of Ranching on the Osage Reservation." *Geographic Review* 62 (October 1972).

Chapman, Berlin B. "Removal of the Osages from Kansas." *Kansas Historical Quarterly* 7 (August/November 1938).

Dodge City Times, 25 January 1879.

Englund, Donald R. "Indians, Intruders, and the Federal Government." *Journal of the West* 13 (April 1974).

Franklin, Benjamin. "Remarks Concerning the Indians of North America." *Real West,* January 1975.

Gabler, Ina. "Lovely's Purchase and Lovely County." *Arkansas Historical Quarterly* 19 (Spring 1960).

Hagan, William T. "Full Blood, Mixed Blood, Generic, and Ersatz: The Problem of Indian Identity." *Arizona and the West* 27 (Winter 1985).

Hansen, Klaus J. "The Millennium, the West, and Race in the Antebellum American Mind." *Western Historical Quarterly* 3 (October 1972).

Hrdlicka, Ales. "The Bearing of Physical Anthropology on the Problems Under Consideration: The Problems of the Unity or Plurality and the Probable Place of Origin of the American Aborigines." *American Anthropologist* 14, n.s. (January–March 1912).

Isern, Thomas D. "Farmers, Ranchers, and Stockmen of the Flint Hills." *Western Historical Quarterly* 16 (July 1985).

Linn, Alan. "Corn, the New World's Secret Weapon and the Builder of its Civilizations." *Smithsonian,* August 1973.

MacNeish, Richard S. "The Origin of New World Civilization." *Scientific American,* November 1964.

Montagu, M. F. Ashley, "An Indian Tradition Relating to the Mastodon." *American Anthropoligist* 46, n.s. (October–December, 1944): 568–591.

Morris, Wayne. "Traders and Factories on the Arkansas Frontier, 1805–1822." *Arkansas Historical Quarterly* 28 (Spring 1969).

"The Native American: A Changing Perspective." *American West,* July 1973.

Parman, Donald L. "The Indian and the Civilian Conservation Corps." *Pacific Historical Review* 40 (February 1971).

Philp, Kenneth R. "Termination: A Legacy of the Indian New Deal." *Western Historical Quarterly* 14 (April 1983).

Rhoades, Robert E. "The Incredible Potato." *National Geographic,* May 1982.

Rohrer, John H. "The Test Intelligence of Osage Indians." *Journal of Social Psychology* 16 (August 1942).

Ryan, Harold W., ed. "Jacob Bright's Journal of a Trip to the Osage Indians." *Journal of Southern History* 15 (November 1949).

Shepherd, William G. "Lo the Rich Indian." *Harper's Magazine,* November 1920.

Shoemaker, Nancy. "Urban Indians and Ethnic Choices: American Indian Organizations in Minneapolis, 1920–1950." *Western Historical Quarterly* 19 (November 1988).

"Silver Lake Early Trade Center." *Oklahoma Rural News,* October, 1978.

Tate, Michael L. "From Scout to Doughboy: The National Debate over Integrating American Indians into the Military, 1891–1918." *Western Historical Quarterly* 17 (October 1986).

Tinker, George "Edward," and C. J. Phillips, eds. "Massacre of Confederate Officers by Osages." *Osage Magazine,* February 1910.

Vietmeyer, Noel D. "America's Forgotten Crops." *National Geographic,* May 1981.

Washburn, Wilcomb. "The Writing of American History: A Status Report." *Pacific Historical Review* 40 (August 1971).

Wheat, Joe Ben. "A Paleo-Indian Bison Kill." *Scientific American,* January 1967.

Zoltvany, Yves F. "New France and the West, 1701–1713." *Canadian Historical Review* 46 (December 1965): 317–319.

PUBLICATIONS OF LEARNED ORGANIZATIONS

Abel, Annie Heloise. "The History of Events Resulting in Indian Consolidation West of the Mississippi River." *Annual Report of the American Historical Association for 1906.* Vol. 1.

———. "Indian Reservations in Kansas and the Extinguishment of their Title." *Collections,* Kansas State Historical Society, 1903–1904.

———. "Proposals for an Indian State. 1778–1878." *Annual Report of the American Historical Association for 1907.* Vol. 1.

Ashcraft, Allan C. "Confederate Indian Department Conditions in August, 1864." *Chronicles of Oklahoma* 41 (Autumn 1963).

Bartles, William Lewis. "Massacre of Confederates by Osage Indians in 1863." *Transactions of the Kansas State Historical Society, 1903–1904.* Vol. 8.

Burchardt, "Osage Oil." *Chronicles of Oklahoma* 41 (Fall 1963).

Busby, Orel, "Buffalo Valley: An Osage Hunting Ground." *Chronicles of Oklahoma* 40 (Spring 1962).

Chapman, Berlin B. "Dissolution of the Osage Reservation." *Chronicles of Oklahoma* 20 (September 1942).

Chappell, Philip Edward. "River Navigation: A History of the Missouri River." *Transactions of the Kansas State Historical Society, 1905–1906.* Vol. 9.

Christianson, James R. "The Kansas-Osage Border War of 1874." *Chronicles of Oklahoma* 63 (Fall 1985).

Connelley, William E. "The Treaty Held at Medicine Lodge." *Collections,* Kansas State Historical Society, 1926–1928. Vol. 17.

Cory, C. E. "The Osage Ceded Lands." *Transactions of the Kansas State Historical Society, 1903–1904.* Vol. 8.

Douglas, Richard L. "History of Manufactures in Kansas." *Collections,* Kansas State Historical Society, 1909–1910.

Finney, Frank F. "The Osages and their Agency During the Term of Isaac T. Gibson Quaker Agent." *Chronicles of Oklahoma* 36 (Winter 1958–59).

Finney, Frank F., Sr. "Progress in the Civilization of the Osage and Their Government." *Chronicles of Oklahoma* 40 (Spring 1962).

Hoig, Stan. "War for Survival." *Chronicles of Oklahoma* 62 (Fall 1984).

Kinnaird, Lawrence, ed. "Spain in the Mississippi Valley. 1763–1794." In three parts, vols. 2, 3, and 4. *Annual Report of the American Historical Association for 1945.*

La Flesche, Francis. *A Dictionary of the Osage Language.* Bureau of American Ethnology. Bulletin 109.

Lockhart, Donald. "Early History of Elk Falls." *Collections,* Kansas State Historical Society, 1928.

Mallery, Garrick. "Pictographs of the North American Indians." *Fourth Annual Report.* Smithsonian Institution. Bureau of American Ethnology, 1882–1883.

Martin, George W. "The Boundary Lines of Kansas." *Collections,* Kansas State Historical Society, 1909–1910.

McGee, W. J. "The Siouan Indians: A Preliminary Sketch." citing J. Owen Dorsey, *15th Annual Report.* Bureau of American Ethnology. Smithsonian Institution.

Mead, James R. "The Little Arkansas." *Transactions of the Kansas State Historical Society, 1907–1908,* edited by George W. Martin. Vol. 10.

———. "The Wichita Indians in Kansas." *Transactions of the Kansas State Historical Society, 1903–1904.* Vol. 8.

Mooney, James. "Calendar History of the Kiowa Indians," *Seventeenth Annual Report.* Bureau of American Ethnology. Smithsonian, 1895–1896.

Morrison, T. F. "The Osage Treaty of 1865." *Collections,* Kansas State Historical Society, 1926–1928. Vol. 17.

"Official Kansas Roster: United States Indian Agencies Affecting Kansas." *Collections,* Kansas State Historical Society, 1923–1925.

Paxson, Frederic L. "The Pacific Railroad and the Disappearance of the Frontier in America." *Annual Report of the American Historical Association, 1907.* Vol. 1.

Pease, T. C., ed. "The French Foundations, 1680–1693." *Collections,* Illinois State Historical Library, French Series. Vol. 1.

Royce, C. C., and C. Thomas. "Indian Land Policy of the United States." *18th Annual Report.* Bureau of American Ethnology. Smithsonian, 1896–97.

Semple, Ellen Churchill. "Geographical Location as a Factor in History." *Annual Report of the American Historical Association for 1907.*

Sibley, George C. "Extracts from the Diary of Major Sibley." *Chronicles of Oklahoma* 5 (June 1927).

Swanton, John R. *The Indian Tribes of North America.* Bureau of American Ethnology. Bulletin 145, 1952.

Tracey, Valerie. "The Indian in Transition: The Neosho Agency 1850–1861." *Chronicles of Oklahoma* 48 (Summer 1970).

Walker, Edwin F. *World Crops Derived from the Indians.* 1953. Vol. 17 (Los Angeles: Southwest Museum Leaflets).

Wedel, Waldo R. *An Introduction to Kansas Archeology.* Smithsonian Institution. Bureau of American Ethnology. Bulletin 174, 1959.
———. "Prehistory and the Missouri Valley Development Program." *Smithsonian Miscellaneous Collections.* Vol. 3. 1948.

UNPUBLISHED MATERIALS

Brief and Argument on Right of Osage Allottees and Purchasers—Mineral Trust, Tulsa, Osage Oil and Gas Lessees Association, December, 1920.
Burns, Louis Francis, ed. "The Elgin Brand Register, 1887–1907." Kansas State Historical Society, Oklahoma City, 1981.
Drew, Mary Lou. Letter. 2 July 1985.
Graves, W. W. 1916, citing *Sedan* [Kansas] *Times-Star,* 23 April 1896.
Justification Brief and Argument of the Osage Tribal Council for Extension of the Osage Mineral Trust Period, November 18, 1963, Exhibit III.
Labadie, George V. *Osage Case for Federal Supervision.* 15 February 1954 (Tribal Council Information Booklet).
Leahy, T. J. Brief and Argument on Right of Osage Allotees and Purchasers-Mineral Trust. Tulsa, Osage Oil and Gas Lessees Association, December, 1920.
Memorandum from Scott Keep to Field Solicitor, Pawhuska, dated September 27, 1979, Copy to Regional Solicitor, Tulsa.
Niebell, Paul M. Letter to D. E. Martin. 6 March 1970.
Osage Council Information Letter. Development of the Osage Reservation and Summary of Special Laws Governing the Osage Tribe.
Parsons, David. "The Removal of the Osages from Kansas." Ph.D. diss., Univ. of Oklahoma, 1940.
Proposal of Fifteen Oil Companies to Council, 5 August 1947, Waterflood.
Statement and Argument by the Osage Tribal Council on Behalf of the Osage Tribe of Indians in Support of Legislation to Extend the Osage Mineral Trust, ca. 1931.
Statement and Argument by the Osage Tribal Council on Behalf of the Osage Tribe of Indians in Support of Legislation to Extend the Osage Mineral Trust [first renewal].
Statement of Facts, In the Matter of Claim of Kingsbery and Holmsley for Relief, On Account of the Wrongful Appropriation by the Osage Nation of Indians of 238 Head of Cattle Belonging to said Kingsbery and Holmsley, in the Years 1874–5.
Thorne, Tanis. "People of the River: Mixed-Blood Families on the Lower Missouri." Ph.D. diss., Univ. of California, 1987.

GOVERNMENT PUBLICATIONS AND REPORTS

Annual Report, Commissioner of Indian Affairs, 1856.
Annual Report, Commissioner of Indian Affairs, 1873.
Annual Report, Commissioner of Indian Affairs, 1875.
Annual Report, Commissioner of Indian Affairs, 1876.
Annual Report, Commissioner of Indian Affairs, 1884.

Annual Report, Commissioner of Indian Affairs, 1886.

Annual Report, Commissioner of Indian Affairs, 1888.

Annual Report, Commissioner of Indian Affairs, 1890.

Annual Report, Commissioner of Indian Affairs, 1891.

Annual Report, Commissioner of Indian Affairs, 1895.

Annual Report, Commissioner of Indian Affairs, 1908.

Annual Report, Commissioner of Indian Affairs, 1921.

Annual Report, Commissioner of Indian Affairs, 1924.

Annual Report, Commissioner of Indian Affairs, 1961.

Annual Report, Department of the Interior, Indian Affairs, 1898.

Annual Report, Department of the Interior, Indian Affairs, Vol. 1, 1899.

Annual Report, Department of the Interior, Indian Affairs, Part 1, 1900.

Annual Reports, Department of the Interior, Indian Affairs, Vol. 1, 1901.

Annual Report, Department of the Interior, Indian Affairs, Part 1, 1904.

Annual Report, Department of the Interior, Indian Affairs, Part 1, 1909.

Annual Report, Department of the Interior, Indian Affairs, 1906.

Brewer, Thomas M. "Maj. Gen. Clarence L. Tinker: A Photographic Tribute." Oklahoma City: Office of History, Oklahoma City Air Logistics Center, Tinker Air Force Base, 1986.

Bureau of Indian Affairs, *Indians of the Central Plains.* N.d.

Bureau of Indian Affairs. *The Osage People and Their Trust Property, a Field Report of the Bureau of Indian Affairs.* Field Report prepared by Jessie Bloodworth. Osage Agency, Anadarko Area Office, 30 April 1953.

Federal Archives and Records Center, Fort Worth, Texas. Region 7. Records of the Osage Agency. Bureau of Indian Affairs (Record Group 75). Records 195–197.

Gibson, Isaac T., "To Enoch Hoag, September, 1873," Report of the Commissioner, 1873.

Miles, Laban J. Annual Report, Commissioner of Indian Affairs, 1879.

——. Annual Report, Commissioner of Indian Affairs, 1880.

——. Annual Report, Commissioner of Indian Affairs, 1882.

——. Annual Report, Commissioner of Indian Affairs, 1884.

——. Annual Report, Commissioner of Indian Affairs, 1889.

——. Annual Report, Commissioner of Indian Affairs, 1890.

——. Annual Report, Commissioner of Indian Affairs, 1891.

Morgan, T. J., Fifty-Eighth Annual Report of the Commissioner of Indian Affairs, 1889.

Opening of Rolls, Senate Hearing on Joint Resolution No. 70, March 1908.

Report of the Commissioner of Indian Affairs, 1856, Letters No. 44 and 45.

Tyler, Lyman S. *A History of Indian Policy.* United States Department of the Interior. Bureau of Indian Affairs. Washington, D.C.: GPO, 1973.

United States. Department of the Interior. Bureau of Indian Affairs. *American Indians and the Federal Government.* N.d.

U.S. House Committee on Interior and Insular Affairs, Subcommittee on Indian Affairs, *Hearing on H. Con. Res. 108,* 83rd Cong., 1st sess., 22 July 1953, p. 15.

U.S. House Committee on Interior and Insular Affairs. *Present Relations of the Federal Government to the American Indian: Hearings,* 84th Cong., 2nd sess., January 1958.

U.S. Senate Committee on Interior and Insular Affairs, Senate Subcommittee, *Osage Indian Tribe of Oklahoma: Hearing on H. Con. Res. 108,* Serial No. 7, 83rd. Cong., 1st sess., 22 July 1953.

U.S. Senate *Documents on Peyote,* S.R. 1399, Part 1, 8 February 1937.

U.S. Senate Committee on Indian Affairs, Subcommittee, *Survey of Conditions of the Indians in the United States: Hearings on S. Res. 79,* 78th. Cong., 1st. sess., 2 and 3 August 1943.

Index

abandonment clause, 404
Abel, Anna, 175, 296
abolition movement, 248
accommodation, 482
Acker Creek, 82
Adair, William P., 311, 351
adaptation, 205, 493
Adena, 4, 21
adoption, 89, 214, 245, 397
adornments, 209
Agency District, 352
agency grass leases, 387
agency reserves, 403
agents, 227
Agrarian Revolt, 461
Agrarian Revolution, 203
agriculture: cultures, concept of land
    ownership, 87; as Euro-American
    food procurement source, 92; Indian
    contributions to, 449, 450–53; as
    supplementary source of food for
    Osages, 91; teaching to Osages, 235–
    36. *See also* farming
Agriculture and Mechanical (A & M)
    College Land Grant Act, 292
Ah ke tah Tun ka (Big Soldier), 212–13
Ah ke ta Ki he ka (Chief Protectors), 18,
    40, 316
Ah ke ta Ki he ka (Soldier Chief), 337
Ah le Pa se Shu tsy (Red Hill Top), 81, 83
Alabaster Caverns State Park, 81, 83

Alaska Purchase Treaty of 1867, 306
Albany Plan of Union, 449, 461
Albuquerque School, 282
alcohol, 366
Algonquian, 16, 21
Allen, Oklahoma, 68
Allen County, Kansas, 52
allotment, concept of individual, 256
allotment, Osage, 481; acreage passed
    into the hands of white men or other
    Indians, 410; areas withheld from allot-
    ment, 403–5; domain in common,
    407–10; end of large-scale grass leas-
    ing, 388; forced, 320; and intruders,
    364; method of allotting, 405–7; and
    mixed-bloods, 326; opposition to, 38,
    400–402; presence of "locaters" on
    the reservation, 407; pressure for, 387,
    401; separation of surface ownership
    from mineral ownership, 400–401;
    and surplus lands, 388; survey issue,
    402–3
Allotment Act of 1906: amendment mak-
    ing all Osages U.S. citizens, 412–13;
    background for, 407–8; drafted by
    BIA-created Osage government, 394,
    405; minerals council, 408–10; setting
    aside of distinction based on parents'
    gender, 399; term of the mineral
    trust, 425
Allotment Commission, 406, 407

aloofness, 464–65, 490
Alva, Oklahoma, 81, 83
amaranth plant, 453
American Board of Commissioners for Foreign Missions, 219, 395–96
American dream, 468
American Historical Association, 25
American history, perception and reality of American Indian, 445–50
American Indian Peyote Church, 363, 496
American Indians. See Indians
American Revolution, 38, 113, 145, 459, 460
Americans. See Euro-Americans
Ancient Society (Morgan), 458
Andreas, A. T., 58
Andrist, Ralph K., 280
animal power, 468, 494
animals, 29
anise, 453
annuity payments, 165, 242, 359, 423; of 1873, 312; of 1878, 177, 346
Annuity Rolls: division between full-bloods and mixed-bloods over, 400; dropping a person from, 398; establishing, 395–400; greed of all persons associated with establishing, 398, 431; inaccuracy of, 242; qualifications, 398–400; residence qualification, 399
Apache of the Plains (Lipan Apache), 28, 34, 109, 110, 132
Appalachians, 149
apron dams, 475
Arapahoes, 277, 350
archaeology, 483
Archaic Age, 4, 9
Arickaree Creek, 278
Arikaree, 144
Arkansas bands: Bear and Panther clans among, 117, 125; Claremore and Black Dog clans among, 67; defense of their territory and rights, 191; move to lower reaches of Neosho-Grand river, 133; population, 243; removal to Kansas, 165; response to intruders, 157; splintering, 125; trouble with Cherokee "Old Settlers" over hunting rights, 154. See also Claremore bands

Arkansas City, 75
Arkansas Post, 45, 74, 106, 117–18, 127
Arkansas River, 5, 74, 77, 79, 80, 84
Arkansas River Mississippians, 10
Arkansas Treaty, 155, 156
Arkansas Valley, 28
Armstrong, William, 214
arrow stories, 20
Articles of Confederation, 149–51, 197, 201
assimilation, 205, 462, 463, 469, 474
Astorians, 325
Atchison, Topeka, and Santa Fe Railway Company, 404
Atlantic Tidewater region, 70
atonement, 262
automobile, and growing demand for petroleum and its products, 417
avocados, 452

Babson, Roger Ward, 29, 499n4
Bad Bird, 60
La Balafre (The Scar), 121
balance of trade, 94
Bancroft collection, 131
band chiefs, 390; empowered by consent of governed, 41; growth in power during Spanish period, 130; last leadership position to be abandoned, 487
band villages, 43
baptisms, 496
Barber County, Kansas, 62
barium, 29
Barnard-Chapman Ranch, 389
Barnsdall, T. N. (Big Heart), 352, 404, 421
Bartlesville, Oklahoma, 79, 84, 335
Bartram, William, 143
Bass Hole, 69

Battle of Arickaree Creek, 277–78

Battle of Claremore's Mound, 67, 119, 194–95

Battle of Duquesne, 101

Battle of New Orleans, 100

Battle of the Washita, 63, 276, 278–80

Bax, John J., 54, 205, 213, 235

Baxter Springs, Kansas, 49, 77, 369

Baxter Springs cattle trail, 77

Beacon on the Plain (Fitzgerald), 208, 253, 260

beans, 453

Bear clan, 41, 117, 125

Beaver, John, 279

Beaver Creek, 82

Beaver's Town, 56, 60

Beede, Cyrus, 357, 358

beef industry. *See* cattle industry

beek, 368

Belle Oiseau (Pretty Bird), 60–61, 64

Bend of the Missouri, 7, 48, 96

Bennett, Joseph, 346

Benton, Thomas Hart, 174

Berry, Brewton, 7

Beyett, Alexander, 305, 329, 337

Beyette, Pierre, 213

Bienvineu, Sam, 337

Big Bone River, 46, 47

Big Caney, 318

Big Cedar village, 51, 61, 66

Big Chief, 261

Big Creek, 60

Big Earth Maker, 66

Big Elk *(O pon Tun ka),* 13–14, 301

Big Foot. *See* Tracks Far Away

Bigheart, Wooster, 329

Big Heart (Barnsdall), 404, 421

Big Hill Creek, 61, 263

Big Hill Joe, 55

Big Hills (Big Bone Osages), 41; and Gray-Horse Fairfax, 352; and removal council, 318, 319; Upland Forest, 61; White Hair, 61

Big House of Mysteries, 15

Big Osages, 7; Claremore bands, 63; close relationship with Quapaw, 44; entrance to Missouri, 72; hunting camps, 62; Osage River, 116; Pomme de Terre River, 11

Big Shrine, 498n35

Big Track. *See* Tracks Far Away II

Big Wild Cat, 63, 278

Bird Creek, 77, 80, 235, 333, 336

Bird Creek District, 352

birth order names, 326

birthrate, 234, 244, 245, 327

Black Bear Creek, 84

Black Bear (Radiant Star) clan: arrow story, 20, 21; and Big House of Mysteries, 15; custodian of the four symbolic knives, 20; resistance of Spanish and Americans on Arkansas River, 17; version of genesis, 14

Blackburn, Oklahoma, 84

Black Dog band: en route camps, 69; hunting camps, 62; independence, 63–64; joining with Claremore bands, 51; Pomme de Terre band, 11; population, 243; saved from attack on Claremore, 67; settlement in Kansas, 46, 49

Black Dog Crossing, 69

Black Dog I (Dark/Black Eagle), 49, 51, 59, 61, 185; on Allotment Commission, 406; band chief, 500n20; chief counselor to Claremore, 64; death and burial, 67; isolation of people from epidemics, 67, 497n14; three great engineering feats, 66

Black Dog II, 51–52, 64, 261

Black Dog Museum, 49

Black Dog's Town (Tally's Town), 61

Black Dog the Younger, 319

Black Dog Trail (second Osage buffalo trail), 49, 66, 69, 71, 75, 77, 82

Black Gold, 417

black gold, 417

Black Kettle, 35, 63, 276

Black Kettle village, 279

black paint, 32, 34
Black Robes, 228
blacksmith and striker provisions, Treaty of 1839, 165
black widow spider, 13
blanket Indians, 357, 358, 359
blood quantum, 395, 396, 399, 483
blood ties, 40
blue, pale, 9
bluestem grass, 24, 28–29, 336, 369
Blue Stem Lake, 430
Bluff City, Kansas, 62
Bluff Creek, 62
bluff paint, 32
Bluff War, 32–33, 34, 89, 96, 426
Board of Commissioner's Missionaries, 348
Board of Indian Commissioners, 313
body painting, 209
Bohéme (vagabond-outcast), 105, 134
Boiling Springs State Park, Oklahoma, 83, 84
Bois de Arc Creek, 80, 82
Bonaparte, Napoleon, 132
bone marrow, 211
"boom hypothesis," 445–46
Boonby, Dodridge (Barnady), 329
botany, contributions to by Indians, 449
Boudinot, Cornelius, 311
Boudinot Mission, 58, 219, 220, 221
Boulanger, Oklahoma, 334
Boulanger-Bowring area, 352
Boulanger Cemetery, 334
boundary line, between Kansas and Oklahoma, 330–31
Bourbon County, Kansas, 75
Bourgmont, Entienne Veniard, 37, 96–97
bow, 19
bow and arrow, superior to firearms in Indian War, 126–27
Bowring, Oklahoma, 339
bow wood, 92
Bradbury, John: Travels, 54, 208
Braddock, Edward, 72, 99, 100, 121
Bradford, William, 446

Brandon, William, 446, 448
brass, 244
brass kettles, 216–17
breech clouts, 209
Briar's Town, 60, 279
Bridget, Sister, 230
Bright, Jacob, 201
British: active among the Northeastern nations, 182–83; colonialism, 94; Indian proposal, 181; means to impose their overlordship, 90; trapping in Old Northwest, 114
Bro Ki he ka/Brucaiguais (Chief to All), 107–8
Brown, Anna, 440, 441
Brown, John, 250
Bruyére, Fabry de la, 97
Bryce, James, 445
buckbrush, 453
Buck Creek, 77
buckeye, 453
Buckmaster, John, 333
buffalo: and bluestem grass, 29; killed by Osage in hunts between 1865 and 1870, 319; passing of, 361–63; southern herd, 24, 62
Buffalo Bull clan (Lo ha), 16, 116, 499n36
buffalo camps. See hunting camps
buffalo fat, 211
buffalo hunts: fall hunt of 1870–71, 345, 346; fall hunt of 1876, 358; long hunts of 1870–1875, 351–52; spring and fall, 43; spring hunt, prolonged, 318–19
buffalo short ribs, 211
buffalo trails: First, 32, 75; Fourth, 79; in Oklahoma, 78; Second (See Black Dog Trail); Third, 77
buffalo tribes, 506n18
buffer zone, between the Euro-Americans and Osages, 161, 163
Burbank pool, 420, 421, 422, 423–24
Burchardt, Bill, 206, 401, 439–40

Bureau of American Ethnology, 12

Bureau of Indian Affairs (BIA): as "big brother," 392–93; bypassing of Congressional land policies, 305; creation of, 198; creation of council to draft Allotment Act, 408; description of Osages, 205; forcing of Osages work for rations bought with their own money, 351; mismanagement of Indian estates, 481; outrage at economic independence of Osages, 359; political power, 258–59; preference given to Euro-Americans, 347; prevention of total extinction of the Osage people, 199; representation of own interest in the Osage town sites, 405; requirement of intruders on new reserve to pay a rental fee to the Osage people, 334; restrictive policies designed to make farmers out of Osage, 372–73; schools, 248; "slush fund," 282; suspension of Osage government, 393–95, 407; veto power of, 152; War Department attempts to reclaim, 331

burial practices, 496, 498n34

Burkhart, Ernest, 441, 442

Burlington Crossing, 75

Burrell, Robert M., 371, 385, 388

Bushnell, Horace, 274

Butler County, Kansas, 74

Butterfield Route (Ox-Bow Route), 248

Cabin Creek, 68

Caddoean Pawnee, 6

Caddos: breaking of 1785 peace agreement with Osages, 111; captured for slave trade, 98; expansion of other peoples into territory of, 28; food trade with Osage, 92; location to immediate west of the Osage Empire, 28; loss of territory to Osage, 32–33, 34; massacre at Claremore's Mound, 194–95; northern, 6; Osage defeat and demoralization of, 113, 115; Reconstruction Council, 267; as sedentary farmers, 28; sheltered by Osage during Civil War, 266; in Spiro Mound area, 5

Cahokia, 11, 48, 95, 96

Caigues Tuajanga, 107

calcite, 29

Caldwell, Kansas, 62

calendar, Osage, 210–11, 500n15

Calhoun, John C., 160, 193

California gold rush, 326, 401

California Trail, 75

Calloway, R. A., 165, 226

calumet, 10

calumet pipes, 60

Camp Holmes, 217

camp reserves, withheld from allotment, 403

Camp Supply, 279

Canadian River, 68, 74, 77, 79

Caney, Kansas, 82

Caney River, 69, 77, 79, 82

Caney River Valley, 335

Canteen Creek, 115

Canville, A. B., 334

Canville Cemetery, 334

Canville's Post, 284

Canville Treaty of 1865, 52, 236, 287; Civilization Treaty, 282–85; communication problems, 284; school lands omission in, 285; unratified treaty of 1863, 281

Cape Girardeau, 35

Cape St. Anthony, 72

Captain, Augustus "Ogeese," 261, 337

captives, 214–15

Carlisle School, 282

Carondelet, Francisco Hector, 109, 123, 124, 126, 127, 128, 129

cascara sagrada, 450

Cashesegra. See Tracks Far Away I

Casquins. See Kaskaskias

cast-iron cookware, 244

Catholic Church, relationship with Osages, 226, 235, 495–96
Catholic missionaries, 226
Catlin, George, 205–6
catlinite (red pipestone), 60, 91
cattail, 453
cattle industry: Osage role in development, 370, 388; problem of distance between source and demand, 368–69
Caya, 11
Cedar Springs, 63
Cedar Vale, Kansas, 77
cemetery gifts, 404
Cemetery Reserve, 403
Central Plains, 24
ceremonial club, 19
ceremonial knife, 19
ceremonial songs, 15
certificate of competency, 405
Cervantes, Miguel de: *Don Quixote de la Mancha,* 103, 505n1
cession. *See* land cession
change, and Osage survival: abrupt, 486; and constancy, 469–70; evidence of, 490–91; nature of, 486–88; recognition of, 489–92
Chanute, Kansas, 52
Chapman, Carl H., 7, 21, 104, 401
Chautauqua County, Kansas, 77, 82
Cherokee Commission, pressure on Osages to Allot, 401
Cherokee Neutral Lands, 51, 163
Cherokee Outlet, 85, 160–61; map of, 162; opening of to homesteading, 369, 370; value of, 342–44
Cherokees: acquisition of Neosho and Verdigris valleys at expense of the Osages, 158–59; and Battle of Claremore's Mound, 67, 194–95; carrying of epidemics to Osage, 238; cholera, 239; claims against Euro-Americans, 157; greed, 339; and hunting on Plains, 506n18; intrusions into Osage territory, 158, 191; move to Arkansas,

191; "New Settlers," 154; objection to price of Osage New Reserve, 343–44; "Old Settlers," 154; opposition to the Indian state, 174; Osage view toward, 401; patent of 1838, 342; removal, 189, 191, 314; Spanish policy and, 114; trail herd tax, 370
Cherokee Strip, 160, 161; map of, 162
Cherokee Tobacco Case, 297–99, 298
Cherokee Treaty of 1866, 321, 336, 341, 342, 343
Cherokee Treaty of 1868, 342
cherts, 29
Chesapeake Piedmont—Blue Ridge area, 3, 22, 43
Cheshewalla, Maud Blackbird, 484
Chetoka *(Tsi To Ka),* 101
Chetopa, Kansas, 81
Chetopa/ *Che To pa (Tsi To pa,* or Four Lodges), 34, 52, 215, 301, 305, 319, 337
Chetopa Creek, 52
Chewere Sioux, 3, 4, 6, 43–44
Cheyenne: Battle of the Washita, 279–80; and the horse, 28; "jumped" reservation, 63; loss of territory to Osages, 35; at Medicine Lodge Council, 277; and Osage hunters, 69; Sand Creek Massacre, 276; Southern, 34, 35; tobacco trade, 109; "War," 321
Cheyenne Autumn, 351
Cheyenne Creek, 79
Chickasaws, 67, 114, 129
child marriage, 360, 361
Chippewas, 429
Chisholm Trail, 349, 369, 371
Chivington, J. M., 276
Choctaw-Chickasaw reserve, 190
Choctaws, 67, 114, 194–95
cholera epidemic, 239, 240
Chouteau, Auguste P., 51, 128, 129, 139, 140, 156, 191, 337
Chouteau, Gesso, 261, 329
Chouteau, Louis J., 261, 338
Chouteau, Peter, 329

Chouteau, Pierre, 142, 144, 154, 155, 191
Chouteau, Sophia Captain (Woman Chief), 279, 325, 443
Chouteau-Revoir (Revard) post, 68
Chouteau's Western Division, American Fur Company, 58
Chovin/Chavin, Santiago, 109
Christianity, 219, 495
Cimarron River, 74, 79, 81
cinchona bark, 450
citizenship: by common soil, 397, 411; by *jus sanguine* (by blood), 411; for mixed-bloods, 329–30; for Osages in Allotment Act of 1906, 412–13; Osages problem of, 411, 432–33
Civilian Conservation Corps, Indian Division, 475
Civilization Act of 1820, 219
Civilization Fund, 163, 282–86, 301, 305, 323, 401, 476
civil rights, 412
Civil War: Confederate Osages, 260–61; Confederate Treaty, 261–63; disastrous effects on Osages, 225, 236, 489, 491; effect on cattle industry, 368; and Euro-American views of the Indian, 198, 253–55; Indian influence in, 258–59; Osages in Union forces, 263; Osage thwarting of Confederate officers, 263–64; raids on Osages during, 236; refugee Indians in Osage territory, 264–67; service rendered to Union by Osages, 259–60, 264
"claims game," 50, 157, 164, 259, 286, 482
claims settlement, Osages, 168, 286, 475–77, 482
Claremore, Oklahoma, 61
Claremore bands (People of the Oaks), 50; Big Hills, 263; climate zone, 24; Earth Chief, 42; majority of the Big Osages, 63; and removal council, 319; request for schools, 218–19; villages of in Oklahoma, 30, 63

Claremore I (Arrow Going Home), 53, 55, 59, 64, 128
Claremore III (Town Maker II), 66, 84
Claremore II (Town Maker), 11, 30, 42–43, 53, 64, 125, 130, 160, 201–2, 218
Claremore's Mound, 61, 66
Claremore's Village, 61, 66–67
Claremore villages, 60–61
Clark, George Rogers, 127
Clark, William, 146, 168, 193
Clarke, Sidney, 293, 306–7
Claymore Creek, 61
clays, 29
cleansing rites, 498n34
Clear Creek, 80
climate: defined, 23; role in the rise and fall of the Osage people, 23–25, 492
Clinton, Missouri, 74
closed tillage, 468
Clovis culture, 3
club, 19
coal, 29, 407
coal oil, 417
coastal cultures, 70
coco, 450
"code talkers," 471
coercive removal, 180
Coffey County, Kansas, 52
Coffeyville, Kansas, 79, 82, 84
Cogisiguedes, 108
Cohen, Felix, 460
colonial powers, acceptance of right to claim and attach American lands, 90
colonization, of Indians, 172
Comanche: carrying of epidemics to Osages, 238, 240; fighting with Osages, 34, 35, 109, 122; and the horse, 28; massacre at Claremore's Mound, 67, 194–95; at Medicine Lodge Council, 277; and the Spanish, 110
Commissioner of Indian Affairs, 229; creation of, 198; Indian policy, 91; on Osage grazing leases, 375; payment to

Van and Adair, 313; work for the railroad, 302

Committee of Twelve, 302

common soil argument, of Osage citizenship, 397

communism, 458

compaction, effects on Osages, 225, 227, 233–34, 237–38

compulsory free education, 247–48

Concordia, Mother, 230

Confederacy, and Osages, 260–61

Confederate Indian Department, 234

Confederate Indians, 265

Confederate Osages, 260–61

Confederate-Osage Treaty of 1851, 261–63, 295

constitutional government: crisis in, 392–94; need for reestablishment, 410; suspension of by Bureau of Indian Affairs, 393–94, 407; two attempts at, 390–92; two forces working against first attempt, 390

Constitution of 1881, 262, 360, 391, 392, 394, 399

constructive change, 486

Contact period, peak in the margin of survival, 488

Continental Congress, 149

continental cultures, 70

Continental Oil Company (Conoco), 421

Continental Trail (Virginia Warrior Path), 35, 46, 50; alternate, 32, 33, 75, 77; branches, 76; in Kansas, 74; in Missouri, 72; Osage denial of use to Euro-Americans, 27

cooking, 207

cookware, 244

Copan, Oklahoma, 79

copper, 244

copper poison, 216

corn (maize), 452; crop, 318–19; culture, 6; and land tenure, 450–51

Coronado, 30, 75, 95

corporate governmental form, 484

Cory, C. E., 297

cosmopolitanism, 27

Côte Sans Dessein, 325

cotton, 450

Council Grove, Kansas, 75

Council Grove Treaty, 160, 164–65, 295

Council of *Ah ke tas,* 54, 55, 130, 315, 316

counterclockwise dancing, 465

counting coup, 213

Coureurs de bois (Runner of the Forest), 105

Coushattas, 194–95

Cowley, Kansas, 317

Cowlitz Prairie, 325

Craig, Captain, 332

Crawfish clan, 66

Crawford, Samuel J., 309, 313

Crawford, T. Hartley, 214

Crawford, Wade, 477

crayfish, 66

credit, 434–35

Creeks, 266

crimes, against Osages, 438–39

Cro-Magnon Man, 483

Crozat, Antonine, 98

Cruzat, Francisco, 108, 114, 121, 181, 182

crystalline quartz, 29

Cucici-nica's band, 60

Cudahy Oil Company, 418

cultural blending, 472–73

cultural borrowing and rejection, 493–94

cultural ethnocentrism, 164, 218, 274

cultural exposure, 492–93

culture, Osages: attraction to ranching, 227, 369–71; aversion to agriculture, 227; awe of symbolic articles, 129–30; calendar, 210–11; ceremonies, 321–22; cultural contrasts with Western civilization, 87–89; cultural persistence, 205; descriptions, 205–6; dress, 209–10; food, 211–12; good water, 202; marriage and divorce, 210; obsession with a long life, 9; opposition to intruders, 88–89; physical feats, 206–8;

religion, 89, 208–9, 487, 495; sense of humor and flair for the dramatic, 359; special traits, 464–66; sun prayers, 8–9; views, 212–14
curare, 450
Curtis, Charles, 338
Curtis Act, 341
Custer, George A., 35, 63, 276, 278, 279–80
cyclonic storms, 492

Dakota Sioux, 6, 7, 21, 144
dancing, 465
Dark (Black) Eagle. *See* Black Dog (Dark/Black Eagle)
Dark (Black) Eagle (prayer eagle), 208
datura, 450
Dawes Act (General Allotment Act of 1887), 383–85; defined the right of nonresident mixed-bloods to allotment, 397; inapplicability to Osages, 341; inclusion of Osages in citizenship provisions, 412
dawn prayers, 498n21
Dean, Charles W., 241
Dearborn, Henry, 140, 142, 144
death rate, of full-bloods vs. mixed-bloods, 327
death sentence, 262
de Bellrive, Louis St. Ange, 101
de Blanc, Louis, 122, 123
de Breuil, Jacobo, 107, 114
decapitation, 89–90, 173, 216
Declaration of Independence, 276
Deep Ford, 80, 336
Deer clan, 15
Defoe, Daniel, 457
De La Croix, Charles, 160, 228
Delano, Columbus, 338
Delaware, 67, 123, 172, 194–95, 266
Delawares, 189
de Lemos, Manuel Gayoso, 128
Deliette, Sieur, 10
Delino, Ignacio, 123, 124, 125

De Maillet, Francis, 228
De Meyer, Peter, 228
De Mun, Jules, 54
Denton, John, 250
Department of Indian Affairs, 198
Department of the Interior, 198, 234
Desert Cultures, 9, 75
De Smet, Peter John, 213, 228, 235
de Soto expedition, 4, 7, 11, 95
De Voto, Bernard, 446
Dexter, Kansas, 62
Dhegiha, 6, 7, 43–44
diamonds, 29
diet, 327, 491
Diminished Reserve, 163, 289, 293, 302, 321; intruders, 308, 309–11
dipping, 371, 385
direct barter, 93
direct democracy, 461
Director of the Hunt, 18
discrimination: against African Americans, 462; against mixed-bloods by full-bloods, 328
disenfranchisement, 412
Division Chiefs: formal limitations and checks on, 41; lodges of, 42; passing away of, 315, 391; threat of constitutional government to, 390
divorce, 210, 360, 361, 437
Doby Springs, 81
dogs, 451, 494
domestic animals, 92–93, 451, 494–95
Donelson settlement, 333–34
Dorn, Andrew J., 198–99, 233, 234, 236, 241, 260, 261, 262, 361
Dorsey, J. Owen, 3, 22
Douglas, Stephen A., 238, 250
Down Under Little Osages, 41, 48, 49
draft notices, 471
Dragoon Expedition of 1833–1834, 217
drinking, 213
drought, 239
Drum Creek, 61
Drum Creek Council, 301, 303

Drum Creek Treaty (Osage Treaty) of 1868, 293–94, 295; background of, 300–301; cause of trouble for Osages after defeat, 311; chicanery, 287–88, 302–3; Civilization Fund error, 284; grants for Kansas schools, 304; last negotiated treaty, 151; negotiation of, 301–3; opposition in the House of Representatives, 305–7; Osage interests ignored by opposition to, 306–7; Osage opposition to, 301, 304–5; protest against, 278, 283

Dry Continental climate, 23–24

Dry Plume, 261, 301, 321, 337

Du Bourg, Louis W. V., 228

Ducharme, Jean Marie, 106

Dull Knife, 278

Dunlap, Robert, 160

Duquesne (Forks of the Ohio), 72

du Tisné, Charles Claude, 95, 97

Eagle Chief Creek (Hu lah Ki he ka Ka ha), 81, 84

Ea hoh ka, 337

early contact period, 490

Earth Chief (Hun ka), 42

Earth Division, 116, 316

Earth Grand Divisions, 17

earthquakes, 44, 506n12

east, as direction of life, 70

East Shawnee Trail, 369

East Tennessee Historical Society Bulletin, 131

Eastwood, Elijah and Abraham, 192

Eatsataneka, Jack, 329

economic imperialism, 90

economics, Indian contributions to, 453–55

economic theory, and the frontier, 455

economy, 91–95; based on hunting and a limited agriculture, 9–10, 28, 87; effects of the trade in hunt products, 94; lack of concept of money, 158; problems caused by too much money, 442–44. See also income

education: beginnings of formal, 218–19; biased account of the American Indian in textbooks, 483; "Indian schools," 282–83; mission schools, 219–20; modern, hampered by low income and remoteness, 483; reform, 247

education fund. See Civilization Fund

Elder Wa sha she clan, 21

Elet, John Anthony, 228

Elgin, Kansas, 69, 77, 82, 330–31, 371

elk, 66

Elk clan, 66

Elk County, Kansas, 74

Elk River, 74

elk's forehead, 13, 14

Elktown, 55

Ellsworth, Henry Leavitt, 213

Elm Creek, 77

E lon schscah (Playground of the Eldest Son), 465

Emerson, Ralph Waldo, 248

emigrant Indians: on former Osage domain in Kansas, 188; on former Osage domain in Missouri, 187; on former Osage domain in Oklahoma, 190; of the Northeast and old Northwest and their respective populations in 1829, 184; from the Northeastern nations, 186

enclosure laws, 87, 388

encomiendo system, 102–3

The End of Indian Kansas, And Then There Were None (Miner and Unrau), 344

English. See British

Enid, Oklahoma, 84

Ennisville, 332

enslavement, of Indians, 102

En Ta pu Pshe (Teach to Grind Corn with Stone), 47

environment, 449

ephedra, 450

epidemics, 230; Black Dog's coping with, 67, 497n14; caused by closer associa-

tion with Euro-Americans, 165; compaction policy as cause of, 225, 233–34, 237–39; early, 239–40; and population, 7, 242; of the 1850s, 240–42, 489
equipment farmer, 286
erosion control dams, 475
Es ad da ua, 350
E spa lo (Spaniard), 113
Estis, Seraphine, 156
ethnocentrism, 164, 218, 274
Eureka, Kansas, 29
Euro-Americans: approach to the Osages vs. that of the Spanish, 142; concept of the strong-leader government, 273; consistent underestimation of Indian populations, 242; convenient fiction of right of occupancy of Indian lands, 200; fear of Osage attack, 144–45; land hunger of, 94–95; Osage fore-knowledge of, 95; views of the Indian, 253–55, 272–73. *See also* Indian policy; Osages, and Euro-Americans
"exploring with the mind," 463–64
extermination, 102
external sovereignty, 147, 152, 200

face paint, 32, 34, 35
Fairfax, Oklahoma, 77, 80, 404
Fall, Albert, 420
Fallen Timbers, 133, 184
Fall River, 74
Falls Creek, 82
family grass leases, 387, 388
famine, 225, 239
farming: glorifying of, 255; methods, 451–52; missions, 68; as a solution to the Indian problem, 255–56
Fawcell, Max, 330, 331
Federal Bureau of Investigation, and Osage murder cases, 441
federal trading factory system, 152, 153, 160, 225, 295
feeder trails, 71

fee simple ownership, 342, 346, 385
fencing, 369
fencing laws, 381
Fenlon Decision, 383
Ferdinandia, 33–34, 62, 75, 77
fertilization, 88
Fey, Harold E., 470
filter dams, 475
"finger talk," 32
Finney, Frank Sr., 345, 357, 392
firearms, role played by in Indian Wars, 126–27
Fire Prairie Treaty, 144, 145, 154, 155
First Buffalo Trail, 32, 75
Fish clan, 15
Fitz-Gerald, John, 329
Fitzgerald, Sister Mary Paul, 55, 59, 240, 251, 253, 260
Five Civilized Tribes, 157, 174, 338, 401, 465
Flathead Tribe, 429
fletching, 100
flint, 19, 20, 29
Flint Hills, 24, 28, 289, 389
flood legends, 44, 498n23
Florer, John N., 403, 419
Folsom culture, 3
food, in Osage culture, 211–12
food crops, 450
food poisoning, 92
food supply: decrease in due to land cessions, 491; Osage sources of, 91; and presence or absence of domestic animals, 494; role of land in, 87
food trade, 92
Foraker, 404
Foreman, Grant, 191, 239
Forest Grove School, Oregon, 282
Forked Horn, 301
Forsythe, Colonel, 277
Fort Arbuckle, 68
Fort Carondelet, 127–31
Fort Clark. *See* Fort Osage
Fort Des Chartres, 101

Fort Dodge Reserve, 289–90

Fort Duquesne, 96, 99

Fort Gibson, 50, 64, 75, 158, 193, 205, 217

Fort Humboldt, 263

Fort Leavenworth, 50, 75

Fort Niagara, 99, 101

Fort Orleans, 96

Fort Osage, 48, 74; closing of, 225, 295; establishment of in Treaty of 1808, 141, 152, 153, 166; federal factory at, 160

Fort Scott, 75

Fort Sill, 216

Fort Smith, 50, 75, 158, 267

Fort Stevenson School, North Dakota, 283

Foster, Edwin Bragg, 418, 419

Foster, Henry Vernon, 418–19, 419–20, 421

Foster leases, 378, 418–19

Fountain of Youth, 457

Four Horsemen, 509n24

Four Mile Creek, 74, 221

fourteen fireplace organization, 14

Fourth Buffalo Trail, 79

Four Winds (Breath of Life) symbol, 7–8

Fox, 47, 48, 96, 122, 123, 144

France, Anatole, 273, 459

franchisement, 412

Francis, John Jr., 331

Franklin, Benjamin, 149, 247, 449

Franquelin, Jean-Baptiste-Louis, 47

Frantz, Frank, 404–5

fraternity, 459–60

Freedman School, 282, 283

free hunting, 72

free passage, 173

free-soilers, 250, 251

free-soil territory, 248

free trappers, 92

French: cession of all of Louisiana to Spain, 101; colonialism, 94; forts, 99; fur traders, 105, 325; means to impose overlordship, 90; Red River expedition, 97; voluntary removal efforts, 175

French and Indian War (Seven Years War), 33–34, 99–101, 148, 149

French-Osages, 402, 473

French Prairie, Oregon, 325

French Revolution, 459

Friend, Peter and August, 192

frontier: and economic theory, 455; Great American, 85; literary themes, 457; thesis, 447; two coexisting, 448

frontier line, 173

Front Range, Rocky Mountains, 24

fry bread, 211

full-blood Osages: birth- and death-rate, 327; decline in, 175, 337; discrimination against mixed-bloods, 328; motivated by enlightened self-interest in allotment issue, 401; opposition to allotment, 386; passing of tribal power to mixed-bloods, 328; suffering after passing of buffalo, 363; two types of, 175–76

fun, in Osage life in the 1920s, 435–37

funeral customs, 350

fur trade, 104–7; assignment of traders, 1794–1795, 108; competition for the Osage trade, 107–9; credit, 434; and depletion of Osage supply of game, 94; Missouri River, 1775–1776, 105; role in defeat of Protestant missionaries, 225; value of, 106–7

fur traders: encouragement of Osages to live by the hunt, 227; French, 105, 325

Gabler, Ina, 159

Gadsden Purchase, 248

Garland, A. H., 385

gas wells, 422

Gate, Oklahoma, 81

Gates, John P., 156, 286

gathering activities, 91

Gemond's Town, 61

generosity, of Osages, 464

genesis story, 12–14, 64

Genoa School, 283

gentile system, 39–42; in 1861, 390; application to all people, 39; clans and subclans, 40; executive branch, 40; organization, 487; rule against marriage within a clan or its subdivisions, 40; split in divisions, 128; weakening of, 125, 132, 487

geographic setting, 23–30

George III, 148, 276

George White Hair, 58, 59

George White Hair IV, 54–55

George White Hair's Village, 58

Georgia Compact of 1802, 177

Getty, George and Jean Paul, 421

Ghost Dance, 363

Gibson, Arrell Morgan, 445

Gibson, Isaac T., 301, 309, 313; appointment of Star Chief as Governor of all Osages, 55; determination to make farmers of the Osages, 335; division of new reservation into five districts, 352; efforts to protect Osages from Vann and Adair, 348; enthusiasm about progress of Osages toward his idea of "civilization," 352–53; erection of schools, churches, barns, mills, blacksmith shops, and agency houses, 348, 352; fight for Osage rights, 199, 348; grass lease arrangement, 349; intent to destroy two tribal chieftain-ships, 315–16; introduction of new tribal organization, 391; investigation of, 348–49; leading of Osage to Silver Lake, 345; love/hate relationship with Osages, 315; on Osage population in 1873, 346; on Osage profit from cattle drives, 370; and price issue of New Reserve, 343; relationship with Osage people, 335–37; and removal act, 317, 318, 339; replacement as Agent, 357; report of 1875, 350; report on the first Osage delegation to Lawrence, Kansas, 349–50

gift giving, after the Removal Council, 322–23

gifts, withheld from allotment, 403–4

Gillstrap's crossing, 318

Gilmore, Samuel, 251

Goethe, Johann Wolfgang von, 469

gold, 93, 94, 258

Golden Age, 9

Golden Triangle, 29

gold rush, 326, 401

good road, 202

Goodskin, John, 443, 444

good water, 202

Gospel of Individualism, 246, 248

government, of Osages, 17–19; changes in over history, 487–88, 491; chart showing mergers and organization of, 5; interim, 394–95; internal politics, 386–88; and natural rights, 38; rela-tionship with United States, 392; reorganization of military govern-ment, 130; superiority to those of Western civilization, 148; three groups of bands, 42; trait of caring for its people, 41. See also constitu-tional government; gentile system

Governor Joe (Star Chief), 228; appoint-ment by Gibson, 55, 315–16; fourth Hunka chief, 56; and intruder settlers, 134; and New Reserve, 337, 339–40; and Removal Council, 318, 320; and Vann-Adair affair, 312

Governor Joe's Village, 61

gradual change, 486–88

gradual emancipation, 248

Grady County, Oklahoma, 69

graft, 259

Graham, Richard, 160

Gra Moie (Arrow Going Home) (Clare-more I), 53, 55, 59, 64, 128

Grand Buffalo Hunts, 18, 43, 62, 238–39, 499n39

Grand Council, 320

Grand Division Chiefs, 17–18, 39, 42, 130, 487

Grand Divisions, 40

Grand Earth Division Chief, 43, 487

Grand Hun ka Chieftainship, 11, 55–56; loss of power during Spanish period, 130; shift to the Arkansas bands, 128

Grand Osage Prairies, 24, 289, 389
Grand Piste (Big Track), 55–56
Grand River, 500n26
Grand *Tsi shu* Chief, 17, 18, 42, 125, 130
Grand War Party, 15, 17, 130
Grange Movement, 290
Grant, Ulysses, 336, 343
grass, bluestem, 24, 28–29, 336, 369
grass leasing, 372, 374–83; agency, 387;
    change in due to conflict over con-
    trol of Osage government, 387; de-
    cline of, 378–83; early, 349; family,
    387, 388; growth of, 375–77; by in-
    dependent ranchers, 381; individual,
    452; leases of 1898, 376; leases of
    1900, 377; leases of 1901, 378, 379;
    leases of 1904, 380, 381; leases of
    1905, 382; only Osages could legally
    enter into, 385; renewal, 374–74; as
    source of Osage income, 358
Gratiot, Sieur, 116
Gra to Me Shin ka (Little Hawk Woman),
    82, 331
Gra to Me Shin ka U su (Little Hawk
    Woman's Grove), 69, 82
Gra to Moh se (Iron Hawk), 54, 55
Graves, W. W., 51, 58
Gray County, Kansas, 74
Gray Horse, 403
Gray Horse-Fairfax, 352
Gray's Point, 72
grazing, 371–73
Great American Desert, 271
Great American Frontier, 85
Great Depression, 433, 474–75
Great Plains, 272, 289
Great Salt Plains, 29, 34
greed: absence of for material things
    among Osages, 485; of Cherokees,
    339; in establishment of Osage roll,
    398, 431; for honors among Osages,
    130, 506n11
Greenville Treaty, 181
Gregg, Josiah, 208

Grema's Town, 61
Griffin, Victor, 363
Griffith, Edwin, 241
Grinde, Donald, 458
Grosse Côte (Big Hill) band, 41, 46
Grosse Côte (Big Hill Town), 66, 243
gross production tax, 427, 429
Grouse Creek, 62, 75
guardianship larceny, 437–38
Guardians of One's Word, 12
guayle, 453
Gulf, Colorado, and Santa Fe Rail-
    way, 370
Gus Strike Axe, 69, 337, 339, 345
gypsum, 29

Haiti, 132
Hale, William K., 441, 442
Hall, Agent, 410
Halley's Bluff, 49, 129
Hamilton, Alexander, 127
Hamlet (Shakespeare), 225–26
Hampton School, 282, 283
Hancock, W. S., 276
Hancock War, 276
Ha pa Shu tsy (Red Corn), 228, 251,
    516n36
happiness, 460
Hard Rope, 263–64; and Confederate
    Treaty, 261; and Drum Creek Treaty,
    301, 305; Medicine Lodge, 351; and
    New Reserve committee, 337; scout
    for Custer, 35, 278–79
hardwood forests, 23
Harmer, Josiah, 183
Harmony Mission, 164, 219, 220, 221
Harmony Mission Journal, 51
Harrington, M. R., 364
Harrison, Benjamin, 384
Harry *Koh pay,* 406
Harvey, Thomas H., 229
Haskell Institute, Lawrence, Kansas, 283
Hatch Act of 1887, 292
Hawk *Wa ho pe* (Hawk Shrine), 16

Hay Town (*Pa she To wan*), 309

Heart Stays Little Osages, 10, 40, 48, 352, 498n23

Heart Stays Trail, 79, 80, 81–83, 83

Heart Stays Village (Little Town), 58

Helena, Oklahoma, 84

Henry, Patrick, 149

Henry Roan Horse, 440–41

Herard, Eugene "Gene," 279

Herard, Paul, 69

Hewins, Edwin "Ed," 374, 375

Hickory Creek, 74

Hickory Station, 345

hides, 94

highest-use argument, 87, 468

highland trail, 73

Hispaniola (Haiti and Santo Domingo), 479

Hoag, Enoch, 313, 319, 320, 338

Ho e ka (snares), 13, 14

Holdenville, Oklahoma, 68

Holmes, 273

homeland, 454

Home Owners Association, 426

Homestead and Preemption Act of 1862, 258, 286, 292

homesteading, 384, 387

homestead selections, 405, 406

Hominy, 84, 403, 404

Hominy District, 352

honors: chief making through, 130; greed for among Osages, 506n11; titles of, 520n16

Hooke, Moses, 142

Hoots, Rosa, 417

Hopefield Missions, 67–68, 219, 220–21

Hopewell, 4

Hopewellian mounds, 6

Hopewellian pottery, 6

"horse bow," 92

Horse Chief, 261

Horse Creek, 81

horsemanship, 207

horses: advent of, 486; changes related to, 490; earliest Osage term for, 498n33; and expansion of mountain peoples, 28; Osage attraction to, 106; technology, 95

Ho ta Moie (Comes Roaring) ("John Stink"), 241

Ho tse He Ka he (Cedar Tree Creek), 83

Ho tse He Pa se (Cedar Tree Hills), 81

Houck, Louis, 11, 54

House in the Middle, 42

House of Mysteries, 15, 16

House of Peaceful Ceremonies, 15

Howard University, 283

Howland, George, 339

Hulah Dam, 334, 345, 430

Hu lah Ki he ka Ka ha (Eagle Chief Creek), 81, 84

Hu lah Tsah, 337

Humid Continental climate: effects on activity of peoples, 25; location of all main Osage villages, 24

Humid Subtropical climate, 23, 24

humor, 213, 436, 456

Hun ka Ah hu tun (*Hun ka,* Having Wings), 13

Hun ka (Earth Chief), 42

Hun ka (Earth/Night People) clan, 6, 11, 14, 52; in the Confederation, 15, 16; knives, 20; warfare as a solution to problems, 21

Hun ka Grand Division, 17

Hun ka (Sacred One), 86

hunting: and food supply, 91; identical to warfare in Osage mind, 18; Indian vs. European, 467; organized, 72. *See also* buffalo hunts

hunting camps: in Kansas, 61–63; in Missouri, 45–49; in Oklahoma, 68–69

hunting cultures, 173; and communal ownership of land, 87; destruction of all, 91; nomadic tendency, 176

hunting rights, 154

Huntington, Ellsworth, 253

hunt products, demand for, 94

Ice Age hunters, 9

ice dam, 44

ideal communities, 246–47

identification cards, 411

illegal leasing, 383, 384

Illinois, 10–11, 11, 96, 123

Illinois district, Osage trade monopoly in, 116

Illinois Hopewellians, 4

Illinois River, 74, 77

Illinois River trail, 77

imperialism, 90, 94, 392–93

income, Osages, 358–59, 433–35; desperate need for annuities from the sale of the 1865 ceded and trust lands, 283; during the 1880s and up to 1906, 358

indentured servitude, 495

Independence, Kansas, 61, 79, 309

Indian Affairs, Laws and Treaties (Kappler), 403

Indian Appropriation Act of 1870, 310–11, 313

Indian Appropriation Bill of 1871, 151, 299, 307

Indian Appropriation Bill of 1880, 324

Indian Citizenship Act, 412

Indian Claims Commission, 475, 482

Indian Cultural Center, Wichita, Kansas, 62

Indian-Knoll culture, 3

Indian land policies, 89–91, 199–201

Indian Nations, location of in 1903, 112

Indian policy, 198–205; casting of Osages in the role of villains, 191; centralized treaty-making, 149; and citizenship, 411–13; clustering of villages near Agencies, 225, 233, 237; contemporary, 481; contempt of officials toward Indians, 274; corruption, 347; cultural policy, 201–5; dependent on enforcement of treaty provisions, 256; dominated by corporate interests after 1850, 201; elements of, 199; end of treaty-making, 292, 299, 307; evolution of attitudes toward the Indian, 273; four solutions that evolved from, 174; goal of removing all Indians from Kansas, 314; government-issued "rations," 347; "Indian Problem," 173; Indian Reconstruction, 267–68; lack of uniformity, 143; land policies, 89–91, 199–201; money involved in, 258; and Osage minerals council, 409; removal, 135, 175–85, 189–95; segregation concept, 149; Supreme Court power to interpret the Constitution, 298; task force on, 462; threat of Osage termination, 477–79; view of Indians as an impediment, 204; War Department near destruction of Osage people, 198, 199. *See also* Bureau of Indian Affairs (BIA)

Indians: concept of harmony with all, 195–97; contradictory relationship with BIA, 481; culture, 466–68; defense of lands forced colonists to unite for mutual defense, 449; derogatory terms used against, 273; as different minority, 462–63; diversity of, 480–81; divided by different views of the slavery issue, 265; effect on economic institutions formed between 1500 and 1900, 446; factionalization under Euro-American influence, 196, 446; and Great Depression, 474–75; histories, 203; independently developed civilization, 448; influence on every Euro-American event up to 1890, 175; lack of written language, 202; and the land, 467–68; perception and reality of in American history, 445–50; political action, 481; population, 175, 204; resistance to change, 468–70; restructuring of political organization, 273; superiority of governments to those of Western civilization, 148; traits, 463–64; unification, failure of, 119–20; wars on the plains, 276–80

"Indian Scare of 1875," 63

Indian state: origin of idea, 172; Osages dream of, 174, 268, 316, 401

Indian Territory, creation, 174, 186–87

Indian Territory Illuminating Oil Company (ITIO), 419

individualism, 93, 248

industrial plants, 450

influenza epidemic, 240

initiative, 461

inland water names, 22

Inshapiungri, 60

intermarriage, 325–26, 447; encouraged by missionaries, 395–96; with the French, 99

internal sovereignty, 147, 152

intruders, on Indian lands, lack of government enforcement against, 256

intruders, on Osage lands: continuing problem on New Reserve, 331–34, 364–65, 367; growing power of, 309–11; Indians, 366; in Kansas Osage reserve, 300, 301, 304, 307–9, 308; misfits and opportunists, 365–66; on Osage land in Missouri, 50–51; Osage methods of dealing with, 134; Osage opposition to, 88–89; settlers, 134; urging for Osage removal, 317

Iowa (Pa Ho tse), 4, 6, 144

Iron Hawk's town, 58

Iron Hawk (White Hair IV), 54, 59, 228

Iroquois, 21, 449, 461

Irving, Washington, 206, 213

Isadawah, 277, 312

Island Man, 216, 217

Isolated Earth People: claim origins on earth, 7; in the Confederation, 15, 16; naming ceremonies, 501n56; stories of, 5–6; traditional name of, 58; unsanitary practices of, 14, 15

J. C. Darling survey, 402

Jackson, Andrew, 135, 154, 239, 314

Jackson, Boyd, 477

James Big Heart, 402, 419

Jasper Exendine, 418

jasperoid, 29

Jefferson, Thomas: attempts to bring about peace among Indian nations west of Mississippi, 143–44; Cherokee removal, 191; on education, 247; frugality, 152; introduction of large scale removal policy, 133, 135, 173, 174, 175, 177–79; Lewis and Clark Expedition, 110; meeting with Osage delegation, 140–42, 505n7; as a natural rights scholar, 37, 461; view of the Indian, 272

Jefferson City, 48

Jennings, Francis: The Invasion of America, 204

Jesuits, and the Osages, 60, 226–30, 233, 234–37, 344, 353

Jimson Weed, 331, 517n38

Jim Town, 331

Joe Boulanger site, 69

Joe Pawnee No Pa she (Not Afraid of the Pawnee). See Governor Joe (Star Chief)

Johnstone Park, 79, 418

johoba, 453

Joliet, 46

Josephy, Alvin M., 448–49

jus solis (by under the sun), 411

justice issues, 155

Ka he Kon se ha (Two Creeks Running Parallel to Each Other), 82

Kansas: in 1862, 252; movement to oust Osage, 391; Osage lands in, 285–90; Osage trails in, 74–77, 76; Osage villages and camps in, 49–63; protection of Medicine Lodge murderers, 350; protest of Drum Creek Treaty, 303–4;

refugee Indian problem in, 265–67;
southern boundary of, 331; statehood,
264, 511n24
Kansas City (Kaw's mouth), 75, 325
Kansas (Kaw): cession of portion north
of the Kansas River, 186; formation,
11; and Indian-Knoll, 3; refusal to
help Osage, 123; splintering off from
Osages, 11, 48, 465; teaching of dance
to Osages, 465
Kansas–Nebraska Act, 238, 246, 248–49,
308, 314, 491
Kansas Territory: formation of, 248; map
of, 249; population growth 1834–
1880, 266; slavery controversy, 62,
225, 238, 250
Ka she Se gra (Tracks Far Away), 55, 64–
65, 68, 128
Kaskaskia, Illinois, 44
Kaskaskias, 11, 48, 95, 96, 102
Kaw (Kansas) River, 75
Kay County Gas Company, 423
Keechies, 266
Keeler, George B., 418
Keep, Scott, 432
Kentucky settlers, 183
kerosene, 417
Keweh ha ka Toby, 329
Kichais, 111, 115
Kickapoo, 122, 123, 189
Ki he ka Ah ke ta (Chief Protectors), 18,
40, 316
Ki he ka Hill, 432
Ki he ka Shin ka (Little Chief), 261, 337
Ki he ka Stet sy (Tall Chief), 337
Ki he ka Wa ti an ka (Saucy Chief),
107, 261
King George's War, 99
Kingman County, Kansas, 62
king's evil, 241
King Williams' War, 99
kinship terms, 458
kinship ties, 40, 459
Kiowa-Apache, 277

Kiowas: calendar, 215, 216; and the horse,
28, 95; at Medicine Lodge Council,
277; Osage massacre of, 34, 215–17
Kipling, Rudyard, 203
Klamath: forest reserves, 478; termina-
tion, 429, 477, 479
knives, 19, 20
Knott, Eliphilet, 247
Koasati, 67
Koch, Albert, 47
Ko ke Se ke ta gra (Approaching Foot
Sounds), 108
Kon sa. See Kansas (Kaw)
Kon sa Ka ha la, 345
Kon za clan, 11, 44–45, 48
Kon za Wa ha pe, 79
Kyle, Mollie, 441

Labadie, George V., 477
Labadie, Sylvester, 504n53
Labette County, Kansas, 74, 221, 285
Labette Creek, 52
La Chapelle, Jean Baptiste Janot/Jeanot
dit, 102
La Flesche, Francis: on Osage character,
205–6; Osage hunting trails, 79–84;
on White Hair, 53
Lafon, Jean (Tracks Far Away I), 55, 64–
65, 68, 128
la Harpe, Bernard de, 97
Lake of the Ozarks, Gladstone Cove, 47
lakes, 430
Lamine River, 74
land, 293–94; as the basis of all wealth,
94; communal ownership of, 87; and
economics, 453–54; frontier, 364; Indian concept of, 87, 256, 484, 526n23;
Indian ownership of in 1980, 452;
Osages' unique position as contributors of land for the use of other Indians, 186–89; passing of, 481–82; personal ownership of, 173; sales, 258;
vs. earth, 454
land cession, 165–71; of 1808, 166–68,

167, 295; of 1818, 160, 168; of 1825, 170, 186, 193; of 1825–1839, 168, 171; of 1865, 281–89; of all Cherokee land claims in Oklahoma, 160; of all Osage lands in Oklahoma, 165; ceded lands controversy, 287–89; opposition groups, 303–9; of Osage lands in Missouri and Arkansas, 186; Osage purchase of portion of Cherokee Outlet, 161; school lands problem, 324; Settler's Protective Association, 288–89; treaties, 296

land forms, 25

Land Ordinance of 1785, 150

land policies, 89–91, 199–201

land tenure, and corn, 450–51

land titles, seizure of by Euro-Americans, 90, 166, 454

language, of Osages, 32, 284; revealing of prehistoric homeland, 22

Lap Land, 161

La Salle Expedition, 10

law: Indian, 462; traditional Osage, 262, 392

Law, John, 98

Lawrence, Kansas, 250

lead, 29, 94, 407

Leahy, Thomas J., 442, 470, 471

lease auctions, 420

Leavenworth, Lawrence, and Galveston Railroad Company, 287

Leclerc, Charles Victor Emmanuel, 132

Le Duc, Baptiste, 115

Lee, R. W., 260

legal problems, and grass leases, 383–85

leggins, 209, 210

Lessert, Clement, 338

Lewis, Meriwether, 143–145

Lewis and Clark Expedition, 110, 139, 143

liberty, 459

life, seven crises of, 21

limestone, 407

Lincoln, Abraham: abandonment of the Osages, 263; decision to take Indian

Territory, 265; ethnic blindness, 256–57; program for the West, 258

linguistic studies, 22

Lipan Apache, 28, 34, 109, 110, 132

Lisa, Manuel, 105

literature: the Indian and, 455–58; Osage, 257

Little Arkansas River, 62, 80

Little Bear, 52–53, 261

Little Bear band, 62

Little Beaver, 261, 278, 279, 305

Little Beaver II, 279

Little Big Horn, 35, 184, 280

Little Bone Osages, 41

"little brothers," 487

Little Caney, 79, 332

Little Chief, 261, 337

Little Earth Maker, 66

Little Hawk Woman crossing, 345

Little Hawk Woman (Gra to Me Shin ka), 82, 331

Little Hawk Woman's Grove (Gra to Me Shin ka U su), 69, 82

Little House of Mysteries, 15

Little Lame Doctor, 337

Little Mouth Forest, 79, 84

Little Osage District, 352

Little Osage-Marmaton, 221

Little Osage River, 48, 75

Little Osages, 30, 352; close relationship with the Missouri and Illinois, 44; Down Under, 41, 48, 49; Heart Stays, 10, 40, 48, 352, 498n23; hunting camps, 62; Kansas splinter, 11, 45, 48; on the Neosho-Grand, 52–53, 133; Saline County site, 49; saving of Kansas from a series of Indian raids, 263–64; site in Bend of the Missouri, 7; strong relationship to the Orr focus of the Oneota aspect, 45; terrain preferences, 10; White Hair, 60, 352

Little Red River, 80

Little River, 77

Little Shrines, 16, 498n35, 499n38

Little Town Below (Village of the Pipe), 51, 55, 58, 59

Littletown (Oswego, Kansas), 55

Little Town Over the River (Little August Ogeese Capitaine) Village, 60

Little Walnut, 74

Little White Hair (*Wa Sop pe* or Black Bear), 55, 59, 300–301, 305, 315

living vs. getting, 466–67

location, of Osages: legends, 21–22; relative, 25–27

Locke, John, 458

lodges, 347

Logan, et al. v. Andrus, et al., 432

Lo Ha (Buffalo Back) clan, 83

London, Jack, 458

long drive, 369, 370–71

Long-Nosed God cult, 5

Long Summer Humid Continental climate, 23

Lookout, Fred, 364, 431

Lorimer, Louis, 126

Lother, Edward, 165

"lots," 421

Loud Clear Voice, 301

Louisiana: British claim, 145; fur and hide trading centers, 105–6; heavy liability to Spain, 131, 449; increase in non-Indian population, 146; population of, 1771, 120

Louisiana Purchase, 152; cause of drastic changes in American Indian policy, 172–73, 175, 184; Osage effect on, 35–37

Louisiana Territorial Act, 179

Loups (Wolf-Pawnee), 182

L'Ouverture, Toussaint, 132

Lovely, William, 159

Lovely Purchase, 159, 168, 169

Machiavelli, Niccolò: *The Prince,* 4

Mack, John, 7

Mad Buffalo (Skiatook), 56, 193

Mad Chief, 329

Magnet Cove, Arkansas, 29

Mah shon ka Tal (Black Dog), 337

Mallet Brothers, 97

Manifest Destiny, 85, 90, 186, 255–58, 274–75

manioc, 450

Mann, Horace, 247

manners, 38

Man of Mystery, 16, 499n36

Manrinhabotso/*Mo he Ah Gra* (Reaches the Sky), 58

manufacturing, Osage, 92

Marais des Cygnes, 75, 221

Marcy, Randolph B., 75, 505n7

margin of survival, cycle of, 488–89

Marie *Me Gra to* (Hawk Woman), 279

Marland, E. W., 423

Marland Refining Company, 423

Marmaton River, 48, 49, 74, 75, 207

marmitons, 207

Marquette, Jacques, 46, 95

marriage, reverse, 326

marriage customs, 210, 359–61, 495

Marshall, John, 461

Martin, Francisco, 107–8

Martin, George W., 331

Marx, Karl, 458

Mary Petronilla, Sister, 230

Maskoutin Indians, 96

Mates Springs, 68

Mathes/Matthews, (William P. "Bill" [Red Corn], 228, 251, 311, 516n36

Mathews, John Joseph, 58, 165, 211, 221, 251, 363, 484

Mathews, Lillian, 484

mauguary, 450

Maxey, S. B., 260

Mayan culture, 6

Mayan morning prayer, 8–9

McCoy, Isaac, 208

McMurtry, William and James, 192

McNickle, D'arcy, 470

measles epidemic, 240

meat-packing business, 368

Medford, Oklahoma, 68
medical plants, 450
Medicine Lodge, Kansas, 62–63
Medicine Lodge Council, 276–77
Medicine Lodge massacre, 63, 350–51
Medicine Lodge Treaty, repudiation
    of, 280
medium of exchange, 93
Me ka Ki he ka (Star Chief). *See* Gover-
    nor Joe (Star Chief)
"melting pot," 468
Membré, 11
Men of Mystery clan, 116, 499n36
Menominee Tribe, 429
Meramac River, 73
mercantilism, and destruction of the
    Osage culture, 93–95
mescal bean, 363–64
"Messiah Craze," 363
mestizo (Spanish-Indian mixed-
    blood), 473
metal cartridges, 127
métis (French-Indian mixed-blood),
    402, 473
Me tso Shin ka (Little Grizzly Bear), 53
Mexican-American War, 168, 248
Mexican ceramics, 6
Miamis, 182
Michel/St. Michel/Mikles, 109
Mid-Continent Oil Field, 29, 418, 422
midden ring, 498n34
Middle Boggy, 77
Middle Waters, 104
Midland Valley Railroad Company, 404
Miege, Bishop, 235
migration concept, 43–45
Miles, Laban J., 199, 358, 374; on child
    marriages, 360; 1890 Commissioner's
    Report, 359; on efforts of passing of
    buffalo, 362; on formation of constitu-
    tional government, 391; on intruders,
    365; on "living poor," 442; on Qua-
    paws, 366; and scalping, 373
Military Supply Road, 75

Milky Way, 14
Millard, Ret, 405
Miller, William L., 405
"Million Dollar" elm tree, 420, 421
Mill's Town, 60
mineral estate, 425, 431; changes in laws
    affecting, 422; reserved from allot-
    ment, 407; shrinking, 429–30
mineral rights, 341, 385
minerals, 25, 28, 29, 166, 258
minerals council, 407, 408–10, 430–33,
    431–32
mineral trust vs. mineral estate, 410.
    See also Osage Mineral Trust
Miró, Estevan, 107, 108, 118, 122, 128, 183
missionaries: blame of Indians for failure
    to become "civilized," 396; Catholic,
    226; encouragement of intermarriage,
    395–96; misdirected efforts, 220; Prot-
    estant, 218, 219; role in failure of mis-
    sions, 221–24
Mission Creek, 339
Mission of St. Francis de Hieronymo
    (Jerome), 509n23
missions: benign peonage, 103; clustered
    along the Neosho-Grand River, 222;
    failure of, 221–26; location of, 220–21
mission schools, 219–20, 220
Mississippian mounds, 4, 6
Mississippian Oneota, 4
Mississippian Phase, of the Late Wood-
    land culture, 4–9
Mississippians, 4; Arkansas River, 10; cul-
    ture, 24; pottery, 6
Missouri: Osage trails in, 72–74; Osage
    villages and camps in, 45–49
Missouri, Kansas, and Texas Railway
    Company, 404
Missourias, 4, 48, 219, 245
Missouri Compromise, 250
Missouri Democrat, 277
Missouri Ozarks, 45
Missouri River, 74
Missouri River fur trade, 1775–1776, 105

Missouri Valley, 28
Mitchell, Francis [Mikles], 329
Mitchell, Joseph [Mikles], 329
Mitscher, O. A., 361, 373, 393
mixed-bloods, 325–30; and allotment,
    386, 401; among the full-bloods, 176;
    creation of separate Osage culture,
    328; cultural blending, 472–74; dis-
    possessed by intruders, 328; distinct
    groups of, 326–28, 402; excessive
    abuse of in removal, 397; harassment
    of, 330; increasing influence in Osage
    affairs, 327, 328, 387; intermarriage
    with both Osage and Kaw, 326; legal
    rights, 397; loss of improved property,
    310–11; non-people, 473–74; Osage
    tribal composition, 474; and United
    States citizenship, 329–30; views
    held by the majority culture toward,
    395–97
mixed marriages. See intermarriage
Mocane, Oklahoma, 81
moccasins, 209
modern Indian, 482
Mogray, Jean Baptiste (Mongrain), 54,
    58, 325
Mogray, Noel (Mongrain), 54, 154, 156
Mo ha Pa se Shu tsy (Red Cliffs), 81
Moh en ka Shin ka (Little Clay), 66
Moh en ku ah ha, 83
Moh he Hun ka (Sacred Knife), 20
Moh he Se e pa blo ka (Round Handled
    Knife), 20
Moh he Shu tsy (Red Knife), 20
Moh he Sop pe (Black Knife), 20
Moh ne Pa she (Not Afraid of the
    Gopher), 67–68
Moh sa He (A Thicket of Arrow Wood), 83
Moh se Kah he (Blacksmith), 153
Moh shon, 86
Moh shon Ah ke ta/ Moh shon ka shay
    (Protectors of the Land), 18, 40, 91, 303
Moh tse Sta Ka ha (Bow Wood Creek), 80

Monks Mound, 6
Monroe, James, 193
Monroney, Mike, 478–79
Mon shou Ka shi, 337
Montesquieu, Charles de, 362, 458;
    The Spirit of Laws, 37–38
Montgomery, Jim, 250
Montgomery County, Kansas, 74
Morgan, Lewis Henry, 458
Morrill, Justin Smith, 292
Morrill, Lot Myrick, 292, 316–17
Morrill Acts, 292
Morrison, Oklahoma, 84
Morrison, T. F., 296
Mo she Scah (I am White), 80
Mo shon Ah ke ta Ka ha (Protector of the
    Land Creek), 82
Mosier, Joseph (Monjeon), 329, 330
mother, importance of, 396
Mottled Eagle clan, 61, 101, 116, 279
mountain man, 362
"mourning" at sunrise, 208
Mourning Ceremony, 373
Muddy Boggy, 77
Murphy, Thomas, 300
muskets, 99
Muskogee, 122
mystic arrows, 21

naming ceremonies, 501n56
Nasuer, John Basil (Bazil Nassier), 156
Natchitoches, 74, 77, 106, 109–10, 117–18
nationalism, rise of, 248
Native American Church, 364
natural gas, 417
natural rights, 37–39, 196–97, 248, 458,
    460–61
Navajo Marines, 471
Naval Reserve, 471
Ne ah he He sko pa (Deep Ford), 80
Nebraska Territory, 248
Ne ha Ka ha (Falls Creek), 82
Ne ka Log ny (Good Man), 520n16

Ne ka To (do) he To won (Good Man Town), 47

Ne ke a Shin ka. See Society of Little Old Men *(Ne ke a Shin ka)*

Nelagony, Oklahoma, 80

Nelagony Creek, 79

Nellie Johnstone, 418

Ne Log ny (Good Water), 79

Ne ne Po sta (Shooting Springs), 80, 83

Neosho Agency, 198, 234, 315

Neosho cession, 163

Neosho County, Kansas, 221, 285

Neosho-Grand River: Claremore bands at, 30; Little Osages on, 52; Osage trails on, 77, 79; Osage village clusters on, 49, 57, 63; White Hair villages on, 51, 52–53, 56–60

Neosho Grand Valley, 28

Neosho Mission, 219, 220, 221, 223

Ne Pe she (Bad Water), 79

Ne scah Lo scah (Place Between Two Rivers), 82

Ne shu Moie (Traveling Rain), 52

Ne Shu tsy (Red River), 33, 74, 77, 80, 106

Ne Shu tsy Shin ka (Little Red River), 80

Ne ske le Ka ha (Saltwater Creek), 80

Ne ske le Ka ske pe, 81

Ne ske le Ne (Saltwater River), 80

Ne ske le U su U gra (Salt Lowland Forest), 80

Neutral Lands idea, failure of, 163

New Deal, 475, 477

Newkirk, Oklahoma, 33

Newman, Tillie Karns, 239

New Reserve, Osages and: agreement on the final reserve, 339–40; appearance of whites to capitalize land and money, 351, 365; attempts to obtain deed from government, 346; boundaries, 346; deed held in trust by government, 346; and development of beef industry, 386; first successful commercial well discovered in, 418; food shortages, 346–47, 350; geographic location, 386; growing conflicts with Euro-Americans on plains, 347; housing problem, 347; importance of access to buffalo, 340; importance of holding land in common, 341; long hunts of 1870–1875, 351–52; loss of 1871–1872 crop, 346; map of, 162; negotiations for, 335–40; petition for a change back to Jesuits, 348; price controversy, 336, 342–44; required payment for government "rations," 347, 351; reserve size and population, 337–38, 340–42; selection committee, 337; social and economic conditions, 352–53; strings attached, 345–46; "thrown into the bluffs," 339

newspapers, 481

New York Indians, and Neosho Agency, 315

Niangua River, 45, 46, 47, 73

Nichols, David, 255

Ninnescah, 75, 77

Nion-Chou Town (Neosho Town), 58

Nix/Nixon, Bill (Red Corn), 228, 251, 516n36

"noble savage," 458

"nobodies," 99

No Heart (Possibly Big Heart), 337

No Man's Land, 161

No ne O pa (Pipe), 59

"non-people," 473–74

No-pa-wah-la/*No pa Walla* (Thunder Fear), 52, 62, 301, 305, 319, 337

Northeastern Nations: background on the removal of, 180, 181–82; removal by exchange, 189

northern Caddo, 6

"northern marches," 46

Northwest Ordinance of 1785, 305

Northwest Ordinance of 1787, 150

Not Afraid of the Pawnee *(Pawnee No Pa she). See* Governor Joe (Star Chief)

No tse Wa spe (Heart Stays), 81
novaculite, 29
Nowata County, Oklahoma, 66
nutrition levels, decrease in, 361
Nuttall, Thomas, 10, 11, 193, 244

oath of allegiance, 262
O'Carter, Peter, 329
occupancy, right of, 200
Octanah School, 282
Office of Indian Affairs, 307
Ohio Company, 182
Ohio headwaters, concentration of
    French forts along, 100
Ohio Hopewellian, 6
Ohio Valley, 22, 44
oil: annuities, 359; discovery of, 417–18;
    leases, 385; lease sales, 419–22; produc-
    tion, 422–25; wells, reactivating, 434
Okesa, Oklahoma, 80
O ke sa (Midway), 7, 13, 14, 350
Oklahoma: Democratic when entering
    the Union, 405; Panhandle, 161; State-
    hood, 379
Oklahoma Territory, 186; Osage trails in,
    77–84; Osage villages and camps in,
    63–68
O la ho Walla (Beautiful Voice), 337
old age, attaining, 495
Old Claremore, 337
old Northwest, Indian Wars of, 182–85
Old White Hair, 59
Omaha, 3, 44
Oneida Community, 247
Oneota aspect, 7, 45, 500n16
Onion Creek, 61
open ranges, 87
open tillage agriculture, 468
O pon (Elk), 14
O pon Tun ka (Big Elk), 13–14, 301
Order of the Dove, 373
origins and early history, Osages: com-
    munities, four basic types of, 42–43;
    compact core area, 25; connection

with Hopewell and Mississippian
    phases of Woodland culture, 7; core
    groups, 30; genesis story, 12–14; gov-
    ernment organization, 17–19; merg-
    ing of five subdivisions to make up
    people, 4, 5, 14; original homeland
    stories, 22; possible invasion from the
    northeast, 7; settlement in hill coun-
    try that adjoined a major river, 10;
    stories of forming the Confederation,
    14–17; stories of origins, 12–22; tech-
    nological developments, 19–21
Orr focus, 7, 45
Ortega, José, 103, 470
Osage Agency, 315
Osage Allotment Act of 1906, 165–66
Osage Boarding School Reserve, 403
Osage Capital, 80
Osage-Cherokee Wars, 191–95
Osage Council: negotiation with the
    Cherokee National Council over
    Outlet lands, 343; oil lease with Fos-
    ters, 419; outlawing of child mar-
    riages, 360; pressure on to allot, 387;
    resolution on extension of the min-
    eral period, 426–27; and Vann-Adair
    affair, 312
Osage County, Oklahoma, 69, 82, 359,
    410; grazing, 389; identical boundary
    with Osage reservation, 268; network
    center of Osage trails, 85
Osage Empire: boundaries, 27–28; end
    of, 297; expansion, 30–35; importance
    of communication among villages,
    41–42; intrusions on during Civil
    War, 264–67; map of, 112; relative lo-
    cation of in the United States, 25–27
Osage-French, 95, 325, 327
Osage Hills, 492
Osage-Irish, 327
Osage Land Company, 407
Osage Little Yellow Flower, 453
The Osage Magazine, 278
Osage Mineral Trust: Agency expenses

paid by Osages, 428–29; extensions, 422, 425–28; operation of, 452; threat of termination, 428–29

Osage Mission, 75, 234–37; official name of, 509n23; Osage Indian School, 230, 233, 235–36; poorly funded, 164

Osage Mission Area, 75

Osage Mission Register, 60, 163, 235, 279

Osage museum, 485

Osage National Organization (ONO), 432

Osage Neutral Lands, 51, 163, 186

Osage Oil Company, 419

Osage Orange, 92

Osage River, 47, 48, 73, 75, 221

Osage River bands, 30

Osages, and Euro-Americans, 95–102; adjustment to Western civilization, 357–58; awareness of the need for change, 225–26; barriers to overland travel and trade, 29–30, 104, 272; blockade of the Missouri and Arkansas Rivers, 447; blockade on the lower Missouri and Arkansas Rivers, 35, 37; blockage of Spanish peace efforts because of territorial concerns, 114–15; compaction into increasingly smaller areas, 225, 227, 233–34, 237–38; conflict of objectives with Spanish, 109–17; development of advance guidelines for dealing with Americans, 133; dislike of the British and Spanish, 101–2, 106; distinction between legal settler and intruder settler, 133–34; disunity as a function of Westernization, 304; effect of views held by Euro-Americans towards the Indian, 253; first Osage delegation to Washington, 140–43; forces working against acceptance of, 228; foreknowledge of French, 95; French and Indian War, 99–101; great spread in adjustment to Western civilization, 400; impact of the Kansas-Nebraska Act, 250–53; influence in costs of Spanish Louisi-

ana, 131–32; internal quarrels, 244; intruders on Osage land in Missouri, 50–51; at Medicine Lodge Council, 277; move away from traditional life after 1849, 198; Osage-Spanish War, 117–21; petition for removal of missions, 223–24; placement under martial law, 63; problem of American citizenship, 411, 432–33; raids on, 192–93; reactions to end of treaty making, 298–99; reaction to the news of Americans taking over Louisiana, 139; relationships with French, 96–99; response to Spanish aggression, 115–17; role in Southeast Kansas, 290; as scouts for Custer, 35, 278–80; Spanish and Osage character, 102–4; Spanish desire to exterminate Osages, 113, 119–20; Spanish embargoes and threats, 105–6, 109, 110, 112, 124; Spanish Paper War against Osage, 121–27; split among Osages about disposition of Euro-Americans, 125; stereotype as wild and uncivilized, 157; "tax collectors," 349; taxing of trail herds, 370; trade with, 10, 45, 89; and transition from French to Spanish, 101–2; Vasquez Affair, 107–9; view of cultural aspects of Western civilization, 87; willingness to accept differences in other people, 463. *See also* Indian policy; treaties

Osages, and other Indian Nations: association with Illinois Indians, 10–11; attacks on emigrant Indians, 134–35; conquest of the Southern Central Plains, 447; deterrent to Indian emigration from the east, 182; fighting the Comanche and Lipan Apache, 109; granting of permission to hunt for food, 19; history of problems with emigrant Indian nations, 173–75; pressure on Caddos, 115; pressures on the Comanche and Lipan Apache, 132;

Quapaws (Arkansas), 56, 113; refuge to Indians during Civil War, 264–67; respect for northeastern people, 123; three attacks upon by other Indians, 121–23

Osages, contributions: in botany and agriculture, 449–53; in economics, 453–55; in formation of the United States, 460–61; in literature, 455–58; place in United States history, 35–39; in political thought, 458–62; service in World War I, 412, 470–71; service in World War II, 471–72

Osage-Spanish War, 117–21

Osage Trace, 50

Osage Tribal Circle, 6

Osage Trust Fund, 358, 402–3

Osage Trust Lands, 289, 293, 316, 323, 514n1

O su ka ha (Those Who Make Clear the Way), 14

Oswego, Kansas (Heart Stays), 81

Otoe-Missouri, 4, 144

Ottawas, 96, 182

Overlees, Frank, 418

overlordship, establishment of, 90

overreachment, 285

Owl Creek, 52

Owl's Village, 60

ox bow lakes, 23

Ox-Bow Route (Butterfield Route), 248

Oxford, Kansas, 62

Ozarks, 488, 492

Ozark Uplift, 27

Ozrow Falls, 77

Pacific University, 282

Pahushan, Marie, 54, 156

Pa hu Te pa (Round Hills), 84

Paillio, Paul (Belieu), 160

Pa le Wa kon ta Ke Ka ha (Medicine Man Creek), 79

Palmer, John H., 418

Panther (Puma) clan, 12–14, 15, 17, 41, 117, 125

papaw, 81

Papin, Joe, 338

Papin, Julia Roy Lessert, 338

Papin, Melicour, 58

Papin's Town, 58

Parker, I. C., 370

Parkman, Francis, 365, 447

parks, 430

Parsons, David, 293, 314

Pa se Shin ka Lo pa (Two Little Hills), 79

Passoni Tanwha/Pasuga/Pasona Town (Ho tse Tun ka or Big Cedar), 51, 61, 66, 67

Passu Ougrin/Pa shon O gre (Those who Came to the Bend of the River), 61, 66

paternalism, 392–93, 462

Pawhuska, Oklahoma, 80, 336, 352, 403, 404

Pawhuska parish, 496

Paw hu Stet sy (Long Hair), 278

Pawnee, 28, 30, 34

Pawnee Deer Creek villages, 82

Pawnee No Pa she (Not Afraid of the Pawnee). See Governor Joe (Star Chief)

Peace Agreement of 1785, 107

Peace Commission, 280

peacemaker clans, 17, 43, 59, 64

pecans, 452

pelage, 92

pemmican, 211–12

Penn, Antoine, 182

Pensecola, Oklahoma, 221

peonage, 94, 103

People of the Middle Waters, 23

People of the Oaks. See Claremore bands

Peorias, 11, 182

Perez, Manuel, 116, 118, 122, 127, 181, 182, 183

personal cleanliness, 238

Pe se (acorns of the red oak), 9

petroleum: in demand as a cheap source of lamp oil, 417; reserves in the Osage fall, 86, 424–25; seeps, 418

Pe tse Moh kon Ka ha (Fire Medicine Creek), 79

peyote, 364

Phillips, C. J., 278

Phillips, Frank, 421

Phillips, Isaac, 383

philosophic contributions, 459–60

Phoenix Oil Company, 419

Physical Divisions, 40–41

physical environment, elements of, 25–30

pictographs, 69

Pike, Albert, 53, 54, 68–69, 260, 261, 271, 505n7

pioneer farmers, 286

pipeline, 419

pipestone, 29, 60, 91

Pixley, Benton, 222–23

Plains Indians: syncophantism, 105; wars upon the Plains after 1865, 272

Plano, 21

plants, 22, 29

plows, 153

pocket gopher, 67

Poland, John Scroggs, 330, 331, 332–34

Pollock, William J., 359, 363–64

polygamy, 360–61

Pomme de Terre River, 11, 45, 46, 47

Pomme de Terre River Big Osages, 11

Ponca, 3, 44; Peacemaker clan, 43, 64

Ponca City, Oklahoma, 80, 82

Pond Creek, Oklahoma, 33, 69, 80, 83, 339, 345

Pontiac: siege of Ft. Pitt, 447; war against British, 148, 149

Pontotoc County, Oklahoma, 68

Ponziglione, Paul M., 58, 59, 235, 237, 251, 362

Poor Pawnee Creek, 33, 69

Pope, John, 332

popular sovereignty, 248

population, Osages, 242–45; in 1873, 346; in 2002, 480; age groups in 1878, 178–81; changing, 386; at contact, 479–80; decline in first year on the new reservation, 346; effect of attrition upon, 244; estimates of, 118–19, 204, 243; growth of through voluntary realignment of loyalties, 244–45; loss of due to epidemics and poor nutrition, 361; on New Reserve, 337–38

Populist Revolt, 201, 285, 290–91, 461

pork, 368

Portable Shrine, 16

portage routes, 325

Portalés, Count, 213

Port of New Orleans, 127

post system, 92

potatoes, 212, 450, 452

Potato River, 47

Potawatomis, 182, 229, 366, 401, 429

Potter, Carroll H., 365

pottery: Hopewellian, 6; at the Little Osage site, 7; Mississippian, 6

Pottowatomie, 96, 123

Power River road, 447

pow wows, 359

Prairie Oil and Gas Company, 419

prairies, 23

prayer eagles, 208

Prehistoric Age, 3–12

preserves, 430

Pretty Bird, 60–61, 64

Price, Henry, 290

Proclamation of 1763, 148–49

pronghorn, 143

property protection, 392

the Prophet, 185

Protectors of the Land *(Moh shon Ah ke ta/ Moh shon ka shay)*, 18, 40, 91, 303

Protestant missionaries, 218, 219

provisions, 302

Pumpkin Creek, 52, 61
purification ceremonies, 238

Quachita, 115
Quaker Agents, 315
Quakers, 309
Quapaw Creek, 366
Quapaws (Arkansas): "big talk" about
    Osages, 113, 124; carrying of epidem-
    ics to Osage, 238; and Illinois, 11;
    intruders, 366; link with Indian-
    Knoll, 3; and Neosho Agency, 315;
    and Osage allotment, 56; pupils at
    Osage Mission, 240; Reconstruction
    Council, 267; related by language and
    origin to Osages, 10
quarantine: fence, 385; regulations, 384;
    on southern cattle, 370, 371, 381
Que, Lizzie, 441
Queen Anne's War, 99
Quivera. See Wichitas

racecourse, at Claremore, 66
racial bias, 253
Radiant Star (Black Bear) clan. See Black
    Bear (Radiant Star) clan
Radisson, Pierre Esprit, 95
Railroad Land Grant Act of 1863, 287–
    89, 292
"railroad ring," 300
railroads, 85; bonds, investment of Indian
    funds in, 258; and ending of long
    drive, 370–71; interests, 248; land
    grants, 151; land sales, 286–88; right
    of way reserves, 403, 404
Rainy Mountain Creek, 215
range program, 475
Reagan, Ronald, 522n6
rebel groups, 9
recall, 461
Reconstruction Council, 267–68
Red Bird, 5
red cedar, 9
Red Cloud, 447

Red Corn, Catherine, 484
Red Corn (Ha pa Shu tsy), 228, 251,
    516n36
Redeagle, George, 329
Red Eagle (prayer eagle), 208
Red Eagle subclan, 498n21
Red Hill Top (Red Cliffs), 81, 83
Redman, Martin, 329
red oak, 9
red paint, 32, 34
"red progressive" movement, 482
Red River (Ne Shu tsy), 33, 74, 77,
    80, 106
Red Rock Creek, 77, 80
referendum, 461
reformers: movement, 246–48; re-
    creation of the Indian in the Euro-
    American image, 254
reign of terror, of 1920s, 439–42
Reiselman, Henry, 228
relative location, 492
religion, Osage, 89, 208–9, 487, 495
removal: Cherokee, 189, 191, 314; decep-
    tion of reform, 481; by exchange,
    189–95; of Northeastern Nations,
    180, 181–82; policy introduced by
    Jefferson, 133, 135, 173, 174, 175, 177–
    79; as U.S. Indian policy, 135, 175–85,
    189–95; and War of 1812, 179–82
removal, Osages, 176–77; death of chil-
    dren and mothers in vast numbers,
    177; detrimental effects of, 195–97;
    excessive abuse of mixed-bloods in,
    397; farewell speech, 345; fund, 322;
    from Kansas, 165, 314–15, 344–45;
    mixed-blood objections to, 328–29;
    nomad and unused-lands arguments
    for, 176–77; prolonged, 317; as result
    of land cession treaties, 296; unique
    nature of, 186
Removal Act of 1870: approval, 321–22;
    and cost of New Reserve, 336, 343;
    Gibson and, 317; and Osage hunting
    rights, 63; school land grants in, 323–24

Removal Council, 317–22; conference with Osage mixed-bloods, 328; convening of, 318; Osage money used to pay the expenses of, 323; Osage questions, 319–20; Osage requested changes, 320–21

Renard. *See* Fox

repeating rifle, 126

Report of the Board of Indian Commissioners, 275–76

Republican Pawnee, 144, 216

Requerimiento, 102

reservation, guaranteed, 256

reservation "jumping," 149

Reservoir Reserve, 403

reservoirs, 429–30

restitution, 459

Retchie, John, 264

reverse marriage, 326

riding equipment, 207

rifle, 100–101

right of occupancy, 200

Rio Grande settlements, 75

Rivar, Josef (Joseph Revard), 109

River of Life, 233

roach, 209

robbery, 208

robes, 210

rocks, 29

Rogers, Will, 456

rolls. *See* Annuity Rolls

Roman Nose, 278

Romanticism, 455–56, 457

Roosevelt, Theodore, 404

Ross, John, 261, 263

round-handled knife, 19

round houses, 364

Rousseau, Jean-Jacques, 458; *Discourse on Inequality,* 460

Royce, C. C., 150

Sac, 47, 48, 96, 122, 123, 144

Sac-Fox War Trail, 48, 72

Sacred Sky, 261

Sac River, 46, 47

St. Ange, 102

St. Clair, Arthur, 54, 121, 183

St. Genevieve, 73

St. Johns Boy's School, 403

St. Louis, 106

St. Louis Girl's School, 403–4

St. Mary's Mission, 251

St. Paul Kansas, 60

St. Regis Seminary, 228–29, 509n16

Ste. Genevieve, Missouri, 35, 115

Salem School, 282–83

Saline County Little Osage site, 49

Saline River, 74

salt, 29

Salt Creek, 77

Salt Creek District, 352

Salt Fork, 68, 77, 83

Salt Plains, 68, 77, 80, 81, 83

Salt Rock, 68

San Bernardo, 33

Sand Creek massacre, 276

Sand Springs, Oklahoma, 68, 77

sandstone, 29

sanitation, 237–38

Sans Nerf (Without Sinew), 219

Sansquartier (Nicholas Royer dit), 102

Santa Fe Railroad, 383

Santa Fe Trail, 35, 75, 164, 295

San Teodoro, 33

Sanze Ougrin, 61

saturation fire, 101

Saucy Calf, 419

Saucy Chief, 107, 261

Saucy *Tsi shu's* Village, 79

Saucy *Tsi shu (Tsi shu Wa ti an ka),* 55

sausages, 211–12

scalping, 101, 373

Schonmakers, John, 230, 235, 236–37, 240, 251, 260, 263

Schoolcraft, H. R., 11, 45

school lands: and ceded lands in Kansas, 285–86; in the Diminished Reserve, question of payment for, 323–24;

grants in Removal Act of 1870, 321, 323–24; omission in Canville Treaty, 285; problem of the compensation for, 323–24

science, faith in, 257

science fiction, 457

Scioto Company, 182

scrofula, 241

scurvy, 240

"searching with the mind," 33

secondary Indian claimants, 187

secondary war clans, 116, 117

Second Buffalo Trail. See Black Dog Trail

Second Indian Regiment, 264

Secretary of the Interior, and Osage minerals council, 409

sectionalism, role in Indian policy formulation, 177

Sedalia-Baxter Springs Cattle Trail (Shawnee Trail), 50, 77, 369

Sedgwick County, Kansas, 62, 74

self determinism, 481

Sells, Elijah, 281

Semple, Ellen Churchill, 25

Seneca, 267, 315

Seneca-Shawnee, 315

serfdom, 94

Serra, Fr. Junípero, 103

Servicemen's Readjustment Act of 1944, 471–72

settlers: carrying of epidemics to Osage, 238; from Kentucky, 183; legal settler vs. intruder, 133–34; in Outlet lands, 369, 370

Settler's Protective Association, 288–89

seven bends of a river, 21

Seven Treaties, 1808–1839, 152–65

Seven Years War. See French and Indian War

Shawnees, 182, 194–95, 266, 267

Shegiha Sioux, 3

shell mount culture, 3–4

shelterbelts, 475

Sheridan, P. H., 272–73, 278, 279, 280

Sherman, William, 277, 280, 332

Shin ka Wa sa (Dark Edge), 60

Sho ka (messenger), 16, 214

Shon tse Lu Sop pe, 84

Shop pe Shin ka (Little Beaver), 261, 278, 279, 305

shopping areas, 435

short grass region, 24

Sibley, George, 22, 62, 68, 204, 243, 244

silver, 93, 94

Silver Lake, 338

Silver Lake Agency, 339

Sinclair, Harry, 421

Sinclair Oil Company, 421

Sing ah Moineh, 66

Sioux: Chewere, 3, 4, 6, 43–44; Dakota, 6, 7, 21, 144

Sisters of Loretto, 230

Sisters of St. Francis, 403

Skelly, William G., 421

Skelly Oil Company, 421

Sky Division, 17, 316

slavery: abolition of, 246; Kansas controversy, 230, 248–49, 266; unknown to prehistoric Indians, 494–95

slave trade, 34, 98

smallpox epidemic, 215, 240–41

Small War Parties, 16–17

Smedts, John Babtiste, 228

Smith, Adam: Wealth of Nations, 455

Smith, Bill, 441

Smith, Edward P., 274

Smith, Reta, 441

Smith, Robert, 140

Smoots Creek, 62

snake root, 453

sneak grazing, 374

Snow Head, 6

Society of Little Old Men (Ne ke a Shin ka), 38; in 1870, 301; erosion of powers, 125, 316, 487, 491; influence, 39; keepers of Osage stories and legends, 12; lessening of power of the Grand Hun ka Chief, 131; loss of power dur-

ing Spanish period, 130, 132; and
Man of Mystery, 16; passing away of,
391; reorganization of gentile system, 17; representation acquired by
achievement and ability, 40; skill of,
264; threat of constitutional government to, 390
soils, 25, 28
soldiers, 18
Son tsa O gre (Those who Came to the
Upland Forest), 61
Son tse Shin ka (Little Upland Forest), 80
Son tse U gre (The Upland Forest), 84
Southeastern nations: adept at feeding
the Anglo-American vanity, 105; removal by exchange, 189
southern buffalo herd, 24, 62
southern Caddo, 6
Southern Kansas Railway, 370
"southern marches," 46
Southern Superintendency, 315
South Grand River, 47, 74
sovereignty, 172, 461; before and after
1815, 151, 152; defined, 147; fear of
loss of, 174; fiction of, 201, 273; internal, until 1815, 151
Spanish: belief in firearms, 127; buffer
status of Louisiana, 109; colonizing
policies, 90, 94, 102–4; desire to exterminate the Osages, 113, 119–20; embargoes and threats, 105–6, 109, 110,
112, 124; establishment of control,
101; fort as a means of controlling the
Osage, 127; fur trading practices, 104–
7; methods to "civilize" Indians, 102–
3; and murder of three Osage chiefs,
128–29; Paper War against Osage, 121–
27; practice of inducement removal
with eastern Indians, 189; problems
fighting the Osages, 118–21; removal
policies, 175; use of Indians as pawns
in the struggle to keep their colonial
empire, 114; willingness to transfer
Louisiana to France, 131–32

Spanish-American War, 393, 471
Spiro, Oklahoma, 5, 24
Spiro Mounds, 5
Spring Creek, 82
spring hunt, prolonged, 318–19
Spring River, 74, 75, 77
stanica, 212
Stanley, Henry M., 277
States' Rights question, 248
stem-cured grass, 374, 375
steppes, 24
Stevens, Hiram, 439
Strahan, Charles, 228
stream courses, 70
Strike Axe, 69, 337, 339, 345
striker, 165
Striking the Earth, 8, 207–8
"stripper" wells, 434
strouding, 210
Stubbs, Mahlon, 339
Sturges Treaty. See Drum Creek Treaty
subdivisions, gentile system, 40
Subhumid Continental climate, 23–24
subject areas, concept of, 89
sunrise, mourning, 208
Superintendent of Public Instruction,
303–4
surface rights, 407
surplus possessions, 362
surveys, problem of payment for, 402–3
survival factors, Osages, 486–96; adjustments in survival base, 487; cultural
aspects, 492–96; geographic aspects,
492; margin of survival, 488–89; nature of change, 486–88; recognition
of change, 489–92
Swan Creek, 45
Swanton, John, 47, 205
sweet potatoes, 450
Swift, Gustavus F., 368, 369
Sycamore Creek, 363
symbolism, role in Osage life, 129–30, 495
Systems of Consanguinity and Affinity of
the Human Family (Morgan), 458

Ta Ka ha (Deer Creek), 33
Talbot, Wallace, 500n21
Tallchief, 261
tall grass region, 24
tallow candles, 94
Tally, 35, 64, 319
"tally sticks," 383
Tally's Town (Black Dog's Town), 61
tanning methods, 92
tattoos, 209
Tawakonies, 115, 122, 266
Tawehash, 122
Tayon, Carlos, 109
Tayrian, Cyprian, 329, 337
Teapot Dome investigation, 420
technologies, 19–21, 88, 95
Tecumseh, 179–82, 180, 185, 195, 196
Te ka ah ka pa na, 329
Teller, Henry Moore, 383
Ten Mile Strip cession, 163
tepary beans, 453
tepee communities, 43, 49
termination, threat of, 477–79, 481
Texas fever, 370
textbooks, biased account of the American Indian, 483
Thayer, Kansas, 52
Third Buffalo Trail, 77
third world people, 274
thirty-seventh parallel, 330–31
Thomas, C., 150
Thompson, Eric, 91
Thoreau, Henry David, 248
Thorny Bush People, 41, 61, 352
Those Who Came to the Bend of the River (Passu Ougrin/*Pa shon O gre),* 61, 66
Those Who Were Last to Come *(Tsi ha she),* 10, 11, 16, 52
Three Forks, 64, 75, 77, 79
Timber Creek, Winfield, Kansas, 62, 75
Timmermans, Peter J., 228
Tinker, Augustus, 516n38
Tinker, C. L., 109, 472

Tinker, George Edward, 247, 437
Tinker, Roy, 439
Tinker, William H., 329, 337
Tinker Hill, 82
Tixier, Victor: *Travels on the Osage Prairies,* 54, 59, 60, 61, 207, 244
tobacco: as industrial and medicinal plant, 450; market, 109; products, 297
Tocqueville, Alexis de: *Democracy in America,* 473
Tonkawas, 28, 67, 115, 194–95
Tonti, Henri de, 10
topeka, 212
To shon He (Papaw Bark), 81
Town Maker (Claremore II), 11, 30, 43, 53, 64, 125; death of, 66, 218; signing of Treaty of 1822, 160; Spanish honors, 130; speech by, 201–2
Townmaker's Town, 61
town site commission, 404, 405
town sites, 403
To won Kon ka He (Go to Meet the Victors Town), 47
Toynbee, Arnold, 203
Tracks Far Away II, 55–56, 64, 128, 130
Tracks Far Away I *(Ko she Se gr)* (Jean Lafon), 55, 68, 128; Grand *Hun ka* Chief, 64–66
Tracks Far Away village, 64
trade: balance of, 94; Euro-American trade with tribes to the West, 92; Osage barriers to overland trade, 104; Spanish embargoes, 105–6, 110, 112; trading posts, 89. *See also* fur trade; slave trade
trade, Osages: dependence on, 487; with Euro-Americans, 10, 45, 89; favorable treatment to the Illinois district, 116; food, 92; in hunt products, effects of, 94; opposition to trade on their western and southwestern territory, 110; Osage monopoly in Illinois district, 116; with other Indian nations, 91–92
trading cards, 435

trail herd taxes, 370

trails, Osage, 69–84; alternate, 71; east-west vs. north-south, 73; entry points into Kansas from Missouri, 75; inter-connecting system, 71; in Kansas, 74–77; left bank preferences, 70–71; map of, 36; in Missouri, 72–74; in Oklahoma, 77–84; pattern of, 69–71. *See also* hunting trails

transcontinental railroad, 248, 250

Transition period, from Spanish to French, 131–35

Traveling Rain, 160

Traver, Santiago, 115

treaties, 147–65; abolition of, 292, 299, 307; acquisition of land areas as motive for, 294; block houses and cabins for influential chiefs, 153; characteristics, 294–97; Council Grove Treaty, 164–65; defined, 147; ending of process of Indian treaty-making, 292, 297–99; making the desires of the United States appear to be a desire for the benefit of the Indian, 152; Proclamation of 1763, 148–49; slanted to corporate interests, 201; treaty annuities, 258; Treaty of 1808, 85, 144, 145, 152–56, 158, 184, 191, 294, 506n16; Treaty of 1815, 146, 156–57, 295; Treaty of 1818, 85, 157–60; Treaty of 1822, 160; Treaty of 1823, 295; Treaty of 1825, 51, 52, 58, 160–64, 225, 226, 229, 295; Treaty of 1837, 217; Treaty of 1839, 165, 229, 295, 317, 342; Treaty of 1861, 261–63; Treaty of 1865, 295, 301, 310, 316–17, 321, 336, 341, 343; Treaty of 1868 (*See* Drum Creek Treaty); Treaty of 1865 (Canville Treaty), 52, 236, 281–85, 287; Treaty of Fort Greenville, 184; Treaty of Fort Pitt, 172; Treaty of Ghent, 146; Treaty of Greenville, 180; Treaty of Medicine Lodge, 277; Treaty of Paris, 101, 145

Tree Sitters, 40, 48

tribal bond, 41, 459–60

tribal education fund. *See* Civilization Fund

tribal museums, 484

Trudeau, Zenon, 123, 125–26, 128, 181

Trumbly, Julian, 405

Tsa non sa Che ha pe, 82

Tse He Tun ka (Bed of Big Lake), 84

Tse le Ke he (Big Lake), 84

Tsi ha she (Those Who Were Last to Come), 10, 11, 16, 52

Tsi She pe a go (Buffalo Range), 81

Tsi shu (Sky People), 6, 9, 15; in the Confederation, 15, 16; Grand Chief, 17, 18, 42, 125, 130; knives, 20; peaceful solutions in preference to warfare, 21; Peacemaker clan, 59

Tsi shu Wa ti an ka (Saucy *Tsi shu*), 55

Tsi Tò ka (Whetstone), 101

Tsi Tò pa (Four Lodges), 34, 52, 215, 301, 305, 319, 337

tuberculosis, 241

Tulsa, Oklahoma, 68

Tumwater, Washington, 325

Turkey Creek, 84

Turner, Frederic Jackson, 173, 286, 308, 447

Turner thesis, 447

Twain, Mark, 309

Twelve o'clock (Chetopah/ *Tse Tò pa* [Four Lodges]), 34, 52, 215, 301, 305, 319, 337

Two Little Hills Trail, 79–81, 82, 83, 84

Tyler, John, 226

typhoid fever, 240

Tzewha-changi, 60

Udall, Stewart, 462

"Ugly American," 494

Ugulayacabe, 128

unallotted Osages, 431, 432

unanimity of action, 490

uncles, 66

Union Army: service rendered to by
 Osages, 259–60, 308; veterans, 308
Union College, 247
Union Mission, 66, 164, 219, 220
Union Mission Journal, 51
United Foreign Missionary Society, 219
United States Congress: House of Repre-
 sentatives, opposition to Drum Creek
 Treaty, 305–7; Senate Committee
 on Indian Affairs, 370; Senate treaty
 ratification debates in closed ses-
 sion, 305
United States Constitution, 297
unity and harmony, 485
unity of sky and earth, 8
universal literacy, 248
Unrau, 344
U pa le, 83
Upland Forest Big Hills, 61
Upland Forest People, 41, 352
Upland Forest Trail, 79, 84
uplifted plateaus, 27
Upper Mississippian phase, 7
Up River People, 44
urban Indian, 482
U su E ha Shin ka (Little Mouth For-
 est), 79
Utes, 216
Utopia theme, 457

vaccination, 241
Valliere, Joseph, 122
Van Assche, Judocus, 228
Van Meter State Park, 48
Vann, Clement N., 311, 351
Vann-Adair claim, 311–13, 348
Van Quickenborne, Charles, 228
Vasbinder, Keno, 383
Vasquez, Benito, 105, 107
Vasquez Affair, 107–9
Verdigris, 30, 49; Osage villages on, 57,
 61, 63
Verdigris Valley, 28, 236

Verhaegen, Peter John, 228
Vernon County, Missouri, 48, 75
Verreydt, Felix Livinus, 228
Vial, Pedro, 110
Village of the Pipe, 51, 55, 58, 59
villages and camps, 39–42, 403; in Kan-
 sas, 49–63; in Missouri, 45–49
Vincennes, 96
Vincentia, Sister, 230
Virginia Warrior's Path, 72
vocabulary, borrowing among Osages
 and Euro-Americans, 456
vote-buying, 288

Wa co Ki he ka (Woman Chief), 56,
 517n26
Wa co Log ny (Good Woman), 520n16
Wacos, 266
Wa ha Ka U le, 79
Wa ho pe songs, 14
Wa Kan ta (The Sovereign Being of the
 Universe), 363
Wakarusa River, 75, 246
Wakarusa War, 238, 246, 250
Wa kon ta, 13, 14
Wa kon ta Ke (The Mysterious Being of
 the Universe), 29
Walker, Francis A., 274–75, 341
walking, Osage trait of, 206, 254
wall dams, 475
Walnut River, 74, 75
walnuts, 452
Walters, Ellsworth E., 420
Wa na she (Director of the Attack), 18
Wa na she Shin ka (Little Soldier), 18
Wa pa he (Pointed Sharp Weapons), 20
war clans, 117
warfare, Osages: complete disregard for
 their lives in combat, 121; experience
 in aggressive warfare, 28; fighting
 force, 119; on the plains, 215–17,
 257; protection of domain against
 uninvited intruders, 18–19, 88–89, 134

War in Kansas, 198, 236, 238, 314, 489

War of 1812, 114, 145–46, 178, 179–82, 295, 325

War Party in Great Numbers (Grand War Party), 15, 17, 130

Wa se Tsu Ho e (Osage name for the Verdigris River), 82

Wa sha she (Water People), 6, 15; arrow story, 21; knives, 20; mother group, 21; as original Osage, 14; peaceful solutions in preference to warfare, 21

Wa she Pe she (Bad Temper), 60

Wa shin Log ny (Pretty Bird), 60–61

Washita River, 69, 79, 216

Wa Sop pe (Black Bear), 59

Wa Sop pe U tsy (Where Black Bears are Plentiful), 84

water, bodies of, 25

water rights, 452

Wa ti An ka (Dry Plume/Dry Feather), 261, 301, 321, 337

Watie, Stand, 260, 264

Wa tse Ki he ka (Star Chief). *See* Governor Joe (Star Chief)

Wa tso Ta Cee (Yellow Animal), 14

Wayne, Anthony, 133, 184

wealth, curse of, 442–44

Weas, 11

Webb, Walter Prescott, 445–46, 454, 458

Webber Falls, 77

Webster-Ashburton Treaty of 1842, 306

Well, John, 192

West, as direction of death, 70

Western civilization: concept of decision by leaders, 196; and Indians, 462–74; Osage cultural contrasts with, 87–89; rationalized the usurpation of Indian sovereignty, 147; superiority of Osage government over, 148; warfare, 257

Westport Landing, 325

West Shawnee Trail, 369

whale oil, 417

"wheel plan," 406

Whiskey Rebellion, 127

white, symbolism of, 9

White Eagle, Oklahoma, 80

White Eagle (prayer eagle), 208

White Hair, 160, 261

White Hair bands, 42, 48, 50; chiefs, 53–55; and removal council, 319; villages of in Oklahoma, 63

White Hair Big Hills, 61

White Hair II, 50, 54, 56–57

White Hair III, 51, 54, 55

White Hair I (Iron Hawk), 53–54, 64, 125, 130; death, 50; at the defeat of St. Clair, 183; peace council in St. Louis, 144

White Hair IV (Iron Hawk), 59

White Hair Little Osages, 60, 352

White Hair's Town, 49, 58, 59, 161, 521n1

White Hair V, 59

White Hair villages, 56–60

Whitehorn, Charles, 440

"white man's burden," 203

White Plume, 59, 123

White River, 11, 45, 73

White Swan ford, 333, 334

Whitman, Walt, 248

Wichitas (Quivera), 28, 122; Osage permission to hunt and reside in Wichita, Kansas, 10, 19, 62, 266; Reconstruction Council, 267; settlement for killing of chief, 350; villages, 74

wickiup, 347

Wild Cat, 329

Wilder, Laura Ingalls: *Little House on the Prairie,* 309, 389

wild food plants, 233

Wilkinson, James, 68, 144

William and Mary College, 247

Williams, Bill, 221–22, 251

willow, 19

Wilson, John, 363

Wilson County, Kansas, 52, 53, 74

Winds clan, 60
Winfield, Kansas, 62, 317
Winnebago, 4
Wochaka Ougrin, 60
Wolf, 52, 321
Wolf's Village, 61
Woodland Indians: agriculture and gath-
    ering, 176; designs of compared with
    Osage designs, 7–9; flood plains as
    preferred terrain, 10
Woodland period, 4
woodsys, 286, 308, 365

Woodward, Oklahoma, 83
Woodward County, Oklahoma, 68
World War II, 101
Wyandot (Huron), 267

yams, 450
Yellow Horse, 261
Younger Brother, 19
Yscanis, 115, 122

Zenobius Membrè, 10
zinc, 29, 94, 407